SHOUT!

PHILIP NORMAN has an international reputation as a chronicler of popular music and culture. *Shout!*, his groundbreaking biography of the Beatles, is a bestseller in both Britain and America. He has also written definitive biographies of the Rolling Stones, Elton John and Buddy Holly.

His memoir, *Babycham Night*, was described by the *Sunday Times* as a 'superb, unforgettable account of an extraordinary childhood' and by the *Daily Express* as 'an amazing collision of comedy and horror . . . the book of his life in every way'.

Also an award-winning writer of fiction, Philip Norman was named one of the original twenty 'Best of Young British Novelists' for his novel *The Skaters' Waltz*. He has published three other novels, two books of short stories and three collections of his newspaper and magazine articles.

Married with a daughter, he lives in London.

Also by Philip Norman

FICTION

Slip on a Fat Lady

Plumridge

Wild Thing

The Skaters' Waltz

Words of Love

Everyone's Gone to the Moon

MEMOIRS

Babycham Night

BIOGRAPHY AND JOURNALISM

The Stones

The Road Goes on Forever

Tilt the Hourglass and Begin Again

The Age of Parody

Your Walrus Hurt the One You Love

Awful Moments

Pieces of Hate

The Life and Good Times of the Rolling Stones

Days in the Life: John Lennon Remembered

Buddy: The Biography

Sir Elton

PLAYS

The Man That Got Away

Words of Love

PHILIP NORMAN

SHOUT!

The True Story of the Beatles

PAN BOOKS

First published 1981 by Elm Tree Books, an imprint of Hamish Hamilton
Published with an afterword 1993 by Penguin Books
Revised and updated edition published 2003 by Sidgwick & Jackson

This edition published 2004 by Pan Books
an imprint of Pan Macmillan Ltd
Pan Macmillan, 20 New Wharf Road, London N1 9RR
Basingstoke and Oxford
Associated companies throughout the world
www.panmacmillan.com

ISBN 978-0-330-51150-6

1 3 5 7 9 8 6 4 2

A CIP catalogue record for this book is available from the British Library.

Typeset by Set Systems Ltd, Saffron Walden, Essex
Printed and bound in the UK by
CPI Mackays, Chatham ME5 8TD

Contents

Part Three
HAVING

Part Four
WASTING

Part Five
LASTING

Acknowledgements

First photo section, pages 1–8: John in garden, Mimi Smith, Julia – Hunter Davies. George and family – Freda Norris. Ringo as a boy, Ringo's parents, Mary McCartney, Michael and Paul – Hunter Davies. Quarry Men – Colin Hanton. Rory Storm and The Hurricanes – Keystone Press. Rooftop cowboys – Keystone Press. Stuart Sutcliffe, Astrid Kirchherr – Sutcliffe family (photographer: Astrid Kirchherr). John and Stuart on the beach – Sutcliffe family. At the Top Ten Club in Hamburg – Jurgen Vollmer. Mathew Street – Pix Features. Cavern Club – Dick Matthews. The band in suits – Albert Marrion. Recording 'Love Me Do' – Rex Features (photographer: Dezo Hoffman).

Second photo section, pages 9–16: wearing art student's clothes – Rex Features (photographer: Dezo Hoffman). Beatlemania – Rex Features. With Ed Sullivan in New York – Rex Features (photographer: Suomen Kuvapalvelu). *Royal Variety Show* – Rex Features (photographer: Dezo Hoffman). Ringo's wedding – Camera Press (photographer: Robert Freeman). George's wedding – Keystone Press. Press conference – Keystone Press. John with Julian at Kenwood – Keystone Press. Allen Klein – United Press International. Linda, Paul, Yoko and John – Camera Press (photographer: Bruce McBroom). John and Yoko – Iain Macmillan. John and Yoko – John Hillelson Agency (photographer: Tannenbaum). Yoko outside Lennon's house – Mercury Press Agency/ Rex Features. Paul and Heather Mills – Rex Features. George with Olivia; Ringo performing – Richard Young/ Rex Features.

Every effort has been made to acknowledge all those whose photographs have been used in this volume, but if there have been any omissions in this respect, we apologise and will be pleased to make the appropriate acknowledgement in any future editions.

We would also like to thank Northern Songs Ltd. for the three lines from the LP *Abbey Road*, 'The love you take, Is equal to the love, You make'; and for the line 'All the lonely people' from 'Eleanor Rigby'.

John alone seemed to get it right, back in the Seventies' bleary dawn when everyone around him was mourning the end of an era, the disintegration of a movement, the extinction of a culture, the death of a dream. 'It's just a rock group split up,' he said with his usual withering bluntness. 'It's not important.'

And, surely, that's what it all comes down to in the end. However talented, innovative, famous – magic, even – the Beatles were fundamentally just a rock group that split up.

Oh, were they?

Prologue

September 2001: Across the Universe

More than two decades have passed since John Lennon died at the hands of a deranged former fan outside his New York apartment. Even those with no special feelings for him or the Beatles recognised the event as a milestone; a moment when craziness and murder moved into previously uncharted terrain. He was only a pop musician, for Christ's sake, coming home late from the recording studio. What cause could possibly be advanced, or grievance assuaged, by blowing him away?

Now, in the city that sheltered John but could not protect him, another such milestone has been reached. Like nothing else in the long history of human cruelty, it will be forever defined and its horrors recalled simply by numbers, like the innocent reading on a digital clock face: 9/11.

Whereas Lennon's end came near midnight on a dimly lit sidewalk, witnessed only by his wife and a handful of chance bystanders, this new kind of annihilation happens at peak commuter time on a glorious autumn morning and is viewed in its entirety on live television. Millions of people, not just in New York but across America – across the world – see those two airliners hijacked by Muslim terrorists fly straight at the twin towers of the World Trade Center. They see the dark lizard shape of each plane merge seamlessly into its chosen satin-silver column, and the blossoming of black smoke on the opposite side. They see the victims – just brokers and financial planners and secretaries, for Christ's sake! – craning from the windows of summit floors beyond any hope of rescue. They see the plunging bodies of those who prefer to jump 80 and more storeys to their death (some in pairs, holding hands) rather than face the holocaust within. It is a real-life disaster movie beyond the worst paranoia of the Cold War years or the most lurid dreams of Hollywood. Minutes later, each tower in turn implodes in a billowy grey cascade, engulfing scores of firefighters and rescue workers, including a priest administering the last rites. The world's greatest skyline is defiled by the hideous semblance of a nuclear mushroom cloud. Where the uttermost symbols of its power and wealth and pride stood half an hour ago, there is now only a charred, Hiroshima-like wilderness.

Armageddon has not come to sunny Manhattan alone. In Washington, another hijacked airliner has ploughed into a ground-floor sector of the Pentagon, the nation's military nerve-centre, incinerating hundreds of service and civilian staff. A fourth plane has been diverted from its kamikaze course, thanks to heroic resistance by its passengers, and has crashed in open country near Pittsburgh, killing everyone on board.

It is America's darkest day since 22 November 1963 when President John F. Kennedy was assassinated in Dallas – the very first of those modern milestones backward to Hell. And, incredibly, in an equivalent national trauma 38 years on, Americans turn to the very same voices their parents and even grandparents once did for consolation. For hope.

On 20 October, a bevy of US and British rock stars give a charity concert in New York for the families of September 11's victims, now finally tallied at close to 3,000. The roster onstage at Madison Square Garden includes Mick Jagger, Eric Clapton, Bon Jovi, Billy Joel and The Who, supported by Hollywood names like Robert de Niro, Leonardo DiCaprio, Harrison Ford and Meg Ryan, plus the city's doughty mayor, Rudolph Giuliani, and representatives of the fire and medical services who have lost their bravest and best.

But the headliner, as always and everywhere, is Paul – now Sir Paul – McCartney. Nearing 60 he may be, a widower with grown-up children and a grandchild, but there is still no other performer on earth with a presence to equal his. Wearing a firefighter's T-shirt, he performs a new song, 'Freedom', written in the aftershock of the atrocity, which now becomes New York's defiant response to the mass murderers from the sky. More poignant still is his rendition of 'Yesterday', not with his traditional sad puppy-dog look but genuinely in tears for the young widows and fatherless children who now 'long for yesterday'. As the show's finale, performers and audience join in the most emollient and prayerful of his Beatles anthems, 'Let It Be'. 'And in my hour of darkness, there is still a light that shines on me . . .'

Even at a moment like this, it seems, Paul and John can't stop competing. To mark the twenty-first anniversary of John's death in two months' time, TNT television had planned a tribute concert, 'Come Together', at Radio City Music Hall, featuring its own cast of fellow musoes and Beatles-addicted Hollywood names, with its proceeds to be donated to the apposite cause of gun-control. But with September 11, 'Come Together' turns into a fund-raiser – in MC Kevin Spacey's words 'to keep John's memory alive and help rebuild New York'. There are reverential cover versions of Lennon tracks, in and out of the Beatles, plus those familiar film clips of him holding forth on long-ago chat shows and loping around Central Park. Dave Stewart and Nelly Furtado duet on 'Instant Karma'. Lou Reed sings 'Jealous Guy'. John's widow, Yoko, and their son, Sean, harmonise with Rufus Wainwright in 'Across the Universe'. The most touching moment is relayed live from the corner of the park that has been renamed Strawberry Fields in his memory. Cyndi Lauper performs 'Strawberry Fields Forever', with candles flickering on the mosaic pavement that bears his one-word epitaph, 'Imagine'. The thoughts of Lennon are written once more on enormous billboards, but this time no one looks exasperated or sniggers behind their hand: IMAGINE ALL THE PEOPLE, LIVING LIFE IN PEACE.

For weeks afterwards, the world's media are consumed by September 11 and its political and economic fallout. America's new President, George W. Bush, declares a 'war on terrorism', raging against his unseen enemy and vowing revenge like Shakespeare's King Lear: 'I will do such things . . . what they are yet I know not . . . but they shall be the terrors of the earth . . .' The Saudi millionaire Osama Bin Laden and his Al Qa'eda organisation are named as the perpetrators of the atrocity and Afghanistan's fundamentalist Taliban government is accused of giving them shelter. Supported by Britain, Russia and a string of uneasy Muslim nations, the world's last superpower sets about bombing Afghanistan, a country scarcely emerged from feudal times. Anti-Americanism sparks riots in Israel's Palestinian territory and Pakistan, and convulses the liberal enclaves of Europe. Across the whole 'civilised' West, stock markets dip, big business panics, airport departure lounges are deserted; every type of negative commercial trend, from a drop in mineral-water sales to a depletion of hotel business in the Lake District, is blamed on '9/11'. With Bin Laden reportedly bent on germ warfare, people grow afraid even to open their morning mail lest it contain spores of lethal anthrax. In New York, the ghastly pit of World Trade Center rubble now known as Ground Zero has not ceased smouldering yet.

Against such a news agenda, there is only one non-9/11 story with the power to lead every TV news bulletin and wipe clean every front page.

On 29 November, George Harrison dies in America after a long battle against cancer, aged 58. The headlines are as monumental as if some statesman on the scale of a Churchill or De Gaulle has quitted the world – as monumental, indeed, as they were after John Lennon's death in 1980. Even the London *Times* splashes the story, reporting that the Queen has added her voice to the chorus of world wide grief. Po-faced British broadsheets employ the same treatment as red-top tabloids: in the *Daily Telegraph*, as in the *Mirror* and the *Sun*, the whole front page is a single picture – moustached George in a rare smile from the 'Let It Be' period and, below, simply a caption: 'George Harrison 1943–2001'.

It is not long since the thirtieth anniversary reissue of *All Things Must Pass*, his triumphant 1970 solo triple album, with additional tracks including a new version of its globally successful single, 'My Sweet Lord'. The song that brought George greatest acclaim, and greatest humiliation, is now released in Britain as a 'tribute' single, its earnings pre-donated to charities he supported. It enters the UK Top Ten at number one. The premier spot on BBC TV's 'Top of the Pops' is a 31-year-old film clip of George playing it live at the concert for Bangladesh, all white suit and earnest beard and Hallelujah and Hare Krishna.

And all over the world, the same bleak little thought comes to old and young alike, in many languages, across countries and cultures with not a single other thing in common:

Only two of them left.

•

I began researching *Shout!* in 1978 when the newspaper for which I then worked was shut down for a year by industrial troubles. Colleagues and friends did their best to talk me out of choosing the Beatles as subject matter. Don't waste your time, they said. The story has been told too many times. Everyone already knows all there is to know.

Despite being a Beatles fan and a writer on London's most chic Sunday colour supplement, I had never considered them to be remotely 'my' subject. Fleet Street, when I arrived in the mid-Sixties, was stuffed with Beatles experts, churning out millions of words each year between them. On such an overloaded bandwagon, how could there possibly be room for me? When, in 1969, an American magazine asked me to write about Apple Corps and its troubles, I almost turned down the assignment on grounds of being under-qualified. However, I decided to brazen it out. The Beatles' press officer, Derek Taylor, liked some pieces I'd written on non-pop subjects and so let me hang around their Apple house for several weeks that summer. I talked to John and Yoko, sat in on photo shoots with George, overheard Ringo on the telephone to Asprey's the jewellers, even got to have breakfast with the terrifying Allen Klein. Without knowing it, I was watching the Beatles break up under my very nose. My article made the cover of *Show* and the *Sunday Times* magazines, was syndicated in various other publications abroad and also begat a short story in my 1972 collection, *Wild Thing*. Then, thinking that was that, I put my notes into storage and moved on to other things.

In 1978, I had published three works of fiction, but never attempted a biography. I chose the Beatles for my debut on a simple basis: which non-fiction story exerted the greatest fascination over the whole human race? It came down to Jesus, Kennedy's assassination and them. I also was tempted to set down a marker in a field where the overwhelming majority of books were shoddily produced paperbacks, retailing the same stale facts in half-literate prose. Pop fans were supposed incapable of reading 'real' books. Non-fans were not supposed to read books about pop. I wanted to have a shot at changing that.

I started my research during Britain's infamous 'Winter of Discontent', when public sector strikes paralysed the nation and the Sex Pistols were an all-too-fitting soundtrack to abandoned schools and hospital wards and piles of uncollected garbage in the streets. Amid the press hoohah over punk, there would still be an occasional rumour of the ex-Beatles putting their solo careers on hold and getting back together. Their old American promoter, Sid Bernstein, kept up his annual full-page advertisement in the *New York Times*, offering them more and yet more millions for a single reunion concert. But no one any longer believed it could ever happen – or would have much relevance if it did. For young pop fans in the late Seventies, life was no longer about love and peace and hedonism, but urban decay, hyperinflation and dole queues. Although the Beatles' music was still ubiquitously played and enjoyed, their day was recognised to have gone for ever.

From the outset I knew that there was little chance of interviewing the former Beatles themselves – doing so, I mean, in the forensic detail required by a biography. The handout from their respective press people had been the same since 1971: what concerned them now was their growth as individuals, not delving back into the past. In reality (as we had not yet learned to say in the late Seventies) they were all in denial. Talking about their Beatles years was almost impossible, even on the shallow level of a television chat show. The same symptoms showed in each of them, even John – the look that still did not quite comprehend; the glib, throwaway lines camouflaging the inexpressable or unthinkable. They were less like superstars than shell-shocked veterans of some terrible war.

At the George V Hotel in Paris, I spent half an hour with Ringo as he drank Mumm champagne (it was his heaviest drinking period) and fulminated about British income tax. At a London press reception for Paul and Linda McCartney's Wings group, I managed to buttonhole Paul and ask for his co-operation. He promised vaguely to 'sit down' with me, but his PR man later conveyed a formal refusal, ending with the words 'Fuck off'. Letters to George's home, record label and film company, HandMade, produced no reply. My best hope seemed to be John in New York, despite the unexplained withdrawal from public life that had followed his *Rock 'n' Roll* album in 1975. There were rumours that he was terminally ill – even that, horror of horrors!, he had gone completely bald. I found out he was living at the Dakota building (a fact not then generally known) and wrote to him there, suggesting I might personally deliver a supply of his favourite Chocolate Oliver biscuits. A polite turn-down came back, signed by Frederick Seaman, 'assistant to John and Yoko'.

I therefore had no alternative but to fall back on the methods of the investigative reporter, piecing the story together like a mosaic from the myriad viewpoints of those caught up in it. I also wanted to use the faculties I had developed as a novelist in evoking the times the Beatles lived through and the social and political forces that helped create the phenomenon they became. At the outset, I made two rules for myself: firstly, never to believe anything I read in a newspaper cutting; secondly, to follow up every lead, however unpromising. I was fortunate early on in securing the help of a young man named Mark Lewisohn, then rejoicing in the title 'Beatles Brain of Europe'. Mark's combination of encyclopaedic knowledge and scrupulous accuracy – not to mention his humorous tough-mindedness toward his idols – would sustain me in an otherwise solitary, unnerving ordeal. I, on my side, take some small credit for discovering the future author of definitive Beatles reference books.

After only a few weeks' digging, it became clear to me that my colleagues and friends were wrong. They didn't know everything there was to know about the Beatles. They knew almost nothing that there was to know. Over time, the story had become like some ancient Norse myth, reduced to a string of worn-smooth legends and half-truths by endless fireside telling and retelling. Yet the whole truth had been out there for anyone who wanted to find it: more unbelievable than the myth; more exciting, more charming, more hilarious, more tragic.

I also realised that, fascinating though the ex-Beatles' input to my book would have been, it was not essential. The fact was that throughout their career, from scruffy obscurity to stupefying fame, they had only the haziest idea of what was happening to them or why. From the moment Brian Epstein started to manage them, he put them inside a protective bubble that afforded security greater than any band ever enjoyed, or ever will, but also kept them largely in ignorance of what was being done in their name. They had no idea how Epstein fiddled and finessed them into the British charts with the weakest of all their A-sides, 'Love Me Do', nor how, later, he finessed and fiddled them into top billing on the *Ed Sullivan Show*, on a night that changed the course of American culture. They had no idea about the millions that were lost through botched contracts for Beatles merchandising, nor about Epstein's tortured private life on the wilder shores of the gay world. And after Epstein's death, somehow that obscuring, anaesthetising bubble remained unbroken. Even John, with all his angry honesty, never got near to the bottom of his Beatles past. Paul preferred – and still prefers – the glossy showbiz version of myth.

Gaining access to the key background figures was no pushover either.

All had been interviewed countless times already: it took the persuasiveness of a cold-calling double-glazing salesman on my part to convince them this book would be different and that I could prompt them to say anything new. I had illuminating talks with George Martin, the Beatles' nonpareil record producer; with Bob Wooler, the Cavern Club disc jockey who gave them crucial early tips about stage presentation; with Pete Best, the drummer they brutally dumped on the threshold of their success. I drank tea with John's aunt and childhood guardian, Mimi Smith, and Irish coffee with Michael McCartney, Paul's younger brother. Brian Epstein's mother, Queenie, and his brother, Clive, gave me their blessing, as did Millie Sutcliffe, mother of the gifted, tragic 'fifth Beatle', Stuart, and his sister, Pauline. I flew to New York to see Epstein's former close friend Nat Weiss, and to Los Angeles to see his old lieutenant, and near-clone, Peter Brown. I travelled to Hamburg to explore the dives and strip clubs where the Beatles cut their teeth as performers, and to track down Astrid Kirchherr, whose photographs gave them their most durable as well as classiest image.

I also unearthed dozens of minor players in the drama who had never been interviewed before; whose stories were still fresh and undistorted by repetition. There was Joe Flannery, the gently hilarious man who had provided Brian Epstein's one and only happy, stable, gay relationship. There was Nicky Byrne, the dapper Chelsea wheeler-dealer who had presided over the merchandising fiasco in America, and Byrne's former business partner Lord Peregrine Eliot, heir to the Cornish earldom of St Germans. There was 'Lord Woodbine', the calypso singer who had accompanied the Beatles on their first trip to Hamburg; Paddy Delaney, the guardsman-like former doorman of the Cavern Club; Tommy Moore, who briefly became the Beatles' drummer although old enough to be their father, but then decided he preferred his former job on a forklift truck. Time and again, my research took me back to Liverpool to stay at the Adelphi Hotel, then still glorious, writing up my notes in its Titanic-sized Palm Court, going to sleep at night under blankets bearing the insignia of the old London–Midland Railway. I grew to love the city: its sumptuous Victorian architecture, its scabrous, surreal humour. Listen to almost any 'Scouser' on the street and you understand all about the Beatles and why they captured the planet. Nowhere else can you be told, as a term of affection, that you are 'as useful as a one-legged man in an arse-kicking contest'.

Writing a biography is impossible without obsession. And I became obsessed, talking about nothing but the Beatles, thinking about nothing but the Beatles, puzzling and worrying at night over tiny missing links in the narrative, developing one muscle in my brain to an inordinate degree while other muscles grew slack. Wasn't it going the tiniest bit too far to list all the stallholders and amusements at Woolton church fête where Paul met John in 1957? Would anyone really care exactly how many steps led down from Mathew Street into the Cavern Club? F. Scott Fitzgerald's comparison of writing with swimming underwater returned to me often in those days, as the Seventies staggered towards their end. Like others of my generation, I remembered how very different the last months of the previous decade had felt; how the joss-scented sunshine, with *Abbey Road* playing through every open window, had promised to go on and on for ever. We hated to leave the Sixties, but everyone seemed to want out of the Seventies: to forget flares and platform heels, sidewhiskers and Socialism, and stride boldly into the new high-tech Tory Utopia of the Eighties promised by Margaret Thatcher.

Ironically, the cusp of the Eighties brought the strongest-ever speculation about a Beatles reunion. In Kampuchea, former Cambodia, millions of refugees were fleeing the war between the country's Vietnamese invaders and Pol Pot's genocidal Khmer Rouge. Over Christmas 1979, it was announced that Paul McCartney would headline a series of concerts at London's Hammersmith Odeon cinema to aid the Red Cross and UNICEF relief effort. When George and Ringo indicated willingness to join Paul onstage, feverish excitement broke out in newsrooms across the hemispheres. But John in New York quickly stamped on any idea that he might complete the reincarnation. Even a personal plea from the United Nations' Secretary-General, Kurt Waldheim, could not move him. 'We [the Beatles] gave everything for 10 years,' he said. 'We gave *ourselves*. If we played now, anyway, we'd only be four rusty old men.'

A few months later, a song came on the radio that sounded vaguely like John – and *was* John, though you had to listen twice to recognise the voice, purged of its old alienating fury and wrapped in a relaxed early Sixties-ish, Motown-ish beat. And soon afterwards, there he was in the flesh, neither ill nor bald, revealing how he had decided to opt out of the rat race and had spent the past five years as Yoko's 'househusband', caring for their new son, Sean. Despite the New Man aura, here was the old John, as dry, droll and helplessly honest as ever. Here he was describing how a sudden urge to create music again had sent him back into the studio to make *Double Fantasy*, an album with Yoko, celebrating their later life together; here he was being photographed with her in the nudity that had seemed grotesque 10 years earlier, but now seemed only natural and rather touching. Here he was aged 40, seemingly reborn and 'starting over' as the song said, celebrating the first step into middle age; the end of the Seventies; the joys of parenthood; the rediscovery of his art; and the continuing freshness and interest of a love affair which, against the whole world's wishes, seemed to have lasted.

I delivered my manuscript to my British publisher in late November 1980, with a warning that there might be more to come. With John so accessible and talkative again, I had high hopes of persuading him to see me before the book went to press. That hope disappeared with a phone call from a friend in New York in the early hours of 8 December.

The scale of the grief after John's murder was, and remains, something unique in modern times. Unlike the mourning for John F. Kennedy 17 years earlier, it was not confined largely to the victim's own homeland. Unlike that for Diana, Princess of Wales 17 years later, it had no taint of hype or media manipulation; no sense, as in the Diana aftermath, that people were reacting in a distorted, even dysfunctional way. It was an utterly spontaneous and genuine outpouring of misery across continents by those who felt they had lost an intimate, inspirational friend. I particularly remember the broken voice of a young New Yorker during the candlelit vigil outside the Dakota: 'I can't believe John's dead . . . he kept me from dying so many times . . .' In a supreme irony that the old truant, rebel and blasphemer would have appreciated, he had become an instant twentieth-century saint.

Millions of fans were now forced to accept, as they never quite had in the preceding nine years, that the Beatles' career really was now over. The result was a re-focus on an oeuvre which had for so long been taken for granted: a new, objective appreciation of its energy and variety, its poetry and humour, its astounding seven-league leaps from aural primitive painting to Michelangelo masterpiece. And reprising one glorious Lennon–McCartney song after another proclaimed a truth that was irrefutable, however disloyal to John's memory: that for all his brilliant idiosyncrasy – his genius even – he was never half so good again as he'd been with Paul, just as Paul was never a quarter as good without him.

All this, of course, was an outcome I had never dreamed of when I began my book against such heavy discouragement two years earlier. Immediately after 8 December, my concerns were the anaesthetising ones of journalism: I had to write a 5,000-word tribute to John for the front of the *Sunday Times* Review section as well as advise on a rushed memorial issue of its magazine. I filed my 5,000 words in the since outmoded Fleet Street manner, dictating it into the telephone as a copytaker at the office typed it. Not until the very end did full comprehension strike me: this was the boy whose life I had lived vicariously from Menlove Avenue and Quarry Bank High School to the London Palladium, Ed Sullivan, Shea Stadium, Savile Row and Central Park West. My final half-dozen words of dictation were checked by an involuntary sob.

Shout! was published in Britain in April 1981, and in the US a couple of months later. It became a best-seller in both countries and was translated into a variety of languages including Estonian. While I was in New York doing promotion, Yoko saw me talking about John on the *Good Morning America* programme and invited me to visit her at the Dakota building. So I did get there after all, albeit five months too late. My conversation with Yoko became an epilogue to the mass paperback edition of *Shout!* It included many surprising sidelights on the Lennons' relationship, and also her observation – made sadly rather than with any bitterness or malice – that 'John used to say no one ever hurt him the way Paul hurt him.'

When Paul read the quote in the British press, he took the unusual step of bypassing his usual PR screen and telephoning me personally at my London flat (having presumably got my number from the PR man who, some months earlier, bade me 'Fuck off'.) Unfortunately, I was out when he phoned, and he left no number for me to call him back. I never did find out what he'd wanted; whether to argue with Yoko's assertion or, more likely, to give me an earful for repeating it.

So that was that, I thought: I'd 'done' the Beatles and proved my point that for a biographer the most banally obvious ideas are generally the best ones. I again put my notes into storage and made plans to move on to other things.

•

Since 1981, I have written three other music biographies (of the Rolling Stones, Elton John and Buddy Holly), two works of fiction, an autobiography and television and stage drama as well as journalism on subjects ranging from Tony Blair's government to the Second World War. But, try as I might, there has been no moving on from the Beatles.

More than 30 years after their break-up, they dominate the headlines almost as much as in their mid-Sixties high noon. Every month or so brings some page-leading fresh twist in the story – a distant cousin of John's now claiming to have been his closest childhood confidant, a Hamburg matron alleging long-forgotten amours with Paul or George, a Sotheby's auction of freshly unearthed memorabilia; a lost letter, a doodled lyric, a fragment of reel-to-reel tape. Books on the Beatles, ranging from muck-raking 'revelations' to scholarly analyses, now run into the hundreds, and go on multiplying all the time. Their old recording studios in Abbey Road, north London, is a shrine rivalling Elvis Presley's Graceland, perennially setting some kind of record for how much mourning graffiti can be crammed onto a single wall. To feed this insatiable appetite, I myself must have written the equivalent of another couple of biographies in newspaper and magazine articles, commentaries, reviews, reconstructions and obituaries, and spoken at least a further one aloud in radio and television interviews. Like it or not, I am tagged as a Beatles 'expert' for good and all. I have come to dread the light that springs into people's eyes at parties when the only alternative to clam-like rudeness on my part is to admit I've written a book about the Beatles. I know that from here on, I shall be allowed to talk about nothing else.

They are, after Winston Churchill, the twentieth century's greatest standard bearer for Britain. When we look back over that lowering and ugly hundred years, only two moments give rise to genuine collective national pride: the one in 1940 when we stood alone against Hitler, and the one in the barely-formed Sixties when four cheeky-faced boys from Liverpool recolonised the world in our name. At times, indeed, they seem to be all we have left as everything once valued about this country slides deeper into neglect and anarchy. Our streets may be overrun by muggers and car-jackers, our public transport a homicidal mess, our hospitals uncaring Third World slums, our schools devalued, our legal system a joke, our police force in retreat, our Royal Family in ruins. But nothing, it seems, can ever tarnish the glory that was John, Paul, George and Ringo.

At the start of their career, they were mocked for choosing a name that suggested an insect. Perhaps the ultimate sign of their fame is that now in the English language, wherever spoken, a small black creepy-crawlie is, by a long way, only the second image the word 'beetle' calls to mind.

Their longevity testifies, of course, to the residual power of the generation that grew up with them: the Chelsea-booted boys and Biba-frocked girls who would one day metamorphose into presidents, prime ministers, captains of industry, television bosses and newspaper editors. Virtually every Briton and American now in their fifties looks back to the same goldenly privileged mid-Sixties youth and cherishes the same clutch of Lennon–McCartney songs, above all, as mementoes of that gorgeous time. Forty years on, shapeless, wrinkled and balding though they may be, they still find it inconceivable that any other generation could embody the state of being young more perfectly than themselves. Hence the post-Sixties culture that compels no one to yield to *Anno Domini*, where even old-age pensioners can still cling to their bath-shrunk Levis and ponytails and mini-skirts. To this worldwide realm of eternal teenagerdom, there is no more instantaneous passport than a Beatles tune.

Yet, immense though the nostalgia market is, it represents only a part of their global constituency. Billions adore them who had no share in their radiant heyday – who, in many cases, were not even born when they ceased to exist as a band. First-generation fans may well smile to recollect how furiously they rejected the pop idols of their own parents; how being a Beatles fan in the early days meant facing a constant barrage of adult disapproval and contempt. Back in the early Sixties, it would have been extraordinary for a young pop addict to share his or her grandparents' fondness for some hit-maker of three decades before, like Harry Roy or Debroy Somers and the Savoy Orpheans. Yet today, grandparents and grandchildren listen to *Revolver*, say, or *Sgt. Pepper's Lonely Hearts Club Band* with the same unreserved delight.

Most potently of all, perhaps, the Beatles are the so-called 'Swinging Sixties' incarnate. Britain has a long tradition of spinning history into fantasy worlds – theme parks of the mind, one might call them – from the knights and damsels of Henry V and the lute-playing buccaneers of Good Queen Bess through the post-horns and stagecoaches of Dickens to the Naughty Nineties, the Roaring Twenties, the 'blitz spirit' of the Second World War. But none of these yearningly recollected, endessly redramatised epochs even begins to compare with what came over stuffy, staid old London between 1964 and 1969. Although every last trace vanished decades ago, millions of foreign tourists annually still come seeking it. You can see them any day of the week, in their drab blue denim crocodiles, from France, Germany, Scandinavia, Japan – everywhere – picking over the souvenir rubbish that now swamps Carnaby Street, treading the no-longer-motley pavements of Chelsea and Knightsbridge, or lurching purposelessly amid the garbage and beggars of the modern West End.

Liverpool, which took so long to recognise its most priceless civic asset, now has a John Lennon International Airport and a permanent exhibition, The Beatles Story, housed in the new Albert Dock development and attracting millions of visitors, that – along with Paul McCartney's Liverpool Institute for the Performing Arts – have set the seal on the city's recent renaissance. Recent donations to The Beatles Story have included the orange-tinted glasses John Lennon wore when writing and first recording 'Imagine', now valued at £1 million. Echoing Scott Fitzgerald's *The Great Gatsby*, there is also a giant replica of the glasses, their lenses showing images of John's major creative influences, the Vietnam War, the peace movement, the 'beautiful people' in robes and beads who are now grandparents and pensioners.

Other vivid decades, like the 'naughty' 1890s or the 'roaring' 1920s seemed grotesque and embarrassing to the ones immediately following. But the Swinging Britain of the Beatles grows more modish the further it recedes into history. When Tony Blair brought the Labour Party back to power as New Labour in 1997, he was marketed as the figurehead of a youthful dynamism, creativity and light-heartedness that evoked the mid-Sixties in almost eerie detail. The jaded and broken-down nation Blair's claque had inherited was rebranded overnight with the Sixties-speak imprimatur of 'Cool Britannia'. As in the days of his Old Labour predecessor Harold Wilson, 10 Downing Street thronged with pop stars, painters, designers and couturiers, all eager to hob-nob with a premier more hopelessly star-struck and camera-hungry even than the shameless Harold.

The concurrent 'Britpop' movement consisted almost wholly of bands in Beatly haircuts playing Beatly songs with Beatly harmonies and enacting shadow plays from Beatles history, one quartet even being shown skipping over a zebra crossing like on the cover of the *Abbey Road* album. The supposed rivalry between the two leading Britpop bands Oasis (working-class northern lads) and Blur (middle-class southern lads) was portrayed in exactly the same terms as that between the Beatles and the Rolling Stones 30-odd years earlier. Psychedelic colours, micro-skirts, long-pointed shirt collars, Union Jack designs on carrier bags . . . suddenly they were all in business again. Never had there been so virulent an outbreak of what psychologists have come to define as 'nostalgia without memory'.

It is often said that 'if you can remember the Sixties, you can't have been there'. But to the vast majority of the decade's survivors whose brains were unaddled by pot or Scotch and Coke, it never felt quite so dreamily enchanted as it is portrayed in retrospect. The age of so-called love and peace saw the world almost as rife as today with natural disaster and human cruelty. As well as free rock festivals, kipper ties, fun furs and white lipstick, it brought the Vietnam War, the Arab–Israeli Six-Day War, the assassinations of John F. Kennedy, Robert Kennedy and Martin Luther King, cataclysmic race riots across America, famine in Bihar and genocide in Biafra. Even as Britain 'swung' with such apparent careless joy, it had to deal with horrors and tragedies like the Aberfan disaster, the Moors murder trial (to this day still unmatched for depraved child-cruelty) and the opening shots of Northern Ireland's later bloodbath. Being a Sixties teenager had sunburst moments, certainly, but also involved long stretches of workaday dullness, unrelieved by modern diversions like mobile phones, text messaging, personal stereos, video games or the Internet.

If we are honest, we must accept the extent to which the heady new freedoms of youth in the Sixties paved the way for the frightening ungovernable world we see about us today. From the happy high of pot and pills and the cosy hallucinations of *Sgt. Pepper's Lonely Hearts Club Band* grew the drug menace that now saturates the most respectable, most rural British communities, turns once bright and happy children into black-and-blue-punctured suicides, litters public thoroughfares and parks with the same foul stew of broken ampoules and needles. From the sexual freedom granted to Sixties boys and girls by the contraceptive pill came the long breakdown in the age-old, civilising influence of the family: the freedom of Sixties children's children in their turn to thieve and vandalise without the slightest fear of parental retribution.

From the great discovery of Sixties youth through the example of the Beatles – that, with a bit of cheek, you could get away with anything – evolved the whole ghastly panoply of modern contempt for convention and self-restraint that encompasses urban terrorism at one extreme and supermarket 'trolley-rage' at the other. Just as John Lennon realised he could get away with cheeking his blue-blooded audience at the 1963 Royal Command performance, so the IRA realised they could get away with blowing up innocent women and children; so successive governments realised they could get away with allowing the national infrastructure to fall into decay; so the police found they could get away with abandoning whole communities; so hospitals found they could get away with ceasing to accord patients basic human dignity; so the legions of murderers, child-molesters and muggers and celebrity-stalkers found they could become ever more arrogantly audacious in their predating; so egotism, viciousness and disregard for others grew to the point where Bin Laden and his fanatics found they could get away with the vileness of September 11 2001. If you seek to pinpoint the exact place in the twentieth century where civilisation ceased moving steadily forward and began taking quantum leaps backward, there can be no other culprit but the Sixties.

Yet, at the same time, one cannot gainsay the decade's many positive, if illusory and short-lived, qualities – its vigour and optimism; its belief that idealism could move the grimmest, rockiest old mountains; its abounding creativity; its ready assimilation of the wildest originality and eccentricity; its childlike sense of discovering the whole world anew. Such are the echoes that Sixties nostalgics, with or without memory, seek most avidly and find most abundantly in the music of the Beatles.

Weary though I may be of discussing the subject, heart-sick as I am at the prospect of writing anything further about it (including this prologue), I cannot pretend that my interest has waned over two decades. For this is the greatest show business story ever told; one whose fascination only deepens as our collective obsession with the joys and horrors of celebrity grows. As a moral tale, it is both utterly emblematic (be careful what you wish for, lest your wish come true) and utterly unique. If it were presented as fiction, with its web of extraordinary accidents, conjunctions and coincidences, no one would believe it. A modern Dickens or Tolstoy would be needed to create such a cast of characters, such a cavalcade of mould-shattering events, such a shading of comedy into tragedy, such a sweeping panorama of social evolution and transformation – though not even Dickens or Tolstoy had the nerve to make any of their heroes actually change the world.

From the moment the Beatles realised they need not fear being overtaken by Dave Clark and the 'Tottenham Sound', there has been no dispute about their being the greatest pop act of all time. No matter how pop's sound and look may develop, or regress, they remain the ideal, the exemplar, the summit to which all performers aspire, whether male or female, singular or plural; their name the ultimate turn-on in the language of promotion, huckstering and hype. There is not a single hopefully seminal attraction of the past three decades, from Seventies glam- and snob-rockers, through punk, disco and new romantics, to today's zombie-strutting boy- and girl- and boy–girl 'bands', whose keepers have not staked their claim to greatness by announcing they have sold more singles or more albums than the Beatles, played to larger combined audiences than the Beatles, had more consecutive hits than the Beatles, stormed the charts more quickly than the Beatles, been mobbed at airports more hysterically than the Beatles, generated more obsessive media coverage than the Beatles. Perhaps the only group to have approached the world-wide stir they created were the Spice Girls in the middle and late Nineties. The highest accolade Ginger, Scary, Posh and Sporty received, or desired, was to be called 'female Beatles'.

The truth is that in purely statistical terms, many later performers can legitimately make one or other of these claims. The Beatles, after all, rose to fame in a music industry as different from the modern one as the Stone Age from Star Wars. Plenty of other acts have shifted more product, counted more heads on their tours and, certainly, earned more money than the Beatles did. Plenty have mimicked their milestone moments – like U2's simulation of their Apple rooftop concert. But none has ever been or could ever hope to be so much loved. Love was what took them to their unbeatable heights but also destroyed them; the terrible, mindless love which ultimately enwrapped them squeezed the vitality from them, like a giant boa-constrictor. That is the power, above all, that endures in those recordings from long-ago Abbey Road in long-ago London. Play any Beatles song (except maybe 'Revolution No. 9') to any group of toddlers in any country and of whatever culture. They will instantly love it.

Posterity thus far has produced only one equivalent object of mass adoration and fascination. From the early Eighties to the late Nineties, the beautiful, brave, batty Diana, Princess of Wales rivalled the Beatles – at times even threatened to overtake them – as the world's favourite icon; no longer pop stars as royalty but royalty as a pop star. In 1995, the reunion that millions had longed for since 1971 actually did happen.

Their long-dormant Apple company announced plans to release the definitive film record of their career which their former roadie, Neil Aspinall, had been compiling for more than a quarter of a century, plus a collective text-autobiography. Paul, George and Ringo reconvened at Abbey Road under their old producer, now Sir George Martin, to provide instrumental and vocal back-up to some Lennon vocal tracks unearthed by Yoko among his archives at the Dakota. But, although the headlines befitted a second Second Coming, they did not shout quite as loudly nor last quite as long as they might normally have done. For this happened also to be the moment when Diana chose to give a television interview, exposing the sham of her supposed 'fairytale' marriage to Britain's future king. A changed world, indeed, when the Fab Four played second fiddle to a Royal broadcast!

Now Dianamania flickers fitfully on and off like faulty neon while Beatlemania blazes stronger than ever. In 2001 an album was released entitled simply *1*, a collection of 27 number one Beatles singles from three decades earlier. It topped the album charts in Britain and America and around the world, selling twice as many copies as their 'concept' masterpiece *Sgt. Pepper's Lonely Hearts Club Band*, and making them *Billboard* magazine's best-selling act of the year above contemporary giants like Britney Spears and J-Lo.

A year later came perhaps the ultimate instance of nostalgia with and without memory as well as delicious full-circle irony. The Queen's Golden Jubilee celebrations reached their climax with a marathon pop concert in the seldom-seen rear grounds – actually, front garden – of Buckingham Palace, featuring every major British pop act of the past half-century from Shirley Bassey to Atomic Kitten. Its twofold purpose was to celebrate Britain's most consistently successful export over 50 years and demonstrate how switched-on and accessible the monarchy had become after its near-fatal bout with 'the People's Princess'.

For the almost one-million-strong crowd that seethed down the Mall like some weird, blue-lit cornfield, there was no contest as to the top of the night's bill. One could almost see them on the giant TV monitors like black and white ghosts, swaggering in to collect their MBE medals in 1965 and, afterwards, boasting of puffing joints in a Palace washroom. It was bizarre to remember what national outrage greeted the award of even so modest an honour to grubby hit-paraders. Tonight, the stage thronged with pop musical knights, all of whom had received their dubbing without the smallest public controversy – Sir Cliff Richard, Sir Elton John and, of course, Sir George Martin, the man who made Beatles music possible, today as beloved a national institution as a great statesman or philanthropist.

The whole night belonged to the old Fab Four as surely as it did to the new Fab Windsors. Here were Joe Cocker and his glorious old throat-ripping cover version of 'With a Little Help from My Friends' from *Sgt. Pepper*. Here was Eric Clapton, paying tribute to his friend George Harrison with 'While My Guitar Gently Weeps' from the *White Album*. And here, to close the show, was Sir Paul again, at yet another uncharted high-watermark of fame and national prestige. Here was the billionaire megastar, showing what a simple working musician he is at heart as he provided back-up piano and vocals for Clapton in the Harrison number. Here he was, leading a million born-again royalists in a mass version of 'Hey Jude' whose 'La-la-la-lalala-la' chorus rolled through the floodlit human seas, both with and without memory, as familiarly as their own heartbeat.

John Lennon was there too, in spirit, albeit more than likely turning a bit in his grave. The concert's closing number – indeed, the backing track for the whole Jubilee – was 'All You Need Is Love', a song even more achingly true of today's world than that of 1967. But now John's countercultural mantra had become an anthem of loyalty to tradition and the status quo, 'God Save the Queen' in all but name: an alternative 'Rule Britannia'.

•

The original *Shout!* ended in 1970, a year before the Beatles' official break-up. There are thus more than three decades to be covered of their respective post-Beatles lives, a story fully as bizarre, if not as light-hearted, as their collective one. Also, since 1981 I have collected much new information about their life together, from both original and new sources and from researching subsequent books, particularly my biography of the Rolling Stones. Hence this revised edition in the fortieth year since Beatlemania descended on Britain.

How different a book would I write if I were starting out now? Some critics felt I gave too much credence to an explanation for Brian Epstein's death never previously raised: that he was artfully murdered by a contract killer in reprisal for the vast sums lost in America through his botched deals on Beatles merchandise. It was a line I could hardly ignore, faced as I was with a source who claimed not only to have heard a murder threat made against Epstein but also to have been informed by phone after the contract had been carried out. Significantly, none of the ex-Beatles ever regarded the theory as too far-fetched. Nor did Epstein's own family, though in their case it may have been preferable to subsequent unsubstantiated claims that he died as a result of a sex-game that went wrong. With hindsight, I think it more likely his death was 'by misadventure', as the coroner recorded.

I must also admit to having suppressed one crucial fact. After Epstein's death, two suicide notes were found shut away in his desk drawer at Chapel Street. They had apparently both been written some little time previously, either for attempts on his own life that he never carried through or as a way of getting attention from his long-suffering associates. Both his brother Clive and his mother Queenie begged me not to mention these notes. At one point I had both of them on the phone at once saying, 'Please, Philip . . . *please*.' They were nice, decent people whom I had no wish to hurt. So I agreed.

Others felt that my judgements of Paul McCartney were too harsh, perhaps even motivated by personal dislike. In the Beatles subculture, one inevitably finds oneself tagged either as a 'John' person or a 'Paul' person. I cannot pretend to be other than the former. Just the same, it was wrong of me – though it won me my initial access to Yoko – to say, as I did on an American TV news programme, that 'John was three-quarters of the Beatles'. I would not question McCartney's huge talent nor deny that, like all of them, he was far nicer than he ever needed to be. But someone so desperately anxious to be liked can never be quite likeable.

Any writer would hope to have improved over a span of more than 20 years. Looking back from here at the original *Shout!*, I see all too many examples of clumsiness and imprecision; indeed, my first instinct was to rewrite the whole book. But its various imperfections do not seem to have stopped people from enjoying it. Apart from updating and correcting, therefore, I've limited myself to toning down the more garish purple passages and sharpening what was too fuzzy before. I was also criticised for dwelling too little on the Beatles' music and that, too, I have tried to rectify.

For all its faults, I do not think any other Beatles book has overtaken it. Peter Brown's *The Love You Make* (1983) was marketed as the sensational revelations of a Beatles 'insider', yet proved curiously uninformative in a large number of areas. The late Albert Goldman's *The Lives of John Lennon* was a jumble of the ordurous untruths and crass misunderstandings peculiar to that author, often contradicting itself ludicrously from one page to the next. Paul McCartney's ghosted autobiography, *Many Years From Now*, contained too many glossings-over of history and too much naked competitiveness with John's ghost to be rated much higher than an inflated piece of vanity publishing. The three ex-Beatles' collective 'autobiography' – in fact just unedited transcripts of their interviews for the *Anthology* TV documentary – featured much fascinating reminiscence, especially from George, but was grossly slanted and selective (every first-generation Beatle wife, for instance, being airbrushed out of the picture in a manner that would have gratified the late Josef Stalin).

I should add hastily that *Shout!* is an impressionistic portrait, not a textbook. For an impeccably accurate day-by-day record of the band, Mark Lewisohn's *The Complete Beatles Chronicle* is unsurpassed and unsurpassable.

It is said that even the most fortunate journalist meets only one truly smashing story in his or her career. The main thing I have learned about biography writing is that it is even more a matter of pure luck. Lucky me to have lit on what the Beatles' irreplaceable publicist, Derek Taylor, rightly called 'the twentieth century's greatest romance'.

PART ONE

WISHING

1

'He was the one I'd waited for'

John Lennon was born on 9 October 1940, during a brief respite in Nazi Germany's bombing of Liverpool. All summer, after tea, people would switch on their wireless sets at low volume, listening, not to the muted dance music but to the sky outside their open back doors. When the music cut off, before the first siren went, you knew that the bombers were returning.

Liverpool paid a heavy price for its Naval shipyards, and for the miles of docks where convoys stood making ready to brave the North Atlantic. The city was Britain's last loophole for overseas food supplies. Night after night, with geometric accuracy, explosions tore along the seaming of wharves and warehouses and black castle walls, and over the tramlines into streets of friendly red back-to-back houses, of pubs and missions and corner dairies with cowsheds behind. During the worst week, so many ships lay sunk along the Mersey, there was not a single berth free for incoming cargo. But in Lime Street, the Empire theatre carried on performances as usual. Sometimes the whole audience would crowd out into the foyer and look across the black acropolis of St George's Hall, to a sky flashing white, then dark again as more bombs pummelled the port and the river.

Mimi Stanley had always worried about her younger sister, Julia. She worried about her especially tonight with more Luftwaffe raids expected and Julia in labour in the Oxford Street maternity home. When news of the baby came by telephone, Mimi set out on foot from the Stanley house in Newcastle Road. 'I ran two miles. I couldn't stop thinking, "It's a boy, it's a boy. He's the one I've waited for."'

She held John in her arms 20 minutes after he was born. His second name, Julia said – in honour of Britain's inspirational Prime Minister, Winston Churchill – would be Winston. Just then a landmine fell directly outside the hospital. 'But my sister stayed in bed,' Mimi said, 'and they put the baby under the bed. They wanted me to go into the basement but I wouldn't. I ran all the way back to Newcastle Road to tell Father the news. "Get under shelter," the wardens were shouting. "Oh be quiet," I told them. Father was there, and I said, "It's a boy and he's beautiful, he's the best one of all." Father looked up and said: "Oh heck, he *would* be."'

Mimi's and Julia's father was an official with the Glasgow and Liverpool Salvage Company. He was aboard the salvage tug which tried to raise the submarine *Thetis* from her deathbed in Liverpool Bay. He had five daughters and brought them up strictly, though he was often away from home salvaging ships. 'We loved Father,' Mimi said, 'but we liked it when he went away to sea and we girls could kick over the traces a bit. If ever there was a boy I had my eye on, I used to pray at night, "Please God, let no one be hurt but let there be a wreck." '

Mimi was slender, brisk and dark, with fine cheekbones like a Cherokee. Julia was slim, auburn-haired, more conventionally pretty. Both loved laughter, but Mimi insisted there should be sense in it. 'Oh, Julia,' she would endlessly plead, 'be *serious*.' Julia could never be serious about anything.

Her marriage to Freddy Lennon in 1938 had been the least serious act of her life. She met Freddy one day in Sefton Park, and commented on the silly hat he wore. To please her, Freddy sent it skimming into the lake. She started bringing him home, to her whole family's great dismay. He was only a ship's waiter, erratically employed: he preferred, in the nautical term for malingering, to 'swallow the anchor'. Julia married him on an impulse at Mount Pleasant Register Office, putting down her occupation as 'cinema usherette' because she knew how it would annoy her father. 'I'll never forget that day,' Mimi said. 'Julia came home, threw a piece of paper on the table and said, "There, that's it. I've married him." '

When war broke out in 1939, Freddy was aboard a passenger liner berthed in New York. The next Julia heard, he had been locked away with the internees on Ellis Island. Later still, he turned up in north Africa. He returned home briefly in 1940 and 1942, then disappeared, it seemed, for good. The shipping line felt obliged to terminate the wages they had been paying direct to Julia.

All her four sisters took a hand in caring for the new baby. But one sister cared specially – the one who, having no babies of her own, ran through the air raid to hold him. From the moment John could talk, he would say, 'Where's Mimi? Where's Mimi's house?'

'Julia had met someone else, with whom she had a chance of happiness,' Mimi said. 'And no man wants another man's child. That's when I said I wanted to bring John to Menlove Avenue to live with George and me. I wouldn't even let him risk being hurt or feeling he was in the way. I made up my mind that I'd be the one to give him what every child has the right to – a safe and happy home life.'

•

The fires ceased falling on Liverpool. The city, though cratered like a Roman ruin, returned to its old majestically confident commercial life. St George's Hall, badly scarred, still stood within its columns, between equestrian statues of Victoria and Albert. Along the docks, the overhead railway remained intact, passing above the funnels and warehouses and branching masts, the horse-drawn wagons and clanking, shuffling 'Green Goddess' Liverpool trams. Business resumed in the streets lined by statues and colonnades and Moorish arches and huge public clocks. At the Pier Head, that broad river front, congregations of trams drew up between the Mersey and its three grey waterside temples; to the Cunard Company, the Docks and Harbour Board and the Royal Liver Insurance Company. The 'Liver building' was still there, its twin belfries soaring higher than the seagulls and crowned with the skittish stone silhouettes of the 'Liver birds'.

Liverpool was still business and banking and insurance, and ships. From the southern headland, under rings of tall cranes, came the rhythmic clout of Cammell Laird's yard where they built the *Alabama*, the *Mauretania*, the *Ark Royal*, the *Thetis*. Across from Birkenhead, brisk river ferries crossed the path of ocean liners, warships, merchantmen and the smaller fry of what was still Europe's busiest shipping pool. Ever and again, from a slipway on the broad river bend, some fresh ungarnished hull would slide backward, and ride there, free of drag-chains, while tug whoops mingled with cheers from the bank.

Liverpool was docks and ships and as such indistinguishable in Britain's northern industrial fogs but for one additional, intermittent product. Liverpool was where music-hall comedians, like Tommy Handley, Arthur Askey and Robb Wilton, came from. Some elixir in a population mixed from Welsh and Irish, and also Lascar and Chinese, and uttered in the strange glottal dialect that simultaneously seems to raise derisive eyebrows, had always possessed the power to make the rest of the country laugh.

Liverpool 'comics' were always preferred by the London theatrical agents. But there was a proviso. It was better for them to lose their Liverpool accents, and omit all references to the city of their origin. No one in London cared about a place so far to the north-west, so grey and sooty and old-fashioned and, above all, so utterly without glamour as Liverpool.

•

Woolton, where John grew up, is a suburb six miles to the south-east, but further in spirit, from the Liverpool of docks and Chinatown and pub signs pasted round every street corner. From Lime Street, you drive uphill, past the grand old Adelphi Hotel, past the smaller backstreet hotels with no pretence at grandeur, past the Baptist temples and Irish meeting halls, and grassed-over bomb sites, turned into eternal temporary car parks, lapping against some isolated little waterworks or church. Eventually you come to a traffic roundabout known by the name of its smallest tributary, Penny Lane. Woolton lies beyond, in wide dual carriageways with grass verges, and mock Tudor villas whose gardens adjoin parks, country clubs and golf courses.

Woolton, in fact, is such a respectable, desirable and featureless suburb as grows up close to any British industrial city. Until 1963, it had only one claim on history. A lord of the same name was Britain's wartime Minister of Food and inventor of the 'Woolton Pie', which boasted total, if unappetising, nourishment for only one old shilling a portion.

The country village which Woolton used to be is still distinguishable in narrow lanes winding up to its red sandstone Parish Church, St Peter's. In 1945, it was still more village-like. It even had its own small dairy farm, to which people would go for fresh milk ladled straight from the churn. The farm and dairy belonged to George Smith, the quiet kind-hearted man whom high-spirited Mimi Stanley had married.

George and Mimi lived at 'Mendips', a semi-detached house in Menlove Avenue, round the corner from the dairy, almost opposite Allerton golf course. Built in 1933, it was a semi-detached villa designed for the aspirational lower middle class, with mock Tudor half-timbering, windows inset with Art Nouveau stained glass and the tiny living-room beside the kitchen grandly described as a 'morning room'. In the years before Mimi and George brought their little nephew, John Lennon, to live here, the house had even had live-in domestics. The untold million future acolytes of the self-styled 'working-class hero' never dreamed he actually grew up in a house with a morning room, Spode and Royal Worcester plates displayed on ledges around its quasi-baronial front hall, and servants' bells in its kitchen.

Julia had settled only a short bus journey away, at Spring Wood. Her man friend, John Dykins, was a waiter in a Liverpool hotel, with children of his own. Every afternoon, she came across to her sister's to see John. He called her 'Mummy'; his aunt he called plain 'Mimi'. 'John said to me once when he was little, "Why don't I call *you* Mummy?" I said, "Well – you couldn't very well have *two* Mummies, could you?" He accepted that.'

From the moment Julia gave him to her, Mimi devoted her life to John. 'Never a day passed when I wasn't with him – just that one time a year when he went up to Scotland to stay with his cousins. And at night, for 10 years, I never crossed the threshold of that house. As I came downstairs, I'd always leave the light on on the landing outside his room. This little voice would come after me, "Mimi! Don't waste light."

'I brought him up strictly. No sweets – just one barley sugar at night – and no sitting around in picturedomes. He never wanted it. He'd play for hours in the garden in summer, in his little swimming trunks. I'd go to the butcher's for pheasants' feathers and I'd make him up like an Indian with gravy browning, and put lipstick for warpaint on his cheeks. And when he said his friends were dead, they *were* dead.

'He never had a day's illness. Only chickenpox. "Chicken pots", he called it. And he loved his Uncle George. I felt quite left out of that. They'd go off together, just leaving me a bar of chocolate and a note saying: "Have a happy day."'

Mimi, for all her briskness, liked nothing better than laughter. Julia had always known how to get her going so that she threw her head back and guffawed, slapping her knee. 'I was very slim in those days. Julia would come in in the afternoon and dance up to me, singing "O dem bones, dem bones—" She'd only got to lift her eyebrow and I'd be off.

'John was the same. I'd be battling with him. I'd send him out of the room, then I'd flop down exhausted in the big armchair next to the morning-room window. He'd crawl round on the path and pull faces at me through the window. He'd come at me like a monster, going "Woooo!" He could get me off just the same way Julia could.'

When Mimi took charge of John she sent him to Dovedale Primary School, near Penny Lane. She took him there each morning, and each afternoon met him at the bus stop, near Penny Lane roundabout. In his class at Dovedale Primary was a boy named Peter Harrison whose younger brother George sometimes came with their mother to meet the three-thirty outpouring from school.

John did well at Dovedale, learning to read and write with precocious speed. He liked sport, especially running and swimming, but was inept at football. The discovery was made that he had chronically poor eyesight. His teachers thought that must be what made his English compositions so unusual. He changed almost every word into another one like it. Instead of 'funds', he would write 'funs'. He loved reading, especially Richmal Crompton's Just William stories about a lawless eleven-year-old. He loved writing and drawing and crayoning. He could amuse himself for hours with books or pencils in the tiny bedroom above the front door that had little space for anything but its red-quilted single bed, undersized wardrobe and one-bar electric fire. Each Christmas, when Mimi took him to the pantomime at the Liverpool Empire, he would endlessly re-tell the experience in stories, poems and drawings. At the age of seven, he began writing books of his own. One of them was called *Sport and Speed*

Illustrated; it had cartoons and drawings and a serial story ending: 'If you liked this, come again next week. It'll be even better.'

At about the same age, while playing on a rubbish tip, John encountered another seven-year-old with a pale pink and white face and fuzzy blond hair. The boy's name was Peter Shotton; his mother kept a small needlewoman's and grocery shop in Woolton village. The encounter quickly turned to combat. 'I'd found out his name was Winston,' Shotton says. 'I was calling out to him, "Winnie, Winnie . . ." He got me down on the ground with his knees on my shoulders. I said: "OK, go ahead and hit me. Get it over with." But he couldn't. He said: "OK, I'll let you off. Just don't call me that name again." I walked away, then I turned round and shouted, "Winnie, Winnie." He was so angry, he couldn't speak. Then I saw his face break into a smile.'

Pete Shotton and John Lennon became inseparable friends. Pete lived in Vale Road, just round the corner from Menlove Avenue. The addition of another Vale Road boy, a mutual acquaintance, named Nigel Walley, added a new dimension. Three of them made enough for a gang.

Nigel went to school with Pete Shotton in Mosspits Lane. He also sang in the choir with John at St Peter's, Woolton. He had often sat in the choirstalls in his white surplice, wriggling with laughter at things which the white-surpliced John dared to do. 'He'd steal the Harvest Festival fruit. And every time the Rector, Old Pricey, climbed into the pulpit, John used to say, "He's getting on his drums now."'

The gang grew to four with the arrival of another Dovedale boy, Ivan Vaughan. Thus constituted, it embarked on its career as the terror of Woolton. One of the earliest games was to climb a tree over the busy main road and dangle a leg down in front of an approaching double-decker bus, then yank it back to safety in the nick of time. If your foot scraped the bus roof, that counted as extra points.

'John was always the leader,' Nigel Walley says. 'He was always the one to dare you. He never cared what he said or did. He'd think nothing of putting a brick through the glass in a street lamp. He'd dare us to go with him and play on the Allerton golf course, trying to hit golf balls across Menlove Avenue. Once, the police came and chased us off. We'd pick up these great clods of earth to chuck at the trains when they went into the tunnel at Garston. Something else was putting stuff on the tram rails to try to derail the trams.

'Shoplifting was another thing. We'd go into a sweetshop run by this little old lady. John'd point to things he said he wanted on the top shelf and, all the time, he'd be filling his pockets from the counter. He did the same at a shop that sold Dinky cars, in Woolton – opposite the Baths. He'd put a tractor or a little car in his pocket while the bloke was looking the other way. We went back to that same shop later on but, this time, John hadn't got his glasses on. He couldn't understand why his fingers couldn't get at the Dinky cars. He couldn't see that the bloke had covered them over with a sheet of glass.

'We'd go to all the garden fêtes in the summer, get under tents and pinch stuff. People would come in, looking for their trays of cakes and buns that we'd eaten. We went to one fête organised by the nuns, and somehow John got hold of this robe and dressed himself up as a monk. He was sitting with some other monks on a bench, talking in all these funny words while we were rolling about under the tent, in tucks.

'Pete was a bit of a bully, always picking on me, so John used to look after me. Whatever he told me to do, I'd do it. "Walloggs", he used to call me.'

Aunt Mimi approved of Nigel Walley. His father was a police sergeant. Mimi thought him a wholesome influence.

•

At the age of 12, John left Dovedale Primary and started at Quarry Bank Grammar School, in Harthill Road, a mile or so from Menlove Avenue. Mimi, distrusting the school outfitter, got his Uncle George's tailor to make his new black blazer with its red and gold stag's head badge and motto, *Ex Hoc Metallo Virtutem* (From This Rough Metal We Forge Virtue). On his Raleigh 'Lenton' bicycle, he would toil up the long hill to school, past old sandstone quarries, long emptied and overgrown. Woolton sandstone built the Anglican cathedral, as well as the many mock-Elizabethan mansions in which Liverpool merchants indulged themselves at the height of their Victorian prosperity.

It was in a local timber baron's Tudoresque 'folly' that Quarry Bank Grammar School was founded in 1922. Despite its newness it was, by the time John arrived in 1952, as steeped in academic lore as any of Liverpool's ancient grammar schools. There was a house system; there were masters in gowns; there were prefects and canings. In later years, after it had produced two Labour Cabinet Ministers – William Rodgers and Peter Shore – Quarry Bank came to be nicknamed 'The Eton of the Labour Party'.

John's Dovedale friend, Ivan Vaughan, had gone on to Liverpool Institute High School. Nigel Walley was now at the Bluecoat School near Penny Lane. Pete Shotton was the only one of the Woolton gang who accompanied him to Quarry Bank. 'We went through it together like Siamese twins,' Pete says. 'We started in our first year at the top and gradually sank together into the sub-basement.

'I remember the first time we both went to be caned. I was really terrified. John wasn't – or if he was, he didn't show it. We were both waiting outside the headmaster's study. John started telling me the cane would be kept in a special case, with a velvet lining and jewels all round it. I was in tucks, even though I was so scared.

'John went in first for the cane. I could hear it – swipe, swipe. Then he came out. What I didn't realise was that there was a little vestibule you had to go through before you got into the head's study. John came out through this little vestibule – though I didn't know it – crawling on all fours and groaning. I was laughing so much when I went in that I got it even worse than he had.'

In John's first year at Quarry Bank, Mimi's husband, Uncle George, died suddenly after a haemorrhage. It was a shock to the whole family to lose the quiet, hard-working dairy farmer who got up every morning without complaint to do the milking and whose only unusual demand of Mimi was his two breakfasts a day. Uncle George had been John's ally when he was in disgrace, smuggling buns upstairs to him behind Mimi's back. Uncle George had bought him the mouth organ John carried in his blazer pocket and tinkered on for hours when he ought to have been doing homework.

Mimi was left alone to cope with a boy whose will was now almost the equal of hers and who, by his thirteenth birthday, seemed to glory in idleness and lawlessness and wasting the opportunities he had been given. From his first moderately virtuous year at Quarry Bank, he gravitated, in Pete Shotton's company, to the bottom of the 'C' stream, and made no attempt to rise again thereafter. The two were perpetually in detention or being sent to the headmaster's study for a caning. Frequently, their exploits were serious enough to be reported to their homes. 'I used to dread the phone going at ten in the morning,' Mimi said. 'A voice would come on, "Hello, Mrs Smith. This is the secretary at Quarry Bank . . ." "Oh Lord." I'd think. "What's he done now?"'

'It was mostly skiving,' Pete Shotton says. 'Not doing the things the others did. We were like wanted men. We were always on the run.'

Rod Davis, a studious boy in the 'A' stream, had watched John and Pete's double act since they were seven-year-olds sitting in a ring at St Peter's Sunday School and John had managed to put a piece of chewing gum into the teacher's hand so that all her fingers stuck together. 'I'd always known him and Pete as the school thugs, dragging on a cigarette they'd got behind their backs, or running into Marks and Spencers and shouting "Woolworths!"'

'John used to turn Religious Knowledge into chaos,' Pete Shotton says. 'One day he cut out all the shiny white cardboard bits from a lot of Weetabix packets and made dog collars for the whole class. When the teacher, McDermott, came in, he was so angry, he couldn't speak. Then he had to start laughing. He made us wear them for the rest of the class.'

The school punishment book records for what diversity of crime J. Lennon and P. Shotton were beaten: 'failing to report to school office'; 'insolence'; 'throwing blackboard duster out of window'; 'cutting class and going awol'; 'gambling on school field during house match'.

'We were in detention once, clearing up the sports field,' Pete Shotton says. 'I found this big envelope full of dinner tickets. You used to pay a shilling a day for a ticket to have your school dinner. These were the used ones that somebody had accidentally dropped. When John and I counted them, we found we'd got the whole school's dinner tickets – about 1,500 of them. And they were worth a shilling each. We sold them off for sixpence each. We were rich. We even gave up shoplifting while that was going on.'

Even John's talent for writing and drawing failed to earn him any good marks or exam distinctions. Only in the last 40 minutes of every day, in the unsupervised 'prep' period, would he show what ability he was relentlessly wasting. He would fill old exercise books and scraps of paper with his cartoons and word play and verse. His nonsense sagas, 'The Land of the Lunapots', and 'Tales of Hermit Fred', were passed to Pete Shotton first, then enjoyed wide under-the-desk circulation. 'He'd do all these caricatures of the masters,' Pete says. 'We'd stick them on bits of cereal packets and make a stall at the school fête where people could throw darts at them. We handed in more money than any other stall – and we still had five times as much in our pockets.'

Often, they would cut school altogether. They would go on the bus to Spring Wood to see Julia, John's mother – now married to the nervous waiter the boys called 'Twitchy', and with a young son of her own. 'Julia didn't mind if we'd sagged off school,' Pete Shotton says. 'She used to wear these old woollen knickers on her head while she did the housework. She'd open the door to us with the knicker legs hanging down her back. She didn't care. She was just like John.'

John, as he grew older, grew more and more fascinated by this pretty auburn-haired woman, so much more like an elder sister than a mother. For Julia did not echo the dire warnings given by Aunt Mimi and Quarry Bank. Julia encouraged him to live for the present, as she did, and for laughter and practical jokes. 'She'd do these tricks just to make us laugh,' Pete says. 'She'd put on a pair of glasses with no glass in the frames. She'd stand talking to a neighbour and suddenly stick her finger through where the lens ought to have been, and rub her eye.'

Julia thought as John and Pete did, and said the things they wanted to hear. She told them not to worry about school or homework or what their lives might have in store.

•

Jim McCartney was no stranger to female admiration. During the 1920s he led the Jim Mac Jazz Band, dapperly outfitted in dinner jackets, paper shirt fronts and detachable cuffs which could be bought then for a penny per dozen. A photograph taken at the time shows a group of girls in silver shoes and stockings, their hair pertly fringed and bobbed, reclining with formal abandon on a dance floor around the Jim Mac drum kit. Among them sits the bandleader with his formal 'dicky-bow', close-cropped hair and his so familiar-looking big brown eyes.

Jim was a cotton salesman working for Hannay's of Chapel Street, Liverpool, an old-established firm of cotton brokers and purveyors to the Manchester mills. His position, for a working-class boy, was a good one; he had risen to it by neatness, diligence and a genuine flair for selling, though he lacked the ruthlessness which might have taken him higher. He had taught himself to play the piano by ear, as any young man did who wished for social grace. The Jim Mac Jazz Band performed at socials and works dances, occasionally even in cinemas. Their biggest engagement was providing incidental music for a silent Hollywood epic, *The Queen of Sheba.* When a chariot race began on the screen, Jim Mac and the boys played 'Thanks for the Buggy Ride'. During the Queen of Sheba's death scene, they played 'Horsy, Keep Your Tail Up'.

Perhaps there were too many of those girls in silver shoes and stockings around the drum kit. At all events, Jim McCartney went through his thirties as a bachelor, working at the Cotton Exchange, playing his spare-time dance music, content for his family to be the hospitable reflection of his married sisters, Millie and Jin.

At the very point where he seemed resigned to bachelorhood, and the impending war seemed to confirm it, Jim McCartney proposed marriage to Mary Mohin. She, like Jim, was of the Liverpool Irish, a slender and gently spoken woman employed by Liverpool Corporation as a district health visitor. Herself in her early thirties, Mary could override the faint objection that Jim did not share her membership of the Catholic Church. They were married in 1941, shortly before Jim's fortieth birthday.

Exempted from military service by partial deafness, he had been transferred from Hannay's to munitions work with Napier's, the firm which produced the Sabre aircraft engine. On 18 June 1942, while Jim was fire watching, Mary gave birth to a son in Walton General Hospital. She had worked there once as nursing sister in charge of the maternity ward, and so received the luxury of a private room. The baby was perfect, with a placid, impish smile and eyes just like his father's. Such was Mary's love for Jim that the more famous saint's name did not receive precedence. The baby was christened James Paul.

His first home was furnished rooms in Anfield, not far from the mass graves where the dead from the dockland blitz had been buried. Jim, no longer needed for munitions work, had left Napier's and become an inspector in the Corporation's Cleansing Department. His job was to follow the dustmen, seeing that they did not skimp their round. The work was badly paid and, to supplement Jim's earnings, Mary returned to her former job as a health visitor. After her second son, Michael, was born in 1944, she took up full-time midwifery.

The process had already begun which was to gouge out the old, shabby, vibrant heart of Liverpool, flattening its bombed streets and scattering their inhabitants wide across an arid suburban plain. Communities whom Hitler could not displace were now induced, by the hundred thousand, to migrate to new estates, dumped down amid transplanted industry, and isolated by walls of dingy open air.

Mary McCartney became a domiciliary midwife on one of the several estates built around Speke's new industrial estates. The rent-free council house in Western Avenue helped to reduce the strain on Jim's tiny wage from the Corporation. The disadvantage was that Mary had to be available 24 hours a day. Her kindness and patience became a legend among people already suspecting they may have been forgotten by the authorities. Little gifts of plaster ornaments or somebody's sugar ration were always being brought to the McCartneys' back door, or left shyly outside on the step.

Her own children, despite the constant pressure, received immaculate care. Jim, who had been somewhat unprepared for fatherhood – and somewhat dismayed by Paul's redness as a newborn baby – could only marvel at the ingenuity with which Mary found time, and money enough, to dress the boys beautifully and feed them with imaginative good sense. Her special concern was that they should speak well, not in broad Liverpool like other children on the estate.

Paul came to consciousness in an atmosphere of worship. His aunts and the neighbours loved him for his chubbiness, his large eyes and amiable, undespotic disposition. The arrival of a little brother, and potential rival, showed him the importance of maintaining popularity. He soon discovered that he possessed charm, and learned early how to put it to use. Though the boys did things together, and were together in normal boyish scrapes, it would invariably be Michael, the more impetuous and turbulent one, who received punishment. Jim McCartney, for all his mildness, was of the generation which believed in hitting children. Michael remembers being chastised by Jim while Paul, who had escaped, stood by, shouting, 'Tell him you didn't do it and he'll stop.' Where Michael would shout and cry, Paul, if his father hit him, showed no emotion. Later, he would go into his parents' bedroom and tear their lace curtains imperceptibly at the bottom.

Though Mary was a Catholic, she preferred to entrust the boys' education to Protestant schools. Paul started in Speke, at Stockton Road Primary. Michael joined him there and, when the classes became overcrowded, both were transferred to Joseph Williams Primary, Gateacre. Here the same contrast was revealed between them. Paul was quiet and law-abiding, and Michael, hotly argumentative. Where Michael found it difficult to absorb learning, Paul came top in almost every lesson with ease. He was especially good at English composition and Art. His handwriting received praise for its clear regularity.

Money remained a difficulty, though the boys never knew it. Jim McCartney had left his job with the Corporation and gone back to cotton selling. This, however, was not the secure trade it had been in prewar days with Hannay's. After a hard week's travelling, Jim would be lucky to find £6 in his wage packet. Mary took a second domiciliary job on the Speke estate, necessitating a move from Western Avenue to another council house, in Ardwick Road. Her husband, worried at the long hours she worked, was relieved when she decided to give up midwifery and return to regular nursing. She became a school nurse, making rounds with school doctors in the Walton and Allerton district.

Bella Johnson met Mary at the central clinic from which both of them worked. A round, little, jolly woman, Bella, too, was finding it difficult to make ends meet. She had been widowed at the age of 36, with two small daughters to educate. This she had done so spectacularly well that one of them, Olive, now worked for the Law Society in Liverpool. The Law Society's offices were only a street away from the Cotton Exchange. On her way to work, Olive used to pass the time of day with Jim McCartney, not knowing that his wife and her mother were colleagues and friends.

Mrs Johnson and Olive got to know the McCartneys well. Bella remembered a family contented and normal, suffused by Mary's gentleness and strength. 'She was a beautiful person: it came from something deep inside her,' Olive says. 'Jim adored her. I remember how he'd sometimes tell us a story he'd picked up from the businessmen at the Cotton Exchange. If it was a bit off-colour, Mary used to look at him and say, "*Husband!*"'

Olive had a small car in which they would all go on weekend trips into the Cheshire countryside. She became a big sister to Paul and Michael, joining in their games, rowing them in a skiff across the lake at

Wilmslow. 'Mary always made us a special treat at tea time,' Mrs Johnson said. 'I'll never forget them. Apple sandwiches with sugar.'

On Coronation Day, 1953, the Johnsons and McCartneys celebrated together at Ardwick Road. The boys had received their commemorative mugs and spoons, and Paul, in addition, had won a book as a Coronation essay prize. They watched, as people did all over Britain in one another's front parlours, the ceremonial flickering over a tiny, bluish television screen.

Michael McCartney sat at his mother's feet, as ever. 'He was the one you always felt you wanted to love and protect,' Olive says. 'With Paul, you loved him but you knew you'd never have to protect him.'

•

Paul passed the Eleven Plus examination without difficulty, and with sufficient distinction to receive a place at Liverpool Institute, the city's oldest grammar school. The honour entailed a long bus journey each day from Speke into Liverpool and up, behind the Anglican Cathedral, to Mount Street, where the Institute's square portico jutted out into steeply plunging pavement. Founded in the 1830s as a Mechanics Institute for deserving artisans, the building had been later divided to form the grammar school and the College of Art. Behind the heavy wrought-iron gates was an interior unchanged since Victorian times, save that the gas lamps, over each classroom door, were no longer lit on winter afternoons. *Non nobis solum*, the school motto runs, *sed toti mundo nati*: 'Not for ourselves only but for the good of all the world.'

Among hundreds of boys, swarming through the green-distempered school thoroughfares, Paul McCartney was not conspicuous, nor wished to be. His black blazer was neat and his hair slicked flat with Brylcreem; he belonged to that co-operative species from which are recruited the collectors of exercise books and operators of window-poles; he was, more or less permanently, head boy in his form. With his classmates he was popular, if a little reserved. They called him, not by his surname or a nickname – just Paul. His close friend Ivan Vaughan was an exception to this attitude of noticeable deference.

He had been put into the 'A' stream, tending as he moved higher to specialise in history and languages. He found most lessons easy, and could get high marks even in Latin if he bothered to apply his mind. He was nonchalant about homework, an embarrassing obligation in a council estate where other boys could do what they pleased at night. On the morning bus into Liverpool, he could churn out an essay still impressive enough to receive commendation from his English master, 'Dusty' Durband. Mr Durband, even so, was aware of the extent to which Paul relied on facility and bluff to see him through. It sometimes failed him, as when he had been given the task of preparing a talk about the Bodley Head edition of Stephen Leacock's works. Paul delivered an impromptu stream of nonsense about the Bodley Head's Elizabethan logo.

He knew what he wanted and, even then, would be satisfied with nothing less. When the Institute put on Shaw's *St Joan* as its end-of-term play, Paul auditioned keenly for the part of Warwick. He did not get it, and had to be content with the minor role of an Inquisitor in the trial scene. The disappointment made him unusually fractious: Mr Durband, the play's producer, remembers shouting in exasperation at the medievally hooded figure which persisted in disrupting rehearsals.

In 1955, when Paul was 13, the McCartneys left Speke and its pallid factory smog. Jim had managed to get a council house in Allerton, one of Liverpool's nearer and better suburbs. It was a definite step up for the family to move into 20 Forthlin Road, a double row of semi-detached houses small and neat enough to pass for privately-owned villas. Mimi Smith's home in Woolton was only a mile or so away, if you cut across the golf course.

For some time, Mary had been troubled by a slight pain in her breast. She did not like to trouble the doctor for fear he would dismiss it as nurse's hypochondria. As she was now in her mid-forties, she and Jim philosophically concluded that 'the Change' must be to blame for the small lump that had appeared. The pain was not great but would not seem to go away.

Paul and Michael were camping with the Boy Scouts that summer. The weather was very wet and cold, and Mary told Bella Johnson, her friend at the school clinic, that she was worried about the boys under canvas. So one afternoon, Olive took Mary and Jim in her car to visit them. On the way home, Mary was in such pain that she had to lie down on the back seat.

'When she got home, she went straight to bed,' Olive says. 'I went up later and found her crying. "Oh, Olive," she said to me, "I don't want to leave the boys *just* yet."'

After a few days' rest, she felt so much better, she began to think that, after all, the trouble was simply over-work. Then the pain returned, so severely that, at last, she consulted a specialist. He sent her at once into hospital – not Walton General but the old city 'Northern', so that he could keep a close eye on her. Breast cancer was diagnosed. She underwent an operation for mastectomy, which was not carried out: the cancer had already spread too far. A few hours later, Bella and Olive Johnson received the news that Mary had died.

Jim McCartney's predicament was one calculated to crush a younger as well as wealthier man. At the age of 53, he found himself bereft of a loving, capable wife and faced with the task of caring for two adolescent boys, all on a wage which still had need of the extra Mary had earned. That, indeed, was the first thing 14-year-old Paul blurted out in the shock of his mother's loss. 'What are we going to do without her money?'

Mary was buried as a Catholic – the wish she had expressed to Jim on her deathbed. Paul and Michael were taken to stay with their Auntie Jin at Huyton, to spare them the funeral and the sight of their father's devastation. Mrs Johnson and Olive moved in to Forthlin Road to be with Jim and to prepare him for the boys' return. Their task, at first, seemed hopeless. All he wanted, he kept saying, was to be with Mary.

2

'Quarry Men, strong before our birth'

1956 was a worrying year for English parents. It seemed that something had gone seriously wrong with the Victorian age. The generation born after 1941, despite exterior differences, lived by much the same rules and values as their parents and their grandparents. It boiled down to a single phrase, the base of Victorianism – they 'had respect'. They had respect for their elders and their betters. They had respect for their country with its Empire, now Commonwealth; its God-given right to be called 'Great' Britain. Having just survived a World War, they had respect for politicians and soldiers. They had respect also for clergymen, policemen, schoolteachers and the Queen. And suddenly, in 1956, they realised that their children did not have respect for them.

The year was one of unparalleled national humiliation. It was the year that the British engaged with France in a ludicrous plan to invade Egypt and were foiled by, of all people, the Egyptians. After Suez, the world would never again function at the behest of British gunboats. We had become overnight a 'second-class power', barely noticed in the new, harsh glare of America and Russia's nuclear cohabitation.

The British language, meanwhile, had been invaded by certain bewildering new words. Of these, the most bewildering was 'teenager'. In Britain before 1956, there were no such things as teenagers. There were only children and grown-ups. Transition took place at 16 when boys put on tweed jackets like their fathers' and girls turned into matrons with 'twinsets' and 'perms'. Conscription, or 'National Service', for two years, completed the male maturing process. The only remission was given to university students, a minority, still largely 'upper class', and thus permitted to behave like hooligans on Boat Race night and other fixed ceremonial occasions.

But there now stalked the streets of Britain young men in clothes as outlandish as they were sinister. The costume, of velvet-trimmed drape jackets, frilled shirts and narrow trousers, was inspired partly by Edwardian fashion – hence the name 'Teddy Boy' – and partly by gunslingers and riverboat gamblers in Hollywood movies. Amid the drab uniformity of postwar Britain, they seemed utterly freakish. Their hair, in a land still Army-cropped, was scarcely believable. A greasy cockade flopped over the forehead, swept back past the ears with constant combing to form two flaps like the posterior of a duck. Their socks were luminous pink or orange. Their shoes had soles three inches thick. They were believed to carry weapons such as flick-knives, razors and bicycle chains. Their other, scarcely less threatening predilection, was for 'coffee bars' and 'rock and roll'.

Coffee bars, to the British of 1956, might just as well have been opium dens. They had sprung up all at once out of the country's Italian population, and also the sudden Fifties' craze for 'contemporary' design. They were dark and filled with basket chairs and foliage; they had names like 'La Lanterna' or 'La Fiesta'; they dispensed, from huge silver machines, a frothy fluid barely recognisable as the stuff which the British were accustomed to boil with milk in saucepans. They were the haunt of Teddy Boys and Teddy Girls, and of jukeboxes. Their jukeboxes united the Teddy-Boy contagion with that of rock and roll.

Rock and roll, as every sensible Briton knew, was American madness such as one saw as a novelty item at the end of the weekly cinema newsreel. Sometimes it was pole-squatting, sometimes dance marathons, sometimes pie-eating contests. Now it was a young singer who did not sing but merely writhed about, pretending to play a guitar, and yet who aroused American female audiences to transports of ecstasy greater even than had Valentino, the screen lover, or Frank Sinatra, the crooner. His songs, or lack of them, and his 'suggestive movements', had scandalised America. When he appeared on American television, he was shown only from the waist up. His name was Elvis Presley. That, too, the British thought, could only happen in America.

Yet the madness seemed to be drifting this way. In 1955, a song called 'Rock Around the Clock' had caused riots in several British cinemas during shows of a film called *The Blackboard Jungle* – significantly, a study of juvenile crime. The singer, Bill Haley, and his 'group', the Comets, had afterwards visited Britain, arriving in London by boat train amid mob scenes unequalled since VE Night or the Coronation.

That had seemed to be a freak occurrence. The country settled back again to its former dull diet of Anglicised American dance-band music – of 'Light Orchestras', crooners named Dennis Lotis and Dickie Valentine, and 'novelty' songs about Italy or little Dutch dolls. Here, at least, there was a powerful guardian of morality and taste. The British Broadcasting Corporation, with its monopoly of all radio, continued to ensure that nothing was played save that in its own image and of its own cold custard consistency.

In February 1956, an Elvis Presley record called 'Heartbreak Hotel' was released in Britain, on the hitherto respectable HMV label. Within days, it had smashed through the crooners and Light Orchestras and little Dutch dolls to first place in the Top Twenty records chart. It remained there for 18 weeks. Another by the same singer followed it, bearing the ludicrous title 'Blue Suède Shoes'; then another, even surpassing that in ludicrousness, called 'Houn' Dog'.

Britain's parents listened, so far as they were able, to the lyric, so far as it could be understood. The vocalist was exhorting some bystander, endlessly and incoherently, not to tread on his blue suède shoes. He was accusing the same bystander, with equal, mumbling persistence, of being a 'houn' dog'. A few people over 20 enjoyed the music, and even recognised it for what it was: an adaptation of American blues, sharing the same honourable origins as jazz. Presley was simply applying blues intonation and phrasing to songs in the white cowboy, or country and western, idiom. He was, in other words, a white man who sang like a black man. The charges of obscenity were ironic. All Presley's blues songs had been purged of their sexual and social content for the white audience's sensitive ears.

To Britain, as to America, the idea that a white man could sing like a black man was intrinsically lewd. It confirmed the malignant power of rock and roll music to incite young people, as jungle drums incited savages, to their newly evidenced violence, promiscuity, disobedience and disrespect. To Britain, as to America, there was only one consolation. A thing so grotesque as Elvis Presley could not possibly last. They said of rock and roll what was said in 1914, when the Great War started. In six months, it would all be over.

•

The headmaster of Quarry Bank Grammar School, Liverpool, considered John Lennon and Peter Shotton to be the worst Teddy Boys among the pupils in his charge. Detentions, canings, even temporary expulsion seemed to have no effect on the insolent-faced, bespectacled boy and his fuzzy-haired companion, whose clothes conformed less and less to school regulation, and who now overtly gloried in their power to cause disturbance. A typical Lennon–Shotton incident occurred when the whole school went into Liverpool to see the film *Henry V* at the Philharmonic Hall. By ill luck, this had been preceded by a Donald Duck cartoon. One did not have to guess from whom, in the tittering auditorium, had come those cries of, 'There he is! There's old King Henry!'

For John, as for most 15-year-olds, rock and roll began as a curiosity manifest among slightly older boys. Pete Shotton and he, on their truant-playing days, would often hang around Liverpool, gaping at the full-dress Teddy Boys – mostly seamen on leave from the big ships – whose disregard for authority was on a scale far more gorgeous than theirs. When *Rock around the Clock*, the first Bill Haley film, reached Liverpool, John went to see it but, to his disappointment, no riot happened. There was just this fat man in a tartan jacket with a kiss curl on his forehead, and saxophones and double basses just like any dance band.

Then, at the beginning of 1956, a friend played him 'Heartbreak Hotel'. 'From then on,' his Aunt Mimi said, 'I never got a minute's peace. It was Elvis Presley, Elvis Presley, Elvis Presley. In the end I said, "Elvis Presley's all very well, John, but I don't want him for breakfast, dinner *and* tea."'

Mimi had been struggling for months to stop her charge from turning into a Teddy Boy. She still sent John to school in blazers that were tailor-made, and saw no reason why these should not do for all social occasions. 'Drainpipe' trousers and drape jackets were, as Mimi constantly affirmed, no kind of dress for a boy who went to Quarry Bank and whose grandfather had been a deep-sea pilot, one of the shipping world's white-collar dandies.

The trouble was that John now spent more and more time out of Mimi's sight with her sister, Julia, his real mother. Julia, as Mimi knew, was too easy-going to worry what John wore. Julia bought him coloured shirts and gave him money to have school trousers 'taken in'. He would leave Menlove Avenue a nice Quarry Bank schoolboy and then, at Julia's, turn into a Teddy Boy as bad as any to be seen around the docks.

The stunning music that went with the clothes was available only with equal deviousness. John listened to it, as thousands did, under the bedclothes, late at night. Since the BBC would not broadcast rock and roll, the only source was Radio Luxembourg, a commercial station, beamed from the Continent with an English service after 8 p.m. The Elvis records came through, fading and blurred with static, like coded messages to an occupied country. Now there were other names and other songs that split open the consciousness with disbelieving joy. There was Little Richard's 'Tutti Frutti'; Bill Haley's 'Razzle Dazzle'; Freddy Bell and the Bellboys' 'Giddy-up-a-Ding-Dong'. The sound came from beyond comprehension; it played, then died out again. You could not catch it, nor sing it nor write it down.

Then, late one night over the hidden radios, a new message came. A banjo-player with the Chris Barber Jazz Band had formed his own small group to record 'Rock Island Line', an American folk song dating back to the Depression or earlier. The number was played in what jazz audiences knew already as 'skiffle', a style originating in the poor Southern states where people would hold 'rent parties' to stave off the landlord, playing music on kazoos, tin cans and other impromptu instruments. The banjoist, Tony – or 'Lonnie' – Donegan, sang in a piercing pseudo-blues wail, set about by elementary rhythm of which the main component was an ordinary kitchen washboard, scraped and tapped by thimble-capped fingers.

'Rock Island Line' began a national craze. For anyone could form a 'skiffle group' simply by stealing his mother's washboard and fixing a broom handle to a tea chest, then stringing it with wire to make a rudimentary double bass. The biggest craze of all, thanks to Elvis Presley, was for guitars. A straitlaced instrument long muffled in orchestral rhythm sections found itself suddenly the focus of all adolescent desire.

As boys pestered throughout Britain, so did John Lennon pester his Aunt Mimi to buy him a guitar. Each afternoon, when Julia paid her daily visit to Menlove Avenue, she, too, would be entreated to give – even lend – him the money. For Julia, as it happened, could play the banjo a little. John's father Freddy had taught her before disappearing overseas. And Freddy's father, so he had always said, used to play professionally in America with a group of Kentucky minstrels.

It was, however, not Julia but Mimi who eventually gave in. One Saturday morning, she put on her coat, checked the money in her purse and told John unceremoniously to come along.

Hessy's, the music shop in Whitechapel, central Liverpool, had an abundant stock of guitars. Frank Hessy, the owner, was sending a van regularly down to London to buy up every one to be found in the Soho street markets. Jim Gretty, his showroom manager, was selling roughly one guitar a minute from the hundreds festooned along the narrow shop wall. Jim was himself a guitarist, Western-style, and each week held a beginners' class in an upstairs room, chalking huge elementary chord-shapes on the wall.

It was Jim who sold Aunt Mimi the guitar which John said he wanted – a little Spanish model with steel strings and a label inside: 'Guaranteed not to split.' 'It cost me £17, I think,' Mimi said. 'I know I resented paying that, even though I'd been giving £12 each for his school blazers.'

From that moment, John was – as they say in Liverpool – 'lost'. Nigel Walley, calling round at 'Mendips', would find him up in his bedroom, oblivious to time or the first soreness of finger-ends split by the steel strings. 'He'd sit on his bed, just strumming,' Nigel says. 'Strumming the banjo chords Julia had shown him, and singing any words that came into his head. After about ten minutes, he'd have got a tune going.'

When Mimi could no longer stand the noise, or the foot beating time through her ceiling, she would order John out of the house, into the little front porch with its walls of Art Nouveau-patterned glass. 'He stood there leaning against the wall so long, I think he wore some of the brickwork away with his behind,' Mimi said. 'To me, it was just so much waste of time. I used to tell him so. "The guitar's all very well, John," I told him, "but you'll never make a *living* out of it."'

•

The first skiffle group he formed had only two members: himself on guitar and his crony Pete Shotton on kitchen washboard, crashing its glass ridges with thimble-capped fingers as the two of them tried out 'Cumberland Gap', 'Rock Island Line', 'Don't You Rock Me', 'Daddyo' and other skiffle classics. They named themselves, in rough-hewn skiffle style, the Quarry Men, after the sandstone quarries dotted around Woolton, and also in unwilling recognition of the school they both attended. The school song contains a reference to 'Quarry men strong before our birth' – a sentiment chorused lustily by John and Pete since it invariably figured in the final assembly of term.

The Quarry Men grew in the image of the gang which had formerly terrorised St Peter's Sunday School. Nigel Walley, now a Bluecoat Grammar School boy, and Ivan Vaughan, from the Liverpool Institute, divided the role of tea-chest bass-player amicably between them. Nigel's first Teddy-Boy clothes had been seized by his policeman father and thrown on the fire, so now he kept all his choicer garments down the road at Ivan's house. Each played bass with the Quarry Men when the other could not be bothered.

Quarry Bank Grammar School supplied a further recruit in Rod Davis, the earnest, bespectacled boy in 4A whose parents had just bought him a banjo. Another Woolton boy called Eric Griffiths came in on the strength of his new guitar, and because he claimed to know someone in King's Drive who owned a full-size set of drums. He took the others to meet Colin Hanton, an apprentice upholsterer who had just begun hire purchase payments on a £38 kit from Hessy's. Colin was two years older than the others but, as he was extremely small, it didn't matter. He was so small, he carried his birth certificate in his pocket, to prove to suspicious pub landlords that he was old enough to be served with beer.

In the group, as in the gang, John was the undisputed leader. His plaid shirt collar turned up, Teddy-Boy style, scowling like Elvis, he monopolised the foreground and the microphone, if there chanced to be one. 'He always used to beat hell out of his guitar,' Rod Davis says. 'He'd always be busting a string. Then he'd hand his guitar to me, take my banjo and carry on on that while I knelt down in the background and tried to fix the string.

'We did all the skiffle numbers that Lonnie Donegan recorded. Right from the start, John wanted to play rock and roll as well; I can remember him singing 'Blue Suède Shoes'. I'd got some Burl Ives records, so we did

'Worried Man Blues'. The only way you could learn the words was by listening to the radio – or buying the record. Records were six bob (30p) each, and none of us could afford that. So John always used to make up his own words to the songs that were popular. "Long, black train" was one of them. Another one went "Come, go with me, down to the Penitentiar-ee". They weren't any worse than the words you were supposed to sing.'

Skiffle contests were happening all over Liverpool, at ballrooms like the Rialto and the Locarno as a cheap way of filling the intervals. In 10 minutes between regular band spots three or four groups would hurry onstage and patter out their brief, invariable repertoire. The Quarry Men entered numerous such competitions, without notable success. One of the groups which continually beat them had as its chief attraction a midget named Nicky Cuff, who actually stood on the tea-chest bass while plucking at it.

Rod Davis's father had a big old Austin Hereford car in which he would occasionally chauffeur them to a skiffle contest. For most of the time, they travelled on buses, with tea chest, drum kit and all.

On Saturday afternoons they met to practise at Colin Hanton's house since his father, a Co-op shop manager, was guaranteed to be absent. Least practising of all was done at Mimi's, for the boys were somewhat in awe of her sharp tongue. Instead, they would go to Spring Wood to Julia's house, where they were always certain of a welcome and a laugh. Sometimes Julia would take Rod's banjo and demonstrate chords and little runs for John and Eric Griffiths to copy on their guitars. Both as a result learned to play in banjo style, leaving the two bass strings untuned. 'We used to practise standing in the bath at Julia's,' Rod Davis says. 'You could get more of an echo that way.'

In 1956, a new headmaster, William Edward Pobjoy, took charge of Quarry Bank Grammar School. At 35, he was young for such a post, and seemed younger with his boyish quiff of hair, and quiet, sardonic manner. Since the new head resorted neither to shouting nor sarcasm, the Quarry Bank heavies believed they were in for an easy time.

Among the information passed on by his predecessor to Mr Pobjoy was that John Lennon and Pete Shotton were the school's leading criminals. 'I was told there was even one master whom they not only used to terrorise, but whom Lennon had actually thumped. The poor man was so ashamed, he begged for the matter not to be reported.'

Mr Pobjoy, in his unobtrusive way, seems to have got the measure of Lennon and Shotton. The punishment book shows that John was caned by him only once. On another occasion, he and Pete were each suspended for a week.

Mr Pobjoy, they discovered with some astonishment, did not disapprove of skiffle. Nor did he try, on the strength of their other crimes, to stamp out the Quarry Men. He encouraged them to do anything more positive than smoking and slacking. Now when John entered the headmaster's office – the timber merchant's circular book room, with finely inlaid shelves, where he had been caned so many times – it would not be defiantly, as before, but to ask Mr Pobjoy, in all humility, if the Quarry Men could play for 10 minutes during the interval at the Sixth Form dance.

Another source of engagements was St Peter's parish church, Woolton. John had sung in its choir and disrupted its Sunday School, and he and Pete Shotton still belonged to its Youth Club, which met in the hall across the road for badminton and ping pong. The Quarry Men would play at the Youth Club 'hops', unpaid and glad of an opportunity to use a stage, and experience acoustics larger than those of John's mother's bathroom. When John broke a guitar string, he was reimbursed from church funds.

The group existed on the most casual basis, expanding and shrinking according to members available. Already there was some dissent between Rod Davis, who wished to play pure folk music, and John with his passion for Elvis. Pete Shotton was in it only for laughs, as he strove to make clear on all occasions. Little Colin Hanton, drumming irregularly, with his birth certificate in his top pocket, was more interested in pubs and pints of Black Velvet. Fights sometimes broke out between the musicians as they were performing, or with members of the audience whose criticisms were untactfully voiced. Fights broke out also if a spectator believed a Quarry Man to be ogling his girl friend, and clambered up among them to take revenge. John Lennon, for some reason, was always the principal target of such attacks, and was seldom averse to using his fists. 'Except if it was a *really* big bloke,' Nigel Walley says. 'Then John'd be as meek as a mouse. He'd always manage to talk his way out.'

'There were these two particular big Teds,' Rod Davis says. 'Rod and Willo their names were. They were the terror of Woolton. Rod and Willo were always looking for us and threatening to do us over. One night when we got off the bus – with all our gear, and the tea chest as well – Rod and Willo were there, waiting for us. They came chasing after us in their long coats, and we scattered. I know we left the tea chest behind on the pavement.'

The tea chest, which Colin's Mum had covered with wallpaper, remained a prominent feature of Woolton village for about a week afterwards. Sometimes it would be standing on the pavement; sometimes it would have migrated to the middle of the road.

The role of bass-player was transferred after this to Len Garry, another

Liverpool Institute boy whom Ivan Vaughan had introduced into the Lennon circle. Nigel Walley, whose consuming interest was golf not skiffle, assumed the duties of manager. With his sun-tanned complexion and shining white teeth, 'Walloggs' was amply suited to a diplomatic role. He took bookings for the Quarry Men and prevailed on local shopkeepers to put advertisements in their windows for no fee. He gave out formal visiting cards which read:

Country. Western. Rock 'n' Roll. Skiffle

The Quarry Men

OPEN FOR ENGAGEMENTS

Summer was just beginning when the Quarry Men played at an open-air party in Rosebery Street. A printer friend of Colin Hanton, who had designed the label on their bass drum, was helping to organise festivities for Rosebery Street's centenary. Though the engagement lay some distance from Woolton – and in a 'rough' district of Liverpool 8 – it was welcomed for the beer it promised, and the girls. The Quarry Men played standing on the tailboard of a lorry, which had to be moved because somebody was ill in the bedroom above. They played in the afternoon, then again in the evening, after strings of coloured bulbs had come alight on the hundred-year-old, back-to-back houses.

Colin Hanton had, as usual, preceded the engagement by going to a pub, producing his birth certificate, and downing several pints of Black Velvet. By himself at the end of the trailer, he played his drums in happy disregard for what John and Eric Griffiths were singing. Pete Shotton, cradling his washboard, wore a long 'Ted' jacket, draped against his bony frame. Rod Davis, on banjo, looked serious, as always.

'I suddenly heard these two blokes talking, next to the trailer,' Colin Hanton says. '"Let's get that Lennon," they said. I told John, and we all jumped off the back of the wagon, and ran into my mate's house: the printer. His mum sat us down and gave us all salad. These blokes that were after us stayed outside, shouting and thumping on the windows. I'd met a girl at the party, so I took my drums and stayed the night at her house. The other lads had to have a policeman to see them to the bus stop.'

•

In Paul McCartney's home, there had always been music. His father, Jim, never tired of recalling those happy prewar days when he had led his own little group, the Jim Mac Jazz Band. The McCartneys still had what all families once used to – a piano in the living-room. Jim had bought it long ago, when money was easier, from the North End Music Stores in Walton Road. Whenever he had a spare moment – which was not very often – he would move the piled-up newspapers off a chair, sit down at the piano, open its lid and play. He liked the old tunes, like 'Charmaine' and 'Ramona' and, his favourite of all, 'Stairway to Paradise'.

Jim's recovery had been marvellous to see. It was as if Mary's quiet competence had somehow been handed on to him. From the engulfing anguish following her death, he had suddenly clicked into a calm resolution that, for Paul's sake, and for young Michael's, home life must manage to continue.

Though housekeeping was mysterious to him, he applied himself doggedly to mastering its every department. He taught himself to cook and sew, to wash and to iron. Each day, after finishing work at the Cotton Exchange, he would hasten to the grocer's and the butcher's, then home to Allerton to tidy the house and cook Paul and Michael their evening meal. His sisters, Jin and Millie, each came in one full day a week to give the house a thorough cleaning. Bella Johnson and her daughter Olive also remained close at hand. When Paul and Michael came in from school, even if the house chanced to be empty, there would be notes left for them about where to find things, and sticks and paper laid for a fire in the grate.

Like Mimi Smith, Jim McCartney did his utmost to prevent there being a Teddy Boy in the family. The trouble was that, being at work all day, he had no alternative but to trust Paul and Michael to go to the barber's on their own and choose clothes for themselves with the money he gave them. In genuine perplexity he wondered how Paul, in particular, was able to return from the barber's seemingly with more hair than when he went, piled up in a cascading sheaf. There were battles, too, over trousers, which, Jim insisted, must not be 'drainies' but of conventional and respectable cut. Paul would bring home a satisfactory pair and show them to his father; then he would smuggle them out again to one of the tailors who specialised in 'tapering'. If Jim noticed anything, Paul was ready to swear that the 14-inch drainies clinging to his ankles were the same pair that his father had sanctioned.

In 1956, Lonnie Donegan and his Skiffle Group arrived in Liverpool to appear at the Empire theatre. Paul and some friends from the Institute waited outside during their lunch-hour, hoping to catch a glimpse of the star when he arrived for rehearsal. He was slightly delayed and, with great consideration, wrote out notes for the factory workers who had waited to see him, explaining to their foremen why they were late back on shift. This testament of how nice a star could be always stayed in Paul McCartney's mind.

It was after seeing Lonnie Donegan that Paul began clamouring for a guitar. He was lucky in having a father only too glad to encourage him to take up any musical instrument. Already in the house, along with Jim's piano, there was a battered trumpet which Paul had tried to learn, but had discarded on being told it would make a callous on his upper lip. For he had now begun to sing – or, at least, to sing in public – without embarrassment. He had always sung to himself in bed at night, not knowing that Jim and Olive Johnson were often listening to him from the bottom of the stairs.

Despite the money shortage, Jim brought home a £15 'cello guitar with violin holes, 'sunburst' colouring and a white scratch plate. Olive Johnson remembers how eagerly he set about trying to teach Paul to play by giving him chords from the living-room piano. 'He'd sit there for hours, shouting, "Come on, Paul. Now try this one!" '

Paul, strangely, made little initial progress. His left-hand fingers found it irksome to shape the patterns of black dots shown in the tuition book, and his right hand, somehow, lacked the bounce necessary for strumming. Then he discovered he could play far better if he fingered the fretboard with his right hand and strummed with his left. He took the guitar back to the shop and had its strings put on in reverse order. The white scratch plate, which carries the strummer's hand down after each chord, could not be moved: it was uselessly upside-down in the way that Paul now held the guitar.

From that moment, he, too, was 'lost'. The guitar became a passion overruling all else in his life. It was the first thing he looked at on waking each morning; at night, after the lights were out, his eyes searched the darkness for the glow of its sunburst face. School lessons; games; bus journeys; the meals his father set in front of him – all were things to be endured and rushed through for the sake of that moment when he could pick up the guitar again, and hear the hollow bump it made, and discover if the chord he had been practising came out clearly this time. He played the guitar in his bath, even while sitting on the lavatory.

From an assortment of 'Play in a Day' tutors, he learned enough chords to play all the skiffle hits. Skiffle bored him after a time: what he really wanted to play were the guitar solos on rock and roll records – the interludes so magically shrill and blurred that one could not analyse them, but only listen as they shivered and wailed around the voice of Little Richard, Carl Perkins or Elvis. 'All Shook Up' was his favourite Elvis record. He played it over and over on the gramophone, his voice in vain pursuit of the wonderful, mumbling incantation; his acoustic guitar strumming in a different key, and universe.

He also bought every new record by the Everly Brothers, a newly popular American act from whom he made the discovery that rock and roll could be performed at a lesser volume, in close, even subtle harmony. For a time, he and another boy, Ian James, modelled their lives on the Everlys: they combed their hair alike, wore matching white jackets and hung around fairgrounds where the fast roundabouts always played the latest American hits; Paul's voice was like Phil Everly's, the higher of the duo, although he would torture it with impersonations of Little Richard, the shrieking exponent of 'Tutti Frutti', 'Rip it Up' and 'Good Golly Miss Molly'.

He even made one or two desultory attempts to involve his younger brother, Michael, in an Everly-style rock and roll act. Michael McCartney, to add to their father's difficulties, currently had an arm in plaster after an accident at Boy Scout camp. It was a serious fracture which paralysed his fingers for several months and forced him to give up learning the banjo Jim had bought him to equal Paul's guitar.

That summer of 1957 – the first after Mary's death – Jim took Paul and Michael for a week's holiday at Butlin's holiday camp in Filey, Yorkshire. There, Paul roped Michael into joining him in an amateur talent contest. They sang an Everly Brothers song that was rather spoiled by Michael's plaster-encased arm. They didn't win the talent contest. 'But after that, we had our first fan,' Michael McCartney says. 'I remember because it was me she fancied and not our kid.'

The skiffle craze had by now seeped into the ancient precincts of Liverpool Institute grammar school. Paul, however, joined none of the newly formed groups, even though his friend Ivan Vaughan repeatedly enthused about one over in Woolton to which Ivan and another Institute boy, Len Garry, belonged. Ivan Vaughan offered to take Paul to meet the leader – a 'great fellow', so Ivan said. But Paul did not commit himself; nor, for that matter, did Ivan. He prided himself on taking only other 'great fellows' to meet John Lennon.

•

The big event in Woolton each summer was a garden fête organised by St Peter's parish church. They made a proper carnival of it, with fancy dress and a procession of decorated floats, representing all the church organisations, that wound through the streets of the old village, gathering up followers for the subsequent gala in the field at the top of Church Road.

The fête planned for 6 July 1957 was to have a particularly elaborate programme. It included, as well as the customary 'Rose Queen' ceremony, the band of the Cheshire Yeomanry and a team of trained police dogs from the City of Liverpool force. This year, too, for the first time, the 'teenagers' of the parish were to be catered for. That Lennon boy had been asked to bring his group, the Quarry Men, to take part in the procession and to perform afterwards at the fête.

The Quarry Men's fortunes were currently at a low ebb. A few days earlier, in common with dozens of other skiffle groups, they had gone into Liverpool to audition for a Carroll Levis 'Discoveries' show at the Empire theatre. The great starmaker Levis had been there in person, selecting local talent for what was presumed to be instant international fame. The Quarry Men had won their audition heat, and then found themselves matched in the final with the group that featured Nicky Cuff, the midget. This other group had played two numbers to the Quarry Men's one and had, on audience response, been declared the winner. 'They were miles better than we were, anyway,' Rod Davis says. 'They all leapt about all over the place. We were the purists. We stood still and didn't even smile.'

Early the next Saturday afternoon, the Quarry Men climbed aboard the gaily bedecked coal merchant's wagon that was to carry them through the Woolton streets. It had been decided that their float should bring up the rear of the procession, to allay any clash of rhythms with the band of the Cheshire Yeomanry. In between, on vehicles borrowed from other local tradesmen, were tableaux representing the Boy Scouts, Girl Guides, Wolf Cubs and Brownies, and the motorised throne on which the 13-year-old Rose Queen sat, in white lace and pink velvet, surrounded by miniature soldiers and attendants.

Just as had been hoped, the Quarry Men brought a large influx of teenagers into Woolton to see the parade. Among them was Paul McCartney. Ivan Vaughan, his classmate at the Institute, had asked him over, although Len Garry, not Ivan, was playing the tea-chest bass in the group that afternoon. Another strong inducement to Paul was the possibility of picking up girls. He cycled over from Allerton, balancing his piled-up hair carefully against the wind.

•

It was a warm, sunny, Saturday garden fête afternoon. Liverpool, its ship towers and grime, seemed remote from the village decked in faded flags, and the little red sandstone church up the hill, in whose square tower the gold clock hands seemed to point to perpetual summer.

Beside the churchyard, a rough track led into the two small parish-owned fields. Of these, the smaller one, on upland near the Boy Scouts' hut, was too uneven for anything but the refreshment marquee. On the lower, larger field were set out stalls purveying handkerchieves, hardware, home-made cakes, fruit and vegetables, and sideshows including bagatelle, egg-hoopla, quoits and shilling-in-the-bucket. Beyond the Scouts' airborne kiddy-ride, a blackened stone wall formed the boundary with another of Woolton's worked-out quarries. A constant patrol of stewards was necessary to ensure that no child climbed over and fell into the deep, overgrown pit.

That Saturday had begun badly for John Lennon. In the morning, coming downstairs at 'Mendips', he had revealed himself to his Aunt Mimi as a full-blown Teddy Boy. His toppling hair, his plaid shirt and 'drainpipes' seemed to Mimi to be a repudiation of all her care, self-sacrifice and sense. There had been a furious row, after which John had stalked out of the house to find Pete Shotton. In between leaving Mimi and climbing aboard the coalman's wagon, he had contrived – in his own estimation at least – to get roaring drunk. The parade, the stalls, the Rose Queen, the opening prayers by the Revd Maurice Pryce-Jones, all reached John through the gaseous mist of several illicit light ales.

Mimi, before she arrived at the fête, seems not to have known of the Quarry Men's existence. 'I'd just got there, and was having a cup of tea in the refreshment tent. Suddenly, in the midst of everything, came this – this eruption of noise. Everyone had drained away from where I stood, into the next door field. And there on the stage I saw them – John, and that Shotton.

'John saw me standing there with my mouth open. He started to make words up about me in the song he was singing. "Mimi's coming," he sang. "Oh oh, Mimi's coming down the path . . ."'

The Quarry Men's big numbers that afternoon were 'Cumberland Gap', 'Railroad Bill' and 'Maggie May', a Liverpool waterfront song in which the references to a famous tart and her beat along Lime Street were, fortunately, incomprehensible to the ladies of the Church Committee. The whole performance was watched keenly by Paul McCartney, standing with Ivan Vaughan next to the little outdoor stage. Paul noticed the tinny banjo chords which the leading Quarry Man played, and how, while singing, he stared about him, as if sizing up or challenging the rest of the world.

While the police dogs were performing obedience trials, Ivan Vaughan took Paul across the road to the Church Hall, where the Quarry Men had made a small encampment of chairs and their coats. They were due to perform again, at a dance that evening, in alternation with the George Edwards band.

Introductions were made, Pete Shotton remembers, a little stiffly. '"This is John." "Hi." "This is Paul." "Oh – hi." Paul seemed quite cocky, sure of himself, but he and John didn't seem to have much to say.' The ice positively splintered when Paul revealed a brilliant accomplishment. 'He actually knew how to *tune* a guitar,' Pete Shotton says. 'Neither John nor Eric Griffiths had learned how to do that yet. Whenever their guitars went out of tune, they'd been taking them round and asking a fellow in King's Drive to do it.'

It impressed John further that Paul knew the lyrics of rock and roll songs all the way through. He himself could never remember words, which was partly why he preferred to make up his own. Paul was even prepared, in his neat hand, to write out all the verses of 'Twenty Flight Rock', which Eddie Cochran had sung in the film *The Girl Can't Help It*. Then, with equal obligingness, he wrote out the words of Gene Vincent's 'Be Bop a Lula'.

As Church Committee ladies washed up in the scullery nearby, Paul borrowed a guitar and launched into his full Little Richard act – 'Long Tall Sally', 'Tutti Frutti' and the rest. As he played, he became aware of someone getting uncomfortably close to him and breathing a beery smell. The Quarry Men's chronically short-sighted leader was paying him the compliment of watching the way he shaped his chords.

•

Paul was not immediately asked to join the Quarry Men. His obvious ability, if anything, weighed against him. He was so good, they reasoned, he would hardly want to throw in with them. John in particular gave the idea what was, for John, prolonged thought. Up to that point, he had been the Quarry Men's undisputed leader. By admitting Paul, he would be creating a potential threat to that leadership. The decision was whether to remain strong himself or make the group stronger. A week after the Woolton fête, Paul was cycling to Allerton across the golf course when he met Pete Shotton. Pete told him that John wanted him in.

Pete's own skiffle career ended soon afterwards at a party when John took away his washboard and smashed it over his head. 'All of us were pissed and larking around. It didn't hurt me. I just sat there, framed by the washboard, with tears of laughter running down my face. I'd known for a long time that I was no good at music – I was only in the group through being a mate of John's. I was finished with playing, but I didn't want to say so, nor did John. This way let me out and it let John out.'

If Pete had not left the Quarry Men at that point, it is doubtful whether Paul and John would have become the close friends they subsequently did. For no two temperaments could have been more unalike. John, dour and blisteringly direct, fought against authority and inhibition in any form. Paul, baby-faced and virtuous, hated to be on anybody's wrong side. Not least of the differences in them was their attitude to the money they earned by playing. Whereas John would – and frequently did – give away his last sixpence, Paul showed noticeable signs of thrift. One of his first suggestions on joining the Quarry Men was that Nigel Walley should not receive equal shares since, as manager, he did not actually play onstage.

What Paul and John had in common was their passion for guitars. They began to spend hours in each other's company, practising, usually at Paul's. John would even let himself be seen in his hated spectacles, the better to understand the chords which Paul showed him. Whole afternoons would pass in the living-room at Forthlin Road, where Jim McCartney had papered the walls with a design of Chinese pagodas. Paul's younger brother Mike would often be there, too, taking photographs of them as they played. One of Mike's pictures records the moment when both were able to play a full six-string chord with the left-hand index finger barring the keyboard. Their faces, as they hold up their two guitars, are rigid with pride and pain.

The other Quarry Men did not take quite so strongly to Paul. 'I always thought he was a bit big-headed,' Nigel Walley says. 'As soon as we let him into the group, he started complaining about the money I was getting them, and saying I should take less as I didn't do any playing. He was always smiling at you, but he could be catty as well. He used to pick on our drummer, Colin – not to his face; making catty remarks about him behind his back. Paul wanted something from the drums that Colin didn't have it in him to play.'

'"Paul was always telling me what to do," Colin Hanton says. "Can't you play it this way?" he'd say, and even try to show me on my own drums. He'd make some remark to me. I'd sulk. John would say "Ah, let him alone, he's all right." But I knew they only wanted me because I'd got a set of drums.'

Even Pete Shotton – still a close friend and ally – noticed a change in John after Paul's arrival. 'There was one time when they played a really dirty trick on me. I knew John would never have been capable of it on his own. It was so bad that he came to me later and apologised. I'd never known him to do that before for *anyone*.'

It was shortly after Paul joined the Quarry Men that they bought proper stage outfits of black trousers, black bootlace ties and white cowboy shirts with fringes along the sleeves. John and Paul, in addition, wore white jackets; the other three played in their shirtsleeves. Eric Griffiths, though also a guitarist, did not have the jacket-wearing privilege. A cheerful boy, he did not recognise this for the augury it was.

Their main engagements were still at church halls like St Peter's in Woolton or St Barnabas', off Penny Lane. A step-up came when a local promoter named Charlie McBain booked them to play at regular dances at the Broadway Conservative Club and at the Wilson Hall in Garston.

The latter was in a district renowned for its toughness and the size of its Teddy Boys, among whom the fashion had lately arisen of going to skiffle dances with leather belts wrapped round their hands. At Wilson Hall one night, a gigantic Ted terrified the Quarry Men by clambering on to the stage in the middle of a number. But it was only to request Paul quite politely to do his Little Richard impersonation.

Nigel Walley had left school and become an apprentice golf professional at the Lee Park course. He continued to act as the Quarry Men's manager and, despite Paul's protests, to draw equal shares: his wallet packed with their visiting cards, he would cycle assiduously with news of a booking from one member's house to the next. Through Nigel, they were even once invited to play at Lee Park golf club. 'They did it for nothing, but they got a slap-up meal, and the hat was passed round for them afterwards. They ended up making about twice what they would have done if they'd been getting a fee.'

At the golf course, Nigel got to know a doctor named Sytner whose son, Alan, had recently opened a jazz club in the centre of Liverpool. Nigel arranged for the Quarry Men to appear there, too, late in 1957. The club was in Mathew Street, under a row of old warehouses, and fully deserved its name, the Cavern. It was strictly for jazz, it allowed skiffle but absolutely barred rock and roll. 'We started doing Elvis numbers when we played there,' Colin Hanton says. 'While we were on stage, someone handed us a note. John thought it was a request. But it was from the Management, saying: "Cut out the bloody rock."'

3

'If I'd just said a few more words, it might have saved her'

John was to leave Quarry Bank school at the end of July 1957. He had taken his GCE Ordinary-level examination and had failed every subject by one grade – a clear enough sign to Mr Pobjoy, the headmaster, that with a little exertion he could have passed every one. Art, his outstanding subject, had been squandered with the rest. The question paper asked for a painting to illustrate the theme 'travel'. John, for the amusement of his exam-room neighbours, drew a wart-infested hunchback.

He sat out that last summer term, stubbornly resistant to all ideas of soon having to make his way in the world. The panoramic school photograph shows him, slumped behind his Slim Jim tie, conspicuous among a Fifth Form with faces otherwise expectant and purposeful. Rod Davis, the Quarry Men's banjo-player, was to enter the Sixth to do Advanced-level French and German. Even Pete Shotton, John's old partner in crime, had, to his teachers' and possibly to his own great surprise, been accepted as a cadet at the Police College in Mather Avenue.

Aunt Mimi's great fear was that, like his father Freddy 30 years before, John would just drift away to sea. 'I remember him bringing home this boy with hair in a Tony Curtis, they called it, all smoothed back with grease at the sides. "Mimi," John whispered to me in the kitchen, "this boy's got *pots* of money. He goes away to sea." I said, "Well, he's no captain and he's no engineer – what is he?" "He waits at table," John said. "Ha!" I said. "A fine ambition!"'

Mimi afterwards stumbled on a plot between John and Nigel Walley to run away to sea as ship's stewards. Nigel says they had got as far as buying their rail tickets to the Catering College. 'I was rung up by this place at the Pier Head,' Mimi said, '. . . some sort of seaman's employment office. "We've got a young boy named John Lennon here," they said. "He's asking to sign up." "Don't you even *dream* of it," I told them.'

Mimi was called to Quarry Bank to discuss with Mr Pobjoy what John might do with his life. Reviewing his meagre school achievements, there seemed only one possibility – his talent for painting, design and caricature. 'Mr Pobjoy said to me, "Mrs Smith, this boy's an artist, he's a bohemian.

If I can get him into the Art College, are you prepared to keep him on for the next twelve months?"' Mimi said that she was.

Quarry Bank's valediction was, in the circumstances, quite kindly. 'He has been a trouble spot for many years in discipline, but has somewhat mended his ways. Requires the sanction of "losing a job" to keep him on the rails. But I believe he is not beyond redemption and he could really turn out a fairly responsible adult who might go far.'

•

Aunt Mimi went with him for his interview at the Art College in Hope Street. 'Otherwise,' Mimi said, 'he'd never have been able to find it. He'd only ever been into Liverpool on the one sort of bus, to the shop opposite the bus stop where he used to buy his Dinky cars.'

On that day, John managed to make himself a relatively unalarming figure, submitting to both white shirt and tie and an old tweed suit that had once belonged to his Uncle George. When he presented himself for enrolment, however, it was in his Teddy-Boy jacket and lilac shirt and the drainpipe jeans Aunt Mimi had forbidden him to wear. He put them on under normal trousers which he stripped off directly he was out of Mimi's sight.

Hope Street bisects the old, elegant, upland part of Liverpool where cast-iron letters on street-ends enshrine the great shipping dynasties of Canning, Rodney, Roscoe and Huskisson. In 1957, the whole district round the Art College was a haunt of painters, sculptors, poets and writers, sharing the faded Georgiana in amity with small businesses, guest houses, junk shops and West Indian drinking clubs. The Anglican cathedral being still unfinished, the principal aesthetic attraction was the Philharmonic Dining-Rooms, a pub fashioned by Cunard shipwrights in crystal and mahogany, where even the Gents' urinals were carved of rose-coloured marble.

Whatever hopes John may have had of a wild bohemian existence were confounded in his first week at college. He had been accepted for the Intermediate course of two years' general study, followed by specialisation in the third and fourth year. To his disgust, he found himself in a classroom again, obliged to study a set curriculum including figure drawing, lettering and architecture. It was, in other words, no different from the school he had just left.

His Teddy-Boy clothes estranged him instantly from his fellow students in their duffel coats, suède shoes and chunky Shetland sweaters with sleeves pushed up to the elbow. At Art College in 1957, no one liked Elvis or rock and roll: what everyone liked was traditional jazz, played in cellars flickering with beer-bottle candlelight. Indeed, the most famous Liverpool group of the moment was the Merseysippi Jazz Band, frequently to be heard on radio as well as at the Cavern Club in Mathew Street. John hated the jazz crowd with their sweaters and their GCE passes.

His tutor on the Intermediate course was Arthur Ballard, a balding soft-spoken man who had once been a middleweight boxing champion. Himself an abstract painter of some reputation, Ballard had no great love for formal teaching and, in fact, held most of his seminars in a tiny pub called Ye Cracke, in Rice Street, where the back room was dominated by gigantic etchings of Wellington greeting Marshal Blücher, and Nelson's death at Trafalgar.

Ballard noticed John Lennon first merely as an ill-at-ease Teddy Boy whose clothes were officially disapproved of and whose posture was less defiant than dejected. 'The students would pin their work up, and we'd all discuss it. John's effort was always hopeless – or he'd put up nothing at all. He always struck me as the poor relation in the group. The rest used to cover up for him.

'Then one day in the lecture room, I found this notebook full of caricatures – of myself, the other tutors, the students – all done with descriptions and verse, and it was the wittiest thing I'd ever seen in my life. There was no name on it. It took me quite a long time to find out that Lennon had done it.

'The next time student work was being put up and discussed, I brought out this notebook and held it up, and we discussed the work in it. John had never expected anyone to look at it, let alone find it funny and brilliant. Afterwards I told him, "When I talk about Interpretation, boy, *this* is the kind of thing I mean as well. *This* is the kind of thing I want you to be doing."'

•

Around the windy corner, in Mount Street, Paul McCartney still daily climbed the steps to the Institute Grammar School. That summer, he had taken two O-levels, passing in Spanish but failing Latin; in 1958, he was due to take six further subjects and then go into the Sixth Form. The ultimate plan, ardently supported by his father, was that Paul should go on to teacher training college. His English master, 'Dusty' Durband, thought this a feasible course. He could imagine Paul one day appearing in the Institute's own staff room, or driving a modest saloon car to and from some small college of adult education.

But Paul's school career, previously so unexceptionable, now grew unsettled and erratic. The presence of John Lennon, literally beyond the classroom wall, affected both his work and his hitherto blameless conduct. More than ever, Mr Durband noticed, he relied on charm and facility to compensate for skimped or unfinished preparation. He had even, unknown to Mr Durband, begun to cut certain classes. There was an internal way from the Institute into the Art College, across a small courtyard beside the school kitchens. John would have told him which lecture room was empty and available for guitar practice. No one in the College thoroughfares looked twice at the big-eyed youth with his black raincoat buttoned up to the neck to hide his Institute tie.

The Quarry Men had been hard hit by the flux of the final school year. Rod Davis was too busy in the Quarry Bank Sixth to have any time for banjo-playing. Nigel Walley had contracted tuberculosis – the consequence, he thinks, of over-work in the cause of skiffle and his golf pro' job. Soon afterwards, Len Garry, the bass player, fell ill with meningitis and joined Nigel at the sanatorium at Fazakerley. 'The other lads used to come and see us on a Sunday. They'd bring their guitars with them, and we'd have a singsong at the end of the ward.'

The skiffle era was by now definitely over. Last year's big names, the Vipers, Chas McDevitt, Bob Cort, even Lonnie Donegan himself, had all dropped the word 'skiffle' discreetly from their billing. In Liverpool, as all over Britain, broom-handles were being restored to their brushes, thimbles returned to maternal work-baskets, and tea chests, decorated with musical notes, left outside for reluctant refuse men. But if thousands of skiffle groups broke up, there were hundreds more with a taste – even a talent – for performing who decided to try their luck with rock and roll.

They had the consolation of knowing that, however bad they might sound at the beginning, they did not sound much worse than professional English rock and rollers. Tommy Steele, launched in 1956 as Britain's 'answer' to Elvis Presley, had set the pattern of cack-handed mimicry. Since then, there had arisen numerous other 'answers' to Presley as well as to the Everly Brothers, Bill Haley, the Platters and Little Richard. There had been Marty Wilde, the Most Brothers, Russ Hamilton, Tony Crombie and the Rockets. Some found hit records and a large following which, for all that, regarded them much as an earlier generation had regarded British films. They were poor substitutes for the real elixir, pumped from its only true source: America.

Liverpool stood closer to America than any other place in Britain. There was still, in 1957, a transatlantic passenger route, plied by ships returning weekly to tie up behind Dock Road's grim castle walls. With them came young Liverpudlian deckhands and stewards whom the neighbours called 'Cunard Yanks' because of their flashy New York clothes. As well as Times Square trinkets for their girl friends and panoramic lampshades of the Manhattan skyline for their mothers' front rooms, the Cunard Yanks brought home records not available in Britain. Rhythm and blues, the genesis of rock and roll, sung by still obscure names such as Chuck Berry and Ike Turner, pounded through the terraced back streets each Saturday night as the newly returned mariners got ready to hit the town.

The Quarry Men knew no friendly Cunard Yank who would bring them American records to copy. They had no money, either, for the new electric guitars and amplifiers now thronging Hessy's shop window. They could not even change their name, as all the other groups were doing. The Alan Caldwell Skiffle Group had become Rory Storm and the Raving Texans. The Gerry Marsden Skiffle Group now called themselves Gerry and the Pacemakers. The Quarry Men stayed the Quarry Men because that was the name lettered on Colin Hanton's drums.

In late 1957, American rock and roll gave struggling ex-skiffle groups in Britain their first friend. His name was Buddy Holly, although at the beginning he figured anonymously in a group called the Crickets. Among the new performers thrown up after Presley, Buddy Holly was unique in composing many of the songs he recorded, and also in showing ability on the guitar, rather than using it merely as a prop. He gave hope to British boys because he was not pretty, but thin and bespectacled, and because his songs, though varied and inventive, were written in elementary guitar chords, recognisable to every beginner.

Paul McCartney had always used his guitar to help him make up tunes. His main objective in the Quarry Men, however, was to oust Eric Griffiths from the role of lead guitarist. One night at the Broadway Conservative Club, he prevailed on the others to let him take the solo in a number. He fluffed it and, later, in an attempt to redeem himself, played over to John a song he had written, called 'I Lost My Little Girl'. John, though he had always tinkered with lyrics, had never thought of writing entire songs before. Egged on by Paul – and by Buddy Holly – he felt there could be no harm in trying. Soon he and Paul were each writing songs furiously, as if it were a race.

•

Sometimes, when the Quarry Men played at Wilson Hall, they would be watched by a boy whose elaborate Teddy-Boy hair stood up around a pale, hollow-cheeked, unsmiling face. The others knew him vaguely as a schoolfriend of Paul's and a would-be guitarist, though he played with no group regularly. His name, so Paul said, was George Harrison, and, in Paul's opinion, he would be extremely useful as a recruit to the Quarry Men. No one, to begin with, took very much notice. For Paul's friend was so silent and solemn and, at 14, so ridiculously young.

Paul had got to know him years before, when the McCartneys still lived at Speke and George used to catch the same bus to school each morning from the stop near Upton Green. Among the shouting, satchel-swinging, homework-copying crowd, George Harrison was known as the boy whose dad actually drove one of these pale green Corporation buses. When Paul, one morning, was short of his full fare, George's mother gave him extra pennies enough to travel all the way into Liverpool.

The Harrisons, Harry and Louise, had married in 1929 when she worked in a greengrocer's shop and he was a steward on ships of the White Star line. The thin, dapper, thoughtful young shipboard waiter proved a perfect match with the jolly, warm-hearted young woman whose mother had been a lamplighter during the Great War. In 1931, a daughter, Louise, was born to them and, in 1934, their first son, Harold junior. Harry quit the sea soon afterwards, braving the worst of the Depression to be nearer his wife and children. After 15 months on the dole, he managed to get a job with the Corporation, initially as a bus conductor. A third child, Peter, was born in 1940, at the height of the Liverpool Blitz.

The family lived then at Wavertree, in the tiny terraced house in Arnold Grove which Harry and Louise had occupied since their marriage. It was here, on 25 February 1943, that Louise gave birth to her fourth child and third son, George. When Harry came upstairs to see the new baby, he was amazed at its likeness to himself. Louise, too, noticed the dark eyes that, even then, cautiously appraised the world.

Though Harry earned little on the buses, he made sure his large family lacked for nothing. Louise was a capable and also a happy mother, whose laughter rang constantly through the house. George, as the baby of the family, was petted by everyone, from his big sister Lou downwards. Accustomed to being the centre of attention, he was, at the same time, independent, solitary and thoughtful. Even as a toddler, he forbade Louise to go with him to school, for fear she would get mixed up with 'all those nosey mothers'. It horrified him to think they might ask her what he did and said at home.

The wartime baby 'bulge' had brought in its wake an acute shortage of space at primary schools. George – like his mother – had been baptised a Catholic, but could be fitted in only at an Anglican infants' school, Dovedale Primary, near Penny Lane. He was there at the same time as John Lennon, two forms below.

In 1954, he went on to Liverpool Institute, where he was put into the form below Paul McCartney. Unlike Paul, however, he soon began to do extremely badly. Alert and perceptive, with an unusually good memory, he developed a hatred of all lessons and school routine. Detentions, even beatings, could not lift the firmly shut barriers of his indifference, and soon the Institute masters found it less fatiguing to leave him alone.

He acquired further disreputability by coming to school in clothes which did not conform to the Institute's regulation grey and black. Already, in admiration of the dockland Teds, his hair was piled so high that a school cap could only cling on precariously at the back. He would sit in class, his blazer buttoned over a canary yellow waistcoat borrowed from his brother, Harry, his desk-top hiding trousers secretly tapered on his mother's sewing machine. His shirt collar, socks and shoes growing pointed all uttered the defiance still hidden in his gaunt face while some master or other, like 'sissy' Smith, was sarcastically making fun of him.

In 1956, his mother noticed him drawing pictures of guitars on every scrap of paper he could find. He had heard Lonnie Donegan, and seen Donegan's guitar. Soon afterwards, he came to Louise and asked her to give him £3 to buy a guitar from a boy at school. She did so; but when George brought it home, he accidentally unscrewed the neck from the body, then found he couldn't put them back together. The guitar lay in a cupboard for weeks until his brother Peter took it out and mended it.

Learning to play, even the first simple chords in the tuition book, was an agonising process for George. Unlike Paul, he had no inherited musical ability; nor was he, like John, a born adventurer. All he had was his indomitable will to learn. His mother encouraged him, sitting up late with him as he tried and tried. Sometimes he would be near to tears with frustration and the pain of his split and dusty fingertips.

His brother Peter had taken up the guitar at about the same time, and together they formed a skiffle group, the Rebels. Their first and only engagement was for 10s each at the Speke British Legion Club. At George's insistence, they left the house one at a time, ducking along under the garden hedge so that 'nosey neighbours' wouldn't see.

The family had moved by now to a new council house, in Upton Green, Speke. It was on his bus journey into Liverpool each morning that George met Paul McCartney. Though Paul was a year older and in a higher form at school, their passion for guitars drew them together. Paul would come across from Allerton to practise in George's bedroom, bringing with him his 'cello guitar with the upside-down scratch plate. George now had a £30 guitar which his mother had helped him buy – a far better one than Paul's, with white piping and a 'cutaway' for reaching the narrow frets at the bottom of the neck.

To pay back his mother, George did a Saturday morning delivery round for a local butcher, E. R. Hughes. One of the houses on his round belonged to a family named Bramwell, whose son Tony had met Buddy Holly during the star's recent British tour. Tony Bramwell would lend George his Buddy Holly records to listen to and copy. Confidence came from the songs built of easy chords, like E and B7; the changes he could do now from one chord to the other; the solo bass runs that, painfully, unsmilingly, he was learning to pick out for himself.

•

Paul introduced him to the other Quarry Men one night late in 1957, in the suburb of Liverpool called Old Roan. 'It was at a club we used to go to, called the Morgue,' Colin Hanton says. 'It was in the cellar of this big old derelict house. No bar or coffee or anything, just a cellar with dark rooms off it, and one big blue light bulb sticking out of the wall.'

The others crowded round George, interested in what they could see of his guitar with its cutaway body. They listened while George played all he had been carefully rehearsing. He played them 'Raunchy', an eight-note tune on the bass strings; then he played the faster and more tricky 'Guitar Boogie Shuffle'.

George was not asked to join the Quarry Men that night. Indeed, they never asked him formally to join. He would follow them with his guitar around the halls where they played, and in the interval stand and wait for his chance to come across and see Paul. Generally, he would have some newly-mastered chord to show them, or yet another solemn-faced bass string tune. If another guitarist had failed to arrive, George would be allowed to 'sit in'.

No one other than Paul took him very seriously. John Lennon in particular, from the pinnacle of 17 years, considered him just a funny little eager white-faced lad who delivered the weekend meat. Even George's ability as a guitarist became a reason for John to tease him. 'Come on, George,' he would say. 'Give us "Raunchy".' George played 'Raunchy' whenever John asked him to, even sitting on the top deck of the number 500 bus to Speke.

The great benefit of letting George tag along was that it brought the Quarry Men another safe house in which to practise. At weekends or on truant days, they could always find refuge at George's. Mr Harrison would be out on the buses, but Louise always welcomed them, never minding the noise. She developed a soft spot for John Lennon, in whom she recognised much of her own scatty humour. She used to say that John and she were just a pair of fools.

Aunt Mimi, by contrast, did not like John to associate with someone who was, after all, a butcher's errand boy, and whose accent was so thickly Liverpudlian. George called at 'Mendips' one day to ask John to go to the cinema, but John, still thinking him just a 'bloody kid', pretended to be too busy. 'He's a real whacker, isn't he?' Mimi said bitterly when George had gone. 'You always go for the low types, don't you, John?'

To Mimi, in her innocence, George – and even Paul – were the bad influences: if John had not met *them*, he would still be happy in ordinary clothes. 'Paul used to wear these *great* long winklepicker things, with buckles on the sides. And as for *George*! Well, of course you couldn't wish for a quieter lad. But one day when I came into the house, there was George with his hair in a crew cut, and wearing this *bright* pink shirt. I told him, "*Never* come into this house with a shirt like that on again."'

With George sitting in more and more, the Quarry Men now found themselves with a glut of guitarists. For, as well as John and Paul, there was still Eric Griffiths, the chubby-faced boy who had been a founder member, and who did not realise his growing superfluousness. At length, the others decided that Eric must be frozen out. Colin Hanton, his best friend in the group, was visited by Nigel Walley and asked to go along with the plan. They still needed Colin or, rather, his £38-drum kit.

'We didn't tell Eric we were going to Paul's house to practise,' Colin says. 'He rang up while we were there. The others got me to talk to him and explain how things stood. Eric was pretty upset. He couldn't understand why they'd suddenly decided to get rid of him. I told him there wasn't a lot I could do about it. I could tell that if they wanted somebody out, he was out.'

•

Between John and Aunt Mimi, the atmosphere had grown increasingly turbulent. Mimi had to support him at Art College for a full year until he qualified for a local authority grant; she therefore felt doubly entitled to pronounce adversely on his clothes, his silly music and the friends who were, in Mimi's opinion, so very ill-attired and unsuitable. Pete Shotton was only one of John's friends who witnessed memorable fights between him and the aunt who so resembled him in strength of will and volatile spirits. 'One minute,' Pete says, 'they'd be yelling and screaming at each other; the next they'd have their arms round each other, laughing.'

Behind Mimi's briskness and sarcasm lay the real dread of losing John. She was only a substitute, as she well knew, for his real mother, her sister Julia. And John, in his teenage years, had grown adept at playing on that fear. After a row at 'Mendips', he would storm out and go straight to Julia's house at Spring Wood, remaining there for days, sometimes weeks on end. With Julia, life was always pleasant and carefree. Having made no sacrifice for him, she bore no grudge against his indolence: she pampered him, bought him unsuitable clothes and made him laugh. Her new man, John Dykins, the nervous waiter John called 'Twitchy', would frequently press on him a handful of the evening's restaurant tips.

Mimi, aware that she was being exploited, sometimes took dramatic measures to call John's bluff. 'They used to keep a little dog called Sally,'

Pete Shotton says. 'John really thought the world of her. One time, when he'd walked out and gone off to Julia's, Mimi got rid of Sally, saying there'd be no one left in the house to take her for walks. That was the only time I ever saw John really heartbroken and showing it – when he came home to Menlove Avenue and didn't find Sally there.'

On the evening of 15 July 1958, Nigel Walley left his house in Vale Road and took the short cut over the stile into Menlove Avenue to call for John. At 'Mendips', he found Mimi and Julia talking together by the front garden gate. John was not there, they said – he had gone to Julia's for the whole weekend. Julia, having paid her daily visit to Mimi, was just leaving to catch her bus.

'We'd had a cup of tea together,' Mimi said. 'I said, "I won't walk to the bus stop with you tonight." "All right," Julia said, "don't worry. I'll see you tomorrow."'

Instead, it was Nigel Walley who walked with John's mother through the warm twilight down Menlove Avenue towards the big road junction. 'Julia was telling me some jokes as we went,' Nigel remembers. 'Every time you saw her, she'd have a new one she'd been saving up to tell you.' About 200 yards from Mimi's house, they parted. Nigel continued down Menlove Avenue and Julia began to cross the road to her bus stop.

Old tram tracks, concealed by a thin hedgerow, ran down the middle of the busy dual carriageway. As Julia stepped through the hedge into the southbound lane, a car came suddenly out of the twilight, swerving inward on the steep camber. Nigel Walley, across the road, turned at the scream of brakes to see Julia's body tossed into the air.

'I can picture it to this day. I always think to myself, "If only I'd said just one more sentence to her, just a few words more, it might have saved her."'

•

There was first the moment, parodying every film melodrama John had ever seen, when a policeman came to the back door at Spring Wood and asked if he was Julia's son. The feeling of farce persisted in the taxi ride with 'Twitchy' to Sefton General Hospital; in the sight of the faces waiting to meet them there. For Julia had died the instant the car had struck her. The shock was too much for 'Twitchy', who broke down with grief and dread of what would now become of him and his children by Julia. Even in the moment of her death, it must have seemed to John that his mother was someone else's property.

The anguish was drawn out over several weeks. The car which killed Julia had been driven by an off-duty policeman. Pete Shotton was working on attachment from Police College in the local CID department which investigated the case. The driver stood trial, but was acquitted. 'I went as a witness,' Nigel Walley says, 'but me being only a boy, they didn't give much weight to what I'd seen. Mimi took it very hard – shouting at the fellow in the dock; she even threatened him with a walking stick.'

John, in the weeks after Julia's death, reminded Pete Shotton of the times they would be caned at Quarry Bank, when John used to fight with all his strength not to let out a single sound of pain. Few people knew the extent of his grief since few understood his feeling for the happy, careless woman who had let her life become separate from his. At College, he would sit for hours alone in the big window at the top of the main staircase. Arthur Ballard saw him there once, and noticed that he was crying.

Elsewhere, if his desolation showed, it would be in manic horseplay with his crony Jeff Mohamed, both in College and at the student pub, Ye Cracke, where John was increasingly to be found. 'They'd come back to College pissed in the afternoon,' Arthur Ballard says. 'I caught John trying to piss into the lift shaft.' Ballard was human enough to understand the reason for such behaviour. But even Pete Shotton was shocked to see how much of the time John now spent anaesthetised by drink. 'I remember getting on a bus once and finding John on the top deck, lying across the back seat, pissed out of his mind. He'd been up there for hours with no idea where he was.'

He had never been short of girl friends, though few were willing to put up for long with the treatment that was John Lennon's idea of romance. His drinking, his sarcasm, his unpunctuality at trysts, his callous humour and, most of all, his erratic temper drove each of them to 'chuck' him, not infrequently with the devastating rejoinder that is the speciality of Liverpool girls. 'Don't take it out on me,' one of them screamed back at him, 'just because your mother's dead.'

Not long after Julia's death, his eye fell on Cynthia Powell, an Intermediate student in a group slightly ahead of his. Cynthia was a timid, bespectacled girl with flawless white skin. Hitherto, if John had noticed her at all, it was merely to taunt her for living in Hoylake, on the Cheshire Wirral, where primness and superiority are thought to reign. 'No dirty jokes please – it's Cynthia,' he would say while she blushed, knowing full well that dirty jokes would inevitably follow.

This was the girl who, nevertheless, found herself drawn to John Lennon with a fascination entirely against her neat and cautious nature. She dreaded, yet longed for, the days when John would sit behind her in the lettering class and would pillage the orderly pattern of brushes and rulers she had laid out for the work. She remembers, too, a moment in the lecture hall when she saw another girl stroking John's hair, and felt within herself a confusion which she afterwards realised was jealousy.

They first got talking one day between classes, after some of the students had been testing one another's eyesight and Cynthia discovered John's vision to be as poor as hers, despite his refusal to be seen in glasses. Encouraged by this, she took to loitering about the passages in the hope of meeting him. She grew her 'perm' out, dyed her mousy hair blonde, exchanged her usual modest outfit for a white duffel coat and black velvet trousers, and left off her own spectacles, with frequently catastrophic results. The bus she caught each day from Central Station regularly carried her past Hope Street and the College stop and on into Liverpool 8.

John approached her formally at an end-of-term dance at lunch-time in one of the College lecture rooms. Egged on by Jeff Mohamed, he asked her to dance. When he asked her for a date, Cynthia blurted out that she was engaged – as was true – to a boy back home in Hoylake. 'I didn't ask you to marry me, did I?' John retorted bitterly.

In the autumn term of 1958, amid much local astonishment, they began 'going steady'. Cynthia's friends – especially those who had already passed through the John Lennon experience – warned her strongly against it. Equally, in John's crowd no one could understand his interest in a girl who, although nowadays had somewhat improved in looks, still had nothing in common with John's ideal woman, Brigitte Bardot. Even George Harrison forgot his usual shyness in John's company to declare that Cynthia had teeth 'like a horse'.

Against these defects there was about her a gentleness, a malleability that John, brought up among frolicsome and strong-willed aunts, had not met in a female before. To please him, she began to dress in short skirts, fishnet stockings and suspender belts which shocked her to her suburban soul as well as giving much anxiety while she waited for him outside Lewis's department store, terrified of being mistaken for a 'totty', or Liverpool tart. For him, each night, she braved the last train out to Hoylake, and its cargo of hooligans and drunks.

She was, even then, terrified of John – of his reckless humour no less than the moods and sudden rages and the ferocity with which he demanded her total obedience. He was so jealous, Cynthia says, he would try to beat up anyone at a party who so much as asked her to dance. He would sit for hours with her in a pub or coffee bar, never letting go her hand. It was as if something stored up in him since Julia's death could be exorcised, or at least quieted, through her.

•

Elvis was tamed. The gold-suited figure whose lip had curled on behalf of all British adolescence, whose proto-punk slouch had altered the posture of a generation, could now be seen meekly seated in a barber's chair preparatory to serving two years in the United States Army. No one yet quite comprehended how much this repentance was a stroke of incomparable showmanship by his manager, 'Colonel' Tom Parker, a one-time huckster at fairs and carnivals. It mattered less to America than to Britain, which Elvis had not yet visited, although rumours of his coming were continually rife. As the Colonel beamed fatly and Elvis shouldered arms, showing what a decent kid he had been all along, England's rockers vowed that, in their eyes at least, 'The King' would never abdicate.

There was some consolation in an upsurge of British rock and roll, and a television show capable of reflecting it. *Oh Boy!* every Saturday night, on the solitary commercial channel, filled a dark stage, as in some Miracle play, with major American performers like Eddie Cochran and Gene Vincent, and their British counterparts, Marty Wilde, Dickie Pride, Duffy Power, Vince Eager and Tony Sheridan. There was also a new young Elvis copy, Cliff Richard, whose lip unfurled at the corner like a faulty window blind, and whose backing group, the Shadows, featured in equal prominence around him, stepping to and fro with their guitars in unison. Their first record, 'Move It', was the first successful British version of American rock and roll with its jungle-like bass rhythm and clangorous lead guitar.

Up in Liverpool, the three guitarists in a group still called the Quarry Men watched *Oh Boy!* every Saturday night, crawling close to the television screen when the Shadows came on, to try to see how they did that stupendous 'Move It' intro. Paul worked it out first and at once jumped on his bike with his guitar to hurry over to John's.

Of all the original, top-heavy skiffle group, apart from John himself, only one member remained. They still had Colin Hanton, the little upholsterer, and the £38 drum kit he was paying for in instalments. They only kept him on, as Colin well knew, for the sake of those drums. Having a drummer, however unsatisfactory, made the difference between a *real* group and three lads just messing around with guitars.

Without Nigel Walley to manage them, their playing was on a haphazard basis, at birthday parties, youth club dances or social clubs, where they would perform for a pie and a pint of ale. To Colin, the ale was consolation for knowing they only wanted him for his drums, and for the increasingly acid remarks made by Paul about his playing.

Both John and George now owned electric guitars. John's was a fawn-coloured Hofner 'Club 40', semi-solid, with two knobs on it, while George had persuaded his mother to help him raise £30 for a Hofner 'Futurama', a cheap version of Buddy Holly's two-horned Fender Stratocaster. But neither could yet afford to buy an amplifier. Better-equipped groups would usually lend them an amp for their orphan guitar-leads. Failing that, George the trainee electrician would wire both his and John's instruments to the club or dance hall's public address system.

In mid-1958, they scraped up 17s 6d (87p) between them to make a demonstration record which, they hoped, might act as a more impressive calling-card than the printed ones in Nigel's wallet. The 'studio' they chose was in the back room of a private house in Kensington, Liverpool, owned by an elderly man named Percy Phillips. The group that day comprised John, Paul, George and a temporary recruit named John Lowe, taking the place of Colin Hanton. Their money bought them a two-sided shellac disc, its A-side a cover version of the Crickets' 'That'll Be the Day' with John singing lead and George rather tinnily reconstructing Buddy Holly's guitar licks. Of far more individuality was John's B-side vocal, a country-ish ballad called 'In Spite of All the Danger', written by Paul with help from George. However, the first duty of all amateur groups in 1958 was to mimic hot sounds in the charts. Their Crickets cover was what they played and replayed, to themselves and anyone else who would listen.

Colin Hanton was still with them when a second chance arrived to become Carroll Levis 'Discoveries'. Again, with every other local group, they presented themselves at the Empire theatre to be auditioned by the great man – this time for his Granada Television talent show. They got through the Liverpool heats, and were booked to appear in the semi-finals at the Hippodrome Theatre studios in Manchester. Before they left they changed their name to Johnny and the Moondogs.

The journey to Manchester was overshadowed by their general poverty. 'We hadn't worked out in advance how much it would cost us to get there by train and by bus,' Colin Hanton says. 'When we got on the bus in Manchester, Paul discovered he hadn't got enough money to get home again. He was panicking all over the place. "What am I going to *do*? This is *serious.*" A bloke stood up at the front to get off and, as he passed Paul, he stuck a two-shilling piece [10p] into his hand. Paul got up and yelled down the bus stairs after him, "I love you."'

Poverty robbed them of their opportunity to appear on television with Carroll Levis's infant ballerinas and players of musical saws. The final judging, on the strength of the audience applause for each act, did not take place until late evening, after the last bus and train back to Liverpool had gone. Johnny and the Moondogs, with no money to spend on an overnight hotel stay, had to leave before the finale.

Colin Hanton appeared with them as drummer for the last time one

Saturday night at the Picton Lane busmen's social club. They had got the engagement through George Harrison's father, who acted as MC there and, with Mrs Harrison, ran a learners' ballroom dancing class. From George's dad had come the important news that a local cinema manager would be dropping in to see whether Johnny and the Moondogs were suitable to put on in the interval between his Sunday picture shows.

'At the beginning, that night went really well,' Colin Hanton says. 'We were all in a good mood – pulling George's leg and saying, "There's George's dad; where's his bus?" It was a real stage they'd put us on, with a curtain that came up and down. The curtain got stuck, so we played six numbers, not five, in our first spot. The busmen and clippies were all cheering, they really dug us.

'In the interval, we were told, "There's a pint for you lads over at the bar." That pint turned into two pints, then three. When we went on for the second spot, we were *terrible.* All pissed. The bloke from the Pavilion never booked us. There was a row about it on the bus going home, and I thought, "Right. That's it. I'll not bother playing with them again."' At the next stop, even though it was before his destination, Colin hauled his drum kit off the bus and did not turn up for any further gigs.

•

For the rest of 1958, Johnny and the Moondogs or the Quarry Men, or whatever they felt like calling themselves, remained poised on the edge of extinction. They would still get together and play, but only at small events like birthday parties, where the lack of a drummer did not count so much. One night, when they all arrived in different coloured shirts, they called themselves the Rainbows. John and Paul would sometimes work as a duo, the Nurk Twins. George regularly sat in with a more stable group, the Les Stewart Quartet at a club in West Derby called the Lowlands.

A short distance away, in the quiet thoroughfare of Hayman's Green, stood a large Victorian house belonging to a family named Best. Johnny Best had originally been Liverpool's main promoter of boxing matches in the city's 6,000-seat stadium. His wife, Mona, was a brisk, dark-eyed woman of Anglo-Indian birth. The couple had lately separated, leaving Mona Best in the big old house with her bedridden mother, her two sons, Peter and Rory, a collection of paying guests and assorted Eastern mementoes including the Hindu idol that flexed its many arms in the front hall.

Peter, her elder son, was then 18, and in the Sixth Form at Liverpool Collegiate Grammar School. An outstanding scholar and athlete, he was also unusually handsome, in a wry, brooding way, with neat, crisp, wavy hair that gave him more than a look of the film star Jeff Chandler. If, in addition, he was somewhat modest and slow to push himself, then 'Mo', as he called his mother, would always be there to back him.

Under the house were extensive cellars, used for storage and the boys' bicycles. Pete and Rory, fatigued by the long summer holiday of 1958, asked Mona Best if they could make a den down there for themselves and their friends. There were so many friends that Mrs Best suggested making the cellar into a real club, like the Lowlands and city espresso bars. For the rest of that year, she, her two sons and a team of potential members redecorated the cellar, installing bench seats and a counter above which, as a final touch, Mrs Best painted a dragon on the ceiling. Her favourite film being *Algiers*, with Charles Boyer, she decided to call the new club the Casbah.

There then arose the question of finding a group to play on club nights. One of the girl helpers mentioned Ken Browne, who played at the Lowlands in Les Stewart's quartet. Ken Browne paid the Casbah a visit while redecorations were still in progress, bringing with him another quartet member, George Harrison. 'George didn't seem to show too much enthusiasm for what we were doing,' Mona Best said, 'but Ken Browne threw himself heart and soul into it. He'd come over and help us with the work at weekends.'

When George came back, he brought with him two other musicians for the Casbah's resident group. 'John Lennon walked in with Paul McCartney, and John's girl friend, Cyn'. We were still painting – trying to get ready for our opening night. John got hold of a paint brush to help us, but he was without his glasses and as blind as a bat. He started putting paint on surfaces which didn't require paint. And all in gloss when I'd told him to use undercoat. On opening night, some of the paint still wasn't quite dry.'

In sedate West Derby, the Casbah Coffee Club caught on with teenagers at once. Mona Best ran it in person, selling coffee, sweets and soft drinks behind the miniature bar. John, Paul, George and Ken Browne played, without a drummer and using Ken Browne's 10-watt amplifier, for £3 a night between four of them. They all grew friendly with the Bests, especially with Pete, the handsome, taciturn elder son who, despite his plan to become a teacher, was keenly interested in rock and roll and show business. The group proved such an attraction that, at weekends, Mrs Best would hire a doorman to keep out the rougher element.

'It all went fine,' Mona Best said, 'until this one night when Ken Browne turned up with a heavy cold. I could see he wasn't well enough to play. I said to him, "Look, you go upstairs and sit with Mother" – he often did that; she was bedridden, you see, and he'd sit and talk to her. I said, "I'll bring a hot drink up to you." But Ken said no, he'd stay down in the club and watch. Just John, Paul and George played, and at the end, I gave them 15s [75p] each. There was a bit of murmuring; then they said, "Where's the other 15s?" "I've given it to Ken," I told them.

'They didn't like that. They wanted the full £3. But it was too late. I'd already given Ken his 15s. There was a bit of arguing and Ken said right, that was it, he'd finished with them. The other three walked out of the club there and then.'

'Pete, my elder boy, had been getting more and more interested, watching the others play. I remember Ken Browne saying to him, "Right. I'm out of that lot. Come on, Pete: why don't you and I get a group up now?"'

•

Twice each week, Arthur Ballard would leave the College of Art in Hope Street to conduct a private tutorial with the student he considered the most gifted of all under his charge. The student, a white-faced, tiny boy named Stuart Sutcliffe, refused to work in College; he had his own cramped studio, in the basement of a house in Percy Street, where Ballard would visit him, bringing a half-bottle of Scotch whisky for refreshment. The tutorial was a morning's talk, during which Sutcliffe never stopped painting. 'He worked with large canvases, which wasn't at all fashionable then,' Arthur Ballard says. 'He was so small, he almost had to jump with his brush to reach the top.'

Among the students, Stu Sutcliffe was something of a cult. His pale, haunted face, topped by luxuriantly swept-back hair, gave him a more than passing resemblance to James Dean, the Hollywood star who had become legendary to that generation for the hectic fame and shortness of his life. Stu was aware of the resemblance, cultivating it with dark glasses and an air of brooding far from his true personality.

He was born of Scottish parents in Edinburgh in 1940. His father, Charles, a senior Civil Servant, moved to Liverpool on wartime attachment to Cammell Laird's shipyard and subsequently went to sea as a ship's engineer. The rearing of Stuart and his two younger sisters was left to their mother, Millie, an infants' schoolteacher. Charles and Millie had a volatile relationship, veering from intense mutual affection to passionate rows, generally on the eve of his departure back to sea. From the earliest age, Millie Sutcliffe said, Stu strove to take on the role of her protector. 'I'd sometimes be sitting in my chair with my head in my hands. Stuart would sit at my feet, looking up at me. "You're tired," he'd say. "Come on, we'll put the little ones to bed, then you and me must have a talk."'

He had entered Art College from Prescot Grammar School, below the normal admittance age, and had quickly revealed a talent of dazzling diversity. His first terms, in addition to prosaic curriculum work, produced notebooks thronging with evidence of a facility to reproduce any style from Matisse to Michelangelo. Derivative as his student work was, it had a quality which excited Arthur Ballard – a refusal to accept or transmit anything according to convention. 'Stu was a revolutionary,' Ballard says. 'Everything he did crackled with excitement.'

Early in 1959, the path of Hope Street's most promising student crossed that of its most uninspired and apathetic one. At Ye Cracke, the student pub in Rice Street, beneath the etchings of Wellington greeting Blücher at Waterloo, and Nelson's death at Trafalgar, Stu Sutcliffe fell into conversation with John Lennon.

The intermediary was a friend of Stu's named Bill Harry, a curly-haired boy who had won his way from a poor childhood in Parliament Street to become the College's first student of Commercial Design. Bill was a prolific amateur journalist, a writer and illustrator of science fiction 'fanzines', and, like Stu himself, an omnivorous reader. They would sit for hours in Ye Cracke, discussing Henry Miller and Kerouac and the 'beat' poets, Corso and Ferlinghetti.

In Bill Harry, John found someone, not stand-offish and superior as he had thought all his fellow students to be, but down-to-earth, friendly, humorous and encouraging. Bill knew already of John's interest in writing, and, one lunch-time at Ye Cracke, asked if there was anything of John's that he could read. He remembers with what embarrassment John dragged some scraps of paper from his jeans pocket and handed them over. Instead of the Ginsberg or Corso pastiche he had expected, Bill Harry found himself reading a piece of nonsense about a farmer that made him gurgle with laughter.

Stu Sutcliffe's effect on John was more complex. For Stu, in 1959, resembled neither Teddy Boy nor jazz cellar habitué. He had evolved his own style of skin-tight jeans, pink shirts with pinned collars and pointed boots with high, elasticated sides. His dress, in fact, was disapproved of by the Art College far more than John's, but was tolerated because of his brilliance as a student.

Stu's passionate commitment to his painting, and to art and literature in all young and vital forms, communicated itself to John in a way that no formal teaching had been able to do. From Stu, he learned of the French Impressionists, whose rebellion against accepted values made that of rock and roll seem marginal. Van Gogh, even more than Elvis Presley, now became the hero against whom John Lennon measured the world.

John's sudden enthusiasm for his College studies to some extent benefited Paul also. Paul, still revising for O-levels at the Institute, was only too glad to join in intellectual discussions, passing himself off as a student from the nearby university. For George Harrison, it was more arduous, since John among his Art College cronies was even more inclined to be witty at George's expense. But he was 15 now, and not such a kid, and learning to answer John back.

This new era revived the group which had been languishing again since the dispute at Mrs Best's. Stu and Bill Harry both sat on the Students' Union committee, and were thus able to get bookings for John, Paul and George to play at College dances. The trouble was, although John and George had electric guitars, they no longer had Ken Browne and his 10-watt amplifier. On Stu Sutcliffe's recommendation, the Students' Union agreed to buy an amplifier for them to use, on the understanding, of course, that it should not be taken away from College.

Stu's interest in rock and roll was a purely aesthetic one. He passionately wanted to join a group as an adjunct to the personal image he had created for himself. As John and he became closer friends, the idea grew that Stu, in some or other capacity, should join John's group. That he possessed no ability on any instrument was not considered a disqualification. If he were to buy a guitar – or, better still, some drums – he surely would be able to learn in the way the other three had. Unfortunately, Stu, with his small grant and his straitened family circumstances, had no money to spend at Hessy's music shop.

In 1959, the biennial John Moores Exhibition took place at Liverpool's illustrious Walker Art Gallery. Mr Moores was the city's commercial patriarch, deriving fortunes from football pools, shops and mail-order catalogues, of which a sizeable part was philanthropically devoted to encouraging the Arts on Merseyside. This was the second Moores Exhibition, offering £4,000 in prize money and attracting some 2,000 entries from all over the British Isles. A canvas submitted by Stu Sutcliffe was one of the handful selected for hanging.

Aunt Mimi remembered John's unfeigned pleasure in Stu's achievement. 'He came *rushing* in to tell me ... "You'll never guess; it's the Moores Exhibition. You must come and see it. And look *nice*!"

'We went to the Walker Art Gallery and John took me up to this enormous painting. It seemed to be all khaki and yellow triangles. I looked at it and I said, "What *is* it?" Well! John got hold of my arm and hustled me outside; I wasn't allowed to see another picture in the show. "How could you *say* a thing like that, Mimi?" He gave his chest a big thump, and bellowed, "Art comes from in here!"'

As well as hanging in one of Europe's principal galleries, Stu's painting was bought, by the great John Moores himself, for £65. 'He'd never really had any money before,' Millie Sutcliffe said. 'I knew he'd got one or two little debts he needed to pay. The rest would see him right, I thought, to buy his paints and canvases for a few weeks.

'His father was home, and went up to Stuart's room while he wasn't there. It was his father who found this thing that Stuart had spent *all* the John Moores prize money on. "That's right, Mother," he said. "It's a bass guitar. I'm going to play with John in his group."'

4

'The bass drum used to roll away across the stage'

In Slater Street, on the edge of Chinatown, there was a little coffee bar, with copper kettles in its window, called the Jacaranda. John Lennon, Stu Sutcliffe and their Art College friends went there almost every day, between classes or in place of them. The coffee was cheap, toast with jam cost only fivepence a slice, nor was the management particular about the time its customers spent wedged behind the little kidney-shaped tables. Whole days could be spent, over one cold coffee cup, looking through the window steam at passing Chinese, West Indians, Lascars, dockers and men going to and from the nearby unemployment office.

To the Jacaranda's black-bearded owner, Allan Williams, John and his friends were 'a right load of layabouts'. Williams had studied them at length while passing coffees and toasted sandwiches through from the back kitchen where his Chinese wife Beryl cooked and kept accounts. He had particularly noticed the slightly-built boy in dark glasses whom the others teased for carrying art materials round with him in a carrier bag. He could not but notice the one called John, who expertly dredged money from the purse of the blonde girl who sat next to him, and could even cajole free drinks and snacks from the more susceptible waitresses.

'The Jac' was not Williams's sole enterprise. He had, in his time, pursued many trades, among them plumber, artificial jewellery-maker and door-to-door salesman. Being a Welshman, naturally he had a voice. Indeed, he had almost trained for the operatic stage. His Welsh tenor was heard, instead, in the Victorian pubs and West Indian shebeens round Liverpool 8, where Williams pursued an energetic, but as yet unspecific, career as a bohemian and entrepreneur.

At intervals, his curly-haired, stocky figure would swagger back along Slater Street to the tumbledown house where, on a capital of £100, he had opened his Jacaranda coffee bar. The 'right load of layabouts' would still be there. Prising their coffee cups away, Allan Williams would remark with heavy sarcasm that *they* were never going to make him his fortune.

•

In the world outside Liverpool, unabated disapproval of rock and roll had worn it into a more acceptable shape. The word was 'rock' no longer, but 'pop'. The taste – again dictated by America – was for cleancut, collegiate-looking youths whose energy had left their pelvic regions and gone into their ingratiating smiles. The British idol of the hour was a former skiffler named Adam Faith, with the looks of a haunted Cassius and a voice which all the artifice of recording engineers could not rid of its heavy adenoids. A ballad called 'What Do You Want?' – or, as Adam Faith enunciated it, 'Puwhat Do Yuh Pwant?' – went to number one late in 1959, using an arrangement of pizzicato violins unashamedly copied from Buddy Holly. Holly lodged no suit for plagiarism, having died in an air crash eight months earlier.

But while Britain listened to Adam Faith and 'pop', Liverpool listened to rhythm and blues. The Cunard Yanks were bringing over records by a new young black performer still confined by his own country to the low indecent level of 'race' music. His name was Chuck Berry; the songs he sang were wry and ragged, vividly pictorial eulogies to girls and cars, the joys and neuroses of American urban life. His verbal felicity and subversive wit had instant appeal for young men who, although white, felt themselves hardly less segregated in their own land from the more privileged and 'glamorous' south. All over Merseyside, in ballrooms, town halls, church meeting houses, even swimming baths and ice-skating rinks, there were amateur r & b groups pumping out Berry's repertoire along with that of other kindred black performers like Little Richard and Fats Domino.

By far and away Liverpool's most adulated group in those days were Rory Storm and the Hurricanes. Rory, a blond, amiable youth known by day as Alan Caldwell, was afflicted by a stammer which, fortunately, vanished when he opened his mouth to sing. He had been an outstanding athlete and swimmer, and would enliven his stage performance by feats of acrobatics and climbing. At the Majestic ballroom in Birkenhead, he would shin up a pillar from the stage to the promenade balcony. At the Tower Ballroom, downriver in New Brighton, he would crawl about inside the 100-foot-high dome. His occasional falls increased his drawing power. His group had lately acquired a new drummer – a slightly-built boy from the Dingle, with mournful eyes, prematurely greying side-whiskers and a habit of burdening his fingers with cheap rings. This drummer's name was Richard Starkey but he preferred, in emulation of his Wild West heroes, to be known as Ringo Starr.

After Rory Storm in popularity came Cass and the Casanovas, a four-man group whose drummer, Johnny Hutch, was the most powerful on Merseyside. They said of Johnny Hutch – as, indeed, he said of himself –

that he could take his brain out and lay it on the table, and his drumsticks would still go on hitting in time.

The Saturday dances over, most of the groups would drive back from the suburbs into Liverpool to congregate at Allan Williams's Jacaranda coffee bar. At night in the basement, there was dancing to a West Indian steel band. Though no alcohol could legally be served, much was drunk in 'spiked' coffee and soft drinks.

Rory Storm, Brian Casser and Duke Duval were personalities whom John Lennon and his followers held in awe. For John's group, such as it was, figured nowhere in the leagues of local favouritism. No less an authority than Johnny Hutch, the Casanovas' drummer, had given his opinion that they 'weren't worth a carrot'.

To begin with, they still lacked a drummer. This wouldn't have mattered so much with a strong undercurrent of bass guitar. But Stu Sutcliffe had only just begun learning to play the big Hofner 'President' bass he had bought with his John Moores prize. The President hung heavy on Stu's slight frame; his slim fingers found difficulty in stretching to the simplest chord-shapes. He would stand turning half-away so the audience could not see how little and how painfully he was playing.

They had had, and lost, one good opportunity at the Casanova Club, a Sunday afternoon jive session in a room above the Temple restaurant in Dale Street. The promoter, Sam Leach, agreed to try them out in support of his resident group, Cass and the Casanovas. But the club members had little time for a group with no drummer and only one small tinkling amp – a group which did not go in for suits and step dance routines like Cliff Richard's Shadows, but instead wore strange, scruffy, 'arty' black crewneck sweaters and tennis shoes, and jumped and leapt in wild asymmetry. And when Paul McCartney began to sing in his high, almost feminine voice, there were titters of amusement from some of the girls.

They did little better at Lathom Hall, out at Seaforth where the Mersey broadens against the rim of Albert Dock. The night's main group were the Dominoes, featuring 'Kingsize' Taylor, a vast youth visible by day cutting up meat in a local butcher's shop. Paul, John, George and Stu had been hired merely to play during the interval. They were so bad that the management ordered them offstage after their second song. When the Dominoes came on again, Kingsize Taylor saw John, Paul and George standing near the stage, each scribbling furiously on a piece of paper. 'They were writing down the words of the songs as we sang them. They'd take turns to scribble down a line each of Dizzy Miss Lizzie.'

They still practised for hours on end, at George's or Paul's house, using a tape recorder of the old-fashioned sort that grew warm after a couple of hours' use. They had no idea of the way they wanted to be.

They knew only that they wanted to be nothing like Cliff Richard's neat, smiling, step-dancing Shadows. A tape has survived of a long, rambling blues sequence with George on lead guitar, his fingers stumbling frequently over half-learned phrases; John and Paul strumming along and Stu Sutcliffe keeping up on bass by playing as few notes as possible. At one point, Paul's voice breaks in impatiently with a kind of impromptu jazz scat-singing. Later there are attempts at various rhythms, first rockabilly, then Latin-American, then a note-for-note copy of the Eddie Cochran song 'Hallelujah I Love Her So'. Suddenly they break into a song which was among the first ever written by John Lennon – 'The One After 909'. The beat lifts; their voices coalesce: for a moment they are recognisable as what they were to become. Then they go back to sitting round while George, painfully, tries to learn the blues.

From the same period, there is a letter drafted by Paul in his scholarly hand, soliciting a mention in some local newspaper after a chance encounter with one of the journalists. The letter claims group accomplishments as much academic as musical; it makes great play with the fact that John goes to Art College, and confers on Paul himself a fictitious place 'reading English at Liverpool University'. Paul's songwriting partnership with John is said to have produced 'more than 50 numbers', among them 'Looking Glass', 'Thinking of Linking', 'Winston's Walk' and 'The One After 909'. To cover every option, the group is credited with a 'jazz feel' and a repertoire of 'standards' such as 'Moonglow', 'Ain't She Sweet' and 'You Are My Sunshine'. 'The group's name,' Paul wrote, 'is . . .' They still had not been able to make up their minds.

Stu Sutcliffe had lately been evicted from his basement in Percy Street for painting all the furniture white. He suggested to John that they both move into their friend Rod Murray's flat in Gambier Terrace, a big, windswept Victorian parade overlooking the Anglican cathedral. The flat was principally floorboards, strewn with records, stolen traffic signs and the mattresses used by various semi-nomadic tenants. Bill Harry, a frequent sleeper in the bath, remembers all-night talk sessions in which Stu and he elaborated their plan to write a book that would give Liverpool the same cultural identity that Kerouac and the 'beat' poets had given America. John Lennon's chief contributions were word games and charades of elaborate craziness.

Though John soon left Gambier Terrace, his friendship with Stu continued. The two were together most of the day, when Paul and George could not escape class at the Institute. They would sit for hours in the Jacaranda, Stu sketching and crayoning while John, with his wolfish smile, cadged coffees from the softer-hearted waitresses. So it came about that

Allan Williams, with his talent for using people, discovered a way of using even two penniless Art students.

Williams was currently engaged in his first major venture as an entrepreneur. He had hired St George's Hall, Liverpool's chief public building, as the venue for an 'Arts Ball', modelled on the Chelsea Arts Ball in London. John and Stu found themselves roped in to design and build the decorated carnival floats whose ritual destruction was the best-known feature of the London event. On the day of the ball, Williams used them as a labouring gang to manhandle the floats across St George's piazza, under the disapproving eye of Victoria and Albert, and into the Great Hall with its mosaic floor, its marble busts of Peel and George Stephenson and its towering pipe organ.

The 1959 Liverpool Arts Ball was an event prophetic of Allan Williams's career as an impresario. The comedian Bruce Forsyth was among VIP guests who watched, not only the ritual destruction of the carnival floats, but also flour and fire extinguisher fights and intermittent attempts to play rock and roll on the Civic organ. At midnight, balloons came down from a web of football goal nets suspended in the ceiling. After that, owing to employee error, the heavy, greasy nets themselves fell on to the heads of the crowd.

•

Among the promoters of British pop music in the late 1950s, none had so potent a reputation as Larry Parnes. It was Parnes who, in 1956, metamorphosed Tommy Steele, 'Britain's first rock 'n' roller', from a Cockney merchant seaman he had spotted strumming a guitar in a Soho drinking club. Tommy Steele's colossal success with British teenagers was due largely to his youthful manager's intuitive brilliance as an agent and image-builder and the jealous care with which, following Colonel Tom Parker's example, he guarded his money-spinning protégé. Though Tommy Steele had now somewhat diminished as a pop attraction, the enterprises of Larry Parnes had prospered and multiplied.

By 1959, Parnes controlled what he himself liked to call a 'stable' of the leading British male pop singers. Most were ingenuous youths from unknown provincial cities who had somehow found their way to London and the 2i's coffee bar in Old Compton Street, hallowed as the place where Larry Parnes had spotted Tommy Steele. Whether they could sing or not, Parnes fashioned them into lucrative teen idols by giving them stage names that combined the homely with the exotic: Billy Fury, Marty Wilde, Vince Eager, Duffy Power, Dickie Pride, Johnny Gentle. A closet homosexual, who made extensive use of the casting couch, he styled his protégés to reflect his own private fantasies, equipping them all with virtually identical blow-waved hair, tight jeans and pointy cowboy boots. It was wonderfully ironic, therefore, that the adult anti-rock and roll lobby should have complained so vociferously about their sexual power over teenage *girls*. Several of them actually lived at Parnes's flat on London's Cromwell Road, directly opposite Baden Powell House, the headquarters of the Scout movement. When not coaching his charges in deportment or stagecraft, Parnes would produce a pair of powerful binoculars and gaze longingly through them at the boy scouts across the road.

As well as furnishing the cast of early TV pop shows like *Oh Boy!* and *Drumbeat*, Parnes used his stable to create self-contained travelling shows which for British fans in places far from London represented the sole chance to see live rock and roll music. Larry Parnes shows played at theatres and cinemas, but also at town halls and rural Corn Exchanges. No audience was too far-flung or insignificant to be visited by the glossy-haired, unflappable young man whom the music business – believing money to be his sole preoccupation – had nicknamed 'Mister Parnes Shillings and Pence'.

Early in 1960, Larry Parnes promoted a tour headed by two imported American stars, Eddie Cochran and Gene Vincent. Cochran, whose 'Summertime Blues' sold a million copies in 1958, was a 21-year-old Oklahoman with the hulking pout of an Elvis run to fat. Vincent was a 25-year-old ex-sailor, famous for his wailing voice, his group the Bluecaps and a classic piece of rock and roll gibberish called 'Be Bop a Lula'. Partly crippled from a motorcycle accident, he performed anchored to the stage by a leg-iron, and irradiating depravity and ill-health. Nor was this present tour destined to build up his constitution.

In Liverpool, as in every city along its route, the Cochran–Vincent show was a sell-out. Larry Parnes himself was at the Empire theatre to watch the wild welcome his artists received, even in this remote corner of the land. Elsewhere, amid the shouting and stamping, three would-be rock and rollers from a group last known as Johnny and the Moondogs strained their eyes to try to see the fingering of Eddie Cochran's guitar solo in 'Hallelujah I Love Her So'. In yet another seat, the proprietor of the Jacaranda coffee bar suddenly perceived that there might be easier ways to a fortune than by attempting to bring the Chelsea Arts Ball to Liverpool. In Allan Williams's own words, 'I could smell money. Lots of it.'

Afterwards, Williams sought out Larry Parnes and, as one impresario to another, invited him back to the Jacaranda. By the end of the night, Parnes had been talked into bringing back Eddie Cochran and Gene Vincent for a second concert, promoted in partnership with Allan Williams at the city's boxing stadium. Half the programme would consist of Parnes acts; the other half would be provided by Williams from among local groups like Rory Storm and the Hurricanes, and Cass and the Casanovas. The concert, lasting several hours, was fixed to take place after Eddie Cochran and Gene Vincent had finished their current tour.

At the very last minute, however, there was a hitch. Cochran and Vincent had appeared at the Hippodrome theatre, Bristol, and were returning to London by road. Near Chippenham, Wiltshire, their hire car skidded and struck a tree. Eddie Cochran – who, by one of those bilious musical ironies had just recorded a song called 'Three Steps To Heaven' – suffered fatal injuries. Gene Vincent and another passenger, the songwriter Sharon Seeley, were both seriously hurt.

A telephone call to Larry Parnes confirmed the news that Allan Williams had heard over the radio. Eddie Cochran would not be able to appear at Liverpool boxing stadium. Gene Vincent, despite fresh injuries added to his residual ones, might be fit, Parnes thought; just the same it would be wiser to cancel the promotion. Williams, having sold most of the tickets, and feeling death to be insufficient as an excuse to a Liverpool audience, insisted the show should go ahead, and feverishly went in search of more local groups to pad out the programme.

His search took him, among other places, to Holyoake Hall, near Penny Lane, and one of the better-run local jive dances. The hall, unlike most, had its own regular compère and disc jockey, Bob Wooler. A clerk in the railway dock office at Garston, Wooler possessed an encyclopaedic knowledge of local bands and their personnel. On his earliest recommendation, Allan Williams booked Bob Evans and the Five Shillings, and Gerry and the Pacemakers, an up-and-coming quartet whose leader, Gerry Marsden, worked on the railway also, as a van delivery-boy.

The Gene Vincent boxing stadium show, jointly promoted by Larry Parnes and Allan Williams, thus, inadvertently, became the first major occurrence of a brand of teenage music indigenous to Liverpool and the Mersey. By an inscrutable irony, the three individuals destined to carry that music into undreamable galaxies of fame were not then considered competent enough to take part. John Lennon, Paul McCartney and George Harrison had to be content with ringside seats and watching Rory Storm, Cass and the Casanovas – even their old rivals, the group that featured the midget Nicky Cuff.

The concert proceeded on a note of rising pandemonium, at the height of which Rory Storm was sent out with his incapacitating stammer to appeal for calm. The show's best performance was unanimously felt to be that of Gerry and the Pacemakers, singing 'You'll Never Walk Alone' from Rodgers and Hammerstein's *Carousel*. No more inappropriate introduction could have been given to the infirm, black leather-clad figure of Gene Vincent himself, who was at last propelled through the ropes into the boxing ring. As the ringside spectators made a rush to join him, Larry Parnes and Allan Williams trotted round briskly, stamping on their hands.

•

It was shortly after this memorable night that John Lennon sidled up to Williams at the Jacaranda's kitchen door, and muttered, 'Hey, Al, why don't you do something for us?' John had been there with George and Stu Sutcliffe after the boxing stadium show when Williams brought the great Larry Parnes back to discuss further co-promotions. Parnes, impressed by the Liverpool music, had hinted at the possibility of using local groups to back solo singers from his stable when touring brought them northward.

Allan Williams, while thinking no more highly of John's group than anyone else did, felt he owed them a favour in return for the Arts Ball floats. Though not prepared to offer them to Larry Parnes, he did agree to help Johnny and the Moondogs become better organised. They, in return, would do such small general jobs as Allan Williams required.

Williams further promised to try to find them the drummer they so chronically lacked. From Cass, of Cass and the Casanovas, he heard of a man named Tommy Moore who sometimes sat in on drums at Sam Leach's club and who, despite owning his own full kit, belonged to no group permanently. Within the week, Tommy Moore had been persuaded by Allan Williams to throw in his lot with Johnny and the Moondogs.

The new recruit was a small, worried-looking individual of 36, whose daytime job was driving a fork-lift truck at the Garston Bottle-making Works. For all that, in his audition at Gambier Terrace, he proved to be a better drummer than any who had ever sat behind Johnny and the Moondogs. When he showed himself able to produce the slow, skipping beat of the Everly Brothers' song, 'Cathy's Clown', even Paul McCartney seemed satisfied.

Tommy Moore began practising with them downstairs at the Jacaranda, in preparation for the work which Allan Williams had promised them when they were good enough. Williams, meantime, used them as odd-job men to redecorate the 'Jac's' primitive ladies' lavatory. John and Stu Sutcliffe were also encouraged to cover the brick walls of their rehearsal room with voodoo-ish murals.

Tommy soon noticed what peculiar tensions were at work within Johnny and the Moondogs. 'John and Paul were always at it, trying to outdo each other. It was them at the front and the rest of us way behind. George used to stand there, not saying a word. And didn't they used to send up that other lad, Stuart! Oh, they never left off teasing him. They said he couldn't play his bass – and he couldn't, though he tried.'

To begin with, Allan Williams would allow them to play to the Jacaranda customers only when his regular attraction, the Royal Caribbean Steel Band, had the night off. Since the cellar had no microphone stands, two girls had to be persuaded to kneel in front of John and Paul, holding up hand mikes attached to a mop-handle and broom. 'I could have retired on what we used to get for playing at the Jac',' Tommy Moore said. 'A bottle of Coke and a plate of beans on toast.'

The great Larry Parnes, meanwhile, had contacted Allan Williams again about the possibility of using Liverpool musicians as backing groups for the solo singers in his 'stable'. It happened that 'Mister Parnes Shillings and Pence' was experiencing difficulty in finding London bands willing to go on tour in the north and Scotland for the rates of pay he offered. When Parnes contacted Allan Williams again, it was with a request that Williams should marshal some local groups for audition as possible sidesmen for Parnes's biggest male pop star, Billy Fury.

The news caused a particular stir in Liverpool because Billy Fury was himself a Liverpudlian. Born Ronnie Wycherley, in the tough Dingle area, he had been a Mersey tugboat hand until two years earlier when his girl friend had sent Larry Parnes some of the songs he had written. Parnes had worked the usual transformation with a tempestuous stage name, a brooding persona and a series of hit records, sung in an Elvislike mumble. Billy Fury, it was further announced, would be coming up to Liverpool with his manager to attend the audition in person.

Every group that frequented the Jacaranda was agog for what seemed a Heaven-sent opportunity. Williams, in the end, narrowed the field down to Rory Storm and the Hurricanes, Cass and the Casanovas, Derry Wilkie and the Seniors, and Johnny and the Moondogs. In Allan Williams's opinion, Johnny and the Moondogs were now ready for something more than decorating the ladies' lavatory.

One pressing requirement, before Larry Parnes saw them, was for a change of name. What they needed was something spry and catchy, like Buddy Holly's Crickets. On an empty page in his sketch-book, Stu Sutcliffe wrote 'The Beetles'. He was not thinking of small black insects but the motorcycle gang led by Marlon Brando in America's prototype youth rebellion film, *The Wild One*. Although *The Wild One* had been banned by the timorous British film censor, pop culture-vultures like Stu and his circle would undoubtedly have known all about it. Coincidentally, Buddy Holly's own group had made the same connection a couple of years earlier and almost named themselves the Beetles before deciding on the Crickets.

'Crickets' were one thing, but 'Beetles', even allowing the Brando precedent, were quite another. No group that wished to be taken seriously in the late Fifties could possibly identify itself with so lowly and unattractive a form of life. Still, the idea was kicked around, undergoing various barely serious mutations along the way. John, unable to resist any pun, turned it into 'Beatles' as in beat music. Stu himself took to spelling it 'Beatals' in the sense of beating all competition. Nonetheless, he is the one who must go down in history as the only true begetter.

However it might be spelt, the name was greeted with the same disbelieving scorn by both their supporters and rivals at the Billy Fury audition. Allan Williams pleaded with them to think of something – anything – else if they didn't want the great Larry Parnes to laugh them into extinction. This opposition had the predictable effect of making John determined now to go on as the 'Beetles', 'Beatles' or 'Beat-als'. A more persuasive voice, however, was that of Brian Casser, lead singer with Cass and the Casanovas. If they had to ally themselves with bugs, Casser urged, then at least stick to the conventional formula of such-and-such and the so-and-so's. Prompted by memories of R. L. Stevenson's *Treasure Island*, he suggested 'Long John and the Silver Beatles'. Though John jibbed at calling himself Long John, the Silver Beatles won the vote.

The place fixed for the audition was a small working-men's club, the Wyvern, in Seel Street, just round the corner from the Jacaranda. Allan Williams had recently acquired the premises with the object of turning them into a plushy London-style 'night spot'. Punctual to the minute, in through the half-demolished foyer walked Larry Parnes, silk-suited and affable, accompanied by the nervy-looking ex-tugboat hand, currently the biggest name in British pop music, who cared rather less for stardom than for the dog and tortoise he was permitted to keep at his manager's London flat.

Down in the basement, the Silver Beatles viewed the competition with dismay. Every group was locally famous, smartly suited and luxuriously equipped. Derry and the Seniors had been well known in Liverpool for years as an authentic rhythm and blues group featuring a black singer, Derry Wilkie, an electric keyboard and a real live saxophone. Johnny Hutch of Cass and the Casanovas was already setting up the sequinned drum kit which he was said to be able to play in his sleep. Rory Storm was there, deeply tanned, with his Italian-suited Hurricanes. Rory's drummer, the little sad-eyed, bearded one, came from the Dingle also, and had been in Billy Fury's class at school. Neither John nor Paul in those days much liked the look of Ringo Starr.

Parnes, sitting with Billy Fury at a small table in the twilight, was impressed by the power and variety of the music. Derry and the Seniors and Rory Storm's Hurricanes were both marked down as strong contenders for the prize. Parnes also favoured Cass and the Casanovas, thanks mainly to their bass-player, Johnny Gustafson, a black-haired, extremely good-looking boy. 'Johnny Gus', in fact, was later called down to London to experience the Parnes star-making process on his own.

The Silver Beatles, when their turn came, made rather less of an impression. 'They weren't a bit smart,' Larry Parnes remembers. 'They just wore jeans, black sweaters, tennis shoes – and lockets.' There was a delay as well, owing to the non-arrival of Tommy Moore, who had gone in search of some stray pieces of drum equipment at the Casanova Club. At length, when Tommy still had not appeared, Johnny Hutch had to be persuaded to sit in with them.

A snapshot, taken in mid-audition, shows the Silver Beatles exactly as Larry Parnes saw them that day at the Wyvern social club. John and Paul occupy the foreground, back to back madly bucking and crouching over their cheap guitars. To the right stands George, his sole concession to rhythm a slight hanging of the head. Stu Sutcliffe, to the rear with his overburdening bass guitar, turns away as usual to hide his inadequate playing. In the background, Johnny Hutch sits at his magnificent drums, showing a great deal of patterned ankle-sock and, very clearly, bored to death.

As to what Larry Parnes thought of them, there are conflicting eyewitness accounts. Allan Williams's version is that both Parnes and Billy Fury were 'knocked out' by the Silver Beatles, excepting Stu Sutcliffe. Parnes would have signed them at once, at £100 per week, provided they would agree to drop Stu. It was John Lennon's curt refusal to betray his friend, so Williams says, which robbed them of their first big chance.

Parnes himself, unfortunately, had no recollection of finding fault with Stu's bass playing. To Parnes, the eyesore of the group was the worried, rather elderly-looking man who arrived halfway through the audition and took over from Johnny Hutch on drums. Tommy Moore had finally made it across town from Dale Street. 'I thought the boys in front were great,' Parnes said. 'The lead guitar and the bass, so-so. It was the *drummer*, I told them, who was wrong.'

What Larry Parnes really wanted, it transpired, were cut-price musicians to accompany his lesser-known artists on tour to Scotland. Cass and the Casanovas were first to be so engaged, as backing group for a gravel-voiced Parnes singer named Duffy Power.

The next letter from Larry Parnes to Allan Williams concerned the Silver Beatles. In mid-May, Parnes was sending another of his stable,

Johnny Gentle, on a two-week Scottish tour. The Silver Beatles could have the job of backing him, for the same as Cass and the Casanovas had received: £18 each per week.

The offer sent the Silver Beatles into transports of elation. Since the Wyvern social club audition, they had thought they'd lost any chance of finding stardom via Larry Parnes. That Johnny Gentle was the least-known of all Parnes's singers did not diminish the excitement of being offered their first work as professionals; of going 'on tour' the way the big names did; of performing in real cinemas and theatres, and staying in hotels the whole night.

All five immediately set about disentangling themselves from their everyday commitments in mid-May. For Stu and John it was simply a matter of cutting College for two weeks. It was less simple for Tommy Moore, whose girl friend set great store by his weekly wage packet from Garston Bottle Works. Tommy pacified her with visions of the wealth he would bring back from across the border.

George Harrison, too, was now a working man. He had left the Institute Grammar School at 16, without O-levels and, for want of anything better, had applied for a job as a window-dresser at Blackler's department store. That vacancy had been filled, but there was another one for an apprentice electrician. To be an apprentice, as his two elder brothers were, represented both a safe and an honourable course. But the only way he could get time off to go to Scotland was to take his summer holiday early.

The greatest ingenuity was shown, as usual, by Paul McCartney. He had to find a method of extricating himself from the Institute Sixth Form where, supposedly, he was deep in revision for his forthcoming A-level exams in English and Art. His friend Ivan Vaughan told him he would be mad to risk those A-levels for the sake of the Scottish tour. Somehow he managed to convince his father that two weeks off in term time would aid his revision by giving his brain a rest.

Before they set off, they decided that to be real pop musicians, they must all adopt stage names. Paul took to calling himself Paul Ramon, thinking it had a hothouse 1920-ish sound. George, whose idol was Carl Perkins, called himself Carl Harrison, and Stu became Stu de Stael, after the painter. John Lennon and Tommy Moore decided not to bother.

They embarked by train from Lime Street, wearing the jeans and black sweaters and tennis shoes that were also their stage outfits, and carrying a selection of borrowed amplifiers which Tommy Moore viewed with deep mistrust. 'The amps got by – just. George was the sparks if anything went wrong. I'd always stand well back while he was fiddling with the plugs. My drums didn't have everything they ought to have had either. I hadn't got a spur to hold the bass drum down. When Paul and John got going in one of their fast Chuck Berry numbers, the bass drum used to go rolling away across the stage.'

The tour struck complications from the start. Duncan McKinnon, Parnes's Scottish intermediary, did not like the look of the Silver Beatles. They liked even less the look of the small van in which they and Johnny Gentle were expected to travel through the Highlands. Nor was there any time to rehearse with Johnny, a handsome young bruiser who, not long previously, had been a merchant seaman putting into Birkenhead.

This particular member of Parnes's stable suffered chronically from stage nerves, which he would attempt to calm by drinking large quantities of lager. Even so, he insisted on taking his turn at the driving because that was the most comfortable seat. On about the second day, somewhat the worse for lager, he drove the vehicle, not at all gently, into the rear of a parked Ford Popular car with a couple of old ladies sitting in it. The impact dislodged all the luggage and equipment from the interior suitcase rack and hurled it on top of Tommy Moore.

Tommy was taken away in an ambulance, badly concussed, with his front top and bottom teeth loosened. That night, as he lay in hospital – it was in Banff, he thought – wearing borrowed night clothes and heavily sedated, the others arrived and hauled him out of bed for the night's performance. He remembers playing the drums, still groggy, with a bandage round his head.

Tommy Moore, with most of his teeth loose, and some pain-killing drugs the hospital had given him, climbed back into the van next morning for the journey onward, to Stirling, Nairn and Inverness. 'I hadn't much idea where we were. I looked out once and saw the big distillery. That's how I knew we'd got to the Highlands.'

According to Larry Parnes, the Silver Beatles went down better than any other backing group he had sent to Scotland. Parnes said that Johnny admitted they were getting more applause than he was, and urged his manager to sign them up without delay. Parnes, however, found the management of solo singers strenuous enough. 'Maybe it sounds silly but I just didn't want the worry of a five-piece group.'

Johnny and the Silver Beatles travelled as far north as Inverness, arriving too early in the morning to go to their hotel. 'We had to walk the streets, and all around the harbour next to the fishing boats,' Tommy Moore said. 'That was the finish as far as I was concerned. I'd had enough of them all – especially Lennon. And I was hungry.'

Their money did not get through to them until the very end of the fortnight. Tommy Moore remembered that on the train journey back to Liverpool he had a couple of pounds in his pocket. 'I went and sat with

Stuart on the journey. He was the only one of them I could stand by that time.'

At Lime Street, Tommy said goodbye rapidly and went to his flat in Smithdown Lane where his girl friend awaited him. 'She said "How much have you brought back then?" I told her, "A couple of quid." "A couple of *quid*!" she said. "Do you realise how much you could have earned in two weeks at Garston Bottle Works?"'

•

For the Silver Beatles, the most important consequence of the Scottish tour was that Allan Williams had at last begun to take them seriously as a group. The Welshman, through his company Jacaranda Enterprises, now looked after several bands, booking them out to dance promoters in Liverpool and 'over the water' on the Cheshire Wirral. The Silver Beatles were added to the portfolio Williams hawked around, in Birkenhead, New Brighton and Wallasey, using the big Jaguar that was well known to the Mersey Tunnel Police.

The Grosvenor ballroom in Wallasey was run by Les Dodd, a small, brisk stationery retailer with bright blue eyes and a back as straight as a slow foxtrot. Les Dodd had promoted strict tempo ballroom dancing at the Grosvenor since 1936, resisting the successive contagions of swing, bebop, skiffle and rock and roll, but by 1960, even he had begun to realise that his customers wanted something more untamed than his regular musicians, The Ernie Hignett Quartet.

For his first reluctant 'Big Beat' dance, on 6 June 1960, Les Dodd paid Allan Williams £10 for a group whose name – if Mr Dodd understood aright – was the Silver Beetles. So he advertised them, together with Gerry and the Pacemakers, as 'jive and rock specialists'. The same display advertisement carried a reassurance that on Tuesday the Grosvenor's strict tempo night would take place as usual.

Not long after Les Dodd began booking them, Tommy Moore decided he had had enough. He had continued as drummer after the Scottish tour, despite the loss of his front teeth, existing on a weekly share-out which, as his girl friend constantly reminded him, could be bettered by almost any type of labouring work. One evening, when the Silver Beatles met before crossing the river to Wallasey, Tommy Moore was not among them. He had gone back to his former, more lucrative occupation of driving a fork-lift truck.

The Silver Beatles, knowing too well the disgrace of being drummerless, tried hard to win back their elderly colleague. En route for Wallasey, they called at the Garston Bottle Works, found Tommy in the yard on night shift and pleaded with him not to quit. Tommy Moore's only reply was to swivel his fork lift away in the opposite direction. Another night, when Tommy was at home, they went to his flat in Smithdown Road and shouted up at his window. His girl friend, resentful of what had been done to her loved one's income and teeth, requested the Silver Beatles to fuck off.

Though Tommy Moore had gone, his drums remained behind. Each week, when they set out for the Grosvenor or for Neston Institute, the drum kit would be taken along. Before the first number, John Lennon would announce half-facetiously that anyone in the audience who fancied himself as a drummer was welcome to come up and have a try. The joke misfired badly one night at the Grosvenor when a huge Wallasey Ted named Ronnie accepted the invitation, sat in on Tommy's drums and produced a din which would have been no worse if he had thrown the kit from the top of a high building. An SOS call brought Allan Williams to the Grosvenor just in time to dissuade the beaming tough from electing himself to permanent membership.

Williams was now booking them into Liverpool halls where gang warfare – between girls no less than boys – was considered essential to a full night's entertainment. At Hambledon Hall or Aintree Institute, there always came a point in the evening, just after the pubs had closed, when up to 50 Teds would come in at once and pass along the jivers, slit-eyed with beer and hope of 'bother'. Most notorious of all were Garston Swimming Baths, known locally as 'the Blood Baths', so violent and gory were the battles fought over the floor that concealed the pool. The gangs, which bore tribal names such as 'The Tiger' or 'The Tank', would sometimes forget their enmities in a common assault on the no less frightening squads of bouncers, equipped with bloodlust and weapons to rival theirs. One legendary bouncer was of such size that he never needed to use his fists. A single jog from his stomach could send an assailant flying. Another, more imaginative promoter employed no stewards other than one little old lady to issue tickets. If a Ted cut up rough, the little old lady would shriek at him, 'You stop that or I'll tell your mum.' These were words to cow the most ruthless Teddy Boy.

Musicians were not immune from attack, particularly if they hailed from a part of Liverpool held in local disfavour, if they played Chuck Berry when the gang preferred Little Richard, or if one of them, however unwittingly, attracted the attention of a local patron's 'judy'. Guitars and drums were frequently smashed and microphone stands turned into clubs and lances if the stage seemed likely to be carried by storm.

The Silver Beatles witnessed their share of violence. At the Grosvenor in Wallasey, a regular uproar took place as local Teds clashed with invading cohorts from New Brighton or Birkenhead. At Neston Institute one night, a 16-year-old boy was booted to death during one of their performances. Even John, who fancied himself as a fighter, now cared more for protecting his guitar when the chairs and beer bottles began to fly, or girls rolled into view on the dance floor, scratching and spitting.

Their luck held until one night in June or July, when Williams had sent them to Litherland Town Hall, a low-lying municipal building in the north of Liverpool. During or after their performance, something was said or implied which upset a faction in the audience. An ambush was laid for the Silver Beatles as they made their way through the car park back to their van. In the ensuing scuffle, Stu Sutcliffe went down and received a kick in the head.

Millie Sutcliffe had waited up for Stu that night. She found him in his room, with blood still pouring from the gash in his head. He told her it had happened after the Litherland dance and that John and Pete Best had come to his rescue, John 'mixing it' so ferociously with the attackers that he broke one of his own fingers.

'There was blood all over the rug – everywhere,' Mrs Sutcliffe said. 'I was going to get the doctor but Stuart wouldn't allow me to do it. He was so terribly adamant. "Mother," he said, "if you touch that phone, I go out of this house and you'll never see me again."'

5

The Great Freedom

The Silver Beatles hit their lowest point in the summer of 1960. Still drummerless, they had given up trying to persuade dance promoters like Les Dodd and Sam Leach to book them. Their only regular engagement was at a strip club, part-owned by Allan Williams, off Liverpool's Upper Parliament Street. Williams paid them 10s each to strum their guitars while a stripper named Janice grimly shed her clothes. At Janice's request, the musicians stuck to 'standards' like 'Moonglow' and the 'Harry Lime Theme', and even gamely attempted 'The Gipsy Fire Dance' from sheet music.

The New Cabaret Artistes Club was run for Williams by a West Indian named Lord Woodbine. Born in Trinidad, 'Woody' earned a varied living as a builder and decorator, steel band musician and freelance barman. His ennoblement – after the fashion of calypso singers – derived from a certain self-possessed grandeur as much as from the Woodbine cigarette permanently hinged on his lower lip.

Lord Woodbine ran his own 'club', the New Colony, in the attic and basement of a semi-derelict house in Berkeley Street. The Silver Beatles played there, too, sometimes in the afternoons, while merchant seamen danced against hard-faced whores, and occasional troublemakers were pacified by the sight of the cutlass which Lord Woodbine kept under the bar.

Williams promised he would make something better happen for them soon. And Williams, by a sequence of cosmic blunders into thousand-to-one chances, did exactly that.

•

It all started when Williams returned to his coffee bar, the Jacaranda, one night and heard silence when he expected to hear the Royal Caribbean Steel Band. The entire band, he was told, had been lured away by a German theatrical agent to appear at a club in Hamburg. Down in the basement, set about by Stu Sutcliffe's voodoo murals, not a single 40-gallon steel drum remained.

To Williams, as to most Englishmen of that era, Hamburg, more than London or even Paris, was a city of breathtaking wickedness. British soldiers stationed after World War Two in Germany brought back extraordinary tales of entertainments purveyed by the Reeperbahn, Hamburg's legendary cabaret district – of women wrestling in mud, and sex displays involving pythons, donkeys and other animal associates. Such things could only be whispered about in a Britain where the two-piece bathing costume was still considered rather daring.

Evidently, along with everything else, there were music clubs along the Reeperbahn. Williams's curiosity was further aroused by letters from various members of the Royal Caribbean Steel Band, showing no remorse at their sudden disappearance but telling Williams guilelessly what a great place Hamburg was and urging him to come across with some of his Liverpool beat groups to share it.

His first idea was to take the Silver Beatles with him to Hamburg on an exploratory trip, but chronic shortage of cash prevented this. Instead, he got them to make a tape recording of their music, in company with Cass and the Casanovas and a local trad jazz band, the Noel Lewis Stompers, to be played to the Hamburg impresarios.

The journey which Williams made was in every sense characteristic. Wearing a top hat and accompanied by Lord Woodbine, he took a cheap charter flight to Amsterdam, intending to proceed to West Germany by train. In one eventful night in the Dutch capital, he succeeded in drinking champagne from a chorus girl's shoe; passing Lord Woodbine off as a genuine English aristocrat; and being thrown into the street after making matador passes at a Flamenco dancer with his coat.

The next evening found him in a similar state, temporarily parted from Lord Woodbine and dazzled by the overarching lights of the Grosse Freiheit, that small but crowded tributary of the Hamburg Reeperbahn, whose name in English means 'The Great Freedom'.

Halfway down the Grosse Freiheit, opposite a Roman Catholic church, Williams stumbled into a downstairs club called the Kaiserkeller. He found it to be decorated in confusedly nautical style, with booths like lifeboats, barrels for tables and a mural depicting life in the South Sea Isles. On a tiny central space, several hundred people danced while an Indonesian group performed Elvis Presley songs in German.

Williams demanded to speak to the proprietor and, after some delay, was shown into the presence of a short, broad-chested man with a quiff of sandy hair, a turned-up nose and a disabled leg which little inhibited his movements. Before the conversation had progressed far, a waiter came in to report a disturbance in the club area. Williams, through the open door, saw a squad of waiters systematically working over a solitary customer. Snatching from his desk drawer a long ebony cosh, the proprietor left the room with an agile, hopping gait, to lend them a hand.

The talk then resumed on amiable lines. Allan Williams introduced himself as the manager of the world's best rock and roll groups. The Kaiserkeller's owner, whose name was Bruno Koschmider, inquired if they were as good as Tommy Steele. Williams assured him they were better than Elvis Presley. For proof he brought out the tape he had made of the Silver Beatles and others. But when it was played on Herr Koschmider's tape recorder, nothing could be heard but scrabble and screech. Somebody, back in Liverpool, had blundered.

•

Having failed, as he thought, to convert Hamburg's Reeperbahn to Liverpool beat music, Allan Williams returned to being a functionary of the great Larry Parnes. The Silver Beatles – or plain Beatles, as they now defiantly called themselves – receded somewhat in Williams's mind. His chief property was the rhythm and blues group Derry and the Seniors, which Parnes had promised work in a summer show at Blackpool. The entire band, in expectation of this, gave up their jobs to turn professional. Then at the last minute, a letter arrived, on elaborately crested Parnes notepaper, cancelling the engagement.

An enraged deputation led by Howie Casey, the Seniors' sax-player, confronted Williams at his Blue Angel Club in Seel Street. Casey was a youth of powerful build, and Williams promised hastily to find them some alternative work. In sheer desperation, he packed the entire five-piece group and their equipment into his Jaguar and headed for the only place he could think of where work for a rock and roll band might magically exist. He was taking them, he said, to the famous 2i's coffee bar in London. There, in the home of skiffle, where Tommy Steele had first been discovered, something or other must surely turn up.

Fortune now smiled upon the agitated Welshman to the ludicrous, implausible extent that Fortune sometimes did. Upon entering the 2i's, whom should he see first but a small, barrel-chested West German gentleman with a quiff of sandy hair, a turned-up nose and a disabled leg not at the moment noticeable. It was Herr Bruno Koschmider, proprietor of the Kaiserkeller Club in Grosse Freiheit, Hamburg.

Koschmider, it transpired, had been deeply impressed by Williams's visit to his establishment, playing unintelligible tapes and boasting of rock and roll groups better than Elvis. Not long after Williams's dispirited return to Liverpool, Herr Koschmider had decided to visit England and hear these wonderful groups for himself. Naturally, however, it was not Liverpool he visited, but London, and the famous 2i's coffee bar.

He had already paid one visit to the 2i's and had signed up a solo singer, Tony Sheridan, to appear at the Kaiserkeller. Sheridan, in fact was a gifted performer, temporarily down on his luck. At the Kaiserkeller, he had been such a sensation that Bruno Koschmider had decided to sack his Indonesian Elvis-impersonators and go over completely to English rock and roll. He was thus at the 2i's a second time, hoping to hire another English group. He had not yet done so when Derry and the Seniors walked in.

It was the work of a few minutes for Williams to get Derry and the Seniors up and playing on the 2i's stage. Despite having had nothing to eat but some stale cake, they performed so well that Bruno Koschmider booked them for his Kaiserkeller club on the spot. They would receive 30 marks each per day – about £20 a week – with travel expenses and accommodation found. A contract was drafted with the help of a German waiter from the adjacent Heaven and Hell coffee bar.

Derry and the Seniors set off by train from Liverpool to Hamburg with £5 between them and no work permits. If challenged, Allan Williams said, the four tough-looking Liverpool boys and their black lead singer should pretend to be students on vacation. The story did not convince German frontier officials and at Osnabruck the entire group was ordered off the train and held in custody until Bruno Koschmider could be contacted to vouch for them.

The next news to reach Williams was a great deal better. Derry and the Seniors, together with Tony Sheridan and his band, were a hit at Herr Koschmider's Kaiserkeller. Together with rapturous postcards from various musicians, a letter arrived from Koschmider himself, asking Williams to send across a third group to play in another of Koschmider's clubs, the Indra.

The group Williams wanted to send was Rory Storm and the Hurricanes. They, however, were already committed to a summer season at Butlin's Skegness holiday camp. Gerry and the Pacemakers, his second choice, did not fancy going abroad. So Allan Williams, rather reluctantly, wrote to Bruno Koschmider, telling him to expect a group called the Beatles.

Shortly afterwards, a letter of protest arrived from the Seniors' lead singer, Derry Wilkie. It would spoil things for everyone, Derry said, if Allan Williams sent over 'a bum group like the Beatles'.

•

The offer came when John Lennon's Art College career was approaching the point of collapse. He had recently sat – or rather half-sat – the exam by which his past three years' work would be assessed. The test paper in Lettering, his weakest subject, was supposed to have been completed in

May, while the Beatles were touring Scotland with Johnny Gentle. Cynthia, John's girl friend, had risked her own College career by doing the paper for him, racked by pains from a grumbling appendix, under a single light bulb at the Gambier Terrace flat.

And yet, for all John's inexhaustible laziness, there were still glimpses of brilliance, in his cartoons and poster designs, which made Arthur Ballard, his tutor, think him worth defending. In Ballard's view, the only logical place for John was the newly opened Faculty of Design: unfortunately, however, he could not convince the relevant department head. 'I had a row with the fellow in the end,' Ballard says. 'I told him if he couldn't accept an eccentric like John, he ought to be teaching in Sunday school. Then I heard from Cyn that it didn't matter because John was going to Hamburg. He'd told everyone he'd be getting £100 a week.'

For Stu Sutcliffe the break with College was more serious, coming as it did at the start of a year's postgraduate teacher-training. Stu at first turned down the Hamburg trip; then John and the others talked him into it. The College subsequently indicated it was willing to accept him on the teaching course as a late entrant.

Paul McCartney obtained his father's consent with typical diplomacy and circuitousness. With A-level exams now past, he technically had no further school commitments. His English teacher, 'Dusty' Durband, was in fact one of the first to hear of the Hamburg offer, just before the Institute broke up for the summer. Mr Durband was sceptical. 'As far as I knew, Paul was going on, as his father wished, to teacher-training college. When he told me about Hamburg, I said, "Just who do you want to be, Paul? Tommy Steele?" He just grinned and said, "No, but I feel like giving it a try."'

Jim McCartney, when told the big news at last, faced a united front consisting of Paul, his brother Michael and Allan Williams, who came up to Forthlin Road to assure him the arrangements were all above board. Though full of misgivings, Jim felt that if Paul were allowed this one jaunt, he might the sooner return to his senses, and to college. He let Paul go at the price of only a minimal pep talk about being careful and eating regular meals.

George Harrison, though even now only just 17, encountered the least opposition from his family. With his father and elder brothers he had achieved the status of 'working man', and was as such entitled to command of his own affairs. The quiet, hard-working Harrison family, besides, had produced its share of travellers. As well as Harry and his sea voyages, there was Louise, George's grown-up sister, now married to an American and living in St Louis. Germany, by contrast, seemed not too distant; if the Harrisons knew of the Reeperbahn's reputation, they were prepared to trust in George's level head. His mother made him promise to write, and baked him a tin of home-made scones for the journey.

One big worry spoiled the collective excitement. It was the same old plaguing worry – they still had no drummer. What would do as backing for a stripper in Upper Parliament Street would not do, Allan Williams told them forcefully, for a big-time, luxurious Hamburg night spot like the Indra Club. The contract with Herr Koschmider specified a full instrumental complement. If the Beatles could not provide one, the gig must be turned over to someone else.

They had been searching, in fact, ever since Tommy Moore had deserted them to return to his fork-lift truck at Garston Bottle Works. The only replacement they had been able to find was a boy called Norman Chapman whom they had overheard one night, practising in Slater Street in a room above the National Cash Register Company. Norman played a few dates with them, happily enough, but then had to join one of the last batches of young Britons drafted into the Army.

Lately, for want of anything better, the Beatles had gone back to playing at the Casbah, Mona Best's cellar club in Hayman's Green. They had not been there since they were called the Quarry Men and had walked out over the docking of 15s from their night's fee.

To their surprise, they found the Casbah thriving. Ken Browne, the bespectacled ex-Quarry Man, now led his own group, the Black Jacks, with Mrs Best's son, Peter, on drums. The Black Jacks were among the most popular groups in that district, drawing even larger crowds to the Casbah than did big names like Rory Storm and the Hurricanes.

Pete Best had just left Liverpool Collegiate Grammar School with abundant GCE passes and athletic distinctions but not so clearcut a plan as hitherto to go on to teacher-training college. The taciturn, good-looking boy, to his mother's surprise, announced instead that he wanted to become a professional drummer. Mrs Best, ever ready to encourage and invigorate, helped him raise the deposit on a brand new drum kit which he had long been admiring in the music department at Blackler's.

That decision taken, nothing much seemed to happen. The Black Jacks were due to disband because Ken Browne was about to move away from Liverpool. No other group had offered Pete a job as drummer, nor was he one to push himself. For several weeks, he sat around at home all day, and at night went downstairs into the club to watch this other group Mo was now booking. Whenever he came in, a little desperate sigh used to run around the girls on the nearer benches.

The Beatles, too, had noticed Pete Best. More specifically, they had noticed his glittering new drum kit. Five weeks after leaving school, Pete was rung up by Paul McCartney and asked if he would like to join them for a two-month club engagement in Hamburg. The question, really, was superfluous. Pete Best said he would.

•

They were to travel to Hamburg by road. Allan Williams had offered to drive them there himself, not in his Jaguar but in a battered cream and green Austin 'minibus' which he had acquired for his Liverpool enterprises. Williams, thinking he might as well make a party of it, invited along also his Chinese wife, Beryl, his brother-in-law, Barry Chang, and his West Indian business associate, Lord Woodbine. On their way through London, they were to pick up a tenth passenger, the waiter from the Heaven and Hell coffee bar, who was returning to Hamburg to become Bruno Koschmider's interpreter.

None of the five Beatles had ever been abroad before. John Lennon, indeed, only acquired a passport within a few days of setting off. Their preparations, even so, were not elaborate. Williams advanced them £15 to buy new black crewneck sweaters from Marks and Spencer and some extra pairs of tennis shoes. For a stage uniform, they now had little short high-buttoning jackets of houndstooth check. Their luggage was the family type, hauled out from under spare-room beds. Paul also brought along a new, very cheap solid guitar and a tiny Elpico amplifier to go with the one that, strictly speaking, still belonged to the Art College. George had the tin of home-made scones his mother had baked for him.

Only one parent was outside the Jacaranda to see them off. Millie Sutcliffe, having said goodbye to Stu at home, followed him down to Slater Street secretly and stood in a shop doorway, watching while the van was loaded and its sides were embellished with a legend, THE BEATLES, in cut-out paper letters stuck on with flour and water paste. For some reason, Mrs Sutcliffe could not stop herself from crying.

At Newhaven, where they were to embark for the Hook of Holland, the dockers at first refused to load the top-heavy conveyance aboard its appointed cross-Channel steamer. John talked them into it just a few moments before sailing-time. The English coast receded amid a chorus of 'Bye Bye Blackbird' from the Anglo-Chinese party clustered at the stern rail.

In Holland next morning, the minibus surfaced among crowds of students on bicycles, some of whom leaned against its tattered sides for support. Williams shared the driving with Lord Woodbine while Beryl, perched on the overheating gearbox, acted as navigator. The five Beatles,

Barry Chang and the German waiter, Herr Steiner, occupied the rear, cut off by a wall of luggage and utensils for cooking along the way. As they headed off across Europe, some more fitful singing broke out.

Like Derry and the Seniors before them, the Beatles were without the necessary German work permits. At the frontier, they, too, planned to pose as students on vacation. They had not proceeded far into Holland before Williams began to doubt if they would get even that far. During a brief stop at Arnhem, John emerged from a shop with a mouth organ which, in Lord Woodbine's words, 'he'd picked up to look at and forgotten to put back'.

The halt is commemorated by a snapshot that Barry Chang, Williams's Chinese brother-in-law, took at the Arnhem Memorial to the dead of World War Two. Paul, in turned-up lumberjack collar, sits with Pete Best and George in front of a marble plinth inscribed with the epitaph 'Their Names Liveth For Ever More'. John is missing from the group; he had refused to get out of the van.

•

They expected a city like Liverpool, and this, in a sense, they found. There was the same river, broad like the Mersey but, unlike the Mersey, crowded with ships and with shipyards, beyond, that seemed to grow out of lush forests. There was the same overhead railway that Liverpool had recently lost, although nothing resembling the same tired cityscape beneath. Not the bomb-sites and rubbish, but tree-lined boulevards, seamless with prosperity; chic shops and ships' chandlers and cafes filled with well-dressed, unscarred, confident people. There was a glimpse of the dark-spired *Rathaus*; of the Alster lake, set about by glass-walled banks and press buildings, and traversed by elegant swans. What was said inside Allan Williams's minibus that August evening would be echoed many times afterwards in varying tones of disbelief. Wasn't this the country which had *lost* the war?

The journey from the West German frontier had been rich in incident. At one point, they were almost run down by a tram, in whose rails Lord Woodbine had accidentally jammed the minibus's front wheels. Allan Williams, taking over as driver on the outskirts of Hamburg, had immediately rammed a small saloon car.

They arrived on the Reeperbahn just as neon lights were beginning to eclipse the fairground palings of the night clubs and their painted, acrobatic nudes. Spotting the narrow road junction, where an *imbiss* belched out fumes of *frikadellen* and *currywurst*, Allan Williams remembered where he was. They turned left into Grosse Freiheit, welcomed by overarching illuminations and the stare of predatory eyes.

Even John Lennon, with his fondness for human curiosities, had not expected an employer quite like Bruno Koschmider. The figure which hopped out of the Kaiserkeller to greet them had begun life in a circus, working as a clown, fire-eater, acrobat and illusionist with 50 small cage-birds hidden in his coat. His dwarfish stature, his large, elaborately coiffured head, his turned-up nose and quick, stumping gait, all made even John not quite like to laugh. Bruno, for his part, was unimpressed by the look of his new employees. 'They were dressed in bad clothes – cheap shirts, trousers that were not clean. Their fingernails were dirty.'

If Bruno was somewhat disconcerting, his Kaiserkeller club brought much reassurance. The exterior portico bore, in large letters, the name *Derry and the Seniors von Liverpool.* A glimpse inside, on the way to Koschmider's office, showed what seemed a vast meadow of tables and side booths, shaped like lifeboats, around the stage and miniature dance floor. The Beatles, their spirits reviving, began to laugh and cuff one another, saying this was all right, wasn't it? Allan Williams reminded them they were not booked to play here but in Herr Koschmider's other club, the Indra.

Further along the Grosse Freiheit, beyond St Joseph's Catholic church, the illuminations dwindled into a region of plain-fronted bordellos interspersed with private houses where elderly *hausfraus* still set pot plants on the upper window ledges. Here, under a neon sign shaped like an elephant, was to be found the Indra Club. Bruno Koschmider led the way downstairs into a small cellar cabaret, gloomy, shabby and at that moment occupied by only two customers. Down here for the next eight weeks, the Beatles would be expected to play for four and a half hours each week night and six hours on Saturdays and Sundays.

Koschmider next conducted them to the living quarters provided under the terms of his contract with Allan Williams. Across the road from the Indra, he operated a small cinema, the Bambi Kino, which varied the general diet of flesh by showing corny old gangster movies and Westerns. The Beatles' lodgings were one filthy room and two windowless cubbyholes immediately behind – and in booming earshot of the cinema screen. The only washing facilities were the cinema toilets, from the communal vestibule of which an old woman attendant stared at them grimly over her saucer of tips.

It was some consolation to meet up with Derry and the Seniors and to learn that, despite munificent billing outside the Kaiserkeller, Liverpool's famous r & b group were also having to sleep rough. 'Bruno gave us one little bed between five of us,' Howie Casey, the sax-player, says. 'I'd been sleeping on that, covered by a flag, and the other lads slept on chairs set two together. The waiters used to lock us inside the club each night.'

The Bambi Kino was not a great deal worse than the cellar of Lord Woodbine's New Colony Club or the Gambier Terrace flat back home in Liverpool. Paul and Pete Best took a cubbyhole each while John, Stu and George flopped down in the larger room. All five were soon asleep, untroubled by sounds of gunfire and police sirens wafted through the grimy wall from the cinema screen.

Their first night's playing at the Indra was a severe let-down. Half a dozen people sat and watched them indifferently from tables with red-shaded lamps. The clientele, mainly prostitutes and their customers, showed little enthusiasm for Carl Perkins's 'Honey Don't' or Chuck Berry's 'Too Much Monkey Business'. The club also bore a curse in the form of an old woman living upstairs who continually 'phoned Police headquarters on the Reeperbahn to complain about the noise. Bruno Koschmider, not wishing for that kind of trouble, hissed at them to turn even their feeble amplifiers down.

Allan and Beryl Williams, Barry Chang and Lord Woodbine remained in Hamburg throughout that inaugural week. Williams, himself comfortably ensconced in a small hotel, did what he could to improve the Beatles' living quarters – it was at his urgent insistence that Bruno provided blankets for their beds. Beryl shopped in the city centre with her brother, and Lord Woodbine, as usual, remained worried by nothing. He sang calypsos at the Kaiserkeller and, one night, grew so affected by its libations that he attempted to dive into the South Sea Islands mural.

Williams, in his conscientious moments, worried about the club he had committed his charges to, and about their plainly evinced hatred of it. On their opening night, they had played the entire four-and-a-half-hour stretch mutinously still and huddled-up. 'Come on, boys!' Williams exhorted them from the bar. 'Make it a show, boys!' Bruno Koschmider took up the phrase, clapping his large, flat hands. 'Mak show, boys,' he would cry. 'Mak show, Beatles! Mak show!'

John's answer was to launch himself into writhings and shimmyings that were a grotesque parody of Gene Vincent on one crippled leg at the Boxing Stadium show. Down the street at the Kaiserkeller, word began to spread of this other group *von* Liverpool who leapt around the stage like monkeys and stamped their feet deafeningly on the stage. They were stamping out the rhythm to help their new drummer, Pete Best, and also to goad the old woman upstairs.

Before long, the rival groups from the Kaiserkeller had come up to the Indra to see them. Howie Casey was astonished at the improvement since their audition as the Silver Beatles in front of Larry Parnes. 'That day, they'd seemed embarrassed about how bad they were,' Howie says. 'You could tell something had happened to them in the meantime. They'd turned into a good stomping band.'

Derry and the Seniors brought with them a wide-eyed, curly-haired youth whom all the Beatles – George especially – regarded with awe. Born Anthony Esmond Sheridan McGinnity, he was better known as Tony Sheridan, a singer and inspired solo guitarist with many appearances to his credit on the *Oh Boy!* television show. His talent, however, was accompanied by habits too blithely erratic to suit the rock and roll starmakers. When Bruno Koschmider hired him, he had been sacked from *Oh Boy!* and most other engagements, and was playing at the 2i's coffee bar for £1 a night. Even now, the British police were hard on his trail in respect of various hire-purchase irregularities.

Anthony Esmond steered the Beatles, past beckoning doorway touts, for an insider's tour of the Reeperbahn's peculiar delights. They saw the women who grappled in mud, cheered on by an audience tied into a protective communal bib. They visited the Roxy Bar and met ravishing 'hostesses' with tinkling laughs and undisguisably male biceps and breast-bones. Two streets away, where a wooden fence forbade entry to all under 18, their companions steered them through the Herbertstrasse, past red-lit shop windows containing whores in every type of fancy dress, all ages from nymphet to scolding granny, smiling or scowling forth, gossiping with one another, reading, knitting, listlessly examining their own frilly garters or spooning up bowls of soup.

The other initiation was into beer. For beer, damp-gold, foam-piling under thin metal bar taps, had never been more plentiful. Derry and the Seniors, when they first opened at the Kaiserkeller, had been allowed beer ad lib in breaks between performing. Though Koschmider had hastily withdrawn this privilege, the nightly allowance still seemed vast to five boys who, at home in Liverpool, had often been hard put to scrape up the price of a half-pint each. Then there were the drinks pressed on them by customers at the Indra; the drinks that would be sent up to them onstage while they played. It became nothing unusual for a whole crate of beer to be shoved at their feet by well-wishers whose size and potential truculence underlined the necessity of finishing every bottle.

Sex was easily available. Here you did not chase it, as in Liverpool, and clutch at it furtively in cold shop doors. Here it came after you, putting strong arms round you, mincing no words; it was unabashed, expert – indeed, professional. For even the most cynical whores found it piquant to have an innocent boy from Liverpool – to lure and buy as a change from being, eternally, bait and merchandise.

The Freiheit provided an abundance of everything but sleep. Sheridan and the other musicians already knew a way to get by without it, just as the barmaids and whores and bouncers and pickpockets did. Someone in the early days had discovered Preludin, a brand of German slimming tablet which, while removing appetite, also roused the metabolism to goggle-eyed hyperactivity. Soon the Beatles – all but Pete Best – were gobbling 'Prellys' by the tubeful each night. As the pills took effect, they dried up the saliva, increasing the desire for beer.

Now the Beatles needed no exhortation to 'mak show'. John, in particular, began to go berserk on stage, prancing and grovelling in imitation of any rock and roller or movie monster his dazzled mind could summon up. The fact that their audience could not understand a word they said provoked John into cries of '*Sieg Heil!*' and 'Fucking Nazis!', to which the audience invariably responded by laughing and clapping. Bruno Koschmider, who had spent the war in a Panzer Division, was not so amused.

At 5 or 6 a.m. – according to subsequent adventures – they would stagger back along the sunny Freiheit, past doorway touts unsleepingly active. Behind the Bambi Kino they would collapse into their squalid beds for the two or three hours' sleep that were possible before the day's first picture show. Sometimes it would be gunfire on the screen that jolted them awake, or the voice of George Raft or Edward G. Robinson.

Hounded into consciousness, they would dash to the cinema toilets while the basins were still clean. Rosa, the female custodian, for all her outward grimness, kept clean towels for them, and odds and ends of soap. 'She thought we were all mad,' Pete Best says. 'She'd shout things at us – *verrucht* and *beknaakt* – but she'd be laughing. We called her Mutti.'

There were now five or six hours to be disposed of before they began playing and drinking again. At the Gretel and Alphons or Willi's Bar, the Freiheit's two most tolerant cafes, they would breakfast on cornflakes or chicken soup, the only food which their dehydrated frames could endure. They would then drift round the corner, through the stench of *frikadelli* and last night's vomit, to the shop on the main Reeperbahn which fascinated John Lennon especially with its display of flick knives, bayonets, coshes, swords, brass knuckledusters and tear-gas pistols.

If not too devastatingly hung over, they might catch a tram into central Hamburg, and stroll on the elegant boulevards, looking at the clothes and the perfumes, the elaborate bakers' and confectioners', the radios and tape recorders and occasional displays of imported American guitars, saxophones and drums. Since their wages, paid out by Bruno on a Thursday, seldom lasted more than 24 hours, such expeditions were usually limited to gazing and wishing. John, however, blew every pfennig he had on a new guitar, an American Rickenbacker 'short arm'.

The daylight hours improved considerably after someone, walking on the dockside, discovered Hamburg's long-established branch of the British Sailors' Society. Investigation proved this rather imposing four-storey building to be the same 'Mission' as on the docks back home in Liverpool, with the same charitable interest in mariners ashore in a foreign port.

Jim Hawke, the resident manager, was a hefty Londoner who had entered Hamburg with the first invading Allied troops and had subsequently done duty as a warder at the Nuremberg trials. In 1960, he and his German wife, Lilo, had been in charge of the Hamburg Mission only a few months. Already, as it happened, they had met Stu Sutcliffe's father, still then a second engineer with the Booth shipping line.

Hawke, a tender-hearted man under his stern exterior, granted the same privileges to Liverpool musicians as to sailors far from home. Most attractive from the Beatles' point of view were the English breakfasts, cooked by an elderly German woman, Frau Prill, who knew the secret of frying real English chips. 'They never seemed to have any money,' Hawke said. 'You could see them carefully counting out the coins. They always had what was the cheapest – steak, egg and chips, which I put on for 2 marks 80 (about 25p). And big half-litre tankards of milk. Some days they'd have an Oxo cube beaten up in milk.

'They were never any trouble – I wouldn't have stood for it in any case. Just nice, quiet, well-behaved lads they seemed. They didn't even smoke then. They'd sit and play draughts or go upstairs for a game of ping-pong with my daughter, Monica. In the room through the bar we had an old piano that had come from the British NAAFI. They used that, or John and Paul did, to help them write their songs. We had a library as well. I'd leave a bag of books for them on the table in front of the settee they always used. They liked reading, but they never took any of the books away. They said they couldn't read very easily where they were staying.

'They'd come in about eleven in the morning and stay until three or four in the afternoon. They'd be quite subdued. I'd look over from the bar and see the five of them, always round that same table, not talking – just staring into space. I've seen the same look on men who've been away at sea in tankers for a long time. Not with it, if you know what I mean.'

•

One bleary-eyed morning when they emerged from the Bambi Kino, a piece of good news awaited them. Bruno Koschmider, bowing at last to the complaints of his customers and the old woman upstairs, was moving them out of the Indra and into his larger, better club the Kaiserkeller.

The Kaiserkeller, at first, threatened to eclipse even John Lennon in noise and spectacle. The noise came from an audience several hundred strong, frequently containing entire ships' companies from English and American naval craft visiting the port. The spectacle was provided by Bruno Koschmider's white-aproned waiters, converging on any outbreak of trouble and quelling it with a high-speed ruthlessness that made Garston 'Blood Baths' look like a game of pat-a-cake. If the troublemaker were alone, he might find himself propelled, not to the exit but into the office of Willi the under-manager, there to be worked over at leisure with coshes and brass knuckles. Finally, as the victim lay prostrate, Bruno himself would weigh in with the ebony night stick from his desk drawer.

Bruno's chief bouncer, a tiny, swaggering youth named Horst Fascher, epitomised the breed. Horst had started life as a featherweight boxer and had represented both Hamburg and the West German national team before being banned from the ring for accidentally killing a sailor in a street fight. It was shortly after serving a prison sentence for manslaughter that he had entered Bruno Koschmider's employment. His squad, nick-named locally 'Hoddel's gang', recruited from his friends at the Hamburg Boxing Academy, were held among the Freiheit's other strong-arm gangs in profound respect.

Horst took the Liverpool musicians – fortunately for them – to his heart. It became an unwritten rule at the Kaiserkeller that if a musician hit trouble, 'Hoddel's gang' would swoop unquestioningly to his aid. Horst showed them the Reeperbahn's innermost haunts and its choicest pleasures; he also took them home to Neuestadt to meet his mother and brothers and taste Frau Fascher's bean soup. All he asked in return was the chance, sometimes after midnight, to get up with the group on stage and bellow out an Eddie Cochran song.

'The Beatles were not good musicians at the beginning,' Horst Fascher says. 'John Lennon was a very poor rhythm guitarist. I remember Sheridan telling me in amazement that John played chords with only three fingers. And always they are funny – never serious. But they steal from Sheridan, from the Seniors, all the time with their eyes. And all the time the bass drum is beating like your foot when you stamp.

'That John Lennon – I loved him, he was mad. A fighter. He is *zyniker*. You say to him, "Hey John . . ." He would say, "Ah, so fuckin' what." Paul was *lustig*, the clown. He gets out of trouble by making a laugh. George was *schuchtern*, the baby one. I could never get to know Stu. He was too strange. And Pete – he was *reserviert*. You had to pull words out through his nose.'

Soon after the Beatles reached the Kaiserkeller, Derry and the Seniors finished their engagement there. The replacement group, brought out from Liverpool by Allan Williams, was Rory Storm and the Hurricanes.

When Rory, relaxed and suntanned from Butlin's, saw the Hamburg living quarters, his stammer totally overcame him. Nor did his drummer, the little bearded one with rings on his fingers, show great delight at having to sleep on chairs covered with old flags. Ringo Starr, like all the Hurricanes, was used to a little more luxury. 'You want to see what the Beatles have got to put up with,' Williams retorted.

Rory Storm's flashiness and acrobatic feats increased the wildness of the Kaiserkeller nights. A contest developed between the Beatles and Hurricanes to see which group first could stamp its way through the already old and half-rotten timbers of the stage. Rory did it at last, vanishing from sight in the middle of 'Blue Suède Shoes'. A case of junk champagne was the prize, washed down with more 'Prellys' at their favourite bar, the Gretel and Alphons.

Bruno Koschmider fumed and fulminated – but they got away with it, as they got away with most things. John got away with standing out in the Freiheit in a pair of long woollen underpants, reading the *Daily Express*. George got away with it time after time in the *Polizei Stunde*, or midnight curfew hour when all under 18 were supposed to have left the club. For their drinking, swearing, fighting, whoring, even vandalising, Grosse Freiheit pardoned them all forms of retribution but one. Williams, the self-styled 'little pox doctor of Hamburg', received many a worried confidence in a back room at the Gretel and Alphons, and, like a connoisseur, held many a beer glass of urine speculatively up to the light.

Pete Best figured in only a couple of shady Beatles exploits on the Reeperbahn. One night, chronically short of cash as usual, John enlisted his help as the group's most seasoned hard man in mugging a drunken sailor and stealing his wallet. Pete himself later confirmed John's account of how the two followed the sailor from a club and managed to put him on the ground. As they started to go through his pockets, however, their victim pulled out a handgun. In fact, the weapon fired only tear-gas cartridges, but neither John nor Pete realised this and, empty-handed, ran for their lives.

Pete played drums well enough – or so it then seemed – hitting his bass pedal in the hard, stomping 'mak show' beat, yet somehow always in a world apart from the unending frontal contest between John and Paul. He was, and knew it, the most handsome Beatle with his athlete's physique, his dark eyes, wry smile and neat, crisp Jeff Chandler hair. Like the girls back home in West Derby, the Kaiserkeller girls were mad about him. Craning their necks to see past John and George, past even Paul, they would scream at Pete Best in English and German to give them a smile.

Being able to speak the most German increased Pete's independence, and he was often away from the Freiheit in the daytime, sunbathing alone or buying new parts for his drums. His fellow Beatles grew accustomed to his absence. They had plenty afoot with Tony Sheridan and Rory Storm and the drummer from Rory's group whom they were growing to like more and more. Ringo Starr, in contrast with Pete Best, was friendly, simple, straightforward and, in his slow, big-eyed way, as funny as even John. They also liked the way he played drums. They were happy with Pete Best's drumming until they began to notice Ringo's.

When Allan Williams next hit town, Paul and John met him, clamouring for his help to find a studio in which they could record. They wanted to try out some numbers with a member of Rory Storm's group, a boy named Wally, whose prodigious vocal range went from bass to falsetto. Pete Best would not be involved. They had also fixed up to borrow Ringo Starr.

The studio Williams found for them was a record-your-voice booth at the rear of Hamburg's main railway station. There, John, Paul, George, with Ringo on drums, backed the talented Wally through two numbers, 'Fever' and 'Summertime'. The man who cut the acetate for their recording mistakenly handed back to Williams first an old-fashioned 78-rpm disc with a commercial message for a local handbag shop on its reverse. Eventually some 45-rpm discs were made, on the booth's 'Arnstik' label, of *The Beatles mit Wally*. Just for a few moments – subtracting Wally – the right four had found each other.

•

Astrid Kirchherr was born in 1938, into a solid, respectable middle-class Hamburg family. Her grandfather, a manufacturer of fairground slot-machines, still owned the factory he had twice seen wrecked by war, and twice painstakingly built up again. Her father was a senior executive in the West German division of the Ford Motor Company. Three generations of Kirchherrs lived together in Altona, a comfortable Hamburg suburb. To Altona people, the dockyard and St Pauli, the Reeperbahn and Grosse Freiheit might as well be on another planet: they are mentioned only to warn children sternly never to stray in that direction.

Astrid Kirchherr was never like other children. At the age of four or five, she would protest when her mother decked her out in the flounces and hair ribbons expected of little German girls. She preferred to wear plain black. She knew that best became her white skin, her large, dark eyes and the blanched-gold hair she would shake free of all encumbrances. Frau Kirchherr visited the infants' school to confirm that the child must have her curious wish.

Already, she had a strongly marked talent for drawing and painting; as she grew older, she would design and make clothes for herself. When the family assembled, as was traditional, to decide her future, her grandfather agreed that there was only one sensible course. Astrid should go to college and study dress design. Possibly that would encourage her to forsake her eccentric ideas for styles more widely acceptable.

She went, not to the State Art College but to a private academy, the Meister Schule. There she met an elegant boy of equally good family, a doctor's son named Klaus Voorman. Klaus, a talented illustrator, passionately loved rock and roll music and wanted to be a designer of pop record covers. He became Astrid's boy friend, also moving in as a lodger at the hospitable Kirchherr house. Their friends were a set known as *exis* – from 'existentialist' – intellectual, beautiful, ascetic and avant garde. Astrid and Klaus were the most beautiful, ascetic and avant garde of them all.

At the Meister Schule, Astrid also struck up a friendship with Rheinhardt Wolf, tutor on the photographic course and a well-known contributor to various Hamburg-based magazines. The perceptiveness with which she commented on his work led Wolf to suggest that Astrid should herself try taking some pictures. These proved so impressive that, at Rheinhardt Wolf's insistence, she changed courses from dress design to photography. After leaving the Meister Schule, she was taken on by Wolf as his assistant.

One late summer evening in 1960, Astrid and Klaus Voorman had quarrelled, and Klaus went off to the cinema on his own. Afterwards, walking about aimlessly, he found himself in Grosse Freiheit. A blast of rock and roll music was issuing from the open door into the Kaiserkeller club. Klaus decided, against all the instincts of his upbringing, to go in and have a look.

The group on stage at the time was Rory Storm and the Hurricanes. Klaus sat down nervously in the tough crowd, and was at once swept away with excitement and delight. He had never been into a club before, and certainly never seen rock and roll played with such crazy ebullience. At a table next to his, some more English musicians, in houndstooth check jackets, with wondrously piled-up, greased-back hair, were waiting their turn to play. In due course this group was announced as the Beatles. Klaus stayed on to watch the whole of their four-hour performance.

Astrid, when he told her about it, was a little disgusted to hear that Klaus had been hanging around dives in St Pauli. He could not persuade her to go back with him to the Kaiserkeller and be shown the amazing music. He went again on his own, determined to get talking to the Beatles if he could. Shy and unsure of his English, he took with him a sleeve he had designed for an American single, the Ventures' 'Walk Don't Run'. In a break between sessions he went over to the leader – so he had already identified John Lennon – and in halting English tried to explain about the design. John only muttered, 'Show it to Stu – he's the artist round here,' indicating the one who had interested Klaus most with his pointed shoes, dark glasses and brooding James Dean face.

By the time Astrid did agree to go to the Kaiserkeller, Stu and Klaus Voorman had become good friends. Klaus brought her in at last one night, dressed in her black leather *exi* coat, white-faced, crop-headed and spectrally cool. When the Beatles began playing, she, too, was instantly won over. 'I fell in love with Stuart that very first night. He was so tiny but perfect, every feature. So pale, but very very beautiful. He was like a character from a story by Edgar Allan Poe.'

The Beatles, in their turn, were flattered by the interest of this in every way beautiful, ghost-eyed girl, so different from the usual Freiheit scrubber. They were still more flattered when, with her few words of English, Astrid asked if she could take their photograph. She met all five of them on the Reeperbahn next day and took them into Der Dom, the city park, where the twice-yearly funfair was in progress. Astrid posed them with their guitars and Pete Best's snare drum on the side of a fairground wagon, then on the broad bonnet of a traction engine.

The photographing over, she asked the five Beatles back to Altona for tea at her home. Pete Best declined; he said he had some new drum skins to buy. The other four readily piled into Astrid's little car. 'They met my Mum – she was as knocked out by them as I was. Directly she saw them, she wanted to start feeding them.'

Astrid took them upstairs to the black and white studio bedroom she had designed for herself. 'I wanted to talk to them, but I knew hardly any English then,' Astrid says. 'John seemed very hard – cynical, sarcastic, but something more than that. Paul smiled – he always smiled and was diplomatic. George was just a baby boy with his piled-up hair and his ears sticking out.

'I wanted to talk to Stuart. I tried to ask him if I could take his picture but he didn't understand. I knew I would have to ask Klaus to help me speak better English.'

The flattery of being photographed by a beautiful blonde German girl was nothing to the flattery bestowed by the photographs themselves. These were not the usual little snapshots knocked off by some bystander, usually at the least flattering possible moment. These were big, grainy prints, conjured by the girl herself from the recesses of her black satin room and showing the five Beatles as they had never imagined themselves before. Astrid's lens, in fact, captured the very quality which attracted intellectuals like Klaus and her – the paradox of Teddy Boys with child faces; of would-be toughness and all-protecting innocence. The blunt, heavy fairground machines on which they sat seemed to symbolise their own slight but confident perch on grown-up life. John, with his collar up, hugging his new Rickenbacker; Paul, with the pout he knew suited him; George uneasy; Pete Best, self-contained, a little apart – each image held its own true prophecy. In one shot, Stu Sutcliffe stood with his back to the others, the long neck of his guitar pointing into the ground.

It was the first of many photographic sessions with Astrid in the weeks that followed. Each time she would pose them, with or without their guitars, against some part of industrial Hamburg – the docks or the railway sidings. She was lavish with the prints she gave them and with invitations to meals at her house. 'I'd cook them all the things they missed from England: scrambled eggs, chips.' All the time, with Klaus Voorman's help, her English was improving.

At the Kaiserkeller, a part of the audience now were *exis* brought in by Astrid and Klaus. It became a fad among them to dress, like the rockers, in leather and skin-tight jeans. The Beatles' music belonged to the same intellectual conversion. Soon the *exis* had their own small preserve of tables next to the stage. And always among them, the girl who followed no style but her own sat with Klaus Voorman, or without him, waiting for the moment, late at night, when John and Paul stood aside and Stu Sutcliffe stepped forward with his heavy bass to sing the Elvis ballad, 'Love Me Tender'.

Astrid made no secret of the pursuit and Stu, for his part, was shyly fascinated. Her elfin beauty, combined with big-breasted voluptuousness, her forthright German ways mingled with a yielding softness, were more than sufficient to captivate any young, inexperienced heterosexual male. Across the barrier of language, they found their passionate artistic and literary beliefs to be one. The talks by candlelight on Astrid's black coverlet quickly led to other delights unenvisaged by a schoolteacher's son from Sefton Park, Liverpool.

Astrid was the initiator and teacher, and Stu the willing pupil. With the skills of the artist and the practicality of the *hausfrau,* she began to model him into an appearance echoing and complementing her own. She did away first with his Teddy-Boy hairstyle, cutting it short like hers, then shaping it to lie across the forehead in what was then called a French cut, although high-class German boys had worn a similar style since the days of Bismarck.

When Stu arrived at the Kaiserkeller that night, John and Paul laughed so much that he hastily combed his hair back into its old upswept style. Next night, he tried the new way again, ignoring the others' taunts. Strangely enough, it was George, the least adventurous or assertive one, who next allowed Astrid to unpick the high sheaf of black hair which had previously so emphasised his babyish ears. Paul tried it next, but temporarily – he was waiting to see what John would do. John tried it, so Paul tried it again. Only Pete Best's hair stayed as before, a crisp, unflappable cockade.

Astrid also began to design and make clothes for Stu. She made him first a suit of shiny black leather jerkin and sheath-tight trousers like the one she wore herself. The other four Beatles so admired it that they at once ordered copies from a tailor in St Pauli. Theirs, however, were of less fine workmanship, baggy-waisted and with seams which kept coming apart. At that point, for the moment, Astrid's influence over them stopped. They laughed at Stu for wearing, as she did, a black corduroy jacket without lapels, based on Pierre Cardin's current Paris collections. 'What are you doing in Mum's suit then, Stu?' became the general taunt.

Astrid's mother, horrified to learn of Stu's living conditions, insisted on giving him his own room, as Klaus Voorman had had, at the top of the Kirchherr house. In November 1960, two months after their first meeting, they became engaged. They bought each other rings, in the German fashion, and went in Astrid's car for a drive beside the river Elbe. 'It was a real engagement,' Astrid says. 'We knew from the beginning that it was inevitable we should marry. And so it should have been.'

Stu, despite his quietness and gentleness, was not always an easy person. At times he could be moody and jealously suspect Astrid of being in love with someone else. His emotion, when angry or passionate, could reach an intensity that was almost like a mild seizure. He suffered, too, from headaches, sudden and violent, that shut his eyes in agony behind the dark glasses which were not, she discovered, entirely for show. Then, with equal suddenness, the fit of pain would pass.

Even Astrid could not affect Stu's life as downtrodden butt of the other Beatles' humour. On stage, they teased and taunted him continually, for his smallness, for his outrageous new clothes, above all for the bass-playing that never seemed equal to their needs. John inflicted the worst treatment of all, even though, as Astrid well knew, a deep friendship still existed between Stu and him. It was in Paul's more bantering tone that the true arrows came. For Paul wanted Stu's job as bass guitarist. 'When John and Stu had a row,' Astrid says, 'you could still feel the affection that was there. But when Paul and Stu had a row, you could tell Paul hated him.'

•

A few yards up the Reeperbahn stood a large semi-underground arena called the Hippodrome. In former days, it had been a circus, featuring horses ridden by naked girls. By 1960, such entertainments having grown unfashionable, the Hippodrome stood, behind its heavy iron portcullis, dark and in decay. Its owner, a certain Herr Eckhorn, decided to hand it on to his son, Peter, who had recently come home from the sea and was anxious to start a music club in competition with Bruno Koschmider's Kaiserkeller.

Young Peter Eckhorn wasted no time in hitting at his intended rival. First, he suborned Koschmider's chief bouncer, Horst Fascher. While still employed at the Kaiserkeller, Horst was helping Eckhorn convert the old Hippodrome, putting in a stage and dance floor and makeshift wooden booths painted the cheapest colour, black. Fascher, in addition, began to sow discontent at the Kaiserkeller, telling Bruno's musicians of the better pay and conditions which Eckhorn's club – the Top Ten – would offer. 'I showed Tony Sheridan out of the back door right away,' Horst recalls with pride. 'That Koschmider went crazy, but what could he do to me? He had too great a fear.'

The Top Ten club opened in November 1960, with music by Tony Sheridan and his original Soho-levied group, the Jets. Eckhorn also wanted Derry and the Seniors, but they were by now so poverty stricken that they had applied to the British Consul in Hamburg for an assisted passage home to Liverpool.

The Beatles stayed on at the Kaiserkeller, although in a mood of increasing restlessness. The Top Ten, with its circus-like dimensions and higher rates of pay, was infinitely more attractive than Bruno Koschmider's nautically inspired basement. Their employer, moreover, stung by Horst Fascher's and Tony Sheridan's defection, grew rabidly proprietorial. With a stubby forefinger, he drew their attention to the clause in their contract which forbade them to play in any other club within a 25-mile radius of the Kaiserkeller. It had reached Bruno's ears that, when visiting the Top Ten, they would sometimes get up and jam with Tony Sheridan on stage.

Before long, Peter Eckhorn had persuaded them to forget the residue of their contract with Koschmider and come across to play for him at the Top Ten. Koschmider, according to Pete Best, hinted that if the Beatles joined Eckhorn, they might not be able to walk with complete safety after dark.

Retribution of a different sort overtook them, however, possibly with some help from Bruno Koschmider. They were about to open at the Top Ten when the *Polizei*, conducting a belated examination of George Harrison's passport, discovered that he was only 17, and too young to be in a club after midnight. For plainly flouting this rule, George was ordered out of Germany. Stu and Astrid put him on the train home, dismayed and lost-looking, with some biscuits and apples for the journey.

The others played a few nights at the Top Ten, with John taking the lead guitar part, or leaving it out, and Paul doubling on a piano that was there. Astrid, Klaus and the *exis* had followed them from the Kaiserkeller; so had Akim Reichel, a dockside waiter who had discovered them first at the Indra. Akim remembers how tired and dispirited the four survivors seemed. They had been on the Reeperbahn, after all, nearly four months. 'They would play sometimes a whole hour,' Akim says, 'sitting on the edge of their amplifiers.'

Peter Eckhorn, as well as paying 10 marks a day more than Koschmider, provided sleeping accommodation above the club, in an attic fitted with bunk beds. Though far from luxurious, and shared with Tony Sheridan's group, it was still a vast improvement on the Bambi Kino. Rosa, the WC lady – who had also forsaken the Kaiserkeller for the Top Ten – was prevailed on by John Lennon to bring coffee and shaving water up to them when they woke in the early afternoon.

In their haste to desert Koschmider, Paul and Pete Best had left most of their belongings in the rooms behind the Bambi. They nerved themselves to go back a few days later, walking in through the cinema foyer without opposition, and finding their property all intact behind the screen. Coming out again, down the dark corridor from their respective cubby-holes, Paul struck a match in order to see. 'There were some filthy old drapes on the wall, like sacking,' Pete Best says. 'Paul caught a bit of that stuff with the match. It wasn't anything like a fire. It just smouldered a little bit.' Paul's version is that, in a spirit of half-hearted vandalism, they set fire to a condom.

Early the next morning, policemen entered the Top Ten club, pounded upstairs to the attic, hauled Pete Best and Paul out of bed, hustled them off to the Reeperbahn's Station 15 and placed them under lock and key. Between them, using their O-level German, they elicited the fact that they were being held on suspicion of trying to burn down the Bambi Kino. 'They only kept us there a few hours,' Pete Best says. 'Afterwards they admitted it never should have happened.'

No charges were pressed – according to Bruno Koschmider, a magnanimous gesture on his part. Even so, Paul and Pete were both immediately deported. The next day found them on a flight to England, minus most of their clothes and luggage and Pete Best's drum kit.

For John and Stu there was no alternative but to follow the others home. Stu made the journey by air, with a ticket paid for by the Kirchherrs. John went on the train alone, carrying his guitar and the amplifier he had not yet paid for, and terrified he wouldn't find England where he had left it.

6

'Hi, all you Cavern-dwellers. Welcome to the *best* of cellars'

He reached home in the early hours of a December morning and threw stones at his Aunt Mimi's bedroom window to wake her. Mimi opened the front door and, as John lurched past, enquired sarcastically what had happened to his £100 a week. And if he thought he was going around Woolton in those cowboy boots, Mimi added, he had better think again. John collapsed into bed, not stirring out of doors for a week afterwards. In a little while, there came a timorous knock at the door of the outer porch. It was his ever-faithful, long-suffering girl friend, Cynthia Powell.

At Forthlin Road Paul found waiting for him a single GCE A-level certificate – in Art – and a father who, luckily, was not the type to crow. Even so, Jim McCartney pointed out, it was time to think about getting a proper job. Paul gave in and registered at the local Labour Exchange. The two weeks before Christmas he spent helping to deliver parcels around the docks on the back of a truck belonging to the Speedy Prompt Delivery Company.

He didn't contact John again until just before Christmas, by which time, to add to the gloom, snow was falling. Snow is never pretty in Liverpool. The two ex-Hamburg desperadoes, with watering eyes and fingers huddled in their pockets, met down in the city for a drink. They could feel through their boot-soles, too, the chill damp of dead-end failure.

Together, they sought out their erstwhile manager, Allan Williams, and found him in equally deflated spirits. Returning from Hamburg the last time, he had decided to open the first Liverpool version of a Reeperbahn beat music club. He had taken over an old bottle-washing shop in Soho Street, and employed Lord Woodbine to effect a brief renovation. The new club was to be called the Top Ten and run by Bob Wooler, the railway clerk and spare-time disc jockey who had helped Williams recruit attractions for his Boxing Stadium concert. Wooler, on the strength of Williams's offer, had even resigned his steady job with the docks office.

Liverpool's Top Ten club opened on 1 December 1960. Six days later, it burned to the ground. Local opinion suspected a 'torch job'.

Only the cellar club in West Derby run by Pete Best's mother remained as a potential gig for Williams's unlucky protégés. Derry and the Seniors had played the Casbah, following their own Hamburg disaster, and had good-naturedly plugged the Beatles' name. When Mona Best gave them their first return booking, a poster was put on the cellar door loyally proclaiming the 'Fabulous Beatles' had returned. George was then contacted – lying low in Speke, he had not realised that John and Paul were home. Stu Sutcliffe, however, remained out of touch with the others until well into the following January.

That first night back at the Casbah showed what a transformation Hamburg had wrought. The months of sweated nights at the Kaiserkeller had given their music a prizefighter's muscle and power; each number was stamped through as if against a Reeperbahn brawl, or in one last attempt to break through Bruno Koschmider's stage. They literally rocked the little club, under the Victorian house, where nothing was drunk wickeder than Pepsi Cola, nothing popped more potent than peanuts, and where no fracas arose that could not be quelled by Mrs Best's vigorous, dark-eyed stare.

A few days later, they were, once more, sitting round Allan Williams's Jacaranda coffee bar. So was Bob Wooler, the disc jockey who had quit his railway job in the expectation of running a beat club for Williams. That job having gone up in smoke, Wooler was now working for a promoter named Brian Kelly who ran regular dances at Litherland Town Hall, Lathom Hall and Aintree Institute.

'They were moaning to me about how little was happening,' Wooler said. 'I'd never heard them before, but I said I'd try to get Kelly to put them on. In fact, I rang him up from the Jacaranda. I asked for eight pounds for them. Kelly offered four; we settled on six.'

Brian Kelly, a somewhat melancholy man employed by the Mersey Docks and Harbour Company, had no overwhelming enthusiasm for rock and roll music. To Kelly, it was a question of simple mathematics. You hired a hall for £5 and by filling it with jivers at 3s (15p) each you showed a profit. As a dance promoter, he possessed one major asset – he did not mind clearing up vomit. Much tended to appear midway in the evening as late-comers arrived from the pubs.

At Litherland Town Hall, on 27 December 1960, Brian Kelly stood in his usual place on one side of the dance area, waiting to go forth with mop and disinfectant. A large crowd was there, curious more than anything to see the group which Bob Wooler had billed dramatically as 'Direct from Hamburg'. Because of this, many people thought they must be German. Among the spectators was Pete Best's young brother, Rory, and a friend of his called Neil Aspinall, an accountancy student who lodged with the Bests. Neil, a thin, serious boy with an impressive cache of O-levels, had never been much interested in rock and roll. He was here tonight only because Rory had said it would be good.

Brian Kelly did not think so. He had booked the Beatles before, in their pre-Hamburg days, and remembered them as very ordinary. He was astonished, when Bob Wooler announced them and the terrible noise started, to see what effect it had on his customers. 'Everyone – the whole lot – surged forward towards the stage. The dance floor behind was completely empty. '"Aye aye," I said to myself, "I could have got twice the numbers in here."'

After their performance, the Beatles emerged into the car park where, a few months earlier, Stu Sutcliffe had been knocked down and kicked in the head. Once again, there was an ambush waiting – but of girls this time, squealing and asking for autographs. Their van had been covered with lipstick messages. Some of the girls who mobbed them still thought they were German and complimented them on speaking such good English.

Amid the general acclaim, they had made two important new friends. One was Bob Wooler, the disc jockey. The other was Neil Aspinall, the accountancy student for whom Fate had ordained a future very different from sitting his Finals.

Wooler became the intermediary for further £6 bookings at Brian Kelly's other weekly dances at Lathom Hall and Aintree Institute. He also became the means of spreading the Beatles' name over wider and wider areas of Liverpool. As a disc jockey, he was an unlikely figure with his round face, his earnest politeness and devotion to word-play and puns. He loved to draft elaborate posters and handbills in which, for example, the initial letters of Litherland Town Hall served additionally to spell 'Lively Time Here', and all the bus routes to the hall would be microscopically detailed. 'Jive Fans!' a Wooler handbill would say, 'This is It!' In neat capital letters, he would draft the evening's running order, murmuring to himself such cautionary slogans as 'Horses for courses. Menus for venues.' Somehow, in the shabby jive halls, he maintained the gravitas of a Roman senator, wagging his large forefinger as he strove to impress on beer-crazed 17-year-olds that punctuality and politeness were the primary virtues of life. Yet his voice, through the microphone, was as rich and relaxed as the best to be heard on Radio Luxembourg.

The Beatles were not interested in punctuality or politeness. But they respected Bob Wooler and recognised that his wagging forefinger often conveyed a valuable point. It was Wooler who advised them to begin playing even before the curtains opened, and who delved among his own record collection for the *William Tell Overture* and suggested using its opening fanfare as their signature tune.

Their other strong supporter was Mona Best. They always met first at the Casbah, setting off on dates in a van driven by Mrs Best's part-time doorman, and usually accompanied by Neil Aspinall, ever ready to leave his accountancy studies to help unload and set up the drums and amplifiers.

Mona Best made forceful efforts on behalf of 'Pete's group', as she considered them. She took their bookings over the telephone, when Pete was not at home to do it: she became, as much as anyone was, their agent and manager. She wrote on their behalf to the BBC in Manchester, requesting a radio audition. The BBC's answer was not discouraging. The Beatles' name would be kept on file.

In Bob Wooler's eyes, too, Pete Best was their principal asset. At Aintree or Litherland, as the first bars of the *William Tell Overture* died away and the crash of guitars began behind still-closed curtains, that shriek of ecstasy, that rush to the front of the stage, was mainly for Pete. At a dance on St Valentine's Day, 1961, Wooler offered the novel idea of moving Pete's drums forward to rank equally with the other three. That night, the girls all but dragged him off his stool and off the stage.

•

One evening just after Christmas, Mrs Best rang up the Cavern Club in Mathew Street, and asked to speak to the owner, Ray McFall. It happened to be a big trad jazz night at the Cavern, starring Humphrey Lyttleton, and, what with the noise, McFall had to press his ear close to the receiver. 'Look here, Mr McFall,' insisted the dulcet voice that sounded both a little Indian and a little Scouse, 'there's this group called the Beatles – you should have them at the Cavern, you know.' McFall replied politely that he'd think about it.

When Alan Synter started the Cavern as a jazz club in 1957, Ray McFall had been the family accountant. In 1959, Synter decided to get out, and McFall took over the lease. It was he, in fact, who had booked John Lennon and the Quarry Men the night they gave offence by playing Chuck Berry numbers. Orders to desist were relayed to them from the man who still looked like an accountant with his light grey suit, his close-shaven cheeks and carefully manicured hands and the small fur hat he wore during winter.

Mathew Street is among the warren of cobbled lanes which once carried goods traffic up from Liverpool docks to their hinterland of dark

Victorian warehouses. By day, the lanes were alive with heavy goods lorries, unstacking and loading in the squeak of airborne hoists. By night, they were empty, but for cartons and cabbage leaves, and the occasional meandering drunk.

Underneath the warehouse at 10 Mathew Street, in 1960, could be found the Cavern Jazz Club. Its entrance was a hatchway, under a single naked light bulb. A flight of 18 stone steps turned at the bottom into three arched, interconnecting brick tunnels. The centre tunnel was the main club area, with a stage against the inner wall and school-like rows of wooden chairs. In the nearer tunnel, the money was taken; in the further one, beyond obscuring pillars, you danced. The best British jazz bands had performed down there, in an atmosphere pervaded by damp and mould and the aroma of beer slops and small, decaying mammals and the cheeses that were kept in the cellar next door.

Ray McFall, though a passionate jazz fan, was aware of rock and roll's growing popularity. The call from Mona Best only confirmed what he had heard about huge and profitable 'beat' dances in out-of-town halls. The short craze for 'trad' was now definitely over, and modern attracted only the earnest, intellectual few. McFall, therefore, decided to let pop into his jazz stronghold, gradually at first so as not to enrage the existing clientele. His first regular group, the Blue Genes, occupied a curious middle ground, playing both rock and jazz, with banjo and stand-up bass. Tuesdays, the Blue Genes' 'Guest Night', became the first break in the Cavern's all-jazz programme.

McFall had noticed how many young office workers in central Liverpool spent their lunch-hour hanging round music shops like Hessy's, and the record department in NEMS, the electrical shop in Whitechapel, round the corner from Mathew Street. It suddenly occurred to him that he could just as easily open the Cavern for dancing at midday as at night. So he began to put on lunch-hour sessions, featuring trad jazz bands in alternation with a beat group called the Metronomes whose singer, Tommy Love, worked in a city insurance office. Derry and the Seniors also got a lunch-time booking after their return from Hamburg.

Bob Wooler, visiting the Cavern one lunch-time, was persuaded by Johnny Hutch of the Big Three to say something into the stage microphone. 'I did it just as the people were going out. I said, "Remember all you cave-dwellers, the Cavern is the best of cellars." I'd prepared that little pun on Peter Sellers's album *The Best of Sellers*. Ray McFall came across. I thought I was going to get a lecture; but instead he offered me the job of compèring the lunch-time sessions.'

Wooler lost no time in urging McFall to hire the Beatles. Paddy

Delaney, the club doorman and an accomplished mimic, would from then on impersonate Wooler's voice and wagging forefinger as he told McFall they would bring in a following of 60, at least.

Delaney, a huge, straight-backed, kind-hearted Irishman, had seen service both in the Guards and the Liverpool Parks Police. He was equally immaculate in his spare-time profession of helping to dissuade Teddy Boys from entering Liverpool's premier dance halls, the Locarno and the Grafton Rooms. In 1959, to oblige his brother-in-law, he agreed to put in one night on the door of the Cavern Club. 'I thought it was a proper place, like the Grafton Rooms, so I turned up smart. I had three dinner suits in those days. I put one of them on with a maroon bow tie, a matching cummerbund with a watermark in it, and three diamond studs in my shirt. I walked up and down Mathew Street three times before I could even *see* the Cavern.'

Paddy Delaney was still there – still in evening dress complete with studs and cummerbund – when the Beatles first played at the Cavern in January 1961. Ray McFall had booked them, tentatively, to appear on a Tuesday, midway through the Blue Genes' Guest Night.

'I'm standing there under the light and I see this lad coming along in a leather jacket, a black polo-necked jersey. I remember thinking to myself, "That's the youngest tramp *I've* ever seen." "Are you a member, pal?" I said to him. He said "I'm George Harrison. I'm in the Beatles." I let him go in, then Paul McCartney came along; then John. Then a taxi came with Pete Best and the drums and their two amplifiers. Just chipboard, those were, no paint or anything, with the speakers nailed up inside.'

Bob Wooler's prophecy was fulfilled. The Beatles brought in at least 60 extra customers, in contingents from Aintree, Litherland and West Derby. The Blue Genes, supposedly the main event of the evening, were totally eclipsed. Paddy Delaney witnessed the furious row upstairs in Mathew Street between Ray McFall and his outraged regular musicians.

McFall was impressed by the door receipts but shocked to the depths of his jazz-pure soul by the Beatles' unkempt appearance. He had thought, after seeing Cliff Richard's Shadows, that groups wore suits. He told Bob Wooler that if the Beatles wanted to play the Cavern again, they must not wear jeans. To this the Beatles replied that Ray McFall could get stuffed. Wooler interceded on their behalf, pointing out to McFall the advantage of block-booking a group which, being 'professional' – that was to say, unemployed – would be available to play lunch-times on any day of the week. 'The Beatles,' Wooler said with pride, 'were what I called the first rock and *dole* group.'

So it came about that, on three or four days each week, the deliverymen and warehouse checkers in Mathew Street witnessed the unprecedented sight of scores of young girls, from city centre shops and offices, in beehive hair and stiletto heels, picking their way down the alleys among the delivery lorries and cast-off fruit crates. By noon, when the session began, a queue would stretch from the corner leading to Whitechapel to the doorway, like a ship's hatch, that would be unnoticeable but for the bouncer who stood there, blocking it with his arm. As the city clocks struck noon, that queue would start to move forward, by degrees, into the hatchway and down the 18 steps to the table where Ray McFall sat, surrounded by soup bowls full of money. Admission cost 1s (5p) to members or 1s 6d (7p) to non-members. Beyond McFall's table was a microscopic cloakroom, tended by a girl named Priscilla White during her lunch-break from a neighbourhood typing pool.

Under the gloomy arches, Bob Wooler's voice would gravely resound in what had become each session's inaugural catechism. 'Hi, all you Cavern-dwellers – welcome to the *best* of cellars.' Wooler broadcast, not from the stage but behind it, in a tiny recess which served also as a changing-room for the bands. The sole ventilation came from the next-door cellar, via a grille which became gradually blocked by a mounting pile of drum kits. A single cupboard served to accommodate the DJ's amplifier and record-playing deck. Between each live session, Wooler sat in this reeking priest hole, playing records from his own large personal collection.

Ray McFall paid the Beatles 25s (£1.25) each per day. For this they did two 45-minute spots at the end of the centre tunnel, on the tiny stage with dead rats under it, and positively no acoustics. The low-arched brick, and the wall of impacted faces and bodies, so squeezed out all empty air that Pete Best's drumbeats rebounded an inch in front of him, making the sticks jump like pistols in his hand. A single Chuck Berry number, in that heat, caused even tidy Paul to look as if his head had been plunged into a water butt. The bricks sweated with the music, glistening like the streams that coursed from their temples, and sending a steady drip of moisture over equipment in which there were many naked wires. Each breath they took filled their lungs with each other's hot scent, mingling uniquely with an aroma of cheese rinds, damp mould, disinfectant and the scent of frantic girls.

For their lunch-time audience, they poured out the vast Hamburg repertoire that could switch crazily from American blues to maudlin country and western; from today's Top Twenty hit to some sentimental prewar dance-band tune. It seemed to Bob Wooler that they took a perverse delight in playing what no rival group would dare to do. 'They had to let you know they were different. If everyone else was playing the

A-side of a record, they'd be playing the B-side. If the others jumped around, they'd decide to stand still like zombies.' Wooler himself possessed a number of rare American singles which he would play as surprise items over the Cavern loudspeakers. One of these, Chan Romero's 'Hippy Hippy Shake', besotted Paul McCartney, who begged to be allowed to borrow it and copy down the words. 'Hippy Hippy Shake' became the climax of their catalogue of sheer stage-stamping rock. A moment later, they would change to the cocktail-lounge tempo of 'Till There Was You', from the stage show *Music Man*, crooned by Paul with the sweat drying on him.

Stu Sutcliffe was back with them on bass guitar, although little more proficient than he had been before the Hamburg trip. 'He'd bop around like the others,' Bob Wooler said. 'But he seemed to know that the others were carrying him.' Stu was hardly noticed by John and Paul in their perpetual contest to be the cynosure of all eyes. They in turn failed to notice how often those eyes would pass over their bobbing heads, to settle on Pete Best. George, on the right, took no part in the clowning, but waited solemnly, biting his lower lip, for the moment when his solo arrived. To his mother, Louise, he explained that he had no time to horse around – it was up to him to keep the music together.

In the intervals, they would go across Mathew Street to the Grapes, a marine-looking pub with scrubbed wooden tables, much frequented by postmen from the GPO in North John Street. There they would sit as long as possible over a fivepenny half of bitter each. The landlady complained they took up seats which might have been more profitably occupied by postmen drinking pints of draught Guinness.

The Cavern provided lunch of a sort – hot soup with mysterious lumps in it; meat pies and rolls and soft drinks. 'Paul borrowed a halfpenny off me once,' Paddy Delaney, the doorman, said. 'He wanted a Coke and a cheese roll; it came to sevenpence halfpenny, and he'd only got sevenpence. "There you are, Paul," I said to him. "Remember me when you're up there, famous."'

Paul's father, Jim McCartney, was the first of their parents to investigate this new epoch. He had noticed the state in which Paul came home from the Cavern, with clothes stinking of mould and a shirt so drenched it could be wrung out over the kitchen sink. Jim was still in the cotton business, working at the Cotton Exchange just round the corner from Mathew Street. Venturing into the Cavern in his own lunch-hour, Jim could not get near enough to the stage to speak to Paul. When he came after that, it would usually be to drop in some meat he had bought to cook for Paul and Michael that evening. Above the din in the band room, he would give Paul careful instructions about when, and at what number, to switch on the electric cooker.

John's Aunt Mimi was less easily placated. Ray McFall, sitting behind his soup-bowl exchequer, was dismayed to be confronted by a lean and angry woman demanding the whereabouts of John Lennon. For Mimi, up to that point, still believed John to be studying at art college. He was on stage at the time, doing a song whose lyrics suddenly changed – as at Woolton fête – to: 'Oh, oh, Mimi's coming. Mimi's coming down the path.' In the break, when he reeled into the band room, he found waiting for him, as well as faithful Cynthia, an extremely grim-faced aunt. 'I said to him, "This is very nice, John, isn't it? This is *very* nice!"'

George's mother also happened to be at the Cavern that day, but in the audience. She would go along and shout and scream for George as loudly as any girl. She saw Mimi going out one day, and shouted exuberantly, 'Aren't they great?' 'I'm glad somebody thinks so,' was Mimi's tart reply.

•

Allan Williams, although busy with his Blue Angel club, was still the sole exporter of Liverpool groups to Hamburg. Early in 1961, he booked Gerry and the Pacemakers to play a two-month session for Peter Eckhorn at the Top Ten Club. It was a well-deserved chance for Gerry Marsden, the smiley little postboy from Menzies Street, who had made such a success at the Boxing Stadium show by singing 'You'll Never Walk Alone'.

Gerry and his group were quiet boys, intent on saving their Hamburg money to buy new equipment. Even so, they brought home enough stories – of Willi's Cafe, the Gretel and Alphons and Jim Hawke's Seaman's Mission – to reawaken the Beatles' addiction to Reeperbahn life. Peter Eckhorn had told them they could go back to the Top Ten any time, subject to police and immigration approval. Pete Best's drums were still there, together with the clothes which he and Paul had been compelled to leave behind in the attic.

Pete, with the approval of the other four, rang up Eckhorn from Mona Best's house in Heyman's Green. Eckhorn instantly gave them a booking, to begin in April, at £40 each per week – exactly twice as much as they had been paid by Bruno Koschmider. Nor would they have to pay Williams his 10 per cent agent's commission, having fixed the engagement without his help. Williams, unaware of this decision, applied to the German Consulate in Liverpool for work permits on their behalf, explaining the circumstances of the Bambi Kino fire, and rendering heartfelt assurances as to their reliability and good character.

Stu Sutcliffe originally had no intention of accompanying them. Guilty at having traded on John's loyalty for so long, he was now perfectly prepared to hand over the role of bass-player in the band to Paul, as Paul so desperately wanted. He was even more full of guilt at having so long neglected his art studies for a career as musician that, clearly, would never lead anywhere. His intention was to accede to his mother's wishes and return to Liverpool Art College to take his teacher-training diploma. On the strength of his previous brilliant record as a student, the College had indicated that he could go back whenever he liked. But now they informed him that he could not be re-admitted. When Millie Sutcliffe made enquiries, she learned Stu was suspected of having stolen the students' union amplifier which the Beatles had appropriated months before.

This unexpected *volte-face* plunged the sensitive Stu into a depression so intense that, for a time, he feared he might never pick up a paintbrush again. His one desire was to get away from Liverpool, with what he saw as its constricting narrow-mindedness, and back to the freedom of Hamburg and the arms of his beautiful fiancée. In exchange for that, a little more humiliation on stage with the Beatles seemed a small price to pay.

•

The Beatles' Top Ten engagement started in April 1961. Thanks to Allan Williams they had proper work permits this time, and proper train tickets, purchased with money sent across by Peter Eckhorn. They arrived at Hamburg Station to be greeted by Astrid in her black leather trouser suit. Even the bashful George did not hesitate to fling his arms around her.

The hours at the Top Ten were, if anything, more punishing than at the Kaiserkeller. They went on at 7 p.m. each night, playing in alternation with Tony Sheridan's band, until 2 or 3 a.m. The club's barn-like size meant they must 'mak show' even more obviously and violently to be seen out in the remoter parts. Now, too, along the front of the stage, there would often be photographers – friends of Astrid and Klaus Voorman – training their long lenses upward and shouting, 'More sveat, boys! More sveat.'

Most of their Kaiserkeller friends had forsaken Bruno Koschmider to work at the new Top Ten. There was Horst Fascher, the Reeperbahn's champion bouncer, just released from another prison sentence and ready, in the Liverpool phrase, to 'worship the bones of their bodies'. There was Rosa, the WC attendant, and her big sweet-jar of 'Prellys'. There were three bold-eyed, powerful barmaids with whom almost everyone had explored the delights of 'muff-diving', 'finger pie' and 'yodelling up the canyon', and who signified when a song had gone down well by setting all the lampshades above the bar counter swinging and jogging.

Astrid continued her flattering habit of photographing the Beatles at every opportunity. She produced studies of them, lounging on the docks or in railway yards, complementing their beardless menace with tugboats, freight wagons or other specimens of German industrial design. She did studio portraits, too, using a technique pioneered by the American Richard Avedon, which gave drama to the face by halving it between shadow and light. George and John were photographed in this way, but not Pete Best – who was genuinely unconceited about his appearance – and, strangely, not Paul. Astrid tended to be with George, whom she mothered, and John, because, as well as being Stu's closest friend, he fascinated her.

It was no coincidence, perhaps, that Stu persuaded John to allow his own steady girl friend, Cynthia Powell, to come out to visit him in Hamburg. Paul's 'steady', a girl named Dot Rhode who worked in a Liverpool chemist's shop, was also invited. The two girls had become friends in their common purdah, squeezing themselves into photography booths for snapshots to send to their lords and masters, or laboriously transcribing the words of the newest Chuck Berry song.

The visit took place in Cynthia's Easter College vacation, and passed off happily, against all the odds. For most of the fortnight, she stayed with the hospitable Kirchherr family. Astrid was nice to her, lent her stunning clothes and drove her down to the Reeperbahn each evening to see the Beatles play. Some nights, she stayed behind, heroically sharing John's bunk in the Top Ten attic, while George snored in the bunk below. Paul and Dot stayed, with Tony Sheridan and other itinerant lodgers, on a harbour barge lent to them by Rosa, the club's lavatory attendant. Most of the meals, as usual, were provided by Jim and Lilo Hawke at the Seaman's Mission. Rosa, walking through the early morning fish market, would steal extra rations for Paul, slipping bananas or sardines into her coat pockets or up her sleeves.

Relations between Stu Sutcliffe and Paul McCartney, meanwhile, grew steadily worse. Paul made no secret of his contempt for Stu's bass playing, and his own conviction that he could do it better. There were rows on the Top Ten stage, behind John's back; one night, Paul's taunts even goaded Stu to physical violence. 'Paul had made some remark about Astrid,' Tony Sheridan says. 'Stu went for him, but he was only a little guy. Paul started beating the shit out of him.'

Stu spent the club intermissions talking wistfully to *exis*, like Peter Markmann and Detlev Birgfeld, who were students at the Hamburg State

Art College. They and Astrid urged him to try to enrol there as a student. Things were especially good just now, they said, as the college had appointed the famous sculptor Edouardo Paolozzi – one of Stu's long-time idols – to run a course of painting and sculpture master classes. Eventually, he was persuaded to go and meet Paolozzi, taking some samples of his Liverpool College work.

A brief glance was enough for Edouardo Paolozzi. He promised to use his influence, not only to admit Stu to the State Art College but also to get him a grant from the Hamburg City Council.

In Paolozzi's class, and in an attic studio which Frau Kirchherr gave him, Stu nerved himself to paint again. And once he had started, he could not stop. His Liverpool work, though accomplished, had always been derivative, slipping in and out of identities that caught his fancy. Hamburg, and the Reeperbahn's dark, sleazy colours, gave him his own line at last. Huge swirling abstracts, like crushed Rio carnivals, like cities crumbling into impacted seas, thronged the canvases that, once again, were almost too tall for him to paint the tops of. Each one, completed in a day or a night, was impatiently stacked aside. Life now seemed too short for the miles his brush had to travel.

For the first month he led a dual life, both studying under Paolozzi and playing at the Top Ten club. At 2 or 3 a.m., he would go into his attic and work there until it was time for class. He existed for days without sleep, borne up by pills and drink and the feverish excitement of his work. The headaches, which had intermittently troubled him, began to increase, in frequency and ferocity. Sometimes the pain would send him into a kind of fit when he would smash his head against the wall or scream at Astrid for some supposed infidelity – then, equally without warning, the anguish would disappear.

He quit the Beatles gradually, without rancour, glad to see how easily they closed ranks behind him. Paul, as Paul had so long wanted, took over bass guitar, borrowing Stu's Hofner President until he could get one of his own. When it came, it was a bizarre new Hofner model, shaped like a violin. Once or twice, for old times' sake, Stu 'sat in' with the Beatles, playing bass alongside Paul. A photograph taken at one such moment shows him half in shadow, his eyes frowning, sightless, as in some study taken a hundred years ago. It was a look that his college tutor, Edouardo Paolozzi, found especially disturbing. 'I felt there was a desperate thing about Stuart. I was afraid of it. I wouldn't go down to that club.'

Though Stu was a Beatle no longer, he allowed himself to be deputed for the job which none of the others fancied. He wrote to Allan Williams in Liverpool, informing Williams of the decision to withhold his 10 per cent commission. It was shabby treatment for a man who, for all his shortcomings, had made genuine efforts on their behalf. Williams wrote back a long and aggrieved letter, threatening to have them blacklisted among theatrical agents, if not deported from Germany all over again. He seems, for once, to have been too hurt to exact retribution. All his written agreements with the Beatles had been destroyed in the fire at his own short-lived Top Ten club. So Williams let the Beatles go.

In Hamburg, meanwhile, a new Messiah had appeared, in Bert Kaempfert, a well-known West German orchestra leader and producer for the German label Polydor. Kaempfert had been to the Top Ten to see Tony Sheridan and immediately put him under contract to Polydor. As a backing group – largely on Tony Sheridan's recommendation – Bert Kaempfert hired the Beatles.

They had gone to bed as usual, Pete Best remembers, just after dawn. At eight sharp, taxis arrived to take them and Tony Sheridan to the recording studio. This, despite Kaempfert's eminence, proved to be no more than the hall of the local infants' school. They recorded on the stage, with the curtains closed.

Bert Kaempfert's idea of rock and roll was to put a drum beat behind tunes familiar to a German audience from their nights of beer and boomps-a-daisy. He had chosen for Sheridan and his backing group material that included two of the world's most boring songs, 'My Bonnie Lies over the Ocean', and 'When the Saints Go Marching In'. Tony Sheridan sang them in a voice still wide-eyed with last night's Prellys, while the 'Beat Brothers' – as Kaempfert had renamed them – rattled off two versions of the same non-arrangement.

The 'Beat Brothers', thrilled just to be in the proximity of disc-making equipment, were content with their subordinate role. They did prevail on Kaempfert, however, to listen to a handful of Lennon–McCartney songs. The great man's verdict was one to which John and Paul were growing accustomed – their songs did not sound enough like the hits of the moment. But Kaempfert was impressed enough to let them cut a disc in their own right. They did 'Ain't She Sweet', one of the standbys from their all-night club act, with John taking the vocal and the old jazz chords rearranged in a style strongly reminiscent of Paul. Kaempfert also liked an instrumental which George had worked out as a parody of Cliff Richard's group, the Shadows. This, too, was taped under the ironic title 'Cry for a Shadow'.

The tracks chosen by Polydor for release were, as might have been feared, 'My Bonnie Lies over the Ocean', coupled with 'When the Saints Go Marching In'. The 'Beat Brothers' had played for a flat fee of 300 marks each (about £26), and so could expect no royalty on the disc's quite healthy German sales. 'Ain't She Sweet' and 'Cry for a Shadow' were still in the Polydor vaults in June 1961, when John, Paul, George and Pete caught the train back to Liverpool.

Stu Sutcliffe did not go with them. He had decided to settle in Hamburg, marry Astrid and continue at the State Art College. His mother shortly afterwards received a photograph of him taken by Astrid in his attic studio, in jeans and gumboots, standing before the easel bearing some new work in headlong progress. The technique was the same that she had used on George and John, splitting the face between light and shadow. In this portrait of Stu, the effect was eerie, his features the palest glimmer against what seemed an encroaching dark.

•

In Liverpool now, beat music raged like a fever. From Mathew Street it had seeped up between the warehouses into Dale Street and through the studded gates of the Iron Door, another long-time jazz stronghold gone over to evening or all-night pop sessions in overt rivalry with the Cavern. The same had happened all over the city, in clubs like the Downbeat and the Mardi Gras, in dance halls formerly dedicated to quicksteps and Veletas. The Riverside Ballroom and the Orrel Park Ballroom, the Rialto Ballroom, the Avenue cinema, even the Silver Blades Ice Rink clamoured for beat groups to fill their Saturday nights. New groups sprang up by the dozen, mutating from older ones, then splitting like amoebae into newer groups still. Now, as rivals to the Beatles at the Cavern, there were the Searchers at the Iron Door. There were Ian and the Zodiacs; Kingsize Taylor and the Dominoes; Faron and the Flamingoes; Earl Preston and the TTs; Lee Curtis and the All-Stars; Dale Roberts and the Jaywalkers; Steve Day and the Drifters; the Remo Four; the Black Cats; the Four Jays. Hessy's music store thronged each day with eager customers for new guitars, new basses and drum kits to be paid for far into a future that had no relevance compared with the finger-sliding, tom-tomming excitement of tonight.

Bill Harry knew every group and every place there was to play. The curly-haired design student from Parliament Street was always to be seen in the clubs and jive halls, talking to the musicians between numbers and scribbling on bits of paper. He kept notes on every new group that was formed and every new venue opened. For him, as for John Lennon, beat music disrupted an Art College course, though in Bill's case, poor family circumstances dictated that even a hobby should be a matter of feverish hard work. He earned extra money by designing stationery for a local printer, and by writing and drawing anything, anywhere, for anyone.

Bill, an inveterate compiler of sci-fi 'fanzines', had long cherished an ambition to start his own music newspaper. For a time, he planned one called *Storyville and 52nd Street*, to cover jazz. Then in 1961, with details of 350 beat music venues in his notebook, another idea occurred to him. He had noticed, on his trips around clubs and ballrooms, how parochial each one was; how little each audience knew of the sheer size and variety of the beat craze. The musicians, too, often had no idea where their friends or their rivals were performing. Bill Harry conceived the idea of a fortnightly beat music newspaper that would serve both as a guide to clubs and halls and an insight for the fans into the lives of their favourite groups.

The paper, launched on 6 July 1961, was christened *Mersey Beat*. A local Civil Servant named Jim Anderson provided its £50 starting capital. Bill Harry was editor, designer, chief reporter, sub editor and advertisement and circulation manager, all while ostensibly studying at the Art College. Each lunch-hour, he would sprint out of College, down the hill to the *Mersey Beat* office, a single room above a wine merchant's shop in Renshaw Street. His girl friend, Virginia, who typed and took telephone calls, was the only other member of staff.

John Lennon's former Gambier Terrace flatmate could naturally be counted on to give the Beatles plenty of space in his new paper. When Bill asked them for photographs, they handed over a pile of the ones Astrid had taken in Hamburg, together with some informal snapshots of John in his underwear, standing on the Grosse Freiheit and reading the *Daily Express*. John's was precisely the kind of Goon Show humour Bill Harry wanted to flavour the *Mersey Beat* editorial. He had never forgotten the nonsense verses which John had shown him during student lunch-time sessions at Ye Cracke. For *Mersey Beat*'s first issue, he asked John to write his own personal account of the Beatles' beginnings as a group. This was produced, Billy Harry remembers, on scraps of paper, with a hangdog, half-embarrassed air. John clearly did not expect his words to be suitable for publication.

Issue number one of *Mersey Beat* had a print run of 5,000 copies. Bill Harry, as well as writing the entire paper, delivered bundles of it personally to 28 Liverpool newsagents. Further stocks went on sale at local dances, at Hessy's music shop and on the record counters of major city stores like Blackler's. One of Bill's best contacts had proved to be NEMS, the electrical appliance shop in Whitechapel which had a record department run by the owner's elder son, Brian Epstein. He showed keen interest in *Mersey Beat*, giving Bill Harry a firm order for a dozen copies.

The first issue carried on its dwarfish front page a picture of Gene Vincent, the American rock and roll star who had visited Liverpool, as the caption admitted, 'earlier in the year'. Bill Harry, unable to afford to make photographic blocks, was compelled to borrow what he could from a local weekly newspaper. Underneath, a story headed Swinging Cilla told how Cilla Black, the Cavern Club's part-time cloakroom attendant, better known along Scotland Road as Priscilla White, had begun to gain confidence as a singer by after-hours appearances on stage with Rory Storm's group and the Big Three.

The right-hand column was given over to John Lennon's article. Bill Harry had printed it complete under its author's heading 'a short diversion on the dubious origins of Beatles, translated from the John Lennon'. What followed revealed little of those origins but much about the boy whose fascination with words coexisted with utter disregard of all normal punctuation and spelling. 'Many people ask what are Beatles? Why Beatles? Ugh, Beatles, how did the name arrive? So we will tell you. It came in a vision – a man appeared on a flaming pie and said unto them: "From this day on you are Beatles." "Thank you, Mister Man, they said, thanking him."'

Mersey Beat was an immediate sell-out. At NEMS in Whitechapel, all 12 copies went within minutes of their appearance in the record department, and Brian Epstein telephoned Bill Harry with an order for two dozen more. The next day, he requested a further hundred. For issue two, published on 20 July, Epstein's order was 12 dozen copies.

Prominent in the first issue, and every one that followed, was a large display advertisement for the Cavern Club, giving details of its lunchtime, evening and, occasionally, all-night sessions. Here, the Beatles' name, varying in type-size from the garish to the microscopic, rotated week by week with that of Gerry and the Pacemakers, Rory Storm and the Hurricanes, Kingsize Taylor and the Dominoes, and also the traditional jazz bands which Ray McFall stubbornly continued to hire.

Though conscientiously filled with news about all groups and their doings, *Mersey Beat* made no secret of its overriding preference. Issue two, when it reached the counter of NEMS record store in Whitechapel, banner-headlined the retrospective hot news of the 'Beatle's' recording session and contract with Bert Kaempfert in Hamburg. Only now did their Liverpool following learn of the existence of the Beatles' music on disc, albeit a little-known foreign label. The story was illustrated by Astrid's photograph of them, with Stu Sutcliffe, on the traction engine at Der Dom. Paul's surname was given, in one of its several *Mersey Beat* versions, as 'McArtrey'.

The paper soon became known, not merely for news about the Beatles but as an extension of the comedy and clowning in their Cavern Club stage act. John, at Bill Harry's encouragement, contributed more nonsense verses and an irregular column called 'Beatcomber', called after 'Beachcomber' in the *Daily Express*. He also wrote and paid for comic small ads, filling a section which would otherwise have been empty, and prolonging Beatle in-jokes for weeks at the modest cost of fourpence a word. 'HOT LIPS, missed you Friday – Red Nose.' 'RED NOSE, missed you Friday – Hot Lips.' 'Whistling Jock Lennon wishes to contact HOT NOSE.'

Mersey Beat flourished, thanks to its thorough coverage and the sprinting energy of its editor. Anyone who placed a large ad could expect a large story to be written about them. If the advertiser could write his own copy, so much the better. It was on this principle that *Mersey Beat*, in its early August issue, published a short article by one of its best customers, Brian Epstein of the NEMS electrical shop, reviewing the new records NEMS currently had for sale. Mostly, he recommended ballads from musical shows like *West Side Story* and *The Sound of Music*. A cursory reference was made to Chubby Checker's 'Let's Twist Again', and the Streamliners' 'Frankfurter Sandwiches'. The closing paragraph was devoted to new John Ogden piano recitals of works by Liszt and Busoni.

Bob Wooler, the Cavern disc jockey, also wrote regularly for *Mersey Beat*. His debut column on 31 August dealt entirely with the Beatles: they were, said Wooler, 'the biggest thing to hit the Liverpool Rock and Roll set up in years'. Among hundreds of groups playing roughly the same r & b material, Wooler pinpointed accurately the novelty in musicians with equal appeal to both sexes – to the boys through their dress and manner; to girls, in Wooler's view, chiefly through the 'mean, moody magnificence' of their drummer Pete Best. Pete, indeed, was the only Beatle singled out by name. Wooler summed them up, with true alliterative relish, as 'rhythmic revolutionaries . . . seemingly unambitious yet fluctuating between the self-assured and the vulnerable. Truly a phenomenon – and also a predicament to promoters. Such are the fantastic Beatles. I don't think anything like them will happen again.' The only other item on the page was the brief column by 'Brian Epstein of NEMS', recommending new releases by Frank Sinatra, the Shadows and the George Mitchell Singers.

Bob Wooler's endorsement in *Mersey Beat* was backed up by ceaseless plugging of their Polydor record, over the Cavern microphone and in the halls where Wooler ran regular dances for Brian Kelly. Such was their drawing power now that Kelly would post bouncers outside their changing-room to stop rival promoters offering them more than £10 per night.

Between the groups, by contrast, there was little competition, save in the sinking of pints and the attracting of 'judies'. Bob Wooler's strict running-order would frequently be confounded by a hybrid semi-orchestra formed of two, or more, groups who felt like jamming together. At Litherland Town Hall one night, the Beatles merged with Gerry and the

Pacemakers to form the 'Beatmakers'. Gerry wore George's leather outfit, George wore a hood, Paul wore a nightdress and Gerry's brother Fred and Pete Best played one drum each.

Three or four nights a week at the Cavern, the queue would move, past Ray McFall's soup bowls, into heat barely describable by those who ever experienced it. 'You could feel it as you went down those 18 steps, climbing up your legs,' Paddy Delaney the doorman, said. 'The lads used to faint as well as the girls.' In the glue of bodies, the only space, apart from the stage, was an area at the opposite end of the centre tunnel where the boys would go and urinate. A girl wishing to get to the Ladies' could often make the journey only by being passed over the heads of the crowd.

For all the 'kicks and kudos', as Bob Wooler alliteratively phrased it, the summer of 1961 ended on a note of anticlimax. The Beatles seemed to have progressed as far as any group could outside the mystic sphere of London. Other local idols, like Rory Storm with his Butlin's holiday camp dates, seemed to be forging far ahead.

John Lennon took out his boredom in writing for *Mersey Beat*, and in letters to Stu Sutcliffe in Hamburg – long letters in pencil on exercise book paper, full of scribble and doodles, poems that started seriously but petered out into self-conscious obscenity, and anguished cries about the 'shittiness' of life. The correspondence could not be shown to Aunt Mimi or Millie Sutcliffe, teeming as it did with swear words and a running joke whereby Stu took the character of Christ and John, that of John the Baptist. It seemed that Stu, by staying on in Hamburg, had done the adventurous and enviable thing.

One letter from Stu mentioned that Jurgen Vollmer, a photographer friend of Astrid's, was soon going to be in Paris on holiday. John and Paul decided on the spur of the moment to use some money John's Scottish aunt had given him to go across to Paris and meet Jurgen. They went without a word to George or Pete Best, and despite the imminence of several important bookings. For almost a week, they lived in Montmartre and hung around the Flea Market, looking for sleeveless jackets like the one Jurgen wore. They also persuaded Jurgen to cut their hair in the 'French' style that Astrid had given Stu and George. They returned to Liverpool to find George and Pete Best disgusted with them; for a time, it seemed that the Beatles were finished. Bob Wooler and Ray McFall persuaded them to continue, each lecturing John and Paul sternly on the need to be reliable.

What did it matter anyway? The Cavern was always there, with another night-long session to trap them underground. Up in Mathew Street, where Paddy Delaney stood in his evening dress, a cloud of steam from the close-packed bodies below drifted out under the solitary light.

PART TWO

GETTING

7

'What brings Mr Epstein here?'

Each Wednesday night in the late 1930s, little Joe Flannery would be dressed in his night clothes and taken to spend the evening at the house of his father's best customer, Harry Epstein. Joe's father, Chris Flannery, was a cabinet-maker, specialising in the heavy sideboards sold at Epstein's Walton Road shop. 'Mr Harry' was a stickler for quality, refusing to accept any piece whose drawers did not slide in as easily upside-down. But on Wednesday evenings, formality relaxed. The Flannerys and the Epsteins drove into Liverpool together to attend the weekly wrestling bouts. Seven-year-old Joe would wait for his parents at Mr Harry's house, playing upstairs in the nursery with the Epsteins' son, Brian.

This other boy was not like Joe. He was slender and delicate; he had a nanny to look after him in his own softly lit upstairs domain. He did not speak like Joe, nor like any Liverpool child. And he had many beautiful toys. Joe, in particular, loved the model coach which Brian had been given to mark the 1937 Coronation of George VI. It was the State Coach in miniature, made of tin but magnificently gilded, drawn by a dozen plumed tin horses, spurred on by liveried tin postillions and grooms.

Brian knew how much Joe loved the Coronation coach. To grant, or arbitrarily refuse, permission to play with it gave him a sensation he slowly recognised as power over someone older and stronger. Though he himself cared little for the coach, he worried that Joe, because of loving it so much, would somehow gain possession of it. So one night while Joe was there, he stamped on it until he had broken it.

•

In 1933, the wedding took place of 18-year-old Malka Hyman to 29-year-old Harry Epstein. The match was approved of, uniting as it did two highly respectable Jewish families and two comparably thriving furniture firms. Harry's father, Isaac, owned the Liverpool shop he had founded as a penniless Lithuanian immigrant at the turn of the century. The Hymans, Malka's people, owned the Sheffield Cabinet Company, mass producing such items as 'The Clarendon', a bedroom suite which, in the Twenties and early Thirties, graced many a suburban English home.

Malka received a comfortable upbringing and a boarding-school education. In 1933, she was a slender, rather refined and artistic girl whose only serious complaint against the world was the way it had Anglicised her given name. Malka is the Hebrew word for queen. So Queenie was what her family, and her new husband, called her.

Her first child was born on 19 September 1934, at a private nursing home in Rodney Street, Liverpool. It was a boy, and as such a cause for rejoicing to grandparents concerned with the perpetuity of business. To Queenie, the baby in her arms was something more beautiful than she had dared to imagine. She called him Brian because she liked the name, and Samuel for the sake of the family and the scriptures.

The new baby was brought home to substance and comfort. Queenie's dowry from her parents was a handsome modern town house in Childwall, one of the smartest Liverpool suburbs. 197 Queens Drive was a five-bedroom residence with bay windows and a sunrise design on the glass over the front door, which a uniformed maid would open to visitors. A nanny became necessary when, in 1935, Queenie gave birth to her second son, Clive John.

The Epstein family shop occupied a prominent place in Walton Road. A row of tall display windows, extending round the corner into Royal Street, offered a range of furniture and home requisites, from sideboards to standard lamps, whose appearance was not especially chic but whose quality and durability could always be relied on. Next door stood the North End Road Music Stores, a little double-fronted shop which had been there since the days when young men and women bought sheet music to sing around the parlour piano. Jim McCartney's was one of the many local families which bought pianos from NEMS on the instalment plan. Subsequently, Epstein's had taken over the little shop, extending its stock to gramophones and wireless sets.

Harry Epstein worked hard, but enjoyed his pleasures and sharing them with his wife. They were keen bridge-players, fond of films and the theatre, well known, in a hospitable community, for the generosity and style of their entertaining. Once a week, they would drive into Liverpool to dine in the Sefton Restaurant at the Adelphi, an hotel then at its splendid apogee. In Ranelagh Place, next to Lime Street, the polished motor cars slid up the ramp. Commissionaires hastened out to welcome them into the majestic, ship-like interior of the entrance hall.

To their two small sons, Harry and Queenie Epstein gave the security, not only of Jewish family life but also of a middle class untroubled, as yet, by any social guilt, For Merseyside, in that time, was racked by unemployment. A few miles from Childwall, on grey and unknown dockyard streets, the men massed at dawn, like livestock, for the favour of even half a day's

Four faces metamorphosed by fame: from Liverpool scufflers to conventional pop idols; from sleek millionaires to psychedelic bandsmen; from lank-haired hippies to trinket-bedecked Caesars, their empire dissolving around them.

Left. John in Mimi's garden
Below, left. Mimi
Below. Julia

Right. George and family

Right. Ringo as a boy
Below, left. Ringo's parents

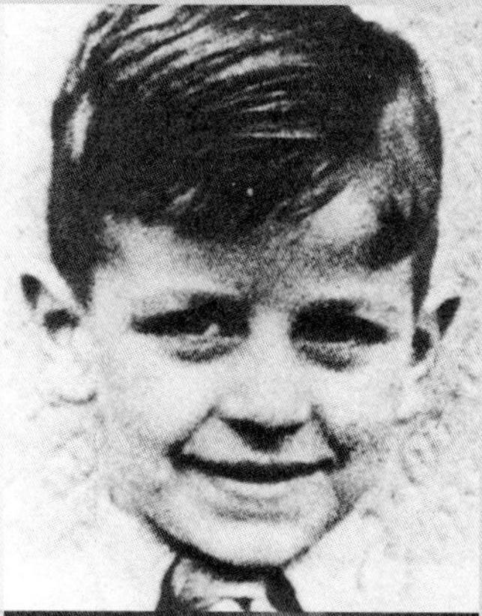

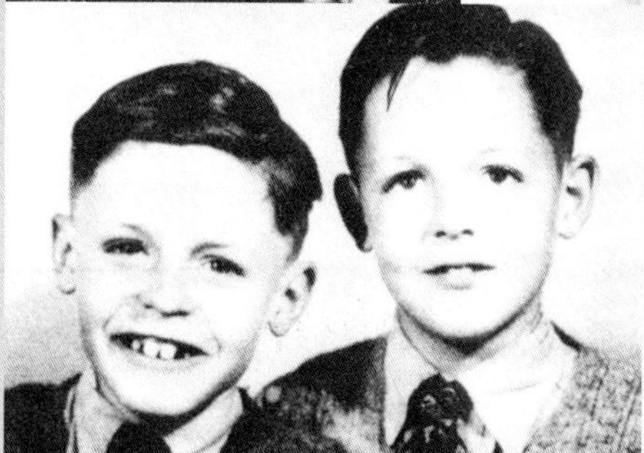

Above. Mary McCartney
Left. Michael and Paul

Earliest known picture of John Lennon's Quarry Men, playing at the Rosebery Street centenary party, summer 1957. 'I could hear these blokes whispering that they were going to get Lennon . . . the lads had to have a policeman to see them to the bus stop'.

Above. Rory Storm, the blithe, blond Liverpool rock 'n' roll showman who, in mid-performance, would athletically shin up a pillar at New Brighton Tower ballroom. His occasional falls increased his drawing power. Extreme right in his group, the Hurricanes, is the sad-eyed drummer still known as Ritchie Starkey, soon to be transformed into Ringo Starr. *Right*. Rooftop Cowboys in Hamburg. Their silver-embossed boots and Gene Vincent caps caused a sensation among polite West German boys.

Above, left. Stu Sutcliffe in 1961. Astrid produced this disturbing double image at a time when Stu's headaches were growing worse, his black-outs more frequent.
Above, right. A rare photograph by Astrid of herself in a mirror, showing the beauty so often kept back behind her camera lens.
Below. On the beach near Hamburg, 1961: Stu (right) the creator and initiator, works on a collage, helped by John, his admirer and disciple.

Above. At the Top Ten Club, Hamburg, 1961: Paul still on the rhythm guitar, George still using the cheap Hofner he saved for, John still uncertain how to comb his hair. *Left*. John and Paul at a boulevard café during their truant trip to Paris in 1961, when Jurgen Vollmer cut their hair as Beatles for keeps. Back in Liverpool, George and Pete almost quit in disgust.

Above. Mathew Street in the heyday of the Cavern Club's lunch-time sessions, the queue stretching back from an entrance that would be unnoticed but for the bouncer's blocking arm. In foreground, right, is Paddy Delaney, the ex-Guardsman who nightly stood watch in cummerbund and pearl-studded shirt.
Below. Paul, John, Pete and George, in the dank days and steamy nights of Cavern Club stardom – a local supremacy chiefly attributed to Pete Best's 'mean, moody magnificence'.

Above. Disgruntled in their new stage suits.
Below. Recording 'Love Me Do', 4 September 1962, under George Martin's critical eye. George Harrison still had the black eye he had received in the Pete Best riots.

work at four and sixpence. Only a mile or so away, ragged children played barefoot on flinty cobblestones. But in Childwall, the nursery lights glowed softly; there was Auntie Muriel or Uncle Mac on the wireless, and thin bread and butter for tea.

Brian left babyhood rapidly, learning to walk by the age of 11 months and to talk soon after that, clearly and interrogatively. In looks he was like his father, dark-eyed and round-faced, with wavy, light brown hair. His temperament was Queenie's, most notably in his love of refinement, and a feeling for style manifest even as a toddler. He would stand in his mother's bedroom while she got ready to go out, and gravely confer with her about which dress and accessories she should wear. Like Queenie he loved the theatre, its world of romance, strange light and make-believe. *The Wizard of Oz*, the first film he ever saw, left him astounded with its wistful fantasy for days. At the same time, he seemed normally robust, hammering wooden shapes into a plywood board at his first kindergarten school, Beechanhurst in Calderstones Road.

In 1940, during the bombing of Liverpool, Harry Epstein moved his family to relative safety in Southport on the West Lancashire coast. Brian attended Southport College, but hated it so much that Queenie transferred him to a smaller private school. Despite his obvious intelligence and alertness, he did not seem to do well there either. But now it was 1944, and safe to move back to Liverpool. Ten-year-old Brian was arrayed in a new black blazer and sent to Liverpool College, the most exclusive and expensive of the city's fee-paying academies.

Before he had reached his eleventh birthday, the College asked Harry and Queenie to remove him. It was alleged that he had done a dirty drawing in the mathematics class. According to Brian, this had been a design for a theatre programme, legitimately adorned by the figures of dancing girls. Privately the headmaster told Queenie that in other respects, too, Brian had proved to be a 'problem child'. He himself was never to forget the shame of sitting on a sofa at home and hearing his father say, 'I don't know *what* we're going to do with you.' The words produced one of the furious blushes by which Brian betrayed even the smallest discomfiture.

He had not sat the Eleven-Plus exam, and so could not be sent to any of Liverpool's excellent grammar schools. His parents were forced to settle for another small private academy which Brian, predictably, loathed. Queenie by now had begun to suspect that the fault might not be entirely on his side. Anti-semitism was a habit in which many otherwise agreeable British people still overtly and comfortably indulged. The nation which had recently pitted itself against the Nazi holocaust saw no harm in using words like 'Yid' or 'Jewboy' and in passing such expressions on to its children. Queenie Epstein knew the lengths to which Brian went at school to hide the fact that his middle name was Samuel.

They decided to try a school that actually welcomed Jewish boys. The nearest that could be found was Beaconsfield, near Tunbridge Wells in Kent. There, despite Queenie's forebodings, Brian seemed to do a little better. He took up horseriding and was encouraged to paint and draw. He made a friend of another Liverpool boy, Malcolm Shifrin, also the son of furniture people. The experiment was so successful that his younger brother Clive came to Beaconsfield to join him.

He continued to show a precocious love of luxury and refinement. Even when quite small, his greatest treat was to go with his mother and father for dinner at the Adelphi. Throughout the boys' infancy, Harry and Queenie sacrificed holidays abroad in favour of annual seaside visits to Llandudno in North Wales, or St Anne's. One wet summer in Llandudno, when Brian was 11, as a change from variety shows, Queenie took him to a concert by the Liverpool Philharmonic Orchestra. From that moment he began to love and learn about classical music. Another year, at St Anne's, the family struck up acquaintanceship with Geraldo, a bandleader famous for his BBC radio shows. Brian was invited to go into Blackpool to watch Geraldo make a recording. Queenie remembers how he sat spellbound in the studio when the red light went on for silence.

His formal education had yet again run into squalls. Shortly to leave Beaconsfield, he was busily engaged in failing the entrance exams for major public schools such as Rugby, Repton and Clifton. At last he was able to satisfy the requirements of Clayesmoore, a small public school still further away, in Dorset. 'As soon as he got there, he started to grumble,' Queenie Epstein remembered. 'Oh, those grumbles of his were enormous.'

Clive, his younger brother, a placid, conscientious, practical boy, had passed through prep school without trouble or complaint. Clive was good at exams, and so easily got into Wrekin College, a public school of the higher echelon in Shropshire. On the strength of Clive's performance, the Wrekin head agreed to accept Brian also.

Wrekin was his eighth school. He stayed there for two years, in a torpor faithfully described in his school reports. His only aptitudes seemed to be for art and – he discovered – acting. He found that he could face an audience without blushing, and that he enjoyed speaking lines. School dramatics brought him friends, at times even won him official commendation. But some worm of reticence, nurtured by all his previous scholastic failures, prevented him from sharing this new success with his parents. Queenie Epstein always remembered driving down to Wrekin to see a school play about Christopher Columbus, and failing to spot Brian where she expected to see him, among the supporting cast. He had not told her, so she did not realise, that he *was* Christopher Columbus.

He left school at 15, without sitting his School Certificate. He had written home that exams were not needed in the career he had chosen. Throughout his final terms, he had come top of his class in art and design. He wanted to go to London and become a dress designer.

Few enough people in 1950 would have wished to see their sons make such a choice of profession. To a northern Jewish family, with its age-old view of filial duty, no more disturbing or wounding suggestion could have emanated from an elder son. Harry Epstein was outraged and made no secret of it; Queenie, though more sympathetic, could see no means of granting Brian's wish within convention. The great scheme was buried quickly, before it could reach the ears of relations.

Another idea, that he might study art, languished as quickly under his father's remorseless practicality. With no exams behind him, no aptitude save that of upsetting his parents, there was nothing left for Brian but to submit to heredity. In September 1950, shortly after his sixteenth birthday, he started work as a furniture salesman in the family's Walton Road shop.

A woman came in to Epstein's that day to buy a mirror. Brian was allowed to deal with her under the critical eye of his parental superiors. By the time the customer left, he had persuaded her that what she really needed was a £12 dining-table.

He was, he discovered, a born salesman. Walton Road was not a grand thoroughfare, nor were they grand people who shopped for furniture at I. Epstein & Sons. This young man who served them, with his dapper suit, solicitous manner and upper-class voice, was decidedly an asset to the shop. Salesmanship awoke in him what eight costly schools could not – the will to work hard and be organised and efficient. He found he enjoyed arranging things for display, and window-dressing. And he was doing something which did not disappoint, but actually pleased, his father.

To his grandfather, he was less pleasing. Isaac Epstein still directed the firm he founded, arriving on the premises each morning as early as 6 a.m. Isaac, having dictated matters for half a century, looked askance on a grandson who boldly arranged dining-room chairs in the shop window with their back to the street, claiming it was 'more natural'.

Upsets with his grandfather became so frequent that, in 1952, his father and Uncle Leslie judged it wiser to remove him temporarily from Isaac Epstein's sight. For six months that year, Brian worked as a trainee with the Times Furnishing Company at their Lord Street, Liverpool, branch. Reports on his progress were consistently favourable. As a salesman, he was smart and efficient; he dressed windows with flair and taste. When his stay with the branch ended, he received a parting gift of a Parker pen and pencil set.

To outward appearances, his position was an enviable one. The son of wealthy parents, adored by his mother, indulged by a father glad to see this new-found business zeal, he seemed, in 1952, the very acme of provincial young bachelorhood. Ample pocket money supplemented his salesman's pay, enabling him to dress with an elegance beyond his 18 years. His suits came from the best Liverpool tailors; his ties were half-guinea silk foulards; he had his hair cut in the salon at Horne Brothers' shop. He belonged to a sophisticated young set which congregated at tennis clubs and cocktail parties, and in fashionable Liverpool haunts, like the Adelphi Palm Court lounge and the Basnett oyster bar. Among this circle he was popular, witty, generous and charming. Girls found him attractive with his wavy hair, his snub nose and delicate mouth and the large soft eyes which did not always look directly into theirs.

But by the time Brian was 18, he realised that, much as he enjoyed female company, he had no wish to share his life with any of the young women whom Queenie and his Adelphi set steered into his path. He must face the fact that he was homosexual.

It was a discovery calculated to fill any young British male of that era with unmitigated horror. In the 1950s, and up to the end of the following decade, homosexual acts between males were still a crime punishable by imprisonment. Only in rarified and enclosed worlds such as show business and couture could homosexuals yet find a measure of tolerance under the humanising term 'gay'. In the everyday world they were loathed, feared and mocked as 'queers', 'bum-boys', 'nancies', 'gingers', 'fruits', 'arse-bandits' and innumerable other heartless synonyms; abused and even attacked with impunity if they betrayed themselves in the smallest detail. For the son of respectable, religious Jewish parents in Liverpool's lingering Victorian twilight, the predicament was infinitely worse. There was never any question of Brian 'coming out', even – or especially not – to his own family. His father was simply unable to grasp such a concept; his more sensitive, intuitive mother may have known the truth even before Brian did, but feared to breathe a word about it to anyone.

•

In 1952, he became eligible for National Service. He was put into the army – not the RAF as he had wished – and sent south to do his basic training in Aldershot. He had hopes of being picked as officer material, but instead became a clerk in the Royal Army Service Corps. He was posted to London, to the RASC depot at Albany Barracks, Regent's Park.

His army life was mitigated by plentiful pocket money from home and comparative liberty after 6 p.m. His mother's sister, his Aunt Frieda, lived in Hampstead, only a mile or so away; he was also within easy reach of the West End. He took to going around like a young Guards officer, with bowler hat, pinstripe suit and rolled umbrella. Driving back into barracks one night, he was mistakenly saluted by the gate sentry, and next morning was put on a charge of impersonating an officer.

The army's reaction to this seemingly trivial escapade was draconian. Brian was confined to barracks and subjected to lengthy medical and psychiatric examinations without ever being told their purpose. His superiors may well have discovered his homoscxuality, which needless to say was absolutely barred from all armed forces in those days. A close business associate would also later suggest that the incident at the barrack gate was no innocent misunderstanding, but that Brian habitually posed as an officer to gain entrance to service clubs like the 'In and Out' in Piccadilly. Whatever the cause, he was declared psychologically unfit for military service and discharged after less than half his two-year term. Although the army could not be rid of him fast enough, it still provided a character reference describing him as 'sober, conscientious . . . at all times utterly trustworthy'.

Within a few months, he was once more a dapper and purposeful young man-about-Liverpool, working hard in the family business – and now with some real empathy and enjoyment. The little NEMS music shop in Harry Epstein's empire had lately widened its stock from pianos and wireless sets to gramophone records. Harry gave Brian the job of organising and running the new record department.

The success he made of it reflected his passion for classical music as well as his new-found business efficiency. Even as a schoolboy he had had his own impressive record collection, housed in a cabinet made specially for him at his Hyman grandparents' Sheffield factory. With his schoolfriend Malcolm Shifrin he was an ardent supporter of the 'Liverpool Phil''. 'Brian's knowledge of music really was impressive even then,' Shifrin says. 'So was his knowledge of the related arts, like ballet. He always *knew* music people – John Pritchard, the Philharmonic's conductor was a friend of his. We drove up twice to the Edinburgh Festival, and Brian introduced me to people there. But I always had the feeling he was a lonely person.'

He was still as addicted to the theatre as he had been in his schooldays. Liverpool's two main theatres, the Playhouse and the Royal Court, were surrounded in those days by half a dozen smaller but flourishing professional repertories. Behind the Royal Court was a genuine stage-door district of pubs and hotel bars which resounded to extravagant greetings in London accents. Brian haunted both the theatres and their adjacent bars in the hope of getting to know stage people. He himself appeared in one or two local amateur productions and, like an actor, acquired the habit of giving away signed photographs of himself to his friends.

Among the actors who befriended him was Brian Bedford, then, at the start of his career, starring in *Hamlet* at the Liverpool Playhouse. To Bedford, Brian confided one night that he hated shop work and Liverpool, and that he, too, wanted to become an actor. Bedford encouraged him to try for an audition at the Royal College of Dramatic Art in London. RADA's director, John Fernald, as it happened, had formerly run the Liverpool Playhouse. Brian auditioned with Fernald and, to his astonishment, was accepted.

The news filled his parents with dismay. In provincial Jewish business circles, 'going on the stage' was hardly less deplorable than becoming a dress designer. All the stability Brian seemed to have acquired was now put away, with his formal suits and ties. 'He'd made up his mind,' Queenie said, 'he was going to be a duffel-coated student. He wouldn't even take his car. We'd given it to him for his twenty-first birthday. A beautiful little cream and maroon Hillman Californian.'

Under John Fernald at RADA, Brian was a more than adequate pupil, sensitive and gentle. 'He didn't have a spectacular talent,' Fernald says, 'but it was a pleasing one. If you think in terms of type-casting, he would have played the second male lead – the best friend in whom the hero can always confide.'

At RADA he acquired – or seemed to – a steady girl friend. Her name was Joanna Dunham; she wore a fur coat dyed red. 'Brian always seemed older than the rest of us,' Joanna says. 'Even though he was only 21. And he drank. That was something hardly anyone at RADA did then, although everyone smoked. Brian would say, just like an older person would, "I *must* have a drink."

'I never thought he had any particular acting talent. There was one time, though, when he *did* surprise me. We had to do a test together for Fernald – a scene from *The Seagull*. We chose the scene between Konstantin and his mother, where Konstantin is adoring to his mother first, then flies into a terrible rage and tears the bandage off his head. The words must have had some special meaning for Brian. As he spoke the lines, I could feel he was getting out of control. When he started tearing the bandage off, I really felt frightened. It was almost as if he were having a nervous breakdown there on stage.'

Brian seems to have tried to make one last stab at heterosexuality by having an affair with Joanna. One night at a party, he got drunk and started to confide in her some of the secrets of his schooldays. 'I felt he seriously wanted to have a relationship with me, and that he was trying to tell me something. He was very pissed and threatened to drive me home. I behaved very badly, I'm afraid. I just ran away.'

Worse was soon to come. At the end of RADA's 1957 Easter term, Brian returned to Liverpool to be with his family during Passover, then returned to London where he'd arranged to spend the rest of the vacation working in a bookshop. One night, as he returned home to his north London flat after seeing a play at the Arts Theatre Club, he exchanged glances and a few words with a young man in the men's lavatory at Swiss Cottage underground station. His interlocutor was a policeman, waiting there to entrap homosexuals in the act of 'cottaging', or seeking sex around public toilets. Despite having committed no offence, Brian was arrested and charged with 'persistently importuning'. When he appeared at Marylebone Magistrates Court later, officers persuaded him to plead guilty, assuring him he'd get nothing worse than a fine or conditional discharge. Only when he'd done so did he realise he was up on a charge of 'importuning seven men'.

A letter, apparently written to his solicitor in the midst of this ordeal, reveals how desperately he had tried to join the sexual mainstream. 'I do not think I am an abnormally weak-willed person – the effort and determination with which I have tried to rebuild my life these last few months have, I assure you, been no mean effort. I believed that my own will-power was the best thing with which to overcome my homosexuality. And I believe my life may have become contented and may even have attained a public success.

'... I am not sorry for myself. My worst times and punishments are over. Now, through the wreckage of my life by society, my being will stain and bring the deepest distress to all my devoted family and few friends. The damage, the lying criminal methods of the police in importuning me and consequently capturing me leave me cold, stunned and finished ...'

In fact, it now seems that Harry and Queenie Epstein did not hear about the case, which would have been unlikely even to figure in any newspaper of wider circulation than the *Hampstead and Highgate Express*. But London was now poisoned for Brian, seemingly for ever. On the eve of his fourth RADA term, over a family dinner at the Adelphi Hotel, he told his parents what they had so much longed to hear. He'd had enough of being a duffel-coated student. He was ready to come home to Liverpool and become a businessman.

For this apparent sacrifice, he was given even further independence within the family firm. His father had bought a small shop in Hoylake, on the Cheshire Wirral, to be stocked with the more exclusive modern furniture which Brian favoured, and run by him on his own. It was his idea that the opening should be performed by a celebrity, 'Auntie Muriel', his childhood radio favourite from BBC Children's Hour.

There now began Brian's uneasy and painful double life. By day, managing Clarendon Furnishings, he was a smart young executive. By night, he was a furtive and self-loathing lawbreaker, cruising the Liverpool darkness in search of others like himself, in constant fear of the police and of no less vigilant 'queer-bashing' gangs. Though the city could not dare harbour anything like a modern gay bar, there were two acknowledged rendezvous under the sheltering wing of the Royal Court theatre. A pub called the Magic Clock (or 'Magic Cock') and an old hotel named the Stork (more usually pronounced 'Stalk') both attracted an exclusively male clientele, dressed always with severe understatement, semaphoring their forbidden brotherhood only with the faintest flicker of eyes or mouths.

But this precarious refuge was not enough for Brian. It was his further misfortune not to be attracted to other middle-class young men like himself, with whom he might have enjoyed discreet and – in that pre-AIDS era – completely safe physical relationships. His taste was for heterosexual men of the artisan class: the very dockers, labourers and merchant seamen who hated 'queers' the most, and most actively sought to do them physical harm. For all their detestation, there were many who habitually posed as 'rough trade', first leading a gay male on, then beating him up in simulated amazed outrage – and later, more often than not, blackmailing him with the threat of exposure to his family or the police.

Some time around 1958, Brian began his first, and probably last, happy emotional affair. One night in the Stork Hotel, he met a tall, dark-haired young man whose evident nerves were kept in check by a quiet, measured Liverpool voice. With mutual astonishment, Brian and he recognised one another. The tall young man was Joe Flannery, the cabinet-maker's son who used to be left in the nursery with Brian every Wednesday night.

The two began a relationship that, from the beginning, was more companionable than passionate. Joe hungered for glamour and refinement, and was as dazzled by Brian's sophistication as he once had been by his beautiful toy Coronation coach. The two would go to the theatre and smart restaurants in Liverpool or sometimes further afield in Manchester. As Joe quickly discovered, Brian still treated his many expensive playthings with utter cavalierness. 'Whenever he was parking his car between two other ones, he never cared if he bumped the one in front or the one behind. "What are bumpers for?" he used to say.'

Driven from home by a homophobic father, Joe had opened a small bric-a-brac shop in Kirkdale Road and taken a flat in Alexander Terrace. Brian would come and have lunch with him in the shop or stay overnight at the flat. Joe bought a 'bed-settee' on the instalment plan for them to share which, out of respect for Brian's family, he did not get from Epstein's furniture shop but from nearby Gerard Kelly's. He still treasures the payments book for it to this day.

He was head over heels in love with Brian, but always accepted that his feelings were not returned with the same intensity. He recognised, too, that Brian still had an insatiable need to 'go downtown' and seek the life-threatening thrills of rough trade. Their flat increasingly became a refuge when these encounters left Brian in no shape to go home to his family. 'He'd sometimes come back at night with his face all bruised and cut and his beautiful Peter England white shirt soaked with blood. "Joe," he'd say to me, "put it straight into the bin."'

His shy, fastidious flatmate came to understand that the danger, the humiliation, the physical pain – even the engulfing shame and self-disgust – of Brian's night forays gave him an excitement he could not live without, try as he might. A horrible excitement lingered even from his worst disaster – the one that had finally unmasked him to his family circle and much of Liverpool also.

He described it all to Joe in quiet moments, as they lay together on the bed-settee. A few months earlier, one of his sexual partners had threatened to go to his family unless he paid a substantial sum. But the blackmail had not stopped there; it had gone on increasing until there was no alternative but to tell the police. In return for a guarantee of anonymity, Brian had agreed to help snare the blackmailer by inviting him to the NEMS shop after hours, where concealed police officers could hear him incriminate himself out of his own mouth. The man had been caught and brought to trial – with Brian giving evidence as 'Mr X' – and had gone to prison, vowing vengeance.

It was evident that Brian derived some queasy thrill from the idea of a convict with a festering grudge against him. 'He used to tell me all the time that somebody was out to get him,' Joe remembers, 'and how his life wouldn't be safe when this person was free again.'

•

The Epstein electrical retail business continued to expand. In 1958, with the start of the television boom, Harry was ready to move into central Liverpool. His first city shop was in Great Charlotte Street, near the Adelphi, and called NEMS after the North End Road Music Stores. Brian ran the record department and his younger brother, Clive, the household electrical side. Once again, at Brian's prompting, there was a celebrity opening, by singer Anne Shelton, the 'Forces Sweetheart'.

The next year, an even bigger singing star, Anthony Newley, opened a second, greatly extended NEMS city centre shop. This one was in Whitechapel, close to Liverpool's banking and insurance district, a narrow street recently developed by a 'parade' of contemporary shops. The Whitechapel NEMS had three sales floors with a fourth for stock rooms and offices.

Brian had worked hard enough and produced profits enough at the Great Charlotte Street NEMS to convince his father that the new shop should have a greatly-extended record department. In the event it had two: the classical on the ground floor, popular in the basement. The Whitechapel street window displayed records with a flair developed in Brian's table and chair arrangements for the Times Furnishing Company. Another of his ideas was to cover the ceiling of the ground floor department with hundreds of LP sleeves.

Before long, NEMS in Whitechapel, rather than Lewis's or Blacker's department stores, advertised 'The Finest Record Selection in the North'. The policy, instituted by Brian, was that no request by a customer must ever be turned away. If the record were not in stock, it must be ordered. An ingenious system of cardboard folders with coloured strings kept Brian constantly abreast of which records were in stock, and which had sold out and needed reordering.

He was now 27, but looked older with his dark suit and his conservative haircut. His staff called him 'Mr Brian'; behind his back they called him 'Eppy'. They laughed a little at his slightly pompous executive airs. But they respected him as a decent and considerate employer, though a niggling perfectionist. If some small things were not right, he could fly into a red-faced tantrum, shouting and stamping his foot. Then, in a minute, he would again be his usual, quiet, charming, courteous self.

If there were occasional whispers about men's lavatories and blackmail and court cases and 'Mr X', they were no more than whispers. Few who saw him by day in Whitechapel could visualise him in circumstances other than driving out to some smart Cheshire restaurant, accompanied by an equally smart young woman. He liked female company and had several passing girl friends. Once, to please Queenie, he even got engaged. The young woman involved was evidently mad about him. Somehow, his mother had noticed; that was always the point when Brian would grow nervous and evasive.

His adventures had brought him the benefit of certain good, long-standing male friends. There was Geoffrey Ellis, a recent Oxford graduate, now working in Liverpool for the Royal Insurance Company. There was also Peter Brown, who had originally run the record department at Lewis's department store, and had afterwards taken over from Brian as manager of the Great Charlotte Street NEMS. A slender, sensitive young man, rejected by his Catholic family in Bebington, Peter was to model his whole existence on Brian's.

By the summer of 1961, Brian was again growing restless. The Whitechapel shop, well-established and smooth-running, absorbed less and less of his attention and energy. The one small innovation that summer had been *Mersey Beat*, Bill Harry's new music paper, with its mutually advantageous record review column by 'Brian Epstein of NEMS'. The column lapsed when Brian went away, as he regularly did, for a long holiday in Spain. In October, the experience and his tan had faded; he was conscious of a vague dissatisfaction. He felt as if he were waiting for something to happen.

•

On Saturday, 28 October, an 18-year-old Huyton boy named Raymond Jones strolled into the Whitechapel branch of NEMS. Brian, that morning, happened to be behind the counter, helping with the weekend rush. He himself stepped forward to serve Raymond Jones, whom he recognised vaguely as one of the crowd of printers' apprentices often to be seen in the shop during their lunch-hour, sorting through the country and western stock. Like a good businessman, he even remembered that Carl Perkins was this particular customer's favourite singing star.

Today, Raymond Jones did not as usual ask for anything new by Carl Perkins. He asked for a single called 'My Bonnie', by the Beatles.

Brian had never heard of the single or the group whose name, in the busy shop, had to be repeated to him: Beatles, with an 'a'. No group of that name, certainly, appeared in the Top Ten chart currently posted on NEMS's front window. No such single had gone into a stock folder, marked by its appropriate coloured string. Raymond Jones could provide no further details of the disc. He had heard about it, he said, at Hambleton Hall, where he and his mates always went on Friday night. The compère, Bob Wooler, had urged them to be sure and ask their record shop for 'My Bonnie' by the Beatles.

The only clue as to the record label was that it 'sounded foreign'. Brian asked if these Beatles were a foreign group. No, Jones replied, they were Liverpudlians, working abroad sometimes, but mainly playing at a cellar club not far from this very shop.

The NEMS policy, that any disc could be ordered, held sway no less on a busy Saturday, to an 18-year-old in jeans and a leather jacket. Brian promised Jones he would investigate the mystery and on his executive notepad wrote, 'The Beatles – check on Monday.' His resolution to do so was strengthened by two further requests for 'My Bonnie', from girls this time, before the shop closed that afternoon.

It was certainly a little odd that Brian had not heard of the Beatles until then. He was, after all, in charge of a shop thronging with their admirers and visited regularly, when at a loose end, by the very Beatles in question. He was contributing to a music paper which mentioned their name about a dozen times in every issue. The Cavern Club itself was only just across Whitechapel and round the corner.

But Brian was 27 and therefore of an age, as well as social background, still untouched by rock and roll music. His interest in it, like his *Mersey Beat* column, had been cultivated purely for business, and with some inner distaste by an ardent devotee of Sibelius and the Liverpool Phil'. And none of his journeys, by day or night, in Liverpool would be likely to take him into Mathew Street.

He was, nevertheless, intrigued to learn of a home-grown group not only available on disc but also in demand by so discerning a customer as Raymond Jones. The following Monday, he began telephoning around NEMS's usual record wholesalers. None could find in its catalogues any record called 'My Bonnie' by the Beatles.

By this stage, with so small a potential profit at stake, any record dealer would have been justified in abandoning the search. Brian, however, partly as a result of the boredom he had been feeling, seized on the challenge of tracking down Raymond Jones's request. If these Beatles truly were a Liverpool group, he reasoned, it would be quicker to go out and find them and ask which label had released their record. Jones, on his next visit, remembers Brian asking in all innocence, 'Where *is* this Cavern Club everyone's talking about?' Only then did he discover it was less than 200 yards away.

Brian's first visit to the Cavern, at lunch-time on Thursday, 9 November, was arranged with typical formality and precision. He rang up Bill Harry, the editor of *Mersey Beat*; Bill then rang Ray McFall, the Cavern's owner, who in his turn instructed Paddy Delaney, the doorman, that Brian was to pass through without the required one-shilling membership card. Paddy remembers seeing Brian that day on his way up Mathew Street, picking his way around the fruit crates and squashed cabbage leaves. 'He had a dark suit on, very smart. And a briefcase under his arm.'

A few minutes later, he bitterly regretted his decision. The warehouse cellar with its dank archways, its dripping walls and dungeon-like aroma bore no resemblance to any club in his understanding of the term. Equally discomfiting was the obvious gulf between him, at 27, and the teenage throng among which, luckily, the darkness hid his intrusion, all but the glimmer of his white business shirt. Bob Wooler's record session was still in progress, with no activity yet down the middle tunnel on what could be seen of the stage. His ears affronted only a little less than his nostrils, Brian decided to wait just a few minutes longer.

What he saw that day was the Beatles giving a routine lunch-time Cavern performance. The club and its audience had become as much a habit as the wild welcome which they scarcely acknowledged, pitching into song after song as if to use time up as fast as possible; in the intervals, talking to each other; wolfing the Cavern snacks that were part of McFall's payment; laughing at private jokes, pretending to cuff one another; at all times picking up and laying down the draggled cigarettes which smouldered dangerously on chairs and amplifier-rims. Then, through the tomfoolery and indifference, would unexpectedly break the pounding, shining sound; the harmony of their grouped faces; the bass and guitars cutting knife-sharp.

On Brian Epstein, their effect was transfixing, but for quite another reason. It is doubtful whether, in those surroundings and with his conservative taste, he could even have begun to appreciate the freshness of the Beatles' music. Rather, it was the sight of four slim boys in form-fitting leather, sweat-drenched and prancing, which held him fascinated. It was a daydream, encountered at midday; a rearing up in public of his most covert fantasies. Most of all, the eye of his secret life watched the boy who seemed most aggressive and untidy, whose off-hand manner and bad language would have affronted the daytime Mr Epstein, but filled the night-time Brian with a scarcely endurable excitement. Though he did not know it then, the one he could not take his eyes off was John Lennon.

At the interval, he pushed his way, briefcase and all, through the middle tunnel to try to speak to the Beatles as they came offstage. He still had no clear idea of why he wanted to meet them or what he might say. Bob Wooler had already mentioned him over the PA system and given a plug to NEMS as the shop where the Cavern bought its records. George Harrison, to whom Brian spoke first, outside the band room, drily enquired, 'What brings Mr Epstein here?'

He stayed at the Cavern through the Beatles' second session, until 2.10 p.m. When he climbed the stairs into daylight again, he had managed to speak to Paul as well as George, and to discover that the record they had made was only as a backing group, and on the Polydor label. He had done his duty, both to NEMS and to Raymond Jones. But by now, a different idea had begun to germinate in his mind.

•

He might have shown less reticence had he known how bored the Beatles themselves were at this moment, and how desperately they, too, were hoping for something to happen.

November 1961 found them in precisely the same position as after their return from Hamburg three months before. They were undisputed kings of the Cavern, and of *Mersey Beat*. They had had the satisfaction of seeing bands which used to condescend to them now avidly copying their r & b repertoire, their clothes and hair and even the types of instrument they played. They had been abroad; they had even made a record, albeit under an alias, which now, it appeared, was selling for actual money in the shops. These were achievements pleasant to contemplate, so long as they did not put their hands in their pockets, to feel the halfpence there, or look down at their shoes, or listen on Saturday morning to the BBC Light Programme, when the Top Twenty was beamed to Liverpool from places still a million miles away.

The one bright spot had been meeting up again with Sam Leach, the promoter who formerly ran the Sunday afternoon sessions at the Casanova club in Temple Street. They liked Sam, as everyone did, for the scope, if not the invariable success, of his concert enterprises. He now ran many – some said, too many – dances all over Liverpool, apparently relishing the continual uncertainty as to whether his door receipts would cover costs. He was a pleasant, big-eyed, scatterbrained youth, always nudging people and laughing.

Sam, even so, was the first local impresario to look beyond the north-west, to London. Realising that no London agent would ever come up to Liverpool, he was planning to start his own record label, and had already booked Gerry and the Pacemakers to cut some demonstration discs in a studio in Crosby. His plan for the Beatles was no less audacious. He would get them on in a hall 'down south', and lure the big London impresarios to see them.

Sam Leach's choice of a southern venue was Aldershot, Hampshire. That glum military settlement, more adjacent to Stonehenge than London, had a dance hall called the Queen's which Sam Leach hired for five consecutive Saturday nights. It wasn't exactly the West End, as he conceded, but it was roughly in that direction. If the Beatles could hit Aldershot in a big enough way, the word might easily spread.

Sam and a photographer friend of his named Dick Matthews made the nine-hour journey from Liverpool to Hampshire in a hired Ford Classic. Following them down the motorway came a van containing the Beatles and driven by one of Sam's bouncers, Terry McCann.

They reached the Queen's Hall, Aldershot, to find four people waiting. 'I'd meant to put an ad in the paper,' Sam says. 'But it hadn't got out.

Maybe I forgot. We went round all the local cafes, telling people, "Hey, there's a dance on up the road." We said we'd let them in for nothing if they came.'

Eventually, eighteen customers had been rounded up. 'The lads said it wasn't worth playing at first, but Paul persuaded them. "Come on," he said. "Let's show we're professionals." '

The Beatles gave those 18 people a two-and-a-half hour all-out non-stop session. When they showed signs of flagging, Paul revived them with his Little Richard act, played to the limit. Dick Matthews, a learned-looking man in a tweed sports jacket, photographed them on the little stage with its wallpapered proscenium, and the half-dozen couples, not all very youthful, jiving under a mirror globe which the management felt it not worthwhile to illuminate. Sam Leach also went among the dancers, pleading with them to look more numerous by spreading out.

Helped by Southern Watney's bottled pale ale and Sam's irrepressible spirits, the evening had its measure of jollity. When the last of the few dancers had gone, John and George, in their thin 'shortie' overcoats, danced a ritual slow foxtrot together. 'Then we had a game of football over the dance floor with ping-pong balls,' Sam says. 'When we finally got outside, there was a great wagon-load of bobbies waiting for us. "Get out of town," they said, "and don't come back." The next Saturday, 210 people came to the dance, just to see the Beatles – but they weren't there.'

Despite the Aldershot fiasco, bright ideas still rocketed around inside Sam's tousled head. He despised promoters like Brian Kelly for the meanness of their dances, with one group only on stage and a finish well before midnight. Sam dreamed of marathon jive sessions, like they were in America, with half a dozen groups or more on a bill lasting into the early hours. Groups were there in abundance all around: Sam needed only an outside sporting chance of being able to pay them.

Earlier that year, he had negotiated with Tommy McArdle the winter-time hire of the New Brighton Tower Ballroom. This gargantuan relic of Victorian seaside splendour – and of an actual tower, higher than Blackpool's – was the largest dance venue anywhere on Merseyside. Its use for rock and roll was spasmodic, ceasing arbitrarily when violence threatened its gilded fabric, or when Rory Storm, climbing up inside the dome, fell to the stage and almost broke through it to the 1,000 seat theatre underneath.

'Operation Big Beat', as Sam Leach called his inaugural Tower night, took place on 10 November 1961, the day after Brian Epstein had walked into the Cavern Club. The Beatles shared the bill with Gerry and the Pacemakers, Rory Storm and the Hurricanes, Kingsize Taylor and the Dominoes, and the Remo Four. Special coaches were provided to transport the Liverpool fans through the Tunnel and down-river to New Brighton's bleak, unfrequented sea promenades.

'It was a real foggy night,' Sam says. 'The Beatles were on at another dance as well, at Knotty Ash Village Hall. They went on at half-seven in the Tower, then over to Knotty Ash, then they came back later for their second spot at half-eleven.' Neil Aspinall, Pete Best's friend, drove them and their equipment in a second-hand van he had recently bought. He had forsaken his accountancy studies to become their road manager for a fee of 5s [25p] from each of them per night.

Operation Big Beat attracted a crowd of 3,500. 'I was that scared,' Sam Leach says. 'I thought maybe I'd not sell any tickets at all. There were hundreds there, even when the Beatles played first at half-seven. When they came back for the half-eleven spot, the kids went wild.' Tommy McArdle, the Tower's general manager, was somewhat less entranced. 'I was ready to ban the Beatles there and then. I caught them behind the stage, poking their fingers through the backcloth. All starry it was and beautiful, and Lennon and them just sticking their fingers through it.'

As Operation Big Beat wore on, and the empty pint glasses formed regiments on the two licensed bars, the Birkenhead faction expressed itself in the customary way. 'I was in the big downstairs bar,' Sam Leach says, 'and I see this fellow get hold of a table and pick it up. He threw it straight at the mirror behind the bar. It went within just a few inches of Paul McCartney.'

Sam rose to the Birkenhead challenge by hiring bouncers in quantities outnumbering the biggest gang. When 50 Teds from Birkenhead paid the Tower a visit, Sam Leach and a hundred bouncers were waiting. One of his regular helpers, a barrel-shaped youth named Eddie Palmer, later grew famous in Liverpool gangland as 'The Toxteth Terror'.

'I got so that I could feel trouble coming,' Sam says. 'There were these four big yobboes in one night that I knew were out to give the Beatles a good thumping. They were up near the stage, all pissed and whispering to each other. I'd got a bouncer behind each one of the four of them. The first moment one of them pulled his arm back, all my four lads pounced at once.'

•

A few days later at the Cavern Club, word was passed to the Beatles that Brian Epstein had come in again. He watched them play and, as before, spoke to them when they came off stage at the break. They still had no idea what he wanted, and so were as inclined as any other Cavernite to laugh at his dark suit and tie and briefcase, and the blush that spread over his face when any of them, especially John, looked him directly in the eye. Even so, they were vaguely flattered to number among their followers this obviously prosperous businessman whose car, it quickly became known, was a new Ford Zodiac.

His aura grew still more impressive when he took to arriving with a 'personal assistant'. Alistair Taylor, an employee in the Whitechapel record shop, had found himself elevated to this mutually flattering post.

All through November, in a roundabout way, Brian was enquiring about the Beatles: about where they played, for whom and at what fee. The idea that he should manage them was one he had not yet articulated, even to himself. It was in a purely theoretical way that he questioned the record company reps, and contacts in London at the big HMV Oxford Street store, about groups and managers and the relationship of one to another. And everyone whom he quizzed unconsciously reiterated the same discouraging fact. People of his age and social background played no noticeable part in British pop music.

Meanwhile, Polydor Records had despatched his order of 200 copies of 'My Bonnie': an event loyally noted by *Mersey Beat.* The record sold moderately well among the Beatles' following, though some – Raymond Jones included – were disappointed to find them only a backing group to Tony Sheridan and billed as 'the Beat Brothers'.

Bob Wooler, the Cavern disc jockey, was one of the first to discover Brian's interest in managing the Beatles, even though his overtures were still muffled by his own embarrassment and uncertainty, and by the Beatles' own elaborate indifference to all outsiders. Wooler, as a close adviser, went with them to the first formal meeting suggested by Brian, early in December. It was to take place on a Wednesday afternoon, directly following their Cavern lunch-time show. Wooler and the Beatles stopped off for beers at the Grapes first, and possibly the White Star, and so did not reach Whitechapel until well after the appointed time. It was early closing day, and they found Brian waiting for them on the darkened ground floor, among displays of home appliances. 'He hated to be kept waiting,' Wooler says. 'That was his first introduction to many hours of being kept waiting by the Beatles. He was quite open by that time about wanting to manage them, but they still wouldn't commit themselves. It was left at, "well, we'll see what happens".'

Equally little encouragement came from those in Brian's own circle to whom he confided his plan. He had already consulted his family's solicitor, E. Rex Makin, hoping for some legal help on the kind of contract he might offer the Beatles. Makin lived next door to the Epsteins in Queens Drive and had known Brian and Clive since their boyhood. He poured scorn on what he termed 'just another Epstein idea'.

The other person Brian sought out was Allan Williams. He had discovered that Williams used to have a contract of some kind with the Beatles, and had been responsible for sending them to work in Hamburg. Visiting the Welshman at his Blue Angel Club, Brian found him still resentful about the commission the Beatles owed him. Williams said he wanted nothing more to do with them, and that Brian was at liberty to take them over. His advice, however, was not to touch the Beatles 'with a barge-pole'.

At another after-hours meeting at the NEMS shop, Brian, blushing furiously, succeeded at last in coming to the point. He told the Beatles that they needed a manager; he was willing to do it; did they want him to? A silence ensued, broken by John Lennon's gruff 'Yes'. Paul then asked if being managed by Brian would make any difference to the music they played. Brian assured him that it would not. There was a second uneasy silence, again broken by John. 'Right then, Brian,' he said. 'Manage us.'

Harry and Queenie Epstein, who had been away to London for a week, returned home to find their elder son in a state of high excitement. He sat them down in the drawing-room and insisted that they listen to 'My Bonnie', telling them all the time to pay no attention to the voice, only to the backing. From Brian's hectic chatter, and the din on a normally well-mannered radiogram, Harry at last extracted the displeasing news that shop business was about to be let slide again. Brian assured his father this was not so: managing the Beatles would require only two half-days each week.

On the Beatles' side, the news spread as rapidly as news in Liverpool generally does. Sam Leach heard it direct from Paul. 'He said there was this millionaire who wanted to manage them.' Sam, though he had been putting the Beatles on regularly at New Brighton Tower, had no contract with them and did not attempt to manufacture one. Nor did Pete's mother, Mona, who had helped to get them on at the Cavern, and pushed them in other ways. She was satisfied Brian knew, as everyone did, that Pete was the Beatles' leader.

Not all the parents were quite so content. Olive Johnson, the McCartney family's close friend, received a call from Paul's father in a state of some anxiety over his son's proposed association with a 'Jew boy'. Since Olive knew the world so well, Jim asked her to be at Forthlin Road on the evening that Brian called to outline his intentions for Paul. 'He turned out to be absolutely charming,' Olive says. 'Beautifully mannered but completely natural. He and Jim got on well at once.'

John Lennon's Aunt Mimi was less easily placated. What worried Mimi about Brian was precisely what impressed the other parents – his charm and position and affluence. 'I used to tackle Brian about that,' Mimi said. '"It's all right for you," I told him, "if all this group business turns out to be just a flash in the pan, it won't matter. It's just a hobby to you. If it's all over in six months, it won't matter to you, but what happens to *them*?"

'Brian said to me, "It's all right, Mrs Smith. I promise you, John will never suffer. He's the only important one. The others don't matter, but I'll always take care of John."'

8

'Elvis's manager calling Brian Epstein in Birkenhead'

Brian, at the outset, foresaw no great difficulty in getting the Beatles a recording contract. As a retailer, he was in regular touch with all the major London companies: Decca, EMI, Phillips and Pye. He had given them all good business in building up 'The Finest Record Selection in the North'. Any of them, surely, would be only too glad to oblige so large and reliable a wholesale customer as NEMS Ltd.

There was a further promising augury. Each week, the old-fashioned broadsheet *Liverpool Evening Echo* published a record review column signed with the pseudonym 'Disker'. Brian, soon after meeting the Beatles, had written to 'Disker', soliciting a mention for them. It turned out that 'Disker' was not based with the *Echo* but was a freelance journalist named Tony Barrow, Liverpool-born but now living in London. As well as his journalism, Barrow worked regularly as a writer of album-sleeve notes for the Decca label.

Tony Barrow wrote back to Brian, saying that as the Beatles had not made a record yet, he could not mention them in 'Disker's' column. What he could do, as a fellow Merseysider, was to recommend them to Decca's 'Artiste and Repertoire' department. The ensuing conversation, strangely enough, was much as Brian had imagined it. 'When I mentioned Brian Epstein,' Barrow says, 'everybody asked "Who?" But when I mentioned NEMS, it was quite different. "Oh, yes – NEMS of Liverpool. *Very* big retailers for us in the north-west."'

The word reached Decca's Head of A & R, Dick Rowe. A large northern record retailer had a pop group he wanted auditioned. It would be tactful, for business reasons, to say 'Yes'. The job was given to a new young assistant in the A & R department named Mike Smith. However, in fairness, the gesture was more than perfunctory. Mike Smith offered to come up to Liverpool to hear the group to best advantage in the club where they usually played. And so, Brian, several weeks before the Beatles had agreed to be managed by him, was able to give them an astounding piece of news. Someone from Decca – from the company that had Tommy Steele, and Buddy Holly, and Little Richard, and the Everly

Brothers, and Duane Eddy and Bobby Vee – was coming into town to audition *them*.

Mike Smith arrived and, after an expensive dinner with Brian, was conducted to Mathew Street, past Paddy Delaney and down the 18 cellar steps to witness the Beatles in their stifling habitat. Their playing impressed the A & R man, not enough to sign them there and then but certainly enough to arrange a further audition for them as soon as possible in London, at Decca's West Hampstead studios. This second test was quickly confirmed for New Year's Day, 1962.

On New Year's Eve, in cold snowy weather, the participants made their separate ways south. Brian travelled down by train to stay overnight with his Aunt Freida in Hampstead. The Beatles set off at midday by road, packed with their equipment in the freezing rear of Neil Aspinall's van. Neil had never been to London before and, striking blizzards near Wolverhampton, lost his bearings altogether. Not until 10 hours later did they arrive in Russell Square, near King's Cross, where Brian had booked them into a small hotel, the Royal. For the rest of New Year's Eve, they wandered round, watching the drunks in Trafalgar Square and trying to find a place to eat. In Charing Cross Road, they met two men who offered them something called 'pot' on condition they could 'smoke' it together in Neil's van. The Liverpool boys fled.

At Decca studios the next morning, they had to wait some time for Mike Smith to arrive. Brian, as ever punctual to the second, reddened at this implied slight, just because they were unknown and from Liverpool. The Beatles, already nervous, became more so when Smith rejected the amplifiers they had dragged with them from Liverpool, and made them plug their guitars into a set of studio speakers.

Brian believed that the way to impress Smith was, not by John and Paul's original songs, but by their imaginative, sometimes eccentric, arrangements of standards. Among the 15 numbers heard by Mike Smith – and preserved for posterity on bootleg singles, stolen later from the master tape – are Paul's versions of 'Till There Was You' and 'September in the Rain'; 'Sheik of Araby', sung by George with jokey Eastern effects; and semi-humorous versions of 'Three Cool Cats' and 'Your Feet's Too Big'. From scores of Lennon–McCartney songs, the only three selected were 'Hello Little Girl', 'Like Dreamers Do' and the recently written 'Love of the Loved'.

The Beatles were far from happy with their performance. Paul's voice had cracked with anxiety several times; George's fingers were stickier than usual; at certain points in Chuck Berry's song 'Memphis', John as lead vocalist seemed to have been thinking of something else. And Pete Best kept up the same drum rhythm, patient rather than cohesive. Only on

'Love of the Loved' had the elements coalesced: Paul's voice at its most appealing within an arrangement both neat and dramatic.

Mike Smith, however, reassured them that the session had gone well. So enthusiastic did the young A & R man seem that, when the Beatles and Brian walked out into the snow that evening, the contract seemed as good as signed. Before their hideous van journey with Neil back to Liverpool, Brian took them to a restaurant in Swiss Cottage and allowed them to order wine.

At Decca, meanwhile, Smith was beginning to have second thoughts. The main reason was another group, Brian Poole and the Tremeloes, which had also auditioned that day and had put up a much better show. His boss Dick Rowe was prepared to let Smith have his head only to the extent of signing one new group.

'I told Mike he'd have to decide between them,' Dick Rowe remembered. 'It was up to him – the Beatles or Brian Poole and the Tremeloes. He said, "They're both good, but one's a local group, the other comes from Liverpool." We decided it was better to take the local group. We could work with them more easily and stay closer in touch as they came from Dagenham.'

•

On 4 January, issue number 13 of *Mersey Beat* published the results of a poll among its 5,000 readers to find Liverpool's most popular group. The Beatles came top, followed by Gerry and the Pacemakers, the Remo Four, Rory Storm and the Hurricanes, Kingsize Taylor and the Dominoes, and the Big Three. The whole front page was devoted to a photograph of the winners in their black leather, cropped to conceal their scruffy shoes, and captioned by the hand that always rendered Paul's surname as 'McArtrey'. In all four Beatles' homes lay piles of December *Mersey Beats* minus the voting coupon on which, like everyone involved, they had voted for themselves.

Mersey Beat knew nothing, however, of the test for Decca in London. Brian would not risk announcing it until the contract had been definitely awarded. The only mention was in 'Disker's' *Liverpool Echo* column, filed by Tony Barrow from inside Decca, where the signs still seemed good. 'I said it was only a matter of weeks before they came down to record their first single.'

Barrow then learned to his astonishment from Dick Rowe's office that the Beatles were to be turned down. The reasons given were that they sounded 'too much like the Shadows', and that groups with guitars were 'on the way out'.

Brian fought Decca's decision as hard as he could. He travelled to

London alone to reason, unavailingly, with Dick Rowe and another Decca man, Beecher Stevens. He also went back to the sales people, reminding them of his position in the retail world. 'I heard afterwards that he'd guaranteed to buy 3,000 copies of any single we let the Beatles make,' Dick Rowe said. 'I was never told about that at the time. The way economics were in the record business then, if we'd been sure of selling 3,000 copies, we'd have been forced to record them, whatever sort of group they were.'

Someone at Decca suggested to Brian the possibility of hiring a studio and a freelance A & R man to supervise a session for the Beatles. He went so far as to contact Tony Meehan, formerly the Shadows' drummer, and now an independent producer. But Meehan proved offhand; besides, the studio hire would have cost at least £100. Brian was not yet prepared to go that far. He walked out of Decca having made the grand pronouncement that his group would one day be 'bigger than Elvis'. The Decca men smiled. They had heard that one so many times.

On 24 January, seven weeks after first approaching them, Brian was finally able to tie the Beatles down to a formal agreement. He had sent away for a sample management contract, and had modified and rewritten the terms in a praiseworthy attempt to make them fairer. The final document, though portentously worded and stuck with sixpenny postage stamps, had no legal validity. Since Paul and George were still under 21, their signatures ought to have been endorsed by their fathers. And Brian forgot to sign his own name.

The four still slightly sceptical and uneasy Liverpool scruffs thus found themselves contracted to a real live 'organisation'. It had been Brian's impressive idea to form a limited company, with his brother Clive, to administer his new charges. He called it NEMS Enterprises, after the family business. Over the Whitechapel branch was a suite of offices which his father allowed him to use, mainly because that would enable him to continue running the record shop downstairs. Harry was determined Brian should keep his promise that managing the Beatles would take only two afternoons each week.

His brisk executive efficiency foundered the moment he first tried to fix the Beatles a booking. Only then did he realise he had no idea how to talk to the rough, tough Liverpool dance promoters on whom they depended for regular work. Tommy McArdle, the ex-middleweight boxer who ran New Brighton Tower Ballroom, was one of many puzzled local impresarios whom Brian suggested should 'come across and have lunch'.

The first booking he managed to arrange was at a tiny seaside cafe on the Dee Estuary over in Cheshire. The profit to NEMS Enterprises, after paying for posters and Neil Aspinall's petrol and sundry expenses, and giving each Beatle his share, was slightly over £1.

Nor had Brian yet realised the quality for which the Beatles were notorious up and down the Mersey – their dedicated unreliability and unpunctuality. He realised it one day when Ray McFall rang up to say that only three Beatles had turned up for the Cavern lunch-time session. Freda Kelly, who worked for NEMS Enterprises as wages clerk and fan club organiser, saw Brian go into one of many subsequent transports of fury. 'There's only *three* of them!' he kept saying. 'Gerry Marsden's singing with them, standing on an orange box so they needn't bother to let the microphone down to his height.'

At night he would drive in his Ford Zodiac to wherever the Beatles were playing – to Neston Women's Institute Hall, to Birkenhead, Wallasey or New Brighton. Since everyone wore dark suits and white shirts to dances in those days, he was not too conspicuous as he walked in. Approaching the Beatles still threw him into a ferment of embarrassment – a circumstance which John Lennon was quick to spot. The more John stared at him, the more Brian would blush and stammer his way into some shaming faux pas. Sam Leach, all innocence, advised John to accept Brian's proposal that they should fly together for the weekend to Copenhagen. 'John nudged me in the ribs,' Sam says. '"Shut up," he went, "Can't you see he's after me!"'

All the time, he was regularly travelling to London to try to interest other record companies in the Beatles. He now had a dozen of their songs on tape from the Decca audition – 'Sheik of Araby', 'Hello Little Girl', 'Three Cool Cats', 'Red Sails in the Sunset', 'Your Feet's Too Big'.

Decca, at least, had given them two auditions. At Pye, at Phillips, at EMI's two prestige labels, Columbia and HMV, interest did not even extend to that. No one saw any future in a group which sounded so unlike the Shadows. Groups other than the Shadows, in any case, were believed to have had their day. The fad now was for solo singers – Helen Shapiro, Jimmy Justice, Frank Ifield. Often, the mere mention of Liverpool was sufficient to glaze over the A & R man's eye. 'You've got a good business, Mr Epstein,' one of them said with a show of kindness. 'Why not stick to it?'

The Beatles would be waiting for him when he got off the train at Lime Street, tired and deflated by yet another supercilious turn-down. He would break the latest disappointing news to them over coffee at the nearby Punch and Judy cafeteria or at Joe's, an all-night 'greasy spoon' where Brian kept a reserved table as grandly as if it were the Ritz. The boys did not reproach him for his continued lack of success; on the contrary, they did their best to lift his spirits and reassure him that next time he was bound to strike lucky. John Lennon would joke that, if no one else wanted them, they'd have to settle for Embassy, the despised cheapo label sold only by Woolworths. Then John would pump up the other three with a time-honoured routine, performed in the cheesey American accents of some 1940s showbiz movie starring Judy Garland and Mickey Rooney:

'Where we goin', fellas?'

'To the top, Johnny!'

'And where's that?'

'To the *toppermost* of the *poppermost*, Johnny!'.

One night, as Brian drank with the Beatles at the Iron Door Club, a tall, dark-haired man came over and shyly introduced himself. It was Joe Flannery, his companion in the nursery and in the later, brief relationship that Joe, at least, had never forgotten. He had not seen Brian since their amicable breakup in 1957, and initially presumed him to be 'downtown' seeking rough trade, as of yore. That definition certainly seemed to apply to at least one of the boys Brian had with him; the slant-eyed, abrasive one who instantly turned the name Joe Flannery into 'Flo Jannery'.

As sympathetic a listener as ever, Flannery soon elicited the fact that Brian now managed a pop group and that all was going far from smoothly. They adjourned for a private drink at the Beehive pub in Paradise Street, where Brian poured out the dual frustration of canvassing London record labels and trying to do business with small-time dance promoters on the Cheshire Wirral. 'He told me he was really cheesed off with everything,' Joe says. 'He was thinking of chucking it all in and going back to learning to act at RADA.'

Joe, as it happened, was managing his younger brother's beat group, Lee Curtis and the All Stars. He offered to work unofficially for NEMS Enterprises, talking to promoters on the Beatles' behalf and negotiating fees. He did it simply out of love for Brian. 'I liked the way Brian spoke on the telephone. He never said "Hello" – just, "Joe . . ." I always liked hearing that.'

The kindly, hospitable Flannery even let them use his pin-neat house as a base camp when gigs ended too late for them to return to their own homes. 'I'd cook them beans on toast or cheese on toast, then they'd go to sleep all around my living-room. Even then, I noticed there was a peck-order. John always took the couch while Paul had the two armchairs pushed together. George didn't seem to need as much sleep as the others, so I'd take him out in my car in the early hours of the morning and teach him to drive.'

On a side table in Flannery's living-room stood a hand-coloured photograph of his mother, taken in the 1920s, her bobbed hair forming a glossy helmet and fringing her eyes. Flannery remembers how fascinated John used to be by the photograph, and remains convinced that his mother, not Astrid or Jurgen Vollmer, was the genesis of the Beatle Cut.

With all these mundane management chores lifted from his shoulders, Brian was free to concentrate on matters he did understand. He understood, for example, how to design a poster, tastefully yet with an impact maximising the Beatles' meagre achievements. When they were booked to play at the Institute hall in Barnston, a small Cheshire village, Brian's posters blazed the advent of MERSEY BEAT POLL WINNERS! POLYDOR RECORDING ARTISTS! PRIOR TO EUROPEAN TOUR!

On the Beatles themselves, Brian began to effect the same transformation – against much the same resistance – as on the display windows of the family's Walton Road shop. He rearranged the four, black-leather, draggle-headed, swearing, prancing Hamburg rockers to reflect his own idea of what a successful pop group ought to be.

To begin with, and most important of all, he told them, they must be punctual. They must not go onstage as a three-piece group, backing Gerry Marsden on an orange box. They must play to a programme, not just as they pleased. They must not shout at their friends, and foes, in the audience. They must not eat or drink beer or wrestle and cuff each other onstage, or make V-signs or belch into the microphone. And if they must smoke, let it not be Woodbines, the working-man's cigarette, but some sophisticated brand like Senior Service.

The black '*exi*' suits they had bought in Hamburg, and worn and slept in for more than a year, were Brian's next concern. Black leather, to most people in 1962, still signified Nazis. He suggested an alternative which John Lennon, at first, doggedly refused to consider. Paul agreed with Brian that they should try it. Paul sided with Brian throughout the whole smartening process. George and Pete Best seemed not to mind, so John reluctantly gave way to the majority. On 24 March, when they arrived for their £25-date at Barnston Institute, each carried a bag from Burton's, the multiple tailor. That night, they took the stage in shiny grey lounge suits with velvet collars, cloth-covered buttons and pencil-thin lapels.

Joe Flannery, having special knowledge, guessed at once what underlay Brian's devotion. He had fallen in love with John Lennon. He was besotted, not by the pretty-faced Paul or Pete but by the boy whose facade of crudeness and toughness touched the nerve of his most secret rough trade fantasies. Joe recognised the look in Brian's eye as he blushed and writhed under John's pitiless sarcasm. 'I've sat for hours with him in the car while he's been crying over the things John's said to him.'

Harry and Queenie Epstein, meanwhile, worried over the time and money Brian was spending, and his neglect of record-shop business in pursuit of his mad idea. To add to their anxiety, he had forsaken his smart lounge suits and white shirts and Horne Brothers ties, and taken to going round Liverpool dressed, like the Beatles, in a leather jacket and black polo-neck sweater. He even came to the Cavern dressed that way, not realising that everyone was laughing at him. 'He was champing a lot, too, that night,' Bob Wooler recalled. 'They'd got him on the pep pills, the ones that dried up the saliva.'

Yet for all his efficiency, his headed notepaper, his expenditure on new lounge suits, his typewritten memoranda to the Beatles concerning punctuality and cleanliness, he still could not move them outside the same old drab hemisphere of Merseyside. No one in London had heard of them, save through a brief mention in the music newspaper *Record Mirror* – and that was through a fan's letter, not through Brian. The *Record Mirror* afterwards sent up a photographer to see them. His name was Dezo Hoffman; he was a middle-aged Hungarian freelance. To the Beatles, he seemed God-like. They all had a bath before they came to Whitechapel to meet him. He shot off rolls of film of them around Sefton Park, and lent them a ciné-camera so that they could film each other, leaping up and down in the spring sunshine, and driving round town in Paul's old green Ford Classic.

The only excitement on their horizon, after Hoffman had gone, was returning to Hamburg. On 13 April, they were to open a new Reeperbahn attraction, the Star-Club. That was the European Tour grandly billed by Brian outside Barnston Institute. Another very grand thing was that they were to go to Hamburg this time by air. Brian insisted on it, knowing what an effect the news would have on *Mersey Beat*'s readership.

He would go to any lengths to convince them that, despite all appearances, a big, wonderful moment was only just around the corner. In Birkenhead, sitting round in the pub next to the Majestic ballroom, he whispered to Joe Flannery to go out of the room, then come back in and say that Colonel Tom Parker, Elvis Presley's manager, was trying to reach him on the telephone. 'They believed it,' Flannery says. 'They really believed that Colonel Parker had been trying to ring up Brian Epstein in Birkenhead.'

•

That Christmas of 1961, while Brian was still wooing the Beatles, their old bass-player Stu Sutcliffe had come over from Hamburg with his German fiancée, Astrid. Stu's friends at the Cavern, like Bill Harry, were shocked by his thinness and translucent pallor. Allan Williams, with typical forthrightness, told him that he looked 'at death's door'.

Stu admitted to his mother that, since settling in Hamburg, in his studio in the Kirchherr house, he had been suffering severe headaches, even occasional black-outs. He had fainted once at Art College, during Edouardo Paolozzi's master class. The news had already reached Mrs Sutcliffe via worried letters from Astrid to Stu's younger sister, Pauline. Astrid feared he was working too hard. For days at a time, she said, he would not come down from his attic to sleep or eat. And the headaches were sometimes so violent, they seemed more like fits. Millie Sutcliffe had described the symptoms, so far as she understood them, to the Dean of Liverpool University Medical School. He told her that she *did* have grounds for concern.

Stu still refused to believe that the headaches were a consequence of anything more than overwork and his and Astrid's round-the-clock Hamburg life. He did agree, for his mother's sake, to see a specialist in Liverpool. The specialist instantly sent him for an X-ray. No appointment could be made for three weeks: by that time, Stu and Astrid had returned to Hamburg.

From January to April, the only news Mrs Sutcliffe received was in Astrid's photographs. One of these showed Stu, seated, stiff as a waxwork, in a bentwood rocking chair next to a marble-topped table crowded with liquor bottles. Another was a close-up of Stu and Astrid together. The face, next to the dark-eyed, ravishing girl, was haunted and brittle. 'When I looked at that,' Millie Sutcliffe remembered, 'something told me that my son was dying.'

In February, Stu again collapsed during an Art School class. This time, he did not return. Astrid's mother forced him to leave his attic and be properly nursed by her in a bedroom downstairs. The Kirchherr family doctor, suspecting a brain tumour, sent him for X-rays. No tumour showed itself. Two further doctors who examined Stu were equally baffled. 'We tried everything,' Astrid says. 'One treatment was a kind of special massage under water. When Stu came home in the afternoon from his massage, he told my mother he'd been looking in an undertaker's window and seen a beautiful white coffin. "Oh, Mum," he said, "buy it for me. I'd *love* to be buried in a white coffin."'

By March, the headaches brought with them spells of temporary blindness. The pain grew so intense at times that Astrid and her mother had to hold Stu down to stop him from throwing himself out of the window. Yet on other days, he could appear quite normal. Astrid would come home from work to find him sitting up in bed, reading, sketching or writing another long letter to John in Liverpool. He was looking forward eagerly to the Beatles' arrival and the opening of the Star-Club on 13 April.

On 10 April, Astrid, at work in her photographic studio, received a call from her mother to say that Stu was much worse, and that she was sending him to hospital. It was the day that three of the Beatles – John, Paul and Pete Best – flew out from Manchester Ringway Airport. George had 'flu, and was to follow with Brian Epstein a day later.

Stu died in the ambulance, in Astrid's arms. 'At half past four,' Millie Sutcliffe said, 'I was in my bedroom at home in Liverpool. I felt as if a great strong cold wind came through that house, lifted me up and laid me across the bed. For 15 or 20 minutes, not a muscle in my body was capable of movement. That was the time, I discovered later, when Stuart was dying.'

The news came in two telegrams from Astrid, out of sequence. The first said he had died, the second that he was seriously ill.

Stu's father was away at sea. Mrs Sutcliffe faced alone the ordeal of breaking the news to her two daughters, getting leave from the school where she was teaching, and booking herself on the first available flight to Hamburg. By chance, it was the one on which Brian Epstein and George Harrison were travelling to join the other Beatles. Brian gave her a lift to Manchester and sat with her on the flight.

At Hamburg Airport, Astrid was waiting with John, Paul and Pete Best. Paul and Pete were red-eyed, but John showed no emotion. With unintended harshness then, the Beatles' and Millie Sutcliffe's paths diverged. Theirs lay to the Star-Club, where they were to open in a few hours. Hers lay to the mortuary, the formal identification of Stu, the receipts to be signed for his clothes, his watch and signet ring.

Cause of death was given officially as 'cerebral paralysis due to bleeding into the right ventricle of the brain'. 'The doctors told us,' Astrid says, 'that Stu's brain was actually expanding – getting too big for the space it floated in. It's a very rare medical condition, but it can happen. Even if Stuart had lived, he would have been blind and probably paralysed. He wouldn't have been able to paint. He would have preferred to die.'

From the mortuary Millie Sutcliffe was taken to the Kirchherr house, to see the room which had been Stu's last home, and the attic where he had worked. Scores of canvases, stacked against every wall, showed with what desperate energy his last months were spent. Mrs Sutcliffe picked up, and never afterwards let out of her sight, the palette on which Stu had mixed his final brilliant colours.

The shock expressed by such eminent figures as Edouardo Paolozzi bore witness to the tragedy that such a talent should be so brutally extinguished. At 22, Stu left behind a body of work in which mere promise already yielded to virtuosity. Those last visions, torn between agony and exhilaration, the blue and crimson carnivals, now left the city whose squalor and glamour had inspired them. So did a sketch of himself

Stu had made at a time when the attacks were getting worse. Both his hands are pressed to a head that is almost a nuclear mushroom cloud of pain and confusion.

Millie Sutcliffe bequeathed Stu's brain for scientific research at the hospital which had been treating him. Eighteen months later, a set of German X-ray plates, taken after his death, were brought across to Liverpool by Astrid. These revealed, for the first time, the presence of a small brain tumour. The Hamburg radiologist had attached a note in English: 'Note the depressed condition of the skull.' Studying the tumour's small shadow, and the cranial depression which seemed to press down on it, Mrs Sutcliffe remembered a night, some three years before, when Stu had been playing bass with the Beatles, and she had found him in his room late at night with blood pouring from his head after being kicked in a scuffle outside Litherland Town Hall.

The Beatles were devastated by Stu's death. Neither George nor Pete Best could stop crying. Paul felt especially bad, remembering his fights with Stu in the past. He tried to find words of consolation for Mrs Sutcliffe but, unfortunately, they did not come out quite right. 'My mother died when I was 14,' he told her, 'and I'd forgotten all about her in six months.'

John alone showed no outward emotion, even though he felt the loss as badly as Stu's own family. To the end of her days, Millie Sutcliffe would bitterly remember his failure to shed a single tear or show his feelings apart from one small detail. He asked for, and was given, the long woollen scarf that Stu used to wear in their winters together among the cold Liverpool streets and alleys.

In fact, John's toughness and pragmatism helped others through the tragedy. 'It was John who saved me,' Astrid says. 'He convinced me, after Stu was gone, that I couldn't behave as if I were a widow. He pretended to be heartless, but I knew what he said came from a heart. "Make up your mind," he told me. "You either live or die. You can't be in the middle."'

Thanks to the efforts of his mother and, after Millie Sutcliffe's death in 1983, his younger sister Pauline, Stu would eventually achieve international renown as a painter who only incidentally happened to have invented the Beatles' name and most abiding image. His work would be shown in prestigious galleries all over the world and form an exhibit at the Rock 'n' Roll Hall of Fame in Cleveland, Ohio; his drawings and sketch-books would feature in the same blue-chip auctions as handwritten Lennon or McCartney lyrics. He would be the subject of numerous books, academic treatises and TV documentaries and, in the mid-1990s, of a British-made cinema film, *Backbeat*, although in a yobbish and foul-mouthed incarnation that few of his contemporaries can have recognised.

In 2001, Pauline Sutcliffe would come forward with further information bearing on her brother's death. Pauline raised the possibility that Stu and John Lennon may have had a brief homosexual relationship – something which would have accounted for the intense emotions between them, both positive and negative, and also for Paul McCartney's intense hostility towards Stu. She went on to claim that while John and Stu were together in Hamburg in May 1961, John had flown into a sudden rage over his friend's poor musicianship, knocking Stu to the ground, then kicking him repeatedly in the head as he lay there. The 'depression' found in Stu's skull after his death was consistent with such an attack – more so, Pauline believes, than with that earlier fight outside Litherland Town Hall when John and Pete Best came to Stu's rescue. She said Stu himself had told her of John's assault, and that, many years afterwards, John himself had owned up to it. To the end of his days, he remained haunted by the thought that Stu's death might have been his fault.

•

Traumatic as Stu's death was for all of them, the Beatles could not stay miserable all the time. They were, after all, the main attraction at the largest and newest of the Reeperbahn beat clubs. It stood in Grosse Freiheit, next door to St Joseph's Catholic Church, in the bowels of what had formerly been a cinema, the Stern Kino. As the Star-Club, it put Koschmider's Kaiserkeller and Eckhorn's Top Ten in the shade. Not that Koschmider or Eckhorn attempted serious competition. The Star-Club's owner, Manfred Weissleder, a huge man with a dusting of golden hair, was the biggest strip-club owner on the Freiheit: he was also, very clearly, a gangster. His sex shows thrived owing to the particular predilection Weissleder had for filming naked girls under water.

During the Star-Club's opening hours, from 4 p.m. to 6 a.m., as many as 15,000 customers could pass through it, most staying long enough to hear their favourite band, moving on to other bars or clubs, then returning later to hear the band's second, third, fourth and fifth spot. After midnight, the place would be swollen by the Freiheit's own population of whores, pimps, strippers and transvestites. To maintain order, Weissleder had recruited Horst Fascher, the Kaiserkeller's old chief bouncer who, luckily for the Beatles, 'worshipped the bones of their bodies'. For the Star-Club Fascher recruited a new and even more deadly 'Hoddel's Gang', including a much-feared one-armed doorman and a waiter named Ali who would instantly floor any troublemaker with a wrestler's drop-kick.

However exploitative – and frightening – Weissleder was a good employer, whose evident power in the Hamburg underworld protected his young British employees from the Reeperbahn's darker perils. Each was issued with a small gilt Star-Club badge which acted as a potent shield in cases of difficulty or danger. 'The usual thing was that you'd be walking along and someone would try to pull you into a doorway and rob you or rip you off,' Liverpool musician Kingsize Taylor remembers. 'But as soon as they saw that badge, and realised you worked for Weissleder, they'd back off straight away.'

The bands were given accommodation in a block of flats above Maxim's Club where Weissleder's strippers and mud-wrestlers also recuperated between shows. 'We were all pretty rough and ready,' Kingsize says, 'but the Beatles were the worst of all. Theirs was the only flat where, if the toilet was occupied, they'd go on the floor, then cover it up with newspaper. When they moved out, Weissleder had to have the whole place fumigated.'

The ringleaders in all the maddest and most pointlessly offensive escapades were John Lennon and Adrian Barber, the Big Three's guitarist who later took a management job with Weissleder. It developed into a kind of contest to see who could be most outrageous. Barber would walk along the Reeperbahn, dragging a hairbrush behind him on a dog-lead. John would come onstage at the Star-Club, goose-stepping and Sieg Heiling, or naked, with a lavatory seat round his neck. Barber bought a pig at the fish market, brought it back to the flats and threw it onto a bed where a fellow musician named Buddy Britten was sleeping. Kingsize Taylor remembers Britten's terrified shrieks and the 'shit coming out of the pig's arse like a flamethrower.'

But even Barber could not match John in the acts of sacrilege that seemed to spring from some profound loathing of his own churchgoing past. On Sunday mornings, he would stand on the balcony of the Beatles' flat, shouting abuse at people walking to services at nearby St Joseph's. In yet another misuse of his art school training, he carved a wooden effigy of Christ on the Cross and attached a water-filled condom to represent an erection. One Easter Sunday, he urinated from the balcony onto the heads of a party of nuns.

'That was the sort of crazy thing you did, full of drink and pills,' Johnny Hutch of the Big Three remembers. 'Before we started playing at night, we'd shake Preludin down our throats by the tubeful. I've seen John Lennon foaming at the mouth, he's got so many pills inside him.'

•

The Beatles were still in Hamburg when, towards the end of April, Brian set off from Liverpool for one last try with the London record companies.

As his train rattled south, he could not even be sure with whom that try should be made. Every label he could find in the NEMS stock catalogue had by now turned the Beatles down. The only hope really did seem to be Embassy, the one everyone laughed at because it was stocked by Woolworth's.

Someone had suggested that, instead of offering the Beatles on tape, he should have a proper 'demo' disc to play to the A & R men. That was what brought Brian, in his smart dark overcoat, to the teeming HMV record shop in Oxford Street. Above the shop was a small recording studio where, for a fee of £1, a tape spool could be converted to an acetate demo.

Brian's luck finally began to change when the studio engineer, a man named Jim Foye, looked up from processing the disc to remark that the music on it was 'not at all bad'. The studio in fact belonged to a firm of music publishers named Ardmore and Beechwood who were in turn a subsidiary of EMI, the record giant from whom Brian and the Beatles had already suffered multiple rejections. So enthused was Foye that he took the demo up to Ardmore and Beechwood, one floor above the studio, and played it to the company's boss, Syd Coleman. Coleman in turn saw 'something' in the demo, asked to see Brian and offered to publish two of the numbers on it, 'Love of the Loved' and 'Hello Little Girl'. He also asked whether the Beatles were signed with a record label, to which Brian's diplomatic answer was 'not yet'. In fact, he nurtured one final hope and had seriously been on the point of auditioning the Beatles with Embassy, the despised 'Woolies' label.

Coleman's deputy at Ardmore and Beechwood, a former singer named Kim Bennett, was so taken with their demo that he suggested recording them as an independent production in the studio below. According to Bennett, Coleman put this idea to EMI's recording head, Len Wood, but the company's rigid internal protocol could not permit its publishing arm to start dabbling in recording. Instead, Coleman sent Brian to yet another EMI subsidiary, the Parlophone label, whose A & R head, George Martin, happened to be a personal friend. According to Kim Bennett, a 'gentlemen's agreement' was made between Coleman and Brian that if the Beatles proved successful, Ardmore and Beechwood would handle their song publishing.

At that time, the only George Martin known outside Tin Pan Alley was a cockney radio comedian specialising in domestic monologues. Nothing could have been more unlike the Parlophone label boss who shook Brian's hand a few days after that chance visit to the HMV shop. This George Martin was tall and gauntly elegant, with a clipped BBC newsreader's accent and the air, Brian himself later said, 'of a stern but fair-minded schoolmaster'.

Martin listened politely to Brian's claim that the Beatles would one day be 'bigger than Elvis'. Like everyone else in the business, he had heard that many times before. Playing the acetate, he could understand why a group partial to 'Sheik Of Araby' and 'Your Feet's Too Big' might not be considered an instantly commercial proposition. But, unlike everyone else, he found things to praise. He said he liked Paul's voice and some of the guitar playing, and the jaunty harmony in 'Hello Little Girl'. He was not excited, merely interested. 'There was an unusual quality – a certain roughness. I thought to myself. "There might *just* be something there." '

Martin agreed to give the Beatles a recording test in June, after their return from Hamburg. It would only be a test, a studio audition like the one they had failed at Decca, and for a label not much in prestige above Embassy. But Brian was never one to downplay things, least of all now. 'Congratulations, boys,' ran the telegram he at once sent to Hamburg. 'EMI request recording session. Please rehearse new material.'

9

'Somebody had to pay for those 10,000 records Brian bought'

When George Martin joined EMI in 1950, people still played 'gramophones' cranked up by handles, and records were heavy black objects one foot in diameter, which broke if you dropped them. Record studios were drab institutional places supervised by men in white coats, and so rigidly formal that not even a jazz drummer could take his jacket off during the recording session.

Young George Martin had joined EMI's Parlophone label as assistant to the head of A & R, Oscar Preuss. He was, even then, suave, elegant and polite. His superiors, in the trade jargon, said he was 'very 12 inch'. They little realised he came from a humble North London background and that his father had once sold newspapers on a street-corner.

He taught himself to play piano by ear, and at school ran his own little dance band, George Martin and the Four Tune Tellers. In 1943, aged 17, he joined the Fleet Air Arm. It was his Navy service which gave him a large social leg-up and also allowed him later to attend the London Guildhall School of Music, to continue his piano studies and take up the oboe. His first job, before joining Parlophone, was with the BBC Music Library. A little of the BBC manner and accent stuck.

EMI in 1950 was a corporation not much different in size and spirit from the BBC. Founded in 1931 as The Gramophone Company, its name changed, as its field diversified, to Electrical and Mechanical Industries. EMI invented the first practicable British television system: it manufactured television sets, medical equipment and weapons systems under contract to the then War Office.

It also made records on a series of labels ingested mostly during the prewar years. Its pride was HMV, the definitive label of wistful dog staring into gramophone trumpet. An HMV dealership in the retail world was as prized as one in Rolls-Royce cars.

No one ever prized the dealership for Parlophone. EMI had bought it in the 1930s as the German Lindstrom label – hence the L label logo which was one day to be mistaken for a £ sterling sign. Within EMI in the Fifties, it was known derisively as the 'junk' label. To Oscar Preuss and his assistant George Martin were left the despised 'light music' catalogue – Sidney Torch and his Orchestra, Bob and Alf Pearson, Roberto Inglez, 'the Latin American Scot'. A sale of only a few hundred copies made any artist viable; to sell a thousand was spectacular. It happened in 1954 when a crooner named Dick James went to number two in the Top Twenty with the theme song from the *Robin Hood* television show.

That year, as it chanced, EMI was in deep trouble. Its chief product, the heavy wooden cabinet TV set, was fast growing obsolete against the new, light, plastic sets coming from Japan. Decca, EMI's great rival, had just introduced the long-playing record, for which EMI's technicians predicted no future other than passing novelty.

In 1954, the EMI chairmanship passed to Joseph Lockwood – not a showbiz man, like his predecessor, but a successful industrialist, big in engineering and flour milling. Lockwood was appalled by the decay of the organisation he inherited. He also quickly decided where the future lay. He ended the production of cabinet TV sets and ordered 20 of the new LP record presses. A year later, in what was considered a foolhardy enterprise, he paid £3m for an established American record company, Capitol.

It was in the flurry of Lockwood's first year as chairman that Oscar Preuss, Parlophone's Head of A & R, retired. By oversight more than anything, George Martin became, at 29, the youngest boss of an EMI label, at a salary of £1,100 per year.

Parlophone, to EMI's bureaucratic mind, remained the 'junk' label. It was simply junk of a different, not unsuccessful kind. Martin, in the late Fifties, went in heavily for comic dialogue records like Peter Ustinov's *Mock Mozart* and Peter Sellers's *Songs for Swinging Sellers.* One of his coups was to recognise what potential cult followings lay in the new generation of London comedy stage revues. He produced live album versions of Flanders and Swann's *At the Drop of a Hat*, and of a four-man undergraduate show, destined to influence comedy throughout the next decade, called *Beyond the Fringe.*

When rock and roll arrived, George Martin shared in the general detestation felt by all trained musicians. It was his duty, however, as an A & R man, to tour the Soho coffee bars for talent. He auditioned and turned down Tommy Steele, preferring to sign up Steele's backing skiffle group, the Vipers. Significantly, in six years up to 1962, Parlophone's only Top Ten hit was a comedy number, 'Stop You're Driving Me Crazy', by the Temperance Seven.

On EMI's Columbia label, the A & R Head Norrie Paramour meanwhile enjoyed virtually unbroken success and gigantic sales with his discovery, Cliff Richard and the Shadows. George Martin did not particularly like the echoey guitar sound which the Shadows had made all the rage. But he did envy Paramour his golden, effortless protégés. Each comedy success for Parlophone was the result of an endless search for new original material. With a pop group, the product was all the same, so Martin thought: you simply sat back and let it happen.

Such was Martin's frame of mind that April day in 1962 when Brian Epstein walked in and played the Beatles' demo. After all their efforts to be otherwise, they would have been enraged by Martin's first idea. Perhaps, he thought, he had found his very own Cliff Richard and the Shadows.

•

On Wednesday, 6 June 1962, the Beatles arrived at EMI's Abbey Road studios in the leafy north London suburb of St John's Wood. Today, the place still looks very much as it did back then: the very last imaginable location for an international record company's creative nerve-centre. Within an expansive front drive stands a plain-fronted late-Victorian townhouse, painted plain white, with a steep flight of stone steps ascending to its front door. The espionage world could hardly have created a more innocent front for the labyrinth of state-of-the art studios, technical departments and offices that lay – and still lie – behind.

The Beatles followed their manager up the front steps in a state of high excitement largely induced by Brian's failure to explain precisely what was to happen today. They believed – as did everyone in Liverpool – that the test was merely routine preamble to recording for Parlophone on the basis of a contract already promised. *Mersey Beat* had said so, even giving July as the month of their first record release and inviting readers to suggest possible titles for issue. They were, in any case, still dazed after Hamburg, the Star-Club and six virtually sleepless weeks.

At Abbey Road studios that day, something entirely unexpected happened. George Martin, that elegant BBC-accented A & R man and the four scruffily-shod Liverpool boys took a liking to one another. Early in their conversation, George Martin happened to mention he had worked with Peter Sellers and Spike Milligan, the founder members of the radio *Goon Show*. 'Goon' humour is dear to most Liverpudlians: in John Lennon's eyes, especially, Martin was instantly raised to near-divinity by his connection with the man who had sung the 'Ying-Tong Song'. He was, besides, agreeably plain-spoken, neither ingratiating nor condescending. John and Paul – and especially George – were soon plying him with questions about the studio and its equipment. Only Pete Best remained, as usual, silent. George Martin does not remember exchanging a word with him all afternoon.

Brian had already sent down a neatly typewritten list of songs which the Beatles could play if required. A large portion were standards, like 'Besame Mucho', since these, Brian thought – mistakenly – had impressed Martin most on the demo tape. There was also the batch of new songs they had written in Hamburg, mostly round the battered piano at Jim Hawke's Seaman's Mission on the docks.

Despite everything else on George Martin's mind, the test he gave the Beatles was exhaustive. Ringed by their puny amps, they stood in the well of the huge studio, attacking song after song, then waiting, in sudden silence, for the verdict of the polite, unexcited voice over the control-room intercom. What they did not realise was that Martin was putting each of them on test individually, to try to see which might be the Cliff Richard he still hoped to find. He could not decide between Paul, whose voice was more melodious, and John, whose personality had greater force. George, and his rather strained, adenoidal voice, figured little in these computations. 'I was thinking that on balance I should make Paul the leader,' Martin says. 'Then I realised that if I did, I'd be changing the whole nature of the group. Why not keep them as they were?'

The question of material remained vexing. Martin still felt that 'Red Sails in the Sunset', 'Your Feet's Too Big' and 'Besame Mucho' were 'too corny'. Nor did he particularly like the songs they had written for themselves. He listened patiently but without inner animation to the one which, plainly, they hoped he would choose as the A-side of their record. Called 'Love Me Do', it was a simple and very brief Lennon and McCartney composition whose loping rhythm served mainly as a showcase for Pete Best's drumming. Its chord structure was basic, its harmony unambitious, its lyric the kind that any cloth-eared beginner might have jotted on an envelope. 'Love, love me do . . . you know I love you . . . I'll always be true . . .' Its only virtue was that at least it sounded glancingly like other 1962 pop songs. But Martin still decided to reserve judgement.

One thing he did know, right from the beginning, was that he didn't want Pete Best. 'At the end of the test, I took Brian on one side and said, "I don't know what you intend to do with the group as such, but this drumming isn't at all what I want. If we do make a record, I'd prefer to use my own drummer – which won't make any difference to you because no one will know who's on the record anyway."' Brian did not protest. Nor did he mention it to Pete, who was packing up his gear as excitedly as the other three.

'If we make a record' was still as far as Martin would commit himself. He liked the Beatles, and felt there was definitely 'something' there. At the same time, he knew that in signing so offbeat and potentially uncommercial a group, he could well risk his own small position within EMI.

Besides, he had a full programme of recording celebrities such as Bernard Cribbins, and a live LP to make at London's first satirical night club, the Establishment.

Not until late July did Brian receive a definite offer. Martin agreed to record the Beatles on Parlophone, subject to the most niggardly contract that EMI's cheese-paring caution could devise. In an initial one-year period, Parlophone undertook to record four titles at a royalty, to Brian and the Beatles together, of one penny per double-sided record. Four further one-year options were open to Martin, each bringing a royalty increment per record of one farthing, or a quarter of an old penny.

•

A few days after the audition, someone said a curious thing to Pete: 'They're thinking of getting rid of you, you know – but they don't dare do it. They're too worried about losing all your fans.'

At about the same time, Bob Wooler, the Cavern disc jockey, making his rounds of Liverpool after dark, came into Danny English's pub to join a meeting in progress between Brian, Paul and George. Wooler, as a long-time confidant, had been specially invited, though for what reason Brian would not say. It soon became clear that Paul and George were both urging that Pete Best should be sacked.

Brian himself held out for some time against sacking Pete. At first, he seems to have thought he could appease all sides by keeping Pete on for live dates but using a substitute drummer on record, as George Martin had suggested. Brian had nothing against Pete – indeed, he relied heavily on him as the group's most punctual and businesslike member. Pete's home in West Derby, and the little coffee club downstairs, continued to be the Beatles' main rendezvous and base camp. An added complication existed in Neil Aspinall, their indispensable van-driver and bodyguard, who was Pete's closest friend. There would also, in the event of unpleasantness, be Pete's mother to contend with. Mona Best, as Brian already knew, was a force one did not lightly provoke.

All through June and July, before word came from George Martin at Parlophone, the plots simmered against a still-unsuspecting Pete. The Beatles – already billed by Brian as 'Parlophone Recording Artists' – were back at their old ballroom haunts, the Grafton, the Majestic in Birkenhead and the New Brighton Tower. It was after a radio appearance in Manchester, on the BBC Light Programme *Northern Dance Orchestra Show*, where he had been literally mobbed by girls, that someone dropped the first hint to Pete. 'They're thinking of getting rid of you, you know.' The thought amused Pete; he even mentioned it jokingly to Brian, who responded by blushing and spluttering 'how ridiculous'. Just the same, when Martin wrote to him in late July, and the Parlophone contract became real at last, Brian took care not to let Pete Best know.

John stayed out of the plot, having a far more urgent worry on his mind. His girl friend, Cynthia, in one of her rare utterances, had informed him that her monthly 'friend' had failed to pay her a visit. Since John and she were virtually living together, in equal innocence of birth control methods, this crucial 'friend's' arrival had long been in considerable jeopardy. Now it was certain, confirmed by a woman doctor whose harshness drove the mild, short-sighted girl to tears. Cyn' was going to have a baby.

John bowed to the inevitable as fatalistically as any north country working man. In that case, he told Cynthia, there was nothing else for it; they'd have to get married. With Cyn's mother away in Canada, the only family member to be reckoned with was John's Aunt Mimi. They put off breaking it to Mimi until the eve of their hastily arranged wedding. Mimi's response was a hollow and heartfelt groan. She had groaned in exactly that way in 1938, when John's mother Julia came home and threw a marriage certificate casually on the table. 'I told them,' Mimi remembered, '"I'll say one thing only, then I'll hold my peace. You're *too young*! There now, I've said it. Now I'll hold my peace for ever."'

August began, and still Pete Best knew nothing of the contract with Parlophone. The Beatles, en route for the Grafton in West Derby Road, were all in Mona Best's sitting-room, waiting for Pete to come downstairs. He did so in high spirits, full of the Ford Capri car he had almost decided to buy. Mrs Best remembered that Paul, in particular, showed unease over the price Pete intended to pay for the car. 'He went all mysterious, suddenly. He told Pete, "If you take my advice, you won't buy it, that's all. You'd be better saving your money."'

On Wednesday, 15 August, they were on at lunch-time in the Cavern. The next night was the first of four major bookings at the Riverpark Ballroom in Chester. Pete had decided to make his own way there, giving John a lift. They both came out of the Cavern and Pete asked John what time he should pick him up tomorrow night. John muttered, 'Don't bother,' and walked away in a hurry. Later, at home, Pete got a call from Brian in his Whitechapel office. 'He said he wanted to see me there tomorrow morning at 11.30. That was nothing unusual. He'd often ask me things about halls or bookings that I knew from the time when I'd been handling the dates.'

Pete's friend Neil Aspinall drove him into the city to see Brian the next morning. 'I went bouncing into Brian's office,' Pete says. 'As soon as I saw him, I could tell there was something up. He said: "The boys want you out of the group. They don't think you're a good enough drummer."

I said, "It's taken them two years to find out I'm not a good enough drummer." While I was standing there, the phone rang on Brian's desk. It was Paul, asking if I'd been told yet. Brian said, "I can't talk now. Peter's here with me in the office."

'I went outside and told Neil. He said, "Right then, that's it. I'm out as well." Brian followed me and asked me if I'd still play the dates in Chester as they wouldn't be able to get a replacement drummer in time. I said OK, I would. We went outside, and Neil went straight away to ring home and tell Mo about it. I just went off and had a few pints – numb. I'd been cut and dried and hung out on the line.'

•

Luck had very seldom favoured the boy who was born Richard Starkey on 7 July 1940, at number 9 Madryn Street, deep in the Liverpool Dingle. The baby was one month late and had to be induced with forceps; as his mother, Elsie, lay upstairs, recovering, the sirens sounded Germany's first aerial visitation. The densely packed Dingle houses had no bomb shelter other than the coal-hole under the stairs. As Elsie, with Ritchie, and three neighbours crouched there, she could not understand why the baby on her shoulder was screaming. Then she realised she was holding him upside-down.

The sad-eyed child they named Ritchie after his father came to consciousness on the tailboard of a removal van as it carried his mother's few possessions from Madryn Street around the corner to a new, even smaller terrace house in Admiral Grove. His father, Ritchie senior, a bakery worker, had by now moved away from home, but continued conscientiously to support his wife and child. He could only send 30s (£1.50) a week, so Elsie herself took work as a barmaid in a pub. Young Ritchie thus spent much of his early childhood at the home of his grandfather Starkey, a boilermaker in the Mersey shipyards. He was a solitary boy, but philosophical and happy with the little that he had. His only reproach to Elsie was the lack of any brothers and sisters, 'so there'd be someone to talk to when it's raining'.

His education was dogged from the beginning by chronic ill-health. At the age of six, after only a year at primary school, he was rushed to hospital with a burst appendix. Surgeons operated in the nick of time to save his life, but he remained in a coma for several weeks. Elsie would come in late, after work at the pub, to peep at the little figure in its hospital cot. He recovered, became his old cheerful self and was about to come home when he fell out of bed while showing a toy to someone. This first absence from school eventually dragged out to a full year.

At eight, consequently, he was unable to read or write. A neighbour's daughter, Mary Maguire, did her best to help him catch up by encouraging him to spell out words from magazines. The operation had left his stomach in a delicate state from which it was never to recover fully. When there was lamb scouse – stew – for dinner, Mary would sit beside Ritchie, carefully picking the onions out of his portion.

When he was 11, his mother began to keep company with Harry Graves, a Liverpool Corporation house-painter, originally from London. Harry and Elsie married in 1953, when Ritchie was not quite 13. He had begun to attend Dingle Vale Secondary School, but was still greatly handicapped by all the lessons he had missed. That same year, he caught a cold which turned to pleurisy and affected one of his lungs. They took him to the big children's sanatorium at Heswall on the Wirral; he remained there for the next two years.

When eventually discharged he was 15 and of school-leaving age. No one remembered him at Dingle Vale Secondary when he went back there for a reference. He could read and write only with difficulty, and the months in hospital had left him thin, weak and sallow. Patches of premature grey were starting to show in his hair and his left eyebrow. His nature, against all the odds, continued cheerful.

The Youth Employment Officer, well accustomed to such lost causes, eventually found him a job with the railway as a messenger boy. He left after six weeks, because they wouldn't give him a uniform, and took casual work as a barman on the ferryboats plying slantwise over the Mersey between Liverpool and New Brighton. Then, thanks to his stepfather, Harry Graves, he was taken on by Hunt's, a local engineering firm, as apprentice to a joiner. The overalls, the slide-rule, the contract binding for years ahead, all promised security for life.

A fellow Hunt's apprentice was a boy named Eddie Miles who lived near the Starkeys in Admiral Grove. When the skiffle craze began in 1956, Eddie and Ritchie started a group to amuse the other apprentices in the dinner-hour. Ritchie, who had always banged and beaten on things, took the role of drummer. Harry Graves bought him his first full kit, paying £10 for it down in London and carrying it valiantly back to Lime Street on the train.

The Eddie Clayton Skiffle Group, as they called themselves, played around the same church hall network as John Lennon's original Quarry Men. Ritchie by now was using brand new drums for which his grandfather Starkey had lent him the £50 deposit. The kit was his passport, around 1959, into Liverpool's most successful amateur group. He joined the Ravin' Texans, afterwards the Hurricanes, the quartet that played while Rory Storm sang and, occasionally, shinned up ballroom pillars. The others nicknamed him 'Rings', because he wore so many, then Ringo as it sounded more cowboyish. 'Starkey' was first abbreviated to 'Starr' at Butlin's holiday camp, so that his solo drumming spot could be billed on a poster as 'Starr Time'.

Until 1961, Ringo belonged to a group far more glamorous and successful than the Beatles. He only got to know them in Hamburg when Rory Storm came over to play the Kaiserkeller and from then on he got to know them well, in many an uproarious bedroom and bar. The Beatles liked him for his droll, harmless humour; for being, in those unreal neon nights, as homely as a Pier Head pigeon. And he was, undoubtedly, a better drummer than Pete Best. The plot to oust Pete dates right back to 1961, when Ringo joined the Beatles as a backing group for 'Wally' in the record-booth at Hamburg railway station.

After Hamburg, Rory Storm's fortunes became somewhat mixed. At one point, he even signed on at his local unemployment office as 'rock and roll pianist'. Ringo had by now given up his apprenticeship; and he, too, spent several weeks on the dole, sitting out vacant days at the Cavern, the Jacaranda or the *Mersey Beat* office upstairs in Renshaw Street. Late in 1961, while sorting through some records, he noticed an LP by Lightnin' Hopkins which gave the singer's birthplace as Houston, Texas. Ringo, who had always adored the Wild West, conceived the idea of emigrating to America. He even wrote to Houston Chamber of Commerce, enquiring about job prospects in that area. The Chamber wrote back helpfully enough, but Ringo lost heart at the sight of the registration forms.

Early in 1962, Peter Eckhorn appeared in Liverpool to recruit musicians for his Top Ten Club. When Brian Epstein priced the Beatles out of his reach, Eckhorn persuaded Ringo to go back to Hamburg with him and join Tony Sheridan's resident band. Eckhorn thought highly enough of Ringo to offer him a permanent job at £30 per week, with a flat thrown in. He was also the special favourite of Jim and Lilo Hawke at the Seaman's Mission. But Ringo felt homesick for Liverpool, Admiral Grove and his mother.

In August, he had rejoined Rory Storm and the Hurricanes and gone south to Skegness with them for their regular summer gig at Butlin's holiday camp. Back in Liverpool, his mother opened the front door one day to George Harrison's pale, unsmiling face. Mrs Graves told him that Ringo wasn't at home. 'Tell him we're trying to get him to join us,' was George's message.

It was John who finally got through to Ringo, ringing up Butlin's and then waiting until Ringo could be found and brought to the camp office phone. The pay as a Beatle, John said, would be £25 per week. In return, Ringo would have to comb his hair forward and shave off his beard. His 'sidies', however, could remain.

Rory Storm was magnanimous over the theft of his drummer. The only stipulation Rory made was that, when Ringo left the Hurricanes to join the Beatles, his pink stage suit was passed on to 16-year-old Gibson Kemp, who had not yet left school and who was so small that the jacket had to be pinned at the back with clothes pegs to make it fit him.

•

Mersey Beat broke the news in its issue of 23 August. Pete Best was out of the Beatles and Ringo Starr had replaced him. According to *Mersey Beat*, the change had been mutually and amicably agreed. The story went on to announce that George Martin was ready at last for the Beatles to go to London and record their first single for Parlophone. They would be flying down with their new drummer for a session on 4 September.

The uproar among Pete Best fans was on a scale far greater than even Bob Wooler had predicted. Petitions signed by hundreds of girls poured into the *Mersey Beat* office, protesting at their idol's banishment. For Ringo's debut as a Beatle, the venue was fortunately quiet and far from Liverpool – the annual dance of Port Sunlight Horticultural Society. But when he first took the stage with them at the Cavern, there were hostile chants of 'Pete Best for ever! Ringo never!' The more besotted of Pete's fans kept a night-long vigil outside the Best family home. When Mona Best opened the front door to pick up her morning milk, she found girls with tear-smudged eye make-up asleep all over her garden.

The following day, in chaos compounded of Pete Best's sacking and several pneumatic road drills, John Lennon married Cynthia Powell at Mount Pleasant Register Office. It was the same place where, in 1938, his mother Julia had married Freddy Lennon, putting her occupation down as 'cinema usherette' for a joke. As on that earlier occasion, no parents were present. Cynthia's mother had come from Canada but gone again; and Aunt Mimi could not bear to see history repeat itself so exactly. Cynthia was given away by her brother, Tony, and Brian Epstein – who had obtained the special marriage licence – acted as John's best man. With insufficient money to buy herself a new wedding outfit, Cynthia went before the Registrar wearing some of Astrid's cast-off clothes. Paul and George were there also, torn between embarrassment and giggles. Much of the service was inaudible, owing to road drills. Afterwards, in pouring rain, they ran across the road for a chicken lunch at Reece's restaurant. Since Reece's had no alcohol licence, the toast to the newly-weds was drunk with water.

Brian had expected the Pete Best storm to fizzle out after a day or so, but he was wrong. When the Beatles turned up at the Cavern Club almost a week later, there were still angry pickets outside. In a stage-door scuffle involving Pete himself – a noted 'hard man' for all his good nature – George received a black eye which ripened spectacularly in the course of the evening's performance. Brian, after this, refused to go to the Cavern unless Ray McFall provided him with a bodyguard. But, being Brian, he did not wholly dislike the notion of being 'the most hated man in Liverpool'.

Pete's mother had already paid him the first of many wrathful and accusing visits. Mona Best was – and remained – convinced that Pete's sacking was due simply to the jealousy of John, Paul and George. 'He'd given them so much with his beat and everything. To a lot of the fans, he *was* the Beatles. I knew that Brian hadn't wanted to do it; he respected Peter too much. None of the others was introduced to Brian's parents; now why was that? Why was Peter the only one?'

The worst affected, after Pete himself, was Neil Aspinall, the Beatles' by now indispensable roadie, whose links with the Best family were now closer than most of their combined circle ever dreamed. Mona Best was still an extremely attractive and vibrant woman and, somehow in the past year, she and her older son's friend, the serious young would-be accountant, had had an affair which had resulted in Mrs Best's becoming pregnant. Just a few weeks before Pete's sacking, on 21 July, she had given birth to Neil's son, whom she named Roag and brought up as a Best, along with Pete and his brother, Rory. In an almost Gilbert and Sullivan twist, the Beatles' driver/bodyguard was also the father of their sacked drummer's half-brother.

Pete understood Neil's conflict of loyalties and had no wish for his friend to suffer on his account. When Neil considered walking out on the Beatles, Pete urged him to stay with them for a few more months at least, to see where they might end up. For a time, the Beatles even carried on using the Casbah as a meeting place before engagements, though they were careful to keep out of Mrs Best's way. 'Then one day Paul knocked on the door and asked me if he could leave his car in the drive. I managed to keep my peace but Kathy, Pete's girl friend, gave John and Paul a damned good talking-to.'

Brian tried to soften the blow to Pete by offering to build a new group around him. What he eventually did was to fit Pete into Lee Curtis and the All Stars, the group managed by Brian's friend and helper Joe Flannery. Joe agreed to accept Pete despite misgivings that his good looks would clash with those of Lee Curtis, Joe's younger brother. The transfer was effected, he remembers, with subtlety typical of Brian. 'First Brian got me to agree to have Pete. Then I had to talk to Pete and say: "I think I can arrange it with Mr Epstein."'

Pete, very naturally, failed to turn up for the first of the Chester

Riverpark ballroom dates. Since Ringo had not yet arrived from Skegness, a substitute drummer had to be found at short notice. Brian solved the difficulty by borrowing Johnny Hutch from the Big Three.

The next big beat show at New Brighton Tower, on 27 July, was presented, not by Sam Leach, but by NEMS Enterprises. The star was Joe Brown, a popular Cockney rock and roller whose song 'Picture of You' was currently high in the charts. Second on the bill were the Beatles. In this way, Brian implanted the idea that Joe Brown, for all his big name, was only a line of type ahead of them. More big names followed, always with the Beatles second on the bill. 'He'd watch the charts all the time and see who was selling most records,' Joe Flannery says. 'When someone like Joe Brown or Bruce Channel came up, Brian would make a big day of it. There'd be an autograph-signing session at the shop, then the show in the evening. American stars used to think that was wonderful. They weren't used to getting that kind of treatment in England, not even in London.'

On 6 September, Brian took a full-page advertisement in *Mersey Beat* to announce a coup which any promoter might have envied. Little Richard, rock and roll's baggy-suited and clamorous founding figure, was currently touring Britain. Brian had negotiated with Richard's London promoters to bring him to New Brighton Tower for one night, on 12 October. The Beatles were second on the programme, together with more Liverpool groups than had appeared in one place since Allan Williams's Boxing Stadium show.

George Martin knew nothing of the Pete Best sacking. He expected Pete to be still with the others when, on 11 September, they came back to Abbey Road studios. Accordingly, down on the floor of Studio Two there waited an experienced session drummer named Andy White whom Martin had engaged to play on the record in place of Pete. When Ringo was introduced to him as Pete's replacement, he saw no reason to depart from his original plan. He knew nothing about Ringo as a drummer, he said, and preferred not to take any chances. White must play on the recording.

After this rather stern beginning, Martin tried to make amends by involving the Beatles in every facet of the recording process. He explained that, due to the wonders of EMI science, they could record their voices and instruments as separate tracks, to be 'mixed' afterwards for optimum texture and balance. He let them record a warm-up number, then took them into the control room to play it back. He asked them if there was anything they didn't like. George said, in his slow, gruff way, 'Well, for a start, I don't like your tie.' 'Everyone fell about with laughter at that,'

Martin says. 'The others were hitting him playfully as schoolboys do when one of them has been cheeky to teacher.'

Martin had decided, after all, to use Lennon–McCartney songs as both the A- and B-side of the single. For the A-side, after much deliberation, he chose 'Love Me Do'. The number had improved since he last heard it, chiefly by the addition of a harmonica riff which John had copied from the Bruce Channel hit 'Hey Baby'. For the B-side, to bring Paul to the fore, Martin chose 'PS I Love You', liking the song for its harmonies, its switch from major to minor chords and the way that John's voice chimed with Paul's on key words through the lyric.

During rehearsals that afternoon, Martin somewhat relented in his attitude to Ringo's drumming. 'He hit good and hard, and used the tom-tom well, even though he couldn't do a roll to save his life.' Ringo himself did not know yet that there was a session drummer waiting to replace him. When it came time to record the 'Love Me Do' instrumental track, Ringo was handed a tambourine and instructed to hit it twice on every third beat. He looked so doleful that Martin relented a little. They would record two versions, Martin said: one with Andy White on drums and one with Ringo. The vocal track would be mixed with whichever version came out best.

The White and Ringo versions became indistinguishable in the quantity of 'takes' that were needed before Martin was content with the instrumental track. The fifteenth attempt finally satisfied him, even though John Lennon's mouth had grown numb with sliding along the harmonica bars. There was a short break; then they returned to do the backing track for 'PS I Love You'. Andy White sat at the drums and Ringo, this time, was given maracas to shake. He later said that he thought the others were 'doing a Pete Best' on him.

At EMI's next 'supplement meeting', when each label head outlined his release plans for the coming month, Martin caused a ripple of amusement by announcing that Parlophone was putting out a single by a group called the Beatles. The general view was that it must be another comedy disc. Somebody even asked: 'Is it Spike Milligan disguised?' 'I told them, "I'm serious. This is a great group, and we're going to hear a lot from them." But nobody took much notice.'

Up in Liverpool, Brian had begun to prepare the Beatles for impending stardom. Freda Kelly from the NEMS office had to go round to each one with a printed sheet for 'Life Lines' – favourite food, favourite clothes, likes, dislikes and so on – just as it was done in the *New Musical Express*. Next to 'Type of car?' Paul wrote 'Ford Classic (Goodwood green)'; next to 'Dislikes?' he wrote 'False and soft people', and next to 'Ambition?',

'Money etc'. George gave his main dislike, ironically, as 'Black eyes', his 'Greatest musical influences?' as Carl Perkins, his 'Ambition?', 'To retire with a lot of money, thank you'. John, using an italic fountain pen, gave his 'Dislikes?' as 'Thick heads, Trad Jazz', his favourite film director as Ingmar Bergman, his 'Ambition?' as 'Money and everything'. Ringo's favourite food was 'Steak and chips'; his 'Likes?', 'Everyone [sic] who likes me'.

On 2 October, a second contract was signed by the Beatles and Brian – a thoroughly legal document this time, and witnessed, as the law required, by Paul's father and George's. The term of the agreement was five years. Brian's share of the earnings was 25 per cent. A further clause – a slip on Clive Epstein's part, hastily rectified soon afterwards – gave each side power to terminate the agreement at six months' notice.

On 12 October, Little Richard and retinue arrived in Liverpool for his show at the New Brighton Tower. The legendary screamer of 'Lucille' and 'Good Golly Miss Molly' was by now slightly toned down in a conventional sharkskin suit, his former wild, greasy locks planed flat to the scalp. But his manner remained as outrageously camp and his mood as wildly unpredictable as ever. With him came his British agent, Don Arden, a stocky, belligerent man who lost no opportunity to stress what a great honour was being done to New Brighton and Merseyside.

Entrepreneurs who have put on Little Richard shows tell blood-curdling stories of his temperament, his unreliability, his bizarre whims and fancies, his refusal in some cases to do anything for the audience but slowly remove his clothes. But on 12 October 1962, when Richard performed at New Brighton Tower Ballroom, something seemed to have happened to put him in a mood of perfect tractability and co-operativeness. 'Brian seemed to be able to do anything with him,' Joe Flannery says. 'When Richard finished his act, something had gone wrong with the mike for the next group, Pete MacLaine and the Dakotas. Brian could even get Richard to walk across, nice as you please, and hand his personal microphone on to Pete MacLaine.' It was rumoured that Brian had won the volatile star over by spending the previous night with him in a room at the Adelphi Hotel. Richard himself firmly denies this, however. 'I didn't even have so much as a *sandwich* with Brian,' he says now.

The Beatles were initially so overcome with nerves at sharing a bill with their greatest soul hero that they couldn't even pluck up courage to ask him to do a photograph with them. Instead, while Richard was on stage, John stood watching him from the wings on one side and Paul photographed the two of them from the wings opposite.

After the show, he was just as seraphically amiable, telling local journalists how much he loved England and Liverpool, posing for pictures with John, Paul, George and Ringo in a tickled-pink group around him. He even gave Paul instruction in the trademark scream he called his 'little holler'. For the rest of his erratic career, he would always maintain, 'The Beatles was my group. I taught 'em everything they knew'.

So powerful was Brian's influence over Little Richard that he was able to bring him back to Liverpool for a second concert, at the Empire theatre on 28 October, to head the existing bill of Craig Douglas, Jet Harris and the Jetblacks, and the Beatles. Brian planned the entire event as a means of giving them their first professional booking at the Empire.

Because it was Sunday, none of the groups was allowed to appear in costume, so they all took off their jackets. The Beatles played in pink, round-collared shirts. For a fan like Freda Kelly it was no less a miracle that they had crossed the gulf from underground clubs to this softly lit, luxurious realm of concert and Christmas panto. 'I remember when the spotlight went on Paul in his pink shirt, and he started to sing 'Besame Mucho'. I thought, "This is *it*. Now they've *really* made it."'

•

'Love Me Do' was released on 4 October 1962, in a week when America's grip on the British Top Twenty had seldom been stronger. Carole King, Tommy Roe, Bobby Vee, Little Eva, Ray Charles and Del Shannon all had new songs making, or about to make, their inevitable ascent. The sensation of the moment was 'Let's Dance' by Chris Montez, prolonging the Twist dance craze which French students had imported into Britain during the summer. Among British artists, the continuing success of Helen Shapiro, Jimmy Justice, Kathy Kirby and Shane Fenton seemed to bear out the Decca prophecy that solo singers were what the teenagers wanted; that guitar groups were 'on the way out'.

EMI themselves seemed to think so. After 'Love Me Do' was released, virtually no effort was made to plug the disc to the trade press or BBC radio, or even EMI's own sponsored Radio Luxembourg show. Newspaper publicity was confined to a single printed handout, copied from the 'Life Lines' which Freda Kelly had drawn up in Liverpool, vouchsafing to indifferent Fleet Street record columnists that Paul McCartney's favourite clothes were leather and suède, that Ringo Starr's favourite dish was steak and chips, that George Harrison's greatest musical influence was Carl Perkins and that John Lennon's 'type of car' was 'bus'.

After his experience with Decca, Brian was taking no chances. He himself had ordered 10,000 copies of 'Love Me Do' from Parlophone. He had been told that was the quantity you had to sell to have a Top Twenty hit.

Though the Liverpool fans loyally bought 'Love Me Do', and though

Mersey Beat's chart made it instantaneously number one, most of the 10,000 copies remained in unopened cartons in a back room of the Whitechapel NEMS shop. 'Brian took me and showed me them,' Joe Flannery says. 'He even made up a little song about all the copies he hadn't been able to sell. "Here we go gathering dust in May," he'd sing.' A few days later, in London, Flannery bumped into Paul McCartney. 'Paul said he was hungry: he'd only had a cake to eat all day. I was amazed. I said, "Paul – how?" Paul said, "Someone had to pay for those 10,000 records Brian bought."'

The first radio play was on Luxembourg, after hundreds of requests from Liverpool. George Harrison sat waiting for it next to the radio all evening with his mother, Louise. She had given up and was in bed when George ran upstairs, shouting, 'We're on! We're on!' Mr Harrison was angry at being disturbed: he had to be up early the next morning to drive his bus.

A few scattered plays followed on the BBC Light Programme, where pop was beginning to creep into 'general' music shows like the early evening *Roundabout*. The best exposure was secured by Kim Bennett of Ardmore and Beechwood, the publishers who had first steered Brian back to EMI and George Martin. By dint of repeatedly nagging a radio producer friend, Bennett got 'Love Me Do' onto the playlist of *Two-Way Family Favourites*, a hugely popular Sunday-morning show playing record requests for British forces overseas. After two appearances there on consecutive Sundays, 'Love Me Do' was shown at number 49 in *Record Mirror*'s top 100. The *New Musical Express*, shortly afterwards, showed it at number 27. Finally, on 13 December, it reached number 17.

For a first record, especially on Parlophone, that was not at all a bad performance. If 'Love Me Do' had not taken the country by storm, it had confirmed George Martin's instinct that the Beatles could be successful singing the right song. He reached that conclusion even before 'Love Me Do' made its brief Top Twenty showing. The second single under their first year's contract was due to be recorded on 26 November.

Though bound to EMI on record for five years, Brian had only a 'gentlemen's agreement' with Syd Coleman of Ardmore and Beechwood that A & B would continue publishing John Lennon and Paul McCartney's song output. He felt disappointed with Ardmore and Beechwood's performance in publicising 'Love Me Do' – though, to be fair, the failure was all on EMI's side – and now confided to George Martin that he'd be seeking new publishers for the Beatles' follow-up single. His initial idea was to go to an American firm, Hill and Range, which held British rights on the Elvis Presley catalogue. Martin's advice was to pick a small firm with a drive to succeed that would match Brian's own. 'In other words, what I told Brian he needed was a hungry music publisher.'

The hungriest music publisher George Martin knew was Dick James, a tubby, amiable, bald-headed man whose office was one first-floor room at the corner of Denmark and Old Compton Streets. Born Isaac Vapnik, James had begun his career as a crooner in the 1930s, as featured vocalist with Primo Scala's Accordion Band. He had sung with leading orchestras, including Henry Hall's and Cyril Stapleton's, and made several records, of which the most famous was the theme song for *Robin Hood*, a children's series on early commercial television. On losing his moderate female fan base along with his hair, he had turned first to song-plugging, then to publishing. In November 1962, he had been in business on his own for one year exactly. Everyone knew Dick James, everyone liked him, but no one yet mistook him for Tin Pan Alley's next millionaire.

In the early 1950s, as a newcomer to Parlophone, George Martin had produced Dick James on several minor hit records including 'Tenderly' and 'Robin Hood'. It was natural, therefore, that when EMI's own publishing company proved deficient, he should approach Dick James informally, both as a possible publisher for the Beatles and also in James's old capacity as a plugger of likely recording material. The first approach, when Martin mentioned 'this Liverpool group' was not encouraging. James laughed his cuddly laugh and echoed, 'Liverpool? So what's from Liverpool?'

The answer, by then, was a disc with at least a toe-hold in the *New Musical Express* Top 100. James heard 'Love Me Do', liked the overall sound but agreed with Martin that the song was 'just a riff'. He promised to use his Tin Pan Alley contacts to find them a good 'professional' song for their follow-up record. This he produced within days, on a demo disc which he played to Martin. The song was 'How Do You Do It?' by a young composer named Mitch Murray. 'As soon as Dick played it to me,' Martin says, 'I started jumping up and down. "This is it," I said. "This is the song that's going to make the Beatles a household name."'

He said the same to the Beatles themselves when Brian brought them back to Abbey Road studios on 26 November. He played them the demo of 'How Do You Do It?' accompanied by his own carefully thought-out ideas on how the song could be adapted to suit them. He was surprised, and not a little irritated, when John and Paul said flatly that they didn't like it, and wanted to do another of their own songs. This apparent wilfulness in the face of an almost certain hit brought a stern lecture from Martin. '"When you can write material as good as this, I'll record it," I said. "But right now, we're going to record *this*."'

His words sent them, chastened, into the studio, to produce a version of 'How Do You Do It?' in which every note, and nuance of John Lennon's lead voice, made plain their lugubrious distaste. George Harrison, halfway through, produced a guitar solo not far removed in scale and ambition from the twanging of a rubber band. Even so, they could not stop a little charm and originality from creeping in.

The song they wanted to record was one of John and Paul's called 'Please Please Me', one fairly slow version of which had already been tried on Martin. Since then, they had worked on it, tidying up the lyric and making it faster. The revised version was now played by Paul and John on their acoustic Gibson guitars while Martin, perched on a musician's high stool, listened critically. Then, as their voices broke together on the 'Whoa yeah', Martin recognised something. His objection was that the song as it stood lasted barely more than a minute. They could lengthen it with an intro on John's harmonica, and by repeating the first chorus at the end.

The first take of 'Please Please Me' was so belligerently alive that George Martin decided to use it, even though Paul had forgotten the words in the first chorus and John, more obviously, had forgotten them in the finale. 'The whole session was a joy,' Martin says. 'At the end, I pressed the intercom button and said "Gentlemen, you have just made your first number one."'

He now had to break it to Dick James that the Mitch Murray song would not, after all, be out soon on Parlophone. 'George rang me up,' James says. 'His words were, "You know that song the Beatles *were* going to record . . ."' James held his head in Tin Pan Alley mock anguish, but agreed to meet Brian Epstein the next day with a view to publishing – and plugging – 'Please Please Me'. It was arranged that Brian would bring an early pressing of the single for James to hear at his Denmark Street office at 11 a.m.

Brian arrived, instead, at 10.20. He had had an earlier appointment with another music publisher, but the man he was supposed to meet had not bothered to keep the appointment. Instead, it was suggested that he play his demo disc to the office boy. He had walked out in fury, and come straight on to Dick James Music. James, to his lasting benefit, was at work already, and able to greet the angrily blushing young man in person.

A single hearing of 'Please Please Me' was enough for James. He loved the song, he told Brian; could he publish it? Brian, a little nonplussed by the shabby office, asked what James thought he could do for the Beatles that EMI's publicity department had not already done. James's answer was to pick up the telephone and call a friend of his named Philip Jones, the producer of the Saturday night television pop show *Thank Your*

Lucky Stars. He told Jones to listen, then put 'Please Please Me' on to his record player and held the telephone receiver near to it. Jones agreed that it was very good. He also agreed, at James's skilful prompting, to put the Beatles into *Thank Your Lucky Stars.* In five minutes, Dick James had guaranteed them exposure on what was – after BBC TV's *Juke Box Jury* – the show with greatest influence over the record-buying public. 'Now,' he asked ingenuously, 'can I publish the song?'

Another reason why George Martin had sent Brian to James was that he knew James to be 'very straight' in financial matters. As a singer, he had himself frequently been done out of large earnings in the days when English artists received no royalty on American sales of their records. Twice in the early 1950s, he had topped the American charts and yet received only £7 each time – the then standard studio fee. The deal he now offered Brian, while not actuated by pure benevolence, was both fair and imaginative.

Under the usual predatory publisher's contract James would have taken 10 per cent of the *retail* price of sheet music, plus up to half of the royalties from radio play and cover versions. Instead, he proposed that a special company be formed within his own organisation but exclusively publishing Lennon–McCartney songs. The company would be called Northern Songs and its proceeds split 50–50: half to Dick James, 20 per cent each to John and Paul and 10 per cent to Brian. It sounded handsome, and it was, notwithstanding the clause that James's own company would take a percentage of Northern Songs earnings 'off the top'. 'Brian said to me, "Why are you doing this for us?"' James recalled. 'What I said to him then was the truth. I was doing it because I had such faith in the songs.'

'Please Please Me' was not scheduled for release until January 1963. In the meantime, the Beatles were committed to return to Hamburg for a two-week engagement at Manfred Weissleder's Star-Club. The booking had been made back in the summer, before George Martin's advent, at rates of pay which no longer seemed attractive. All four, besides, felt they had had their fill of the Reeperbahn. Also, for the first time, they would be away from home during both Christmas and New Year's Eve. The clincher was an offer from Manfred Weissleder to Brian of 1,000 deutschmarks in 'brown bag money' that wouldn't have to be declared for income tax.

On 2 December, a severe jolt was sustained by the Beatles' collective ego. Brian, through sheer effrontery, had managed to get them into what was then known as a 'package' show of pop acts currently enjoying Top Twenty success. He had discovered the private telephone number of Arthur Howes, the country's biggest tour-promoter, and had rung up

Howes one Saturday afternoon at home in Peterborough. Arthur Howes, a veteran at the agency game, smiled a bit when he heard the name of the group on offer, but was fair-minded enough not to refuse them without a trial. He offered to put them on for one night only at the Embassy cinema, Peterborough, in a show headed by Frank Ifield, the Australian yodeller.

The appearance was an unmitigated flop. The staid East Anglian audience had come to see Frank Ifield, not four unknowns from the north; they had come to worship suntan and upswept hair, not eccentric fringes, and to hear sentimental ballads, not Chuck Berry and Carl Perkins music. Total silence followed every perversely loud number. But something about them appealed to Arthur Howes; he told Brian that the disaster was not all their fault, even making a small offer for the option of using them in future package shows.

On 18 December, with the worst possible grace, they set off for Hamburg and what would be their farewell performance at the Star-Club. 'Please Please Me' was just beginning to show in the Top Twenty; rather than vanishing abroad, they felt they should be on home territory, taking every possible opportunity to promote the single. It was not much consolation that sharing the Star-Club's Christmas bill would be Carl Perkins, one of their earliest rock 'n' roll idols, whose easygoing numbers, like 'Honey Don't' and 'Matchbox', had proved ideal for giving Ringo a stab at singing lead.

By now the Beatles' place as darlings of the Reeperbahn had been somewhat usurped by Kingsize Taylor and the Dominoes, the high octane r & b band who had taught them so much at Merseyside gigs like Lathom Hall. 'Kingsize' Taylor, the towering, throaty-voiced butcher's apprentice was an uncomplaining workhorse for Weissleder and other German promoters, sometimes playing sets of up to 12 hours duration with just 15 minutes' break each hour. However, after several incidents with tear-gas guns in the flats above Maxim's Club, Weissleder had felt it safer to move all his British bands into a small hotel, the Pacific. There Kingsize and the Beatles celebrated their reunion by pelting one another with grapes.

The Star-Club's barn-like acoustics made it impossible for the bands to hear themselves while they played. To help him and his colleagues check their sound-balance, Kingsize Taylor left a tape-recorder running throughout much of that 1962 Christmas show. So was accidentally preserved for posterity the fullest and most vivid record of the Beatles' soon-to-disappear stage act. Audibly drunk, fluffing words and notes, shouting back to hecklers in pidgin German, they lurch through some 20 songs in their old, undisciplined mixture of rock 'n' roll classics, country songs, middle-of-the-road ballads and show tunes – 'Your Feet's Too Big', 'Red Sails in the Sunset', 'Besame Mucho', even Marlene Dietrich's 'Falling in Love Again'. Kingsize and the Dominoes had been featuring a new soul number, the Isley Brothers' 'Twist and Shout', which – keeping up Lathom Hall tradition – the Beatles have instantly 'stolen with their eyes', reproducing even the Dominoes' added guitar break.

On Ray Charles's 'Hallelujah I Love Her So', the lead vocal is warbled by an unfamiliar voice that makes Ringo Starr sound Caruso-like by comparison. It is Horst Fascher, the Star-Club's lethal bouncer. They let Horst (and also his brother Freddy) have a go onstage in return for 'getting the beer in'.

10

'Four frenzied Little Lord Fauntleroys who are earning £5,000 a week'

The winter of 1962–3 was Britain's worst for almost a hundred years. From December to mid-March, the entire country disappeared and a snow-levelled tundra took its place, stretching from north to south, silent and motionless but for snowploughs trying to locate the buried motorways. With the blizzards came Siberian cold that froze the English Channel, annihilated old people and the Essex oyster beds, wiped out the zebra at Whipsnade Zoo, turned milk into cream-flavoured sorbet and caused beer to explode spontaneously in its bottles. South-west England was completely cut off; indeed, there seemed at one point a sporting chance that Wales would never be seen again. As usual in Britain, winter was the last thing anyone had expected and, as usual, the British responded to chaos with cheerfulness. A year of unprecedented uproar, of unparalleled outrage, thus began with a feeling that everything in Britain was much the way it had always been. Everyone talked, and talked, about the weather.

On 12 January, the nation, still snowed into its homes, provided a bumper audience for ABC-TV's Saturday night pop show *Thank Your Lucky Stars*. The show was popular for two reasons – its teenage record critic 'Janice', and the imaginative studio sets that were built around singers and groups as they mimed, not always accurately, their latest Top Twenty disc. 'Janice's' peculiar magic was a thick Birmingham accent in which, awarding some new release maximum points, she would invariably say: 'Oi'll give it foive.'

A certain act on *Lucky Stars* that night had caused some perplexity to the show's producer, Philip Jones, and his set designer. Jones had kept his promise to his friend Dick James to book the Beatles in the same week that 'Please Please Me' was released. Jones had not met them until the afternoon they arrived at ATV's Birmingham studios, after driving straight down from a tour of Scottish ballrooms. 'We'd no idea how to present them,' Jones says. 'In the end, we just gave up. We decided to put each one of them inside a big metal heart. It was obvious that the song, not our set, would be the thing that sold them.'

The four metal hearts framed a pop group such as no British teenager south of Lancashire had ever seen before. Their hair was not blow-waved into a cockade; it fringed their eyes like the busbies of Grenadier guardsmen. Their suits buttoned up to the neck, completely concealing their ties. The front three figures did not, as was usual, step to and fro: they bounced and jigged with their guitar necks out of time. One, unprecedentedly, played a Spanish guitar; another held a bass guitar like a stretched-out violin, its skinny neck pointing leftward rather then rightward, in completely the wrong direction. All four compounded their eccentricity by refusing to look stern and moody, as pop stars should, but by grinning broadly at the cameras and each other. The song they performed was largely inaudible, owing to the screams of the studio audience – all but for the moment where, with one extra zesty 'Whoa yeah', their voices toppled into falsetto. Then, six million snowbound British teenagers heard what George Martin, on his musician's stool, had heard; what Dick James in his Tin Pan Alley garret had heard; what Philip Jones had heard even down the telephone. It was the indefinable yet unmistakable sound of a 'number one'.

The same week brought enthusiastic reviews of 'Please Please Me' in the music trade press. Keith Fordyce, a leading Radio Luxembourg disc jockey, said in *New Musical Express* that 'Please Please Me' was 'a really enjoyable platter, full of vigour and vitality'. The *World's Fair* thought the Beatles had 'every chance of becoming the big star attraction of 1963'. Brian Matthew, compère of *Thank Your Lucky Stars* and BBC radio's *Saturday Club*, and the country's most influential commentator on pop music, delivered the ultimate accolade, calling them 'musically and visually the most accomplished group to emerge since the Shadows'.

The national press, however, still maintained an attitude of scornful indifference to teenagers and their music. One exception was the London *Evening Standard* which on Saturdays published a full page by its young pop columnist, Maureen Cleave. A friend of Cleave's, the Liverpool-based journalist Gillian Reynolds, had been urging her for months to come up and write something about the Beatles and the Cavern Club. Late in January, just as 'Please Please Me' was about to enter the Top Ten, Maureen Cleave travelled to Liverpool to interview them for her *Evening Standard* page. On the train she met Vincent Mulchrone, the *Daily Mail*'s chief feature-writer, bound on the same assignment.

The Beatles were in Liverpool to play a one-nighter at the Grafton Ballroom before leaving on the Helen Shapiro package tour. Mulchrone and Cleave were taken by Brian to see the queues which, as usual, had formed outside the Grafton two hours in advance of opening-time. Some of the girls told Cleave they hadn't bought 'Love Me Do' when it first appeared for fear the Beatles would become famous, leave Liverpool and never return.

The interview which followed was like none Maureen Cleave had ever done with a pop group. 'The Beatles made me laugh immoderately, the way I used to laugh as a child at the *Just William* books. Their wit was just so keen and sharp – John Lennon's especially. They all had this wonderful quality – it wasn't innocence, but everything was new to them. They were like William, finding out about the world and trying to make sense of it.'

'John Lennon,' Cleave wrote, 'has an upper lip which is brutal in a devastating way. George Harrison is handsome, whimsical and untidy. Paul McCartney has a round baby face while Ringo Starr is ugly but cute. Their physical appearance inspires frenzy. They look beat-up and depraved in the nicest possible way.'

The piece caught the knockabout flavour of their conversation – John's threat, for instance, to lie down on the stage like Al Jolson during the Helen Shapiro tour, and Paul's rejoinder that he was too blind to see the audience anyway. In John, Cleave found a fellow-devotee of the William stories. 'After the piece came out, John said to me, "You write like that woman who did the William books." For me, it was like being told one wrote like Shakespeare.'

They had been hired to tour with Helen Shapiro by Arthur Howes, the promoter who saw them die the death at Peterborough but who had, even so, kept an option with Brian to re-book them. This Howes now did, for a bottom-of-the-bill fee of £80 per week. The tour was to last throughout February, visiting theatres as far south as Taunton, Shrewsbury and, once again, Peterborough.

It was by no means one of Arthur Howe's major package tours. Helen Shapiro, who had enjoyed spectacular success as a 14-year-old schoolgirl, was now considered, at 16, to be somewhat past her best. The Beatles, at any rate, found her awesomely star-like with her chauffeur-driven car, her dressing-room TV set and constant, ferocious chaperonage.

She was, as it happened, a friendly girl who preferred to dodge her chauffeur and chaperone and travel with the Beatles and other small fry on the bus. Her chief memory is of snow, and of John Lennon, next to her, pulling his cripple face at passers-by through a clear patch in the frosted window. 'He would never sit still – none of them could. They'd always be writing songs or fooling about or practising their autographs. Paul, I remember, used to practise his a lot. They didn't have any give-away photographs of themselves, so they used to practise signing across pictures of me.

'Paul was the PR. He was the one who came up to me on the tour and said, very nervous, "Er – we've written this song, we wonder if you'd like to do it." It was "Misery".'

In Carlisle, after they had returned to their hotel, someone came up to Helen and invited her to a Young Conservatives dance in progress in the hotel ballroom. Feeling cold and bored, she decided to accept. The Beatles also decided to accept. The Young Conservatives door steward saw them all coming down the corridor, taking long steps and snapping their fingers in chorus like a *West Side Story* 'Jets' routine. They got past the door steward but were then, stiffly, asked to leave. The Beatles' leather jackets had caused offence and outrage.

Next morning, the *Daily Express* reported that the famous schoolgirl pop star Helen Shapiro had been ejected from a dance in Carlisle. Sympathy was entirely with the hotel, the Young Conservatives, and with the schoolgirl star herself, since the incident had obviously not been her fault. It was the leather jackets worn by her companions that gave the story the whiff of sordidness which was Fleet Street's only interest in printing stories about pop musicians.

On 16 February, while they were still iced into the tour bus with Helen Shapiro, *Melody Maker*'s Top Twenty showed those reprehensible leather jacket wearers' record 'Please Please Me' at number two. That meant another journey south through the snow, to appear a second time on *Thank Your Lucky Stars*, on BBC radio's *Saturday Club* and EMI's own *Radio Luxembourg Show*. On 2 March, the snows were beginning to melt. *Melody Maker*'s chart showed 'Please Please Me' at number one. Brian spread the paper out on his desk in Liverpool, and Olive and Freda and everyone crowded round to look. It was true.

•

Liverpool could not believe it. Letters poured into the NEMS office, written on complete toilet rolls, on cardboard hearts four feet high, on cylinders of wallpaper. There were also celebratory offerings of life-size cuddly toys, 'Good Luck' cakes from Sayer's, sacks of charm bracelets, brooches, eternity rings, jelly babies, even – from one fan with dockyard connections – a live tarantula in a specially ventilated box. 'Luckily, I never opened it,' Freda Kelly says. 'I took one look inside the box and ran. Brian sent me out to find a home for it at the School of Tropical Medicine.'

In his third-floor front office, Brian sat, amid ringing telephones, with a pretence at coolness that, for once, deceived no one. 'I'd never seen him so excited,' Freda says. 'It was the first thing he said to anyone who rang up. "Have you heard about the boys?" If anyone came to see him, it was the first thing out of his mouth: "Have you heard about the boys?"'

George Martin heard the news with elation, but also deep thought. The Beatles were doing this week what the Kalin Twins had done in 1957, what the Allisons had done in 1960 and what the Brook Brothers had in 1961. Any A & R man could reel off a list of such 'one-hit wonders', raised to freakish fame on a single song, then instantly forgotten. Martin's concern was to capitalise on a success which, according to the statistics of the business, had only the smallest outside chance of happening twice.

The way you capitalised on a number one single in 1962 was to rush-release an LP record of the same name. It was a simple, shameless catchpenny device to persuade the teenage public to buy the same song again, but at £1.50 instead of 62p. For few, if any, listened to the supporting tracks, knowing all too well what they would be. They would be 'standards', hastily recorded in an insincere attempt to pass off some perishable, new, blow-waved zombie as an 'all-round entertainer'.

Martin's instinct was that he could do something better with the Beatles' first LP. He was, after all, distinguished as a producer of live stage recordings. He considered, but abandoned, the idea of taping them live at the Cavern. His gamble was that they would be able to pour out the excitement anywhere. 'What you're going to do,' he told them on 11 February at Abbey Road studios, 'is play me this selection of things I've chosen from what you do at the Cavern.'

In one 13-hour session, Martin pushed them through enough songs to complete the 14-track LP. The numbers were those, like 'I Saw Her Standing There', which John and Paul had knocked up long ago to get them through a Hamburg night, mixed with American soul songs like 'Chains' and 'Baby It's You'. Martin, once again, confined himself to editing, shaping, rearranging and dovetailing. He added a piano intro – played by himself – to 'Misery', and the double-tracking of Paul's voice through 'A Taste of Honey'. George and Ringo, in fairness, were given the lead vocal on one song each. George's was a new Lennon–McCartney composition called 'Do You Want to Know a Secret?' He sang it in thick Liverpudlian, barely managing its falsetto line. Ringo, with even less of a voice, still managed to give an infectious joy to 'Boys', the old Cavern show-stopper. The finale was 'Twist and Shout', the Isley Brothers song with which their stage act always closed. 'John absolutely screamed it,' Martin says. 'God knows what it did to his larynx because it made a sound like tearing flesh. That *had* to be right on the first take.'

It was the same performance they were giving each night in a different English town, on tour once again for the Arthur Howes Organisation. Howes had booked them – before 'Please Please Me' reached number one – for the same £80 per week they had got for the Helen Shapiro tour. By now, any promoter would have paid ten times that fee. Brian Epstein would not renege on his agreement with Howes.

Two American singers, Chris Montez and Tommy Roe, were supposed to be the tour's joint stars. It soon became obvious to Arthur Howes that neither was getting applause on the same scale as the Beatles. Their wages did not increase but their billing did. The running order was changed so that they, and 'Twist and Shout', closed the show each night.

On 22 March, the release of their album, 'Please Please Me', provoked fresh interest from the music papers. Even the jazz-oriented *Melody Maker* welcomed what every reviewer agreed was not the usual cash-in LP dross but a run of songs each in its own way different and surprising. For the first time it became apparent that the Beatles were songwriters on a scale unknown among performers of pop music. Record buyers, previously, had cared little about who *wrote* the songs they liked. On the back of the 'Please Please Me' sleeve were helpful notes (by 'Disker', the *Liverpool Echo* columnist) detailing which of the songs were the Beatles' own and also acknowledging their debt to American groups like the Shirelles and songwriters like Goffin and King. The front cover photograph showed four figures in Burgundy-coloured stage suits, grinning cheerfully down from a balcony in what seemed to be a block of council flats. No one seen in the Top Twenty since Tommy Steele had made so overt a declaration of being working class.

By now their personalities as well as their records were reaching a national public. Two BBC radio pop shows, *Saturday Club* and *Easy Beat*, brought them to London during the Tommy Roe tour, to play in the studio what they were to play on stage that evening, a hundred miles away through the sleet and slush. In London, their faces were still unknown: they could walk as they pleased, with Dezo Hoffman their *Record Mirror* friend, around Shaftesbury Avenue and Berwick Market, and eat at Hoffman's favourite restaurant, the Budapest in Greek Street. Dezo also showed them how to work the new cameras he persuaded a Soho shop to give them in exchange for a signed photograph. Dezo Hoffman saw the same reaction everywhere that he had felt on his first trip up to Liverpool. The Beatles were something that pop musicians had never been before. They were witty, lively, intelligent; they charmed and tickled and excited all who met them. Brian Matthew, the *Saturday Club* compère, strove in vain to keep up his usual BBC manner against John Lennon's devastating ad libs. 'I was introducing them on one show, going through the usual thing of asking them about the music. I'd just come back from holiday in Spain. As I was talking, John leaned across and said into the microphone, "Brian's nose is peeling, folks."'

To George Martin, John was like a precocious child, only half-aware of the joltingly funny things he said. 'I remember we were having dinner out one night, and the waiter brought *mange-tout* peas. John had very evidently never seen such a thing before, but I said he ought to try them. "All right then," he said, "but put them over there, not near the food."'

Brian, too, was spending much of every week in London. His father could hardly object to that now. The Whitechapel record shop ran smoothly under Peter Brown's management, and the office upstairs in Olive Johnson's charge. Olive was the McCartney family friend whom Paul's father had first consulted about Brian. She had afterwards left her job with the Law Society to join NEMS Enterprises as his 'personal assistant'.

In London he still had no base other than his favourite hotel, the Grosvenor House. 'He'd walk into my office,' Dick James said, 'and tell me he'd been offered this date for the Beatles at £200. I'd say: "Tell 'em to double it." Brian would come back in amazement and say, "It worked." "Next time," I'd say, "tell 'em to double that figure again."'

In early 1963, a South London impresario could still book the Beatles for £30 to play for dancing at Wimbledon Palais. Brian's chief concern seems to have been to ensure them a full summer's work, even if the follow-up record to 'Please Please Me' did not make the charts. He struck up a regular business arrangement with Larry Parnes, still a leading impresario despite the virtual eclipse of Billy Fury and the rest of his 'stable' by the Mersey tidal wave. Parnes and Brian had Jewishness as well as concealed homosexuality in common and became good friends, though their mutual intransigence thwarted Mister Parnes, Shillings and Pence's plan to build a series of Sunday concerts around the Beatles at the end of Great Yarmouth pier. 'I was offering £30 per show and Brian wanted £75,' Parnes remembered. 'He told me that if I'd meet his price I could have an option to do shows with the Beatles and all the other NEMS acts for the next five years. In the end, he came down from £75 to £35. I went up to £32. I wouldn't budge and neither would he.'

The Beatles unquestioningly went wherever Brian told them, however small the fee or insignificant the venue. Perhaps the most bizarre was arranged after a pupil at Stowe, the Buckinghamshire public school, wrote and asked if they could perform for him and his schoolmates. It helped that the pupil was David Moores, a scion of Liverpool's Littlewoods stores family (and a future chairman of Liverpool football club). For £100, the Beatles performed two 30-minute sets in the school's Roxburgh Hall, watched by boys and teachers seated in orderly rows as if listening to a visiting bishop on Speech Day. Afterwards, they were given tea and a conducted tour of the school. This with one hit already behind them and another one ('From Me to You') due to be released the following week.

NEMS Enterprises, Brian decided, must have solicitors in London as well as Liverpool. Characteristically, he chose the most expensive and fashionable of West End law firms specialising in show business clients. The Beatles were now on the books of M. A. Jacobs of Pall Mall, in company with such illustrious past litigants as Marlene Dietrich and Liberace. The firm's senior partner, David Jacobs, was himself a fashionable figure, to be seen tirelessly ministering to his clients' needs at the Savoy or Dorchester. He was, like Brian, cultivated, immaculate, Jewish and a homosexual.

Already, a spot of bother had arisen which required urgent consultation with Jacobs. The owner of a Hamburg club was threatening to hold a Beatle responsible for making his daughter pregnant. Jacobs referred the matter to counsel, who advised a quick settlement. It was the first of countless such claims, consultations, visits to counsel and recommendations to settle out of court. With David Jacobs, Brian formed a shield around the Beatles that would not be lifted so long as he or Jacobs remained alive.

•

Early in March, every national and provincial newspaper in Britain received a publicity handout announcing the record debut of a second group managed by NEMS Enterprises. Journalists who bothered to read the handout learned that the group was called Gerry and the Pacemakers, that it recorded on EMI's Columbia label, that it shared the same management as another successful group, the Beatles, and that it came from the same city, Liverpool. For the first time since its birth in Britain's industrial dawn, Liverpool was deliberately invoked as a source of excitement, glamour and novelty.

Brian Epstein was hardly the first to see potential in Gerry Marsden, the ex-messenger boy from Ringo Starr's neighbourhood who had led a successful group on Merseyside since 1958. But no one before Brian had taken the trouble to harness Gerry's boundless energy, nor to dress him in a suit instead of sweaters and jeans, and stop him smoking Woodbines, and tell him to 'project'.

Gerry's first single was 'How Do You Do It?' the song which the Beatles had rejected in favour of 'Please Please Me'. He and the Pacemakers came across from Hamburg to record it, in blissful unawareness that the mutinous John Lennon version was anything other than a helpful demo. Gerry's jaunty treatment confirmed what George Martin had said all along – the number was a natural hit. It reached number one on 22 March. The music papers realised that two hits from the same source constituted a 'sound'. From now on there was constant reference to the Liverpool or the Mersey Sound.

The Beatles' third Parlophone single, 'From Me to You', released on 12 April, had a similarly stylish publicity send-off. The smallest local paper in Britain received the NEMS handout, written by Tony Barrow and designed much as Brian used to draw up his posters for dances at New Brighton Tower. Instead of the usual glossy studio pose, the Beatles were shown with their instruments on the deck of a Mersey tugboat. Underneath was Brian Matthew's potent declaration that they were 'visually and musically the most exciting group since the Shadows'.

The song had been written by John and Paul on the bus during the Helen Shapiro tour. It was 'Please Please Me', a little slower, with the falsetto repositioned, and its reviews proved no more than lukewarm. Most of the music papers thought they had 'gone off' since 'Please Please Me'. Keith Fordyce said the new record was not even as interesting as 'Love Me Do'.

On 27 April, 'From Me to You' was number one, well on the way to selling half a million copies and earning a Silver Disc. 'How Do You Do It?' by Gerry and the Pacemakers was still at number three. Everyone who watched television or listened to radio in Britain had heard of the Mersey Sound.

•

Four days earlier, in Sefton General Hospital, Liverpool, Cynthia Lennon had given birth to a son. The labour was long and painful; the delivery became complicated when the umbilical cord was found to be wrapped round the baby's neck. His father knew nothing of these anxieties, being still out on tour in the Chris Montez show. Not until a week later did John visit Cynthia, and even then he had to wear a crude disguise to avoid the fans waiting outside. He held his son in his arms, watched by a grinning crowd through the glass cubicle wall.

The baby was called Julian, the nearest John could get to his mother's name, Julia. His obvious delight at becoming a father encouraged Cynthia to visions of happy domesticity in Woolton, where they were to occupy the whole ground floor of Mimi's house. The visions evaporated when John told her that Brian had asked him to go away on holiday to Spain. Cynthia, recognising that she had no real say in the matter, assented with a show of cheerfulness.

This holiday, in May 1963, was Brian's first and only public declaration of his feelings towards John. It was made in the euphoria of seeing two of his groups in the Top Twenty, when all other impediment to happiness seemed to have been swept away; why not this last intractable one? Close friends like Olive Johnson advised against it, in vain. The two of them flew off to Brian's holiday haunts, leaving Liverpool to gossip as it pleased and Cynthia to take care of the baby. Years later, John as good as admitted that, in their Spanish hotel, Brian finally plucked up courage to make sexual advances to him and that, with his kind and resigned heart, he did not resist. But matters went no further than 'a hand job'.

Recently, Brian's attention had become focused on another, far more conventionally beautiful young man. Billy Ashton – or Kramer as he was known in the dance halls – led a group of Bootle boys called the Coasters, rated third in *Mersey Beat* newspaper's popularity league. Brian paid £50 to acquire Billy from his original manager, an elderly gentleman named Ted Knibbs who had rehearsed the nervous Adonis by making him sing, standing on a chair.

Billy J. Kramer, with the new suits and initial letter which Brian had bestowed on him, was then brought to London for a recording test by George Martin at Parlophone. Martin gave his opinion that, for the first time, Brian had made a mistake. Though the youth was undoubtedly good looking, his voice was erratic and his personal magnetism rather slight. Brian, however, insisted that 'my Billy' should be allowed to record.

Billy J. was duly taped, backed by a Manchester group the Dakotas, singing the Lennon–McCartney ballad 'Do You Want to Know a Secret?' If George Harrison's voice had cracked on the falsetto line, Billy J. Kramer's broke into smithereens. Martin concealed the worst of it by double-tracking the vocal and filling in the cracks with his own piano accompaniment. The record was released on 26 April; by mid-May every Top Ten chart showed it at number two.

That Brian had no idea of what the Beatles were already becoming is amply shown by his activities with NEMS Enterprises during the summer of 1963. Formerly, his desire had been to become a Beatle; to merge his existence, if only spiritually, with theirs. Now he began to see them merely as brand-leaders in an empire of Liverpool artists, founded and ruled over paternalistically by himself. One of the NEMS handouts, indeed, showed all of them, the Beatles, Gerry and Billy J., the Pacemakers and Dakotas, as disembodied heads encircling Brian's in a schoolmasterly mortar-board.

By June, he had signed up the Big Three and the Four Jays, another popular Cavern group, with 22 O-level passes between them, now renamed the Fourmost. He wanted a ballad singer to complement all the groups: Tommy Quigley, a freckle-faced boy he had seen at the Queen's Hall, Widnes, was even now being groomed, as Tommy Quickly, to fulfil that destiny. One group he was dissuaded from signing was Lee Curtis and the All Stars, even though their manager was his great friend Joe Flannery. The Beatles vetoed the idea, apparently because Lee Curtis, Joe's brother, was too handsome. When the two groups appeared together, Paul McCartney would never sing any songs that Lee had in his repertoire.

NEMS Enterprises now had a London office and the services of a full-time publicity man. Tony Barrow, in fact, had been industriously writing handouts for Brian since late 1962, still carrying on his PR work for Decca and his 'Disker' column in the *Liverpool Echo*. Brian's offer of £36 per week was exactly double what Barrow earned as a freelance. Another young PR man gave him some journalists' names and addresses to copy out in exchange for a cheap lunch.

One of Barrow's first jobs was to reorganise the Beatles' Fan Club, which Freda Kelly still ran from the NEMS office in Liverpool. Freda could no longer cope with the applications for membership, running into tens of thousands, and the sacks of letters, inscribed toilet rolls, soft toys and other Beatles-inspired greetings which poured daily into her office and her home. Barrow divided the club into a northern region, run by Freda in Liverpool, and a southern region, run from Monmouth Street by a girl named Bettina Rose. It was Barrow's idea to invent a national secretary, 'Anne Collingham', whose duplicated signature appeared on every newsletter. To girls all over the British Isles, 'Anne Collingham' was real, and revered as an intermediary between their idols and them.

NEMS Enterprises also briefly encompassed a 19-year-old hustler of Anglo-Dutch parentage named Andrew Loog Oldham who had previously worked as a PR man for Larry Parnes, Don Arden and the designer Mary Quant. Meeting Brian on the set of ABC-TV's *Thank Your Lucky Stars* show, Oldham wangled a £25-per-month retainer as an additional publicist for NEMS. To his chagrin he found this did not mean working with the Beatles; merely with subordinate Epstein discoveries like Gerry and the Pacemakers and Billy J. Kramer.

In April 1963, unable to make further headway with NEMS, Oldham gave up his retainer and decided to strike out as a manager on his own. A tip-off from a friendly music journalist led him to the Station Hotel in Richmond, Surrey, where a band called the Rolling Stones played Chicago-style rhythm and blues, fronted by a sweater-clad sometime economics student then known as 'Mike' Jagger. Scenting the odour of raw sex, Oldham offered to manage them despite having neither previous experience nor funds to back up such a venture. So he went back to Brian Epstein, offering 50 per cent of the Stones in exchange for some office space and minimal cash investment. But Brian felt he already had more than enough bands and singers on his plate, and thus missed the chance to run both of the greatest supergroups of all time.

Oldham brought the Beatles to see the Stones at the Station Hotel, and introduced the two bands afterwards. Despite their cultural differences, the homespun northerners and the more worldly, cynical southerners instantly struck up a rapport. In the Stones' rebelliousness and sartorial free choice, the Beatles all too clearly saw themselves as they had been before Brian cleaned and tidied them up. John particularly admired the Stones' then leader Brian Jones for his multi-faceted instrumental talent, especially on harmonica. 'You really play that thing, don't you?' he said to Jones wistfully. 'I just blow and suck.'

The Beatles were now making their first-ever tour as top of the bill, headlining over Gerry and the Pacemakers and the American country star Roy Orbison. Orbison was such a hero of theirs that they felt almost guilty to see him take the subordinate slot on the bill, with his dark glasses, huge quiff of hair and sub-operatic arias like 'In Dreams' and 'Only the Lonely'. Another new performing hazard derived from George's recent faux naif remark to a press interviewer that one of his major passions in life were children's jelly babies. As a result, the Beatles were welcomed on stage not only by demented feminine screams but also by lime, orange or blackcurrant jelly babies in hails thicker than locusts, that stung unpleasantly whenever they connected with human flesh.

Up until this point, their solitary road manager – or 'roadie' – had been Neil Aspinall, the one-time accountancy student whom they had got to know through Pete Best. For the first three tours, Brian had left everything connected with the band's welfare to him. It was he who drove them from town to town, carried in their guitars and amplifiers, and saw that they had food, sleep and stage suits, if necessary tending to the latter with a portable iron. Brusque and hollow-cheeked, with hair already thinning, Neil – or 'Nell' as the Beatles called him – was both friend and servant, their equal, yet their errand boy.

In May 1963, after overwork had reduced Neil's weight by three stone, Brian took on Mal Evans as assistant road manager. Mal was a hefty Liverpudlian, formerly employed as a Post Offfice engineer and part-time Cavern Club bouncer. Despite his size, he was gentle, amiable and filled with the romance of rock and roll. At 28 he was noticeably older than the Beatles and Neil; he was also married, with a newborn baby son. 'He had a lot of sleepless nights, wondering if he should go on with them,' his widow, Lil Evans, says. 'I didn't want him to. I told him, "You're a person in your own right – you don't need to follow others." But he was starstruck.'

John's Aunt Mimi, having been a seagoing pilot's daughter, did her best to cope with the growing chaos of life at 'Mendips'. Though Cynthia and the baby were living downstairs, all Mimi had seen of John for weeks were the suitcases of sodden stage shirts he would leave for Cyn' and her to wash. The telephone rang continuously; at the front gate there was a permanent picket of girls. 'And if I left the back door open,' Mimi said, 'there wouldn't be a teacup or a saucer left in the kitchen.'

In Speke, Harry and Louise Harrison faced similar problems in their little council house. The fans were there when Harry left for work in the morning; they queued at the bus stop, hoping to stop his bus. In the Dingle, little Elsie Gleave was frankly bewildered by what had happened to her Ritchie. One minute he was on the dole; the next, he had so much money, his mother wondered if it was all quite honest. 'I remember her coming to me in a terrible state,' Olive Johnson says, 'because she'd found pound notes left all over Ringo's dressing table. He didn't have a bank account until Brian opened one for him.'

Because of the siege of fans at Forthlin Road, Paul's 21st birthday, on 18 June, had to be celebrated at his Auntie Jin's in Birkenhead. The large family party was augmented by John Lennon and Cynthia, Ringo and his girl friend Maureen, George, Brian and Bob Wooler. It was, as Paul had wanted, a typical Liverpool booze-up, riotous and noisy, with children underfoot and Jim McCartney's piano renditions of sentimental evergreen songs. Unfortunately, the hard-drinking, sharp-tongued Wooler chose the occasion to voice some caustic speculation about John's relationship with Brian, as apparently corroborated by their recent Spanish holiday. John flew into a rage and set about Wooler with his fists, breaking the portly DJ's nose and bruising several of his ribs. The incident was smoothed over with profuse apologies and an ex gratia payment for damages to Wooler, though it still somehow managed to leak into the tabloid *Sunday Mirror*. But John and the Beatles were still too obscure in the adult world for it to generate much interest, let alone the deluge of follow-up stories that would have resulted today.

Liverpool was currently undergoing a hectic visitation by London A & R men, all eager to sign up their own Beatles and Pacemakers. In July, the Pye label released 'Sweets For My Sweet' by the Searchers, long resident at the Iron Door Club. When 'Sweets For My Sweet' went to number one, the A & R invasion of Liverpool became positively desperate. Any group would do so long as it talked Scouse, played rhythm and blues, buttoned its jackets high and combed its hair forward. The man from Oriole signed Faron's Flamingoes, Rory Storm and the Hurricanes, Earl Preston and the TT's; the Fontana man took the Merseybeats and Howie Casey and the Seniors; the Pye man took the Undertakers and the Chants.

Merseyside's new modishness was not confined to pop, but affected every sphere of British entertainment. Comedians who had once been told to disguise their Scouse accents now used them as an irresistible *schtick*, notably Beatle-fringed young Jimmy Tarbuck, a former habitué of the Cavern Club and friend of the Beatles, and Ken Dodd who poured out a never-ending stream of Liverpool goonery about 'Diddy Men' and 'tickling sticks' and a seemingly mythical place called Knotty Ash. Arty and poetic Liverpool also received a look-in when Paul McCartney's younger brother Michael joined with poets Roger McGough and John Gorman in a trio called the Scaffold, scoring hits with unlikely material like the cub scouts' campfire song 'Gin-Gan-Goolie'. The city that had once been the furthest possible point from all things fashionable had even inspired a 'Mersey Look' for metropolitan dolly-birds to complement the Mersey Sound – Lennon caps, wet-look PVC coats and striped scarves marked 'Liverpool' or 'Everton'.

The south's Merseymania brought salvation, at least, for Dick Rowe of Decca Records who had passed on the Beatles, albeit after two exhaustive auditions. In April 1963, Rowe agreed to judge a talent contest in Liverpool, hoping vainly it might produce some facsimile of the band he now so wished he hadn't turned down. To make him even more uncomfortable, one of his fellow judges turned out to be none other than George Harrison. But it was to prove a blessing in disguise. During the evening, George happened to tell him about the 'great' r & b group that Andrew Loog Oldham had just found playing behind the Station Hotel in Richmond, Surrey. Dick Rowe left Liverpool there and then, dashed down to Richmond and offered Oldham's discovery a contract, so winning dual immortality as The Man Who Turned the Beatles Down and The Man Who Signed the Rolling Stones.

Whatever new northern hit act came along, Brian Epstein's NEMS stable always seemed to take another giant leap ahead. In June, Gerry Marsden was again number one with 'I Like It'. In July, Billy J. Kramer did the same with 'Bad To Me', another Lennon–McCartney song, skilfully doctored by George Martin. At one point, the first three Top Ten places were occupied by NEMS acts – Gerry, Billy J. Kramer and the Beatles' 'From Me to You'. To this day, no other pop impresario has matched the achievement.

In August, to lessen disruption at the Whitechapel shop, Brian moved NEMS Enterprises to Moorfields, a couple of streets away, near the old Liverpool Exchange station. The new offices, situated above a joke shop, had a 'reception area' decorated with blow-up photographs of all the NEMS acts. Freda Kelly's friend, a deep-voiced Irish girl named Laurie McCaffery, was taken on as receptionist and switchboard operator. Another new arrival was Tony Bramwell, George Harrison's childhood friend, as office boy.

The Beatles were doing what all pop groups hoped for in summer.

They were at the south coast resort of Margate, appearing with Gerry and the Pacemakers at the Winter Gardens theatre. Dezo Hoffman came down from London to photograph them in their swimming trunks and socks, sunbathing on the terrace of their modest seafront hotel. They did not look like a group with the country's best-selling single *and* album. Hoffman also filmed them, as he had in Liverpool, this time skylarking on the beach in striped Victorian bathing suits. Another visitor was the publisher of *Beat Monthly*. Brian had agreed to let him start a separate publication dealing exclusively with the Beatles and their fan club. 'What are you going to find to write about us every month?' Paul McCartney asked him.

They had already been back to Abbey Road studios to record their fourth Parlophone single for George Martin. The song, 'She Loves You', was in the Lennon–McCartney tough-tender mode that previously had been confined to B-sides. For the first time in any British pop song by male vocalists, its subject was not a girl but another boy – a friend who couldn't or wouldn't see how much his girl cared for him. Cupid's message, however, was not delivered by a quiet word in his ear but by an affirming shout of 'She loves you, yeah, yeah, yeah!' that could have been heard from the top of the Liver Building. John and Paul played it over on their acoustic guitars and, as usual, Martin had an editorial suggestion – why not move the first verse back and start with the chorus? Once again, in their instinctive way, they had hit on melodic effects far outside the usual pop scale. The ringing last chord of 'She Loves You', their producer informed them to their surprise, was a major sixth, reminiscent of Forties big bands like Glenn Miller's. Martin even worried if the song's ending might be a little corny. But he had no such doubts about its beginning.

•

Britain, that wet and windy summer, had been enjoying a sex scandal unrivalled since the reign of Edward VII. A cabinet minister, John Profumo, holding no less an office than Conservative Secretary of State for War, had been caught out in a sexual liaison with a 22-year-old 'model' named Christine Keeler. The affair was enriched by Miss Keeler's extremely wide circle of men friends, which included sundry West Indians; a property racketeer; a seedy osteopath named Stephen Ward; and – most piquant of all – the Naval attaché at the Russian Embassy in London. It was the possibility that Britain's War Minister shared the same courtesan as a Russian spy which drew Secret Service attention finally to Profumo's sexual habits. Questioned in Parliament, he at first denied the impropriety; then – faced with imminent police and press disclosures – he admitted that he had 'misled' the House of Commons.

The Profumo Affair provided Fleet Street with a saga of almost infinite dimensions. From the unhappy minister, an avenue of sleaze stretched in one direction to the Notting Hill slums, where Keeler's ex-lover, Peter Rachman, would set dogs on his unco-operative tenants; in the other direction, it implicated the cream of British aristocracy, the Astor family, on whose Cliveden estate Profumo had made his fatal acquaintanceship. By midsummer, all Britain seethed with rumours of sexual perversion on every level of public life. It was variously claimed that another cabinet minister had been caught receiving fellatio in public; that 'up to eight' High Court judges had been involved in a sex orgy; and that at a fashionable dinner-party, one of the country's most eminent politicians had waited at table, naked and masked, with a placard around his neck reading: 'If my services don't please you, whip me.'

Months passed, the summer worsened, the Profumo affair ran on, and on. Christine Keeler disappeared, then reappeared. Profumo resigned in disgrace. Stephen Ward was arrested for living off immoral earnings. Every newspaper front page, day after day, steamed with the torrid, frequently horrid, doings of Christine Keeler and her associate, Mandy Rice-Davies. And gradually the surfeit of sex and scandal passed the limit which even the British public could absorb. Attention moved away from Profumo and on to the Prime Minister who had so indolently accepted the lie of his fellow aristocrat. Harold Macmillan, after 11 years in office, was re-examined in a new and searching light. What it revealed was scarcely credible as a twentieth-century politician. A dusty old man in a walrus moustache hummed and hawed in the accent which had ruled Britain for a thousand years, but which now signified only complacency, crassness and the natural conspiracy between men who shared the same public school and club.

No newspaper will ever admit to there being too much news. But to Fleet Street, in the summer of 1963, that condition was perilously close. Stephen Ward committed suicide on the eve of his trial; then, five days later, a second colossal story broke. A mail train on its way from Scotland to London was waylaid and robbed of £2½m, the largest haul in criminal history. The search for the gang was then pushed off the front pages by Macmillan's belated resignation and the struggle within the Tory party to choose his successor. By the end of September, every editor in Fleet Street was longing for a diversion from this incessant heavy news – something light; something unconnected with the aristocratic classes; something harmless, blameless and, above all, cheerful.

•

The *Daily Mirror* found the answer first. The *Mirror* in those days belonged to the same publishing group as *Melody Maker*, Britain's oldest-established music newspaper. On 11 September, *Melody Maker* announced the results of a poll among its readers to find the year's most popular record artists. The Beatles – who had barely scraped into the 1962 poll – came out as top British group. Billy J. Kramer was named in the same poll as 'Brightest Hope for 1964'.

As well as a fraternal story about the poll, the *Mirror* ran a two-page profile of the Beatles by its acerbic show-business columnist, Donald Zec. Under the headline 'Four Frenzied Little Lord Fauntleroys Who Are Earning £5,000 a Week', Zec described the scenes he had witnessed among young girls at a Beatles concert in Luton, Bedfordshire. He afterwards had the Beatles to tea at his flat, an ordeal which they survived with high spirits enough to drain all vitriol from the columnist's pen. They were, Donald Zec said, 'as nice a group of well-mannered music makers as you'll find perforating the eardrum anywhere'.

Other papers, too, were awakening to the existence of a population whose chief interest was not over-sexed cabinet ministers but a particular 'pop' record – as sub-editors still rendered it – whose wild 'Yeah, yeah, yeah' chorus kept piercing the summer static. For 'She Loves You', having gone straight to number one on advance orders of half a million copies, was still there, almost two months after its release. Radio disc jockeys like Brian Matthew no longer even bothered to announce it. 'Do you realise,' Matthew frequently enquired of his listeners, 'how many songs in the current Top Ten are written by, if not sung by, the Beatles?'

To Brian Epstein, this was still no more than a facet of success on every front. Brian's big autumn project was the launch of NEMS Enterprises' first female artiste. Priscilla White, the Cavern Club's gawky cloakroom girl, now renamed Cilla Black, was to be, not a discovery like the Beatles and Gerry but a *creation*, wrought by Brian's own feminine taste. For weeks, he had lavished attention on Cilla; on her clothes, her hair, her make-up. He had taken her to George Martin, and Martin – privately thinking her a 'Cavern screamer' – had recorded her singing the Lennon–McCartney song 'Love of the Loved'. Tony Barrow, in Monmouth Street, was producing the usual stylish NEMS press release, describing Cilla's recherché taste for wearing men's jeans, and relaying Cavern Club slang like 'gear', 'fate' and 'endsville'.

On 13 October, the Beatles were due to appear on British television's top-rated variety programme, *Sunday Night at the London Palladium*. The show went out live on Sunday nights from the famous old, gilt-encrusted theatre, in Argyll Street, just off Oxford Circus. In form it was straight music hall, with jugglers, trampolinists, a 'Beat the Clock' interlude in which members of the audience underwent ritual self-humiliation, and finally a top-of-the-bill act which was quite likely to be the pop singing sensation of the moment. At the end, the entire cast stood on a revolving platform among chorus girls and giant letters spelling out SUNDAY NIGHT AT THE LONDON PALLADIUM.

News of the engagement had circulated among Beatles fans and there were girls waiting in Argyll Street that Sunday morning when the Beatles arrived at the Palladium to rehearse. The photographer Dezo Hoffman, who accompanied them, counted 'about eight girls. The car drew up – we went inside, no trouble.' Since rehearsals lasted all day, the Beatles were provided with a roast lamb lunch in their dressing-room. While they were eating it, a group of girls ran into the auditorium and had to be ejected.

The show that night broke all precedent by putting on its top-of-the-bill act first, for a few seconds only. Bruce Forsyth, the compère, then appeared and stuck out his long chin. 'If you want to see them again,' Forsyth taunted, 'they'll be back in 42 minutes.' That final, short, inaudible performance, before they hurried aboard the revolving stage, was watched by an audience of 15 million.

Next morning, every mass-circulation British newspaper carried a front-page picture and story of 'riots' by Beatles fans outside the London Palladium. 'Police fought to hold back 1,000 squealing teenagers,' the *Daily Mirror* said, 'as the Beatles made their getaway after their Palladium TV show.' Both the *Daily Mail* and *Daily Express* had pictures of the four Beatles peeping out in supposed dread of a mob, this time said to number 500. 'A Police motorcade stood by,' the *Mirror* continued, 'as the four pop idols dashed for their car. Then the fans went wild, breaking through a cordon of more than 60 Policemen' (20, the *Express* said). 'With engines racing, the cavalcade roared down Argyll Street and turned into Oxford Circus, heading for a celebration party at the Grosvenor House hotel.'

This official outbreak of Beatlemania in Britain has certain puzzling aspects. In every case, the published photograph of those '1,000 squealing teenagers' was cropped in so close that only three or four could be seen. The *Daily Mail* alone published a wide-angle shot – Paul McCartney and Neil Aspinall emerging from the Palladium, watched by one policeman and two girls.

'There were *no* riots,' Dezo Hoffman says. 'I was there. Eight girls we saw – even less than eight. Later on, the road managers were sent out to find the Beatles a girl each, and there were *none*.'

11

'Even the jelly babies are symbolic'

In 1963, the simple fact was, Britain's population had become unbalanced by a vast surplus of people under 18. The decline in infant mortality, together with the mysterious non-appearance of a Third World War, had allowed an entire generation to grow up virtually intact. They were the babies born after 1945 and raised in a Britain struggling to transform itself from postwar drabness to the material well-being so long observed and envied in America. Cars, radio sets, washing machines, all the luxuries still cherished by their parents were, to these young people, simply the mundane furniture of life. Television spread the whole world before them, to be casually viewed and judged. In 1960, the kindly Macmillan Government abolished the two-year period of compulsory military service that had shaped young men's lives since the end of the Second World War. For those between 16 and 21, no obligation remained save that of spending their ever increasing pocket money on the amusements demanded by their ever quickening glands.

Pop music was the most obvious sign of youth's growing economic power. What had begun in 1956 as a laughable, disreputable adolescent outburst was now an industry turning over £100m each year. The attitude to teenagers remained largely unchanged: they were, as in 1956, a puzzling, fractious element of the population, endlessly deplored and advised by politicians, headmasters and clergymen. They were also a market, undreamed of in size and potential, to be wooed and cajoled by the retail trade at every level.

The British teenage girl of early 1963 faithfully reflected the numerous boom industries who battled for her weekly pay packet. Her hair, teased up into a huge hollow bouffant, or 'beehive', represented hours spent at the hairdressing salon and in arduous private backcombing and curling with Carmen heated rollers. Her face was deathly white, but for two coal-black eyes embellished with false lashes like those popularised by the singer Dusty Springfield. She wore trousers, or 'trews' with loops under each foot, but more usually a formal dress with a wasp-tight waist and a full skirt ballooned by starch-stiffened petticoats into the semblance of an outsized tea cosy. Her shoes, invariably matching her handbag, were white or beige with 'winklepicker' points and the stiletto heels that had wrought destruction on polished dance floors across the land.

Her boy friend was an even more interesting sight – for young males were gradually reviving the conventions of the fifteenth and sixteenth century in dressing as colourfully as females. He might be a Mod, a faction which went in for ostentatiously neat Italian suits and trilby hats and rode about on Vespa or Lambretta motor scooters. He might, on the other hand, be a Rocker, the heirs of the Fifties 'Teds' who favoured the macho look of early-Elvis rock and roll, draped themselves in black leather, decorated themselves with tattoos and aspired only to do a 'ton' (100 mph) on their thunderous motorcycles. The Mods and Rockers had sprung up in 1963, simultaneously and with an instant mutual loathing of one another. All that summer, in innocent seaside resorts like Clacton and Margate, their set-piece battles had surged back and forth, trampling daytrippers, deck chairs and children's sand castles.

In autumn, the Mod–Rocker war was eclipsed by a new kind of teenage excess that was not new but was louder and wilder than Britain had ever known it before. Television and cinema newsreels added live pictures to those appearing daily in all the national papers. The pictures showed girls in their hollow-spun bouffants and spectral make-up, their black eye make-up running in rivulets down their faces. The sound was of incessant screaming.

•

Girls had screamed for pop stars before, but never quite like this. Never – as they did at the Beatles' ABC, Cambridge concert – hunched into a foetal position, alternately punching their sides, covering their eyes and stuffing handkerchieves and fists into their mouths. Later, when the curtain had fallen and the last dazed girl had been led through the exits, a further difference from the screams that greeted Valentino became manifest. Hundreds of the cinema seats were wringing wet. Many had puddles of urine beneath them.

Such scenes had been commonplace for six months already: the difference now was that newspapers reported them. Fleet Street had realised that the Beatles were more than a momentary diversion – they were a running story of guaranteed reader interest. The riots faked in Argyll Street were to be seen, ten times more spectacularly, along the route of their current package tour. On 26 October in Carlisle – the small border town they had last seen as nobodies with Helen Shapiro – 600 fans queued for 36 hours to buy tickets. When the box office opened, the queue moved forward with such ardour that nine people were crushed and had to receive hospital treatment.

Fleet Street's initial line was simply reporting on the girls' hysteria. It changed the moment someone took the trouble to visit the Beatles' dressing-room. There, in the tiny space hemmed in by teacups and stage suit bags, the 'Street' men found what every journalist craves and what he will distort the plainest fact to manufacture – good 'quotes'. For when John and Paul got going no one had to invent the dialogue.

'How long do you think the group will last, John?'

'About five years.'

'Are those wigs you're wearing?'

'If they are, they must be the only wigs with dandruff.'

'What kind of guitar is that, Paul?'

'It's a Hofner violin bass. Here, take a look.' The bass – now widely copied by other groups – would be tossed into the startled questioner's lap.

'Are they expensive?'

'Fifty-six guineas. I could afford a better one but I'm a skinflint.'

Ringo, still unsure of himself, would be coaxed forward to say a mordant word or two. If asked why he wore so many rings on his fingers, he replied it was because he couldn't get them all through his nose. 'I don't like talking,' he explained. 'Some people gab all day and some people play it smogo. I haven't got a smiling face or a talking mouth.'

George, unless specially asked for, would remain apart, his hollow face cupped in a high black polo neck, his eyes under the Beatle fringe not happy. He would tune guitars assiduously, John's as well as his own, despite knowing they had not the remotest chance of being heard. Even at this early stage, the fan uproar, the flailing screams and toys and jelly babies were a source of detestation to him.

Certain journalists, on the strength of past favours, were exempt from the moments when Neil Aspinall, at a secret signal, would clear the Beatles' dressing-room of the press. Maureen Cleave from the *Evening Standard* was one such: John Lennon called her 'the Just William woman'. Another was Ray Coleman, from *Melody Maker*. The Beatles liked 'MM' because it troubled to discuss their musicianship as well as the riots. Coleman, a quiet, clerkly figure, would stand in the wings, telling John the words of songs which, even though John himself had written them, he could barely remember from day to day. Usually, when he ran on stage, the words would be written on the back of his hand.

Peter Jones, of *Record Mirror*, found himself in the most difficult position. Jones had written the first article about the Beatles in a national publication; he was now contributor-in-chief to their fan magazine, *Beatles Monthly*. He was at once privy to their most intimate moments and sworn to secrecy concerning all that might have shown them, not as cuddly toys, but as ordinary, imperfect human beings.

The papers did not mind revealing that all four of these new national role models, especially George, were heavy smokers. But on other matters, Peter Jones had to remain silent. He could say nothing about the hatred they already felt for performing night after night, and how Neil Aspinall sometimes literally chased them from their dressing-room into the wings. Jones could not mention the rows they frequently had with one another, or with Brian. Nor could he make even the vaguest mention of what everyone in the Beatles' entourage called 'the girl scene', the sexual encounters with young women, hand-picked from their night's audience or stage-door crowd, that continually went on in hotel bedrooms or bathrooms or out-of-the-way theatre passages or toilets.

'At times,' Jones says, 'they could pick on someone for a kind of corporate cruelty that was absolutely merciless. Down on the south coast, there was this old journalist who went into the swimming pool with them while some photographs were being taken. All four of them really set on this quite elderly guy – pretending it was all fun, but it wasn't. They were so rough with him, they actually broke one of his toes.'

Such stories, if written, would not have been printed. Fleet Street had settled on its view of the Beatles – the four happy-go-lucky Liverpool lads who looked absurd, but knew it, and whose salty one-line witticisms seemed to epitomise the honesty of the working classes, blowing through the seedy lies of the Profumo upper crust. 'You *had* to write it that way,' an ex-*Daily Mirror* man says. 'You knew that if you didn't, the *Sketch* would and the *Express* would and the *Mail* and the *Standard* would. You were writing in self-defence.'

Within a week of the London Palladium Show, Britain's attitude to the Beatles had completely changed. No longer were they just a silly pop group which incited teenagers to be even sillier than usual. They were also, unprecedently, endowed with wit and intelligence. The inclusion among their cover versions of several songs originally recorded by American girl groups – notably the Marvelettes' 'Please, Mister Postman' and the Cookies' 'Chains' – underscored their Liverpool toughness with appealingly paradoxical sensitivity. Whatever the prejudice engendered by their hair and clothes, it vanished as soon as their voices began to speak, in what was half-remembered, through ages of music hall and radio, as comedy's natural dialect:

'None of us has quite grasped wharrit's all about yet. It's washin' over our 'eads like a yuge tidal wave—'

'—I don't s'pose I think mooch about the future. Though, now we have made it, it would be a pity to get bombed—'

'I get spasms of being intellectual. I read a bit about politics. But I don't think I'd vote for anyone. No message from those phoney politicians is coomin' through to me.'

'—We've always 'ad laughs. Sometimes we find ourselves gettin' hysterical, especially when we're tired. We laugh at soft things that other people don't get – we call it "The Cruelies"—'

'Is it true that you were turned down by Decca?'

'A guy at Decca turned us down.'

'He must be kicking himself now.'

'I 'ope he kicks himself to death.'

On 16 October, an announcement was made which both confirmed their new status beyond any doubt and brought Fleet Street northward in a still more maddened pursuit. The Beatles had been chosen to appear in the Royal Command Variety Performance in London on 4 November. Bernard Delfont, the organiser, told reporters he had picked them on the insistence of his 10-year-old daughter. Buckingham Palace, to which the list went for approval, offered no objection.

•

Late in October, Brian Epstein moved his entire organisation from Liverpool to London. 'It happened at about a week's notice,' Tony Bramwell says. 'Eppy walked in and said he was going south – were we coming?' Tony, Alistair Taylor, Laurie McCaffery the switchboard girl, immediately went home to pack. Freda Kelly's father refused to let her go, although she pleaded. Almost the entire staff managed to reassemble itself in London to greet Brian when he arrived, looking as if he had expected nothing else.

The new NEMS office was in Argyll Street, only a few doors away from the London Palladium. Brian drew great satisfaction from being so close to this famous old theatrical monument. He drew equal satisfaction from his new cable address: Nemperor, London. It was Bob Wooler, the Cavern's pun-loving disc jockey, who had once said to him on the telephone, 'Is that the Nemperor?'

Brian now had his own London flat, in a fashionable block in William Mews, Knightsbridge. One of the first people he took there was Brian Sommerville, an old friend of his who had recently left the Royal Navy and was now working in Fleet Street. 'The flat was very Brian,' Sommerville says, 'all white walls and black leather cushions. While I was there, he showed me a proof of the Beatles' new LP cover. He was already starting to suggest that we might work together.'

Once installed in the new flat, Brian began to entertain lavishly. David Jacobs, his solicitor, had introduced him to many of the showbusiness celebrities for whom Jacobs's firm also acted. He developed a particular friendship with Lionel Bart, the East End ex-skiffler who had won, and was rapidly losing, a fortune as a composer of West End musicals. He loved all 'show people' and in their cocktail chatter found a measure of security. Show people did not care who was, or was not, 'gay'.

He had, as his success grew more hectic, placed increasing reliance on Jacobs and on his accountants, Bryce, Hanmer and Isherwood of Albemarle Street, Mayfair. Bryce, Hanmer were, in fact, a Liverpool firm whose London office made a speciality of theatrical clients. Dr Walter Strach, one of the firm's senior members, a gaunt and melancholy Czech, thus found himself, in late 1963, charged with the responsibility of finding London accommodation for all four of the Beatles. Total secrecy was maintained, to evade the fans and to keep the rents within reason.

For John and Cynthia, a flat was rented in Emperor's Gate, Kensington, just behind the Cromwell Road terminal where, in those days, one could check in for flights from Heathrow airport. Thanks to the almost psychic powers of detection bestowed on Beatles fans, the hideaway became instantly and universally known. Girls waited all day, as well as most of the night, around the pilastered front porch, even venturing into the hallway, if the front door was left open, to settle down with blankets, sleeping bags and vacuum flasks. Across the road was a student hostel with a balcony that looked directly into the Lennons' flat. Whenever Cyn' looked, she would see figures hanging over the balcony and waving. Six flights up, without a lift, she spent days at a time, with baby Julian, in conscientious isolation.

George and Ringo moved together into a flat lower down in the William Mews block where Brian lived. Old ladies, carrying Pekinese dogs, looked askance at the girls who instantaneously took up station on the front steps. Brian was torn between excitement at having two Beatles so closely under his wing and terror that George and Ringo might 'find out' what, in any case, they had known about him for years. Even when he asked them to one of his gay parties, he seems to have hoped they would view the all-male gathering as no more than coincidence. 'Do you think they noticed?' he later anxiously asked a friend.

As to the living arrangements of Paul McCartney, not even the most tenacious journalistic doorstepper could hazard a guess. Whereas George and Ringo's address, like John's, would invariably be specified in newspaper reports, Paul, since leaving the President Hotel, could only be said ambiguously to be living at 'an address in Central London'.

Four months earlier, at a pop concert in the Albert Hall, the Beatles had met a young actress called Jane Asher, herself on the way to becoming a celebrity through her appearances on the BBC TV show *Juke Box Jury.*

The Beatles crowded round her in their usual way, all four instantly proposing marriage. The others guessed at once that such a 'classy' girl, red-haired and madonna-like, would appeal strongly to the socially ambitious Paul. They had asked her back to their hotel for a drink and, after some winking and nudging, had left Paul and her alone in the bedroom. It quickly transpired that Jane, as well as being only 17, was still a virgin. When the others came back, she and Paul were sitting there, deep in discussion about their favourite kinds of food.

Jane's background, as much as her chaste beauty, fascinated Paul. Her father, Sir Richard Asher, was a noted psychiatrist. Her mother, a professional musician, had taught George Martin the oboe. Her brother Peter belonged – as did Jane herself – to a teenage top drawer which played its rock records in the studies of elegant town houses and formed the earliest clientele of the music clubs and 'boutiques' now springing up in the West End and Chelsea. Since heeding his mother's plea not to talk like other estate children, Paul McCartney had dreamed of worlds like this.

The fans knew that Paul and Jane were often seen together, at parties or the theatre. The Ashers' house in Wimpole Street was plagued by telephone gigglings and breathings which Sir Richard could not shut off because the line belonged to his surgery. What few people knew, even within the Beatles' entourage, was that Paul now spent all his time in London with the Ashers. Returning from the Continent late one night, he had missed his connection to Liverpool, and Jane's mother had offered him the spare room. That room was now permanently his.

To young men long used to staying out all night, London in 1963 offered many diversions. The old West End 'night spots', with their clientele of debutantes and Guards officers, were giving way to 'with it' clubs like Wips, whose advertisement promised 'pirhanas in the dark above London's skyline . . . black velvet and new faces . . . music, strong, hard and moody'. In Soho, for a brief season, flourished the Establishment Club, named for all the hapless official targets, from Royalty downward, flayed nightly by the satirists in its floor show. In Mayfair, handily close to George and Ringo's shared flat, was the super-posh Saddle Room, kept by the television 'personality' Hélène Cordet, from which the two Beatles would often return home to Williams Mews by horse-drawn carriage. Just off Leicester Square was the Ad Lib – its very name a declaration of London's unlimited treats – where pop stars mingled with their own kind and excluded outsiders in the same way that Pall Mall gentlemen's clubs had for the past two centuries.

Newspaper acquaintances, like Ray Coleman, who ran into the Beatles after dark at the Ad Lib, could be sure both of an eventful night and of a large bill to be camouflaged among expenses. 'None of them ever seemed to have any money,' Coleman said. Peter Jones, the journalist in closest contact with them, received an impression, not so much of Liverpool thrift as of spasmodic insolvency. 'If I was on my way to see them, I'd ring up first. Often they'd say, "Here, pick up some food for us on the way, will you?"'

The fact is that, although the Beatles were Britain's biggest-selling pop group, their income was – and for a long time remained – astonishingly small. The records now selling in millions earned them, under their original Parlophone contract, a farthing per double-sided disc. Their concert appearances, richly profitable to promoters and cinema circuits, often realised barely enough to cover their travel and hotel expenses. For Brian was still letting them work at rates agreed to months previously.

At Bryce, Hanmer and Isherwood, Dr Strach's first act – after sorting out certain small tax difficulties arising from their Hamburg days – was to form the Beatles into a limited company for which the grave Czech gentleman himself acted as both treasurer and secretary. It was to Strach that the bills for their flats and living expenses came. In those days, the Doctor remembered, his main concern was to amass a reserve of money to pay income tax after – as must invariably happen – the Beatles had stopped earning money as pop stars. The residue of their earnings, therefore, simply lay in bank accounts, expecting that evil day. For meals, drinks, the suits and shirts and boots they wore once and then discarded, they turned to Neil Aspinall, their road manager, and the float Neil always carried. Larger expenditure was discouraged by the black-suited figure whom, without much conviction, the Beatles called 'Uncle Walter'.

Dr Strach remembers how Brian Epstein strove at every step to make his dealings with the Beatles fair. 'He always worried that he might be taking advantage of them. He came to me once and said he wanted to give them a piece of *his* company, NEMS Enterprises. He gave them 10 per cent of it, so they would get back some of the 25 per cent they paid him. Brian didn't have to do that, but he wanted to. He was a decent, honest, average human being.'

Punctilious in small matters, and small amounts, Brian could not adjust his sights to the bigger and bigger commercial prospects now materialising on every side. At the same time, his pride would not allow him to ask advice from older, more experienced people in the same business. Resolutely he did every deal for the Beatles in person, never revising a payment scale still based more on Liverpool's values than London's. And among his pursuers, the word rapidly spread. Brian Epstein – in the American entrepreneurial phrase – was not 'street wise'.

In the autumn of 1963, he received an offer for the Beatles to appear in their first feature film. This was already a recognised way of capitalising on pop music success – simple 'exploitation' movies in which the thinnest background was given to the regurgitation of Top Twenty hits for a cinema audience. United Artists, the company which approached Brian, were at that stage chiefly interested in sales of a Beatles soundtrack album.

UA had already hired Walter Shenson, an independent American producer, based in London, with some reputation for making successful low-budget comedy films. Shenson agreed to meet Brian, together with Bud Orenstein, UA's office head in London, to discuss the terms under which the Beatles would be allowed to appear.

'I knew Bud Orenstein well,' Walter Shenson said. 'So I went over to his flat before Brian arrived to talk over the deal that we'd be prepared to make. I knew nothing about pop music or managers. I said: "What do you think he's going to ask for?" The film was low budget, with not much to pay in advances. Bud and I agreed it would be fair to offer Brian and the Beatles 25 per cent of the picture.

"Then Brian came in. He seemed very nice. We put to him the fee we'd thought of – the Beatles would get a salary of £25,000 to work on the picture – and he agreed to that. Then we asked him, "Mr Epstein, what would you consider a fair percentage of the picture?" Brian thought for a minute, then he said, "I couldn't accept anything less than seven-and-a-half per cent."'

•

Uproar spilled over into the Beatles' first European tour – a series of concerts in Sweden from 24–29 October. Self-possessed Swedish girls now jigged and shrieked as wildly as any Cavernite, and sensible Swedish boys wore their hair in what Scandinavian newspapers called the 'Hamlet' style. At a concert in Stockholm fans rushed the stage, breaking through a 40-strong police cordon and trampling George Harrison momentarily underfoot. Between concerts, Paul wore a disguise so effective that not even the other Beatles could recognise him.

Their return to London on 29 October showed them for the first time the full extent of their British following. At Heathrow airport, as their aircraft taxied to a stop, a concerted scream broke out from hundreds of girls massed along the terminal's terraced roof. The invasion had thrown the whole airport into a chaos in which such other celebrities as Britain's Prime Minister, Sir Alec Douglas Home, and the newly-elected Miss World passed by, totally unnoticed.

The Royal Command Variety Peformance is an institution dating back to Queen Victoria, whose little dour face masked a fondness for theatrical glamour and who would 'command' all the latest entertainers, like

'Buffalo Bill' Cody, to give private performances for her and her family at Windsor. From this had evolved an annual Royal charity gala featuring a marathon bill of top entertainers that gave the West End its most glamorous night of the year and was later seen by the rest of the nation on TV. In 1963, the Queen could not attend, being heavily pregnant with her fourth child, the future Prince Andrew, and her place in the Royal Box was to be jointly filled by Queen Elizabeth the Queen Mother and Princess Margaret. The Beatles were placed seventh on a 19-act programme that included Marlene Dietrich, comedians Charlie Drake, Harry Secombe and Eric Sykes, the self-styled 'Red-Hot Momma' Sophie Tucker and the dancing pig puppets Pinky and Perky.

But there was no question as to the night's real draw. Long before dusk, on that raw afternoon, 500 policemen had been drafted to duty outside the Prince of Wales theatre, off Leicester Square, where the usual crowd, assembled to glimpse the 'Royals', was swollen by several thousand girls, screaming and chanting, 'We want the Beatles'. Marlene Dietrich, a legend of 30 years' standing, was able to enter the stage door, unrecognised. But when the Queen Mother herself appeared, waving and smiling, followed by Princess Margaret and her photographer husband Lord Snowdon, a basic British instinct asserted itself: the screaming and chanting changed to applause and cheers.

Brian Epstein, in all the hurry and excitement, very nearly found himself without the evening clothes that are de rigueur at a Royal performance: his dinner jacket, he remembered, too late, was hanging in the wardrobe at home in Liverpool. To add to the tension, he was due to fly to America the next morning. His parents, Harry and Queenie, sitting in the audience, had almost resigned themselves to not seeing him when, just before curtain-up, in his hastily fetched tuxedo, he lowered himself into the empty seat next to theirs.

The Beatles, cooped up with Neil and Mal Evans in a dressing-room no more munificent than usual, were also evincing signs of strain. Their spot in the show was brief – four songs near the end, surrounded by carefully rehearsed bows. What Brian feared more than musical slip-ups was that, despite his entreaties for decorum, some ad lib would be made, offensive to Royal ears. John had already threatened one ghastly ad lib if the audience proved unresponsive: 'I'll just tell 'em to rattle their fuckin' jewellery.'

Brian's fears proved groundless. The audience of stiff-shirted showbiz notables and their wives could not have been more susceptible to the Beatles' insouciant charm and the cheekiness which by instinct they measured out in precisely the right amount. Paul struck the exact note at once, surveying the dignified dark and saying, 'How are yer – all right?'

A joke between songs, about 'Sophie Tucker our favourite American group' produced a ripple of confirming laughter. Then it was John's turn, to announce the final number, 'Twist and Shout'. The line which had jangled Brian's nerves in the dressing-room came out as a perfect mingling of impudence and deference: Will people in the cheaper seats clap your hands? All the rest of you, if you'll just rattle your jewellery . . .'

The next day's papers were unanimous. 'Beatles Rock the Royals', said the *Daily Express*. 'Night of Triumph for Four Young Men', said the *Daily Mail*, roguishly adding, 'Yes – the Royal Box was stomping'. It was reported that the Queen Mother had listened to 'Twist and Shout' with every appearance of enjoyment and that Princess Margaret had definitely leaned forward, 'clapping on the off-beat'. John's little joke was quoted everywhere, as was the banter overheard later when the Beatles stood in the Royal receiving line. Asked by the Queen Mother where they were appearing next, they had together murmured 'Slough'. 'Oh . . . that's near us,' Her Majesty replied with such warmth as to suggest she might seriously consider popping over from nearby Windsor Castle to catch the gig.

The *Daily Mirror*'s coverage of scenes outside and inside the Prince of Wales theatre bore the simple headline 'Beatlemania!' The *Mirror* simultaneously gave the epidemic a name and offered its six million readers this deeply infected diagnosis.

> YEAH! YEAH! YEAH!
>
> You have to be a real sour square not to love the nutty, noisy, happy, handsome Beatles.
>
> If they don't sweep your blues away – brother, you're a lost cause. If they don't put a beat in your feet – sister, you're not living.
>
> How refreshing to see these rumbustious young Beatles take a middle-aged Royal Variety performance by the scruff of their necks and have them Beatling like teenagers.
>
> Fact is that Beatle People are everywhere. From Wapping to Windsor. Aged seven to seventy. And it's plain to see why these four cheeky, energetic lads from Liverpool go down so big.
>
> They're young, new. They're high-spirited, cheerful. What a change from the self-pitying moaners, crooning their lovelorn tunes from the tortured shallows of lukewarm hearts.
>
> The Beatles are whacky. They wear their hair like a mop – but it's WASHED, it's super clean. So is their fresh young act. They don't have to rely on off-colour jokes about homos for their fun.

To say that Britain, in November 1963, succumbed to an all-excluding obsession with a four-man pop group – even one which had made Royalty smile – would be palpably absurd. The mania was Fleet Street's; it therefore appeared to blanket the land. In a single week after the Royal Variety Performance, the *Daily Express* ran five front-page stories indicative of Beatlemania at every compass-point. Its chief rival, the *Daily Mail*, soon afterwards ceased bothering even to use the name 'Beatles' in headlines. A small cartoon logo of four fringed heads gave all the identification that was needed.

Naturally, the press soon winkled out the fact which Brian had striven so to conceal – that John Lennon was married, with a baby son. The fans, however, far from resenting Cynthia, seemed to regard her as part of John's inexhaustible originality. She continued, nonetheless, to exist in the deepest hinterland, at the top of the Emperor's Gate flat or some sternly defined public corral, fenced off by a road manager's shoulder.

The scope of Fleet Street coverage was widening from theatre sieges and screaming and the cheeky things they said. On 10 November, the first school headmaster sent the first teenage boy into public martyrdom for sporting a Beatle haircut. On 18 November, the first vicar invoked their name, requesting them to provide a tape of 'Oh Come All Ye Faithful, Yeah Yeah Yeah' for his Christmas congregation. Two days later occurred the first Parliamentary mention. A Labour MP in the House of Commons demanded that police protection for the Beatles should end. On the *Express* editorial page there appeared a prophetic cartoon. The Prime Minister, Sir Alec Douglas Home, genuflecting before the Beatles, asked: 'Gentlemen – could we persuade you to become Conservative candidates?'

The quality papers, traditionally aloof from such proletarian topics, now weighed in with purportedly scientific analyses of the Beatles' effect on teenage girls. The *Observer* published a picture of a Cycladic fertility goddess which, it was maintained, 'dates the potency of the guitar as a sex symbol to about 4,800 years before the Beatle era'. The livelier-minded *Sunday Times* commended the Beatles for enriching the English language with words from their private slang – like 'gear' and 'fab' – which were now in fashionable use. The *Sunday Times* went on to examine Beatlemania in a style and vocabulary that were to be widely imitated. '"You don't have to be a genius," says a consultant at a London hospital, "to see the parallels between sexual excitement and the mounting crescendo of delighted screams through a stimulating number like 'Twist and Shout', but at the level it is taken, I think it is the bubbling, uninhibited gaiety of the group that generates enthusiasm."'

The habit quickly spread of consulting the medical profession, especially its psychiatric branch, for opinions which would lend scientific weight to the orgies of chortling prose. And doctors and psychiatrists, sensing regular fees, were careful to pronounce nothing unfavourable.

Not even the *News of the World* could find anything in Beatlemania against which to caution its credulous readership. Psychologists, the *NotW* said, in its usual comfortably inexplicit way, had been trying to discover why the Beatles sent teenage girls into hysteria. One of them had come up with this explanation:

> This is one way of flinging off childhood restraints and letting themselves go . . . the fact that thousands of others are screaming along with her makes the girl feel she is living life to the full with people of her own age . . . this emotional outlook is very necessary at her age. It is also innocent and harmless.
>
> The girls are subconsciously preparing for motherhood. Their frenzied screams are a rehearsal for that moment. Even the jelly babies are symbolic.

EMI hastened to release the second Beatles LP, recorded by George Martin in mid-July and incubated through autumn until sales of the first album, and its spin-off EPs, should finally subside. This second album, *With the Beatles*, appeared on 22 November. Never before had a pop LP been released, not to cash in on a Top Ten single but on the strength of its overall content. Advance orders alone totalled 250,000 copies – more than for Elvis Presley's biggest-selling album, *Blue Hawaii*.

By far the most striking thing about *With the Beatles* was its cover. Brian had for months been showing his proof copy to friends and asking anxiously what they thought. Gone was the look of the *Please Please Me* album – the cheap, cheeky faces, looking down from high-rise flats. A top London fashion photographer, Robert Freeman, had shot the Beatles, heads and shoulders only, in black and white. Faces halved by shadow, hemmed in by their fringes and high polo necks, they could have been a quartet of young actors or art students. It was the same technique Astrid had used to photograph Stu Sutcliffe three years before in Hamburg, in her black and silver room.

A week later came their fifth single, 'I Want to Hold Your Hand', which advance orders of one million copies placed instantly at number one. The pre-Christmas air seemed to transmit little other than that loping, handclapping beat. The album, meanwhile, had its independent existence in the stunning combination of Lennon–McCartney songs like 'All My Loving' and 'It Won't Be Long', with Chuck Berry's 'Roll Over Beethoven', Berry Gordy's 'Money', and other r & b songs so little known to the general pop audience, it was thought the Beatles must have written those also. 'Disker's' sleeve notes put the matter in perspective.

Never again would pop music be considered the prerogative only of working-class boys and girls. *With the Beatles* was played not only in council houses but in West London flats, in young ladies' finishing schools and in the blow-heated barns where country squires' daughters held their Christmas dances.

•

On 5 November, the day after the Royal Command show, Brian Epstein flew to New York, accompanied by Billy J. Kramer, that handsome but awkward young man. Landing at the airport still called Idelwilde, they drove in a yellow cab towards the magic skyline which reveals itself at first in miniature like the crest on a souvenir ash tray. Brian, on the drive, was full of what Broadway plays they would see in between his several very important business meetings. These meetings, Billy J. gathered, were the merest preliminary to the Beatles' instant subjugation of the North American continent. Even if Brian himself ever believed this, he ceased to do so as the cab entered Manhattan and the streets became sheer glass on every side.

America up to now had regarded the Beatles as it regarded every British pop performer – an inferior substitute for a product which, having been invented in America, could only be manufactured and marketed by Americans. The view was reinforced by the half-century in which American artists, through every musical epoch, had dominated the English market as against only one or two freakish incursions by English acts travelling the other way. In the same fashion now, American pop music dwarfed its English counterparts in size and wealth, in the complexity of its chart systems and the corollary role of hundreds of independent radio stations. Even so big a British name as Cliff Richard had attempted only one American tour, half-way down the bill, amid deafening indifference. The British, it was agreed in the boardrooms of Manhattan, should stick to the things they knew best, like whisky, woollen sweaters and Shakespeare.

America in late 1963 had already ordained the new direction of teenage music. Three brothers from California, Brian, Carl and Dennis Wilson, and their cousin Mike Love, known collectively as the Beach Boys, were already internationally famous for their close-harmony songs hymning the West Coast pleasures of surf-riding, drag racing and crewcut, freckled sex. That 'surfing' sound, like previous pop styles, reflected a nation still jingoistically confident in the perfection of all its values; whose new young President, John F. Kennedy, had precisely the same sun-healthy, college-fresh appeal.

George Martin had found the anti-British barrier impossible to penetrate, even though, thanks to Sir Joseph Lockwood's entrepreneurial drive, EMI owned the American Capitol label. When 'Please Please Me' went to number one in Britain, Martin had immediately sent it to Jay Livingstone, Capitol's boss in New York. Back from Livingstone came the reply, 'We don't think the Beatles will do anything in this market.'

Martin, to his great annoyance, was therefore obliged to hawk 'Please Please Me' around other American labels in direct competition with Parlophone's own parent company. It was finally accepted by Vee Jay, a small Chicago-based firm. Released by Vee Jay in February, 'Please Please Me' had instantly vanished without trace. The same happened in May with 'From Me to You'. Martin offered it to Capitol, who gruffly refused it; issued by Vee Jay, it rose no higher than 116th in *Billboard* magazine's chart.

In August, when 'She Loves You' began its eight-week blockade of the British charts, Martin appealed for the third time to Jay Livingstone, and was again told that in Capitol's opinion the Beatles had no prospects in America. Instead, 'She Loves You' was issued by a small New York label, Swan. The sound engulfing the British Isles did not even penetrate the *Billboard* Hot 100.

One American entrepreneur at least – a tubby, sentimental New York agent named Sid Bernstein – disagreed with Capitol's prognosis. Bernstein worked for the General Artists Corporation, America's largest theatrical agency, but, having a thirst for culture, spent his leisure time attending an evening course on the subject of 'Civilisation'. 'Our teacher had told us to study the British way of life as a great democracy comparable with our own. He said the best way to study England was to read the British newspapers. That was how I first heard about what the Beatles were doing over in Europe.'

Quite early in 1963, Bernstein says, he was telling his superiors at GAC that the mania he had read about in the British press could happen in New York City. 'I could see what they were, and that they were going to be monsters here. I wanted them.'

Brian arrived in New York, unaware that Sid Bernstein had been trying for several weeks to contact him by transatlantic phone. 'I couldn't sell the idea to anyone at GAC,' Bernstein says, 'so I decided to make it my own independent promotion. I had already booked Carnegie Hall, the most famous auditorium in New York. You couldn't get Carnegie Hall unless you made the reservation months ahead. I chose 12 February 1964 – Lincoln's birthday. The lady I dealt with at Carnegie Hall had a thick Polish accent. "The Beatles?" she said, 'Vat are they?' I knew that Carnegie Hall would never allow a pop concert to happen in its famous auditorium. I said, "They're a phenomenon." "Oh, a *phenomenon*," she said, thinking that was maybe a type of string quartet.'

Brian had only one friend in New York. Geoffrey Ellis, the Liverpool estate agent's son, was still working there for the Royal Insurance Society. Geoffrey had not seen Brian since he was home on holiday in 1962 and Mrs Epstein confided to him that the family were 'letting Brian get this group thing out of his system'. Geoffrey was astonished to see what a *real* impresario Brian had made himself; how earnestly he dissuaded Billy J. Kramer from buying a cheap shirt, 'because it's not your *image*, Billy'.

Dick James, the music publisher, had recommended him to Walter Hofer, an attorney who already acted for James's company in New York. Hofer, hospitable and an Anglophile, at once invited Brian up to his office on West 57th Street. 'From the beginning he was full of questions,' Hofer remembered. 'How did American TV work? How did the radio stations work? While he was in town, I gave a cocktail party for him, which was a disaster. No one had ever heard of Brian Epstein. No one came but a few people from Liberty Records, because Billy J. Kramer was signing with them.'

Similarly, no one at Capitol Records Inc. recognised the severely dapper young Englishman who came in to see their Director of Eastern Operations, Brown Meggs. Brian had called in person to try to persuade Capitol to give the Beatles an American release. With him he had a demo of the song which John and Paul, working in the basement of Jane Asher's house, had striven to invest with 'a sort of American spiritual sound'. And, indeed, to Capitol's hypersensitive ears, the song did have something which three consecutive British number ones had lacked. Brown Meggs, after much corporate deliberation, agreed that Capitol would release 'I Want To Hold Your Hand'. Even so, it was made clear to Brian, the company did not expect a great response. The release date was 13 January 1964.

Brian's other appointment was to meet a little sharkskin-suited, elderly man with heavy jowls, a gruff voice and an air of misanthropy often detectable in those renowned as talent spotters and arbiters of the public taste. At the Delmonico Hotel, Brian Epstein, for the second time, found himself face to face with the great Ed Sullivan.

For 20 years, Sullivan's CBS television show had been famous for breaking new entertainers, not in New York only but across the whole American continent via hundreds of local stations served by the CBS network. Sullivan, a former sports journalist, combined an uncanny instinct for the sensational with an air of bewilderment that his fellow Americans could find such things remotely entertaining. It was Sullivan who had booked Elvis Presley to sing 'Houn' Dog' on condition that the cameras showed him only from the waist up. Sullivan's introduction then was simply a shrug and the words: 'America, judge for yourselves.'

Ed Sullivan had been aware of the Beatles since his recent talent-spotting trip to Europe, when he and Mrs Sullivan were among many travellers at Heathrow airport inconvenienced by their homecoming from Sweden. He had asked to meet them, and been sufficiently impressed to offer Brian a tentative booking on his show early in 1964.

Sullivan's idea at that stage was to use the Beatles as a minor novelty item in a show constructed around some established American entertainer. Brian, however, insisted they should receive top billing. The Sullivan show's producer, Bob Precht – who happened also to be Ed Sullivan's son-in-law – remembers how surprised both he and the great man were by this unforeseen tactic. Top billing was conceded against a deal otherwise far from munificent. 'I said that if we were going to pay the Beatles' air fares out here,' Precht says, 'we ought to get more than one appearance out of them.' It was agreed that the Beatles should appear in two Ed Sullivan shows, on February 9 and 16, and should record more songs to be used in a subsequent transmission. The fee for each appearance would be $3,500, plus $3,000 more for the taping. 'Even for an unknown act,' Bob Precht admits, 'that was about the least we could pay.'

If America had not fallen, it was at least prepared to listen. Brian had that much to comfort him when, a day or two afterwards, he and Billy J. Kramer flew back to London. He had persuaded Capitol. He had persuaded Ed Sullivan. Short of the fatigue, the phoning back, the waiting and the compromise, these would seem dazzling achievements. And halfway over the Atlantic, as he read the British papers, Beatlemania grew audible again.

America, if Brian had only known it, was already his – was moving nearer his unconscious grasp as, far away in Texas, the mechanism of a high velocity rifle was cleaned and checked, and a vantage-point selected. America fell to him on the morning in Dallas that the presidential motorcade set off on its route, supremely confident and open to the sunshine, and the kerbside ciné-enthusiast turned his camera towards the limousine which carried a young man's unprotected head. This was 22 November, the day the Beatles' second album went on sale in Britain. Late that afternoon, the news began to come through which, for every English person, hardly less than every American, would fix in the memory for ever the exact time, place and circumstances of hearing it.

•

For their winter tour, through the deepening blizzards of national dementia, Brian entrusted the Beatles to his friend Brian Sommerville, the ex-Naval officer turned Fleet Street journalist. Tony Barrow, NEMS' original Press Officer, now had more work than he could handle alone. It was therefore fixed that Barrow should represent Gerry, Billy J. Kramer,

Cilla and the Fourmost while Sommerville – or rather, Sommerville's one-man PR company – acted exclusively for the Beatles. Small, plump, already balding, he had the aspect of a country squire and a quarterdeck brusqueness which did not at once endear him to his new charges.

The tour was the most arduous one yet – six weeks of one-night concerts at Gaumont, ABC or Odeon cinemas in a zigzag course from Cambridge to Sunderland. At the same time, they were rehearsing their pantomime sketches for a special NEMS Christmas show in London, at the Finsbury Park Astoria. In Liverpool in one 24-hour period, as well as their two evening concerts, they taped appearances for two television shows and performed for a convention of the Beatles Northern Area Fan Club. John and Paul were also working on a dozen new songs for the film that Walter Shenson wanted to shoot the following spring.

In university city or Midland industrial town, the procedure was invariable. Mal Evans went in first, driving the van with their equipment through the blue avenues of waiting police. At dusk, by vainly circuitous routes, would come the Austin Princess limousine containing the Beatles, Neil Aspinall and Brian Sommerville. They would go straight to the theatre, remaining in the dressing-room until the performance while Neil brought in food or pressed their stage clothes and Sommerville stood guard testily outside. As soon as the curtain fell, Sommerville would shoo them, in their damp suits, out through the police ranks to their beleaguered car. By midnight, they would be trapped inside some provincial hotel which, more often than not, would have stopped serving dinner at 9 p.m. On many nights, all they could get to eat were dishes of cornflakes.

In Lincoln, Ringo developed earache and had to be rushed to hospital, disguised in an overcoat, hat and spectacles which, as one reporter noted, 'made him look like Brecht being smuggled out of Germany'. Near Doncaster, their car ran out of petrol and they had to thumb a lift in a lorry. In Sunderland, they escaped from the theatre by running into the adjacent fire station, sliding down the firemen's pole and escaping in a police car while one of the engines rushed out to create a diversion.

In Liverpool, the Empire theatre had been commandeered by the BBC for a special edition of *Juke Box Jury* featuring all four Beatles as panellists. Disgruntled technicians, faced with this unprecedented journey outside London, were heard muttering that BBC must stand for 'Beatle Broadcasting Corporation'. Before the show, the Beatles mischievously rearranged their name cards so that George Harrison sat behind the one reading 'John Lennon'. As panellists, they were not only far funnier and livelier than the usual ageing disc jockeys and empty-headed starlets; they also displayed a depth of musical knowledge seldom, if ever, heard on that show before. When the Swinging Blue Jeans' version of their old

Cavern show-stopper 'Hippy-Hippy Shake' was played, George remarked what a big fan he was of the song's composer, Chan Romero. At that time, the only 'Chan' most teenage record-buyers had ever heard of was Charlie.

The advantage of Brian Sommerville as publicist was that he spoke in an upper-class voice, in a tone to which policemen, commissionaires and other potential obstacles almost all automatically responded. The Beatles, hemmed in as tightly by authority figures as by screaming fans, recognised the need for someone, like Sommerville, peppery and abrasive. 'I had a good relationship with John; he called me "old baldy-something-or-other". Paul and I got on well enough, though I always found him rather two-faced. Ringo was just Ringo. I did have one serious fight with George. He never regarded me with anything but muffled dislike.'

Throughout the tour, Sommerville was left totally in charge, to screen the press seeking interviews, sign the hotel bills and negotiate strategy with theatre managers and the police. Brian would appear at irregular intervals, in his overcoat and polka-dotted scarf. 'He'd float into the dressing-room, usually with a piece of paper for them to sign,' Sommerville says. 'But if there was any trouble, you could count on Brian to be miles away. He had this wonderful knack of being able to disappear during a crisis.'

Backstage rows were frequent between Brian and Sommerville. It irked Brian to see anyone close to the Beatles but himself. He even suspected Sommerville of trying to usurp his own growing fame as their mentor and mouthpiece. 'Brian already saw himself as a star in his own right,' Sommerville says. '*He* wanted to do the things they did, like appearing on *Juke Box Jury*. He was hurt because he hadn't been asked to chair the special Mersey edition of *Thank Your Lucky Stars*. The worst rows we had were after I'd made some comment, and the press quoted me instead of Brian. "You had no right to do that!" he'd say.'

And yet, at times, Brian would seem unable to pluck up courage to go into the Beatles' dressing-room, but would stand out in the auditorium, suddenly as distant from them as the furthest screaming girl. 'I saw him once,' Sommerville says, 'in one of those northern ABCs, when the curtains opened and the scream went up. He was standing there with tears streaming down his face.'

•

It had become clear at an early stage, to various sharp-eyed people, that the Beatles were capable of selling far more than gramophone records by the million. Beatlemania demonstrated as never before to what extent young people in Britain were a 'market', gigantic and ripe for exploitation.

From October 1963 onward, Brian Epstein carried in his wake a little trail of businessmen, coaxing, cajoling, sometimes begging to be authorised to produce goods in the Beatles' image.

Merchandising as a concept was largely unknown in mid-twentieth-century Britain, even though the Victorians had been adept at it. Walt Disney, that peerless weaver of dreams into plastic, was imitated on a small scale by British toy manufacturers, producing replicas of television puppets. Pop singers until now had lasted too short a time in public esteem to sell any but the most ephemeral goods.

No precedent existed, therefore, to warn Brian that there were billions at stake. He saw the merchandising purely as public relations – a way to increase audience goodwill and keep the fan club happy. He worried about the fan club and keeping it happy.

The first Beatles products catered simply for the desire, as strong in girls as in boys, to impersonate their idols. In Bethnal Green, East London, a factory was producing Beatles wigs at the rate of several thousand each week. The hairstyle which Astrid's scissors had shaped for Stu Sutcliffe became a best-selling novelty, a black, fibrous mop, hovering just outside seriousness, 30s (£1.50) apiece. A Midlands clothing firm marketed collarless corduroy 'Beatles jackets' like the one Astrid had made for Stu; the one which the Beatles at the time despised as 'Mum's jacket'. Girls, too, wore the jackets, the tab-collar shirts, even the elastic-sided, Cuban heel 'Beatles boots', obtainable by mail order at '75s 11d (£3.80), including post and packing'.

Christmas 1963 signalled a fresh avalanche of Beatles products into the shops. There were Beatles guitars, of plastic, authentically 'autographed', and miniature Beatles drums. There were Beatles lockets, each with a tiny quadruple photograph compressed inside. There were red and blue Beatles kitchen aprons, bespeckled with guitar-playing bugs. The four faces and four signatures, engraved, printed or transferred, however indistinctly, appeared on belts, badges, handkerchieves, jigsaw puzzles, rubber airbeds, disc racks, bedspreads, 'ottomans', shoulder bags, pencils, buttons and trays. There was a brand of confectionery known as 'Ringo Roll', and of Beatles chewing gum, each sixpenny packet warranted to contain *seven* photographs. A northern bakery chain announced guitar-shaped 'Beatles cakes' ('Party priced at 5s') and fivepenny individual Beatles 'fancies'.

Brian, in the beginning, personally examined the products of each prospective licensee. In no case, he ruled, would the Beatles directly endorse any article. Nor would they lend their name to anything distasteful, inappropriate or overtly exploitive of their fans. And, indeed, parents who had scolded their children for buying trash were frequently surprised by the goods' quality and value. The Beatles jacket was smart, durable and well-lined. The 'official' Beatles sweater ('Designed for Beatles people by a leading British manufacturer') was 100 per cent botany wool, hardly extortionate at 35s (£1.75).

Soon, however, unauthorised Beatles goods began to appear. Though NEMS Enterprises held copyright on the name 'Beatles', infringement could be avoided simply by spelling it 'Beetles'. The vaguest representation of insects, of guitars or little mop-headed men, had the power to sell anything, however cheap, however nasty. Even to spot the culprits, let alone bring lawsuits against them, meant a countrywide invigilation such as no British copyright-holder had ever been obliged to undertake. NEMS Enterprises certainly could not undertake it. And so, after one or two minor prosecutions, the pirates settled down, unhampered, to their bonanza.

By late 1963, the merchandising had got into a tangle which Brian had not the time nor the will to contemplate. He therefore handed the whole matter over to his solicitor, David Jacobs. It became Jacobs's job, not only to prosecute infringements, where visible, but also, at his independent discretion, to issue new manufacturing licences. Prospective licensees were referred from NEMS Enterprises to Jacobs's offices in Pall Mall. Since Jacobs, too, was deeply preoccupied with social as well as legal matters, the task of appraising designs, production strategy and probable income was delegated to the chief clerk in his chambers, Edward Marke.

Among the other cases currently being handled by M. A. Jacobs Ltd were several claims for damages by the relatives of passengers lost aboard a cruise ship, the *Lakonia*. The waiting-room where these bereaved litigants sat also served as a dumping ground for cascades of Beatles guitars, plastic windmills and crayoning sets. Mr Marke, though a conscientious legal functionary, knew little of the manufacturing business. So David Jacobs, in his turn, looked round for someone to take on this tiresome business of making millions.

His choice was Nicky Byrne, a man he had met at one of the numerous cocktail parties he attended. Byrne, indeed, was rather a celebrated figure at parties, of which he himself gave a great many at his fashionable Chelsea garage-cum-flat. Small, impishly-dapper, formidably persuasive, he had been variously a country squire's son, a Horse Guard trooper and an amateur racing driver. His true avocation, however, was membership of the 'Chelsea Set', the sub-culture of debutantes, bohemians, heiresses and charming cads which, since the mid-Fifties, had flourished along and around the King's Road.

Nicky Byrne was not a totally implausible choice, having in his extremely varied life touched the worlds of show business and popular retailing. In the Fifties, he had run the Condor Club, in Soho, where

Tommy Steele was discovered. His wife, Kiki – from whom he had recently parted – was a well-known fashion designer with her own successful Chelsea boutique.

The offer from Jacobs was that Byrne should administer the Beatles' merchandising operation in Europe and throughout the world. He was not, he maintains, very eager to accept. 'Brian Epstein had a very bad name in the business world at that time. Nobody knew who was licensed to make Beatles goods and who wasn't. I got in touch with Kiki, my ex-wife, to see what she thought about it. I mentioned this company firm in Soho that was meant to be turning out Beatles gear. Kiki said, "Hold on a minute." She'd had a letter from a firm in the Midlands, asking her to design exactly the same thing for them.'

Nicky Byrne was eventually persuaded. He agreed to form a company named Stramsact to take over the assigning of Beatles merchandise rights. A subsidiary called Seltaeb – Beatles spelt backwards – would handle American rights, if any, when the Beatles went to New York in February to appear on the *Ed Sullivan Show*.

Five partners, all much younger than Nicky Byrne, constituted both Stramsact and Seltaeb. One of them, 26-year-old John Fenton, had already been doing some merchandising deals of his own via David Jacobs. Two others, Mark Warman and Simon Miller-Munday, aged 20 and 22 respectively, were simply friends of Nicky's who had been nice to him during his break-up with Kiki.

Nicky Byrne's most picturesque recruit, after himself, was 23-year-old Lord Peregrine Eliot, heir to the Earl of St Germans and owner of a 6,000-acre estate in Cornwall. Lord Peregrine's qualification was that he had shared a flat with Simon Miller-Munday. Although extremely rich, he was eager to earn funds to recarpet his ancestral home, Port Eliot. For £1,000 cash, His Lordship received 20 per cent of the company.

Only Malcolm Evans, the sixth partner, a junior studio manager with Rediffusion TV, had any definite professional ability of any kind. Evans had met the others at a Nicky Byrne party, the high spot of which was the pushing of a grand piano through the Chelsea streets. 'Nicky had got the entire Count Basie Orchestra to play at his party,' Evans says. 'I remember that they were accompanied on the bagpipes by a full-dress pipe major from the barracks over the road.'

The contract between Stramsact-Seltaeb and NEMS Enterprises was left to Jacobs to draw up, approve, even sign on Brian's and the Beatles' behalf. 'I was at my solicitor's, just round the corner,' Nicky Byrne says. 'He told me, "Write in what percentage you think you should take on the deal." So I put down the first figure that came into my head – 90 per cent.

'To my amazement, David Jacobs didn't even question it. He didn't think of it as 90 per cent to us, but as 10 per cent to the Beatles. He said, "Well, 10 per cent is better than nothing."'

•

Christmas, far from diverting the mania, actually seemed to increase it. The Beatles *became* Christmas in their fancy dress, playing in the NEMS Christmas Show at Finsbury Park Astoria. One of the sketches was a Victorian melodrama in which George, as 'heroine', was tied on a railway line by 'Sir Jasper' (John) and rescued by 'Fearless Paul the Signalman'. They had acted such plays and farces for years among themselves. Mal Evans, their second road manager, stood by, laughing, as all did, at the good-humoured knockabout fun; Mal had just received a savage tongue-lashing from John for having lost his 12-string 'Jumbo' guitar.

Beatles records made the December Top Twenty literally impassable. As well as 'I Want to Hold Your Hand' at number one, it contained six songs from the *With the Beatles* LP – indeed, the album itself, with almost a million copies sold, qualified for entrance to the *singles* chart at number fourteen; the customary seasonal gimmick record was Dora Bryan's 'All I Want for Christmas is a Beatle'.

Two anxiously awaited messages, that Christmas, went out to the British nation. The first came from Queen Elizabeth, speaking on television from Balmoral Castle. The second came from four young men, unknown a year ago, speaking to their 80,000 Fan Club members in a babble of excited voices. They sang 'Good King Wenceslas' and wished their subjects 'a very happy Chrimble and a gear Near Year'.

'An examination of the heart of the nation at this moment,' the London *Evening Standard* said, 'would find the name "Beatles" upon it.' Under the heading 'Why Do We Love Them So Much?' columnist Angus McGill said it was because 'like well-bred children they are seen and not heard'. Maureen Cleave, in another article, could only conclude that 'everybody loves them because they look so happy'.

In marketing terms, the figures they represented were still barely believable. 'She Loves You' had sold 1.3 million copies; 'I Want to Hold Your Hand' had sold 1.25 million. They had transformed the British music industry from complacent torpor to neurotic – though still unavailing – competitiveness. A tiny record label called Parlophone, once noted for Scottish dance bands, towered over the frantic A & R men with a run of success, unequalled to this day. For 37 weeks out of the past 52, George Martin had had a record at number one. He was currently reading a memo from his EMI superiors explaining that he would not this year qualify for the staff Christmas bonus.

Pop music was legitimised – and not only socially. At the end of December, a ballet, *Mods and Rockers*, was scored with Lennon and McCartney music. *The Times* published an article by its classical music critic, William Mann, who pronounced John and Paul to be 'the outstanding English composers of 1963' for qualities of which they were probably unconscious. In their slow ballad 'This Boy', Mann detected 'chains of pandiatonic clusters', and in 'Not a Second Time', 'an Aeolian cadence – the chord progression which ends Mahler's "Song of the Earth"'. He further noticed their 'autocratic but not by any means ungrammatical attitude to tonality . . . the quasi-instrumental vocal duetting . . . the melismas with altered vowels . . .' That one article raised for all time the mental portcullis between 'classical' and 'pop'; it also ushered in decades of sillier prose.

No Englishman, however cantankerous, could any longer profess ignorance on the subject. Not even Field Marshal Lord Montgomery, hero of El Alamein, who, speaking from the garden where he still kept Rommel's desert caravan, threatened to invite the Beatles for the weekend 'to see what kind of fellows they are'.

•

1964 began on a note of post-Christmas acidity. In the Top Twenty, 'I Want to Hold Your Hand' yielded its number one position to a non-Lennon–McCartney song, 'Glad All Over', by the Dave Clark Five. Since the Five all came from the same north London suburb, they were greeted as harbingers of a 'Tottenham Sound'; they had 'crushed' the Beatles, several front-page headlines said. The *Daily Mail* published a cartoon in which a group of girls contemptuously regarded one of their number. 'She must be really old,' the caption ran, 'she remembers the Beatles.'

As a prelude to America, they were to visit Paris. Brian had booked them a three-week engagement at the Olympia theatre, beginning on 15 January. The crowd which massed at Heathrow to see them off descried only three Beatles being herded out to the aircraft. Ringo Starr, the newspapers said, was 'fogbound' in Liverpool. Ringo, in fact, most unusually, was having a fit of temperament and had declared he wasn't fookin' coming. Across the Channel, further large and small hitches waited.

The Olympia, a wholly Parisian cross between cinema and music hall, was operated by a wily French promoter named Bruno Coquatrix. For three weeks of nightly Beatles shows, Coquatrix was paying Brian Epstein a fee which did not cover their travel and hotel expenses – particularly since Brian, with typical expansiveness, had booked the entire entourage into the expensive George V hotel. To offset the loss, Brian Sommerville did a publicity deal with British European Airways. The Beatles were issued with special inflight bags lettered BEAtles. For carrying and prominently displaying these, they and their guardians received three weeks' unlimited air travel between London and Paris.

Brian justified the low fee, once more, against the publicity value. France, until now, had remained noticeably indifferent to Beatlemania. He was determined that the Beatles should conquer Paris, and that Paris should be in no doubt concerning who had engineered that conquest. Before the journey, he asked Dezo Hoffman the photographer to print up 500 giveaway pictures of himself. Hoffman persuaded him this was not a good idea.

A vast contingent of British journalists went to Paris to cover the event. This time, the *Daily Express* led the field, having signed up George Harrison to 'write' a daily column. The writing was actually to be done by Derek Taylor, a Hoylake-born *Express* reporter, formerly the paper's northern dramatic critic. This cultural background, no less than his Italianate good looks, recommended Taylor to Brian for what was a deliberate attempt to give George a share of the limelight. 'It will be *nice* for George,' Brian told him. 'John and Paul have their songwriting and Ringo is – ah – rather new.'

The George V's foyer thronged with expectant photographers, hungrily noting the comings and goings of various important stakeholders in the quartet. George Martin, their record producer, had flown over to supervise a German language recording of 'She Loves You'. Dr Strach, their accountant, was there; so was Walter Shenson, their prospective film producer, accompanied by Alun Owen, a Liverpool playwright whom the Beatles themselves had requested as scriptwriter. Nicky Byrne, of the Stramsact company, was there to arrange large deals, so he expected, for Beatles merchandise in France and throughout Europe.

As well as variety acts such as jugglers and acrobats, the Beatles shared the Olympia bill with two singers whose French following greatly exceeded theirs. One was Sylvie Vartin, France's own turbulent pop *chanteuse*. The other, Trini Lopez, was an American with a huge Continental chart success called 'Lemon Tree'.

Lopez's manager, Norman Weiss, instantly sought out Brian at the George V. Weiss worked with the American General Artists Corporation, whose former associate, Sid Bernstein, had already booked Carnegie Hall in New York in the hope of being able to present the Beatles there. February 12, the date of Bernstein's booking, was only three days after their first *Ed Sullivan Show*. Weiss, therefore, concluded the deal at last on Sid Bernstein's behalf. Brian agreed that the Beatles would give two concerts at Carnegie Hall, each for a flat fee of $3,500.

They themselves were very different now from the four boys in George Martin's studio, earnestly doing everything their producer told them. Martin, waiting at EMI's Paris studio to supervise their German language recording of 'She Loves You' ('Sie Liebt Dich'), was coolly informed by telephone that the Beatles had decided not to come. He stormed over to the George V, to find them lounging round their suite while Paul's girl friend, Jane Asher, poured out tea. Such was Martin's schoolmasterly wrath that all four scattered in terror to hide under cushions and behind the piano.

On the eve of their first concert, while the French and English press jostled for position outside, John and Paul slept until 3 p.m. Dezo Hoffman in the end accepted the hazardous job of waking them. 'I told John, "*Paris-Match* is waiting. They want to do a cover story." "*Paris-Match*?" John said. "Are they as important as the *Musical Express*?"'

Emerging into the Champs Elysées in a circle of retreating lenses, they found Paris rather less than ecstatic at their arrival. According to Hoffman, very few passers-by even recognised them. The British press made a valiant attempt to stimulate Beatlemania, posing John and Paul at a pavement cafe and hedging them in among waiters and reporters. Vincent Mulchrone remarked on the prevailing apathy in his dispatch to the *Daily Mail*. 'Beatlemania is still, like Britain's entry into the Common Market, a problem the French prefer to put off for a while.'

Backstage at the Olympia the following night, naked violence broke out after the French press had had the Beatles' dressing-room door slammed in their faces. French photographers, especially those who have served in theatres of war like Algeria and Indochina, are not so easily discouraged. A fierce scuffle followed in which Brian Sommerville received a rabbit punch and Brian – who tried to interpose himself with outstretched arms and a querulous, 'No – not *my* boys!' – was shoved backwards by a burly French pressman who was simultaneously treading on his toes.

The show ran late, as French shows invariably do, and the Beatles did not go on stage until well after midnight. Trini Lopez, who had closed the first half hours before, seemed much more like top of the bill. To add to their unease, a glimpse through the curtains showed the audience to be almost entirely male. 'Where's all the bloody chicks then?' they kept asking in agitation.

During the performance, their usually reliable Vox amplifiers broke down three times. George, enraged by his fading guitar, began to complain openly of sabotage. Neither John nor Paul made any attempt to speak French, and the audience, for its part, evinced boredom towards Lennon–McCartney songs. All they seemed to want were rock and roll numbers like 'Twist and Shout', which they greeted with cries of '*un autre, un autre*'. At one point, a strange chant became audible. 'Ring-o', it sounded like. 'Ring-o, Ring-o.'

The reviews, next morning, were tepid. *France-Soir* called them *zazous* (delinquents) and *vedettes démodées* (has-beens). According to Nicky Byrne, the effect on merchandising prospects throughout Europe was swift and disastrous. Galeries Lafayette the department store decided, after all, not to fill an entire window with Beatles goods. Nor did Lambretta, the Italian motor scooter corporation, proceed with its plan to market a special model with a Beatles wig for a saddle.

The barbs of *France-Soir*, in common with everything French, had ceased to matter to the *zazous* and their entourage several hours earlier. Dezo Hoffman, eating dinner at a small restaurant with Derek Taylor, received an urgent summons back to the George V. Both returned, to find the Beatles' suite in a state of eerie quiet.

'Brian was there as well,' Hoffman says. 'He was sitting on a chair and the Beatles were sitting on the floor around him. He said the news had come through that "I Want to Hold Your Hand" was number one in the American Top Hundred. The Beatles couldn't even speak – not even John Lennon. They just sat on the floor like kittens at Brian's feet.'

12

'They've got everything over there. What do they want *us* for?'

Early on 7 February 1964, when the New York streets were still empty but for snow and steam and fast-bouncing cabs, a disc jockey on station WMCA sounded the first note of impending madness. 'It is now 6.30 a.m., Beatle time. They left London 30 minutes ago. They're out over the Atlantic Ocean, headed for New York. The temperature is 32 Beatle degrees.'

•

America's interest, until the eleventh hour, had remained no more than cursory. The American press is at the best of times notoriously parochial; and these were the worst of times. Since 22 November, there had been only one newspaper story in America; only one picture, on an amateur's ciné film, endlessly replayed up to that same frozen frame. A young man, next to his wife in an open car, slumped sideways as the bullets tore into him.

Just before a Christmas holiday which very few Americans felt disposed to celebrate, Walter Hofer, the New York attorney, sat in his office on West 57th Street. Hofer, like many New Yorkers, had the habit of perpetual work. It was one way, at least, to shut out the dull, slow, directionless feeling that, since President John Kennedy's assassination in Dallas, had shrouded Manhattan like a fog.

'Out of the blue, I got this call from Capitol Records. They wanted to know, was it right that I acted in New York for a British company called NEMS Enterprises? I told them, yes I did. They said they were trying to find out who controlled the publishing on a song called "I Want to Hold Your Hand" by this British group, the Beatles.'

Capitol, prepared to release that unknown British group's record into the sluggish post-Christmas market, had received some puzzling news from out of town. A disc jockey in Washington DC, working on station WWDC, had somehow obtained a copy of 'I Want to Hold Your Hand', and was playing it on the air amid a commotion of interest from his listeners. The record had come not from Capitol but direct from London via the disc jockey's girl friend, who was a stewardess with British Overseas Airways.

'Capitol wanted to get clearance on the publishing side, to be able to ship a few hundred copies into the Washington area,' Walter Hofer remembered. 'In fact, I had to tell them that the publishing rights had been sold to another company, MCA. Sold for almost nothing, it so happened, just to give the song any foothold that was possible over here.'

While Capitol tried to resolve this trifling matter, a second, identical commotion was reported, from Chicago. A radio station was being besieged by enquiries after playing a song called 'I Want to Hold Your Hand' by this British group, the Beatles. Apparently it had been sent on tape from a friend of the disc jockey's at WWDC, Washington. From Chicago, by the same fraternal taping process, it moved west again, to St Louis.

In New York, as the pavement Santas pessimistically clanged their bells, a drastic change was ordered in the marketing strategy of Capitol Records. A week earlier, Brown Meggs and his colleagues had been uneasy about a prospective pressing for 'I Want to Hold Your Hand' of 200,000 copies. Now three entire production plants – Capitol's own and that of CBS and RCA – were alerted to work through Christmas and New Year to press one million copies.

•

By the time the news reached Brian Epstein in Paris, sales were closer to 1.5 million. The night disappeared, after speech had returned, in a wild spree of drinking and piggyback-riding and a restaurant party, joined by George Martin and his wife-to-be Judy Lockhart-Smith, when Brian so far forgot himself as to sit and be photographed with a chamberpot on his head.

Next morning, the American press were there en masse. *Life* magazine's London bureau chief, having planned to slip over to Paris merely for lunch, found himself, to his dismay, assigned to write the week's cover story. Equivalent responsibilities had suddenly devolved on representatives of CBS, Associated Press, the *New York Times* and *Washington Post.* The Beatles, roused from sleep at 1 p.m., were brought in to meet the first deputation, still in their dressing-gowns.

The deputation, crop-haired and collegiate-looking as all good American media types ought to be, saw at once what element in the story their readers would find of consuming but abhorrent fascination.

The *New York Times* tried to put it tactfully.

'Who does your hair while you're in Paris?'

'Nobody does it when we're in *London*.'

'But where did those hair-do's . . .'

'You mean hair-don'ts,' John said.

'We were coming out of a swimming bath in Liverpool,' George said, amid earnest note-taking, 'and we liked the way it looked.' So the story went out on the AP and UPI agency wires.

The most celebrated journalistic visitor was Sheilah Graham, F. Scott Fitzgerald's last love and one of America's most widely syndicated columnists. She waited an hour and a half while the Beatles underwent medical examinations for their forthcoming film.

At length, only George put his serious face around the door. 'Why – hello, dear,' Miss Graham said, rising. 'Now tell me quickly – which one are you?'

•

Nicky Byrne and his Seltaeb partners were already in New York. They had gone ahead of the Beatles to set up merchandising deals according to the 90–10 per cent contract in their favour. Nicky Byrne wore an overcoat with an astrakhan collar. Lord Peregrine Eliot wore a scruffy leather jacket belying his ancestral home with its 130 chimney stacks.

New York by this time, late in January, made only one kind of sound. Every radio station every few seconds played a Beatles record. Capitol had now also released the *With the Beatles* LP – renamed *Meet the Beatles* – and, to their blank astonishment, had seen it go instantly to the top of the album charts.

Nicky Byrne and his Seltaeb young men took accommodation at the elegant Drake Hotel and offices on Fifth Avenue. Within hours, they were besieged by manufacturers seeking a part in what the American business world already recognised as the biggest marketing opportunity since Walt Disney had created Mickey Mouse.

The procedure was that Seltaeb, having satisfied themselves as to the suitable nature of the merchandise, issued a licence in exchange for a cash advance against 10 per cent manufacturing royalties. An early licensee, the Reliant Shirt Corporation, paid £25,000 upfront for exclusive rights to produce Beatles T-shirts in three factories they had bought for the purpose. Three days after the T-shirts went on sale, a million had been sold.

At Seltaeb's Fifth Avenue office, three or four presidents of major American corporations would obediently wait in line outside Nicky Byrne's door. With magnificent hauteur, Byrne refused to talk business with anyone below the rank of president. Not the least confusion among these urgent supplicants arose from the knowledge that one Seltaeb director they might deal with was an earl. Lord Peregrine Eliot, more than once, was buttonholed by an anxious, 'Say, listen Earl—'

Within a week of setting up in New York, Nicky Byrne received an offer of $½m for Seltaeb from Capitol Records. 'They were willing to pay the money straight into the Bahamas,' he remembers. '*And* they were willing to let us keep a half-interest in the company. But I turned them down. Part of the deal was that they were going to get me one of the top American merchandising men – a man who'd worked for Disney and who'd since retired. Then I found out that Capitol had no intention of persuading this man to work with us. I turned them down because they'd lied to me.

'Capitol wouldn't take no for an answer. They tried *everything* to get me to sell. They'd checked out my background and found out about my interest in motor racing. At our next meeting, when I said I still wouldn't sell, the Capitol man said, "Just take a look out of the window, Nicky." Down in the street, there was one of the most exclusive Ferraris ever made – the 29. Only one had come into America, to be driven by the North American Racing Team. This was it – it had mechanics standing beside it. "That's yours, Nicky," I was told, "if we can do this deal."

'I said, "But it's not as easy as that. I've got five partners." The Capitol man turned round and said, "Joe! Get five more of those." '

•

At Capitol Records, $50,000 was hastily allocated for a 'crash publicity program' leading up to the Beatles' arrival on 7 February. Five million posters and car windscreen stickers were printed with the cryptic message 'The Beatles Are Coming'. A four-page life story was circulated, with promotional records, to disc jockeys across the continent. Certain stations also received tapes of 'open-end' interviews, pre-recorded by the Beatles, with spaces left for the disc jockey's questions. Capitol executives, like so many repentant Scrooges, were photographed in Beatles wigs.

The *Ed Sullivan Show*, meanwhile, had received 50,000 applications for the 700-odd seats at its transmission on 9 February. CBS had a greater number even than for Elvis Presley's first appearance in 1957. There was similar massive demand for the Beatles' second appearance for Sullivan, a week later, in a special show broadcast from the Hotel Deauville, Miami. Not a seat remained for their first American concert, at the Washington Coliseum, nor for Sid Bernstein's two concerts at Carnegie Hall. Mrs Nelson Rockefeller was one of numerous celebrities whom Bernstein hoped to accommodate by putting extra seats on the stage.

And yet for all this brisk commercial activity, nothing had been done to connect the manifest excitement of American teenagers with the Beatles' physical presence on American soil. A film clip of them, shown on NBC's *Jack Paar Show*, brought confident predictions, notably from the *New York Times*, that, although the Beatles might be coming, Beatlemania definitely was not. 'For all Capitol and CBS cared,' Nicky Byrne says, 'they were just going to walk off the plane and go to their hotel. Nobody would even have known they were in America.'

Byrne, as a merchandiser of Beatles goods, had his own reasons for desiring something more. 'I kept ringing London to say, "Look here, Capitol are hopeless, nobody's doing *anything* in the way of publicity." I couldn't get hold of Brian Epstein at all. He'd completely disappeared. So had David Jacobs.'

As 7 February drew near, Nicky Byrne decided to take the initiative. He enlisted the help of a T-shirt manufacturer and of two New York radio stations, WMCA and WINS. 'Every 15 minutes, the same announcement was made over the air. A free T-shirt for every kid who went out to the airport to meet the Beatles.'

•

The objects of all this ferocious manoeuvring were seen off from Heathrow Airport by 1,000 banner-waving fans whose screams Cynthia Lennon mistook, in her innocence, for the noise of their waiting Pan Am jet. Cynthia was to accompany the party and, such was the momentousness of the occasion, even received permission to be photographed by the press corps which packed the VIP lounge. No departure from Britain had so mingled national acclamation and hope since Neville Chamberlain's flight to Munich in 1938.

The greater part of Pan Am flight 101 was occupied by the Beatles and their entourage. They themselves sat in the first-class cabin with Brian, Cynthia and a new friend, the American record producer Phil Spector. Certain favoured press friends also travelled first class, such as Maureen Cleave from the *Evening Standard*, and a *Liverpool Echo* journalist, coincidentally blessed with the name George Harrison. Harrison, when he retired from Fleet Street in the 1950s, had thought himself out of the 'rat race'. Now he found himself bound on the world's biggest assignment, with expenses, which, for the thrifty *Echo*, was equally phenomenal.

In the economy cabin sat Dezo Hoffman and the two road managers, Neil and Mal, already deep in their task of forging Beatle signatures on thousands of give-away photographs. Scattered among the other press, and eyeing each other just as balefully, was a contingent of British manufacturers with ideas for new lines in Beatles merchandise. Unable to contact Brian Epstein on the ground, they hoped he would prove more accessible at 30,000 feet. Notes were passed to Brian throughout the flight, and endorsed with a polite refusal.

The Beatles, though resolutely laughing and larking, all showed signs of terror at what lay ahead. None could be convinced they were any different from previous British entertainers who had taken on America, and lost. The example of Cliff Richard was frequently mentioned. George, on a visit to his elder sister in St Louis, had seen Cliff's film *Summer Holiday* relegated to a drive-in second feature. Nor did the work permits Brian had obtained make them feel very special. The H2 classification allowed them to play, within a strict two-week period, 'so long as unemployed American citizens capable of performing this work cannot be found'.

Paul McCartney strapped himself tightly into his safety belt, not unbuckling it throughout the whole flight. To Maureen Cleave and Phil Spector he confessed the same unease that George did to his namesake from the *Liverpool Echo*. 'He mentioned all the big American stars who'd come across to Britain,' Harrison says. 'He'd been across, unlike the others; he knew what the place was like. "They've got everything over there," he said. "What do they want *us* for?"'

America, at first, presented only the normal aerial view of coast and long piers and the snow-flecked scrubland up to the runway edge. Even after the wheels struck tarmac, no particular welcome was visible save in the earmuffed men who walked backwards, signalling with their small round bats. Then, as the terminal buildings came into view, the prospect dramatically changed. Five thousand people waited like a mural beyond the thick window glass. 'The Beatles had no idea it was for them,' Dezo Hoffman says. 'They thought the President must be going to land in a minute.'

The opening of the door let in a sound which made Heathrow and its cataclysms seem merely decorous. Not only were there more fans than the Beatles had ever seen before: they also made twice the noise. Screaming, they hung over balconies and retaining walls; screaming, they buckled against a 100-man police cordon, oblivious to peril or pain. Blended with the shriek was the shout of photographers, equally possessed, who approached the aircraft clinging to a hydraulic crane. As the Beatles, somnambulistically, began to descend the steps, a girl on the terminal's third outside level flung herself into space and hung there on the arms of two companions, crying: 'Here I am!' Near the bottom step stood the first intelligible New Yorker, a policeman. 'Boy,' he was heard to remark, 'can they use a haircut.'

Brian Sommerville, their Press Officer – who had arrived two days earlier – advanced through the uproar, accompanied by Pan Am officials, not the least of whose concerns was to cover up the Beatles' BEAtle inflight bags. As the remaining passengers descended, each received from

Capitol Records a 'Beatles kit' consisting of a 'signed' photograph, an 'I Like the Beatles' badge and a Beatles wig. The Beatles had by now reached the customs hall, where every item of their luggage was examined. In one direction, several hundred howling girls were chased back by police and security men; the other way, about 1,000 more flung and flattened themselves like insects against the plate-glass wall.

On the first floor of the main terminal, where 200 journalists waited, Brian Sommerville began to show his quarterdeck irascibility. The photographers, massed in front of reporters and TV crews, were making too much noise for any formal question to be heard. Sommerville, after several more or less polite injunctions, grabbed a microphone and snapped: 'Shut up – just shut up.' The Beatles concurred, 'Yeah, shurrup.' This produced spontaneous applause.

The New York press, with a few exceptions, succumbed as quickly as the fans. Within minutes, one svelte and sarcastic woman journalist was babbling into a telephone: 'They are absolutely too cute for words. America is going to just *love* them.' On another line, an agency reporter began his dispatch: 'Not since McArthur returned from Korea . . .' Meanwhile, in the conference room, their 198 colleagues continued the interrogation which was supposed to have been ironic and discomfiting but which had produced anything but discomfiture. The Beatles were at their flash-quick, knockabout, impudent best.

'Are you going to have a haircut while you're in America?'

'We had one yesterday,' John replied.

'Will you sing something for us?'

'We need money first,' John said.

'What's your secret?'

'If we knew that,' George said, 'we'd each form a group and be managers.'

'Was your family in show business?' John was asked.

'Well, me dad used to say me mother was a great performer.'

'Are you part of a teenage rebellion against the older generation?'

'It's a dirty lie.'

'What do you think of the campaign in Detroit to stamp out the Beatles?'

'We've got a campaign of our own,' Paul said, 'to stamp out Detroit.'

Outside the terminal, four chauffeur-driven Cadillacs waited. The Beatles, ejected rather than emerging from the rear entrance, were each lifted bodily by two policemen and thrust into a Cadillac. Long after they had returned to England, their arms would still bear the marks of this helpful assistance. Paul, in addition, had a handful of his hair wrenched by a photographer, to see if it was a wig. 'Get out of here, buddy,' a policeman told the leading chauffeur, 'if you want to get out alive.'

•

Outside the Plaza hotel on Fifth Avenue stretched a sea of screaming teenage humanity on which a squad of mounted policemen bobbed as ineffectually as corks. Reservations had been made a month earlier in the individual names of Lennon, McCartney, Harrison and Starr, four 'London businessmen'. At the time, the hotel checked only as far as to ascertain their 'good financial status'. Directly the true nature of their business became known, a Plaza representative went on radio, offering them to any other New York hotel that would take them.

As the four Cadillacs sped in from Kennedy among their weaving and shouting and grimacing motorcade, the Plaza strove valiantly not to capitulate. The Palm Court served tea, as usual, with violin music, though the orchestra leader was vexed to receive requests for Beatles songs. Waiters moved among the pillars and heaped pastries, discreetly requesting the odd errant guest to remove his Beatles wig.

The Beatles and their party had been allocated the hotel's entire twelfth floor. A special force from the Burns Detective Agency was on duty around the clock, to screen all arrivals and conduct periodic searches in the floors above, where some female fans had climbed several hundred fire stairs to lie in wait. A bevy of under-managers ran around, fearful, as well they might be, for the hotel's cherished fabric. When a photographer asked John to lie down on a bed and show his boots, a Plaza man interrupted, 'Oh no – *that's* not the image we want to project.' 'Don't worry,' John reassured him. 'We'll buy the bed.'

Interconnecting suites, 10 rooms in all, had been provided for the Beatles, their solitary wife, their two autograph-manufacturing road managers and their overworked publicist. Only Brian had separate accommodation, on the Central Park side, far away from everyone else.

One of the first to get through the security was Geoffrey Ellis, Brian's old Liverpool friend, the Royal Insurance man. 'The whole scene was extremely surrealistic,' Ellis says. 'The Beatles were all sitting round with transistor radios in their ears, listening to their records playing and watching themselves on television at the same time.'

All the evening TV news bulletins carried the airport scenes as top story, though not all expressed unqualified delight. On NBC, Chet Huntley, the celebrated 'front man', quivered with bilious distaste. 'Like a good little news organisation, we sent three cameramen out this afternoon to cover the arrival of a group from England, known as the Beatles. However, after surveying the film our men returned with, and the subject of that film, I feel there is absolutely no need to show any of that film.' A dissident radio station, WNEW, repeatedly observed that 'I Want to Hold Your Hand' made some people want to hold their noses.

On every other pop frequency, Beatles' voices could be heard, conversing in pre-recorded form or as they had spoken a few minutes earlier, live from their hotel suite. Fast-talking disc jockeys found them an easy target, instantly friendly and funny and willing to endorse anything or anyone. The great success in this field was scored by Murray 'the K' Kaufman of station WINS; having first interviewed the Beatles by telephone, he arrived in their suite, accompanied by an entire girl singing group, and was seldom, if ever, got rid of thereafter.

The strain was beginning to tell already on Brian. First, there was a furious dispute with Brian Sommerville over the room arrangements, which ended with Sommerville threatening to resign. Then Brian came into the Beatles' suite, crimson with anger. Among the products they had obligingly endorsed by telephone were several bootleg recordings of their own music, smuggled out of England and now on sale in the New York shops. 'Brian screamed at them for what they had done,' Dezo Hoffman says. 'They listened to him like naughty children. He still had some authority with them then.'

Shortly after their arrival, George went to bed, complaining of a sore throat. He had been unwell in Paris, too, dictating his *Daily Express* column – as he was to continue to do – without mention of the disconcerting French habit of administering medicines in suppository form. His elder sister, Louise, who had just arrived from St Louis, moved into the Plaza to nurse him.

The other three, despite the crowds outside, managed some limited after-dark movement. Paul visited the Playboy Club, leaving subsequently with a Bunny girl. The Lennons and Ringo, under Murray the K's garrulous protection, went to the Peppermint Lounge, finding it 'the home of the Twist' no longer; its resident group were imitation Beatles. Later, John and Cynthia scuttled back past the photographers, their two heads covered by a coat. Ringo did not return; it was feared for a time that he might have been kidnapped. He returned in the early hours, unaware of the frenzied unease he had caused.

The next morning, it drizzled. Twelve floors below, the crowds and police horses still struggled together in a muted chant of 'She Loves You'. Brian, in his sequestered drawing-room, made a series of urgent telephone calls. The first was to Walter Hofer, the attorney, on West 57th Street. Hofer, at this time, was not sure if he was still NEMS' New York lawyer. 'Brian told me, "You're our attorney – we need you over here." He gave me the job of dealing with all the Beatles' fanmail. I put my usual messenger service to work on it. Later on, I got this call from the messenger. "Mister – I'm 77 years old! There's 37 sacks of mail here."

'We set up a special department in another hotel to deal with it. One of the letters that was opened had come from Lyndon B. Johnson. Another was from the manager of the Plaza. "When are you guys going to settle your check?" it said.'

An urgent appeal went to Capitol Records for a temporary secretary to help Brian in New York and travel on with the British entourage to Miami. Through their classical music department Capitol found Wendy Hanson, an imposing blonde who had until recently been personal assistant to Leopold Stokowski. 'I had to fight my way into the Plaza through all this pandemonium,' Wendy says, 'and there, absolutely cut off from it all, was this baby-faced young man, *drenched* in Guerlain. "Hello, my dear," were his first words. "Would you like some tea?"'

The Beatles, meanwhile – minus George – sat in a limousine packed so close among keening girls, the chauffeur could get in only by crawling across the roof. John Lennon, in dark glasses and Bob Cratchit cap, was asked if all this bothered him. 'No,' he replied in all innocence, 'it's not our car.'

At the Ed Sullivan Theatre on West 53rd Street, a set had been constructed of half a dozen inward-pointing white arrows. The programme designer explained to a posse of journalists his desire 'to symbolise the fact that the Beatles are *here*'. Even for the rehearsal, with Neil Aspinall standing in for George, three high-ranking CBS executives were turned away at the door. Sullivan himself was all amiability, rebuking his musical director for having told the *New York Times* the Beatles would last no longer than a year, and threatening to put on a Beatles wig himself if George was not well enough for the transmission. He became a little less affable when Brian approached him and said grandly: 'I would like to know the exact wording of your introduction.' 'I would like you to get lost,' Ed Sullivan replied.

The *Ed Sullivan Show* on 9 February was watched by an audience of 70 million, or 60 per cent of all American television viewers. At the beginning, a congratulatory telegram was read out from Elvis Presley. Conditioned as they were to hyper-unreality, this event still gave pause to Liverpool boys who had listened to 'Houn' Dog' under the bedclothes, and struggled to learn the words of 'All Shook Up' as it was beamed from its inconceivable Heaven.

For a generation of young Americans, only weeks after the Dallas horror, it would be another – but infinitely happier – moment fixed forever in their memories. And, whether their destiny was to turn into famous pop stars, film directors, industrial magnates, politicians and even presidents, or simply suburban dads and moms, the same image would be eternally etched on their memories, its slightly distorted monochrome image and warbly sound-quality somehow enhancing the rush of incredulous delight. Not only New York, the Bronx, Brooklyn, New Jersey and Queens, but Chicago, Philadelphia, Washington, Pittsburg, San Francisco and Los Angeles, the snowbound midwest, the southern swamps and bayous and the far-western prairies, all succumbed to the same instant, laughing adoration of those four little, jiggling figures with their shiny suits, preposterous hair and indefatigable smiles. Like some rare entomological specimen, each Beatle was given a subtitle bearing his name. John's caption said 'Sorry girls – he's married'.

The *New York Herald Tribune*, next morning, called them '75 per cent publicity, 20 per cent haircut and 5 per cent lilting lament'. The *Washington Post* called them 'asexual and homely'. The *New York Times* carried reviews by both the television and the music critic. The former judged the Beatles 'a fine mass placebo' while the latter, anxious to out-obfuscate William Mann, discovered in 'All My Loving' 'a false modal frame . . . momentarily suggesting the mixoldyian mode . . .' Earl Wilson, the *New York Post* columnist, was photographed at the head of his afternoon's paragraphs in a bald wig. From UPI came the news that Billy Graham, the evangelist, had broken a lifetime's rule by watching television on the Sabbath.

On that one night, America's crime rate was lower than at any time during the previous half-century. Police precinct houses throughout New York could testify to the sudden drop in juvenile offences. In all the five boroughs, not one single car hubcap was reported stolen.

•

The nervous plans, the small-scale hopes, the little deals for cut-price fees, all coalesced in a moment that was miraculously right. America, three months earlier, had been struck dumb by a great and terrible event. America now found her voice again through an event which no psychiatrist could have made more therapeutically trivial. That voice was in itself therapeutic, reassuring a suddenly uncertain people that, at least, they had not lost their old talent for excess.

It was a moment when the potential existed for a madness which nothing indigenously American could unleash. It was a moment when all America's deep envy of Europe, and the eccentricity permitted to older-established nations, crystallised in four figures whose hair and clothes, to American eyes, placed them somewhere near Shakespeare's Hamlet. It was a moment simultaneously gratifying America's need for a new idol, a new toy, a pain-killing drug and a laugh.

On the morning after the *Ed Sullivan Show*, the Beatles were brought to the Plaza hotel's Baroque Room to give a press conference that was itself record-breaking, both in size and fatuousness. Even superior organs like *Time* magazine and the *New Yorker* stiffened themselves to the task of determining whether Beatle hair was correctly described as 'bangs' and their footwear as 'pixie boots'. The *Saturday Evening Post* had sent a photographer with $100,000-worth of equipment to shoot a cover. The *New York Journal-American* had sent Dr Joyce Brothers, a psychologist with flicked-out blonde hair and her own television show. Dr Brothers had her pulse humorously taken by the Beatles and afterwards reminded her readers that 'Beatles might look unappetising and inconsequential, but naturalists have long considered them the most successful order of animals on earth'.

However patronising, insulting or plain clueless the question, the answer would be the same disarming mixture of angel-faced politeness and needle-sharp wit. As well as new music, the Beatles were inventing what would one day be known as sound bites. 'Either they're employing the most marvellous concealed gag man,' Maureen Cleave cabled the *London Evening Standard*, 'or Bob Hope should sign them up right away.'

'What do you think of the Playboy Club?' Paul was asked.

'The Playboy and I are just good friends.'

'Why aren't you wearing a tie?' a woman journalist snapped at George.

'Why aren't *you* wearing a hat?' he fired back.

The inquisition continued all day, without a break for lunch. Instead, some plates of hotel chicken were brought in. 'I'm sorry to interrupt you while you're eating,' a woman reporter said, 'but what do you think you'll be doing in five years' time?'

'Still eating,' John replied.

'Have you got a leading lady for your movie?'

'We're trying to get the Queen,' George said. 'She sells.'

'When do you start rehearsing?'

'We don't,' John said.

'—oh yes we do,' Paul put in.

'We don't, Paul does,' John amended. Some papers had already discovered the fact that among the other three, Paul was referred to as 'the star'.

The American press, in its wild scramble, paid little attention to the other young Englishman, in a polka-dotted foulard scarf, who stood at one side, observing the scene with what the *New York Times* described as 'a look of hauteur'. Even when Jay Livingstone – the same Capitol boss who had said, 'We don't think the Beatles will do anything in this market' – stepped beamingly forward to present them with two million-sale Gold

Discs, Brian still did not allow himself the relaxation of a smile. 'He had ice water in his veins before,' another Capitol man remarked. 'Now it's turned to vinegar.'

Actually Brian's 'hauteur' – like the seeming cool imperturbabality with which he had greeted Wendy Hanson – was nothing but a front. A far more accurate index to his feelings were his frequent mysterious bursts of weeping or the furious, red-faced rows he kept having with Brian Sommerville. For the ever-increasing size and fury of the Beatles' American hurricane only made Brian more and more aware of his inability to manage it.

For example, he had presumed that the only Beatles records available to their new American fans would be the brand-new product on Capitol. But, inevitably, the other US labels that had released Beatles' songs when they were nobodies now hastened to cash in on their success. The Chicago Vee-Jay label, which had grudgingly put out 'Please Please Me' a year earlier, re-released it and within a day saw it rocket to number three. The MGM label even got hold of 'My Bonnie', which the Beatles had recorded long ago in Hamburg as 'the Beat Brothers' with Tony Sheridan. These unauthorised, but genuine, Beatles releases were bad enough, blocking the ascent of official Capitol releases up the charts and earning almost nothing in royalties, but even worse were the number of counterfeit Beatles groups – known as 'Beetles' or 'Bugs' – already recording and being bought by fans in mistake for the genuine article. One unscrupulous producer had even talked his way into the Beatles' suite and tricked them into taping an endorsement for his particular poor facsimile of themselves.

Only now, too, was Brian starting to realise what a catastrophic deal had been made on his behalf with Nicky Byrne's Seltaeb merchandising company. In the aftermath of the *Ed Sullivan Show*, Beatles goods were pouring into the New York shops. REMCO industries had already produced 100,000 Beatles dolls. Beatles wigs were flopping off the production line at the rate of 35,000 a day. The over-indulged American child could choose from a range including Beatles masks, pens, bow ties, 'Flip Your Wig' games, edible discs and 'Beatle nut' ice cream. Agreement was reportedly pending between Seltaeb and a major cola company. Woolworth's and Penney's were negotiating to put 'Beatles counters' in hundreds of their stores, coast to coast. The *Wall Street Journal* estimated that by the end of the year $5m worth of Beatles goods would have been sold in America.

Nor was it reassuring to observe the progress around New York of the man whose company's share of the profits would be 90 per cent. For Nicky Byrne did business on a magnificent scale. His lunches took place at the Four Seasons or the New York Jockey Club. He had two chauffeur-driven limousines, on 24-hour standby, and a private helicopter. His style quickly communicated itself to the five young men from Chelsea who were his partners. Lord Peregrine Eliot has pleasant memories of dropping into the Seltaeb office, once or twice a week, to draw a $1,000 bill from petty cash.

Nicky Byrne argued – and still argues – that it was the only way to do business with large American corporations. He is equally firm on a point later to be disputed – that as the money in manufacturers' advances poured into Seltaeb, the 10 per cent due to Brian and the Beatles was paid over to them within seven days.

'When Brian arrived in New York, I'd just banked $97,000. So, of course, I handed a cheque to Brian for $9,700. He was delighted at first. "Now," he said, "how much of this do I owe you?" "Nothing, Brian," I said. "That's your 10 per cent." He was amazed and furious all at the same time. "But this is *marvellous*, Nicky," he was saying – because he'd been told I'd fixed the airport business. "How did you *do* it, Nicky – but you had no *right* to do it! But it was marvellous, Nicky . . ."'

Having proved his talents as a fixer with the Kennedy Airport crowds, Byrne remained on hand throughout the tour, pushing Beatles records on the radio – at one point, he claims, even buying off a photographer who had obtained some pictures of Brian in his secret gay life and was threatening to make them public.

'Brian said, "You must work for *me*, Nicky – I'll make you a president, I'll give you a thousand a year." I said, "A thousand a year? Oh come *on*, Brian . . ." Then all of a sudden I realised he was crazy.'

•

On 11 February, the Beatles were to fly to Washington to give their first American concert, at the Coliseum sports arena. The booking had been made for Brian by Norman Weiss, of the General Artists Corporation, to help offset the loss on the overall trip. Brian had also accepted an invitation from the British Ambassador to a function as yet unclearly defined. 'Is it true,' the press kept asking them, 'that you're going to a masked ball?' By coincidence, Sir Alec Douglas Home, who had succeeded Macmillan as Britain's Prime Minister, was also due in Washington for talks with Kennedy's successor, Lyndon Johnson. On hearing of the Beatles' imminent arrival in DC, Sir Alec wisely postponed his own until the day afterwards.

The morning of their departure, snow began falling thickly on New York. Led by George, the Beatles flatly refused to fly in a 'fookin' blizzard'. They were, however, amenable to travelling by train. A private carriage was sought, and miraculously appeared in the magnificent shape of an

Edwardian sleeping car from the old Richmond, Fredericksburg and Potomac Railroad. This equipage drew out of a shrieking Pennsylvania Station, carrying, with the Beatles and their entourage, dozens of journalists, several TV crews and the egregious Murray the K. Cynthia Lennon, disguised by sunglasses and a brunette wig, was almost left behind on the platform.

At Washington's Union Station, 3,000 teenagers flung themselves against the 20-foot-high wrought-iron platform gates. Seven thousand more filled the Coliseum, an arena with the stage in the centre, like a boxing ring. While the Beatles performed, Brian Sommerville had to keep running out to turn them in a different direction. The Washington fans, having read George Harrison's joke about liking jelly babies, resolutely pelted the stage with America's version, the jelly bean – often not troubling to remove them from the packet – as well as buttons, hair rollers and spent flash bulbs. A policeman near the stage philosophically screwed a .38 calibre bullet into each of his ears. And Brian Epstein, once again, was noticed standing and weeping.

The British Embassy visit had been arranged by Brian Sommerville, an old shipmate of the Naval attaché there. The Beatles agreed to go only because Brian thought it would be good for the image. Upon arriving, they were greeted by the Ambassador, Sir David Ormsby-Gore, pleasantly enough. What followed was extremely unpleasant, though not atypical of Foreign Office social life. Men in stiff collars and their gin and tonic wives pushed and struggled for autographs, at the same time exclaiming in patrician amusement, 'Can they actually *write*?' One cawing female produced nail scissors and cut off a piece of Ringo's hair. The purpose of this visit, they discovered, was to announce the prizes in an Embassy raffle. When John Lennon demurred, a group of young F.O. types formed threateningly around him. Ringo, touching his shoulder, said pacifically, 'Come on – let's get it over with.'

The story, when reported in the British press, caused a major Parliamentary incident. A Conservative MP, Joan Quennell, called on the Foreign Secretary, R. A. Butler, to confirm or deny that the Beatles had been manhandled by Embassy personnel. Mr Butler replied that, on the contrary, the Beatles' manager had written to Lady Ormsby-Gore, 'thanking her for a delightful evening'.

At the White House, meanwhile, Sir Alec Douglas Home had arrived for his talks with President Lyndon Johnson. The Beatles in fact largely helped break the ice between a big, folksy Texan and a tweedy, skeletal Scottish earl who otherwise might have found small talk difficult. 'I like your advance guard,' Johnson quipped. 'But don't you think they need haircuts?'

And in New York, the promoter Sid Bernstein sat on the staircase at Carnegie Hall, listening to an uproar which made even the framed portraits of Schubert and Ravel jig slightly on the corridor wall. His 'phenomenon', mistaken by that Polish lady for a string quartet, had in one night recouped Sid Bernstein the losses suffered in promoting the 1960 Newport Jazz Festival. Celebrities like David Niven and Shirley MacLaine had unsuccessfully begged him for tickets to the Beatles' Carnegie Hall concerts. Mrs Nelson Rockefeller, with her two daughters, had waited half an hour just for a peep into the dressing-room.

'After the second concert,' Bernstein says, 'I walked with Brian across to Madison Square Garden. We looked inside the old Garden arena. Seventeen thousand seats. I knew the Garden wanted the Beatles; they could have had tickets printed in 24 hours. I offered Brian $25,000 and a $5,000 donation to the British Cancer Fund. I knew he was tempted. But he gave me that little smile he had. "Sid," he said, "let's save it for next time."'

•

Next morning, the police barricades were removed from the front of the Plaza hotel; its elegant lobby grew quiet but for the headlines on the news-stand counter. 'Britain's Boy Beatles Buzz By, Bomb Bobbysoxers.' 'Audience Shrieks, Bays and Ululates.' A large sum of money, which CBS had paid into the hotel for the use of the Beatles party, was found to be untouched. Nobody even knew it was there.

The Beatles were aboard a National Airlines jet, bound for Miami and their second *Ed Sullivan Show*, their course to the south-west plotted by a flight engineer in a Beatles wig. On landing, they were greeted by a crowd of 7,000 which smashed 23 windows and glass doors inside the terminal building.

At the hotel, each Beatle was decanted into his own lofty, luxurious, three-room prison cell. For the Deauville, like the New York Plaza, was in a state of screaming siege. Two enterprising girls had themselves wrapped in two parcels addressed to the Beatles, but were apprehended before they could be delivered.

George Martin, who happened to be in America on a business trip, came to see them in Miami, bringing his wife-to-be, Judy Lockhart-Smith. Martin watched the Beatles rehearse in bathing trunks in the hotel ballroom, and later repay Ed Sullivan's $3,500 with a performance destined to break every record in audience ratings for televised entertainment. So far as such things can ever be computed, 75 million Americans watched the *Ed Sullivan Show* that night. During the transmission, from the hotel's Mau Mau Club, a girl next to George Martin broke off sobbing and bouncing to stare at him in surprise. 'Do *you* like them, *too*, sir?' she asked.

Another widely oversubscribed photo opportunity took place at the 5th Street Gymnasium where Cassius Clay – still some years from renaming himself Muhammed Ali and embracing Islam – was in training for his impending World Heavyweight title fight against Sonny Liston. Even John could not compete with the loose-limbed young giant whose every word defied America's unwritten rule that even famous black people must conduct themselves with slavish self-effacement. The Beatles pretended to spar with Clay for the camera and smiled complicitly when he gave his so-quotable verdict that they might be 'the greatest' but he was still 'the prettiest'. Long-suffering Ringo even found himself picked up and flourished aloft by the soon-to-be champ.

Their only escape from the crowds and press was a day spent at the beach-side mansion of a Capitol Records executive. Sergeant Buddy Bresner, a Miami cop who had befriended them, arranged for them to escape from the Deauville in the back of a butcher's truck while other policemen brought decoy guitar cases out through the front lobby.

George Martin and Judy joined them for that first real respite since they had sunbathed on the seafront at Margate. Brian was there, too, with his temporary assistant, Wendy Hanson. The householder, though absent, had left an armed bodyguard to look after them. Their protector barbecued steaks for them with a cigarette in his mouth, his shoulder holster clearly visible. 'Brian was complaining about all the bootleg records that were coming out,' George Martin remembers. 'Suddenly, this tough-looking guy who was barbecuing our steaks leaned forward and said: "You want we should take care of them for you, Mr Epstein?" It was a *very* sinister moment.'

PART THREE

HAVING

13

'One more stage, one more limo, one more run for your life'

The scene is an oak-panelled room deep in the hallowed precincts of an ancient and illustrious Oxford college. Before the open fire stands the Principal, an elderly gentleman both scholar and diplomat, conversing in mellifluous undertone with his junior dons and one or two of his most favoured students. A cold buffet supper, garnished by the rarest wines from the college cellars, is attended by white-jacketed servants. From a distance, through the historic courtyards and cloisters, a clock may be heard, civilly striking the hour.

The 15th-century oak door opens, to admit the Beatles. They are wearing, as always, dark suits, deep-collared shirts and boots with elasticated sides. Their manner, as they meet the college Principal, the tutors and undergraduates, is deferential yet impudent. A servant offers Paul McCartney champagne in a silver goblet: Paul says he would rather have milk. George Harrison surveys the spread of smoked salmon and beef fillet buffet, then beckons to a retainer. 'Have you got any jam butties?' he asks. 'I'll trade you an autograph for a jam butty.'

The scene comes, not from *A Hard Day's Night* but from life. It happened at Brasenose College in March 1964 arranged by a still unknown self-publicist named Jeffrey Archer. It is recorded in the *Daily Mail*, in a vast picture spread and a story running to three columns. Nothing evokes more powerfully Britain's mood in early 1964 than the *Mail*'s hyperbolic triumph at this coup; its writer's mixture of jocular indulgence and history-witnessing earnestness.

The Beatles were no longer a teenage fad: they had become a national obsession. Far from self-destructing in the way everyone had predicted, their fame somehow fed on its own freakishness, passing more and still more previous limits of celebrity.

Anyone, in however unrelated and elevated a sphere, could command instant attention simply by mentioning their name. The usually rarified *New Statesman* published an editorial headed 'The Menace of Beatledom'. The literary peer Lord Willis denounced them as 'a cheap candy-floss culture-substitute' – as if his own television creations such as *Dixon of*

Dock Green had not been precisely that. In his regular Sunday soapbox orations at Hyde Park Corner, the Methodist cleric-peer Lord Soper asked, 'In what aspect of the full life of the Kingdom of God can we find a place for the Beatles?' Even Royalty was beginning to recognise them as a national asset on a par with – well, Royalty. The Duke of Edinburgh, in an address to a youth conference, called them 'good blokes'. Buckingham Palace even let it be known that an American fan had written to the Queen, congratulating her on having John, Paul, George and Ringo among her subjects. A lady-in-waiting had written back, regretting 'that it is impossible for the Queen to tell you how to get in touch with them.'

The Variety Club of Great Britain named them, collectively, Show Business Personality of the Year. Wax effigies of them in their round-collar shirts were put on show among world leaders and film stars at Madame Tussauds. They became an entry in the *Encyclopaedia Britannica.* It was all like a game, played with the roguish connivance of ancient institutions, to see in what unlikely surroundings the Beatles would turn up next, unawed by any grandeur, disarming the pomp of ages with a request for a jam butty.

In April, a literary luncheon, more heavily subscribed than any that Foyle's bookshop had run since the age of Shaw and H. G. Wells, commemorated John Lennon's entry into authorship. The little drawings and verses he used to doodle under his Quarry Bank desk – and still did at odd moments backstage – appeared as a slim volume entitled *John Lennon In His Own Write.* It was, said the *Times Literary Supplement,* 'worth the study of anyone who fears for the impoverishment of the English language'. Other critics saw, in the book's myopically mispronounced, punning fragments, the influence of Edward Lear and James Joyce. 'Do you,' a radio interviewer asked John, 'make conscious use of onomatopoeia?' 'Automatic pier?' John echoed. 'I haven't the faintest idea what you're talking about.'

It was thought shocking, but forgivably so, when the Foyle's luncheon received no speech from the guest of honour. John, who arrived with Cynthia, deeply hung-over after a night at the Ad Lib, had not realised he was supposed to say anything. Urged to his feet, he could only mumble, 'Thank you. It's been a pleasure.' An obliging press translated this into the more Beatle-like: 'You've got a lucky face.'

The 'Mersey Sound' pumped out by George Martin from Abbey Road studios represented a mere fraction of the teen music from far-flung British locations that now filled the charts, sometimes under names that made 'Beatles' look positively conventional. There was also a 'Manchester Sound', spearheaded by the Hollies, whose spiralling harmonies were analysed by musicologists with almost the same earnestness as the Beatles' own. There was a 'Tyneside Sound', spearheaded by the Animals and their epic-length version of an old bordello-blues number, 'The House of the Rising Sun'. There was a 'Birmingham Sound', spearheaded by the Applejacks, a 'Scottish Sound', spearheaded by Lulu and the Luvvers and the Poets, an 'Irish Sound', spearheaded by Them, featuring the young (but never youthful-looking) Van Morrison.

London and the south, meanwhile, fought back to regain their old cultural ascendancy with a Shepherds Bush Mod group called the High Numbers, soon to be transmogrified into The Who; with Soho blues stars like Georgie Fame, and with a thousand and one eager young r & b bands from which would eventually emerge Eric Clapton, Elton John and Rod Stewart.

Ironically, the group destined to become the Beatles' greatest rivals owed their start to the Liverpudlians' native friendliness and generosity. On the day of their Variety Club awards back in 1963, John and Paul had been riding through Soho in a taxi when they spotted Brian's erstwhile teenage publicist Andrew Loog Oldham walking along with a preoccupied frown on his face. Oldham had gone on to manage his Richmond discoveries, the Rolling Stones, after Brian passed on them. But, to his disappointment, they had so far failed to make themselves – and him – rich by writing their own songs *à la* Beatles.

Their first release, a cover version of Chuck Berry's 'Come On', had barely registered in the charts. At this very moment, Oldham had left them at a club in Great Newport Street, vainly arguing about what to record as a follow-up. Overcome with frustration and annoyance, their young manager had gone out for a breath of fresh air – and the first people he happened to meet were John Lennon and Paul McCartney. 'The conversation really did go like this,' Oldham recalls. '"'ello, Andy. You're looking unhappy. What's the matter?" "Oh, I'm fed up. The Stones can't find a song to record." "Oh – *we've* got a song we've almost written. The Stones can have that to record if yer like."'

The song was 'I Wanna Be Your Man', a tongue-in-cheek blast of r & b destined to be sung by Ringo on the *With the Beatles* album. With an obligingness Oldham still marvels at to this day, John and Paul turned their taxi around, accompanied him back to the Stones' rehearsal room and finished off the song so that the Stones could record it with minimum delay. One can read it as kindliness or as hard-hearted opportunism, since John and Paul at this point both saw their ultimate destiny as songwriters rather than performers. Like so many early Lennon–McCartney songs, 'I Wanna Be Your Man' proved wonderfully adaptable to non-Beatles treatment, in this case providing a perfect frame for Mick Jagger's sneery-punk voice and Brian Jones's palpitant slide guitar. By December 1963, it was headed for the UK Top Ten and the Stones were off the launch-pad at last.

This huge glut of pop had long ago proved too much for the British Broadcasting Corporation, whose music radio output remained limited to a few strictly controlled slots on what it still rather condescendingly called the Light Programme. Now, that hitherto impregnable bastion of the Establishment was also to be challenged. The challenger was a young Irish entrepreneur named Ronan O'Rahilly, a colourful figure around the London scene, well known to Brian Epstein and the Beatles. On Easter Day 1964, O'Rahilly's 'pirate' station, Radio Caroline, began transmitting continuous pop, with slick American-style disc jockeys and jingles, from a small ship anchored outside Britain's territorial limits, beyond the jurisdiction of the Wireless Telegraphy Act that enshrined the BBC's radio monopoly. The public's response to getting what it, rather than the Light Programme, wanted was instantaneous. Radio Caroline won a huge listenership and gave the signal for a whole armada of rival pirate stations to begin operation from various offshore moorings as far north as the mouth of the River Clyde.

On pirate wavelengths, as everywhere, the Beatles were pre-eminent. Their new single, 'Can't Buy Me Love', had become the first record ever to go to number one simultaneously in Britain and America, and that before a note of it had been heard. Advance orders from America alone exceeded three million copies.

Their first film had been shot during the six weeks between their return from America and their departure on a tour of Europe and the Far East. Rather than confecting an artificial plot, their scriptwriter Alun Owen had sensibly opted to show them just as they were, four astonished lads perpetually on the run, with seasoned British comedy actors in supporting roles like Norman Rossington as Norm', their manager, and Wilfred Brambell, from television's top sitcom *Steptoe and Son*, as Paul's grandfather. Owen's script largely reproduced the four's own private badinage, with an acknowledged steal from W. S. Gilbert in the running joke about Brambell being 'a clean old gentleman'. Location filming took place in north London, in instalments rarely lasting longer than about 10 minutes. 'Wherever we set up, the word would instantly get out that the Beatles were there,' director Richard Lester remembers. 'After about three takes, we'd all have to run for our lives.'

Within this simple formula, Lester managed to give the film both the gritty honesty of working-class dramas like *Saturday Night and Sunday Morning* and the surreal artiness of something French or Italian. In its most memorable sequence, aboard an old-fashioned British Railways corridor train, the Beatles played 'I Should Have Known Better' inside the guard's van's metal cage – first to an audience of glamorous gym-slipped 'schoolgirls', then as a soundtrack to their own private card game. Lester's history with the Goons' *Running, Jumping, Standing Still Film* also came to the fore in a speeded-up comedy sequence recalling Mack Sennett's silent-movie *Keystone Cops*. Escaping their pent-up life, the Beatles gambolled onto an open sports field and began to hold imaginary running and sack races. Not even Cliff Richard had presented so pure an image of pop-star innocence.

The film was supposed to have been called Beatlemania. Then, at the last minute, a far better and more Beatle-like title offered itself in a favourite phrase of Ringo Starr's. Whenever a round of performing, recording, partying and fleeing from fans had been particularly crazy, Ringo, in an unconscious paraphrase of Eugene O'Neill, would say it had been 'a hard day's night'. The eponymous album that came with the film was the first to consist entirely of Lennon–McCartney compositions, including 'If I Fell', 'I'm Happy Just to Dance With You', 'I Should Have Known Better' (with 'yeah yeah yeah' mutating into 'hey hey hey') and the title track with its gloriously long and irrelevant guitar coda. The material had mostly been written months earlier, between *crêpes flambées* at the George V. Yet the album evoked the film, just as the film caught Beatlemania at its maddest and happiest.

The film received a West End premiere in July, attended by Princess Margaret and her photographer husband, Lord Snowdon. 'There was a big party afterwards,' Walter Shenson says. 'Nobody thought that Princess Margaret would agree to come to it, so no one invited her. I said we should at least *ask*. It turned out that she and Lord Snowdon had an engagement for dinner but that they'd love to be asked to stop in for a drink first.

'We were all in the ante-room, having drinks before going in to the food. George Harrison gave me a look and whispered: "When do we eat?" I told him, "We can't until Princess Margaret leaves." She and Lord Snowdon had this other engagement but they stayed longer and longer at the Beatles' party, having drinks, chatting. Finally George went across to Princess Margaret and said "Ma'am – we're starved, and Walter says we can't eat until you leave." Princess Margaret just burst out laughing. "Come on, Tony," she called out. "We're in the way."'

A second premiere took place in Liverpool, accompanied by a civic welcome from the Lord Mayor. 'The Beatles were nervous wrecks about that,' Walter Shenson says. 'Even though they'd just come back from a world tour, they were scared about that appearance in Liverpool. "Ah," they kept saying, "you don't know what people are like up there."'

They drove in from Speke Airport, along the same Woolton avenues where Paul used to cycle with his guitar on his back, and where John would struggle along with the Quarry Men, carrying a tea chest. All the way, between bus stops, crowds stood, waving and cheering. Paul, to his particular pleasure, recognised 'Dusty' Durband, his English teacher from the Institute. And there, beyond what used to be Uncle George's dairy, was the red sandstone tower of St Peter's, where the annual fête would soon be held.

There was a civic reception at the Town Hall, then the four former black-leather troglodytes from Mathew Street emerged onto the balcony with the Lord Mayor and other dignitaries to wave to the cheering throng below. Unbeknownst to them, and the adoring media, the crowd was not composed entirely of well-wishers. A few hours earlier Brian Epstein had heard that leaflets were circulating throughout Liverpool naming a Beatle as father of a young child recently born to one of their Cavern Club seraglio. Helped by his brother Clive, Brian had tracked down the claimants and managed to buy their silence.

•

It was the year they conquered the world, but did not see it. For them the world shrank to a single dressing-room, buried under continents of screaming. More than once, on their zigzag flight down back-alleys between the hemispheres, they would ask which country this was. 'It all looked the same to them,' Tony Bramwell says. 'One more stage, one more limo, one more run for your life.'

In June they toured Scandinavia, Holland, the Far East and Australasia. Ringo Starr was having his tonsils out and missed three-quarters of the journey; in his place sat Jimmy Nicol, a session drummer small and obscure enough to scotch any rumour of permanent change. Nicol drummed with them until Melbourne, where Ringo rejoined: history from then on relates nothing further of Jimmy Nicol.

Among the entourage for the tour's Far East and Australian segment was John's Aunt Mimi. In Hong Kong, the police cleared a path for her, crying, 'John Mama, John Mama.' The sight of Adelaide and 300,000 fans, the largest Beatles crowd ever, proved too much for Mimi's nerves: after glimpsing New Zealand, she flew home to Woolton. 'I got into trouble,' Mimi said, 'for telling an Australian TV man that John used to be bad at arithmetic when he was at school. So, on TV, this man said to him, "If you're bad at maths, how do you count all that money you're earning?" "I don't count it," John said, "I weigh it."'

In August, they returned to America to find Beatlemania so rampant as to make the British and European variety seem muted by comparison. At one point in April, the first five places in *Billboard* magazine's Top 100 records were Beatles records. *A Hard Day's Night*, opening in 500 cinemas across the country, had earned $1.3m in its first week. Cinema showings were accompanied by as much screaming as a live concert.

The Beatles, travelling in their own private Lockheed Electra, performed in 23 cities, crossing and recrossing American airspace on a journey totalling 22,441 miles, or more than 600 miles per day. At times they did not know if they were in Jacksonville, Baltimore, Denver, Cincinnati, Detroit or Atlantic City. Everywhere, there were mayors and senators and senators' wives, and sheriffs and deputies; there were the town's most exclusive call girls; there were handicapped children, lined in wheelchairs near the stage, and later brought into the Beatles' dressing-room as if to see or touch them might work a Lourdes-like miracle. The sight always filled John with horror, awakening the fear of disability and disfigurement he had always tried to sublimate by pulling village-idiot faces and shambling around like the Hunchback of Notre Dame. In the four's private language, long before political correctness outlawed such words, 'cripple' came to mean anyone in the dressing-room who was making themself unwelcome. A murmur of 'Cripples, Neil' to their roadie would be the signal for the room to be unceremoniously cleared, to their own seeming regret.

In San Francisco, at the Hilton hotel, a woman guest was robbed and pistol-whipped, her cries unheard in the noise greeting the Beatles' motorcade. At Love Field, Dallas, fans broke through the police barrier, climbed on to the aircraft wings and belaboured the windows with Coke bottles. Later at the hotel, a chambermaid was kidnapped and threatened with a knife unless she revealed the location of the Beatles' suite; other girls had to be rescued from the air-conditioning shaft. In Los Angeles, the post-concert escape plan featured an armoured truck, all four tyres of which proved to be flat. In Seattle, as the Beatles left the stage, a girl fell from an overhead beam, landing at Ringo's feet. In Cleveland, they were physically dragged offstage while mounted police charged the arena, lassoing 200 fans together in a giant net. In New York, the whole of Riverside Drive was cordoned off for their passing; in Toronto, they came in from the airport at 3 a.m., past seventeen miles of continuous parked cars. Each day the madness differed yet remained the same. It was cops and sweat and jelly beans hailing in dream-like noise; it was faces uglied by shrieking and biting fists; it was huge amphitheatres left littered with flashbulbs and hair rollers and buttons and badges and hundreds of pairs of knickers, wringing wet.

Out of the itinerary of chaos, a single figure came to personify that '64 American tour. His name was Charles O. Finley; he owned a baseball team, the Kansas City Athletics. He first approached Brian Epstein in San

Francisco, offering $100,000 if the Beatles would give an additional concert at his baseball stadium in Kansas City. He said he had promised Kansas City they would have the Beatles. Brian replied that the tour could not be extended.

Charles O. Finley did not give up. He reappeared in various other cities, increasing his offer by degrees to $150,000 if the Beatles would let him keep his promise to Kansas City. At length, in Seattle, as it became clear to Brian and Norman Weiss that the tour might not quite cover its gigantic overheads, Charles O. Finley and Kansas City took on a new significance. It was up to the Beatles, Brian said, and whether they were willing to sacrifice one of their few rest days. The Beatles, playing cards with George Harrison of the *Liverpool Echo*, said they would leave it up to Brian. So, at the rate of £1,785 per minute, Charles O. Finley and Kansas City were not disappointed.

In New York, a brisk sale was reported in tinned Beatles' breath. In Denver, the bedlinen they had used at two stopover hotels was bought by a business consortium and placed, unlaundered, in a maximum security bank vault. The sheets were cut into three inch squares and sold at $10 per square, each one mounted on parchment and accompanied by a legal affadavit swearing it to have once formed part of a Beatle's bed.

•

John Lennon started to put on weight. The face, under the Beatles fringe and the mocking, shortsighted eyes, grew rounder – more contented, so Cynthia hopefully thought. Cyn' did not know what happened on tour, nor did she want to know. When she read the letters John received from girls, she laughed them off as he did, doing her best to mean it. She hoped that between tours he would settle down to his unenforced obligations as husband and father. And for a time, that did seem to please him – just staying in at night after Julian was asleep, smoking, reading, doodling, endlessly playing the same Bob Dylan records.

Paul McCartney was more and more often to be seen escorting Jane Asher to Belgravia parties and West End first nights. It clearly gave him huge satisfaction that Jane was not only a 'classy bird' but also now becoming a celebrity in her own right as a stage and film actress and a panellist on television's *Juke Box Jury*. With her tumbling red hair and his cheeky Beatles grin, they made a perfect couple and seemed totally wrapped up in each other – unless some big star appeared on the horizon to divert Paul's attention. 'Paul and Jane came out to a dinner party with my wife and me one night,' Walter Shenson said. 'Joan Sutherland the opera singer just happened to be there. Paul zeroed in on her at once. He left

Jane with me and my wife and stayed talking to Joan for the rest of the evening.'

George Harrison had begun dating Patti Boyd, a 19-year-old model with a quirky, gap-toothed smile who had played one of the schoolgirl nymphets in *A Hard Day's Night*. Pale and waif-like, Patti was the archetype of 1964 high fashion. She now became an object of hatred to George's fans, who booed and jostled her, even once tried to beat her up.

Equally rough treatment was suffered in Liverpool by Maureen Cox, Ringo's 'steady' since Cavern Club days. Maureen worked as a hairdresser: on many occasions, the very head she was shampooing would be uttering threats at her via the mirror. At last, Maureen, too, became public, visiting the hospital where Ringo was having his tonsils removed. A dark-haired, rather undernourished girl stood on the London pavement in bewilderment, clutching a carrier bag.

The Beatles gave entertainment also for the millions they were presumed to earn; for existing, like boy maharajahs, in clouds of spending money. George, it was reported, had changed his E-Type Jaguar for a white Aston Martin like Paul's. Ringo, fresh from his driving test, now drove an Italian Facel Vega. John, who had not yet learned to drive, owned a Rolls-Royce, a Ferrari and a Mini Minor. Their adoption of such consumer status symbols gave vicarious pleasure; their verdict on unattainable luxury was earthily reassuring. An entire newspaper article was based on the revelation that George had tasted his first avocado. 'I've had caviar and I like it,' he told Maureen Cleave, 'but I'd still rather have an egg sandwich.'

All four spent with diminishing pleasure but at increasing speed, in the few seconds possible before the shop became a riot. John, while filming in Bond Street, ran into Asprey's silversmiths through one door and out through another having managed to spend £600. All day, wherever they were, they bought themselves presents, scarcely heeding the accumulation of presents behind them: the suits by the dozen, shirts by the hundred, the ciné-cameras, projectors, watches, gold lighters, the Asprey's silverware and cocktail cabinets shaped like antique globes. Asprey's was as good as Woolworth's, Ringo said – they had everything spread out in the open so you could see it.

The clouds of ready money bought new homes for their families according to pop star precedent. John's Aunt Mimi left Woolton for a luxury bungalow near Bournemouth, overlooking Poole Harbour. Jim McCartney, now retired from the Liverpool Cotton Exchange, moved out on to the Cheshire Wirral to enjoy the house, the wine cellar and the racehorse which Paul had given him. Harry and Louise Harrison gave up their Speke council house for a bungalow in the country near Warrington. Only Ringo's mother, Mrs Graves, said she was happy where she was. She stayed in the Dingle at Admiral's Grove, and her husband, Ringo's stepfather, continued to paint Corporation lamp-posts.

The acquisition of country houses and estates for the Beatles themselves took place in late 1964, in the spirit of yet another swift shopping trip. Again, the task devolved chiefly on Dr Strach, their accountant. Strach lived in Esher, Surrey, and so concentrated his search around that semi-rural haven of accountants and stockbrokers.

For John and Cynthia, Dr Strach found 'Kenwood', a £30,000 mock-Tudor mansion on the select St George's Hill estate at Weybridge. 'Sunny Heights', a similar, closely adjacent property was earmarked for Ringo after his – as yet unannounced – marriage to Maureen Cox. The idea at that stage seems to have been for all four Beatles to live together in a mock-Tudor, topiary-encircled compound around a fifth property owned by Brian Epstein. It was one of Brian's more impossible dreams to have them in his sight for always; to know that John was literally at the bottom of his garden.

For John, that location could not have been more unfortunate. A mile or so from Weybridge, in the kitchen of an Esher hotel, an elderly dishwasher was even now working up courage to step forward and claim the leading Beatle as his son and heir. It was, indeed, Freddy Lennon, the father John had last seen at the age of four, when Freddy sailed away from Liverpool to north Africa.

Aunt Mimi had always feared that Freddy might turn up again – though not in this terrible way, selling his life story to *Tit Bits* and *Weekend* magazine. 'When they told me who it was,' Mimi remembered, 'I felt a shock run right through my body to my fingertips and the tips of my toes.'

A meeting was arranged between John and Freddy – only one. When Freddy called at 'Kenwood' later, he had the door slammed in his face. Subsequently, via the Beatles' accounts, he received a flat and a small pension. He resold his life story for diminishing fees and even made a pop record entitled 'That's My Life'. Julian Lennon did not acquire a long-lost grandfather.

Nor at Weybridge did there materialise Brian's hoped-for village of Beatles mansions. George broke the pattern by buying a bungalow on a different stockbroker estate, at Esher. And Paul, though offered several properties in the district, refused to commit himself yet. The house which Paul bought, and everything in it, was to be the result of minute social calculation. 'He telephoned me one night,' Walter Shenson said, 'but it was my wife he wanted to speak to. They talked for a long time. Paul was asking about a red velvet couch he'd seen at our house. He wanted to know where he could get one made exactly like it and how much it would cost.'

Patti Boyd was discovering that to be a Beatle's girl friend was like joining a cell of Resistance fighters. Her initiation had been when she and George and the Lennons attempted a weekend at a 'secret' hotel in Ireland, and awoke next morning to find the world's press loud-hailing them down the telephone. Patti and Cynthia left the hotel disguised as chambermaids and concealed in two wicker laundry hampers.

That summer, in a bid to go on holiday, they split into two groups. Paul and Jane with Ringo and Maureen flew to the Virgin Isles by way of quick airline changes at Paris, Lisbon and San Juan, Puerto Rico. The Lennons, George and Patti were sighted variously in Amsterdam, Vancouver – where a radio station incited local teenagers to form 'Beatles posses' to hunt them down – then Honolulu and Papeete, Tahiti. From Papeete they put to sea in a cabin cruiser stinking of diesel oil and largely provisioned with potatoes. The vessel at once ran into heavy seas, causing Cynthia to be sick in the nearest receptacle: her new flowered sun hat.

Drugs occurred, like everything else, in almost wearisome profusion. The need dated from Hamburg and the months without sleep; it remained, amid the dizzying fame, to prop their eyes open through each night's arduous pleasure. Now the pills were bright-coloured, like new clothes and cars – French Blues, Purple Hearts, Black Bombers and Yellow Submarines. The habit grew in their growing boredom with everyday pleasures. More exciting than worship or sex, champagne or new toys, was to swallow a pill, just to see what would happen.

In 1964, in certain fashionable London circles, a curious after-dinner ritual was beginning to take place. A member of the party, upon a certain conspiratorial signal, would take out a small plastic bag, a cigarette-rolling machine such as previously used only by the poorest classes, and a packet of similarly proletarian Rizla cigarette-papers. With much thumb-twisting and paper-licking, a meagre, loosely-packed cigarette would be made. It would be passed round the table for each guest to puff, with a deep inhalation, then handed on to the next as reverently as if it were a portion of the Host.

Marijuana, resin of the Indian hemp or cannabis plant, had been used in England hitherto chiefly by West Indian immigrants to allay, with its languorous fumes, the misery of their Brixton tenements. Now, as 'pot' or 'hash', the ancient Oriental dream substance became the latest social accessory. That it was also strictly illegal, under laws which had cleansed the drug-crazy Victorian age, bothered no one very much at first.

The Beatles had been initiated into pot-smoking in 1964. The tell-tale medicinal fragrance of marijuana joints hung about the set of their second feature film, *Help!* 'They were high all the time we were shooting,' the director, Richard Lester, says. 'But there was no harm in it then. It was a happy high.'

It was a laugh, even better than earning millions, to watch the awkward little cigarette rolled; and to breathe down the sweetish smoke that made laughing even easier. It was a laugh to see what characters began to sidle up, their mouths twitching with the promise of even more sensational pleasures. 'I saw it happen to Paul McCartney once,' Richard Lester says, 'the most beautiful girl I've ever seen, trying to persuade him to take heroin. It was an absolutely chilling exercise in controlled evil.'

Early in 1965, George Harrison took John and Cynthia Lennon and Patti to a dinner-party given by a friend of his. 'I'll always remember,' Cynthia says, 'that when we walked into this man's drawing-room, there were four lumps of sugar arranged along the mantelpiece. We all had a delicious dinner with lots of wine. When coffee came, one of the four sugar lumps was put into each of our cups.

'It was as if we suddenly found ourselves in the middle of a horror film. The room seemed to get bigger and bigger. Our host seemed to change into a demon. We were all terrified. We knew it was something evil – we had to get out of the house. But this man told us we couldn't leave. We got away somehow, in George's Mini, but he came after us in a taxi. It was like having the Devil following us in a taxi.

'We tried to drive to some club – the Speakeasy, I think it was. Four of us, packed into the Mini. Everybody seemed to be going mad. Patti wanted to get out and smash all the windows along Regent Street. Then we turned round and started heading for George's place in Esher. God knows how we got there. John was crying and banging his head against the wall. I tried to make myself sick, and couldn't. I tried to go to sleep, and couldn't. It was like a nightmare that wouldn't stop whatever you did. None of us got over it for about three days.'

Their host had playfully dipped their coffee sugar into a substance which, although widely used in mental hospitals and on prisoners of war as a truth serum, was so new as a 'pleasure' drug that it had not yet been declared illegal. It was a man-made substance, odourless and colourless; its chemical name, lysergic acid diethylamide, was usually shortened to LSD.

•

Britain, meanwhile, had changed governments and prime ministers. The General Election of October 1964 had swept the Conservatives from power after 13 years and brought back the Labour Party for only the fourth term in its history. Supreme power had passed from an obscure Scottish laird to a plump, white-haired man who smoked a pipe and holidayed in the Scilly Isles, and about whom little else was known other than that he represented the constituency of Huyton, near Liverpool.

Harold Wilson – Yorkshire-born, a Merseysider only by electoral accident – restored Labour to office largely with the pop idiom used by teenagers and would-be teenagers. 'Let's Go With Labour!', the decisive campaign slogan, borrowed pop music's pre-eminent image – that of being galvanised, as by music, into keen and exhilarating life. Such was the 'New Britain' which Mr Wilson promised, in language as attuned to the mass mood as any juke-box hit – 'a hundred days of dynamic action' . . . 'a dynamic, expanding, confident, above all purposive Britain' . . . 'forged in the white heat of the technological revolution'.

There was, however, another side to Harold Wilson. It had become visible, though not yet diagnosable, the previous April when, as Leader of the Opposition, he had presented the Beatles with their Variety Club award at the Dorchester Hotel. It was perhaps the most astute act of his political career to telephone Sir Joseph Lockwood, Chairman of EMI, and offer to grace the occasion as a 'fellow Merseysider'. Not that the Beatles recognised Mr Wilson as such – or, indeed, recognised him at all. John Lennon, mistaking him for the Variety Club's 'chief barker', and getting confused with Barker and Dobson toffee, mumbled: 'Thank you, Mr Dobson.' But Mr Dobson did not mind. His face, in the double-page newspaper spreads, wore the smile of one who had discovered a great secret.

Britons who had feared the Socialist menace wondered how, for instance, such an apparition could possibly conduct his regular and necessary meetings with the Queen. Yet conduct them the apparition did, with every sign of confidence. And despite technology's white heat, the old familiar State apparatus went on functioning as before. Early in 1965, just as today, the Queen's official birthday was marked by a distribution of honours. Just as today, the Queen herself merely put a signature to the list drawn up by her Prime Minister.

On 12 June, it was announced that the Beatles were each to receive the MBE – Membership of the Most Excellent Order of the British Empire. One northern newspaper headlined the story: 'She Loves Them! Yeah! Yeah! Yeah!'

The Beatles, recuperating from their second European tour, awoke to find a throng of press, eager to ascertain how they would feel at being entitled to walk in State processions behind peers of the realm and hereditary knights but in front of baronets' younger sons and 'Gentlemen of Coat Armour'.

They felt confused.

'I thought you had to drive tanks and win wars to get the MBE,' John Lennon said.

'I think it's marvellous,' Paul McCartney said. 'What does that make my dad?'

'I'll keep it to dust when I'm old,' Ringo Starr said.

'I didn't think you got that sort of thing,' George Harrison said, 'just for playing rock and roll music.'

In Harold Wilson's Britain, as would become abundantly clear, you did. The country had elected its first Beatle Prime Minister.

•

The Wilson Age, which had promised such starkness, such austere purpose, was to produce, instead, an interlude of frivolity unmatched since Charles II sat on the English throne. Newly Socialist Britain in 1965 is remembered, not for 'white heat' or 'driving dynamism' but for shortsighted euphoria and feather-headed extravagance. It is remembered above all for a hallucination which descended on England's capital city, brilliant at first, but in quickly fading, tawdry colours – the hallucination of 'Swinging London'.

Swinging London was born at a moment when government debts at home and abroad had brought the country to the edge of economic ruin. Yet the hard times, so earnestly promised by Mr Wilson, were nowhere visible. All that could be seen was a spending boom registered on the now familiar gauge of teenage fashion. London girls, whey-faced and crop-headed, now tripped along in black and white Op Art dresses terminating scandalously far above the knee. The boys who queued outside the Marquee Club wore 'hipster' trousers and spotted or flowered shirts. Opulence was the rage, and offered to all through Sunday colour-supplement ads for 'pure new wool', 'real cream – pour it on thick', the 'unashamed luxury' of sleekly packaged, though inexpensive, after-dinner mints. Magazines like *Town* and *Queen* mirrored the new preoccupation with taste and style, publishing extravagant picture stories on emergent arbiters of fashion whose extreme youth and humble backgrounds were invoked, almost unconsciously, as a parallel with the Beatles'. Fame, almost equalling that of pop stars, descended on the fashion model Jean Shrimpton, the photographer David Bailey, the clothes designers Mary Quant and John Stephen, whose menswear shops were already transforming a West End backwater called Carnaby Street.

Swinging London was a look – of short skirts, floppy hats, white rabbit 'fun' fur – it was also, at the beginning, an attitude. That attitude, to a great extent, came from the Beatles. As they had looked, wide-eyed, around the strange world of their celebrity, so young Londoners now looked round a capital whose ancient sedateness seemed suddenly hilarious. The essence of Swinging London was in happening against a tolerant background of non-Swinging London – of black taxis, red buses, Grenadier Guardsmen, the sacred monuments and statues past which the young, outrageously dandified, zoomed laughingly in open-top Mini Mokes; the Union Jack itself translated to a novelty kitchen apron or carrier bag. The essence was audacity, like the Beatles'; it was certainty that, because they had got away with it, everyone could.

Swinging London was also big business like none before or since. All summer, in the West End around Carnaby Street, in Chelsea around the King's Road, in formerly down-at-heel byways of Fulham and Kensington, there sprang up 'boutiques', as clothes shops were now called; there sprang up hairdressers offering the Beatles or Mary Quant bobs; bistros, serving newly fashionable cream-laden dishes, windows jumbled with the latest crazes in Victorian bric-a-brac. A rash of new clubs vied with the Ad Lib to attract those who, in the yearning terminology of that hour, were 'the with-it set', the 'new faces', the In-crowd.

The innermost In-crowd, the ultimate clique, continued to be the Beatles. Their hair now sculpted and razored, their clothes one jump ahead of Carnaby Street, they were the model, and their songs the background, for boutique shopping, bistro-dining, feather boa-wearing, Swinging London life. They, together with Union Jacks and wooden headed dolls and Great War recruitment posters, were founding effigies in the Pop Art vogue, born of the period's child-like brilliance and bric-a-brac. *Queen* magazine reported in July that Peter Blake, London's leading pop artist, was employed on a major study of them, while the sculptor David Wynne was casting their heads in bronze for what was predicted to be 'one of the most profound English philosophical portrait sculptures of the 20th century'.

Their second film, *Help!*, is Swinging London personified – part-music, part-colour-supplement travelogue, part-Pop Art strip cartoon. Again the producer was Walter Shenson and the director, Richard Lester. Again the theme was the Beatles' private life – not real life this time but a fantasy one such as their song lyrics and public clowning had led their fans to half-imagine. The opening sequence shows John, Paul, George and Ringo each entering a front door in four identical terraced houses. Within is a communal 'pad' equipped with vending machines, a sunken floor, a grass carpet and a cinema organ.

Various writers, among them the dramatist Charles Wood, had laboured on a plot which, in its final, much-rewritten form, dealt with the efforts of a Hindu murder sect to recover a ring stuck on Ringo's finger. No less appropriate to the moment, the cast included character actors, like Eleanor Bron and Roy Kinnear, well known from fashionable television 'satire' shows. There being no restraint on budget now, the action moved from London to Salisbury Plain, where the Beatles performed inside a ring of Centurion tanks; then to Austria and the Bahamas.

The West End premiere, in Princess Margaret's by now almost inevitable presence, brought reviews hailing the Beatles as 'modern Marx Brothers'. They had, in fact, prepared for their role by studying the Marx Brothers' classic *Duck Soup*. Ringo Starr received special praise for a 'Chaplinesque' performance recognisable to everyone around him as just Ringo being Ringo on camera. On the sleeve of the soundtrack album, four ski-clad Beatles semaphored a title song which had been number one in Britain for most of the two preceding months.

Their evolution into national treasure received an extra boost through the growing notoriety of the band they'd helped find a first foothold in the charts. After initially trying to market the Rolling Stones as ersatz Beatles, Andrew Loog Oldham had hit on the brilliant wheeze of turning his discovery into anti-Beatles, shattering every convention of charm and family-friendliness that John, Paul, George and Ringo had laid down for all pop groups. The Stones did not smile, but sneered. Their hair was not barbered into neat fringes, but left to hang in Byronesque tangles over their ears and collars. They did not perform in shiny stage uniforms, but in the same unmatched, unpressed clothes they had worn to the gig. Their music was not tuneful and catchy like the Beatles', but charged with an animal fury and sexuality that goaded their audiences to violence and vandalism like nothing seen since the earliest days of rock and roll.

Oldham realised that a huge segment of the teenage pop audience felt they had 'lost' the Beatles to their parents, even their grandparents. Boys who attended school with Stones-style hair down to their shoulders were now being sent home with instructions to get it 'cut neatly like the Beatles'. From the five hitherto law-abiding Stones, their teenage manager fashioned rebels and outlaws whose subliminal message was they'd never sell out in the same way. A series of publicity stunts staged by Oldham had turned the Stones into a national scandal that obsessed the media almost as noisily as Beatlemania once had. They were the bêtes noirs of every pulpit-thumping clergyman, youth leader and columnist for a catalogue of crimes that ranged from urinating in public to refusal to ride the revolving platform on TV's *Sunday Night at the London Palladium*. And, just as Oldham had predicted, the more the grown-up world mocked and reviled them, the more teenagers adored them.

Pop fans not just in Britain and America but the world over now polarised into two camps. It was the first question whenever one raver met another: 'Are you Beatles or are you Stones?' To reply Beatles meant that one was essentially conventional and law-abiding; to reply 'Stones' meant that one gloried in anarchy, subversion and free love. 'The Beatles want to hold your hand,' famously wrote the New York journalist Tom Wolfe, 'but the Stones want to burn your town.' Wolfe, of course, had no idea that the squeaky clean Fab Four had been no less averse to a bit of town-burning in their Liverpool and Hamburg days.

The Stones, too, had now conquered the States and were enjoying a run of huge hit singles, latterly co-written by their vocalist Mick Jagger and lead guitarist, then known as Keith Richard. Jagger, the former shy student, under Oldham's influence had become a star in his own right, focusing the band's insolence and provocativeness in his strutting, girlish body and enormous, rubbery lips. What few people outside the Ad Lib club realised was that, although polar opposites and deadly rivals in public, the Beatles and the Stones were privately the best of friends. John, in particular, admired Jagger and Richard as well as envying them their licence to speak and behave as they chose. As time went on, the two bands would even co-operate, making sure they did not release a new single at the same time and so impede each other's progress up the charts.

The Beatles' investiture as MBEs was performed by the Queen on 26 October 1965. Swinging London was thus united with Buckingham Palace in a spectacle whose solemn pomp and hilarious incongruity spoke prophecies of the Wilsonian honours system. Mr Wilson's wheeze had not been universally applauded. Several MBE-holders, together with sundry OBEs and BEMs, had returned their decorations in protest that an honour hard won through war or sub-postmastership should be given to what one outraged naval hero described as 'a gang of nincompoops'. Colonel Frederick Wagg announced his resignation from the Labour Party and cancellation of a £12,000 bequest to party funds. The general delight showed that Mr Wilson had achieved his object: to reflect the Beatles' popularity upon himself. No single commentator expressed surprise that, despite achievements which nowadays would probably have taken him into the House of Lords, Brian Epstein received no honour of any kind.

Crowds even larger than those which await royal births and deaths collected along the palace railings and around the Victoria Monument's winged chariot to watch the Beatles take their place in the hierarchy of State. Once again, real life had exceeded any scriptwriter's fantasy – in the cries of 'God save the Beatles' as they entered by the Privy Purse Door; in the Lord Chamberlain's official, 6 ft 3 ins in knee breeches, who instructed them how and when to bow; and, finally, the white and gold State ballroom, and the long red carpet leading to the regal figure destined, on this occasion, to play only a bit-part.

Later at a press conference, holding up their rose-ribboned silver crosses, they were asked their opinion of Buckingham Palace. Paul McCartney replied that it was a 'keen pad'. They had been to other palaces of course – such as the San Francisco Cow Palace. And the Queen? They liked her, Paul said – she had been 'like a mum'. The Queen had asked how long they had been together and Ringo had replied, 'forty years', at which Her Majesty had laughed. 'Were you scared?' John was asked. 'Not as much as some others in there,' he replied. 'What will you do with your medal?' 'What do people usually do with medals?' Paul replied. Paul would later claim – or, at least, strongly hint – that they had been created Members of the Most Excellent Order of the British Empire in a happy haze of a marijuana joint, quickly puffed by turns in a mahogany-lined palace washroom.

In Birmingham that same day, Princess Margaret was opening the new offices of the *Birmingham Post and Mail*. The first issue off the new presses had the Beatles' Investiture as its lead story. Glancing at it, the Princess made what seemed like a veiled comment on the most inexplicable absentee from her sister's Honours List. 'I think MBE must stand for "Mr Brian Epstein."'

•

At the end of 1964, a New York business syndicate had offered Brian £3½m outright for the Beatles. He was also considering an offer for NEMS Enterprises from the powerful British Delfont Organisation. 'What shall I do? Shall I take it?' he would ask, resting his forefinger along his cheek as the paper millions danced around him.

The Beatles, though the most colossal element in Brian's success, were by no means the only one. Gerry and the Pacemakers had remained consistently popular and were themselves now making a feature film. Even greater had been the impact of Cilla Black, the Cavern Club's metamorphosed cloakroom girl. Strangely unsuccessful with Lennon–McCartney material, Cilla made her breakthrough with a song which Brian found for her in America: the Burt Bacharach ballad 'Anyone Who Had a Heart'. Hit records continued into 1965 for Cilla Black, as they did for Billy J. Kramer, the Dakotas and the Fourmost.

Success beyond exaggeration had brought obvious personal wealth. Brian's suits came from Savile Row, his shirts – of pure monogrammed silk – from Jermyn Street: his presence had the crispness of new banknotes, the cool fragrance of cologne and triumphant deals. In Chapel Street, Belgravia, he had a Georgian house, furnished with fastidious taste, glittering with ceremonial silver, pale with white gold and quiet with excellent art. There he maintained a domestic staff befitting a young lord, and entertained with a generosity and thoughtfulness that few of his guests have ever forgotten. He took pains, for instance, to notice which brand of cigarettes each visitor smoked, and to ensure that brand would be next to his or her place at dinner. When George Martin married Judy Lockhart-Smith, each table setting was marked by Brian's gift of 'M' monogrammed silver napkin rings – not the conventional dozen but 11, commemorating the number present.

It was the same solicitousness that Brian devoted to all his artists at the beginning – the finicking, almost feminine perfectionism which chose Cilla's dresses and worried over Billy J.'s tendency to plumpness; which sent telegrams on first nights, placed flowers and fruit and champagne and portable TV sets in dressing-rooms; which provided hairdressers, tailors, doctors, lawyers; which, in a thousand, almost unnoticed ways, eased gawky Liverpool boys and an even gawkier Liverpool girl into their roles as international celebrities.

The Beatles came first, and everyone knew it: the Beatles were not in Brian's head but his heart. Whatever desire he had once felt for John Lennon had changed, amid the world's worship, into a quadruple infatuation, an affair with an image he had created, yet still doted uneasily on. To be with them, or a few paces behind them, represented his life's only absolute happiness. On their return from America late in 1964, he had gone up to Liverpool; he was in his old office, talking to Joe Flannery, his long-time friend and confidant. 'We made an arrangement to meet for coffee the next morning,' Flannery says. 'That night, the Beatles flew into London airport. Next day, I was with Brian in his office, the television was on – and there was Brian with the Beatles on the screen. He'd driven all the way down to London to meet them at the airport, then all the way back up to Liverpool to keep his appointment with me. He had to be with them. He could never let go.'

Yet he was never quite at ease with them, always a little nervous of going into their dressing-room unless to impart some further astounding piece of news. Even after all this time, for all his triumphs, a barbed comment from John could still cut him to the heart. George Martin remembers such a moment, late one night at Abbey Road studios while the Beatles and Martin were working on a track that stubbornly refused to come right. 'Brian appeared in the control-room with one of his boy friends – and did something I'd never seen him do before. When John had finished a vocal track, Brian switched on the intercom and said, "I don't think that sounded quite right, John." John looked up at him and in his most cutting voice said, "You stick to your percentages, Brian. We'll take care of the music."'

The publicists he employed tended to bear the brunt of his possessiveness where the Beatles were concerned. Brian Sommerville's tenure came to a stormy end on the first American tour when he committed the sin of being quoted by name in a news story about the band. Brian screamed at him, then tried to make him sign a written oath of anonymity in all future dealings with the media. Sommerville refused, dissolved his freelance arrangement with NEMS and went off to read for the Bar.

In his place Brian took on Derek Taylor, the Hoylake-born *Daily Express* reporter who had ghost-written George Harrison's articles from Paris. Among the Fleet Street scrimmage, Taylor had caught Brian's eye with his Italianate good looks and droll, idiosyncratic speech. He joined NEMS in April 1964, initially as Brian's personal assistant. 'I suppose it was because he fancied me that I got the job,' Taylor admitted, 'even though, in all the time I knew him, he never so much as laid a finger on my knee.'

Earlier in 1964, Brian had agreed to write his autobiography for a London publisher, the Souvenir Press. Taylor's first NEMS job, even before he had quite left Fleet Street, was to ghost-write Brian's life story on the basis of one weekend with him and a tape recorder at the Imperial Hotel, Torquay. The result was the evasive yet strangely honest self-portrait which he called *A Cellarful of Noise*, but those in his inner circle retitled *A Cellarful of Boys*.

As the Beatles' Press Officer, for the first of three terms, Taylor stood in the firing-line of Brian's proprietorial obsession. 'I'd been told he could be cruel. I only realised it when I came to organise a Fab Four press conference. Brian didn't want it to work. If I made a mess of it, even though the Beatles would be in that mess, he'd be happy – because I'd gained no control over them. He said, "Go ahead – but this is doomed. I look forward to speaking to you about it afterwards." I joined in April; here he was in May, treating me with *massive* cruelty.'

In 1964, during the Beatles' second American tour, Brian met Nat Weiss, a pale, cautious New Yorker who until then had earned his living as a divorce lawyer. Over the next three years, Weiss became to Brian what a few male friends, like Joe Flannery and Peter Brown, were – an adviser, a confidant and, with increasing frequency, a means of rescue.

The Brian who revisited Nat Weiss in 1965, however, was still the languid, immaculate young Englishman who loved New York and its arrant luxury, who bought clothes extravagantly up and down Fifth Avenue, who had a weakness for the Waldorf Hotel, French toast and American chef's salads, and whose large intake of alcohol, especially cognac, seemed to produce only greater euphoria. 'When he was high,' Weiss says, 'he'd pile the furniture up. He'd put chairs on top of tables and then more chairs on top, just to see the effect. Moving furniture was always a thing with Brian.

'But however high he was, he'd never talk about the Beatles. I've seen him at parties when people tried to broach the subject. Brian would suddenly change – it was as if an icy shutter had come down.

'Anything he ever told me was in the strictest confidence, over lunch or dinner. To Brian, the relationship with the Beatles was something mystical – he himself used that word. He believed there was a chemistry between the five of them that no one else could understand. They weren't a business to Brian: they were a vocation, a mission in life. They were like a religion to him.'

Weiss came as close as anyone did to Brian in those three tumultuous years. His memory is deeply affectionate, admiring and perplexed. For with Weiss, as with even his most intimate companions, Brian Epstein defied understanding. 'He wasn't a Jekyll and Hyde character – he was Jekyll and Hyde and about twenty other people besides.'

He was, on one hand, the ice-cool young tycoon who sat in Walter Hofer's office, saying nothing, only listening, while big brash New York promoters bludgeoned him with their bonhomie, but at the first inconsistency politely interrupting '... but I thought you said a minute ago ...' He was the businessman whose integrity seemed born of an earlier age, whose handshake was as good as a contract, who treated the unknown teenage masses of Denver or Cincinnati with the same scrupulous fairness as customers in his family's Liverpool shop. 'He always insisted that concert promoters should never take advantage of the fans – that tickets always had to be kept as cheap as possible.'

But always there was the other Brian, contradicting each strength with a weakness, each cool-headed triumph with a peevish, destructive temper tantrum, each provident care and precaution with a reckless and fearful risk.

There was the Brian who, with the whole world at his feet, spent time and energy in buying up *Mersey Beat*, the little Liverpool music paper, simply for the pleasure of settling old scores among local musicians and promoters. There was the Brian who, unable to adjust his mind from Liverpool shopkeeping values, attempted to woo people like Nicky Byrne and George Martin into his employment by promising them 'a thousand a year'. There was the Brian who, as paper millions whirled around him, hardly realised what tangible millions were slipping through his grasp.

The Beatles' 1964 American tour, though buoyed up on cash advances larger than any in entertainment history, had eventually done little more than cover its gigantic overheads. To make matters worse the US Internal Revenue had become uneasy about all the dollars which, reputedly, were to be removed from the country. Under a long-standing Anglo-American tax treaty, the Beatles' tour earnings were liable only for British Income Tax. The US authorities nonetheless obtained a New York court order, freezing $1m in concert proceeds while 'clarification' was sought.

Still worse was the position with Seltaeb, the American merchandising company of whose projected multimillion dollar earnings from Beatles buttons, masks, ice cream and more than 150 other items, NEMS Enterprises' share was fixed at 10 per cent.

In August 1964, the original ludicrous Seltaeb–NEMS contract was renegotiated. The Beatles' royalty from goods in their image rose to 46 per cent. Relations between NEMS and Seltaeb's English president, Nicky Byrne, deteriorated sharply in the process. They deteriorated still further when Byrne's lawyers informed him that some American manufacturers were turning out Beatles merchandise on licences granted, not by Seltaeb in New York but by NEMS direct from London.

As a further complication there was strife within Seltaeb, among Byrne's young English partners. Lord Peregrine Eliot, after six months of 'good lunacy' as he describes it, received a distinct impression that neither the Beatles nor Uncle Sam had been paid the sums due to them and that, under tax treaty law, Uncle Sam might seek to annexe his Cornish ancestral home, Port Eliot. So, while Nicky Byrne was in London, Lord Peregrine and Malcolm Evans, another Seltaeb partner, instituted court proceedings against him. They claimed that Byrne had failed to pass on Beatles royalties while at the same time spending $150,000 for his own 'comfort and benefit'. The comforts alleged included hotel bills running into thousands of dollars, two Cadillacs and chauffeurs on 24-hour standby and charge accounts for his girl friends at costly Fifth Avenue stores.

At the same time, NEMS began a lawsuit against Seltaeb for alleged non-payment of $55,000 in merchandise royalties. Nicky Byrne entered a counter-suit claiming breach of contract and damages of $5m.

The NEMS–Seltaeb dispute entered the pre-trial stage of a legal epic destined to last three years, accumulate three tons of documents and dissipate fortunes which no one can ever accurately compute. For the confusion over licences had caused panic among America's litigation-wary retailers. Woolworth's and Penney's instantly cancelled orders together worth $78m. The total of business lost among the lawsuits, in that one year alone, must be closer to $100m.

•

NEMS Enterprises, meanwhile, had swollen to literally unmanageable size. For Brian, while on the one hand struggling to contain the Beatles phenomenon, continued to sign up any new act which caught his increasingly capricious fancy. Sounds Incorporated, Cliff Bennett and the Rebel Rousers, Paddy, Klaus and Gibson, and the Rustiks – each in turn received the now familiar NEMS treatment of new suits, stylish press handouts and, if fortunate, a Lennon–McCartney song. It did not occur to Brian that his eye could be at fault; that he mistook mere competence for Beatles-size talent; that often his new discoveries only obtained record contracts on the strength of what he had discovered before.

Nor did Brian now have the assiduous energy of 18 months ago. The arrival of Peter Brown from Liverpool in 1965 allowed him to delegate much day-to-day routine to the slim young man who, in so many ways, became his surrogate presence. He had also persuaded his other Liverpool friend Geoffrey Ellis to quit the insurance business and join NEMS, ultimately as a director. The arrival of Vic Lewis, an established London agent, completed the transformation from one-man company to multi-faced, impersonal 'organisation'.

The change was felt most keenly by the Liverpudlians who had followed Brian to London, and now found his attention withdrawn from all but the Beatles and Cilla. Tommy Quickly, his intended solo 'sensation', lost hope of ever seeing the Top Twenty. Billy J. Kramer put on weight, unreproached. The Fourmost bemoaned their lack of songs to record. The Big Three so hated the prissy image that Brian had given them, they were publicly threatening to 'fill him in'. Gibson Kemp, of Paddy, Klaus and Gibson, supplemented his weekly £15 NEMS salary by working as an office-cleaner.

It was partly this accumulating discontent which led Brian, during 1965, to move away from NEMS' Argyll Street offices to a small command post of his own in Stafford Street, near Piccadilly. There he planned to devote himself only to top-level management – in other words, the Beatles. The move was made with elaborate secrecy: only Peter Brown and Geoffrey were supposed to know his new address. 'Brian spoiled that,' Geoffrey Ellis says, 'by immediately ringing up his 20 closest friends and telling them where he was.'

With him to Stafford Street he took Wendy Hanson, the high-powered, ebullient English girl whom he had wanted as his personal assistant since she had worked for him briefly in America the previous year. Wendy had subsequently come to Europe 'because of a man in Paris'; the man having proved difficult, she found herself able to accept Brian's offer. She remained with him, despite many attempted resignations, until the end of 1966.

Her job in principle was to provide anything a Beatle wanted, from new Asprey's luggage for Ringo to a Coutt's bank account for Paul;

from Jane Asher's birthday cake at Maxim's in Paris, to the whole of the Harrods store kept open after hours for the Beatles as had only been done hitherto for Royalty. There was also the continuing job, for which Wendy's experience among turbulent operatic tenors and prima donnas had only half-prepared her, of trying to organise Brian.

'We were in Nassau while the boys were filming *Help!*; it had all got a bit dull, so Brian decided to go to New York for the weekend. Pan Am couldn't seat us together on the flight, which made Brian *furious*. There and then he wrote a letter to Pan Am, saying "The Beatles will never use this airline again". When we got to New York, there were, I promise you, 20 Pan Am officials, bowing and scraping on the tarmac.

'The next morning we were supposed to leave for London. Pan Am sent their own limo to the airport to fetch us. I was downstairs in the lobby with all my bags – no Brian. I waited and waited. Still no Brian. Eventually, I went up to his room. There he was, still in bed with not one of his 13 suitcases packed.

'All the way to the airport, the limo driver was in radio contact with Pan Am: "We're just crossing the river," I could hear him saying. "We're five miles from Kennedy . . ." They got us on to the flight with literally seconds to spare – in fact, they threw our bags into the compartment after us. Then, as we were taxi-ing along the runway, Brian looked at his watch. "Hm," he said. "Half a minute late in taking off. Typical."'

The move to Stafford Street, far from concentrating Brian's mind, presaged a deterioration which, for the moment, only Wendy Hanson noticed. Wendy, increasingly, found herself left alone with the hot line the Beatles used to communicate their wishes and whims. When they asked for Brian, she would have to admit he had not been in to the office that day.

The trouble was partly insomnia, inherited from his mother and fostered by London's extravagant night haunts. A relentless gambler, he was known to lose up to £12,000 in one roulette or chemin-de-fer session at the Curzon Club. The price was a small one for the company of waiters, croupiers, the rolling ball, the click of cards from the shoe. At dawn or later, dosed with pills on top of the night's brandy, he might, if he was fortunate, fall asleep. The sleep became ever more difficult to penetrate from the office where, at 4 or 5 p.m., he would still have not made an appearance.

The trouble, above all, was an emotional life into which fame and money had brought no fulfilment. It was the helpless heart, still lost to any loutish 'rough trade' boy: the beatings-up, the thefts and petty blackmail. It was the pimply young Guardsmen who left Chapel Street at dawn; the steel-hatted construction worker calling to see him at the New

York Waldorf at 5 a.m. It was the fear, reborn each horrified morning, that the police, the press – but, most frightful of all, the Beatles – would 'find out'.

That the Beatles had not yet found out remained a hallucination with Brian, despite grins exchanged behind his back, and despite John Lennon's occasional brutal puncturings of the masquerade. 'What shall I call this book of mine?' he had wondered aloud after finishing *A Cellarful of Noise*. John, fixing him with a merciless eye, replied, 'Queer Jew'.

Despite this underlying malaise, the Beatles' 1965 American tour seemed once more to confirm Brian's power to take the Beatles beyond even their wildest dreams. On both their previous two tours, they had hoped to meet their idol Elvis Presley and thank him in person for his cordial welcoming telegram. But the visits had been too short and their schedule too insanely crowded for anything to be worked out. This time around it happened that when they hit the West Coast in August, Elvis would be in Hollywood, shooting one of the three films he was obliged to make each year. All four entreated Brian to move heaven and earth, if necessary, to procure them an audience with the King.

A meeting was arranged between Brian and Presley's manager, Colonel Tom Parker, at the Colonel's permanent office at Paramount Studios, which was exotically furnished with mementoes of his personal symbol and totem, the elephant. The crafty old carnival huckster offered his pale young British visitor a lunch of pastrami sandwiches, little suspecting how many times his name had been taken in vain to spice up fictitious phone-messages for Brian in Birkenhead pubs.

Colonel Parker being amenable to Elvis meeting the Beatles, their roadie Mal Evans was dispatched to finalise arrangements with Joe Esposito, Elvis's road manager and head honcho of his protective body-guard, the legendary 'Memphis Mafia'. 'Mal was a huge Elvis fan', Esposito remembers. 'He turned up at the studios all dressed up in a suit and tie. When Elvis said "Hi" to him and shook his hand, Mal was a nervous wreck.

'We sent cars to fetch the Beatles and bring them to the house in Bel Air where Elvis was living. I rode over in one car with George and Ringo; in the other one were John, Paul and Brian. It was all supposed to have been a secret, but the Colonel had tipped off one of the radio stations and when we arrived there were hundreds of screaming kids outside.

'When we showed the Beatles into the living room, Elvis was in his bathrobe and playing a bass guitar. All four of them were tongue-tied to meet him . . . even John could hardly speak. Finally Elvis said "Well, if we're just going to sit here looking at each other all night, I'm going to bed."

'That broke the ice a little bit and they started playing roulette together – all but for George, who got high as a kite on grass out beside the pool.'

The '65 tour included the Beatles' greatest performing triumph – one which still found Brian apparently centre stage and in full control. It occurred on 23 August, when a helicopter containing the Beatles, Brian and Tony Barrow tilted down through the New York twilight and the pilot pointed out Shea Stadium, though they could already hear the roar of it, and see the flashes of unnumbered cameras pointed hopefully into the sky.

Brian was there at the New York Met's baseball ground, to witness the concert which, though it grossed $300,000, earned only $7,000 for its promoter, Sid Bernstein. He is there in the film that was made, standing near the stage, nodding his head in time a little jerkily, looking out to the terraces at 55,000 people – in seats kept cheap at his insistence – then back to the four figures for whom 55,000 voices are screaming, with their military-style khaki tunics, their hot foreheads and still unwearied smiles.

'If he'd been an ordinary manager, Shea Stadium couldn't have happened,' Nat Weiss says. 'None of it could have happened the way it did. It all only happened that way because it was Brian Epstein's fantasy.'

14

'This is it. This is the last one ever'

At the beginning, two boys in travel-creased shirts would stand in front of George Martin, playing the new song they had scribbled in an old school exercise book. Martin even then saw two personalities at war. A song would be John's aggression held in check by Paul's decorum; it would be Paul's occasionally cloying sentiment cut back by John's unmerciful cynicism. Yet Paul loved all-out rock and roll, just as John could be capable of brusque tenderness. Examples of total collaboration were rare. More often, one would write half a song and then come to the other for help with the chorus or 'middle eight'. The formula was established that whoever had written most of the song took the lead vocal, the other providing harmony. That harmony derived its freshness and energy from the contest being waged within it.

Collaboration was dictated, in any case, by close confinement in tour buses, dressing-rooms and, later, aircraft; the pressure of songwriting to order in spaces cleared among newspapers, teacups and the debris of 'the road'. From the early, simple 'yeah yeah' hits up to the *Hard Day's Night* album, the songs, whether by John or Paul, are chiefly redolent of a common life on the run. Nor was it still absolutely certain that Lennon–McCartney songs were what the public wanted. Their next, and fourth, album, *Beatles for Sale*, reverted largely to their old Liverpool and Hamburg stage repertoire: Chuck Berry's 'Rock and Roll Music'; Carl Perkins's 'Honey Don't'; Little Richard's 'Kansas City'; Buddy Holly's 'Words of Love', a track on which their fans first discovered their almost uncanny powers of mimicry. By covering the songs of these and many others of their rock and soul idols, and openly acknowledging their creative debt, they had reactivated several careers previously in the doldrums, notably Berry's and Perkins's and Holly's posthumous one. It was thanks to them also that knowing about pop history for the first time became cool.

The importance of George Martin cannot be over-emphasised. First of all, he signed them. Second, he did not cheat them. Third, he did not adulterate them. It would have been easy for him, as all-powerful record producer, to insist that each release should carry a B-side composed by himself. Martin happened to be of the rare breed who are content to use their talents in improving other people's work. To Lennon and McCartney, he was the editor which all creative promise strikes if it is lucky. He took the raw songs; he shaped and pruned and polished them and, with scarcely believable altruism, asked nothing for himself but his EMI salary and the satisfaction of seeing the songs come right. As the songs grew more complex, so did Martin's unsung, unsinging role.

Paul McCartney was, of the two, the more obviously 'natural' musician. Much came from heredity, and the Jim Mac Jazz Band. He had an instinctive grasp of harmony, a gift of phrasing which raised the bass guitar in his hands to an agile, expressive lead instrument. Already proficient in guitar and drums, he was now taking formal piano lessons. Paul developed by following rules, a notion altogether repugnant to John Lennon. John's music was, like his drawing, bereft of obedience and straight lines, but honest and powerful in a way that Paul's never dared to be.

Innovators though they had become, they were still as wide open to outside influences and quick to absorb other people's good ideas as they had been in far-off days when they'd sit in Paul's front room, copying Buddy Holly and Carl Perkins. They still looked as eagerly to America, where scores of new ensembles with round-collared suits and fringes now adopted Beatle-ish names (the Turtles, the Byrds, the Monkees) and used Beatle-ish harmonies and humour to claw back the Scouse-borrowed music of their native land. Even the new habit of calling the former groups 'bands' came from John, George, Paul and Ringo, who would often collectively sign themselves 'The Beatles – a band', like tuba- and triangle-players from some Yorkshire mining village or the Salvation Army. Many American bands went so far as to adopt Liverpool accents and use Liverpool phrases, despite blissful ignorance as to their meaning. One Monkees song, for instance, was to come out in the US as 'Randy Scouse Git' (hastily changed to 'Alternate Title' for its British release).

But the most significant of Britain's American converts to rock was Bob Dylan, formerly a folk-singing reincarnation of 'travellin' man' Jimmie Guthrie and chief standard bearer for the emergent 'protest' movement. Then one fateful day, on his car-radio, Dylan heard the Animals' Newcastle-on-Tyne version of New Orleans' 'The House of the Rising Sun'. There and then Dylan abandoned acoustic protest songs like 'Blowin' in the Wind' and 'A Hard Rain's Gonna Fall' for electric-powered rock, thereby instantly turning the form into one without limitations of subject, expression or length.

Dylan had also been an early convert to the Beatles, although at the time crediting them with rather more daring than they possessed. When they first met him, he told them how blown away he'd been by the 'druggy' line in 'I Want to Hold Your Hand' – 'I get high, I get high!' John and Paul had to explain rather sheepishly that they'd actually sung 'I can't hide, I can't hide!'

John, in particular, now waited for every new Dylan release, hungry for the next giant leap in experimentation it was bound to bring. He also kept a weather eye on the Beach Boys, whom Beatles records had prompted to abandon simple surfing chants for complex urban chorales, developing the harmonic genius of their leader, Brian Wilson. In 1965, too, there was a rising New York band, the Lovin' Spoonful, whose lead-singer/songwriter John Sebastian worryingly seemed to possess the humour of Lennon and the romanticism of McCartney inside one Beatle-shaggy head.

The soundtrack album for *Help!* brought the disparate characters of John and Paul, for the first time, into open contrast. On the one hand, there were unmistakably 'John' songs, like 'You've Got to Hide Your Love Away', written under Bob Dylan's influence: sardonic and world-weary, idylls of the morning after. On the other hand there was Paul's solo performance of a ballad he had been playing around with for weeks under the provisional title of 'Scrambled Eggs' but hadn't liked to bring to the studio because he couldn't believe its melody had never been used before. Now titled 'Yesterday', it was performed by Paul alone, accompanied by a classical string quartet and no other Beatle vocal or instrumental embellishment whatever. It was immediately 'covered' by a leading British ballad-singer Matt Monro, the first of some 2,000 recorded versions.

Rubber Soul, their second album that year, reflected a widening schism belied by the four Carnaby-look Beatles, still barely distinguishable from each other, in its modish fisheye-lens sleeve. Paul and John were by now leading separate – and, as it proved – mutually inimical lives. John's was the dominant presence, through songs that were fragments of current autobiography – the boredom, in 'Nowhere Man', of sitting at home in his Tudor mansion; the edgy lust of 'Norwegian Wood', a description of infidelity in some London girl's flat. From Paul came 'Michelle', a love song as sweet and untroubled as his affair with Jane and half its lyrics translated into French as if to impress the highbrow Asher family.

EMI's Abbey Road studios, whatever other amenities they lacked, were an ideal hideaway. London's northbound traffic sped in total indifference past the plain-fronted white house with its neat gravel driveway and high front steps. Only the commissionaire, eyeing the fan pickets posted respectively at the IN and OUT gateway, hinted at anything discordant with St John's Wood, acacia bushes, retired publishers and Austrian au pair girls.

In the house's rubber-silenced hinterland, Studio Two, that once strictly rationed Holy of Holies, was now consecrated almost exclusively to the Beatles' use. George Martin likewise no longer looked in his diary to see whether or not he could fit in a session. When the source of EMI's current £3m profit felt an urge to record, Martin and his engineer, Norman Smith, obeyed the peremptory summons.

Gone, too, was the producer's old clock-watching authority. Studio Two at Abbey Road became in effect a rehearsal room where new Beatles songs took shape by methods increasingly prodigal of time and expense. Four-track recording, which had replaced two-track at Abbey Road in late 1963, altered the entire concept of an album session. Whereas *Please Please Me* had been blasted off in one 13-hour marathon, *Rubber Soul* grew over several weeks as a 'layering' of rhythm, vocal and instrumental tracks, any of which could be erased and re-recorded. Both John and Paul, in their different ways, embraced these new technical possibilities. Each built his own private studio where demo tapes could be produced as a guide to the final Abbey Road version. Both ran through George Martin's domain as through a toyshop, alighting with rapture on this or that novelty of sound. They must have *that* on the track, they would say. Martin, the trained musician, Norman Smith, the trained engineer, would reply that it couldn't work. Then they found it did work. Studio procedure was to be changed for all time by this whim of iron.

At a certain moment in each session, Martin would leave John and Paul and cross the cable-strewn floor to George Harrison, waiting apart from the others, unsmiling with his Grecht rehearsal guitar. George would then play to Martin whatever solo he had worked out for the song. If Martin did not like it, he would lead George to the piano, tinker a little phrase and tell him to play that for his solo. Such was the origin of the guitar in 'Michelle'. 'I was,' Martin admits, 'always rather beastly to George.'

In George the world's ecstasy had as yet produced no answering lift of inspiration. He played lead guitar as he always had, earnestly, a little ponderously. He took his turn at lead singing in a voice whose thick Scouse seemed to mask an underlying embarrassment. Latterly, goaded into action by John and Paul's stupendous output, he, too, had begun to write songs by himself rather than in partnership with either of the other two and with titles unwittingly echoing his rather testy and impatient nature: 'Don't Bother Me' . . . 'Think for Yourself' . . . Each new album, in fairness, featured a song by George – just one. He was also learning the Indian sitar, an instrument which Richard Lester had added for comic purposes to a scene in *Help!* 'Norwegian Wood' was the first Beatles song to benefit from the wiry whining and wailing of George's sitar.

As for Ringo, he sat patiently in a corner of the studio, waiting to be called to sing his song or drum as directed; whiling away hours when he was not needed in card games with Neil and Mal.

•

Their UK tour in the winter of 1965 included their last-ever performance in Liverpool – though no one realised this at the time. They had intended to visit the Cavern Club and perform under its reeking stone arches, just for old time's sake, but Brian talked them out of the idea for their own safety. John felt particularly enraged at being unable to move about as he pleased even in his home city. He longed to meet Bill Harry and his other Art College cronies again at Ye Cracke and have a quiet pint or two under the mural of Wellington greeting Marshal Blucher at the Battle of Waterloo.

Had they made it to Mathew Street, they would have found the Cavern still much the same as when they'd played there, even though it was now world famous as 'the club that broke the Beatles' and to play there was the objective of every band seeking to follow in their footsteps. There were still the same stone steps, the same reeking arches, the same mingled odours of cheese rind and sweat. Outside, Paddy Delaney the doorman still stood in his dinner jacket and cummerbund, often now greeting celebrities such as Rex Harrison and Lionel Bart as they disembarked from chauffeur-driven limousines.

The Beatles' last Liverpool concert also was their last chance to revisit the Cavern. Its owner, Ray McFall, had got into financial difficulties and, a few weeks later, suddenly announced to Delaney that the bailiffs would be coming in the following morning. The members tried to prevent this by holding an all-night session, then blocking the steps with chairs and setting off all the fire extinguishers. Police sympathetically cleared the demonstrators then escorted Delaney out in a guard of honour, his immaculate dinner jacket white with foam. The warehouse was demolished soon afterwards, and the tunnels beneath, with all their Beatles echoes and memories, obliterated by a car park.

The Beatles' European and world tour of summer 1966 brought them another, slightly more satisfactory homecoming. The concerts included one in Hamburg, though this time they had to play for only 30 inaudible minutes at the city's Ernst March Halle sports arena rather than all night on the Reeperbahn. 'Don't try to listen to us,' John told the German support band. 'We're terrible these days.'

There were backstage reunions with old Hamburg friends like Bert Kampfaert and Bettina, the Star-Club barmaid whose friendly nails had raked so many pale young Liverpool backs. John even found his way to

Jonhannasbollwerk to see Jim and Lilo Hawke at the seaman's mission and eat a nostalgic plate of Frau Prill's real English chips. To the disappointment of all four, the visitors did not include Horst Fascher, the bouncer whose killer punch had protected them on so many bloodthirsty Star-Club nights. Horst was again in jail, serving a term for manslaughter. At their concert, the Beatles dedicated 'Roll Over Beethoven' to him, remembering how he loved to step in as their ad hoc vocalist whenever John or Paul were too pissed.

There was also a reunion with Astrid Kirchherr, the woman who had so crucially helped to create the image that now obsessed the world. Astrid's photographs of those tough-tender child rockers, sitting on the fairground traction engine, had appeared in newspapers and magazines throughout the world without any credit – or fee – to her. 'It was one of a bundle of prints I'd sent over to Liverpool,' Astrid says now. 'Later on, when it turned up in the media, it was credited to UPI. I didn't sue them; what would have been the point? To me, it was just a photograph of some friends.'

Astrid told the Beatles she'd now given up photography, thinking herself not good enough. She had taken a job in a female drag bar, dancing as required with the 'men'. In her black-draped bedroom, there was still a blow-up portrait of Stu Sutcliffe above her head. Candles burned night and day in memory of the fifth Beatle whom no one but his mother and sisters in Liverpool now seemed to remember.

•

The tour's stop after Hamburg was Tokyo, via the polar route. Because of a typhoon-warning their aircraft was forced to land in Anchorage, Alaska. Nat Weiss in New York was roused from sleep by Brian's voice on the telephone, demanding with some petulance, 'Who *owns* Alaska, Nat? And can you recommend a nice place to stay?'

Their two Tokyo concerts, at the Nippon Budo Kan (Martial Arts Hall), were, not surprisingly, the best-organised of the Beatles' performing career. The promoters explained to Brian that any riot would have brought dishonour upon themselves. Accordingly, the 9,000-strong audience had 3,000 police to guard them. Backstage, the Beatles were provided with geisha girls, a perpetual tea ceremony and a Japanese road manager for liaison. Between concerts, in the 24-room Presidential Suite at the Tokyo Hilton, a private bazaar was spread, of radios, cameras, happi coats and painting sets. The Beatles all bought inks and calligraphy brushes and, having nothing intelligible to watch on television, produced a garish mural on one huge sheet of paper that was later given to the Japanese fan club.

They expected something similar in the Philippines. They were charmed, as are all newcomers to Manila, by a miniature Texas set down among tropical islands; by the skyscrapers, specially earthquake-proofed, the shanties and juke boxes and brilliant jeep taxis, the jungle foliage reflected in a speed cop's Harley Davidson. After dark, as the bats bounced like shuttlecocks against the rim of Manila Bay, shotgun blasts at random bespoke South-East Asia's most uninhibited autocracy.

The Philippines in those days were still the fiefdom of President Ferdinand Marcos and his wife Imelda, a woman long celebrated for her vanity, her enormous wardrobe and unscrupulous use of her husband's absolute power. Herself a Beatles fan, Mrs Marcos had arranged a lavish garden party at Malacanang, the presidential palace, to introduce them to 300 hand-picked government officials and their families. The invitation delivered to Tony Barrow, however, gave no hint of these elaborate preparations: even Brian saw no particular necessity to attend.

Manila's English language newspapers next morning carried the banner headline BEATLES SNUB PRESIDENT. When a President happens also to be a military dictator, his wounded feelings naturally evince widespread sympathy. The concert promoters sympathised by refusing to pay Brian Epstein the Beatles' concert fee. Other citizens sympathised by telephoning death threats to the British Embassy.

Brian, horrified by the furore, did his best to make amends. He asked to appear on Manila television the following night to explain that no snub had been intended. The transmission was almost wiped out by heavy static which, coincidentally, vanished as soon as Brian's apology came to an end.

Departure from Manila Airport on 5 July was accompanied by ugliness unenvisaged even outside Litherland Town Hall. Deprived of all police protection, the Beatles party dashed for the aircraft through a concourse of jeering customs officers; they were jostled, even punched and kicked. The KLM flight for New Delhi took off only after lengthy negotiations between Brian and a Philippines Income Tax official who refused to let them go until they had paid £7,000.

En route back from New Delhi to London, exhausted, disillusioned, bruised physically as well as mentally, the Beatles told Brian that was it, they'd had enough. When this tour finally wound its way to an end, there would be no more.

•

The news so devastated Brian that his whole body erupted in a painful case of hives. Suffering from total exhaustion he fled to an hotel in Portmeirion, the Welsh resort where he had always found a measure of relaxation and quiet. He had barely settled down there when Nat Weiss telephoned from New York to tell him that Beatles albums were being ritually burnt in Nashville, Tennessee.

The previous February, in one of her regular Beatles reports for the London *Evening Standard*, Maureen Cleave had asked John his views, if any, on organised religion. His response gave little hint of a past life in the choir of St Peter's Church, Woolton. 'Christianity will go. It will vanish and shrink . . . we're more popular than Jesus now. I don't know which will go first – rock and roll or Christianity.' He had nothing against Jesus, he went on, but the disciples were 'thick'. 'They're the ones that ruin it for me.'

In Britain, the remark passed unchallenged – indeed, unnoticed. Such was not the case five months later when, on the eve of the Beatles' American tour, Maureen Cleave's interview with John was reprinted by a teenage magazine, *Datebook*. What in the *Evening Standard* piece had been merely an aside was headlined on *Datebook*'s cover: a stray ad lib transformed to vaunting sacrilege. John Lennon was claiming that the Beatles were 'bigger than Jesus Christ'.

In cheerily godless Britain with its enfeebled Protestant Church – already reeling under the mockeries of young satirists like Peter Cook and Alan Bennett – the remark had seemed no more than flippant and rather foolish. But to the core of old-fashioned, literal-minded Christianity that runs through America, it was no more or less than outright blasphemy. In fundamentalist Southern states, even the most avid female Beatles fans had no doubt as to whom they owed greater loyalty. The Tennessee radio station that invited shocked and disillusioned teenagers to cast their Beatles albums on to public bonfires was just one of hundreds originating similar protests throughout the country. One outraged community installed rubbish bins labelled 'Place Beatle Trash Here'; another brought in a tree-crushing machine to pulp the offending vinyl. Pastor Thurmond Babbs of Cleveland, Ohio, threatened to excommunicate any of his flock who attended a Beatles concert on the approaching tour. Their music was banned on 35 radio stations, from Ogdenburg, New York, to Salt Lake City, Utah.

The outcry added further fuel to what was already extreme disenchantment with the 'British Invasion' of pop bands who had followed the Beatles' triumphal path across the Atlantic. Now, the product being offered to America's youth was no longer innocent and charming 'Hamlet' fringes, pixie boots and deft one-liners. It had become a seemingly unstoppable procession of shaggy-headed and unsmiling yahoos who seemed to compete with each other in the tunelessness of their music and the mayhem of their performance. It was The Who, led by their anarchic, windmill-armed leader Pete Townshend, who ended each set by smashing his guitar to smithereens as though urging his audience to do the same to the concert hall. It was a new three-man group named Cream, the first ever to lose the definite article, whose drummer, Ginger Baker, delighted in firing off sticks like guided missiles to hit watching police or security men. Above all, it was the Rolling Stones, whose shaggy hair was popularly supposed to be teeming with vermin, whose equally 'filthy' lyrics had to be bleeped on television and whose recent US smash, 'Satisfaction', was apparently a hymn to the joys of playing with yourself.

Worse even than that was the new mood growing up among America's own young music-makers, the singers and groups whom the Beatles had galvanised into new energy and experimentation barely two years earlier. Under the leadership of Bob Dylan, American pop had ceased to be about high schools, drive-ins and junior proms and become as much a medium of protest and ridicule as acoustic folk had ever been, but now reaching an infinitely wider audience. The hitherto unchallenged war in Vietnam, racial intolerance, white suburban snobbery, urban decay, even the prospect of impending nuclear destruction, all now found their way into the charts in songs that sold by the billion. Until this moment, every type of American mass culture had reassured its citizens that their country was infallibly the good guy. Now the mocking voices of Dylan, Joan Baez, the Byrds and a hundred other insurrectionists broke the news that it had become the bad guy, not in folkies' harsh monotone but in seductive commercial hooks and harmonies, set about by electric pianos, wistful flutes and zithery 12-string guitars.

The Beatles were not in any sense political or subversive. But there was no doubt that they had changed, radically and disconcertingly, from the instant charmers who had whooped 'Yeah yeah' on the *Ed Sullivan Show*. The single they released early in 1966 – unconnected to any album, and a double A-side – bore the unmistakable stamp of Bob Dylan, and many others besides. Paul's contribution was 'Paperback Writer', a vague satire against hack journalism and the mass media, set about by Pete Townshend-esque guitar chords and intricate harmonies with more than a nod towards the Beach Boys. 'Rain' was by John, echoing the Byrds as they had sounded in their smash cover version of Dylan's 'Mr Tambourine Man', but with his own special air of being pressured and persecuted almost beyond endurance: 'When the rain comes, you run and hide your head . . . you might as well be dead . . .' Its closing babble of gibberish was added late at night in his private studio, by drunkenly running the vocal chorus backwards.

As usual, advance orders took 'Rain/Paperback Writer' instantly to number one in Britain and America. Only after 1½ million copies had been taken home and played did some little uncertainty arise. 'Paperback Writer', which received most radio play, frankly mystified American fans with its allusions to a man named Lear and the *Daily Mail.* A suspicion formed, even if no one dared yet to say it, that the Beatles were not infallible.

A further bloody mess of controversy was just around the corner. To promote their American tour, Capitol had issued a compilation album of songs from *Help!* and *Rubber Soul*, plus three from the new British album still awaiting release. The title of this hybrid, reflecting its most lyrical McCartney contribution, was *The Beatles – Yesterday and Today*. Any promise of gentle nostalgia was dispelled by a full-colour sleeve on which the Beatles, wearing white butchers' overalls, nursed dismembered and decapitated toy dolls and brandished bloody joints of meat.

The 'butcher sleeve', as it became known, was the Beatles' own art directing concept. Sean O'Mahony, editor of their fan club magazine, had been present at the photographic session and had covered his eyes in dismay when the props were brought in. Such was their power by then that Brian's misgivings were overruled. The gruesome tableau appeared first in England, on the cover of *Disc* magazine. Capitol Records, cowed by their former lack of prescience, agreed that it would probably be a winner. Seven hundred and fifty thousand sleeves had been printed before the first calls came in from disc jockeys almost retching over their advance copies. The sleeve was then axed, together with all the promotional material, at a cost of $200,000. A special staff spent one weekend extracting each of the 750,000 discs from its butcher sleeve and inserting it into one hastily improvised round a picture of the Beatles leaning on a cabin trunk. In many cases, to save trouble, the new sleeve was simply pasted over the old.

As to which Beatle had proposed the bloody joints and limbless dolls, there was never any serious doubt. The banned cover, a bitterly resentful John Lennon said, was 'as relevant as Vietnam'. His tone, people noticed, was neither cheeky nor funny.

Meanwhile, John's 'bigger than Jesus' remark continued to be denounced from pulpits across the world. Both the Spanish and South African governments issued official condemnations though the latter, still ostracised for its racial policies, did not carry excessive moral weight. The Pope added his disapproval via the Vatican newspaper *L'Osservatore Romano*, which declared that 'some subjects must not be dealt with profanely, even in the world of beatniks'.

Though debilitated with hives as well as groggy from a bout of flu, Brian flew to New York ahead of the tour party in an attempt to calm, at least, the American furore. Nat Weiss remembers how his anxiety and distress when he got off the plane were not just about the huge sum of tour earnings at stake. 'He really cared most about the possibility that the Beatles would suffer abuse – that they might even be in danger,' Weiss says. 'The first question he asked me was: "What will it cost to cancel the tour?" I said: "A million dollars." He said: "I'll pay it. I'll pay it out of my own pocket, because if anything were to happen to any one of them, I'd never forgive myself."'

Using all his powers of diplomacy, Brian assured the American press that John had intended no sacrilege, but only wished to express 'deep concern' at the decline in spiritual values. It was announced that when the Beatles arrived on 12 August, John himself would formally apologise. He did so at a press conference in Chicago, pale and nervous – for the hate mail that he had been receiving had badly shaken him. 'I'm sorry I opened my mouth,' he said. 'I'm not anti-God, anti-Christ or anti-religion. I wouldn't knock it. I didn't mean we were greater or better.'

So began the tour destined to be the worst, if not yet officially last of all. To add to the general unease, a famous American clairvoyant had predicted that three of the four Beatles would die soon in an air crash. Though the prophecy was later retracted, it cast a lingering tremor over the constant shuttle-flights. Mal Evans was convinced he would not survive the tour, and spent one journey between concerts composing a last letter to his wife, Lil, and his new baby daughter, Julie.

All four Beatles became conscious for the first time of a threat which had worried Brian since the American tours began – that, some night, in some huge, oval human sea, someone might be hiding with a high-velocity rifle. In each big city stadium, grinding out the numbers they could no longer hear, they felt themselves endangered now by something other than dangerous adoration. At Memphis, their first concert south of the Mason-Dixon Line, the backstage fear was palpable as sweat. On television earlier that day, a portly wizard of the Ku Klux Klan had promised that, if they went onstage, the Klan would fully justify its name as a terror organisation. Instead of jelly beans, rubbish began to land on the stage. Halfway through the performance, a firecracker exploded. Brian, for one hideous moment, thought it was a rifle shot.

Almost every major venue along the tour route seemed to bring its own peculiar curse. In Washington DC, the Beatles had to play in competition with a race riot a few blocks away. At the Los Angeles Dodger Stadium, scores of innocent fans were manhandled by security staff and attacked by baton-wielding police. In Cincinnati, the concert promoter tried to economise by building a stage with no roof or canopy. Just before the Beatles went out to play, a downpour of rain began. They could not have gone ahead without serious risk of electrocution. 'The whole audience – 35,000 screaming kids – had to be turned away,' Nat Weiss says. 'They all got passes for a show the next day but, for a while, it really looked ugly out there. All the Beatles were frightened. Paul, I know, was physically sick.'

The final concert of the tour was on 29 August at Candlestick Park, San Francisco. 'Brian told me it was the end in San Francisco,' Nat Weiss says. 'He was dejected. "This is it," he told me, "this is the last one ever."'

The day was to be even more terrible than Brian anticipated. For some months past, he had been living with an American youth known as 'Dizz' whom, in his first grand infatuation, he had even signed as an artist with NEMS Enterprises. But the relationship had proved too stormy, and physically violent, even for Brian's taste. Unlike previous partners, Dizz proved recalcitrant when shown the door and had threatened to tell the whole story to the Beatles unless given a substantial sweetener. Through Nat Weiss, Brian had paid him $3,000 in exchange for a promise to stay off this present tour, when one single further word of bad publicity would have been disastrous.

By the time the tour party reached Los Angeles, however, Brian had started to hanker for Dizz again. Against Weiss's pleas, he was brought to LA, put up in a bungalow at the Beverly Hills Hotel and invited to the Beverly Hills house where Brian and Weiss were based.

On 29 August, after the Beatles had left for San Francisco, the two returned to the house to discover that both their briefcases had been stolen. Weiss's merely contained business papers, but Brian's was a compendium of drugs, homosexual correspondence and pornographic pictures, plus a hefty sum in cash, skimmed off the tour's concert receipts, which he had intended to share among the Beatles as a bonus. While the money was of little consequence, the briefcase's other contents put a lethal blackmail weapon into any ill-wisher's hands. Brian was so convulsed with terror and dread that he dared not even leave the house.

So, to his lasting remorse, he missed the Beatles' last live concert. He never forgave himself for not being at Candlestick Park, on that night of all nights, to watch over the four boys in his charge.

•

Britain, that summer of 1966, had little cause to feel pleased with itself or the world. The year, barely half-expended, could already chalk up the varying torments of a General Election and a national shipping strike. The pound ailed; inflation kept briskly on the ascent. The re-elected Wilson Government stood revealed, not as dynamic or purposeful but merely another set of politicians, with the usual capacity to bungle and vacillate. Rhodesia, having seceded from British rule a year earlier, still thumbed a derisive nose at her fuming mother country across the world. From still further afield came noises which penetrated even the age-old British indifference to what was still vaguely thought of as the Orient. America began bombing the North Vietnamese cities of Hanoi and Haiphong. A war hitherto faint and far-flung ceased to happen comfortably out of earshot.

There was, however, bright sunshine. The British, as they had in the past forgotten pestilence, famine, the Great War, Hitler's bombs and the Suez Crisis, now just as easily forgot Mr Wilson, Vietnam and the Pay Freeze under the influence of weeks of unbroken summer. So 1966 was to pass into popular remembrance: not for crises, both present and promised, but for blue skies, soft breezes, and for two events – the only two – which fortified that ephemeral happiness.

On 30 July, England won the World Football Cup, audaciously snatching the vital goal in the last seconds of the final against Germany. Old wartime animosities doubtless assisted the fervour with which, on another hot summer evening, the victorious team was welcomed home to London. Footballers looked like pop singers now; they grew their hair, wore trendy clothes and received the approbation of great men. For Harold Wilson, naturally, was there, puffing his pipe as smugly as if England's winning goal had originated in a Cabinet memorandum.

The second, even more potent source of national esteem owed its origin to America's *Time* magazine, which had only recently got around to noticing the Swinging London phenonemon that, in fact, had peaked more than a year earlier. On 13 April, *Time* had devoted its cover and a breathless 12-page report to London as 'the Style Capital of Europe', a judgement with which other American mainstream magazines like *Life* and the *Saturday Evening Post* were quick to agree. As a result, London was experiencing an influx of American visitors unknown since the Second World War. Hitherto, crossing the Atlantic had always been prohibitively expensive, creating Britain's image of the American tourist as a cigar-chewing plutocrat with a guidebook. But now a coincidental drop in transatlantic air fares allowed thousands – millions – of American students, even schoolchildren, to come across under their own steam and experience the staid old capital's new short-skirted, strange-scented wonders. Almost without exception, the first question these visitors asked on touching down at Heathrow was 'Where can I find the Beatles?'

On 5 August, an album appeared in the record shops which, were it not for the fact that approximately one million copies had been ordered in advance, might have seemed to stand little chance of being noticed on the shelves. Its cover, amid its rivals' Carnaby colours, was plain black and white: a collage of photo-fragments spiralling through what looked like palm fronds but proved on close inspection to be hair, encircling four silhouetted faces so instantly recognisable, it was not thought necessary to print their collective name. Who else in the world would announce themselves in graphics reflecting the smartest magazines? Who would call a record album simply *Revolver*, investing even that commonplace pun with the sleekness of some new-minted avant garde? Who but the Beatles would have confidence colossal enough to be so chastely downbeat?

Revolver was not presented in the usual patchwork album style but as a continuous, cohesive performance, as if they had chosen Abbey Road's Studio Two as a substitute stage. There was, first of all, to underline this, some stagey coughing and throat clearing. Then came 'Taxman', not a love song but a bitter satire written as well as lead-sung by a chronically bitter George Harrison, railing against the huge portion of the Beatles' earnings due in income tax under jolly Mr Wilson. There was 'Eleanor Rigby', sung by Paul alone with a string octet: a song more like a short story, evoking Paul's Irish Catholic roots, about a lonely woman picking up other people's wedding rice. There was John's 'I'm Only Sleeping', answering back Paul's sentimental conscience with a paean to unrepentant apathy. There was the contrast of George's sitar-squibbly 'Love You To' and the stunning, simple charm of Paul's latest Jane-idyll, 'Here, There and Everywhere'. There was 'Yellow Submarine', a song for children (as it seemed) perfectly suited to Ringo's happy drone, accompanied by slurpings and gurglings, ringing ships' bells, a sub-aqueous brass band and commands from the bridge in a John Lennon funny voice; and then John's non-funny voice, in 'She Said She Said', among graffiti-like guitar phrases, saying 'I know what it's like to be dead'.

On side two, to glorify the weather, there was 'Good Day Sunshine'. There was 'And Your Bird Can Sing', more lucid Lennon nonsense, and Paul's pretty, self-pitying 'For No One'. There was Doctor Robert, the first of many in-jokes and concealed references to be planted in Beatles music: a sly dig at one of the upmarket medical men who kept them supplied with pills. There was George's 'I Want to Tell You', with its wonderful message to pampered, unharassed and fully-employed 1966 teenagers that it was still OK to feel flat and dissatisfied (or 'hung up') the way George did; and then Paul's 'Got to Get You into My Life', a soul song as neat and brassy and rousing as ever came out of Memphis or Chicago.

The Beatles, in fact, were not the first to nail down Swinging London in sound. Four months earlier, the Rolling Stones' *Aftermath* album had created very much the same King's Road and Carnaby Street feel, thanks mainly to the multi-instrumental talent of Brian Jones, whose intuitive sitar-playing made George by contrast sound as though his fingers were all thumbs. But no one looked to the Stones to catch the zeitgeist, whereas for the Beatles it was now almost a duty to be in step with the nation's destiny. Thus *Revolver* became the perfect aural snapshot of Britain's greatest triumph since 1940, a moment that would be still unequalled and revisited as often as its soundtrack was replayed half a century later.

If they were not quite the first to distil the present, they made up for it by prophesying the future soon to dawn. It was there on *Revolver*'s seemingly aberrant closing track, 'Tomorrow Never Knows', a Ringo saying transmuted by John into a weird melange of backward-played tapes, his once exuberant lead voice flattened to near tunelessness. 'Turn off your mind, relax and float downstream ... Lay down all thought, surrender to the void ... Or play the game Existence to the end. Of the beginning ...' Like England World Cup victories, the days of 'She loves you, yeah, yeah, yeah' were over for good and all.

•

The four who stopped running, who stood still at last in 1966, looking curiously about them, were beings such as the modern world had never seen. Only in ancient times, when boy Emperors and Pharaohs were clothed, even fed, with pure gold, had very young men commanded an equivalent adoration, fascination and constant, expectant scrutiny. Nor could anyone suppose that to be thus – to have such youth and wealth, such clothes and cars and servants and women, made for any state other than inconceivable happiness. For no one since the boy Pharaohs, since the fatally pampered boy Caesars, had known, as the Beatles now knew, how it felt to have felt everything, done everything, tasted everything, had a surfeit of everything; to live on that blinding, deadening, numbing surfeit which made each, on bad days, think he was ageing at twice the usual rate.

It was as little comprehensible that to command such fame as Beatles might not be enough: that each, in the stupendous collective adoration, felt himself to be overlooked as an individual: that each on his own should long to test the reality, or otherwise, of his independent existence.

•

John Lennon seemed the most determined – and best qualified – to make an individual career. That autumn, with Neil Aspinall, he detached himself from the other three to appear in a new film, *How I Won the War*, directed by the now extremely fashionable and financeable Richard Lester. It had been clear to Lester, even in the harmless knockabout of the two Beatles films, that John had serious possibilities as a screen actor. This view was confirmed when *How I Won the War* went on release and John's portrayal of Private Gripweed was singled out for critical praise. 'I told him then he could do anything he wanted in films,' Richard Lester says. 'But he wasn't interested. It came too easily to him. He despised it.'

The Beatle who had vanished into Private Gripweed was never to re-emerge. He kept his hair cropped short – a renunciation already front-page news throughout the world. He took to wearing the glasses he had always hated, perversely choosing little owl-eyed frames like those prescribed for him at primary school in the 1940s.

Under the cropped hair, the granny glasses, the clothes that tended increasingly towards flowered scarves and loose waistcoats, much of the same old John remained. The same impossible vagueness still caused him to forget the words of his own songs, his ex-directory telephone number, even his Aunt Mimi's Christian name. The same impossible generosity would still press on anyone his last cigarette or whatever was in his pocket, whether sixpence or a thousand pounds. The same blistering sarcasm and silly puns kept those around him suspended between terror of his contempt and helpless, incredulous laughter. The same old John would try anything once, whether a new author, a new painter, a new liquor, a new vegetable or a new permutation of sex. Among his acquaintances in this period was Jonathan King, recently in the charts with 'Everyone's Gone to the Moon', a song he had writen and recorded while still a Cambridge undergraduate. One night, he and John rounded off an evening out with two female pick-ups, intending a 'foursome'. But, as King remembers, 'John and I ended up enjoying each other'.

When he came off the road in 1966, John's life seemed to hold so many possibilities. Publishers wanted him to write for them. Print engravers and greeting card companies urged him to draw for them. Art galleries – now springing up in London almost as rapidly as boutiques – begged him to attend their private views. Art seemed to engage his whole attention for a time. He would drive up from Weybridge two or three times a week in the rainbow-daubed Rolls-Royce whose Scottish chauffeur also used it as an occasional doss.

Newest of all the new little West End galleries was the Indica in Mason's Yard, run by Marianne Faithfull's ex-husband, John Dunbar. In November 1966, the Indica was hanging an exhibition called 'Unfinished Paintings and Objects by Yoko Ono'. The artist, a Japanese-born American, enjoyed minor notoriety in London for having recently exhibited her photographs of various unclothed human bottoms.

The night before the Indica exhibition opened, John arrived to look at it. He spent quite a long time over the Unfinished Paintings and Objects, particularly a painting attached to the ceiling with a ladder up to it, and an apple unembellished but for a price ticket saying '£200'. Later on, John

Dunbar sent Yoko across to talk to him in hopes he might turn out a useful patron. She proved to be very small and dressed entirely in black, her rather grim little face almost obscured by clouds of black hair. Instead of speaking, she handed John a card on which was written the single word 'Breathe'.

Next day, he was back in the small living-room in one corner of the mansion which had taken nine months to decorate; folded up inside the small sofa he preferred to all his pastel-upholstered acres. He would lie there for hours, watching television or half-watching it, glancing at books and papers, then throwing them aside. He could lie there all day, not speaking to Cynthia, not seeming to notice Julian, his trance penetrable only by some scrap of nonsense from a TV quiz, some stray paragraph from the *Daily Express*, some costly and purposeless toy like his 'nothing box', a black plastic cube in which red lights winked on and off at random. He could spend hours in trying to guess which of the red lights would wink on next.

Late at night, if no excursion was happening, he would unfold himself from the couch and wander away to his studio, the guitars, the Vox organ, the 10 linked-up Brunel tape recorders. Cynthia knew she would not see him again that night. Next day, she would have to keep the house quiet until early afternoon, when she took up his breakfast tray.

Sitting downstairs with her drawing or her needlework, cowed by the feuding between Dot, the housekeeper, and the general factotum's wife, afraid to go outside the grounds in case some photographer saw Julian; thrifty, soft-spoken, eternally hoping for the best, Cyn' was the same person she had always been.

•

Paul, the most committed performer, the most addicted to worship, the one who had worked the hardest at being a Beatle, now found himself at something of a loss. His first act, after the touring stopped, was to take a long and, for him, extravagant sabbatical. With Mal Evans – whose wife Lil still waited patiently at home in Sunbury-on-Thames – he set out on a long road safari across Africa.

His future, Paul announced on returning, would be concerned with all-round cultural self-improvement. He felt – as, indeed, both John and George did – that being a Beatle had been a form of missing life. The A-level Institute boy was excited, too, by London's increasing artistic bustle. 'People are saying things and painting things and writing things that are great,' he told the *Evening Standard*. 'I must *know* what people are doing.'

In this endeavour, as in all Paul's private life, his girl friend Jane Asher was the main stimulus. Jane, unlike the other Beatles women, possessed complete independence: now 21, she had her own highly successful stage and film career. With her angelic looks went a strong mind and forthright manner which curtailed Paul's ego, deflated his superstar pomposities and made her a companion altogether preferable to any of the brainless beauties who clustered adoringly round him. He made a point of seeing all Jane's plays, wherever the run happened to start. It was in Bristol, waiting to see Jane in a play, that a shopfront name gave him the idea for 'Eleanor Rigby'. His best love songs had been written for Jane: in the feather-light 'Here, There and Everywhere' she is an almost tangible presence.

His first project apart from the other Beatles was the composition of theme music for a new British comedy film, *The Family Way*. *Newsweek* magazine – which otherwise would hardly have noticed such a minor piece – considered his score 'neat and resourceful'. He had already begun producing records – for Peter and Gordon, the duo featuring Peter Asher, Jane's brother; for a group called the Escourts; and for Cliff Bennett and the Rebel Rousers when they covered his song 'Got to Get You into My Life'.

He had chosen a house at last: not in stockbroker land with the other Beatles but in Cavendish Avenue, St John's Wood. The district epitomised his cultural and social ambitions and was also conveniently close to the EMI studios. The house, discreetly large, was enclosed by high walls and protected by electronic security gates. With it, Paul acquired the accessory status-symbols of a married couple: butler and cook. An Old English sheepdog named Martha roamed the extensive garden which, despite his family's protests, he resolutely neglected.

As far as the press and public were concerned, the most interesting thing about Paul's self-improvement programme was the point in it when he and Jane Asher would announce their engagement. Jane had helped him to decorate and furnish the new house although, with a nicety characteristic of both, she did not officially live with him there.

Each of them had grown adept at fending off the same old, microphone-thrusting question. 'I certainly would be most surprised,' Jane said, 'if I married anyone but Paul.' And Paul himself, caught yet again outside his electronic gates, looked up from his Aston Martin with the geniality that never seemed to falter, listened to the question, considered and replied: 'Just say that when you asked me that, I smiled.'

•

George, so it seemed, was even more at a loss. He had been a Beatle ever since the age of 15. All his adult life had been spent running or, with his gradually more magnificent guitar, his mop-top framing his pale, wary face, just standing there.

For the final year of touring, if not longer, George had actively hated his Beatle existence. On the outside, it might appear pure gold: on the inside, it bristled with snubs and slights – the heavy patience of George Martin in the studio; the stifling profusion of John and Paul's partnership which allowed him, if he was lucky, one song per album; the realisation that in their eyes he was still what he had been in Liverpool, the kid just tagging along.

His unvented rage he turned upon the adoring world. While Beatlemania was still a laugh to the others, to George it was an affront against the musicianship he had so laboriously taught himself. His fame seemed to have brought him only money and a terrible touchiness – a suspicion, already voiced in one song lyric, of 'people standing round who screw you in the ground'. His wife Patti – they had married in January 1966 – virtually gave up her modelling career lest, in George's eyes, people should try to exploit him through her.

It had been with the idlest curiosity, on the *Help!* film set, that George first heard Indian sitars playing a burlesque version of the Beatles' own song 'A Hard Day's Night'. *Help!* was, of course, a goonish romp about Eastern mystics in pursuit of a sacrificial jewel. The finale was a pitched battle between Beatles and dacoits in the surf along a Bahamas beach while a many-armed Hindu idol lolled in the offshore swell. As Richard Lester remembers, no one quite knew if it was part of the script or not when, in the midst of shooting, an Indian suddenly rode up on a bicycle and handed each Beatle a small religious book.

From the joke film property and the Indian on the bicycle grew the earnest passion which was to make George Harrison the least recognisable Beatle of all. He acquired a sitar of his own and began to play it, initially as if it was a guitar. Clumsy as his first experiments were, they gave him something he had never had before – a definite and distinctive contribution to what the Beatles did in the studio. For not even George Martin could be snooty about sitars. The sound tentatively used on *Rubber Soul* was one of the prime elements, and praised as such, in *Revolver*. Henceforward it was recognised that when a group of Indians walked in and squatted down, balancing their strange, giraffe-necked instruments against the ball of one bare foot, that was when George took over and gave orders. In 1966, at a dinner-party, he met Ravi Shankar, the Indian sitar virtuoso who offered to visit his bungalow in Esher and give him private tuition.

He had already been to India once, briefly, on the run from the

Philippines. In autumn 1966 – after what he at least firmly regarded as the Beatles' last appearance – he returned there with Patti for two months' sitar study under Ravi Shankar. He also met Shankar's spiritual teacher, or guru, who explained to him the Law of Karma – the Buddhist principle of inevitability. He and Patti travelled to Kashmir, where they witnessed religious festivals and conversed with students and holy men.

Just as he had once obsessively applied himself to his £3 guitar, George now devoted his life to sitar practice. In this period, indeed, he rarely touched a guitar outside the recording studio. He practised day and night, sitting on the floor in his Indian tunic with Ravi Shankar's instructions playing on tape.

George, too, was now regularly taking LSD. For him, the mental landscape the drug produced was one he had already seen. It was the India of mystic sounds and mystic beings, able to levitate or lie on spikes or bury themselves: the India which, in sight and touch and voice and clamour and calm, was the furthest distance you could go from being a Beatle, wearing a suit and singing 'Yeah, yeah, yeah'. He who had always kept his mind shut tight against all schooling, now began to devour books about yoga and meditation. The books promised a state he had so far found unattainable – of perfect pleasure, 'enlightenment' and peace. He need not worry then about the taxman and who was screwing him; about who recognised him, or failed to recognise him; about the girls who climbed into the garden he cultivated like a northern working man and broke the tops off his roses.

•

Only Ringo seemed to know for certain what he wanted. He wanted to stay at home with Maureen and their new baby, Zak. They called the baby Zak because it was the name Ringo had wished for when small. Life for Ringo was still that simple, even when he stood in the grounds of 'Sunny Heights', looking across his landscaped garden to the wall half-constructed by his own building company, and at his cars, the Facel Vega, the Land-Rover, the Mini Cooper, and at the house itself with its miles of soft furnishings, its white carpets, its six TV sets, its ciné equipment, billiard table and one-arm bandit. He would remember his childhood in the Liverpool Dingle and all those lonely hospital beds, and think: 'What's a scruff like me doing with all this lot?'

•

Even as separate householders and individual millionaires, they could not stop being together. No wife, no girl friend yet had broken the inexplicable bond between four individuals who had not only grown up together but also helped each other through an ordeal none but that four understood. The habit continued of doing things, wearing things, buying things, having crazes for things in unison. When John took to wearing glasses, the others did. Paul and John, during the New Delhi stopover, bought sitars like George's. All took simultaneously to baggy-sleeved flowered shirts, high-buttoning frock coats, wide-brimmed hats and loosely-tied scarves. And early in 1967, on the upper lips of all four, there appeared identical small curved moustaches.

Just as on tour, the people closest to them were the two fellow Liverpudlians who, as road managers, had so long formed their only bulwark against the world. Neil – or, as John called him, 'Nell' – Aspinall, the nervous, clever ex-accountancy student, and Mal Evans, the inoffensive ex-bouncer, continued to fill a role necessary to each Beatle and the four as a unit. Neil and Mal went where the Beatles went, wore what the Beatles wore, smoked what the Beatles smoked: for their not over-large salaries they remained perpetually on call to provide any Beatle with any of life's necessities, from a transcontinental chauffeur to a tray of tea and toast. Mal's wife, Lil, in Sunbury, did not see him for weeks at a time. Neil – paradoxically in the service of such masters – was starting to lose his hair.

Similarly, the close friends each Beatle had tended to be friends acquired collectively, in Liverpool or Hamburg. There was Tony Bramwell, George's childhood acquaintance, who had progressed from NEMS office boy to stage manager of Brian's latest venture, the Saville theatre. There was Terry Doran, another Brian friend, his partner in Brydor Cars, but welcome in every Beatles home for his willingness to go anywhere, fetch anything, and his talent to amuse. There was Klaus Voorman, their art student friend from Hamburg, the boy whom Astrid forsook for Stu Sutcliffe. Klaus now played bass guitar in the Manfred Mann group but had stayed close enough to his former Hamburg mates to design the *Revolver* album sleeve. There was also, intermittently, Pete Shotton, John Lennon's old school and skiffle crony, whom John had recompensed for the night he smashed Pete's washboard over his head by buying a supermarket for him to run in Hampshire.

Creatively, the band seemed to be coasting – little dreaming it was just the calm before the storm. Though committed to make a third film for United Artists, they could not agree with Walter Shenson, their producer, over a script. John, especially, complained that in *Help!* they had been 'extras in our own film'. One idea was that they should make a Western; another was that they should play the Three Musketeers; another – the one that Shenson thought most promising – visualised them as four living facets of the same personality. As with the previous two films,

Shenson looked around for a 'quality' writer. A script was commissioned from Joe Orton, the young working-class dramatist whose macabre comedies *Loot* and *Entertaining Mr Sloane* had each been huge West End successes.

Orton visited Brian Epstein at Chapel Street to discuss the project. Paul, who had much admired *Loot*, was also there. 'I'd expected Epstein to be florid, Jewish, dark-haired and overbearing,' Orton wrote in his diary. 'Instead, I was face to face with a mousey-haired, slight young man. He had a suburban accent. Rather washed out. Paul was just as in the photographs. Only he'd grown a moustache. "The only thing I get from the theatre," Paul M said, "is a sore arse" . . .'

Orton, typically, produced an outrageous script entitled *Up Against It* in which the Beatles were to be portrayed as anarchists, adulterers and urban guerillas. After a long delay, the script was rejected without comment. 'An amateur and a fool,' wrote Orton angrily of Brian. 'Probably he will never say Yes. Equally he hasn't the courage to say No. A thoroughly weak, flaccid type.'

During November, the Beatles had returned to Abbey Road in what proved an abortive attempt to make an end-of-year follow-up to *Revolver*. All that appeared that Christmas was a cut-price collection of Beatles Oldies-but Goldies and the traditional zany disc message to their fan club.

What with one thing and another these days, they seemed to see almost nothing of Brian. From various intermediaries like Peter Brown and Geoffrey Ellis, they had heard that he was 'depressed'. But at that moment, the thought concerned them rather less than what in hell they were going to put out as their next album, if anything.

15

'I don't think there was any hope for him since the day he met the Beatles'

For those whose blessed good fortune it was to grow up in the 1960s, the year to be remembered above all is 1967. Already in the twentieth century, moments of especially purblind human delusion had been symbolised by summers – the 'long Edwardian summer' before the First World War; the hot summer of still trusting to Hitler's essential good intentions in 1939. But none of those could compare, nor ever will, to 1967's so-called 'Summer of Love'.

Internationally, the world had probably never had less love in it. America's 'limited' military intervention to support South Vietnam's friendly government against the Communist north had swollen into an all-out conflict, demanding huge resources in machinery and men and remorselessly laying waste one of the most beautiful countries in South-East Asia. It was the first war of the television age, and one in which America's military had yet to learn the most fundamental techniques of news management. European TV crews flocked to record a conflagration in which women and children, often of stunning beauty and grace, perished by the thousand. Horrific images were beamed into every Western living-room: of helicopter gunships strafing rice paddyfields, of toddlers blistered from head to toe by a state-of-the art incendiary called napalm, of a US Army spokesman declaring in all earnestness, 'In order to save this village, it was necessary to destroy it.'

America, for the first time in her history, found herself involved in a war she could not win; a war which, even more bewilderingly, was opposed by many Americans. A wave of pacifist feeling swept the country, not among cranks and beatniks only but among the ordinary teenagers now liable for military service. 'Protest' as a concept left the lunatic fringe, spreading through formerly peaceable universities, spreading also into the black ghettoes whose young men were impartially called on to fight for a system which still oppressed them. Pop music was a reflection – even aggravation – of the new rebellious mood. Bob Dylan's bitter mockery, the sweet reproaches of Joan Baez, became the spur to anti-war demonstrations and marches, and the ever increasing numbers who fled 'the military draft' to Canada or Europe.

So the American Dream began to dissolve. Yet that bitter awakening, ironically, produced its own short, golden reverie in a city harbouring more American dreams than most. Like the first settlers and the gold-seekers, like the Zen Buddhists of the early Sixties, like Kerouac and his 'beat' poets, America's dissenting youth in 1967 turned their eyes to that side of the republic where the ocean began and, in particular, where the ocean's space and freedom seemed reflected in the city of San Francisco.

San Francisco's run-down Haight-Ashbury district had long ago been settled by a homespun and bewhiskered 'hippy' community. That community now swelled with the arrival of draft-dodgers, disaffected students and social drop-outs by the thousand. Fresh hippy colonies sprang up along the North California coast, around Berkeley University and in remote beach hamlets like Big Sur. The environment, with its natural beauty and leisurely policing, was ideally suited to resignation from all conventional American life. More and more came to share the hippy heaven: to grow their hair, put on flowing robes and walk barefoot; to speak softly, behave meekly, offer each other flowers, and 'turn on' by means of the small, limp cigarettes that somehow became more special the more mouths had previously dragged on them.

Marijuana was the badge of hippy brotherhood, the odour most common in hippy refuges, the initiator of the hippy belief that through drugs lay a path to higher wisdom and humaneness. A middle-aged university physicist, Dr Timothy Leary, was already their leader – or guru – following his dismissal from Harvard for experiments into the 'psychedelic' (literally, mind-expanding) properties of LSD. Leary and his academic converts led the awakening interest in drug-inspired literature, from Byron to Aldous Huxley, and of drug-sanctioning Eastern religions. Joss sticks were thus tentatively lit in California, and Buddhist prayers phonetically intoned. Astrology became a youth fad to rival the hula hoop. It was through astrology most of all that wisdom became available: an age-old wisdom settling, in the pot smoke, over woolly and impressionable minds. An entire new vocabulary evolved to distinguish the hippy from his persecutor, the 'beautiful' from the short-haired and workaday, the divine souls who 'turned on', 'tuned in', 'freaked out' and 'blew their minds' from the residue of unenlightened humanity.

Musicians, being natural converts, blew the hippy happening like pollen across America. By early 1967, San Francisco groups like Jefferson Airplane and the Grateful Dead were bringing the first rumours to British youth – of Haight-Ashbury and Big Sur and a huge outdoor concert at

Monterey; of harsh new metal sounds and flashing lights; of a new dream world which young Britons, having no Big Sur, only Margate and Llandudno, supposed they must be content to experience at second-hand.

•

On 17 February, Parlophone released two new Beatles songs: 'Penny Lane' and 'Strawberry Fields Forever'. The tracks had been recorded late in 1966, for the album that was to surpass *Revolver*: with a lightweight ditty called 'When I'm Sixty-Four', they represented the sum of almost three months' work. Since a single was long overdue, George Martin had no choice but to sacrifice the two three-minute productions that, each in its own way, had involved more time and expense than most entire LPs. The 'double A-side' formula was less a boast than a political necessity, since one side was wholly John's and the other entirely Paul's: the weight of creativity packed into each only emphasised what a gulf lay between them.

Strawberry Field was the name of a Salvation Army children's home John remembered from his Liverpool boyhood. The song he had named after this childhood landmark began with the air of a nostalgia trip ('Let me take you down, 'cause I'm goin' . . .) then dissolved into LSD hallucinations, intensified still further by chronic myopic pun-making ('Nothing is real. And nothing to get hungabout'). The lyric was a stream of semi-consciousness conjuring forth all the elements in John's character – now loftily philosophical, now angry, now fearful, now sarcastic, now despairing, now wearily resigned – see-sawing between the surreal and the colloquial ('Er, yes but it's all right . . .'), in total adding up to nothing that remotely resembled a Salvation Army children's home nor a field of strawberries, yet destined to imprint each obscure image and clouded thought on the listener with the burning-brand indelibility of Blake's 'Jerusalem'.

Paul's 'Penny Lane', by contrast, recreated with photographic clarity a part of Liverpool well known to all the Beatles, the place where Aunt Mimi used to see John off to Dovedale Primary and where the Quarry Men had played their earliest gigs at the little hall called 'Barney's'. It mentioned the traffic roundabout, the fire station, the barber's with its shop-window portraits of satisfied customers; it had a cast of characters including the fireman with his loyal 'picture of the Queen', and a 'pretty nurse' like Paul's own much-missed mother, 'selling poppies from a tray'. It evoked the 'blue suburban skies' and 'pouring rain' of their Liverpool childhood, the 'four of fish' (i.e. four-pennyworth) they would order at their local chippie, the 'finger pie' (poking at a girl's crotch with a forefinger, then sniffing it) that was their ultimate sexual thrill before they were old enough to make love in earnest. It was surrealism from a rational mind, as recognisable yet mysterious as looking at someone else's family snaps.

As an arranger, Martin's only guide was Paul's enthusiasm for the piccolo trumpet passage in Bach's 'Brandenberg Concerto'. David Mason of the London Symphony Orchestra stood by in Studio Two with his piccolo trumpet while Paul hummed the notes he wanted and Martin inked them into a score.

'Strawberry Fields' proved an even greater test of the producer's ingenuity. The song, as John first played it on acoustic guitar, was a simple, reflective melody. With the other Beatles added, it changed to the heavy metal style they were already absorbing from the San Francisco psychedelic groups. John liked it that way at first but then, a few days later, asked Martin to produce a softer arrangement with trumpets and cellos. In the end, he could not decide between the two versions. He said he liked the beginning of one but preferred the ending of the other. Martin had to find a way of splicing half the heavy metal version with half the orchestral one. To his lasting credit, no one noticed the join.

With each song came a colour film sequence, designed to be shown on television pop shows in place of the band themselves. Rather than the usual straight performance shots, however, these were mini-fantasies heightening the mood of the music, with the Carnaby-coloured Beatles appearing as actors rather than musicians. For 'Strawberry Fields', they were shown romping through a landscape that was actually Knole Park, the Kentish stately home, playing tag around an oak tree, and seated around an open-air dinner table laid with candelabra, being waited on by footmen in stockings and powdered wigs (one of whom, in an unwitting moment of truth, was their roadie, Mal Evans). For 'Penny Lane', they were seen riding white horses through cobbled streets that actually belonged to London's East End, with intercut shots of the real Penny Lane, still scarcely altered since their childhood. The age of pop video starts here.

Self-surpassing talent, given in double measure, resulted in the first Beatles single since 1962 which did not reach number one in the Top Twenty. It climbed to second place, but was just pipped for the top spot by a middle-of-the-road ballad containing no innovation whatever: Engelbert Humperdinck's 'Release Me'.

The fact was, the Beatles now had an influence no longer measurable by the Top Twenty alone. George Melly, the jazz singer and critic and a fellow Liverpudlian, reviewed 'Penny Lane' as poetry: it was, he said, a true evocation of Liverpool in the 1950s with 'great sandstone churches and the trams rattling past'. The imagery worked with no less power on those who had never seen Liverpool, and barely remembered the Fifties: those for whom Penny Lane's 'blue suburban skies', like Strawberry Fields' acid-swirling bridle-path, became a mirage eclipsing even that of San Francisco. You heard it even better, people said, when you were high.

•

Late in 1966, at his Belgravia home, Brian Epstein tried to commit suicide with an overdose of sleeping tablets. Fortunately, both his secretary, Joanne Newfield, and his chauffeur, Brian Barratt, were on hand to thwart him. Barratt broke down the double doors to his bedroom while Joanne telephoned for Dr Norman Cowan, the physician who had been regularly treating him. The three managed to keep Brian conscious until they could get him to his usual clinic.

The attempt was kept secret among those, like Joanne or Peter Brown, who were privy to his homosexual life and so familiar with its *leitmotif* of despair. Doomed love affairs with brutal boys had driven him often to the brink before. But always before he had had the means to recover: to convince himself, as no rational argument could, that his life still held pleasure and purpose.

For Brian, that pleasure and purpose were extinguished on 29 August 1966, when the Beatles gave their last concert in Candlestick Park, San Francisco; when Brian, terrified and preoccupied as he was that day, would have given anything to unravel the years and the wealth and be back at Barnston Women's Institute, watching four boys arrive with their new stage suits in Burton's carrier bags.

On the homeward flight, he had almost let his unhappiness show. 'What am I going to do now?' he kept saying. 'Shall I go back to school and learn something new?'

The Beatles, for five years, for the centuries contained in each of those years, had been his all-eclipsing passion. He had lived for them, and through them, with an intensity granted to few born under his unlucky star. He had loved them, not shamefully, not furtively, but with an idealism which millions found fit to share. That love was as the painter for his canvas, the parent for his children, the lost soul for its salvation. Having been hardly noticed, it was not rejected with any great show of regret.

He remained the Beatles' manager; a celebrity in that due proportion. He was, indeed, rather more often in the papers nowadays since their submersion in private projects and recording. Was it true they had started to break up? Quite untrue, Brian patiently said. They were simply resting. After what they had been through, who could blame them? Just before

Christmas 1966, when an infants' school in the Welsh village of Aberfan was engulfed by a coal-tip, several public voices as good as demanded that the Beatles do a live show to help raise funds for the bereaved families. The concept of the charity benefit pop concert was then an unknown one and, much as all four sympathised with Aberfan's plight, they rejected what seemed a further move to turn them into national public property. As ever, Brian was there to explain the position on their behalf and stop the media criticism from rising above a mutter.

He might convince the press, but he did not deceive himself. A bond was broken which had, in any case, been so fragile, composed of arrangements, schedules, timetables and notes. Despite the years and miles he had travelled with them, despite a fame and reckless wealth to equal theirs, he had no point of communication with them but a contract. Once their talent outran his efficiency, Brian Epstein had no further part to play. With all else that was to be heard in their brilliant new music, Brian could hear the sound of his own doom.

He was, to outward appearances, still the epitome of that youthful success associated with Swinging London. Not yet 32, he controlled an entertainment organisation which, as well as the Beatles, represented some of the best-known names in show business. His personal wealth was estimated, by the *Financial Times*, at £7m. Outside 13 Chapel Street, his red Rolls-Royce or his silver Bentley convertible stood in the mellow Belgravia sun.

NEMS Enterprises, though administered by many hands, still owed its main direction to Brian's personal business judgement, that strange mixture of rashness and prescience. In 1965, he had bought the Saville Theatre in Shaftesbury Avenue, impervious to objections that it was just a few yards on the wrong side of the West End. The building appealed to Brian with its Art Deco exterior, its boxes with private ante-rooms in which leopard-skin couches stood. At the Saville, he planned to put on straight plays in alternation with Sunday night pop shows. 'We brought the Four Tops over from America, on the Sunday before their big record, "Reach Out, I'll Be There", went to number one in Britain,' Tony Bramwell says. 'Brian paid them $32,000 for a £2,000 gross at the Saville. Then, of course, he was able to bring them back to do a seven-week British tour.'

His passion for theatre led Brian to subsidise the Saville through seasons of excellent, barely profitable productions, both drama and dance. He spent a fortune on the place, much of it unnecessarily – as with his insistence on taking out all the existing seats and replacing them with more comfortable ones. He had his own box there, and his own private bar. At the Saville, he could play theatrical impresario right to the borderline of his true desire, undimmed since his RADA days – that one night on the lit stage, the leading man who entered left, through French windows, would be Brian himself.

The fantasy recurred in various projects with which, after August 1966, he attempted to fill his life. There was, for instance, his plan, in partnership with the disc jockey Brian Matthew, to build a new theatre-cum-record studio in Bromley, Kent. He also dabbled in bullfighting, his other surreptitious passion. He put money into a film about El Cordobes and became a sponsor of the English matador Henry Higgins.

These ventures were not for profit, since he had more than enough money: they were symptoms of Brian's desperate wish to find some other role than entrepreneur and businessman. He wanted to be creative, as the Beatles were – to establish by any possible means that credential for re-entry into their world. So he tried to produce a record, for the Liverpool singer Rory Storm. He had always felt guilty at having poached Ringo Starr from Rory's group. He even tried directing a play, *Smashing Day*, at the New Arts theatre. John Fernald, his old RADA teacher, had been supposed to direct it but had fallen ill. 'Brian took over and really threw himself into rehearsals,' Joanne Newfield says. 'He was totally involved, right up to the evening of the dress rehearsal. All the cast were waiting in their costumes – but no Brian. He'd forgotten all about it.'

Joanne had joined NEMS originally as secretary to Brian's assistant, the high-powered Wendy Hanson. She inherited Wendy's job in late 1966, when Brian closed down his Stafford Street office and announced he would be working entirely from Chapel Street. Sitting upstairs, under two life-size David Bailey portraits of her employer, Joanne was first to see the marked change in Brian's dress and habits. His clothes grew more flamboyant, his gestures more overtly camp: it became a struggle for Joanne to keep him to his business engagements. 'I'd find notes for me in the morning, asking me to get him out of appointments – meetings or lunches. I once had to cancel Bernard Delfont four times.'

One business matter had so harried and tormented Brian that he now refused even to think about it. In New York, the lawsuit against Seltaeb, the merchandising company, was about to enter its third year. The huge delay – caused largely by Brian's failure to attend pre-trial examinations – had seen Nicky Byrne's claim for 'lost' revenues rise, as the Beatles grew still more famous, from $5 to $22m. The Beatles themselves even now knew nothing of the millions – perhaps billions – that their name had generated but that Brian had been unable to catch.

His other NEMS artists – apart from 'my Cilla' – had long ago ceased to absorb his energy. Gerry Marsden was in a West End musical; Billy J. Kramer and the Fourmost had gone to other agencies. Brian was in fact actively seeking a business partner who could ultimately take over the whole NEMS operation from him. He had already offered a controlling interest to Larry Parnes, which Parnes turned down because the deal would not include the Beatles. Instead, Brian turned to Robert Stigwood, a ruddy-faced Australian who, since his arrival in London, had built up an impressive roster of emergent pop acts. Stigwood became NEMS' joint managing director, pending his acquisition of a majority shareholding. Among the new clients he brought into the company were Cream, the Moody Blues and Jimi Hendrix, a young blues guitarist from Seattle whose explosive virtuosity had turned even modern legends like Eric Clapton and George Harrison into besotted disciples. Also under Stigwood's wing was a trio of fellow antipodeans called the Bee Gees, until then thought not to have a prayer because their name sounded too much like the Beatles.

Brian himself was now rarely to be seen in the daylight hours. Joanne Newfield, arriving at Chapel Street each morning, would find her day's instructions in the note pushed under his bedroom door – a note written at dawn in amphetamine wakefulness, before the antidote drug plunged him into sleep. Sometimes, pushed under the door, there would be a pile of money, won on his perpetual journey round the Mayfair gambling clubs. 'Jo . . .' one note said, 'Please bank my happiness . . .'

With luck, and a little extra dose, he would not have to open his eyes until mid-afternoon. Joanne knew he had surfaced when the intercom in his bedroom was switched on. 'When he first got up, he always felt terrible – hung over from drink and pills. He'd take some uppers to get over that. At about five o'clock, he'd be full of life. He'd come in and say, "Right. Let's start work."'

The mounting depression, the chemicals warring within him, produced fits of irrational anger which drove Joanne many times to the point of resignation. Like others before her, she could never quite bring herself to do it. 'The smallest thing could send him half-crazy. I got him a wrong number once, and he literally went berserk. He threw a whole tea tray at me. Another time, it was my birthday: he was terrible to me all day. The next day, I found this note. "Jo – good morning. Better late than never. Many happy returns of yesterday. Be a bit tolerant of me at my worst. Really, I don't want to hurt anyone . . ."'

Several times he made a determined attempt to pull himself together. He began seeing a psychiatrist and, on at least two occasions, went into a drying-out clinic in Putney. For one period of several weeks, a doctor and a nurse took up residence at Chapel Street. The nurse went out one afternoon, and Brian escaped. He was missing for two days. No one thought of looking for him where he was more and more to be found – in the dismal trysting alleyways of Piccadilly Underground station.

At other times it seemed he could find satisfaction only by creating a bizarre facsimile of his own mother, or at least the all-encompassing security she had once given him. Among his secret ports of call was a dominatrix in Mayfair whose clients also included several senior figures in the Conservative party. Her main task was to gratify the almost conscious death wish that still remained a strong part of Brian's sexual make-up while simultaneously making him feel childishly coddled and secure. He would lie in a rubber coffin while she read the newspapers out loud to him.

Life could still return to normal, as when his mother came down from Liverpool for a visit. Paradoxically, spells of conventional illness put him back on the rails. 'I looked after him when he had glandular fever,' Joanne Newfield says. 'He had a bout of jaundice as well, when Queenie came down to stay. Brian got into a good routine then and really seemed to enjoy it. I remember one Saturday afternoon how thrilled he was that he and Peter Brown had been out to Berwick Market to buy fruit. Brian thought this was wonderful. He'd done something normal – something just the same as other people did.'

Early in 1967, he made a second attempt to kill himself with a drug overdose. The Beatles were by then deeply involved in recording their new album. Brian had let an early pressing of 'Strawberry Fields'/'Penny Lane' be stolen from Chapel Street by one of his boy friends. Shortly afterwards, the words 'Brian Epstein is a queer' were scrawled on the garage door in lipstick. 'He did once confide in me how hopeless his private life was,' Joanne says. '"I'm no good with women and I'm no good with men," he told me. He was in absolute despair that day.

'The doctor told me once that Brian was like a collision course inside himself. He could only be terribly happy or terribly unhappy. If there was any depression or misery, Brian would be drawn helplessly into it. The Beatles caused that happiness, and they caused that unhappiness. I don't think there was any hope for him since the day he met the Beatles.'

The Sixties' increasingly tolerant atmosphere did little to ease his particular problems. In London at least, homosexuality had lost much of its Victorian stigma, thanks mainly to the fact that even ragingly hetero young men with their long hair, velvet suits and ruffle-fronted shirts personified the traditional notion of 'queers'. Nineteen sixty-seven was to see the decriminalisation of homosexuality *per se*, with sexual acts permitted between consenting adult partners in private. But Brian's tastes left him still miles on the wrong side of the law; besides, for someone in his public position and of his parentage and religious background, it remained as impossible as ever to come out of the closet.

America still held vestiges of happiness. With his lawyer friend Nat

Weiss he had formed a separate company, Nemperor Artists, to represent NEMS acts in New York. Weiss had himself gone over to artist-management, handling groups like Cyrkle, whose song 'Red Rubber Ball' Brian had correctly judged a million-selling US single. Nemperor Artists had another new signing, of talents as yet unrealised – Brian Epstein. He virtually gave the company to Nat Weiss so that Weiss could become *his* agent.

The portly, rather strange New Yorker had become Brian's most loyal, long-suffering friend. There were difficulties in that city, too, after encounters with predatory boys around Times Square. One day, when Brian was due to be interviewed on radio WORFM, Nat Weiss found him drugged almost insensible with Seconal tablets. Weiss, somehow, revived him and delivered him to the studio.

That interview, with the long-time Beatles adherent Murray the K., has survived on an hour-long tape in Nat Weiss's possession. It is remarkable less for the subjects covered than for the tenacity with which Brian, once on the air, fought his way back from his Seconal coma. At the beginning, he can scarcely even speak. But slowly, his voice frees itself, his thoughts unstick. He can articulate what everyone – what he most of all – has hoped to hear. The Beatles and he remain as close as they have ever been. 'There hasn't been so much as . . . a row.

'At the moment they're doing great things in the studio. They take longer nowadays, of their own volition, to make records. They're hypercritical of their own work. Paul rang me the other day and said he wanted to make just one small change to a track.

'I hope "Penny Lane" and "Strawberry Fields" are going to prove a thing or two. And certainly – *certainly* – the new album is going to prove more than a thing or two.'

'So – there we go,' are Murray the K.'s sign-off words. 'It's good to know the Beatles are still together. Eppy is still together . . .'

•

There had been moments at Abbey Road studios during the past four months when George Martin wondered whether the Beatles might have gone too far this time. There was, for instance, the time they asked him to provide farmyard noises, including a pack of foxhounds in full cry. There was the matter of the Victorian steam organs, the 41-piece orchestra with no score to play, and the hours spent searching for a note which only dogs could hear. At such times, the Beatles' record producer feared this new album would end, if it ended at all, merely by baffling its listeners.

Early 1967 had found them in the now familiar position of having to out-do the rivals they themselves had created. After *Revolver*, every other creative mind in pop was awakening to the possibilities of an album that was not just a compendium of past hits but a self-contained work on a definite theme, its tracks working interdependently like movements in a classical concerto. Two post-*Revolver* productions from across the Atlantic that had taken the Beatles' idea several notches further on were largely responsible for driving them back into the studio. One was the Beach Boys' *Pet Sounds*, an almost Mozartian montage of multi-dubbed harmonies and counterpoint, recorded almost single-handedly by Brian Wilson while the rest of the band were out on tour. The second, even sharper goad was *Freak-Out* by a new Californian group called the Mothers of Invention: one of the first ever 'double' albums, pungent with the iconoclastic wit of their leader, Frank Zappa, and embellished with quasi-comical sound effects and scraps of conversation.

The Beatles had originally meant their answer to *Pet Sounds* and *Freak-Out* to be an album in the most literal sense, each track a snapshot of Liverpool as they remembered it from childhood. But, having completed 'Penny Lane' and 'Strawberry Fields Forever', they found their enthusiasm for the idea beginning to wane, and simply turned over those two unmatched pearls to Martin for release as their next single. Afterwards they continued recording songs with no theme save the things they were currently doing, the newspapers they chanced to be reading, the London whose language and fashion they continued both to dictate and reflect. The newest London craze was for Victorian militaria, sold in shops with ponderously quaint names like I Was Lord Kitchener's Valet. So one night, the Beatles met to rehearse a new song, in that same vein of moustachioed whimsy, entitled 'Sgt. Pepper's Lonely Hearts Club Band'.

'It was Paul's number,' Martin says. 'Just an ordinary song, not particularly brilliant as songs go. When we'd finished it, Paul said: "Why don't we make the whole album as though the Pepper band really existed, as though Sergeant Pepper was doing the record. We can dub in effects and things." From that moment, it was as if Pepper had a life of its own.'

That life stemmed at first from simple enjoyment. They relished the idea that the four most famous pop musicians in the world should create mock bandsmen as their alter ego, and present their music in the faux-naif setting of a children's circus and pantomime. Then, as the sessions progressed, there was born in both musicians and their producer that special life, that sensation comparable only with walking on water, which comes from the certain knowledge that one is making a masterpiece.

Its strength lay in the fact that, to all four Beatles, the vision was the same. All four were now converted to the LSD drug. Even Paul McCartney, the cautious, the proper, had finally given in. LSD is said to have beneficial effects only if used among close friends. In *Sgt. Pepper* it did not move the Beatles to brilliant music only: it also restored them to a closeness they had nearly lost in the numbness of being adored by the whole world. It would be remembered as their best record, and also their very best performance.

Martin had no idea about the LSD at the time. The Beatles, in deference to their schoolmasterly producer, kept even innocent joints out of his sight, puffing them furtively in the 'gent's toilets'. Martin was, in any case, fully occupied with trying to reconcile an infinity of new ideas with his by now antiquated and inhibiting four-track recording machine. As the kaleidoscope blossomed and expanded, Martin and his engineer Geoff Emerick cadged extra sound channels by dubbing one four-track machine over another.

Martin had taught the Beatles much: he learned a little, too, in reckless spontaneity. The song which set the circus atmosphere was 'Being for the Benefit of Mr Kite', a John Lennon composition suggested by the words of an old theatre bill he had bought in an antique shop. Martin's instructions as arranger were to provide 'a sort of hurdy gurdy effect'. He did so by means of assorted steam organ sound effect tapes, cut into irregular lengths, thrown on the studio floor, then re-edited at random. The result was a dream-like cacophony, swirling about the Lennonesque big top where 'summersets', rather than somersaults, are executed, and 'tonight Henry the Horse dances the waltz'.

Martin, indeed, found his last reserves melting in admiration of a song like John's 'Lucy in the Sky with Diamonds', whose images – of 'tangerine trees', 'marmalade skies', 'newspaper taxis' and 'looking-glass ties' – were dazzling enough to a man with his middle-aged senses intact. It did occur to him sometimes that John looked rather strange, if not actually unwell. One night, in the aftermath of an acid trip, he looked so ill that Martin had to take him up on to the studio roof for air. Later, Paul took charge of him, driving him home to Weybridge and keeping him company in the hoped-for restorative of turning on yet again.

For Paul, *Sgt. Pepper* was a chance to experiment still further with the vein of narrative realism he had found in 'Eleanor Rigby' and 'Penny Lane'. Among the treasures he brought to the table was 'Lovely Rita', a cod love song to a 'meter maid', America's more seductive term for a female traffic warden, its tweeness diluted by the background of yearningly ironic 'ooohs' and 'aaahs' from John. 'When I'm Sixty-Four' found Paul looking forward to barely conceivable old age, a Darby-and-Joan vision of 'doing the garden', 'renting a cottage in the Isle of Wight', and grandchildren named 'Vera, Chuck and Dave'.

His most ambitious offering was 'She's Leaving Home', the story of a young woman nerving herself to leave her dependent parents and elope with 'a man in the motor trade'. Introduced by a rippling harp, the song unfolded like one of the new, gritty working-class plays to be seen on black and white TV – the young woman stealing away from home at daybreak, 'leaving the note that she hoped would say more', then her mother discovering her loss with a cry of 'Daddy! Our baby's gone!' It was a small – perhaps not-so-small – masterpiece from a humane and understanding heart, only slightly marred by its composer's imperiousness when the moment came to cut it. As usual, Paul had produced a 'head-arrangement' which needed George Martin to turn into a formal orchestral score. When Martin could not do the job at twenty-four hours' notice, as Paul wanted, he found himself summarily dropped in favour of an outside arranger.

Paul, at least, had no doubt that every song the Beatles were recording formed a link in the overall concept. 'This is our *Freak-Out*', he kept saying. But Ringo was to have a different recollection. 'After we'd done the original Sergeant Pepper song, we dropped the whole military idea. We just went on doing tracks.'

If they were not quite following the original plan, they were working together with a harmony, unity and enjoyment they had seldom known before, and never were to again. George, as usual, was given his moment of control when Indian musicians came in to help record his latest sitar epic, 'Within You, Without You'. Ringo was called from the sidelines ('I learned to play chess during *Sgt. Pepper*,' he would later say) to do a vocal for 'With a Little Help from My Friends', the song destined to be given the crucial place after the overture. The roadies Neil and Mal took an active part, helping to operate the numerous sound effects and even playing back-up harmonicas. Martin watched beamingly from the control room, still convinced that all these dazzling pyrotechnics were fuelled by no stimulant stronger than tea.

Indeed, the album's stand-out masterpiece, 'A Day in the Life', represented a John–Paul collaboration like none since early Beatlemania. The idea had been suggested to John by the death in a car crash of Tara Browne, youthful heir to the Guinness fortune and a friend of both the Beatles and the Rolling Stones. When he first played Martin an acoustic guitar sketch of the song, with its references to 'a lucky man who made the grade and blew his mind out in a car', Martin already felt the hairs prickle at the back of his neck. Unable to finish the lyric, John turned to Paul for something to fill its middle-eight. Paul provided a scrap of an unfinished song about getting up late and running for a bus, as cheery and everyday as the rest was bleak and apocalyptic. The bridge between the two parts was a long drawn-out cry of 'I'd love to turn you on!', which they knew was asking for trouble. But there could be no pulling back now.

The song's finale, John told Martin, had to be, 'a sound building up from nothing to the end of the world'. That was the night Martin faced the 41-piece symphony orchestra and announced that what they were to perform had no written score. All he would tell them were the highest and lowest notes to play. In between, it was every man for himself.

The song, in its final form, was taped at Abbey Road amid a gala of pop aristocrats such as Mick Jagger and Marianne Faithfull. The orchestra wore full evening dress and also carnival disguises distributed by the Beatles. One noted violinist played behind a clown's red nose; another held his bow in a joke gorilla's paw. Studio Two thronged with peacock clothes, Eastern robes, abundant refreshments and exotically tinted smoke. The four Beatles sat behind music stands playing trumpets, with Brian leaning on a chair back among them. Their moustaches had aged them: it was Brian, in this last photograph with them, who suddenly looked like a boy.

As with every masterpiece, the hardest part was letting go. They had tailed as well as topped the album with *Sgt. Pepper*'s theme song, adding a reprise of the 'Lovely Rita' backing vocal that left John's grin floating in the air like a bespectacled Cheshire cat's. Recognising that 'A Day in the Life' was something quite apart from even the most recherché of the other tracks, they had turned it into a devastating afterthought, followed by a multiple crash of piano chords – like the totalling of Tara Browne's car – that would slam the collection shut like a sarcophagus. They had worked from 7 a.m. to 3 p.m. simply to produce a brief snatch of gibberish to be heard from the record's normally mute play-out groove. As they stood around the microphone, a drug-dazzled Ringo suddenly remarked 'I think I'm going to fall over', and toppled forward, to be caught like a doll in Mal Evans's arms. The final touch was a note at 20,000 hertz frequency, audible only to the fine-tuned hearing of dogs.

The album sleeve, as much as its music, perfectly evoked the hour of its coming. The pop artist Peter Blake was commissioned to design a frontispiece as up-to-the-minute as its four subjects were, and as heedless of convention or expense. The Beatles, holding bandsmen's instruments and dressed in satin uniforms, pink, blue, yellow and scarlet, stood mock-solemn behind their own name spelled in flowers, set about by a collage of figures representing their numerous heroes. The group included Bob Dylan, Karl Marx, Laurel and Hardy, Aleister Crowley, Marlon Brando, Diana Dors, W. C. Fields – every fashionable face from the pantheon of Pop Art pseudo-worship. There were also private jokes, such as the Beatles' own ludicrous wax effigies from Madame Tussaud's, a stray Buddha and a doll with a sign reading 'Welcome Rolling Stones'. In one corner, next to Aubrey Beardsley, above Sonny Liston's head, the face of Stu Sutcliffe, the Beatle who was lost, peered out from a snapshot fragment of some long-forgotten Hamburg night.

EMI initially rejected the design, fearing that those among the assembly who were still alive would object to their likenesses being used in this way. The Beatles appealed directly to the company's chairman, Sir Joseph Lockwood, who informally consulted two of the country's most eminent lawyers, Lord Goodman and Lord Shawcross. 'Both Shawcross and Goodman said the same,' Sir Joseph recalled. '"Don't touch it," they said. "*Everyone* will sue."

'Paul McCartney talked me into allowing it. "Ah, everyone'll love it," he said. "All right," I said, "but take Gandhi out. We need the Indian market. If we show Gandhi standing around with Sonny Liston and Diana Dors, they'll never forgive us in India." So the Beatles agreed to take Gandhi out.'

EMI further stipulated that the Beatles should indemnify them to the tune of some £20m against possible legal trouble. In addition, Brian had to undertake to get clearances from as many of the 62 celebrities as possible. Wendy Hanson, his former assistant, was brought back specially to undertake this marathon of the transatlantic telephone. As she later remembered, most of them were only too flattered and delighted to be asked.

Sgt. Pepper had taken four months and cost £25,000 – an unheard-of sum in those days, more than twenty times the cost of the Beatles' debut album. Its packaging also was something altogether new, reflecting that age of conspicuous consumption. Instead of the usual single 'envelope', it came in a double segment that opened like a book. On the back, replacing the traditional leaden sleeve notes, the lyrics of every song were printed in full. Inside with the record was a sheet of cut-out novelties, figments of the Beatles' own comic-book childhood transformed to the last, or next, word in Pop Art – a jovial Victorian army sergeant picture card, a paper moustache, two badges and a set of NCO's stripes.

One other feature of the cover passed unnoticed by EMI's lawyers, nor was it picked up by the keen eye of Lord Shawcross or Lord Goodman. In the foreground of the garden where Sergeant Pepper's band and their companions stood grew a flourishing row of what looked like marijuana plants.

•

The landmark events in each era, those strokes of history so monumental that people recall for ever afterwards exactly where they were and what they were doing at the time, are generally tragedies. The outbreak of world wars, the passing of sovereigns or statesmen, the from-nowhere annihilations of John F. Kennedy, John Lennon and Diana, Princess of Wales, the wanton mass slaughter of '9/11': such have been the moments that, for billions across the globe for their remaining lifespan, recall exactly the circumstances they were in, the clothes they wore, the faces that looked disbelievingly into theirs on first hearing the news.

Only the blessed Sixties generation have such a moment to remember, not marked by open-mouthed horror and incredulity but open-mouthed delight and exaltation: the moment in June 1967 when they first listened to the Beatles' *Sgt. Pepper's Lonely Hearts Club Band*. The memory in this case is uniform to all: how they rushed to their record store to buy it, how Peter Blake's cover dazzled and delighted them as no album design ever had before, how they first opened its book-like flap and drew out the disc with its shiny virgin grooves and green Parlophone label, how at the first play they simply couldn't believe it, and had to play it again and again and again.

Musically its conquest was total. It equally entranced the most avant garde and most cautious; both fan and foe alike. The wildest acid freak, listening in his mental garret to 'Lucy in the Sky with Diamonds', could not doubt that his mind had been blown to undreamed realms of psychedelic fancy. Nervous old ladies, listening to 'When I'm Sixty-Four' in their front parlours, would never be frightened of pop music again. Sergeant Pepper's cabaret show, with its twanging mystery and workaday humour, its uppercut drive and insinuating charm, invited the elderly as well as the young, the innocent no less than the pretentiously wise. On drama critic Kenneth Tynan, the most rigorous cultural commentator of his age, and on Mark Lewisohn, an eight-year-old in Kenton, Middlesex, the effect was the same. Tynan called *Sgt. Pepper* a decisive moment in the history of Western civilisation. Mark Lewisohn stood in the garden as it played, shaking his head wildly while trying not to dislodge the cardboard moustache clenched under his nose.

In America, where the album appeared one day after its UK release, critical hyperbole climbed to Gothic heights. The *New York Times* announced that *Sgt. Pepper* heralded 'a new and golden Renaissance of Song'. *Newsweek*'s reviewer Jack Kroll compared the lyrics with T. S. Eliot: 'A Day in the Life', he said; was 'the Beatles' *Waste Land*'. Some of the more woolly headed American commentators classed the album as an almost religious experience and the Beatles as deities – this time with none of the fundamentalist backlash John had caused with his 'bigger than Jesus' remark. 'I declare,' said Dr Timothy Leary, high priest of hippydom, 'that the Beatles are mutants. Prototypes of evolutionary agents sent by God with a mysterious power to create a new species – a young race of laughing freemen . . . They are the wisest, holiest, most effective avatars [God incarnations] the human race has ever produced.'

Others saw things rather differently. By the time *Sgt. Pepper* was released, the adult world had moved on somewhat from its initial amused tolerance of the 'swinging' one. Concern was growing about the use of drugs among young people and the degree to which pop music encouraged, even exhorted it. A growing body of opinion now called on pop stars to recognise their position as vastly influential role models and to set a good rather than exultantly bad example to their millions of impressionable fans.

Before *Sgt. Pepper* there had been occasional controversies over pop lyrics deemed to be 'suggestive', like the Rolling Stones' 'Let's Spend the Night Together'. Now for the first time – thanks to the helpful provision of its lyrics in cold print – an album attracted as much notoriety as a subversive eighteenth-century pamphlet. The BBC took the lead by banning 'A Day in the Life' for a list of 'overt' references to drug-taking, some readily sustainable but others merely the products of overheated bureaucratic imagination. Obvious fair game were the 'man who blew his mind out in a car', the references to 'smoke' and 'dream' in Paul's middle section and, of course, the mischievous cry of 'I'd love to turn you on'. But the '4,000 holes in Blackburn, Lancashire', now interpreted to mean mass heroin needle-marks, had simply been John using a news item that caught his fancy. Even the final 'sound like the end of the world', created by classical violinists in clown noses and gorilla-paws, was accused of symbolising an addict's first chaotic joy after a fix.

More dubious subtexts were eagerly sought and quickly found on the album's other tracks. Paul's 'Fixing a Hole' – a song plainly about little more than DIY – was condemned as another heroin allegory. The Ringo track 'With a Little Help from My Friends' caused such a furore in America with its reference to getting high that Senator – soon to be Vice-President – Spiro T. Agnew led a public campaign to ban it. In 'She's Leaving Home', the 'man from the motor trade', in reality Brian Epstein's car-sales partner Terry Doran, was thought to be a euphemism for an abortionist. Even the tracks with no alleged narcotic subtext were credited with a role in turning nice normal teenagers into mumbling, shiftless freaks. The ultra-right wing John Birch Society even announced that the Beatles were part of a Communist conspiracy and warned that *Sgt. Pepper* showed 'an understanding of the principles of brainwashing'.

But by far the greatest furore arose from the realisation that 'Lucy in the Sky with Diamonds' was a mnemonic for LSD. Since the song clearly could have only one author, it was John who received the bulk of the condemnation for advertising the substance that now dominated every media drug scare story and representing its effect in attractive terms of 'tangerine trees and marmalade skies'. John protested that the song had nothing to do with LSD, but had been inspired by a painting his son Julian had done at school. 'What's that?' John had asked, and Julian had replied, 'It's Lucy in the sky with diamonds.' Had the story come from anyone without John's love of verbal jokery, it might have been more believable.

For the millions of hippies now dropping out across America, and their ever-increasing British brethren, *Sgt. Pepper* very quickly became more than a gramophone record. In their quasi-religion of love and peace, it became an almost sacred text, its random tracks elevated into a gospel more cohesive than even Paul McCartney had ever dreamed, its casual in-jokes and spur-of-moment sound effects interpreted as coded symbols, messages and philosophical observations on the deepest matters of life and death. Even the fragment of electronic gibberish in the play-out groove was subjected to intensive analysis and eventually pronounced to be saying 'Fuck me like a superman', whatever cosmic profundity that might imply.

If the Beatles had hated the mindlessly screaming fans of four years back, they hated the mystery and message-seekers more. John, especially, denied with increasing bitterness that his songs had any hidden or mystical meaning. 'I just shove a lot of sounds together, then shove some words on,' he said. 'We know we're conning people, because people want to be conned. They give us the freedom to con them.'

A month earlier in the Beatles' fan magazine, a correspondent had expressed the view of the huge other audience they still had. 'I know that if Paul took drugs, I'd be worried sick,' the letter-writer said. 'But I know he's too sensible.'

It was, however, the most cautious and image-conscious Beatle who, a fortnight after *Sgt. Pepper*'s release and on the eve of his 25th birthday, admitted to *Life* magazine that he had taken LSD. The admission was possible since acid had only recently become illegal. Paul, while stressing the pluperfect tense, spoke nonetheless as an enthusiast. 'It opened my eyes,' he said. 'We only use one-tenth of our brains. Just think what we'd accomplish if we could tap that hidden part.'

The outcry was even more ferocious than over Sergeant Pepper's alleged illegal pharmacopoeia. The Beatle who had hitherto been looked on as pop music's best ambassador was denounced, in the *Daily Mail*, as 'an irresponsible idiot'. Intercessionary prayers were offered by Dr Billy Graham to prevent the world's innocent youth from rushing to emulate him. Paul, protesting he bore no such responsibility, did his best to disarm his attackers with good old Liverpool humour. Taking drugs, he said, was 'like taking aspirin without a headache'. On television he was asked if he didn't feel it irresponsible to broadcast that endorsement to such a huge audience. Paul very reasonably answered that the television company was doing no less by interviewing him in prime-time. 'It's *you* who've got responsibility not to spread this. If you'll shut up about it, I will.'

Soon afterwards came news of an even more unlikely acid-head. Brian Epstein, the Beatles' apparently well-bred and respectable manager, came forward with John and George in a supportive phalanx to admit having taken LSD about half a dozen times 'before it became illegal'. Among those who read the news (oh, boy) was the Beatles' supreme idol Elvis Presley, soon to forsake Hollywood schlock and return to live performance. Once the standard bearer for rebellious youth, Elvis now looked with horror on the drug counterculture (in which he did not include his own massive narcotics intake, those all being supplied on doctors' prescriptions). Indeed, the King now sported the honorary badge of a Federal Narcotics Agent and, later, would personally urge America's new President, Richard M. Nixon, not to let the Beatles into the country again.

Within a few days, the whole controversy had been eclipsed by an event which established the Beatles as a literally astral presence as well as demonstrating the schizophrenic nature of the BBC. To demonstrate the ever developing marvels of satellite broadcasting, the Corporation initiated a programme called *Our World*, made jointly by itself and TV networks in 13 other countries, and broadcast live as a symbol of international amity in tune with hippy love and peace. The same BBC that so recently had damned 'A Day in the Life' as a drug addict's guidebook now saw nothing contradictory in presenting the Beatles as stars of *Our World*'s British segment, representing the Corporation, the country and the theme 'artistic excellence'. And, however terminally pissed off with the Corportion they might feel, the Beatles could hardly resist such a showcase for a new song.

The broadcast took the form of a party – now more correctly called a happening or a love-in – in Abbey Road's Studio One. The Beatles in flower-power gear performed their specially written number perched on stools and wearing headphones as if caught in the act of recording. Among the privileged crowd who sat around them were Mick Jagger, Marianne Faithfull, Keith Moon of The Who, Eric Clapton of Cream, Patti Harrison, Jane Asher and Paul McCartney's brother, Michael.

The new song was called 'All You Need Is Love', a foot-stomping chant seemingly designed to contain no shades of meaning or hidden symbols or messages whatever. In a Scouse accent, of course, the crucial word came out as 'loov', suggesting something rather more edgy and ironic than the usual bland flower-child articulation. 'All you need is loov,' sang John, between chews on a wad of gum, 'Loov, loov. Loov is allyerneed . . .' A 13-piece orchestra was on hand to provide sound effects that included the opening trumpet fanfare of 'La Marseillaise' and a sarcastic Lennon reprise of 'She loves you, yeah, yeah, yeah'. At the end, balloons and party streamers were showered on to the set, and members of the pop royalty present walked rather self-consciously up and down with placards saying 'love' in various languages while others danced a conga around the studio floor.

The performance went out to 31 countries and was watched by approximately 500 million, a global audience destined not to be surpassed until the Live-Aid concert of 1985 and the death of a still unknown princess.

•

That hopeful message to the world was unfortunately lost on the British police who, in response to mounting pressure from Fleet Street, Parliament and the Church, had chosen 1967 for an all-out assault on the drug-guzzling counterculture. Their intended victims presented invitingly soft targets, not least the group who had most outraged public feeling with their hairiness, surliness, sexiness and refusal to mount the revolving platform on *Sunday Night at the London Palladium.* In February, an 18-strong police task force had raided the Sussex home of the Rolling Stones' lead guitarist Keith Richard while Mick Jagger, Marianne Faithfull and a number of other upmarket underground figures were spending the weekend there. A thorough search of the premises and everyone present had revealed four illegal amphetamine tablets in the pocket of a coat belonging to Jagger. George and Patti Harrison had also been among the party, but had left just before the police arrived. It would later be alleged that the raiders had waited for them to get clear, because to bust a Beatle was still considered tantamount to defiling a national treasure.

The subsequent trial of Jagger and Richard, each for about the most minor drug-offence in the book, gave a dark and ugly descant to that summer of flowers and bells and joss sticks and multicoloured *Sgt. Pepper* satins, when 'all you need is loov' seemed woven into the very sunshine. Tried and convicted at Chichester Quarter Sessions the following June, Richard was sentenced to a year's imprisonment and Jagger to three months, while Marianne Faithfull achieved notoriety as 'the girl in the fur rug' who had allegedly been the centrepiece of a group-sex orgy. A rumour swept Britain that when the police burst in, Jagger had been licking a Mars bar lodged in Marianne's vagina. It was the Profumo scandal all over again, just moved down an age-group and a class.

The affair took on some of the qualities of an LSD hallucination when

Britain's most pro-Establishment newspaper, *The Times*, rallied to Jagger's and Richard's defence, criticising their vengeful public humiliation and plainly excessive sentence in an editorial headed by a quotation from William Blake, 'Who Breaks A Butterfly On A Wheel?' Both Stones were freed on appeal, Jagger being then helicoptered to take part in a televised discussion with assorted Establishment grandees, including the editor of *The Times*, about 'what today's young people really want'. His next act was to join Richard and the other Stones in the studio to produce their own sarcastically Beatles-themed message to their late persecutors, a song called 'We Love You' with anonymous back-up vocals by John Lennon and Paul McCartney. The Beatles and Brian lent them further support on 24 July as signatories in a full-page *Times* advertisement calling for the legalisation of marijuana.

In early August came another portent of how the Summer of Love's seemingly limitless sunshine was soon to turn rancid. The playwright Joe Orton, so nearly scriptwriter of the Beatles' third film, was battered to death by his jealous lover Kenneth Halliwell, who then himself took an overdose of sleeping pills. John Lennon's 'A Day in the Life', about the 'lucky man who made the grade', was Orton's funeral music.

•

Visiting Nat Weiss in New York that spring, Brian had felt a strong premonition of death. 'He was sure his plane would crash on the journey home,' Weiss says. 'I persuaded him to take the flight – which, in fact, was delayed a long while on the runway at Kennedy.' The jet finally took off, leaving Nat Weiss with Brian's last wish, scribbled in a note at the airport coffee shop. His last wish concerned the packaging of the Beatles' new album: 'Brown paper bags for *Sgt. Pepper*'.

When Weiss came to London a few weeks later, Brian was back at the drying-out clinic in Putney. The attorney drove to visit him with Robert Stigwood, his Australian heir-apparent at NEMS Enterprises. According to Weiss, Brian now regretted his decision to let Stigwood buy control of NEMS. 'Stigwood had the option to buy, but they were still joint managing directors. Brian was telling Stigwood to do things, but it was obvious that Stigwood had no intention of doing them.

'While I was with Brian, a big bouquet of flowers arrived from John Lennon. The card from John said, "You know I love you – I really mean that." When Brian read it, he just broke down.

'He begged me to stay on until he got out of the clinic, but I had to go back to New York. That was the last time I saw him.'

Not even Nat Weiss could comfort Brian in the dread which had begun to torment him – the dread foreshadowed in early summer when

Cilla Black announced her intention of leaving NEMS Enterprises. Cilla disliked Robert Stigwood; still more had she been offended by the loss of that feminine solicitude with which Brian had built up her career. The emergency cleared Brian's head. There were meetings with Cilla at Chapel Street: he apologised, was charming – from the haunted, drug-exhausted night-being, enough of the old Brian returned to persuade Cilla, at least, not to leave him.

But the greater, unassuageable dread remained. In October 1967, Brian's five-year management contract with the Beatles ended. He had reason – or thought he had – to believe it would not be renewed.

There had been signs for many months that Paul McCartney, in particular, was discontent with Brian's management. Their relationship, in any case, was never easy. Paul, with his looks, was the one Brian *ought* to have loved: he always felt he owed Paul compensation because he had chosen John. The worst moments of all for Brian, worse even than John's sarcasm, were when Paul decided, in his smiling way, to play the prima donna. 'Paul could get to Brian the way none of the other three could,' Joanne Newfield says. 'Whenever I saw him put down the phone really upset, he'd always been talking to Paul.'

At the beginning, it was always George, in his dour Liverpool way, who cross-examined Brian closest over business deals. As George absorbed himself in spiritual things, Paul took over, with more unsettling effect, as Brian's chief inquisitor. 'He'd come into Chapel Street, doing his business Beatle bit,' Joanne says. 'That always worried Brian. They never had a row, but you could see he was uneasy when Paul was there.'

Brian had hoped to please Paul, above all, in the new recording deal with EMI and American Capitol that he had negotiated the previous February. This replaced EMI's risible 'penny per record' for a 10 per cent royalty on singles and albums, rising to 15 per cent after 100,000 and 30,000 copies respectively. In America, the royalty was 10 per cent, rising to 17½ per cent. The deal, in fact, transformed the economics of the record industry. No longer would record companies be able to sign impressionable young men to miserly contracts with the excuse of its being 'standard practice'.

But Paul, rather than giving Brian the longed-for congratulations, had instead been full of the new recording contract negotiated for the Rolling Stones by the manager who had taken over from Andrew Loog Oldham – a New York businessman named Allen Klein. Faced with the threat of losing the Stones to another label, Decca had agreed to pay an unheard-of advance against future royalties of $1.25 million. In all the years that the Beatles had been sending EMI's profits through the roof, it had not occurred to Brian to demand any money upfront.

Paul was also mainly responsible for a feeling within the Beatles that they had now outgrown their need for a manager in the old proprietorial sense. Certainly, *Sgt. Pepper*, that multi-hued testament to their infallibility, had been made to a large extent against Brian's wishes. By now, too, rumours were beginning to filter out of NEMS, and through each Beatle's personal court, that even as that kind of manager, Brian had made serious long-term mistakes. They were starting to hear about Seltaeb and Nicky Byrne; the 90 per cent merchandising contract given to five strangers; the millions of dollars which had been allowed to blow away.

Brian, on his side, made strenuous efforts to prove that they did still need him. He took special trouble over the arrangements for Paul McCartney's first private trip to America. It was, ironically, the trip which Paul used to formulate much of a future for the Beatles in which there would be little room for anyone named Brian Epstein.

To one person, the impresario Larry Parnes, Brian finally confessed what he could still barely articulate in his own mind. 'He told me the Beatles were leaving him,' Parnes said. 'He was losing Cilla and he was losing them. The Beatles were giving him notice.'

His support of Paul in the LSD furore revealed how fervent was Brian's desire to stay at one with the Beatles. And, indeed, it brought him closer to them – certainly, closer to Paul – than for many months. Soon afterwards at Kingsley Hill, he threw a weekend party to which the Beatles and their women drove together, packed into John's psychedelic Rolls. When the Rolls stopped at traffic lights, people crowded round to try to see through its darkened windows. It was a day that Cynthia Lennon was to remember with horror. Brian's party, at the house where Churchill used to meet his wartime Chiefs of Staff, turned into a mass LSD trip. Cynthia took some herself, for only the second time, in her fast-failing attempts to keep up with John. The result was a horrendously bad trip in which she almost jumped from a second-storey window onto the heads of the beautiful people below.

In July, the Beatles began to think of leaving England and setting up in hippy-commune style on their own private Greek island. All of them and their wives took a lengthy boat cruise, looking at possible sites to buy. The plan went as far as negotiations with Greece's fascist military government and with the British Treasury – who gave permission in principle for them to transfer the purchase price abroad – before being dropped in favour of the next big idea. Brian took no part in the plan and pretended mild amusement at it. 'I think it's a dotty idea,' he wrote to Nat Weiss, 'but they're no longer children, and must have their own sweet way.'

The fatherly tone is poignant, considering the moment. His own father, Harry Epstein, the hard-working, straight-dealing, uncomplicated

Liverpool businessman, had died suddenly of a heart attack, aged 63. It was his second within only a few weeks. When news of the first one reached Brian, at a party, he did not think it sounded serious enough to return home immediately.

The bereavement, paradoxically, had a stabilising effect: it forced him out of his own depression into concern for his family – in particular his mother, Queenie, widowed after 34 years of marriage. From the age of 18, she had known no existence other than as Harry's wife. After her religion, it was to her elder son that she turned for support. Brian was comforted to realise that someone in the world truly needed him.

He spent several days with Queenie in Liverpool, surprised to discover how a city which had once seemed so dully provincial now soothed and reassured him. After Harry's retirement, his parents had moved from their Queen's Drive house to a more convenient bungalow. Brian visited their old next-door neighbour Rex Makin and sat in Makin's garden, staring at the house with the sunrise over its front door, thinking of the father who had returned from the shop one afternoon to find him sent home from school, and whose angry words were still etched on his son's memory. 'I simply don't know *what* we're going to do with you.'

He wrote to Nat Weiss from Liverpool, mentioning his plan to come to New York on 2 September. Weiss, as his agent, had arranged for him to present a series of chat shows on Canadian television. Brian was excited by this opportunity to test himself as a performer. In comforting his mother, he had himself evidently drawn comfort from the Jewish religion. 'The week of Shiva [mourning] is up tonight,' his letter to Weiss continued, 'and I feel a bit strange. Probably good for me in a way . . .'

His mother came to London to stay with him on 14 August. The idea was that she should move down to London permanently, to be near Brian and her sister, his Aunt Frieda. For the 10 days of her visit, Brian forced himself to keep to a normal routine. Queenie would wake him each morning, drawing his bedroom curtains as she used to when he was small, and they would have breakfast together in his room. Brian would then work a conventional office day with Joanne. Each night, he stayed in, watching television with Queenie, rarely going to bed later than 11 p.m. Joanne had never seen him so quiet and apparently content.

Mrs Epstein returned to Liverpool on Thursday, 24 August. That evening, at the Hilton hotel, sitting on a bedroom floor and staring devoutly upward, the Beatles embarked, three days prematurely, on their post-Brian era.

A letter to Nat Weiss was in the post – a cheerful note concerning arrangements Weiss was to make for Brian's American visit, such as the chartering of a yacht and tickets to a Judy Garland concert. There was also mention of Eric Anderson, a folk singer whom Brian wanted to put under contract. '. . . till the 2nd', the letter ended, 'love, flowers, bells, be happy and look forward to the future . . .'

Enclosed was a colour snapshot, taken on the roof at Chapel Street, of a young man – hardly more than a boy – in striped trousers and a frilled shirt open to the waist. His hair was long; it fell in a fringe over his eyes. Four days before his death, Brian at last became what he had striven hardest to be: a Beatle.

•

The new era took a form already long familiar to London Underground travellers. For it is on tube station walls that advertisements for Indian Holy men and their spiritual crusades in Britain commonly appear. Among this bearded, cross-legged platform-wall fraternity, the most clearly recognisable was the Holy Man named Maharishi Mahesh Yogi. In 1967, after a decade of regular visits, the Maharishi – or Great Saint – could claim some 10,000 British converts to his doctrine of Spiritual Regeneration. A still larger number recognised him in the way they recognised chocolate vending machines, posters for Start Rite shoes and illuminated signs to the Central or Bakerloo line.

It was, ironically, not George Harrison but his model wife Patti who brought the Beatles and the Maharishi together. Patti had joined the Spiritual Regeneration movement in February after hearing a talk by one of the guru's lieutenants. George, although immersed in Hindu religious study since his Indian expedition, had found no real direction as yet. He had been to San Francisco and – accompanied by Derek Taylor, now a fashionable Hollywood publicist – had strolled among the Haight-Ashbury hippies. There he found less love and peace than beggars and souvenir stalls. He had also been in contact with a British-based guru, who persuaded him to go down to Cornwall and climb a hill, with equally disappointing spiritual results.

In the week before August Bank Holiday, Patti Harrison read that the Maharishi Mahesh Yogi had come to London, to deliver a single lecture before retiring from his crusade and devoting himself to a 'life of silence' in India. The valedictory lecture was to take place at the mystic's hotel, the Park Lane Hilton, on Thursday, 24 August. Patti made George contact the other Beatles and persuade them to attend.

Amid the small 7s 6d (37p) per head audience of the faithful, four Beatles garbed as flower-power aristocrats listened while a little Asian gentleman, wearing robes and a grey-tipped beard, described in his high-pitched voice an existence both more inviting and more convenient than mere hippydom. The 'inner peace' which the Maharishi promised, and which seemed so alluring to pleasure-exhausted multi-millionaires – not to mention the 'sublime consciousness' so attractive to inveterate novelty-seekers – could be obtained even within their perilously small attention span. To be spiritually regenerated, they need meditate for only half an hour each day.

Maharishi Mahesh Yogi, despite a highly developed nose for publicity, did not know the Beatles were in his congregation until after the lecture, when they sent a request to speak to him in private. There and then, acting as a group, they offered themselves as his disciples. The Holy Man, for whom 'tickled' would be an insufficient adjective, invited them to join him the next day on a course of indoctrination for the Spiritually Regenerated at University College, Bangor, north Wales. The Beatles said they would go.

They did subsequently contact Brian and ask him to join the party. He, too, had been showing some interest in Indian religion. Brian said he had other plans for the Bank Holiday weekend, but that he'd try to get down to Bangor later during the 10-day course.

The next day, an incredulous mob of reporters and TV crews saw them arrive at Euston station and climb aboard the dingy blue and white train that now had to serve instead of their usual private jet. Also in the party, thanks to a spur-of-the-moment decision, were the country's favourite anti-Christ and scarlet woman, Mick Jagger and Marianne Faithfull. Cynthia Lennon missed the train; when she arrived at the barrier, the ticket inspector mistook her for just another fan and refused to let her through until after the guard's whistle had blown for departure. As Cyn' sprinted vainly along the platform, John leaned from his compartment window, laughing and calling, 'Run, Cindy, run!'

It was the first journey they had ever made without Brian – without even the two protective road managers. John compared it to 'going somewhere without your trousers'. They all sat rather guiltily, wedged into one first-class compartment, afraid to venture so much as to the lavatory. They then had a second audience of the Maharishi, who occupied his own first-class compartment, squatting on a sheet spread over British Rail's green upholstery. He held up a flower – the first of many – and explained that its petals were an illusion, like the physical world. In a telling simile, he compared Spiritual Regeneration to a bank, from which its practitioner could always draw dividends of repose.

It had become apparent by now that the Maharishi considered himself fully as great a star attraction as the Beatles, and believed the crowds and media attention to be on his account rather than theirs. As the train finally limped towards Bangor station, another frantic multitude and battery of television cameras came into view on the platform. The Beatles, with no shield of roadies to protect them, were all for staying on the train a couple of extra stops, then returning to Bangor by taxi. With his beatific smile, the Maharishi told them to stick close beside him and they'd be all right.

That night the Beatles' party found themselves ensconced with the Maharishi's 300 other conference students, in the spartan bedrooms of a teacher training college. Later they went out to the only restaurant open late in Bangor – a Chinese. Only after a long and rowdy meal did they realise they weren't carrying enough money between them to pay the bill. In London, any restaurant would have pressed the dinner on them gratis, but Chinese waiters in a remote north Wales seaside resort were clearly a somewhat different proposition. Things had begun to look decidedly tricky when George prised open the heel of one of his sandals and produced a wad of £10 notes he had secreted there.

The following day, the Beatles used a press conference with their new guru to announce that they had given up taking drugs. 'It was an experience we went through,' Paul McCartney said. 'Now it's over. We don't need it any more. We think we're finding new ways of getting there.'

One of the journalists present was George Harrison, their old *Liverpool Echo* acquaintance – for Bangor is just in the *Echo*'s circulation area. Harrison was with them the next afternoon – Sunday – as, fully initiated into Spiritual Regeneration, they strolled around the college grounds.

'There was a phone ringing inside,' Harrison said. 'It rang and rang. Eventually, Paul said, "Someone had better answer that." He went in and picked up the phone. I could hear him speaking. "Yeah," he said. "Yeah . . ." Then I heard him shout, "Oh, Christ – *no*!" '

•

That Friday, Brian had suddenly asked Joanne his assistant down to spend the Bank Holiday weekend at his house in Sussex. He also told her to invite a mutual friend of theirs, the Scots singer Lulu. But he had left it too late: both Lulu and Joanne herself had other arrangements. As Brian did not seem too disappointed, Joanne presumed he would be entertaining a large house party. 'He went off on his own on the Friday afternoon. He seemed really bright and happy that day. He'd put the top of the Bentley down. He was waving to me as he drove off.'

At Kingsley Hill, other disappointments waited. A young man whom Brian had hoped to know better that weekend would not, after all, be able to make it. Peter Brown had not arrived yet. He was still in London, trying to get Cynthia Lennon off to Bangor by car. Peter, and Geoffrey

Ellis, from the NEMS office, would be the only house guests. They were old friends and familiar companions. Brian, after two quiet weeks, had looked forward to more exciting company.

The three had dinner served to them by Brian's Austrian butler. Afterwards, in an evidently restless mood, Brian began telephoning numbers in London that supplied what we would now term rent boys. But all were fully booked. Brian grew more edgy and irritable and finally announced he was returning to London. Peter and Geoffrey were not offended, nor particularly surprised. Walking out was a habit of Brian's. Peter went with him out to the Bentley and told him he oughtn't to drive after the wine he'd drunk with dinner. 'Brian said I wasn't to worry. He'd be back in the morning before I woke up.'

By this time, one of the agencies he'd contacted had found three boys and dispatched them on the sixty-mile journey to Sussex in a black London cab. But Brian was now well on his way back to London.

Geoffrey Ellis telephoned Chapel Street shortly after midnight to confirm that he had arrived safely. Up to then, Peter and Geoffrey had half-expected him to reappear at Kingsley Hill after a drive round the countryside. The call was taken by Antonio, Brian's Spanish town butler. Antonio said that Mr Epstein had come in a little time ago and had gone straight upstairs. He tried the intercom to the master bedroom, but got no reply. Peter and Geoffrey were reassured. Brian had managed the car journey safely and had obviously succeeded in falling asleep.

When Peter and Geoffrey got up, late on Saturday morning, Brian had not returned. They thought of ringing Chapel Street, but decided to let him sleep. At about five that afternoon, the telephone rang. It was Brian. He told Peter he had been asleep all day and was still very drowsy. Peter said that if he was returning to Sussex, it would be safer to take the train. Brian agreed to telephone just as he was setting off so that Peter could collect him by car at Lewes station. Peter waited all Saturday evening for his call.

By Sunday morning, Antonio and his wife Maria were beginning to be worried. Brian was still in his room. The Spanish couple had heard nothing from him since breakfast time the previous day. Nor had he gone out, as was his habit, after dark. The Bentley was still as he had left it on Friday night. At the same time, they knew his irregular ways and how angry he could be. A lengthy discussion in Spanish ensued before Antonio decided to take the initiative.

He telephoned Peter Brown in Sussex first, but Peter had gone with Geoffrey Ellis to the village pub. He then telephoned Joanne Newfield, Brian's assistant, at her home in Edgware. Joanne had helped cope with Brian's two suicide attempts: she had also seen several false alarms. She drove at once from Edgware through the Bank Holiday silence to Chapel Street. 'The moment I walked in,' she says, 'I felt uneasy.'

Ceaseless hammering on Brian's door and buzzing of his bedroom intercom brought no reply. Even then, they hesitated to break down his door. They had done so, unnecessarily, once before and Brian had been furious. By this time a doctor had arrived – not Brian's regular Dr Cowan but another man who understood his case. Peter Brown had rung up again from Sussex and was waiting on the line for news.

Antonio and the doctor broke down the bedroom suite's outer double doors. Beyond the dressing-room lobby, the curtains were drawn. Brian lay on his side amid the litter of documents and correspondence spread over the bed. Joanne approached and shook him. 'Even though I knew he was dead, I pretended to the others that he wasn't. "It's all right," I kept saying, "he's just asleep, he's fine."

'The doctor led me out of the room then. Maria was there, screaming, "Why? Why?" Peter Brown was still holding on on the phone.

'A little while after that, something really strange happened. We broke into Brian's room at about two o'clock. At three o'clock, the *Daily Express* rang up and said, "We've heard that Brian Epstein's terribly ill. Is there any truth in it?" Only the four of us knew what had happened and none of us had contacted any press. It was never explained how the story got out to the papers.'

Reporters and photographers were already massed in Chapel Street when Peter Brown and Geoffrey Ellis arrived from Sussex. Alistair Taylor, the NEMS office manager, had been sent for, and also Brian's solicitor, David Jacobs. Peter Brown got through to Bangor and broke the news to Paul. Then he telephoned Brian's brother Clive in Liverpool. Joanne heard Clive shout: 'You're lying! You're lying!'

Brian's body was taken away in a makeshift police coffin. Joanne attacked a photographer who pointed his camera at it. 'I just couldn't bear the thought of people seeing Brian in a thing like that.'

By early evening, there were television pictures of the Beatles leaving the Maharishi's conference through forests of microphones and lights. 'How do you feel,' they were asked, 'about Brian Epstein's death?' It emerged that they had been to see the Maharishi again and had been told that Brian's death, being of the physical world, was 'not important'. Their faces, even so, looked ravaged among the garlands and the bells. 'He was a lovely fella,' John said bleakly.

The story was told in full on Bank Holiday Monday in newspapers read at the seaside or in back gardens. 'Brian Epstein Death Riddle: Valet Finds Pop King in Locked Bedroom'. It was widely assumed – and still is – that he committed suicide. The story gained weight – not instantly, since Fleet Street still shunned the word – when his homosexuality became public knowledge. To the larger British public in 1967, that was reason enough to want to die.

•

The inquest, on 8 September at Westminster Coroner's Court, found that Brian had died from an overdose of Carbitrol, a bromide-based drug which he had been taking to help him sleep. That the overdose had not been all at once but cumulative, over two or three days, seemed to rule out the possibility of suicide. The suggestion was that Brian, in a gradually more drowsy state, had not realised he was exceeding the proper dose. The police inspector called to Chapel Street reported having found 17 bottles of various pills and tablets in his bathroom cupboard, in his briefcase and beside his bed.

Nat Weiss travelled from New York to attend the inquest, bringing with him Brian's last letter – the one which seemed so full of confidence in the future. The Coroner, Mr Gavin Thurston, recorded a verdict of accidental death from 'incautious self-overdoses'.

One person who knew him, and also knew well a particular burden he carried, remains convinced that Brian's death was neither accident nor suicide. According to this, necessarily anonymous, ex-associate, Brian was the victim of a murder contract taken out on him three years earlier in America after the Seltaeb merchandising fiasco.

In 1964, certainly, any number of American businessmen bore him a bitter grudge. The confusion over manufacturing licences, and consequent cancellation by the big stores of $78m worth of Beatles merchandise, caused several manufacturers to lose a fortune. 'One man even had a heart attack and died. I was at a meeting when Lisson said he was going to kill Brian Epstein. I thought it was just American bullshit. I said, "No – wait until the courts have finished with him."'

In August 1967, the courts had finished. The $22m lawsuit between NEMS and Nicky Byrne had been settled for a cash payment of $10,000 to Byrne – enough to buy himself a yacht and sail off to start a new life in the Bahamas.

Just before he left New York, Nicky Byrne received a mysterious telephone call. 'This man's voice, very low, very polite, said: "Mr Byrne. I understand that your suit against Brian Epstein is settled, is that right?" I said: "Yes, and what's it got to do with you?" But whoever it was just hung up.

'In August, I was in Florida – actually on my boat – and I got another call. That same very quiet, polite voice. "Mr Byrne," it said, "you're going to hear soon that Brian Epstein has met with an accident."'

No one has ever explained those two telephone calls to Nicky Byrne, nor explained the curious fact that Brian's death was known in Fleet Street less than an hour after Joanne Newfield burst into his darkened room.

For the murder theorists there is one further and deeply significant detail. The signature on the Seltaeb contract – the signature which gave five strangers 90 per cent of Beatle merchandise royalties, and so ensured the back-tracking litigation which followed – was that of Brian's solicitor David Jacobs. In the autumn of the following year, Jacobs was found in his garage hanging by a length of satin from one of the beams. The inquest verdict was suicide. But several of his friends and associates were later to remember that in his last weeks alive he had seemed profoundly upset and worried about something.

•

Brian's funeral, at Long Lane Jewish cemetery in Liverpool, was a private family affair. To his mother's distress, he was not buried next to his father but in a separate avenue of undecorated memorials. The Beatles did not attend. George Harrison sent a sunflower which Nat Weiss threw into the open grave.

Five weeks later, a memorial service was held for Brian at the New London Synagogue, St John's Wood. It was only a short walk from there to Paul's house and Abbey Road and the studios where Brian ushered in the Beatles to meet George Martin on that summer day long ago in 1962.

The Beatles did attend this time, as did George Martin, Dick James and scores of people who were wealthy and well known only because of the young man who came down from Liverpool in his Crombie overcoat; who blushed easily and never went back on a promise; who could be ecstatic but never happy; who somehow caught the lightning and then somehow let it go. The rabbi's text was chosen from the Book of Proverbs. 'Sayest thou that the man diligent in his business, he shall stand before kings.'

•

Jewish cemeteries as a rule do not permit flowers. But after the funeral, a tall, quietly spoken man visited the rabbi at Long Lane synagogue and obtained special dispensation to lay a small posy on Brian's grave each year on his birthday. It was Joe Flannery, his one-time companion in the nursery: the one-time lover who'd never fallen out of love with him.

PART FOUR

WASTING

16

'We've got to spend two million or the taxman will get it'

Since Brian had died without making a will, his whole estate passed automatically to his mother, Queenie. Nor was it worth anything like the £7m commentators had estimated. Lush living had absorbed – even exceeded – a vast yearly income which had never been left to accumulate for one second into capital. What Brian did not spend on himself, on other people or on the roulette table, he invested into offshoot companies and loss-making personal projects, like the Saville theatre. Towards the end, shortage of ready money had led him to borrow heavily from NEMS Enterprises. His debt to his own company was found to be in the region of £150,000. His final cash estate was realised chiefly through the sale of his two houses, his cars, paintings and artworks. The residue, after death duties, was a little more than three-quarters of a million pounds.

Mrs Epstein, bereaved within six weeks of both her husband and elder son, was in no state to face the complexities instantly arising from her inheritance. It fell to her younger son, Clive, to try to sort out Brian's tangled business affairs. Clive, as co-founder of NEMS Enterprises, took over the chairmanship, pending discussions on the company's future.

Tony Bramwell, George Harrison's friend, visiting NEMS a few days after Brian's death, found the half-dozen directors in a state of total confusion. No one at NEMS realised yet that Brian had virtually sold the company to his Australian associate, Robert Stigwood. 'They were all squabbling about who was going to manage the Beatles,' Bramwell says. 'It sickened me. I just walked out.'

Despite Brian's depleted personal wealth, his estate was liable to taxes, based on NEMS' current value, of some half a million pounds. Word quickly leaked on to the London Stock Exchange that, to meet the estate duty, the Epsteins would have no choice but to sell NEMS. It was rumoured that an offer would be made, linking NEMS with Brian's 10 per cent holding in Northern Songs, the Lennon–McCartney publishing company.

Since Brian's death the Beatles had had several further, apparently fruitful, sessions with the Maharishi. They were now full members of the

Spiritual Regeneration Movement and, as such, liable to pay a week's earnings per month to support it. They had also undertaken to visit their guru's academy in India, to further their studies and ultimately to qualify as 'teachers of Meditation'.

At Buckingham Palace the same week, the Queen held a levée for the Council of Knights Bachelor, whose members included Sir Joseph Lockwood, Chairman of EMI. As Her Majesty entered the room, she called out to Sir Joseph: 'The Beatles are turning awfully *funny*, aren't they?'

A few days after Brian's funeral, the four of them met Clive Epstein at Brian's house in Chapel Street. Queenie, too, had insisted on being there. 'All the boys turned up in suits, out of respect for Queenie,' Joanne Newfield says. 'We all sat around Brian's sitting-room, having tea together. It felt so strange – as though nothing had happened at all. I half-expected Brian to walk in, just the way he used to, and join us.

'It was all too much for me. I just burst into tears. George looked at me very sternly and said, "You're not crying for Brian. You're crying for yourself." '

At that and subsequent meetings, the Beatles agreed to accept Clive as Brian's successor, at least for the two months until their contract with NEMS expired. What they most emphatically did not want was any managerial relationship with Robert Stigwood. Lengthy consultations followed with Lord Goodman, the country's most eminent lawyer, who had latterly acted for Brian as well as for EMI. As a result, Stigwood was persuaded to relinquish his option on NEMS. He departed with some £500,000, plus half the NEMS artists roster – among them the Bee Gees, Cream and Jimi Hendrix – to set up, with spectacular success, on his own.

A new company, Nemperor Holdings, was formed to administer NEMS in what Clive Epstein promised would be 'a programme of vigorous expansion'. Vic Lewis, the ex-bandleader, became managing director. Clive, as Chief Executive, commuted back and forth from Liverpool, conscientiously trying to fill his elder brother's shoes.

Peter Brown, at the Epstein family's request, lived on for a time at Brian's Chapel Street house. His resemblance to Brian, and the consequent reliance of Queenie Epstein on him, seemed to guarantee his accession to the role he had so long understudied. He took over Brian's desk and Brian's assistant – even certain of Brian's little executive affectations. 'Brian used to have this habit of dropping all the music papers on the floor and saying, "I've finished with these now," ' Joanne Newfield says. 'A few days after he took over, Peter did exactly the same thing and used exactly the same words.'

It was Brown who now had the direct line to all four Beatles and who, in a voice so very like Brian's, passed along the inter-Beatles message he had just received. Paul wanted to have a meeting, just among themselves, to discuss future projects and plans. Could they all meet up on 2 September at Paul's house?

•

The girls who stood outside Paul's Cavendish Avenue house had never been formally introduced. They knew each other only as syllables, breathlessly gasped out in the running and jumping and climbing and neck-craning of the campaign they pursued in common. There was Big Sue and Little Sue, and Gayleen, and Margo, and 'Willie' and 'Knickers'. Others came and went, or were shooed away, having tried to pre-empt the space allotted by mutual agreement between those half-dozen perennials. Waiting there, day after day, night after night until dawn, as days turned into months, as months lengthened to years, they somehow never did discover one another's surnames.

They waited outside Paul's because he was their favourite Beatle, but also because his house, being only a short walk from Abbey Road studios, was the recognised listening-post for all Beatles intelligence. Pilgrimages would be made at intervals to John's mock-Tudor Mansion in Weybridge or George's Esher bungalow. But always the trail led back to St John's Wood and the big black double gates whose electric security lock, as time passed, grew less and less of an impediment.

Bored to distraction as the Beatles were by their female following, they could not help but marvel at the almost psychic power which enabled these hard-core fans to shadow or waylay them. At Paul's house or Abbey Road, or any ad hoc rehearsal or film-editing rendezvous, Peter Brown's secret call would bring the four together under the scrutiny of those same half-dozen, rather red and breathless faces. 'They used to shout at us, "How did you *know*?" Margo says. 'Paul always called us The Eyes and Ears of the World.'

Margo, a brisk, jolly and otherwise deeply rational girl, worked as a children's nanny in Kingsbury, North London. Both job and location had been chosen for their convenience to the greater purpose which brought Margo to London from the Lincolnshire seaside town of Cleethorpes. She arrived in 1968, looked after her two charges conscientiously for 48 hours, then made her way to St John's Wood. For the next two years, with only the most necessary intervals, Margo stood and waited outside Paul McCartney's house.

The other Beatles had their own faithful followers, usually identified by a nickname: 'Sue John' or 'Linda Ringo'. 'We all respected John,' Margo says. 'We were a bit afraid of him really. Ringo would come along and you'd never notice him until someone said "That was Ringo". George always seemed to hate us. He'd push past us and even try to tread on our toes or kick us. He seemed very unhappy in those days.'

The main objective, however, remained that Beatle who was not only the most irresistibly good-looking but also the most patiently amiable and accessible. Margo had first noticed this quality in 1964 while chasing the Beatles' limousine down Monmouth Street, when Paul leaned out of a window and shouted, 'Run, girls, run!' There was also a time outside the Scala Theatre, during filming of *A Hard Day's Night*, when he emerged to talk to Margo and her cousin in one of his several disguises. 'This man came up to us with blond hair and a clipboard. He told us where to go if we wanted to see the next day's filming. It was only when he said "Ta-ra" that we realised it was Paul.'

So, every day of the week, Margot, Big Sue, Little Sue, Gayleen, 'Willie' and 'Knickers' waited in Cavendish Avenue with their hungry eyes and small Instamatic cameras. They photographed Paul in the early morning as he came out to walk Martha the sheepdog on Hampstead Heath. They photographed him late at night, returning from holiday, his sunburned nose shining eerily in the flashbulb glow. They photographed him driving out, with Jane or without her, in the Aston Martin or Mini Cooper; then, hours, even days, later, they photographed him driving back in again.

Paul, for his part, presented token discouragement. The front gates would be thrown open suddenly, and the Aston Martin would roar out and away up Cavendish Avenue. The girls were by then so fit, they could beat the car on foot over at least the distance to Abbey Road studios. 'We all got very tough as well,' Margo says, 'through being thrown down the EMI front steps by Mal Evans, the roadie. But we understood that he was only doing his job. At other times he'd be concerned for us, standing out there in all weathers. At heart he was an incredibly gentle person.'

The bulk of the snapshots, however, showed Paul, in his endlessly-changing suits and shirts and scarves and waistcoats, pausing at an entreaty: turning and smiling. The face – in real life slightly asymmetric – became for the cheapest Instamatic what it was in the glossiest magazines. Frequently, too, he would be in a mood for conversation. One snapshot from the hundreds shows him playing with a monkey one of the girls had brought. It bit his finger a moment afterwards. 'We told him once we could see him from the back of the house, sitting on the loo,' Margo says. 'We stood him on a flowerpot to show him we were telling the truth.'

Each of the girls, by tradition, brought Paul gifts of varying usefulness. 'I gave him three peaches in a bag once,' Margo says. 'He'd eaten one of them by the time he got down the Abbey Road front steps. Another time, we shouted out, "What do you want for your birthday?" He thought for a minute, then he said, "I haven't got any slippers."' The slippers were ceremonially handed over in front of massed Instamatics.

The vigil broadened in scope after someone discovered under which flowerpot Paul was accustomed to hide his back-door key. Selected parties then began letting themselves into the house while he was absent, and moving from room to room in hushed wonder at the opulent chaos mingled with working-class formality: the lace-covered table, the Paolozzi sculpture, and the ranks and ranks of clothes. They would bring away some memento – small at first – a tea towel or a handful of lavatory paper.

'The American girls were worst,' Margo says. 'They started nicking his clothes.' The English girls, though refusing to pilfer, felt their scruples waver when offered a share in the booty. Margo acquired a pair of Paul's underpants and a spotted Mr Fish shirt. Some Harris tweed trousers were also brought out as a communal prize to be worn reverently, by rota. The hems would be shortened for Little Sue, then lengthened again so that Big Sue could have a turn at wearing them.

•

Six months earlier, Paul had written a song, or the beginning of one, called 'Magical Mystery Tour'. It was to have been put on the *Sgt. Pepper* album: it had been arranged, rehearsed, even partially recorded before Paul conceded that it did not quite fit into Sergeant Pepper's cabaret show. The track was held over – indeed, it was forgotten until early September, and the meetings to decide how the Beatles were to begin the era after Brian.

The idea, like the song, was Paul's. He had been thinking in his whimsical way about little charabanc buses, setting out with coy trepidation on Mystery Tours from British seaside towns. He had been thinking, too, of Ken Kesey's Merry Pranksters, an American hippy troupe which, two years earlier, had journeyed by bus through the Californian backwoods, buoyed up by LSD diluted into thirst-quenching Kool-Aid. Tom Wolfe's chronicle of their journey, *The Electric Kool-Aid Acid Test*, recorded, among other things, what visions the Pranksters experienced by taking acid during a Beatles concert in Los Angeles. So, yet again, something they had originally inspired came floating back to them almost unrecognisably as a new idea to copy and adapt.

Paul's plan was to hire a coach and set out on a real life Mystery Tour, as the Pranksters had, to see what adventure – what 'magic' – would be extracted from the unsuspecting English countryside. They would take cameras and film it, Paul said, but this time direct the film for themselves. He showed the others the scenario he had written – or rather, drawn. It was a neatly-inscribed circle, segmented with what were to be the visual high-points. In one segment, Paul had written 'midgets'; in another, 'fat lady'; in yet another, 'lunch'.

The prospect, as Paul outlined it, was generally appealing. At last they would be able to make a film unhampered by Walter Shenson, Dick Lester and all the petty restraints which had made *Help!* and *A Hard Day's Night* so tedious and disappointing an experience. Film-making, as they well knew, was easy enough. All you needed was money and cameras, and someone saying 'Action!'

So exhilarating did the project – and other projects – seem that they decided to postpone their pilgrimage to the Maharishi's Indian ashram until early 1968. John and George gave their first television interview for two years, appearing on the *David Frost Show* to explain their new-found religious beliefs. Even about Transcendental Meditation they were pithy and funny: they seemed calm, cheerful and restored to sanity. Best of all, they no longer incited Britain's gullible youth to experiment with LSD. The *Daily Sketch* spoke for all in noting maternally, 'It's nice to see the roses back in the Beatles' cheeks.'

Certainly, it was simple enough to hire a luxury coach and commission the best graphic artists to design placards reading MAGICAL MYSTERY TOUR, though not quite so easy to make the placards stick to the coach's highly polished sides. It was easy to hire actors to play the characters specified in Paul's diagram – a fat lady, a midget, a music-hall funny man. It was easy to engage cameras, and three crews to operate them, and to persuade a sprinkling of journalists and NEMS employees to go along as extras. Forty-three people eventually boarded the coach which, early in September 1967, in a secrecy somewhat compromised by its insecurely fixed MAGICAL MYSTERY TOUR placards, headed out of London along the Great West Road towards a still unspecified destination.

Chaos set in from the beginning. The Magical Mystery Tour, far from floating off into a psychedelic sunset, laboured sluggishly and all too materially around Britain's summer holiday routes, hounded by a cavalcade of press vehicles, surrounded at every random halt by packs of sightseers and fans. Encountering a sign to 'Banbury', they followed it, to see if Banbury had a fair. It didn't, so they turned round and headed for Devon.

The journey, it became quickly evident, held neither magic nor mystery: only poignant reminders of how things used to be when Brian Epstein looked after the travel arrangements. Aboard the coach, becalmed in traffic jams, or trying to register at hotels that were not expecting them, everyone realised at last what a protective shield had been wrenched away. Neil Aspinall realised it, trying to apportion overnight rooms among midgets and fat ladies squabbling over who had to double up with whom. 'When Brian was alive, you never had to worry about any of that. You'd just ask for 15 cars and 20 hotel rooms and they'd be there.'

They reached Devon and started back, still vainly trying to extemporise quicksilver comedy from the all too mundane disorganisation and bad humour. Nothing was explained to the actors or even the cameramen. The script was anything that anyone happened to say.

'We missed the tour ourselves in the end,' Neil Aspinall says. 'We were too busy driving. We drove all the way to Brighton and finished up just filming two people on the beach. What we *should* have been filming was the chaos we caused – the bus trying to get over this narrow bridge, with queues of traffic building up behind us, and then having to reverse and go back past all the drivers who'd been cursing us, and John getting off in a fury and ripping all the posters off the sides.'

The climactic scenes were filmed on a disused airfield in West Malling, Kent. There, under Paul's direction, a scene was improvised with 40 dwarfs, a military band, a football crowd and a dozen babies in prams. The coach, by now looking decidedly careworn, swerved round the pitted runway with limousines in hot, but unexplained, pursuit. That was the finish of the *Magical Mystery Tour*.

It was the finish, that is to say, but for the editing, which took 11 weeks. 'Paul would come in and edit in the morning,' Tony Bramwell says. 'Then John would come in in the afternoon and re-edit what Paul had edited. Then Ringo would come in . . .' When not editing and re-editing, they would stand in the cutting room, having singsongs with a toothless Soho street busker who carried a port bottle balanced on his head.

The print eventually passed by all four Beatles was then handed to NEMS Enterprises for distribution. NEMS' response was indecisive. 'It was like giving your film to NBC and CBS and all the networks at once,' Neil Aspinall says. 'Everyone came up with a different comment. "Couldn't you do it this way?" "Couldn't you do it *this* way?"' NEMS eventually sold the British rights to BBC Television, even though the film had been shot in colour and BBC TV, to all but a select handful, was still black and white. BBC 1 announced that it would be shown on Boxing Day, 1967.

The Beatles had been at Abbey Road since mid-September, recording material for an EP to accompany the film. Their pre-Christmas single, however, was a separate track, 'Hello, Goodbye,' written by Paul, in which a grandstand of overdubbed voices chanted a lyric so simple as to be almost inane and so inane it appeared subtly ironic. 'You say goodbye and I say hello. Hello, hello. I don't know why you say goodbye, I say hello. Hay-la! Hey-hello . . .' By early December, 'Hello, Goodbye' was number one in Britain and America. The Beatles continued to walk upon water.

Magical Mystery Tour was launched by a party whose lavishness showed no doubt of *Sgt. Pepper*-like success. The Beatles specified fancy dress. John came as a Teddy Boy, accompanied by Cynthia in Quality Street crinolines. George Martin came as the Duke of Edinburgh, Lulu as Shirley Temple and Patti, George's wife, as an Eastern belly dancer. John, that night, made no secret of powerfully desiring Patti Harrison. He danced with Patti time after time, leaving Cynthia so disconsolate in her crinolines that Lulu was roused to sisterly indignation. The climax of the party was the moment at which a little ringletted Shirley Temple, clutching an immense lollipop, confronted the chief Beatle in his greaser outfit and berated him for being so mean to his wife.

Fifteen million British viewers, on the dead day after Christmas, tuned their television sets hopefully to BBC 1 and *Magical Mystery Tour*. Expecting a miracle, they beheld only a glorified and progressively irritating home movie. The four donned crude animal costumes to perform 'I Am the Walrus', a song inspired by Lewis Carroll's nonsense poem about the 'Walrus close behind us . . . who's treading on my tail'. The Beatles themselves were only intermittently visible sitting among 43 freaky passengers on the bus or as four red-robed wizards, messing around in a chemistry lab. Paul, in one of the few professionally directed sequences, sang 'Fool on the Hill', against a background of French Riviera mountains and sea. George, squatting Indian style, sang 'Blue Jay Way', repeating the line 'don't be long' 29 times. A lengthy abstract interlude, devoid of its colour, became merely puzzling cloud-drifts and icebergs. The finale was one more idea that no one had quite bothered to think through. 'Let's do a Busby Berkeley sequence,' Paul had said. The Beatles, in white tailcoats, descended a staircase, singing 'Your Mother Should Know', while ballroom dancing teams whirled in aimless formation beneath.

The *Daily Express* TV critic received front-page editorial space next morning to declare that never in all his days of viewing had he beheld such 'blatant rubbish'. The unaminous decision of the British critics was picked up by American papers like the *Los Angeles Times* ('Beatles Bomb With Yule Movie') and brought speedy cancellation of the film's US television deal. The BBC meanwhile, took belatedly old-maidenly fright at John's lyrics for 'I Am the Walrus' – especially the references to 'knickers' and 'yellow matter custard', i.e. snot – and denied it any further airplay.

For the first time since they'd worn leather jackets at a Young Conservatives dance, the Beatles found themselves being collectively slagged off in every newspaper they opened. It came hardest of all to the one who'd initiated the whole catastrophe, drawing a clock face and trusting to his Pied Piper magic to do the rest. 'Dusty' Durband at Liverpool Institute Grammar School could have cited many similar instances long ago when Paul McCartney did insufficient preparation.

Now, too, it came home to them with full force what life was like without Brian to protect them and clear up the messes they made. 'If Brian had been alive, the film would never have gone out,' Neil Aspinall says. 'Brian would have said "OK, we blew £40,000 – so what?" Brian would never have let it happen.'

•

John Lennon's old schoolfriend, Pete Shotton, had long felt a distinct impression that John was trying to tell him something. Pete still lived in Hampshire, managing the supermarket John had bought him: on visits to John in London, he could not but notice what larger business preparations were afoot. 'I'd known John so long and had so many laughs with him, he could never come out with anything straight. He'd just grin across the room and say: "When are you coming up here to work then?"

'Eventually he did come out with it. He said he wanted me to come to London and run a boutique the Beatles were opening. He said: "We've got to spend two million or the taxman will get it."'

Dr Walter Strach, their chief financial adviser, had many times implored Brian to invest the colossal Beatle earnings simply left on deposit at various British banks. Socialism had as yet closed few of the Tory loopholes for channelling money abroad into tax-exempt trusts and companies. Brian would never do it, partly through a naive respect for capital, partly from a belief that to take money abroad was unpatriotic. 'After the Beatles got their MBEs,' Dr Strach remembered, 'Brian always insisted they had to be whiter than white.'

It was therefore on 'Uncle Walter's' advice rather than Brian's that individual Beatles made personal investments, such as John's Hampshire supermarket and Ringo's brief, unsuccessful foray into the building trade. On one occasion, all four came to Strach, eager to put money into a washing-machine company run by a bearded young tycoon named John Bloom. The doctor takes credit for talking them out of involvement with one of the decade's more spectacular financial crashes.

Strach figured in the single attempt during Brian's lifetime to divert Beatles money from its huge liability under British income tax. In 1965, the proceeds from *Help!* were paid directly into a Bahamian company, Cavalcade Productions, formed jointly by the Beatles and the film's producer, Walter Shenson, and administered by Dr Strach as a temporary resident in Nassau. 'That was why we shot part of *Help!* in the Bahamas,' Shenson admitted. 'It was a goodwill exercise to persuade the Bahamian authorities we were an asset to their business community.' Unfortunately, the *Help!* proceeds were banked entirely in sterling. When Harold Wilson devalued the pound in 1967, Cavalcade Productions lost approximately £80,000.

Towards the end of his life, Brian had been considering more complex measures to protect the Beatles' accumulated fortunes. His concept was not much different in essence from that which would soon spectacularly emerge – a corporation built around the Beatles which would both lighten their personal tax liabilities and give them control of their own work at every level, from songwriting to recording, even distribution, marketing and retailing. Brian had also visualised a string of 'Beatles boutiques' or pop supermarkets, selling records and clothes.

In addition to their original company, Beatles Ltd, the four were now incorporated into a partnership, Beatles & Co. The manoeuvre took place in April 1967 as a means of providing each with some quick capital. Beatles Ltd paid £800,000 for a share in the partnership. By this absolutely legal method of selling themselves a share in themselves, each Beatle received £200,000 and, later on, a tax demand to match.

In 1968, they had joint reserves of around £2m which, after the taxman's punitive bite of 90-plus per cent, would leave scarcely enough to buy them each a new Mr Fish shirt. Far better, their advisers agreed, to write off the money as a business loss. And if they could have a little fun – even do a little good – in the process, so much the better.

•

Simon Posthuma and Marijke Koger were beautiful people from Holland. Couturiers and interior designers, famous for their Amsterdam boutique Trend, they had migrated to London in 1967, hoping to widen their activities to the theatre. Among their first patrons were a pair of publicists named Barry Finch and Simon Hayes whose clients at the time included Brian Epstein's Saville Theatre. By this means, Simon and Marijke gained access to the Beatles' circle, where their exotic clothes and dreamy, Dutch-accented hippytalk made an immediate impression. So successful were they, both as stage designers and Beatles friends, that they brought their former Amsterdam boutique partner, Josje Leeger, over from Holland to join them. The three, plus PR man Barry Finch, then formed themselves into a design group named The Fool.

All through the Summer of Love and the still-affectionate autumn that followed it, The Fool enjoyed the quasi-royal status of designers and couturiers to the Beatles. They made the costumes for the 'All You Need Is Love' television sequence. They painted a piano and a gipsy caravan for John and designed a fireplace for George's Esher bungalow. They began to appear in newspaper fashion spreads as heralds of an era to follow wasp stripes, PVC and mini-skirts. 'Simon,' explained the *Sunday Times*, 'is dressed to represent Water. His jacket is glittering Lurex in bluey, greeney colours; his trousers are blue velvet. Marijke is Nature, in blue and green, and has a pastoral scene on her bodice. Josje is Space, her midnight-blue trousers covered with yellow appliqué stars.' To the *Sunday Times*, Simon explained that The Fool was a name with meaning beyond the obvious one. 'It represents Truth, Spiritual Meaning and the circle, which expresses the universal circumference in which gravitate all things.'

In September 1967, The Fool received £100,000 to design a boutique for the Beatles and stock it with their own exotic garments and accessories. It was Paul, the most dandified Beatle, who announced 'a beautiful place where you can buy beautiful things'. It was Paul who strove to think of a name befitting the new boutique's ideal of chaste elegance, and who found inspiration in a Magritte painting he had recently bought as well as the general idea of a hippy Garden of Eden. The others agreed: they would call their boutique, simply, Apple.

The summer had produced another Beatles friend. His name was Alexis Mardas. He was a young, blond-haired Greek who had come to Britain knowing only two people: Mick Jagger and the Duke of Edinburgh.

Nicknamed Magic Alex by Lennon, Mardas was an inventor of electronic gadgets with ideas which, he believed, could revolutionize twentieth-century life. There was the transistorised hi-fi; the 'scream' built into a gramophone record to prevent illicit taping; the force field around a house which would keep intruders at bay with a wall of coloured air. His ideas appealed to the Beatles' thirst for novelty and their endless quest for protection against a cheating, importunate world.

Meanwhile, in Baker Street, a respectable eighteenth-century corner house, not far from Sherlock Holmes's mythical consulting rooms, was being transformed to a condition which might have baffled even Holmes. The Fool hired gangs of art students to help them cover the side wall along Paddington Street with psychedelic patterns, whizzing and whirling around what seemed to be the face of an enormous Red Indian. Magic Alex was also there, designing floodlights.

All the Beatles relished the novelty of setting up a shop. The prettiest, swingingest, girls – among them Patti Harrison's sister, Jennie – were recruited as staff. Pete Shotton left his Hampshire supermarket to oversee the arrival of oriental fabrics and exotic jewellery ordered in profusion by

The Fool. 'John would come in every day,' Pete says. '"You've got to put a partition over here," he'd say. Then Paul would come in and say, "What's that partition here for? Better move it over there."'

The Apple boutique opened on 7 December 1967, with a lavish party and fashion show. 'Come at 7.46,' the invitations said. 'Fashion show at 8.16.' In the elegant, sweating crush, sipping apple juice, only two Beatles were visible: John and George. Ringo was abroad, playing a small part in the film *Candy*, and Paul had decided to go away to his farm in Scotland.

Within a few days, the pattern of trading had been established. Hundreds of people came to Baker Street to look at the Apple boutique, and look inside it. There was no obligation to buy, or to consider buying. Garments began rapidly to leave the premises, though seldom as a result of cash transactions. The musk-scented gloom, where feather boas hung helpfully from bentwood hat-stands, was a shoplifters' paradise.

•

It was upstairs from the Apple boutique that the empire named Apple initially took root. On the first floor, in a snow-white office, Terry Doran, 'the man from the motor trade', ran Apple Music, intended nucleus of the Beatles' own independent publishing and recording company. On the second floor, Pete Shotton administered Apple Retail, comprising the boutique, and men's tailoring and mail order subsidiaries. Pete also did much of the hiring for the other Apple provinces springing up almost daily. For the empire, unlike its symbol, did not ripen at leisure. It appeared all at once like a conjuring trick at the imperious clap of four multimillionaires' hands.

Its purpose – to begin with, at least – was clear and concurring in all four multimillionaires' minds. It was to be *theirs*, rather than administered on their behalf. It was liberation from the control of 'men in suits', as John Lennon called the irksome powers at NEMS, Northern Songs and EMI. It was to prove that people of less than middle age, without stiff collars or waistcoats, were capable of building and running an organisation. Apple was to be the first triumphant annexation by youth's living apotheosis of all the power and riches which youth had generated. It was to be free and easy and open-handed; above all, in that poignant Sixties word, it was to be 'fun'.

Magical Mystery Tour, in 1967, was the first production credited to Apple Films. Among future productions, it was announced, would be a film starring Twiggy, the model; possibly a screen version of the hippy world's most sacred text after *Sgt. Pepper*, J. R. R. Tolkein's *The Lord of the Rings*. Simultaneously there appeared an Apple Electronics division, run by Magic Alex from a laboratory financed by the Beatles. Alex was to design an entire recording studio for them: meanwhile, his Hellenic wizardry would be applied to such marketable novelties as luminous paint, domestic force fields and plastic apples with miniature transistor radios inside.

In January 1968, Beatles Ltd changed its name to Apple Corps Ltd. 'It's a pun,' Paul explained patiently. 'Apple *Core* – see?' Neil Aspinall was appointed Managing Director and Alistair Taylor, General Manager. The board of directors included Peter Brown and Harry Pinsker, head of Bryce, Hanmer, Brian Epstein's old Albemarle Street accountants.

The new divisions, and their newly appointed directors and managers quickly spilled over from the Apple shop into a suite of offices in Wigmore Street, a quarter of a mile away. Here were established Apple Records, with Jane Asher's brother, Peter, as A & R man, and Apple Publicity, run by Derek Taylor, the idiosyncratic Press Officer whom the Beatles had wooed home from Hollywood for his second term of serving them. Also at Wigmore Street, Neil Aspinall exchanged his time-honoured role as roadie for that of office manager, finally making use of his teenage accountancy training.

In these early days, a stark contrast emerged between friends of the Beatles, working for a moderate salary, and impressive outsiders, recruited to senior executive positions at almost any figure they cared to name. Pete Shotton, whose weekly take-home pay was £37 10s, found himself approving munificent salaries for Denis O'Dell, Head of Apple Films; Ron Kass, Head of Apple Records; and Brian Lewis, lawyer in charge of Apple contracts. 'As soon as they arrived,' Pete says, 'they started going out to lunch. I'd be left with a toasted sandwich from the cafe across the road.'

•

In February, in the midst of Apple's blossoming, John and George, with Cynthia and Patti, flew to India to begin their much postponed religious studies under the Maharishi Mahesh Yogi. The advance party also included Patti's sister, Jennie. Paul and Jane followed soon afterwards, with Ringo, Maureen and a consignment of baked beans which Ringo had brought as insurance against the curry-eating weeks ahead.

The ashram to which their guru beamingly welcomed them was not devoid of worldly comforts. Situated in verdant foothills above the Ganges at Rishikesh, it was a settlement of stone bungalows, with English hotel furniture, telephones and running water. A high perimeter fence and padlocked gate kept out sightseers, beggars, *sadhus*, wandering cows and the clamour of everyday worship at the *ghats*, or Holy bathing places, along the river bank. The Maharishi himself occupied an elaborate residence equipped with a launching pad for his private helicopter.

Apart from the Beatles, an impressive netful of personalities had been trawled to sit at the Maharishi's feet. They included Mike Love of the Beach Boys; Donovan, the English folk singer, and his manager, 'Gipsy Dave'; and the film actress Mia Farrow. All put off their pop hippy finery, the girls to dress in saris, the boys in *kurta* tunics, loose trousers and sandals. At Mike Love's example, both John and George started to grow beards. John even experimented with a turban, though he could not resist the temptation to pull Quasimodo faces when wearing it.

The Maharishi took pains to ensure that ashram life would not be too stringent for his star disciples. The chalets were comfortable – like Butlin's, Ringo said – and the food, though vegetarian, was ample; there were frequent excursions and parties. The Lennons were presented with Indian clothes and toys for their son, Julian, and George's 25th birthday was celebrated by a seven-pound cake. Obliging houseboys would even smuggle the odd bottle of forbidden wine into the Beatles' quarters.

Even so, the schedule of fasting, chanting and mass prayer quickly proved too much for Ringo Starr. He left Rishikesh with Maureen after only 10 days, complaining that his delicate stomach couldn't take the highly spiced food and that he missed his son.

The others showed every sign of sticking out the course for its full three-month duration. Fleet Street journalists who had infiltrated the stockade reported seeing this or that Beatle seated contentedly at a prayer meeting, feeding the monkeys that inhabited the trellises or aimlessly strumming a guitar. It emerged that they were holding a contest among themselves to see who could keep up non-stop meditation the longest. Paul led the field with four hours, followed by John and George with three-and-a-half each. They were also using the unwonted peace and immobility to write songs for their next album.

At regular intervals, Neil Aspinall would fly out from London to report the latest progress in setting up Apple, and the position of 'Lady Madonna', the single they had left for release in their absence. Neil was also making arrangements for Apple Films to finance a production in which the Maharishi himself would star. 'We had a meeting about it in his bungalow,' Neil says. 'Suddenly, this little guy in a robe who's meant to be a Holy Man starts talking about his two-and-a-half per cent. "Wait a minute," I thought, "he knows more about making deals than I do. He's really into scoring, the Maharishi."'

Paul, who filmed most of his and Jane's nine-week stay, remembered their Rishikesh experience as being very like school, with the teachers delivering long, boring sermons and the pupils nudging each other and trying not to giggle. As he told John later, 'We thought we were submerging our personalities, but really we weren't being very truthful then. There's a long shot of you walking beside the Maharishi, saying "Tell me, O Master," and it just isn't you.'

It was in the ninth week, after Paul and Jane had decided to leave, that John himself began showing signs of restlessness. 'John thought there was some sort of secret the Maharishi had to give you, and then you could just go home,' Neil Aspinall says. 'He started to think the Maharishi was holding out on him. "Maybe if I go up with him in the helicopter," John said, "he may slip me the answer on me own."'

By the eleventh week, despite trips above the Ganges in the Maharishi's helicopter, the answer still had not come. Furthermore, it began to be whispered that the Maharishi was not so divine a being as he had seemed. There was also a rumour that his interest in Mia Farrow might not be spiritual only. Even George, the guru's most impassioned disciple, seemed to be having second thoughts. So, to Cynthia's dismay, John decided they were going home.

He led the way into the Maharishi's quarters and announced his decision, characteristically mincing no words. The guru, for all his quick-wittedness, seems to have had no idea that the lights had changed. When he asked 'Why?' John would say only, 'You're the cosmic one. You ought to know.' At this, he said later, Maharishi Mahesh Yogi, The Great Soul, gave him a look like 'I'll kill you, you bastard.'

John, in fact, was convinced for a long time afterwards that the Maharishi would wreak some sort of Transcendental vengeance. He told Cyn' it was already starting when, on the way back to Delhi, their taxi broke down, and they both stood panic-stricken, trying to thumb a lift as the Indian dusk with its thousands of staring eyes closed in around them.

•

The Maharishi, his teachings and flowers and Transcendental gurglings were dismissed as utterly as last month's groupie or yesterday's Mr Fish shirt. 'We made a mistake,' Paul said. 'We thought there was more to him than there was. He's human. We thought at first that he wasn't.' Into another airport microphone, George concurred: 'We've finished with him.' The Holy Man was left in his mountain fastness to cogitate upon a mystery as profound as any offered by Heaven or Earth. Had the Beatles, or had the Maharishi Mahesh Yogi, been taken for the bigger ride?

Last month's ashram-dwellers were this month's corporate executives, flying to New York with their numerous, highly paid lieutenants to unveil Apple Corps to the most crucial of its prospective markets. The first board meeting was held aboard a Chinese junk, cruising round the Statue of Liberty.

At press conferences and on the NBC *Johnny Carson Show*, John and Paul explained the revolutionary but also philanthropic motives which would guide the Beatles' business. 'The aim,' John said, 'isn't just a stack of gold teeth in the bank. We've done that bit. It's more of a trick to see if we can get artistic freedom within a business structure – to see if we can create things and sell them without charging five times our cost.'

Paul said that Apple's aim was 'a controlled weirdness . . . a kind of Western Communism'. It was he who announced the newest sub-division: an Apple Foundation for the Arts. 'We want to help people, but without doing it like a charity. *We* always had to go to the big men on our knees and touch our forelocks and say, "Please can we do so-and-so . . .?" We're in the happy position of not needing any more money, so for the first time the bosses aren't in it for profit. If you come to me and say, "I've had such and such a dream," I'll say to you, "Go away and do it."'

In other words, the Apple Foundation for the Arts would grant struggling unknown artists in every genre the finance and fulfilment they had been denied by a mercenary, unsympathetic, middle-aged world. Paul designed a proclamation to that effect, issued via full-page advertisements in the British music press. Alistair Taylor, Apple's general manager, was coerced into posing for a photograph weighed down with the impedimenta of a one-man band. 'This man has talent!' ran Paul's caption. 'One day, he sang his songs into a tape recorder and, remembering to enclose a picture of himself, sent the tape to Apple Music at 94 Baker Street. You could do the same. This man now owns a Bentley.'

The response was as anyone but a Beatle might have predicted. An avalanche of tapes, of novels, of plays and poems and film scripts and synopses and scenaria, of paintings, etchings, sketches, lithographs, sculptures, designs, blueprints, working models and other, less easily classified submissions fell at once, with a huge, soft, slightly deranged thud upon Apple's Wigmore Street office. Many were delivered in person, the artists electing to wait the short time necessary before they received their bursaries from the Apple Foundation for the Arts. The reception area all day thronged with creative, insolvent humanity, from ethnic bards to seaside Punch and Judy men, reminding Richard DiLello, a young San Franciscan working for the Press Office, of nothing so much as the VD clinics back home in his native Haight-Ashbury. Brighter even than hope of penicillin shone the belief that the Beatles meant it: that behind those very partition walls even now, they were reading, listening, looking, nodding and saying, 'Yes. Go away and do it.'

They were certainly there, though not engaged precisely as imagined. They had a big corner room in which open house was kept for the fellow rock stars and friends who dropped in continuously to wish Apple luck and drink, and smoke, its health. John and Paul each kept more or less regular office hours, enjoying the novelty of a fixed destination, a desk and secretaries. John employed an astrologer named Caleb to cast a daily horoscope for senior staff, and guide major policy decisions by consulting the *I Ching Book of Changes.* Paul's concern was that people arrived on time in the mornings and that there was enough lavatory paper in the Ladies'.

It was pleasant, now that they themselves could rise no higher, to act as sponsors of new, young pop talent to join them on their very own Apple record label. Terry Doran had made the first signing – a teenage group named Grapefruit, and launched to the music press on an avalanche of Fortnum and Mason grapefruit in special presentation boxes. A second group, The Iveys, was Mal Evans's discovery. George had his own protégé, a fellow Liverpudlian named Jackie Lomax; in America, Peter Asher had found a raw-boned singer songwriter named James Taylor. Twiggy the model also kept telling Paul about a sweet little Welsh soprano named Mary Hopkin, the longest consecutive winner of the television *Opportunity Knocks* talent show.

By June 1968, Wigmore Street could no longer contain all this bright, bustling activity and expansion. Neil Aspinall was given half a million pounds and told to find Apple a larger orchard.

Within a few days, Neil found 3 Savile Row, a five-storey Georgian house standing deep in the heartland of bespoke tailoring and dealers in hand-made cigarettes. The house knew something of show business: it had previously been owned by Jack Hylton, the theatrical impresario, who in latter days ran it as the Albany Club. On its left, Gieves, the military tailors, guarded the crevice into Regent Street. To its right stretched timbered casements, displaying Royal warrants, in which elderly men with tape measures still toiled around the waistlines of peers and archbishops.

Savile Row was never to be quite the same again.

•

Throughout June and July, the Beatles' new business occupied them to the exclusion of almost everything else – including music. In the past six months, indeed, they had been to Abbey Road only to record a new single, 'Hey Jude', and some tracks for a project about which they felt zero enthusiasm. The problem of what to do as their contracted third film for United Artists had finally been solved by a compromise that mercifully spared them from having to go in front of the cameras again. A cartoon feature film would be made, featuring their music and themselves as principal characters but with voices overdubbed by actors. The theme would be their song 'Yellow Submarine', which since its 1966 release – despite its association with ochre-tinted pep pills – had become one of the best-loved airs in Britain. Tiny tots were taught to sing it in kindergartens. Strikers chanted it on protest marches, changing 'We all live in a yellow submarine' to 'We all live on bread and margarine.'

The Beatles' lack of involvement in the film was hardly conducive to enthusiasm in recording songs for its soundtrack and subsequent album. To be sure, they regarded it as a dustbin for second-rate tracks. 'It'll do for the film,' John would say whenever a song had not come up to expectations. Even after recycling 'Nowhere Man' and 'All You Need Is Love', they found they hadn't enough material for even one album side. So George went away for an hour and wrote 'Only a Northern Song', a sarcastic reference to the publishing company and the low standard to which its product seemed to have sunk. George Martin in the end had no option but to make up a side two of Beatles songs scored as orchestral pieces by himself. For the first time ever, the Beatles had given short weight.

Surprisingly, however, *Yellow Submarine* turned out to be an artistic triumph. Scripted by Erich Segal – soon to hit the fiction jackpot with *Love Story* – it translated Beatles lyrics and Beatles allusions into genuinely appealing and inventive fantasy about the inhabitants of a dream world called Pepperland and its oppression by killjoy invaders called Blue Meanies. Through it floated four little cartoon Beatles with the same characters and much the same childlike insouciance as in *A Hard Day's Night* and *Help!* and voices that could easily have been mistaken for their real ones. The film opened in London on 17 July. Though patronisingly reviewed and – amazingly – denied a general release – it proved popular with fans, restoring much of the goodwill that *Magical Mystery Tour* had lost.

At Baker Street, meanwhile, the Apple boutique was sliding into chaos. Its psychedelic mural had been scrubbed away, after petitions by local tradespeople, leaving behind what was, after all, just another clothes shop, distinguished only by the ineptitude of its management. Despite their alleged boutique experience in Holland, The Fool seemed to have no idea how to run a business, and borrowed many of the choice items of stock for their own use. Shoplifting raged on, barely noticed by assistants, some of whom regularly fiddled up to £50 each week on top of their wages. A new head of Apple Retail, John Lydon, was desperately trying to stop the rot. Stern memos went out to The Fool, warning them to take no more garments off the premises and forbidding any further expenditure without direct authorisation.

At the end of July, Pete Shotton was called to a meeting at Paul's house. 'John told me, "We've decided to close the shop down. We're tired of playing shops." '

The Apple boutique liquidated itself on 30 July by the simple process of giving away its entire stock. A dozen policemen fought to control the riot in Baker Street as hundreds grabbed at Afghan coats, Indian beads, Art Deco ashtrays and whatever shop fittings could be wrenched loose. The Beatles and their wives had already gone in privately for first pick, gleefully carrying off the choicer spoils with no sense that it was their own property they were plundering. To the media, Paul repeated John's remark, with an almost Napoleonic twist: 'The Beatles are tired of being shopkeepers.'

Bright, fresh, apple-green carpet now covered all five floors at 3 Savile Row. On 11 August, Apple Records released four inaugural titles on the label whose logo was a perfect Granny Smith apple. Teams of photographers, designers and typographers, not to mention fruiterers, working in London and New York, had laboured for six months, rejecting whole crops, to produce that stunningly crisp and explicit motif. When you turned the record over, you saw the same apple, cut into a heart-shaped creamy half. As a final touch, Alan Aldridge, London's highest-paid pop illustrator, contributed the 'copyright reserved' message in hand-drawn italic script.

The Beatles' new single, 'Hey Jude', was accompanied, in a shiny black presentation box, by three of the talents now under their wing: Mary Hopkin, Jackie Lomax and the Black Dyke Mills brass band. Paul had produced Mary Hopkin's ballad 'Those Were the Days', and conducted the Black Dyke Mills band's performance of his own composition, 'Thingummybob'. George had written and produced Jackie Lomax's song 'Sour Milk Sea'. The young Press Officer Richard DiLello was given the job of delivering one boxed set each to the Queen at Buckingham Palace; the Queen Mother at Clarence House; Princess Margaret at Kensington Palace; and the Prime Minister, Harold Wilson, at 10 Downing Street.

By far the greatest augury of Apple was the Beatles' appearance together on television, for the first time in two years, to perform 'Hey Jude' on the *David Frost Show*. The studio audience came and stood round them as Paul, at his piano, sang the wistful wounded ballad that turns, midway, into an anthem seven minutes long. At the Abbey Road session, all the 40-piece symphony orchestra had joined in that final mesmeric la-la chorus. So did the studio audience – and much of the country – join in tonight. It was as though the Beatles were reaffirming their oneness with their audience and with each other, instead of just beginning their drift into chaos and bitter enmity.

17

'Your finances are in a mess. Apple is in a mess'

Cynthia Lennon knew there was no hope left for John and her. The marriage survived only because John could not be bothered to end it. For months, Cyn' had been little more than a prisoner in the mock-Tudor mansion at Weybridge, with its miles of untrodden pastel carpet, its unused gadgets, its antique globe cocktail cabinet from Asprey's, its suits of armour and medieval altar-pieces. By day she looked after Julian: at night she watched television, wondering if she would see her husband on it. She did yards of embroidery, and took up drawing and painting again. She slept alone in the huge master bedroom, often awakening to find only her half of the bed disturbed. She would then nerve herself to voyage through the house to look for John among the empty bottles, the scattered album sleeves and the groggy, sprawling figures of whatever new strangers he had brought home at dawn.

Sometimes, at her embroidery when the house was quiet, Cyn' would speculate on the type of woman John ought to have married. In this, as in all else about him, she faced impenetrable mystery. She could think only of Brigitte Bardot, his adolescent passion whom Cynthia herself had tried so hard to copy. And Juliette Greco, who was not at all pretty and who played the guitar and sang like a man. His unknowable strangeness used to disappear, at least, when they made love. But that had stopped happening more than a year ago.

Cyn' knew John could suffer bouts of depression – desperation even – that were entirely separate from his outward success. One such 'trough' had been in 1965, at the height of Beatlemania, when no one thought to ask why the idol of millions would write a song called *Help!* Another, still deeper trough came in 1967, in the months before he met the Maharishi, when John, under Dr Timothy Leary's influence, tried to 'destroy' his ego by expanding it to ludicrous proportion. He would arrive at Abbey Road dressed like Sabu the Elephant Boy in a cloak, curly slippers and a turban. At a dinner-party given by Jane Asher, a guest happened to ask for an ashtray. John crawled under the table and invited her to flick her ash into his open mouth.

Now, in early '68, Cynthia felt another trough beginning. So far as she could divine, it had something to do with student riots – the savage street warfare in Paris, West Germany, even London's own elegant Grosvenor Square. John, in some obscure way, felt himself a part of this worldwide change from lisping hippy Love and Peace to brick-hurling activism. The Underground looked on him as a potential leader, to join Tariq Ali and Daniel Cohn-Bendit and the others whose 'charisma', in the modish word, was akin to that of rock stars. He had even written a song called 'Revolution', but then, apparently, lost his nerve. One version said 'You can count me in'; the other said 'You can count me out'. Part of him wanted to be a pamphleteer, a rabble-rouser, a street fighter. The larger part was still buttoned into his Beatle self, still forged to a corporate smile, still fearful of what his Aunt Mimi might read about him in the press.

Occasionally, summoning up her courage, Cynthia would ask him if he had found someone else. John always vehemently denied it. He still did not think in remotely that way of the Japanese woman he had met two years ago at John Dunbar's Indica Gallery, and who, instead of speaking, had handed him a card inscribed 'Breathe'. And yet, as the months passed, as his restlessness grew to match the outside world's, for some unfathomable reason he could not get Yoko Ono off his mind.

•

The woman whose name in English means 'Ocean Child' was born seven years before John, in February 1933. On her mother's, Isoko, side, she could trace her ancestry back through a line of wealthy bankers and aristocrats to a Japanese emperor. Her father, Keisuke Ono, was a talented classical pianist who had opted to abandon his dream of turning professional to work in a bank. One of Yoko's earliest memories was of her father spreading out her fingers to see if she might become the classical pianist he had wanted to be.

Keisuke's career prospered, and Yoko was brought up in sheltered luxury with her younger brother, Keisuke, and sister, Setsuko. Her mother was fanatical about cleanliness, often insisting that seats should be disinfected before Yoko was allowed to sit in them. At the same time, her mother encouraged Yoko to be hardy and self-sufficient. As a tiny tot, if she happened to slip and fall, the household servants had instructions not to help her but to let her get up by herself.

Yoko spent the Second World War in Tokyo, frequently in terror from bombing attacks, though spared the horror of the Atom Bomb attack on Hiroshima that completed Japan's annihilation. Keisuke's bank job had taken him to America frequently before the war, and in 1945, when Yoko was 12, he decided to move his family there permanently and settled with them in the New York suburb of Scarsdale. Yoko attended the highly respectable and conventional Sarah Lawrence College, where she studied art and musical composition. At the age of 18, she outraged both her family and Sarah Lawrence by marrying a Japanese musician and going off to live with him in a Greenwich Village attic.

Here she fell in naturally with the crowd of avant-garde painters, sculptors and poets who collected around the anaemic figure of Andy Warhol. Warhol's dictum that art should aim principally to surprise, or even shock, found a willing convert in Yoko. In direct lineage with his Campbell's soup cans, she became known for works seemingly designed to stir people into bewilderment, if not outright fury, that they should be presented as 'art' at all. One of her creations was an 'eternal time clock', showing only seconds and encased in a sound-proof perspex bubble attached to a doctor's stethoscope. Another was a 'book' called *Grapefruit*, a collection of cards bearing one-line 'instructional poems'.

She came to England in 1966, to attend a symposium entitled 'The Destruction of Art'. Swinging London was in full bloom, and ripe for events and happenings such as she had staged in New York. She settled in London, with her second husband, an American film maker, named Tony Cox, and had a daughter by him, Kyoko. She received the mild notoriety the era so freely bestowed by photographing naked human bottoms and, later, wrapping the Trafalgar Square lions in white canvas. She had not, however, heard a single Beatles record until that night at the Indica when John Lennon walked in on her 'Unfinished Paintings and Objects Show', and John Dunbar sent her across to chat him up as a likely sponsor.

Shortly after their first meeting, she asked John to finance her next exhibition, at the Lisson Gallery in north London. This new Yoko Ono event was entitled 'The Half Wind Show', because everything was in halves. There was half a chair, half a table, half a bed, half a pillow, half a washbasin and half a toothbrush. Like the apple with its £200 price ticket, the idea delighted John's sense of the absurd. He put up the money but recoiled in horror when Yoko suggested his name should appear in the catalogue. Instead, the show was credited enigmatically to 'Yoko plus Me'.

She also sent John her book, *Grapefruit*, with its enigmatic messages, like 'Bleed' or 'Paint Until You Drop Dead'. John, alternately puzzled and fascinated, kept the book at his bedside. While organising yet another happening, entitled 'Dance Event', Yoko sent him further message cards: 'Breathe' or 'Dance' or 'Watch the Light Until Dawn'. At this stage, she was something of a joke between John and Cynthia. They looked at each other rather helplessly, after a Meditation session in London, as Yoko determinedly climbed into the psychedelic Rolls to sit between them.

John met her again at different galleries and again was unaccountably disturbed. He could not explain the disturbance: it occurred in an unused organ, his mind. It was unrelated to his inbred northern concept of servile womanhood. It was something he had only ever felt for men – for the tough, mad Liverpool Teds who could make even him defer and keep silent. Yoko Ono, quite simply, did things that John Lennon did not dare.

He began to look out for her across rooms. He would stand with her and simply listen while the little white face, in its clouds of black hair, poured forth ideas bent on only one purpose: to challenge and upset the conventional, complacent art world. 'As she was talking to me, I'd get high, and the discussion would get to such a level, I'd be getting higher and higher. Then she'd leave, and I'd go back to this sort of suburbia. Then I'd meet her again, and my head would go open, like I was on an acid trip.'

He did make one outright move on Yoko in this period, though unfortunately it had about as little finesse as propositioning a groupie in his Beatles touring days. 'John had invited me to the recording studio,' Yoko remembers. 'He suddenly said, "You look tired. Would you like to rest?" I thought he was taking me to another room, but instead we went off to this flat – I think it belonged to Neil [Aspinall]. When we got there, Neil started to fold this sofa down into a bed. Maybe John thought we were two adults: we didn't have to pretend. But it was so sudden, so crude, I just rejected it. I slept on the divan, I think, and John went into another room.'

He considered asking Yoko to join the pilgrimage to Rishikesh, but couldn't pluck up courage enough to do it. Instead, she went off to Paris, feeling – as she now says – 'like we'd never get started'. He wrote to her there from India – long, rambling letters like the ones he used to send to Stu Sutcliffe. Yoko replied with further message cards. 'I'm a cloud,' one card said. 'Watch for me in the sky.'

It was at Rishikesh, ironically, that Cynthia felt a small revival of hope for her marriage. She, at least, remained convinced that the Maharishi was a power for good and that only envious whispers were turning the Beatles against him. In India, John seemed calmer and happier than Cyn' had ever known him. He began writing songs, about childhood and his mother, Julia, that Cyn' could again understand. Then, on the plane back to England – still half-fearful of the Maharishi's revenge – he told Cyn' something which caused her vast astonishment. He told her that, over the years, he had not been completely faithful to her.

Back in Weybridge, their estrangement deepened. Cynthia even suggested, rather wildly, that John would be better off with someone like Yoko Ono than with her. She begged to go with him to New York for the

Apple launching, but he refused. In May, he packed her away on holiday to Greece with Jennie Boyd and Magic Alex. His old school crony Pete Shotton came down to Weybridge to keep him company.

'We were just sitting round together one night.' Pete says. 'John suddenly asked me, "Don't you feel like having a woman around again?" Then he said, "I've met this woman called Yoko. She's Japanese." Yoko came over and John took her off to listen to his tapes. I just went to bed.

'When I got up the next morning, John was sitting in the kitchen, eating boiled eggs. He said he hadn't been to bed. Then he said, "Will you do us a favour? Would you get us a house?" I said, "What do you want a house for?" "To live in," he said. "With Yoko. This is it." '

When Cyn' walked in to Kenwood unexpectedly a few days later, she found John and Yoko seated together, with the curtains drawn, in a sea of dirty cups and plates. Both looked nonchalantly up at her and said: 'Oh, hi . . .' A pair of Japanese slippers, standing neatly on an upstairs landing, opened the gentle, shortsighted girl's eyes at long last.

•

The Beatles first became aware of Yoko at Abbey Road studios. They could hardly do otherwise. She did not stay, as was proper – as was womanly – in the control room. She came down onto the sacred floor of the studio, where none but Beatles and their closest male aides were allowed, and settled herself down at John's side. Paul, George and Ringo exchanged eloquent glances but – for the moment – said nothing. They could not have survived so long as Beatles without a deep tolerance of one another's fancies and blind spots. They expected John to tire of this soon, the way he tired of everything. They tried not to notice Yoko, and referred to her obliquely as 'Flavour of the Month'.

She was still there, however, as Apple grew and its divisions multiplied. She had now left Tony Cox and her daughter Kyoko to live with John, at Kenwood first, then in London, at Ringo Starr's Montagu Square flat. Pete Shotton drove them around, glad to have been superseded as John's 'personal assistant'. Such was Yoko's introduction to Sir Joseph Lockwood, the EMI chairman, at a boardroom lunch with all four Beatles, Neil Aspinall and Apple Executive Ron Kass. In the visitor's book after her name, John wrote 'female'. 'This little white figure followed the Beatles in,' Sir Joseph said. 'She sat further down the table with my assistant, but hardly said a word all through the meal. Afterwards, my assistant told me she'd had a tape recorder running all the time.'

Her first night with John at Kenwood had begun an artistic partnership that was to perplex and enrage the world. When Yoko first arrived John played her all the experimental tapes he had made, knowing they were useless for Beatles albums. After the final tape, Yoko said, 'Let's make one of our own.' It was only as dawn broke that they got around to first making love.

In the character that everyone believed so uninhibited and audacious, Yoko found bottomless wells of shyness and self-doubt, exacerbated by years of having to keep his mouth shut as a cuddly moptop. 'He was a genius, but he had this huge inferiority complex. He was brilliant as an artist, but he didn't think he was capable of it. Like, when someone wanted to do an exhibition of his lithographs – he was just too scared to get started on the drawings. We both took mescalin, and then he tried. I told him, "That's brilliant, it's beautiful." John said, "But it's only a circle, like a child would do." I said "Maybe it's childish, but it's still beautiful."

'It was the same when he was asked to write a sketch for *Oh! Calcutta!* [a soft porn stage show compiled by drama critic Kenneth Tynan]. "What am I going to write?" John kept saying. I said, "Write that thing you told me about when you were a boy and you used to masturbate." He and his friends all used to masturbate, shouting out the names of sexy actresses – then suddenly John or one of them would shout, "Frank Sinatra!" So he made that the sketch and it was marvellous.'

The obsessive jealousy with which John used to guard Cynthia from other men was now passed on to Yoko. 'Jealous! My God! He wrote a song, "Jealous Guy", that said it all,' Yoko remembers now. After we got together, he made me write out a list of all the men I'd slept with before we met. I started to do it quite casually – then I realised how serious it was to John. He didn't even like me knowing the Japanese language because that was a part of my mind that shut him out. He wouldn't let me read any Japanese books or newspapers.'

Despite her seemingly unquenchable self-belief, Yoko had her insecurities, too. 'When I met John, I was self-conscious about my appearance. I thought my legs were the wrong shape and I used to try to cover my face with my hair. He told me, "No, you're beautiful, your legs are perfect, tie your hair back and let people see your face."'

At other times, the compliments seemed more back-handed, although he seriously wanted to convey to Yoko he'd met no one with her toughness and audacity since the 'Teds' at Garston's Blood Baths. 'I used to tell him "I think you're a closet fag, you know." Because he often said, "Do you know why I like you? Because you look like a man in drag. You're like a mate."'

In June 1968, their first collaboration went on public show. It was a sculpture consisting of two acorns, one labelled 'John by Yoko Ono', the other 'Yoko by John Lennon, Sometime in May 1968'. The acorns, symbolising peace and simplicity, were to be buried as an 'event' at the National Sculpture Exhibition in the grounds of Coventry Cathedral.

John and Yoko, both dressed in white, drove to Coventry in John's white Rolls, accompanied by their newly appointed 'art adviser', Anthony Fawcett. Outside the Cathedral they were met by a canon, who informed them that objects could not be buried in consecrated ground and that, in any case, acorns were 'not sculpture'. Yoko flew into an impressive rage, demanding that leading British sculptors be instantly telephoned to vouch for her artistic integrity. Someone actually got through to Henry Moore's house, but he was out. As a compromise, the acorns were buried on unhallowed ground, under an iron garden seat. Within a week, they had been dug up and taken by Beatles fans as souvenirs. Two more acorns were buried; a security firm mounted 24-hour guard on the seat that marked the spot.

On 18 July, a stage adaptation of John's book *In His Own Write* opened at the London Old Vic theatre. The play had been heavily censored by the Lord Chamberlain's office, for its blasphemous reference to 'Almighty Griff', and disrespect to such world statesmen as 'Pregnant De Gaulle' and 'Sir Alice Doubtless-Whom'. Fleet Street, by now perceiving a still racier story, were out in force in the summer downpour. When John arrived with Yoko and Neil Aspinall, he was surrounded by press raincoats and challenging cries of 'Where's your wife?'

The girls who stood outside Abbey Road studios – and now also outside 3 Savile Row – made no secret of their instant hatred of Yoko. 'Every time we saw her, we shouted awful things,' Margo says. '"Yellow!" "Chink!" Subtle things like that. We all felt so sorry for Cynthia. Once, outside Abbey Road, we'd got this bunch of yellow roses to give Yoko. We handed them to her thorns first. Yoko took them and backed all the way down the stairs, thanking us. She hadn't realised they were meant to be an insult. Nor did John. He turned back and said, "Well, it's about *time* someone did something decent to her."'

In July, John's first art exhibition opened in London, at the fashionable Robert Fraser Gallery. Its title, inspired by the hackneyed message on British street maps, was 'You Are Here': it acknowledged its motive force with a dedication 'To Yoko from John with love'. It began with the release of 360 white balloons into the sky above Mayfair. Each balloon bore the printed message: 'You are here. Please write to John Lennon, c/o the Robert Fraser Gallery.'

To reach the exhibition, one had to walk through a display of charity street collection boxes in the shapes of pandas, puppets and disabled children. The only other items were a circular piece of white canvas, lettered, 'You are here', and John's hat lying on the floor, its upturned brim inscribed: 'For the artist. Thank You.' When some art students sarcastically contributed a rusty bicycle, John immediately put that on show also.

The critics were scornful. They said what was to be many times repeated – that if John had not been a Beatle, he would not have dared put such rubbish on show. In this, at least, the critics erred. So long as he was a Beatle, he never dared do anything.

Many people who picked up the white balloons responded to John's invitation to write to him. Their letters, for the most part, combined racial slurs against Yoko with advice concerning the sanctity of wedlock. 'I suppose I've spoiled me image,' John said. 'People want me to stay in their own bag. They want me to be lovable but I was never that. Even at school I was just "Lennon".'

Cynthia, meanwhile, had found herself ruthlessly cauterised from his life. Magic Alex was deputed to travel to Italy, where Cyn', her mother and Julian were staying, and announce that John intended to divorce her. 'Alex was waiting for me one night when I got back to the hotel. He told me John was going to take Julian off me and send me back to my mother in Hoylake.

'When I got back to England, I tried to have a meeting with him and discuss things. The only way I could get in touch with John was to make an appointment with him through Peter Brown at Apple. And when I finally did meet him, Yoko was there. He insisted she should stay while we were talking.'

John, at the outset, intended to divorce Cynthia for adultery supposedly committed in Italy. Despite his own countless infidelities, he was still mortified – as he told his Aunt Mimi – that Cynthia should have slept with someone else. The petition was dropped when it became clear that Yoko had become pregnant. Cynthia sued for adultery, and was granted a decree nisi in November 1968.

A few weeks earlier, as Cyn' was alone and helplessly contemplating the future, Paul had paid her a surprise visit. With him he brought a song he had written on his way in the car – it was for Julian, he said, although the title was 'Hey Jude'. He gave Cynthia a single red rose, then said, in the old carefree Liverpool way, 'Well, how about it, Cyn'? How about you and me getting married now?' She was moved that Paul should think of her, and grateful for his gesture of friendship and encouragement.

•

Sometimes, in a surge of ecstasy, the girls on watch outside 7 Cavendish Avenue would approach the black security gates and buzz the Entryphone.

As a rule, the voice that answered would belong to Jane Asher, Paul's long-time girl friend. The voice was serious but tolerant and always polite. So Jane was, too, on the hundreds of occasions when she answered the front door. The girls appreciated that civility and patience. Far from resenting Jane, they felt their angelic Beatle was in deserving hands. They were Jane's admirers in a small way, as well as Paul's. They grew their hair long like hers, washing it only in Breck shampoo, because that was the brand Jane advertised on television; pressing it out straight on their mother's ironing boards.

Everyone close to Paul liked Jane and acknowledged her beneficial influence. For, in her clear-voiced way, she was as down to earth as any Liverpool girl. Alone of the entire female race, she refused to pamper and worship Paul. If Jane disagreed or disapproved, she said so. She could curb his ego, his use of charm as a weapon – rather as John curbed the syrup in his music – and yet do it in a way that commanded respect and a maturing love.

That the relationship had lasted five years was due principally to Jane's skill in avoiding the worst of the Beatles madness, and her insistence on following her own successful film and stage career. When Paul and she met, it was with the freshness and appreciativeness of new lovers. Paul's farm, near Campbeltown, Argyllshire, was their usual retreat. Paul had done the painting and decorating, even knocked up some rudimentary furniture. There, in the uncurious hills, they walked and rode; they talked and read by lamplight and washed in the kitchen sink, and Jane cooked appetising vegetarian dishes. Each time they left, she would pack the remnants thriftily away in plastic bags.

For Paul, it was the best of two highly pleasurable worlds. His life with Jane provided domesticity, and the refinement and social standing he craved. In her absence, his life reverted to that of Britain's most hotly pursued bachelor. His casual affairs were conducted with such diplomacy and discretion that Jane never suspected anything. So it might have continued but for a theatre tour that ended prematurely, and a witness who suddenly found herself with a legitimate reason to press Paul's Entryphone.

Margo Stevens, the girl from Cleethorpes, was just beginning her second year of standing outside 7 Cavendish Avenue. She preferred to begin her vigil late at night, when the picket was thinning or absent altogether. She would arrive at about 10 p.m., always with some gift for Paul – fruit or a miniature of whisky – on the offchance of handing it to him as he came home late from the studios or a club. She had been standing there so long, Paul vaguely recognised her now. She knew how to open the security gates by kicking them, and had done so once for him when he could not find his key. Latterly, on the recommendation of his housekeeper, Rosie, he had even trusted her to take Martha the sheepdog for walks on Hampstead Heath.

'It was a summer day: we were all standing there as usual,' Margo says. 'Jane was on tour with a play, and Paul brought home this American girl, Francie Schwartz. He waved to us as they drove in. Later on, another car turned into Cavendish Avenue – it was Jane. She'd come back to London earlier than she was supposed to. We did our best to warn Paul. Someone went to the Entryphone, buzzed it and yelled, "Look out! Jane's coming!" Paul didn't believe it. "Ah, pull the other one," he said.

'Jane went into the house. A bit later on, she came storming out again and drove away. Later still, a big estate car drew up. It was Jane's mother. She went inside and started bringing out all kinds of things that were obviously Jane's – cooking pots and big cushions and pictures.

'We all thought after that they must have finished with each other for good. But the next day, a whole crowd of us were in Hyde Park. Who did we run into but Paul and Jane. They were walking along, holding hands and eating ice lollies.'

Early in 1967, Jane went on tour in America again with the Bristol Old Vic company. Apart from Paul's visit, to celebrate her 21st birthday, they were separated for almost five months. When Jane returned, she found Paul deeply involved in the creation of *Sgt. Pepper* and in LSD. She herself would have nothing to do with acid, and said so bluntly. Paul could not convince her of what she was missing.

Brian Epstein's death was a heavy blow to Jane. She, too, found comfort in the Maharishi: she went with Paul to Rishikesh and felt the experience to have been rewarding. With LSD banished, their understanding returned. Paul, at long last, made ready to commit himself. They announced their engagement at a McCartney family party on Christmas Day, 1967.

The following June, they were back up north for the wedding of Paul's younger brother, Michael. Jane opened in a new play that month and Paul, as usual, attended the opening night. All between them seemed normal until mid-July, when *Yellow Submarine* received its gala premiere. Paul arrived alone at the cinema and at the party which followed. Two days later, on a television chat show, Jane was asked a casual question about their wedding plans. She replied that Paul had broken off the engagement and they had parted.

'Hey Jude', the song which brought such comfort to Cynthia Lennon, was Paul's expression of his own deep personal unhappiness. The words, for once, were not facile and neat; it was a song written honestly, in pain. It moved even John as no song of Paul's ever had before. 'Hey Jude, don't be afraid, you were made to/go out and get her', seemed to John to be a message of encouragement for Yoko and him. 'I took it very personally,' he admitted. '"Ah, it's me!" I said when Paul played it. "No," he said, "it's *me*." I said, "Check. We're both going through the same bit."'

The news that the most adorable and adored Beatle was now on the market again sent a seismic wave of excitement through the young womanhood of the Western world. Paul clearly could have his pick of anyone he wanted, and in a million hairdressers' shops and club powder-rooms debate raged furiously as to which breathtakingly beautiful starlet or model would be the lucky one. In the event, his choice was to be almost as baffling as John's had been.

A year or so earlier, an American photographer named Linda Eastman had called at Brian Epstein's office to show her portfolio of rock star portraits in hopes of getting further work from the Epstein stable. She was a coltishly built New Yorker with rather unkempt blonde hair and a dour, unsmiling face. Peter Brown, who dealt with her, knew her already as a regular backstage at American rock venues like New York's Fillmore East. 'She was just an ordinary girl, like so many you saw around then. She'd arrived in London, saying she wanted to photograph the Beatles. I let her in on the *Sgt. Pepper* session, which was a big thing because only fourteen photographers were allowed from the whole world's press.'

Brown next met Linda one night when he was with Paul McCartney and some other rock figures at the Bag O' Nails Club. He introduced Paul to Linda and, as he remembers, 'That was it. The two of them just went off together.'

•

Linda Eastman did not belong, as many supposed, to the Eastman family whose enormous wealth derived from Kodak photographic film and Eastman colour film stock. Her father Lee, a New York lawyer, had taken the surname to replace one more directly announcing his Jewish immigrant antecedents. But for this gentrification, Paul's future wife as well as his late manager would have borne the surname of Epstein.

Lee Eastman had built up a highly successful New York practice, specialising in music copyright and also representing several of America's leading painters. His wife, Louise, was independently wealthy through her family connection with Linders' department stores. Linda and her brother John grew up in the affluent environment of a house in Scarsdale and a Park Avenue apartment. Linda became accustomed to mixing with the stars whom her father represented, among them the songwriter Hoagy Carmichael and the cowboy action-hero Hopalong Cassidy.

Louise Eastman died in an air crash when Linda was eighteen.

Resisting all opportunities to exploit her father's social connections, she married a geologist named John See, moved with him to Colorado and gave birth to a daughter, Heather. The marriage quickly failed, however, and Linda returned to New York with her baby daughter, by now determined to make her name as a photographer. She got a job with *Town and Country* magazine, Manhattan's equivalent of the *Tatler*, and became a familiar face backstage at the Fillmore East and at photo calls for pop bands flying in from Europe. Her abilities as a photographer were not rated very highly; she was known, rather, as a high-class groupie who used her camera to get on close – sometimes very close – terms with male pin-ups like Mick Jagger, Stevie Winwood and Warren Beatty.

She did not see Paul between the *Sgt. Pepper* session and May 1968, when he came with John to New York to inaugurate Apple. Linda was at the launch party with her journalist friend, Lilian Roxon. On Lilian's advice, she slipped Paul her telephone number. They met at Nat Weiss's New York flat and afterwards in Los Angeles. Paul returned to London but a few weeks later, telephoned Linda and asked her to come and join him.

He brought her home to Cavendish Avenue in his Mini-Cooper, late one summer night. Margo Stevens was on watch by the gates, as always. 'A few of us were there. We had the feeling something was going to happen. Paul didn't take the Mini inside the way he usually did – he parked it on the road and he and Linda walked right past us. They went inside and we stood there, watching different lights in the house go on and off.

'In the end, the light went on in the Mad Room, at the top of the house, where he kept all his music stuff and his toys. Paul opened the window and called out to us, "Are you still down there?" "Yes," we said. He must have been really happy that night. He sat on the windowsill with his acoustic guitar and sang 'Blackbird' to us as we stood down there in the dark.'

Linda was certainly a startling change from the carefully back-combed and immaculate Jane. Hers was the New York 'preppy' style, still so unknown in Swinging Britain that it seemed like no style at all – shapeless dresses below the knee, flat-heeled tennis shoes, even ankle-socks. Nor was she nice, the way Jane always had been, to the girls who eternally monitored Paul's comings and goings from Cavendish Avenue and the Apple offices. 'We could tell that she viewed us as a threat,' Margo remembers. 'Every time they appeared together Linda would cling to Paul's arm as much as to say, "*I've* got him now." None of us could understand what he saw in her. She was hairier than he was.'

For all her seeming unkemptness, Linda had an irresistible appeal to the social-climbing Paul – the aura of Manhattan's aristocracy that, in its way, is as rarified and exclusive as London's. She was certainly beautiful, with her fine-chiselled cheekbones and straw-blonde hair, though she always seemed utterly unconcerned about her appearance. Most importantly, she idolised and deferred to Paul as Jane had always firmly refused to do. Clinging to his arm, she would gaze up at him with awe and say what an honour it would be to bear his children.

Her daughter, Heather, helped to cement the bond between them. Paul had always adored children. His final parting with Jane arose from their disagreement over when to start a family. After meeting Heather, an insecure, rather lonely six-year-old, he insisted she be brought to live at Cavendish Avenue. He delighted in playing with her, reading stories and drawing cartoons for her and singing her to sleep at night.

Linda, meanwhile, was bringing about changes in Paul that Margo and the other girls viewed with deep resentment. They knew, from their illicit journeys round the house, how fastidious he had formerly been. 'He used to shave every day, he always wore fresh clothes and he smelled delicious. Rosie, the housekeeper, told us he insisted on having clean sheets on his bed every night.

'We heard from Rosie how different Linda was. We hardly recognised Paul once she'd got hold of him. He started to put on weight – and he got so scruffy. I'll swear he didn't wash his hair for three weeks at a time. He never shaved, never wore anything but this old Navy overcoat. He could go on the bus down to Apple, and no one would recognise him. Some of us thought we saw him in Oxford Street one day. We followed this real tramp in a Navy overcoat all the way down Oxford Street, thinking he was Paul.'

•

In May, the Beatles had met at Abbey Road to begin their first album for release on their Apple label. John and Paul between them had a backlog of some 30 songs, mostly written during their stay in India. George had been earnestly composing; even Ringo had a tune of his own to offer. With so much material to hand, it was decided to use a format common enough in classical recording but unprecedented in pop. The collection would appear as two LP discs packed into a single dual-envelope sleeve. Not even *Sgt. Pepper* started in such an atmosphere of energy and abundance.

Things began to go wrong on the very first day, when John Lennon walked into Studio One, his arm protectively encircling a small, frizzy-haired figure, dressed all in white. He had not, it seemed, grown tired of Yoko Ono. He was, if anything, more incomprehensibly obsessed by her.

As before, Yoko showed no awareness of studio protocol. She settled herself among the Beatles, cutting herself and John off from the other three by the neck of his guitar. His hair centre-parted like hers, his eyes aslant behind pebble glasses, he was even starting to look a little Japanese.

They whispered together, constantly and secretively, all through the session. Most unbelievably, when John took off his headphones, laid aside his guitar and went off to use the men's lavatory, Yoko still trotted at his heels. 'That wasn't me pursuing John, the way everyone thought,' she says now. 'That was John's terrible insecurity. He made me go out to the men's room with him. He was afraid that if I stayed in the studio with all those other guys, I might go off and have an affair with one of them.'

The awkwardness deepened as John and Paul strummed over to each other the finished songs they proposed the Beatles should record. This interchange, so often the flashpoint for brilliance, now produced only non-committal nods. To Paul, John's new music seemed harsh, unmelodious and deliberately provocative. John, for his part, found Paul's new songs cloyingly sweet and bland. For the first time, Lennon and McCartney saw no bridge between them.

The album that resulted was, therefore, not the work of a group. It was the work of soloists; of separate egos, arguing for prominence. Paul and John each recorded his own songs in his own way, without advice or criticism from the other. George – apart from his own individual sessions – withdrew into a resigned neutrality. Ringo, in his acoustic hutch, bent his drumsticks as far as possible with the ever-changing currents. Sometimes, Ringo did not even bother to turn up.

From John came music equally full of resentment and defiance and lingering terror of opening his mouth too wide. 'Sexy Sadie' was a satire on Maharishi Mahesh Yogi ('What have you done? You made a fool of everyone?') but heavily camouflaged for fear that the Holy Man might still be able to put some kind of Transcendental hex on him. 'Revolution' was a chant in sympathy for the student protest now breaking out all over the world, yet in two minds whether the composer himself was quite ready to take to the barricades. 'Happiness Is a Warm Gun', inspired by an American firearms magazine, swiped in the approximate direction of the Vietnam holocaust. 'Glass Onion' satirised over-earnest Beatles fans with cross-references to earlier lyrics, even a false clue: 'The Walrus was Paul'. The straightforward rock pieces, like 'Yer Blues', were one-dimensional and charmless, the playing turgid, the singing harsh and somehow vindictive. Nowhere was his conversion more evident than in the track called 'Revolution 9', a formless length of electronic noise interspersed with vocal gibberish, which Paul – and everyone else – tried unavailingly to cut from the finished album.

Paul's tracks were neat, polished, tuneful and, in their way, as unbalanced and incomplete – 'Martha My Dear', a song for his sheepdog; 'Rocky Raccoon', an unfinished Western doodle; 'Honey Pie', a glutinous Twenties pastiche. In each, somehow, the most noticeable element was John's missing 'middle eight'. Only in 'Blackbird', briefly and beautifully, did Paul's gift succeed in editing itself. 'Back in the USSR', too, was totally successful, a Chuck Berry-style rocker with Beach Boy harmonies which briefly restored the old familiar grin to John's face. In that, as in a few more songs to come, their matchless combination somehow survived in an individual effort. Paul could have written John's song 'Julia'. It was his memorial, 10 years too late, to the mother whose laughter gave the timbre to his own. But Julia in the song bore another name: 'Ocean Child'.

It was while Lennon fought McCartney on 'Ob-la-di, Ob-la-da' and 'Revolution 9' that George Harrison suddenly and surprisingly gathered strength as a composer and performer. His tally of four songs on the finished 30-track list was the highest John and Paul had ever permitted. As their joint control dwindled, so George's presence increased: his voice, gathering confidence, sounded somehow like John's *and* Paul's. His 'Savoy Truffle' was, after 'Back in the USSR', the album's best piece of rock and roll. 'Piggies', a black nursery song against meat-eaters, was mordantly humorous. Best of all was 'While My Guitar Gently Weeps', a heavy rock lament, with searing guitar phrases played by George's friend Eric Clapton, of Cream. Clapton could not believe at first that the Beatles needed anyone but themselves.

All this happened amid a constant drip of argument and bad feeling which, strangely enough, took heaviest toll on the Beatle whose placid temper was so often a strength and rallying-point. Ringo, halfway through the sessions, emerged from behind his acoustic screens looking tired and morose. He was playing badly, he said, and generally 'not getting through'. To John first, then to Paul, he announced he was resigning. The others, tactfully, did not try to stop him. A week at home with Maureen and Zak and his new baby son, Jason, restored him to his old equanimity. When he returned to Abbey Road, Paul and George had covered his drums with Welcome Back messages and flowers.

They had been working on the, still untitled, double album for five months. For all that time, by night as well as day, Margo Stevens and the other girls had waited and watched the Abbey Road front steps. 'We stuck it out through all weathers,' Margo says. 'We were as tough as old boots in the end. When they came in to record, we'd sleep out on the pavement. People who lived in Abbey Road saw us when they came home from work at night. In the morning when they left for work, we were still there. I got so tough, I could sleep in all weathers. When I woke up one morning, there was snow all over me.'

Margo, on these all-night watches, shared a sleeping bag with Carol Bedford, a Texan girl to whom George Harrison had once actually said 'Hello'. 'Normally the Beatles would go in to record around midnight,' Carol says. 'They'd finish around 4 a.m. So we could count on at least four hours' sleep. But once they all came out suddenly at about 2.30. Margo and I woke up – we tried to stand up but we couldn't undo the zipper on our sleeping bag. Both of us were hopping round the pavement, shrieking and trying to undo the zipper while the Beatles stood there, laughing at us.'

George Martin had done all he could as adviser and editor. To Martin, the 30 songs, or song fragments, on tape reeked of the argument and self-indulgence that had gone into their making. Vainly he pleaded with John and Paul to drop the double album idea; to lose the scribble, like 'Goodnight' and 'Revolution 9'; to cut out all the linking, meaningless shouts and murmurs and pull the 14 best titles together for a Beatles album like *Revolver*, packed end-to-end with quality. The answer was no. On that, at least, all four agreed.

'One night, we were all outside – we could tell they'd nearly finished,' Margo says. 'It got to about three in the morning. We could see John through a window, playing with a light cord hanging from the ceiling. "Come *on*, boys," we were all saying, "it *has* been five months." Then they all came out and down the steps. It was all over.'

As a tribute to their five-month wait, Margo and the others were then taken into the empty Studio One, to hear a playback of 'Back in the USSR', and to pick up and take home as cherished souvenirs the apple cores and crisp packets littering the floor.

•

The doorman at Apple was a thickset, heavily genteel young Cockney named Jimmy Clark. He was, so people said, a discovery of Peter Brown's. He wore a stiff collar, tight-fitting trousers and an exquisitely cut dove-grey morning coat. On fine days he would bask on the Apple front step, his hands in his coat tails, watching the girls who eternally watched the house. His job was to prevent unauthorised entry via the front door or the area steps to the basement studio. He would block the rush and repel it with his large, starch-cuffed, shooing hands. To the resultant boos and insults, Jimmy Clark would grin and bridle delightedly like a cat under the grooming brush.

It was, even so – as hundreds discovered – quite easy to enter the Apple house. Provided that one arrived by taxi and that one carried no banner or other sign of Beatles fanaticism, one was generally assumed to have legitimate business with Apple Corps. The girls fell back, unenviously. Jimmy Clark sardonically stood aside. The white front door yielded to a gentle push.

The front hall was much as in any half-million-pound Georgian house. To the right sat a receptionist, instructed, like all Apple staff, to believe in the bona fide of all visitors. Into a telephone, white as the *White Album*, she would murmur the information that so-and-so was here. She would then smile. 'OK, you can go up. You know the way, don't you?' Everyone knew the way, up the green-carpeted stairs, past the framed Gold Discs, too numerous to count, and the soft-lit oil painting of two honey-coloured lion cubs.

One did not, if one were scrupulous, try any of the doors of offices on the first floor. One climbed on, past more Gold Discs, to Derek Taylor's second floor Press and Publicity office. This room, in the mornings, was bright with sun and furniture polish. In the late afternoon, it grew dark and bewildering. The only light came under the window blinds and from two projectors which beamed a psychedelic light show of bright-coloured, writhing spermatozoa shapes, travelling in perpetuity across the opposite wall. Though dark and filled with obstructions, the room was exceedingly busy. One crossed the projector beam, conscious of many shaggy heads turning, like anxious topiary hedges, in the gloom.

None but the specially important or importunate caller immediately approached Derek Taylor's desk. If one were merely a journalist, one sat initially on a small outlying sofa, behind Taylor's second assistant, Carol Paddon, and next to a tray of water into which several plastic birds endlessly dipped their beaks. Presently, one might move across to the small white button-backed sofa that led directly into Taylor's presence. Already, one would have been offered tea, Scotch and Coke, a cigarette or perhaps something stronger. As each of Taylor's visitors got up and left, one wriggled towards him another few inches. Eventually one would be seated immediately to the right of his huge scallop-backed wicker chair. The slender man with his neat hair and moustache and quiet, indiscreet voice, would lean over on the wicker arm that was to become split and broken with hours of leaning and listening.

Press Officers by their very nature pursue journalists. It was Derek Taylor's unique accomplishment to be a Press Officer whom journalists pursued. Journalists from every newspaper, magazine, wire service and radio and TV network in the Western world pursued him, as a means of access to the Western world's longest-running headline story. They pursued him also because Taylor, strangely enough, was not a monster. He was amiable, sympathetic, polite to a degree which would ultimately seem miraculous. As an ex-journalist himself, he believed that journalists should get their story. It was simply a matter of time, he always said; and of choosing a moment when one or other 'Fab' would be amenable.

Two side doors connected the Press Office with other Apple departments. On Taylor's right was the door to a downstairs kitchen where two cordon bleu-trained debutantes supplied meals to the directors and executive staff, and refreshments to all. On the left was a cupboard, presided over by Taylor's hippy assistant, Richard, and popularly known as the Black Room. It had been used initially as a dumping ground for the entire – and entirely unread – cache of novels, poems, synopses, plans, blueprints submitted from all over the world as projects deserving support by the Apple Foundation for the Arts. Several thousand manuscripts lay there, forgotten as absolutely as the nearby row of high fashion shoes which Derek Taylor had brought home from Hollywood. What the Black Room principally contained were boxes of LP records by Apple artists, cases of wines, spirits and soft drinks, and cartons of Benson and Hedges cigarettes.

Another amenity of the Press Office – as of every other office in the building – was drugs. The presence of the West End's major police station only a couple of hundred yards away did not prevent 3 Savile Row's staff from puffing joints as casually as they sipped tea. 'Upper' and 'downer' pills of every colour, compounded by the costliest amateur pharmacists, were to be found in desk drawers, along with the envelopes, glue and stapling-guns. A certain secretary had been nominated to gather up the entire stock and flush it away in the ladies' lavatory if ever Savile Row's boys in blue should decide to pay a surprise visit (which, amazingly, they never did). Another female employee brought in regular consignments of hash brownies which she had baked herself at the home she still shared with her parents and grandmother. Finding some left to cool in the family kitchen, her grandmother innocently sampled one and remained unconscious for the next twenty-four hours.

'Press', under Derek Taylor's tolerant regime, was a term of almost infinite elasticity. It described virtually anyone who came to Apple with the ghost of an excuse for sharing in the Beatles' artistic Utopia. It encompassed the sculptress who wanted money to produce 'tactile' figures in leather and oil; and the French Canadian girl, frequently prised from the basement windows, who wanted money to get her teeth capped. It corralled in the same potentially creative ambit a showman who wanted money to do Punch and Judy shows on Brighton beach, and an Irish tramp who wanted money to burn toy dolls with Napalm as an anti-war gesture in the King's Road.

It encompassed, most of all, the hippies, who simply wanted money

Refined by Brian Epstein from a Liverpool art student's clothes and a Hamburg girl's hairdressing scissors: the image that at last seized and besotted the world.

Beatlemania, 1964: a madness newly diagnosed, with an underlying good humour that would last for several years.

Above. February 1964: with Ed Sullivan in New York. 'I would like you to get lost,' Sullivan told Brian.

Below. The Beatles leap, yet again, for press cameras during rehearsals for the *Royal Variety Show*. Brian, extreme right, waits on tenterhooks.

Right. Brian, ever the best man, at Ringo's wedding to Maureen Cox (top), and George's to Pattie Boyd. He had done the same for John and Cynthia in 1962.

Below, left. Jane Asher
Below, right. Cynthia Lennon

Clockwise, from top left. Neil Aspinall
Mal Evans
Derek Taylor
David Jacobs
Dick James
Peter Brown

Below. After the investiture, 1965: the Beatles deliver MBE quips, watched by Brian and Neil Aspinall.

Right. John with Julian at Kenwood, 1966: the Nowhere Man, still afraid to break out of the palace.

Below. John with George Martin listening to the *Sergeant Pepper* playback: acid-drenched, sparkling visions from his voyage through LSD.

Bottom. 1968: pilgrims at Rishikesh with their mirthful guru. The group also includes Mia Farrow and Donovan. Daily competitions were held to see who could meditate longest.

The Georgian town house where Apple's empire rose and rotted. The 'vibes' made it first glow rosily, then turn pale with fear.

April 1969: Pipe-puffing, statesmanlike Allen Klein tries to reassure the City about his involvement with the Beatles' Northern Songs takeover bid. The press conference, one paper said, 'must have set some kind of record for unprintable language . . .'

Linda with Paul, Yoko with John: an infrequent, uneasy quartet. Ringo does his best to keep up the conversation.

Right. 1969: Paul marries Linda on a bleak day for the young women of the Western world.

Below, right. 1969: the Two Virgins, unashamed, unabashed, undefeated. John has found a partner he needs more than he needs Paul McCartney.

Below. January 1969: The cold, chaotic Apple rooftop session. 'Four musicians playing as no four ever would again.'

Top. John, with Yoko in New York two years before his death, 'our love is still special . . .'
Above, right. Yoko at the official opening of 251 Menlove Avenue, John's old house which she bought in 2002 and donated to the National Trust.
Above, left. Paul and Heather Mills outside the main gates of Castle Leslie in Scotland, on the eve of their wedding.
Below, left. George Harrison and wife Olivia at the Festival of Speed Cartier Lunch.
Below, right. Ringo performing at the Cowdray Concert for the Tibet House Trust in June 2002.

and who flocked to Savile Row in every type of flowing garment and every degree of dreamy-eyed incoherence. Several times each week, the call would come to Apple from Heathrow Airport's Immigration department, announcing that yet another beautiful person had arrived from California with beads and bells, but without funds or definite accommodation, to look up his four brothers in Karma and Sergeant Pepper. At 3 Savile Row, an entire San Francisco 'family', complete with breast-fed baby, waited to accompany John and Yoko to found an alternative universe in the Fiji Isles. There was also a mysterious Stocky, who said nothing, but perched all day on a Press Office filing cabinet, drawing pictures of genitalia. He was harmless enough, as Derek Taylor always said.

The spirit of Apple in those days is best summed up, perhaps, in a moment when Taylor's desk intercom chirped yet again. 'Derek,' the receptionist's voice said, 'Adolf Hitler is in Reception.'

'Oh, Christ,' Taylor said. 'Not that asshole again. OK, send him up.'

•

It was a consequence of the hippy age's mingling superstition and vanity that young, fashionable people, in the young, fashionable music industry of the late Sixties, endowed themselves freely with what amounted to psychic powers. Judgement of a person was made according to what vibrations – or 'vibes' – he gave off by his presence and mood. So the people who came to 3 Savile Row were judged not by the legitimacy or sincerity of their purpose but by their good or bad vibes. A person visiting Apple in a beard and sandals, holding a lighted joss stick, portended good vibes. A lawyer, tax official or policeman portended bad vibes. Colloquies of people, such as board meetings, created vibes proportionately stronger. It was mainly under the influence of these ever-changing, ever-unpredictable vibes that 3 Savile Row, during the next year and a half, alternately glowed with happiness and grew pale with fear.

To start with, the vibes were nearly all good. 'Hey Jude', the Beatles' most successful single ever, had sold almost three million copies for their own Apple label. 'Those Were the Days', by Mary Hopkin, the little Welsh girl Paul had taken up, was number one in Britain and number two in America. Apple's other new signings, James Taylor, Jackie Lomax, the Iveys – and, a 'prestige' acquisition, the Modern Jazz Quartet – were all receiving an energetic and expensive launch as the Beatles' favoured protégés.

There had been some bad vibes, admittedly, over the Apple boutique, The Fool and their extravagance, and the undignified scrimmage for give-away merchandise. Nor were the vibes entirely amiable downwind of the house, among Savile Row's bespoke tailors and outfitters. Dukes and bishops in their fitting-rooms looked on appalled at the day-long riot, the banners and chanting, the shrieks whenever a white Rolls-Royce appeared. But, in general, the West End treated Apple with indulgence. The scene around the front steps made even passers-by with bowler hats and rolled umbrellas smile.

Best of all were the all-powerful vibes given off by the Beatles' own frequent presence in the Georgian town house, directing their luscious new empire with a zest that infected each member of their ever multiplying staff. Though largely invisible within Apple, their presence was unmistakable. There would be the commotion on the first-floor landing, the tightly shut door to Neil Aspinall's office, or Peter Brown's. There would be the wakefulness surging suddenly through the Press Office as Derek Taylor answered his intercom. There were the familiar kitchen orders – a one-egg omelette for Ringo; cheese and cucumber sandwiches for George; for John and Yoko, brown rice, steamed vegetables, chocolate cake and caviar.

Bad vibes from the outside made their first major strike on the afternoon of 18 October. Laurie McCaffery, the deep-voiced telephonist who had followed NEMS down from Liverpool, put through a call to Neil Aspinall from someone who declined to give his name. In a moment, John Lennon's voice came on. 'Imagine your worst paranoia,' John said. 'Well – it's here.' He and Yoko were in police custody, charged with possessing cannabis.

They had been camping out at Ringo Starr's Montagu Square flat when the bust happened, shortly before midday. Six policemen and one policewoman had arrived with a search warrant and a sniffer dog, which had nosed out approximately one and a half ounces of cannabis. There was an additional charge of obstructing the officers during their search. John and Yoko were now being held at Marylebone police station.

Paul at once sought the help of Apple's most powerful ally, Sir Joseph Lockwood, Chairman of EMI. 'As soon as Paul contacted me, I rang Marylebone police station,' Sir Joseph said. 'John picked up the phone. "'Ello," he said, "Sergeant Lennon here." "Now stop all that," I said. "You've got to plead guilty. We'll get Lord Goodman on it. Oh no, we can't: he hates drugs. Anyway, you must plead guilty."'

After a preliminary court appearance, John and Yoko were released on bail. They emerged from Marylebone Magistrates Court into a forest of press cameras and a 300-strong crowd. John's slight figure, hemmed in by scowling police helmets, hugged Yoko tightly to him. Though his martyrdom was self-inflicted and self-aggravated, there began to be something almost chivalrous in the way his slight body shielded Yoko's even slighter one.

The case was due to be heard in full on 27 November. That date had special irony for a Press Office bracing itself to deal with another John Lennon event whose vibes had already shown themselves practically combustible.

John had been determined from the start that Apple Records should be a medium for his and Yoko's experiments in avant garde electronic music. The first album they had produced together was now ready for release. Entitled *Unfinished Music No. 1 – Two Virgins*, it consisted mostly of the tapes they had made during the first night they had ceased to be virgins, at least with one another. Early in October, John had handed to Jeremy Banks, Apple's 'photographic co-ordinator', the picture he wanted used as the album cover. Banks immediately shut it in his desk drawer: for some days afterwards, he could be seen surreptitiously peeping at it. The picture had been taken by John himself in the Montagu Square basement, on a delayed action shutter. It showed him with Yoko, their arms entwined, both – as word swiftly circulated – 'stark bollock naked'.

The vibes were precisely as expected. EMI flatly refused to distribute *Two Virgins* unless the sleeve were changed. John appealed direct to Sir Joseph Lockwood, but this time 'Sir Joe' stood firm. '"What on earth do you want to do it for?" I asked them. Yoko said, "It's art." "In that case," I said, "why not show Paul in the nude? He's so much better looking. Or why not use a statue from one of the parks?"'

The eventual compromise was that EMI would manufacture the album but that it would be distributed by The Who's record label, Track, and the offending cover would be hidden inside a brown paper outer envelope. The same deal was done in America through a label called Tetragrammation. While 30,000 copies sat in a New Jersey warehouse awaiting distribution, they were confiscated as obscene material by the local police.

From here on, good and bad vibes bombarded Apple Corps with even greater capriciousness than the London weather.

On 22 November, the double album was released whose enmities and unevenness faded in the breathtaking novelty and simplicity of its appearance. Originally, its cover was to have been created by Alan Aldridge, Swinging London's leading 'graphic entertainer' and a popular figure in the circle that included the Beatles, the Stones, Jimi Hendrix, The Who and Cream. Aldridge had proposed a design like an advent calendar, each window of which opened to show a scene from a song on the album – but the cost had been beyond even what EMI were prepared to spend. Instead, it was decided to go for stupendous understatement. The album would be packaged in pure, plain, shiny white, its only title a small, crooked diestamp, 'The Beatles'. Each cover also bore a serial number, making a select limited edition of the first two million copies pressed. On opening the double sleeve, one found only more tasteful austerity: a list of the 30 tracks on one side, four small, separate portraits of the musicians on the other.

The reviews were of snow-blinded ecstasy. In the *Observer*, Tony Palmer wrote that Lennon and McCartney stood revealed as 'the greatest songwriters since Schubert'. Palmer's review, more than any other, perpetrated the belief that the *White Album* (so its public soon renamed it) represented conscious artistic enterprise; that, by going to the opposite extreme of *Sgt. Pepper*, the Beatles had touched a new, stark, self-surpassing virtuosity. That *Sgt. Pepper*'s abiding quality was cohesion and that the *White Album*'s was disorganisation quite escaped most critics' ravished ears. The quality most evident throughout, he wrote, was 'simple happiness'. Even *Revolution 9* could not qualify his belief that the Beatles dwelt on 'shores of the imagination others have not yet sighted'.

The day the *White Album* was released, Yoko lost the baby she had been expecting. Her room at Queen Charlotte's Hospital had a second bed in which John himself lay, propped up with pillows. Throughout the emergency that ended in Yoko's miscarriage, he refused to leave her. When the second bed was needed for another patient, he spent each night in a sleeping bag beside her on the floor.

Their drugs case was heard a week later at Marylebone Magistrates Court. John pleaded guilty, assuring the bench that Yoko had nothing to do with acquiring or using the cannabis. He was fined £150, with £21 costs. On the charge of wilful obstruction, no evidence was offered. His counsel, Martin Polden, asked for leniency for someone who had given pleasure to millions with his music. 'An ounce-and-a-half of compassion,' Polden said, was not too much to ask.

It was on that very same day that Apple, having no other choice, released the album which could not be advertised in any music paper and could be bought only like pornographic literature in a plain brown paper bag. On its front cover, the two virgins proclaimed their commitment to each other and their new agenda with a view of John's penis and of Yoko's breasts; on the back, they stood hand in hand, looking over their shoulders and showing their bare bottoms.

•

The success of Apple Records was unquestionable. But what of the other divisions? Six months had passed since Paul had announced that wide-ranging creative prospectus. Apple Films had yet to make a film. The

Apple Press had yet to publish a book. Apple Retail, after the boutique disaster, was virtually moribund. The Apple Foundation for the Arts was something people preferred not to recollect. Occasionally, when a Press Office employee went into the Black Room and pulled out another case of wine, the huge, unread pile of manuscripts would totter and slide a little, then once more settle to rest.

Numerous subsidiary projects had been floated on the seas of Beatles cash. As a rule, these represented the whim of an individual Beatle: they lasted as long, and no longer, than that Beatle's flickering enthusiasm. Paul had at one stage been keen on an offshoot called Zapple, a label which would release 'spoken word' records by modish Underground writers like Ken Kesey and Richard Brautigan. Kesey – the original Merry Prankster, progenitor of the *Magical Mystery Tour* – was brought to London, given an IBM golfball typewriter and invited to write a 'street diary' of his impressions. By then, Paul's enthusiasm had moved elsewhere. There was no one else to read Ken Kesey's street diary. He returned to California, leaving his IBM typewriter at the front desk.

Apple's design consultant was Alan Aldridge, who would be called in to Derek Taylor's office several times a week and handed an outsize joint called a B-52 before being asked to come up with plans for an apple-shaped record player, an apple-shaped transistor radio or a jokey letterhead for Taylor's own Press Office headed 'Lies from Apple' and illustrated by a picture of a pear. 'I also designed some wallpaper based on "Lucy in the Sky",' Aldridge remembers now. 'The idea was to come up with colours that would make people get high just by looking at them.'

Expenditure ran on at a dizzy rate which was, by Beatles standards, entirely normal. Only now, more people than four were spending and consuming. The tea, the coffee, the Scotch and Coke, the VSOP brandy, the Southern Comfort, the Benson and Hedges Gold dispensed so liberally in Derek Taylor's office were but the visible, obvious part of the largesse poured out by Apple to its visitors and its staff. From a kitchen stocked by Fortnum and Mason, endless relays of food came forth – hot meals, cold meals, cold wine, sandwiches, champagne. Junior staff shared liberally in the beano. A certain brand of vodka favoured by the Apple High Command could be bought only at a restaurant in Knightsbridge. Since the restaurant did no off-sales, two Apple office boys would be sent there to eat an expensive lunch and bring back the vodka. One of the kitchen girls remembers a certain Friday afternoon when a £60-pot of caviar had been ordered from Fortnum's for Yoko, who did not arrive after all. Two girls spread the £60-worth of caviar on a single round of toast, and ate a slice each.

Only after three Apple secretaries had had their pay packets stolen on the same day was it realised that Apple's open-handedness now extended to casual passers-by. 'Security' as a principle barely existed. That beautiful people, clad in kaftans and emitting good vibes, could stoop to theft simply did not seem possible. Meanwhile, LPs, hi-fi speakers, television sets, IBM typewriters, any movable part of the green and white decor, continued to vanish: not through the back door – there wasn't one – but through the front door in broad daylight, before hundreds of staring eyes. Post Office messengers who brought in the sacks of fanmail were methodically stripping off the roof lead and carrying it away in the empty mailbags.

The Beatles' accountants were still, as in Brian Epstein's day, Bryce, Hanmer Ltd of Albemarle Street. Harry Pinsker, the head of the firm, supervised Apple's financial affairs and also sat on the Apple Corps Board. When John and Yoko appeared nude on the *Two Virgins* album cover, Pinsker, and four other directors, resigned. Apple's day-to-day accounting was then delegated to a junior partner, Stephen Maltz. For a few weeks, Maltz worked at 3 Savile Row, attempting to control its vast outgoings. He resigned in late October in a five-page letter to each of the Beatles, warning of dire consequences if they could not find a way to curb Apple's expenditure.

By that time, the company had gobbled up the million pounds set aside to launch it. It had devoured a further £400,000, the second instalment of the £800,000 which the Beatles had realised by selling themselves to their own company. All four had heavily overdrawn their corporate partnership account: John by £64,858, Paul by £66,988, George by £35,850 and Ringo by £32,080. All four, in addition, were facing personal Income Tax liabilities of around £600,000 each.

'As far as you were aware,' Maltz wrote, 'you only had to sign a bill and pick up a phone and payment was made. You were never concerned where the money came from or how it was being spent, and were living under the idea that you had millions at your disposal.

'Each of you has houses and cars . . . you also have tax cases pending. Your personal finances are in a mess. Apple is in a mess.'

The Beatles by then could see that Apple was in a mess. They could even, however reluctantly, see why. They had all shared Paul's vision of 'Western Communism' – of young people, freed from turgid conventional business methods, managing their own affairs on the pure, simple dynamo of their own young energy. The lesson of the past six months was that young people were no less greedy, dishonest, avaricious and incompetent than middle-aged ones. Maltz's letter and grim warning only confirmed a suspicion, growing even in John's mind, that turgid, conventional business might have something to recommend it after all. In particular, their thoughts turned towards the very concept which Apple had meant to disown. Someone, they agreed, had better become the boss.

At 3 Savile Row, despite all the high-paid executives in their elegantly appointed offices, no one was quite the boss. Ron Kass, the Head of Apple Records, probably came the closest. But Kass did not have, as Peter Brown did, the direct hotline to all four Beatle hides. Peter Brown held expansive managerial lunches. But Neil Aspinall, who never ate lunch, held the post of Managing Director. Neil, their former road manager, was the Beatles' oldest, closest friend; it was his very closeness and trustworthiness which prevented him from seizing full executive power. He simply took on a workload which on several occasions caused him to be physically sick.

If Apple was to have a boss, the Beatles decided, it must be a big boss. It must be the biggest, bossiest boss that the land of business and bosses could provide.

As so often in such matters, they sought guidance from the biggest boss on their horizon: Sir Joseph Lockwood, Chairman of EMI. Sir Joe's advice was to bring in the head of a merchant bank. He himself offered to approach one of the City's most powerful merchant banks, on their behalf. A meeting was arranged between Paul and the bank's Chairman, Lord Poole, who at that time also happened to be giving financial advice to the Queen.

Sir Joseph accompanied Paul to the Lazard's meeting. 'He'd come along without a tie of course. So Lord Poole took off his tie and jacket and we sat down to lunch. At the end, Lord Poole said, "I'll do it. And what's more, I won't charge you anything." The Queen's financial adviser was offering to sort out the Beatles – for nothing! But the Beatles didn't bother to follow it up.'

Another highly symbolic approach – by John this time – was to Lord Beeching, the man who 'reorganised' British Railways by shutting down huge lengths of them. The 'Beeching Axe' was not available to be wielded at Apple. Beeching, however, listened sympathetically to the tales of chaos and then offered one wise – and prophetic – recommendation: 'Get back to making records.'

Meanwhile, Christmas was coming. So were the Hell's Angels. The former was to be celebrated with a party for Apple employees' children organised by Derek Taylor in Peter Brown's sumptuous first-floor office. The latter were motorcycling heavies from San Francisco whom George Harrison had asked to drop in whenever they happened to be passing through London.

At first, it was rumoured that the entire San Francisco chapter of Hell's Angels had decided to take up this invitation. The deputation, however, proved to be limited to only two, though sufficiently terrifying,

Angels, one named 'Frisco Pete, the other Billy Tumbleweed. With them they brought two Harley Davidson bikes – shipped from California at Apple's expense – and a harem a dozen strong. They and their retinue were reportedly en route for Czechoslovakia 'to straighten out the political situation'.

First, 'Frisco Pete and Billy Tumbleweed straightened out Apple, partaking of hospitality made still more liberal by the terror their looks inspired. Carol Paddon, in the Press Office, was one of several Apple girls who mastered the knack, when a Hell's Angel hand went up her skirt, of smiling with ghastly good humour. Naturally, it would have been discourteous, not to say dangerous, to exclude the two visitors from the Apple children's Christmas party.

The party, in Peter Brown's office, featured seas of jellies, blancmange and a conjurer named Ernest Castro. Afterwards there was to be a grown-ups' party, with John and Yoko officiating as Father and Mother Christmas. Of the lavish buffet which Apple's cordon bleu cooks had prepared, the centrepiece was a 42-lb turkey, guaranteed by its suppliers to be The Largest Turkey in Great Britain.

The party proved a fitting climax to Apple's Golden Age. John, sitting on the floor with Yoko, a white Santa Claus beard covering his dark one, was bewildered to find himself menaced by both 'Frisco Pete and Billy Tumbleweed. The Hell's Angels resented what they felt was unnecessary delay in starting on The Largest Turkey in Great Britain. When the music journalist Alan Smith tried to intervene, 'Frisco Pete felled him with a single punch. Smith's toppling body struck John as he was raising a teacup to his lips. Father Christmas sat there, protecting Mother Christmas, with tea dripping down his spectacles.

18

'The Beatles are the biggest bastards in the world'

Until 1969, the British public at large had never heard of Allen Klein. They had heard only of Alan Klein, a young Cockney songwriter briefly famous during the early Sixties for a number entitled 'What a Crazy World We're Livin' in'. To be sure, when the Klein named Allen first began to impinge on their consciousness, many people initially mistook him for the Klein named Alan, whom they remembered as young, wiry and humorous: a kind of bargain-basement Lionel Bart. Not until Allen Klein's stunning coup had put him on every national front page did the realisation dawn that he was in fact a 38-year-old New Yorker whose shortness, tubbiness and total absence of neck gave him a more than passing resemblance to Barney Rubble in *The Flintstones*.

Klein did not originally set out to manage the greatest pop act the world had ever known. He was born in New Jersey in 1932, the son of an impoverished kosher butcher. His mother died when he was still a baby and his father, unable to cope, gave him and his sister into the care of Newark's austere Hebrew Shelter Orphanage. In later years, when his father remarried and his new stepmother proved unsympathetic, Allen was boarded out with an aunt. This fact was to prove crucial years later, during perhaps the most important business conference of his whole career.

His young manhood, as Klein himself liked to recall, was one of almost Dickensian hardship, endeavour and self-denial. He worked as a clerk for a firm of New Jersey newspaper distributors, at the same time holding down two or three other part-time jobs to pay for a course in accountancy at the Lutheran Uppsala College. As he sat in class there, he would often be so exhausted that his head would drop forward onto his arms. Yet whenever the teacher posed a problem in mental arithmetic, he would still always be first to rattle out the answer.

After graduating from Uppsala, he married his college sweetheart and set up as the newest and hungriest of Manhattan's million-and-one accountants. His vocation made itself clear when he accepted a small retainer to handle the finances of Buddy Knox, a teenage pop idol who had a nationwide hit with 'Party Doll' in 1957. Klein discovered that Knox's record company had failed to pay a substantial part of what they owed him in royalties. An equally interesting discovery was the mixture of guilt and confusion on the faces of the label executives when Klein confronted them with these discrepancies. The upshot was that Knox received what he was owed and Klein received $3,000 in commission, enough to buy him and his wife Betty their first-ever new car.

Klein thereafter specialised in clients from the pop music world, making each the same bluntly seductive offer: 'I can get you money you never even knew you had.' He would ferret it out in the same way he had for Buddy Knox, trapped in ponderously slow accounting systems, or in unpaid performance fees or miscalculated royalty returns. He would then confront the miscreant company in the role of avenging angel, threatening legal action or criminal prosecution if the deficiencies were not instantly made good. Even record companies who dealt conscientiously with their artistes could not be sure that Klein wouldn't find something to stretch them on the rack. 'If a corporation is big, it *has* to make mistakes,' was his maxim. 'There's no big organisation in the world that doesn't have something to hide.'

The technique worked with spectacular success for the singing husband and wife Steve Lawrence and Eydie Gorme, for Bobby ('Splish-Splash') Darin and most notably Bobby ('Blue Velvet') Vinton, whom Klein approached at a mutual friend's wedding and asked 'How would you like to make $100,000?' Within just a few days, that very sum in ferreted-out fees and back royalties was paid into Vinton's bank account. Among these grateful clients, he became known as 'the Robin Hood of Pop', though Klein himself never claimed such dashingly altruistic motives. Despite his general orthodoxy in religious matters, he chose as his desk-top motto a slightly amended version of Psalm 23: 'Yea, though I walk through the Valley of the Shadow of Death, I will fear no evil, for I am the biggest bastard in the valley.'

In 1964, he took over the affairs of Sam Cooke, a talented soul singer then riding high on the Twist dance craze. Klein negotiated an unheard-of $1 million advance for Cooke from the RCA label, though unhappily the singer did not live long to enjoy it. A year later, he was shot to death in a Los Angeles motel while in the company of a lady other than his wife.

When the Beatles conquered America in 1964, Klein looked on with the same hungry, helpless eyes as a hundred other indigenous agents and managers. A couple of months afterwards, on a trip to London, he called on Brian Epstein to offer Sam Cooke as a support act on the Beatles' soon-to-follow second US tour. During the meeting, with typical chutzpah, he also offered himself as their financial consultant, implying that the same huge sums in unpaid royalties could be prised from their record companies as from Bobby Darin's and Bobby Vinton's. Brian did not take the suggestion seriously. But Klein came away boasting that he would 'have' the Beatles, even setting a deadline of Christmas 1965. Meantime, he occupied himself in hoovering up other significant names from the so-called British Invasion: the Dave Clark Five, the Animals, Herman's Hermits, Donovan and, finally, the Rolling Stones.

Klein's acquisition of the Stones showed his unerring ability to spot the most vulnerable points in his prospective quarry. He had observed how the band's young manager, Andrew Loog Oldham, cast himself as a star equally as glamorous as Mick Jagger, and also how much Oldham longed for wealth and status symbols to equal those of his one-time employer, Brian Epstein. Meeting Oldham in London in mid-1965, Klein's opening gambit was, as usual, devastatingly simple. 'Andrew,' he said, 'whaddaya want?'

'I want a Rolls-Royce,' Oldham replied.

'You got it,' Klein told him.

The dazzled Oldham thereupon dropped his existing partner, Eric Easton, and hired Klein as his personal business manager, so giving the New Yorker effective control of all the Stones' financial dealings. The move, as it happened, came midway through Oldham's and Easton's negotiation of a new contract for the Stones with Decca records, one which as usual promised royalty payments only after the records had been sold. Klein weighed into the negotiations with all the tactics that had made him feared in New York. The upshot was that a stunned Decca found themselves agreeing to pay the Stones an advance of $1.25 million.

Following this apparent huge coup on their behalf, the supercilious, super-cool Stones were as enraptured by Klein as Steve Lawrence and Eydie Gorme ever had been. They were also impressed by his organisation of their 1966 American tour and announcement of a three-movie deal aimed at making them just as big on the big screen as the Beatles. Not the least exhilarating feature of Klein's management was a rumoured direct connection with the underworld, which Klein himself always firmly denied while being obviously not displeased by it. One of his closest associates, a promotion man named Pete Bennett, dressed just like a mafioso in sharkskin suits and shades, and was given to patting his left armpit as if a holstered handgun were secreted there.

The Stones naturally were not slow to extol the achievements of their new miracle man to their good friends, the Beatles. That wonderful $1.25 million Decca advance in effect quite eclipsed the new contract with EMI which Brian Epstein negotiated for the Beatles early in 1967, and further complicated the always fraught relationship between Brian and Paul McCartney. Ironically, in view of later events, Paul suggested that Klein be hired to do for the Beatles what he had for the Stones. Rumours spread of an impending merger between Klein's company and NEMS, negotiated by a so-called 'third man', which Brian angrily dismissed as 'rubbish'.

By 1967, Klein's control of the Stones was absolute and exclusive. Relations between the band and Andrew Loog Oldham, which had seriously declined during Jagger's and Richard's drugs trial, hit rock bottom as the Stones struggled to finish *Their Satanic Majesties Request*, the album intended to be their 'answer' to *Sgt. Pepper*. One day, goaded beyond endurance by their slipshod playing and unfocused attitude, Oldham walked out of the studio, never to return. Klein subsequently bought out his management share for around £1 million.

Brian's death might have seemed the perfect moment for Klein to move in on the Beatles. Yet he continued to bide his time and watch from afar the confusion among Brian's too many heirs-apparent. Among the plans swirling round in late 1967 was an ambitious – and rather sensible – one whereby the Beatles and Stones would have shared the same UK front office and jointly financed their own recording studio at North London's Camden Lock. Mick Jagger approached Peter Brown to see if he would act for the Stones, as he did for the Beatles, as ambassador, fixer and social secretary. But Klein violently opposed the idea, and flew straight over from New York to scotch it. There was a meeting, also attended by Clive Epstein, when Klein struck Brown as 'a rather hysterical, unstable person. Then he realised I wasn't trying to take over the Stones, and calmed down a bit. As he walked out, he suddenly turned to Clive and said, "How much d'ya want for the Beatles?"'

Across the Atlantic, meanwhile, Klein's reputation as a ruthless opportunist and wheeler-dealer was reaching new heights. He had recently acquired Cameo-Parkway, a record label once successful with Twist king Chubby Checker but now on the edge of bankruptcy. No sooner had Klein bought the label than its shares rose steeply in value, from $3 to more than $75 each. He was suspected of 'talking up' Cameo-Parkway's share-price by inventing rumours of impending lucrative takeovers or mergers with larger organisations, like the British music firm Chappells. As a result, the New York Stock Exchange suspended dealings in Cameo-Parkway shares and ordered an investigation by the Securities and Exchange Commission. Cameo-Parkway's stockholders also began legal proceedings against Klein, enraged, among other things, by the $104,000 per year salary he had awarded himself as Chief Executive. In the event, Cameo-Parkway were to make only one significant acquisition: the Allen Klein accounting company. Klein took himself over in reverse, naming the resultant entity ABKCO Industries (the 'ABK' part standing for Allen and Betty Klein.)

As 1968 drew to a close, and Apple stood revealed as a bottomless financial pit, Klein's dream of winning the Beatles seemed as far away as ever. The Rolling Stones had extolled his genius to them time after time, without result. He himself had put in a telephone call to John Lennon, but John could not be bothered to accept it. They had also met briefly, in December 1968, when John and Yoko took part, with Eric Clapton, The Who and other pop luminaries, in the Stones' Sgt. Peppery *Rock 'n' Roll Circus* film. But Klein, surprisingly, made no attempt to capitalise on the meeting and John barely glanced at the tubby little man with his unfashionable greased-back hair, cardigan and pipe.

Not until the following January did Klein's moment come – when he picked up *Rolling Stone*, the new 'intelligent' music paper named after his first supergroup protégés, and saw the story splashed all over it. John had said that, if the Beatles carried on spending money at their present rate, he'd be 'broke in six months'.

•

With Paul McCartney, the need to breathe was scarcely more important than the need to perform. It was a need which transcended mere vanity and his love of his own bewitching, beguiling, melodic power. He would sing and play for as many, or as few, people as happened to be there when the impulse came that was as natural as breath. Once, on a car journey with Derek Taylor, he stopped in a Bedfordshire village and played the piano in a village pub. He would sing softly through the dark to the girls on watch outside his house. Late in 1968, he and Linda spent a week with friends in Portugal. His hosts noticed a phenomenon unchanged since a decade ago in Forthlin Road, Liverpool. Even in the lavatory, Paul could not stop singing and playing his guitar.

Paul had always felt that by giving up road tours and retiring into album work, the Beatles had broken faith with the public to whom, fundamentally, they owed everything. So he began arguing with renewed persistence after the *White Album* was finished. He had lately – at Linda's encouragement – grown a thick, dark, uncultivated beard. It might have been a keen and determined young schoolmaster who sat in the Apple boardroom, urging the other three that their next project together ought to be a return to playing live concerts.

The chief deterrent, as Paul himself acknowledged, was simple stage fright. It was more than two years since the Beatles had last faced an audience together. In that time, only John had given anything like a live performance, in the *Rock 'n' Roll Circus* film. He had also appeared at the

'Alchemical Wedding', a Christmas rally of Britain's hippies, mystics and drop-outs, though that merely meant sitting with Yoko inside a plastic bag on the stage of the Royal Albert Hall.

Paul kept up the pressure, reminding them of stage fright successfully overcome in the past. Hadn't it been the same when they suddenly took a step up from Liverpool and Hamburg clubs to the grandeur of Leicester's de Monfort hall? And when they had made the quantum leap from the London Palladium to Shea Stadium? John and Ringo seemed persuadable but not George. Nothing, he said, could make him go back to the witless screaming and frantic running of the Beatlemania years. Paul agreed that going back on tour in the old way would be unendurable. They would play only a few, carefully selected live dates; perhaps only a single one. 'But we've got to keep that contact somehow. And it's what we do best.'

In the end, they agreed on a compromise. Rather than giving a live performance, they would make an album that was like a live performance – an album shorn of all studio artifice, reliant only on their abilities as singers and musicians, simple and powerful and honest enough to reach back over the years to their original, punching power in the Cavern Club. To underline the point, they went to George Martin – now a freelance producer, soon to launch his own independent AIR studios – and asked, or rather begged, him to work for them again. It was their obvious sincerity rather than any fee that persuaded Martin to put his new career on hold and try to recreate the spontaneity and 'honesty' of the *Please Please Me* album. 'They said they wanted to go right back to basics,' Martin says. 'They wouldn't use any overdubbing. They'd do the songs just as they happened.'

The simple resolve of four musicians, however, was now subject to the complexities of Apple Corps, and its still unused subsidiaries, Apple Films and Apple Publishing. It was decided that the making of the album must be made into a film, and that film and record sessions should be described in an illustrated book to accompany each album. The climax of the film would be the live performance Paul wanted, at a location still to be decided.

The arrival of a film crew, led by director Michael Lindsay-Hogg, gave additional scope to Paul's ideas. At one point, with Lindsay-Hogg's encouragement, he proposed giving the concert in a Tunisian amphitheatre; at another, he suggested making the whole album live in Los Angeles. George vetoed both suggestions as 'very expensive and insane'. Another of Paul's schemes was to record at sea, on board an ocean liner. George objected that the acoustics would be impossible and that anyway they'd need two liners rather than one. As the argument flew back and forth, John was heard to mutter, 'I'm warming to the idea of doing it in an asylum.'

The project's working title – symbolic of their desire to rediscover their roots – was *Get Back*. At John's suggestion, they even posed for a photograph looking down from the same balcony as on the cover of their first chirpy, working-class LP.

Rehearsals began on 2 January 1969, at one end of a cavernous sound stage at Twickenham film studios. Michael Lindsay-Hogg's camera crew were already in position to film Mal Evans, the perennial 'roadie', carrying in amplifiers and cymbal-stands, and Paul testing the grand piano, still in his hobo-ish tweed coat, a half-eaten apple before him on the polished lid.

The cameras ran on as Paul, each morning, strove to make the other Beatles forget their dismal surroundings, the unaccustomed daylight playing and the constant, numb-fingered cold. His resemblance to a schoolmaster grew, even as the class grew more plainly recalcitrant. 'OK – right. Er – OK, let's try to move on.' He went and sat with George, as with a backward and also stubborn pupil, tracing with his arm the sequence he wanted George to play. 'You see, it's got to come down like that. There shouldn't be any recognisable jumps. It helps if you sing it. Like this—'

Resentment was not yet in the open. Paul worked conscientiously to provide a falsetto counterpoint to John's 'Across the Universe'. John played chords as instructed to a pretty little Paul tune that would one day become 'Maxwell's Silver Hammer'. They even, spasmodically, enjoyed themselves. John got up, and Yoko did not follow him: Paul and he sang 'Two of Us', burlesquing like teenage Quarry Men. When George played over 'I Me Mine', a new song in turgid waltz time, Paul and Ringo tackled it gamely. John and Yoko, two meagre, white-clad figures in gym shoes, waltzed to it together across the cable-strewn floor.

As well as the new material, they continually ran through old songs from Liverpool and Hamburg: the Chuck Berry and Elvis and Little Richard songs they had always played to warm up before performing or recording. They even resurrected a Quarry Men song, 'The One After 909', written by John and Paul on truant afternoons in Jim McCartney's sitting-room with the Chinese pagoda wallpaper and the *Liverpool Echo*s piled under the dresser. 'We always hated the words to that one,' Paul said. '"Move over once, move over twice. Hey, baby, don't be cold as ice . . ." They're great, really, aren't they?'

Whatever glow these memories awoke soon died again in the cold and general discomfort. Nor did playing the old songs seem to bring the new songs any nearer to satisfying Paul. 'We've been going round and round for an hour,' he complained wearily at one point. 'I think it's a question of either we do it or we go home.'

As Paul talked to George, a row started. 'I always hear myself – annoying you,' Paul said. 'Look, I'm not trying to *get* you. I'm just saying "Look, lads – the band. Shall we do it like this?"'

'Look, I'll play whatever you want me to play,' George cut in. His voice silting with resentment, he continued: 'Or I won't play at all. Whatever it is that'll please you, I'll do it.'

At lunch time on 10 January, George said he had had enough. He was tired of being 'got at' by Paul. He was quitting the Beatles, he said. He got into his car and drove home to Esher.

It was a temporary flare-up, and recognised as such. George knew, and the others did, that he could never resign with an album half-finished. And, sure enough, when a business meeting took place at Ringo's a few days later, George turned up as usual. Work on the album resumed after Paul gave an undertaking not to get at George or try to teach him the guitar. And, they all agreed, they had had enough of Twickenham studios. They decided to move straight into their own studio – the one which Magic Alex had been designing and assembling in the basement of the Apple house.

George Martin had already visited the basement but found the studio unready, lacking a console. It could be made fit for recording only by silencing the air conditioner, which thumped and wheezed in the corner, and by bringing in heavy consignments of sound equipment on hire. This done, the Beatles and their film crew tried again. Billy Preston, a gifted American performer who was George's protégé, joined the sessions as organist. What with the film crew, and this or that friend and acolyte, there was scarcely room in the basement to move. Yoko sat by John, as always, reading or embroidering. When Paul arrived – managing to make an entrance even through that narrow basement doorway – he brought Linda's little daughter, Heather, riding on his shoulders.

The album that would finally be released as *Let It Be* in fact contained only the tiniest fraction of what the Beatles recorded in that crowded basement during January 1969. More than a hundred songs, by every artist they had ever admired or copied, and also from every epoch of their own career, piled up on spools destined never to be released, or even listened to, again. It was as if, to rediscover themselves as musicians, they were putting themselves through the kind of endurance test that Hamburg used to be; seeking to renew themselves with music that stretched back to their collective birth. They even recorded 'Maggie May', the Liverpool sailors' shanty which John sang at the Woolton fête that day in 1957 when Paul McCartney cycled across from Allerton to meet him.

It was after they stopped jamming and returned to today's material that the breakdown always came. Determined to be 'honest', to forsake all artifice, they still wanted from George Martin what he had always given them: a flawless final product. 'We'd do 60 different takes of something,' Martin says. 'On the 61st take, John would say, "How was that one, George?" I'd say, "John – I honestly don't know." "You're no fookin' good then are you," he'd say. That was the general atmosphere.'

Ironically, the best and happiest song on the finished album was one which grew out of random studio ad-libbing. Paul gave it the shorthand name 'Loretta': only later did it receive the album's original title of 'Get Back'. Several versions of Paul's vocal were taped, including one that sarcastically made 'Get Back' a warning to Asian immigrants in the tones of the racist lobby inspired by Enoch Powell. Another featured John as lead singer, giving the song a bitter drive and bite that even Paul's best version lacked. Halfway through the John version, both he and Paul suddenly tailed off into silence: it was Ringo, redeeming himself at last in George Martin's eyes, whose quick-witted drum solo forced them back again on target.

The film crew, with 28 hours of footage, finally packed up and left. The Beatles themselves did so a few days later, leaving behind an aural rag-bag that not even Paul could face hearing, let alone editing down to 14 songs. John was all for putting out the album as it stood: a confession of their own internal chaos. 'It'll tell people, "This is us with our trousers off, so will you please end the game now?"'

For the benefit of the film crew, they had already given their much debated live performance – not in Tunisia or LA or on an ocean-going liner, but on one arbitrarily chosen afternoon on the roof of the Apple house. In keeping with the atmosphere of reticence and self-deprecation, no one knew about the event but their own employees and a few close friends. They little realised they were creating yet another scene to be replayed, and many times imitated, in decades to come, as passers-by stopped to stare up in amazement at the electric din erupting in the sky; as traffic between the bespoke tailors' shops ground to a halt; as policemen appeared, at last, from nearby Savile Row station; as the law decided it must put a stop to it, and a thickset sergeant crossed the road to knock sternly at Apple's white front door.

•

It was, in fact, a British music paper, *Disc*, that had first broken the story now blazoned all over American *Rolling Stone*: John Lennon Says Beatles In Cash Crisis. *Disc*'s editor Ray Coleman, a long-time Beatles follower and friend, later received an angry dressing-down from Paul on the stairs at Apple for having run the original piece. 'This is only a small company and you're trying to wreck it,' Paul shouted. 'You know John shoots his mouth off and doesn't mean it.' Coleman had been close to the Beatles long enough to recognise what was off or on the record.

So it proved when the world's press poured over the Apple threshold, asking for further and better particulars. John confirmed what he had told Ray Coleman – that Apple was losing some £20,000 a week to its myriad hangers-on, and that he personally calculated he was 'down to my last £50,000'. George, as a rule the closest one in money matters, was equally willing to talk. 'We've been giving away too much to the wrong people – like the deaf and the blind,' George said. 'This place has become a haven for drop-outs. The trouble is, some of our best friends are drop-outs.'

The story that the Beatles were going broke somewhat abated the Apple orgy. It also placed the honest, and rather underpaid, regular staff members under the same stigma as predatory Hell's Angels and larcenous visitors. Paul, in a thoughtful PR gesture, sent round a morale-boosting letter to all Apple artists and employees. 'In case you're worried about anything at Apple, please feel free to write me a letter, telling me about the problem. There's no need to be formal. Just say it. Incidentally, things are going well, so thanks – love, Paul.'

The news that Allen Klein, the Rolling Stones' manager, was in London and wanted to see the Beatles with a view to helping them, did not at first seem vastly portentous. When Klein's first call reached Apple, they were still immured at Twickenham studios, refusing to see anyone. It was simply another message from the hundreds left hanging in the psychedelic twilight of Derek Taylor's Press Office. 'Allen Klein! What the fuck does he want, man?' 'How the fuck should I know?'

That Klein's message should have reached John Lennon was surprising enough. What was still more surprising was John's instant agreement to meet him, as requested, at Klein's suite in the Dorchester Hotel. John went without telling the other Beatles, accompanied only by Yoko, and, as he later admitted, petrified with nerves.

Klein played the scene perfectly, meeting John and Yoko alone in his room, wearing a sweater and sneakers, the nearest to their hippy threads that he could muster. Having expected a one-dimensional businessman, John found a fan of more than usual devotion, for Klein knew by heart every Beatles song dating back to the very start of their career. He showed an instinctive grasp of the Beatles' peculiar problems, and had clear and forceful proposals for remedying them. He impressed John with his straightforward manner and the blunt New York wit that put him spiritually not far from a Liverpudlian. The fact that he, too, had lost his mother in early childhood and been boarded out with an aunt cemented the bond between them.

By the end of that first meeting, John had made up his mind. There and then he wrote a note to EMI's Chairman, Sir Joseph Lockwood: 'Dear Sir Joe – from now on, Allen Klein handles all my stuff.'

Sir Joseph read the note with a bewilderment shared by others to whom John announced his adoption of Allen Klein. For so far as their closest associates knew, the Beatles had already decided on the man who would rescue them and Apple Corps from chaos.

Late in 1968, Linda had taken Paul McCartney home to New York to meet her family. He had met her father, the elegant Lee Eastman, and her brother, John, a bright young Ivy Leaguer, already a partner in the family law and management practice. He had surveyed the list of show business VIPs and renowned painters whom the Eastmans represented, and tasted the high-caste Manhattan life that formed the highest rung of his ascent from a little terraced house in Allerton. By the time he returned to London, he had decided that Eastman & Eastman were the solution for both the Beatles' management and Apple.

Paul having prepared the ground on both sides, John Eastman flew to London to meet the other Beatles a few weeks later. They were not bowled over – first, because Lee hadn't thought it worthwhile to show up in person; second, because John came across as rather immature and over-eager. No one was impressed by his efforts to make up to John and Yoko with arty talk about Kafka. Also, it was known to everyone inside the Beatles' circle, though not yet to anyone outside it, that the Eastman and McCartney families were soon to be joined by matrimony. Nevertheless, a letter signed by all four Beatles authorised John Eastman to act for them in contractual matters. By the time Allen Klein appeared, Paul's soon-to-be brother-in-law had begun an ambitious plan to consolidate their dwindling reserves.

NEMS Enterprises, Brian Epstein's original management company, still hung, ghost-like in the Apple firmament. Under its new name, Nemperor Holdings, it continued to receive the Beatles' earnings and to deduct Brian's 25 per cent before passing on the residue to Apple. Yet NEMS had long since ceased to exercise control over them as agents and managers. The bond was purely technical – and sentimental, since Brian's mother, Queenie, was NEMS' main shareholder and his brother Clive was Chairman. The Beatles themselves still held the 10 per cent share in NEMS allotted to them by Brian's tender conscience.

The Epsteins, on their side, while wishing to retain control of NEMS, still faced the bill for half a million pounds in estate duty which Brian's cash assets had nowhere near covered. Clive Epstein, for all his dutiful efforts to expand NEMS, knew he had no ultimate course but to sell the company. What restrained him was his sense of obligation – to Brian's memory, to his mother, to the remaining Liverpool artists; to everything in fact but his own fervent desire to return to Liverpool's quieter business climes.

Late in 1967, Clive had received an offer for NEMS from the Triumph Investment Trust, a City merchant bank with a reputation for aggressive takeovers. At that stage, however, NEMS, transformed into Nemperor, was committed to a 'programme of vigorous expansion'. The expansion proved less than vigorous, and a year later, pre-empting a rumoured bid by the British Lion Film Corporation, Triumph's Chairman, Leonard Richenberg, made a second approach to Clive Epstein. This time, Clive was ready to accept Richenberg's offer.

John Eastman's plan was that the Beatles themselves should buy up NEMS, matching Triumph's offer of one million pounds. Sir Joseph Lockwood at EMI had agreed to advance the entire sum against future royalty earnings. Clive Epstein, feeling that the Beatles had a moral right to the company which Brian had launched on their name, notified Leonard Richenberg that the sale to Triumph was off.

It was at this point that John met, and adopted, Allen Klein. George and Ringo, who met Klein soon afterwards, were struck, as John had been, by Klein's forthrightness and his thorough grasp of the Apple problem. They did not instantly accept him as their saviour, but they were willing to listen. Paul was not. He attended only one meeting with Klein, and walked out soon after it had begun.

The plan agreed by the other three was that John Eastman and Klein should *both* work as advisers to Apple. Eastman was to follow up the NEMS deal while Klein looked into their financial position with special regard to EMI's £1m loan.

The Eastmans, father and son, made no secret of the disfavour with which they regarded Allen Klein. They were quick to inform Paul – as Leonard Richenberg had independently discovered – that Klein was viewed with suspicion in New York because of the Cameo-Parkway affair; that some 50 lawsuits decorated the escutcheon of Klein's company, ABKCO Industries; and that Klein himself currently faced 10 charges by the US Internal Revenue Service of failing to file Income Tax returns.

To George and Ringo that was less important than the stunning promise Klein held out to them. He would go into Apple and clean up the mess. He would also make each of them wealthy in a way that even they, in their clouds of ready cash, had never imagined possible. He had a way of characterising money as some dragon-like entity which had slain Brian Epstein, with his paltry £7m gross, but which Allen Klein, with his

ABKCO sword, knew the secret of vanquishing. 'You shouldn't have to worry about money. *You* shouldn't have to think about it. You should be able to say FYM – Fuck You, Money.'

George and Ringo responded, as John had, to Klein's pungent fiscal imagery and down-to-earth manner. They liked him for the brusqueness he did not trouble to moderate, whatever the company. John Eastman, by contrast, wavered between urbane bonhomie and spluttering rage. It was a trait shared by his father, who had at length flown over from New York to meet the Beatles and Klein together at Claridges Hotel. A few minutes after the meeting began, Lee Eastman rounded on Klein and began to shout abuse at him. The outburst was, in fact, skilfully engineered by Klein, to reveal Lee Eastman as an hysteric and himself as the stolid underdog. John, George and Ringo naturally sided with the underdog.

Clive Epstein, meanwhile, had begun to suspect that selling NEMS to the Beatles was a process that might drag on for months. He therefore reopened negotiations with Leonard Richenberg and Triumph, though stressing he would still prefer to accept the Beatles' offer. He undertook not to sell for three more weeks, to give them time to conclude their bid.

But the Beatles' advisers were by now bogged down in internecine warfare. Klein claimed that the Eastmans were blocking his access to vital financial details within Apple. John Eastman accused Klein of imperilling the deal by boasts that he could get NEMS 'for nothing' on the strength of sums owed to the Beatles in back payments. Though the deadline had not expired, it clearly would not be met. Clive Epstein sold out to Triumph, for a mixture of cash and stock, on 17 February.

John Eastman flew back to New York. The Beatles continued discussions with Allen Klein – minus Paul. Instead, Paul would send along his lawyer, a Mr Charles Corman. The others were amused at first that such a personage was meant to fill Paul's place at the board table. They would ask Mr Corman why he hadn't brought along his bass guitar.

•

On 11 March, Apple's Press Office issued a brief communiqué confirming the rumour it had for weeks been vigorously denying. Paul McCartney *was* to marry Linda Eastman. The ceremony would take place the following day in London, at Marylebone Register Office.

The bombshell exploded, among other places, in a small house in Redditch, Worcestershire, where Jill Pritchard, a travelling hairdresser, was giving one of her regular customers a shampoo and set. 'Even before I heard it on the radio,' Jill says, 'I had a sort of premonition it had happened. I remember looking at the customer's little girl and wondering how she'd react.

'It was just a short announcement on the BBC News. I finished the shampoo and set, then I drove straight home and packed a little overnight bag. I'd got a bit of money that I'd always kept put by for an emergency. I got a friend to ring up my mum later and tell her where I'd gone. Then I drove to New Street Station in Birmingham and left my car on a No Waiting sign. I bought myself a ticket to London – first class, so I wouldn't have to sit and cry in a compartment full of people.'

Late that night, wet-eyed and still carrying her suitcase, Jill Pritchard walked up Cavendish Avenue and joined the large, stunned crowd which had gathered there. The first girl she spoke to was Margo Stevens. 'Is *she* in there?' Jill asked. Thousands of girls throughout Europe and America found it similarly impossible to articulate Linda's name.

'We all knew it was going to happen,' Margo says. 'We even knew Linda was pregnant. We'd seen the prescription that Rosie, the housekeeper, collected for her. But we kept hoping Paul would get out of it somehow. He was upset because we were taking it so badly. He'd come out to the gates to talk to us earlier in the day. "Look, girls," he said, "be fair. I had to get married some time." '

Every British newspaper, the day after Paul's wedding, carried pictures of the same desolately weeping girl. It was Jill Pritchard, the travelling hairdresser from Redditch. Photographers whirled her this way and that for most of the afternoon, shouting, 'Go on – cry. You'll be in the papers.' When Paul drove back with Linda after the ceremony, grief began to turn to violence. The security gates were forced apart; the front door was kicked and wads of burning newspaper were pushed through the letterbox. After that, the police appeared and told everyone to disperse.

Margo, Jill and the other regulars, drained of all emotion, adjourned to the nearest pub. 'We heard later from Paul's housekeeper Rosie that he was really upset about us,' Margo says. 'He was standing just inside the front door, saying, "I *must* go out and talk to them again." But when he did come out, none of us was there any more. He couldn't believe we'd all gone away, so Rosie said. When he came back into the house, he was almost in tears.'

That same night, a squad of police officers raided George Harrison's Esher bungalow, and found a total of 570 grains of cannabis. George was in London, recording his friend Jackie Lomax; when he returned he found the officers sitting with his wife Patti, watching television and playing Beatles records. By an unkind coincidence, the name of the sniffer dog was 'Yogi'.

•

Eight days later, at the British Consulate on the Rock of Gibraltar, John and Yoko were quietly married. John wore a crumpled white jacket, an apostle-length beard and tennis shoes. Yoko wore a wide-brimmed white hat, a matching mini-dress and outsize sunglasses that made her face as expressionless as a panda's. They had decided on marriage suddenly while on holiday in Paris, and chosen Gibraltar as being 'quiet, friendly and British'. Peter Brown made the arrangements from London, and himself flew out to be best man. John and Yoko posed for pictures with the consulate staff, saw what little of Gibraltar there was to see, then flew back to Paris to own up to the international press. 'We're going to stage many happenings and events together,' Yoko said. 'This marriage was one of them.'

The Beatles' American fan club organiser issued an appeal for tolerance of what the whole world greeted as John's worst aberration yet. 'I know this news is shocking. Please try to understand that we should at least give Yoko the same chance we are giving Linda, and that Maureen and Patti got. If it makes John happy, I suppose we should all be enthused too.'

Their honeymoon was the first of Yoko's promised happenings: it also inaugurated their campaign to promote that much desired but fast-fading hippy commodity, Peace. To promote the cause of peace they announced they would spend seven successive days in bed, at the Amsterdam Hilton hotel.

Most of the press who instantly converged on Amsterdam believed that the newlyweds had actually offered to make love in public. To their disappointment, they found John and Yoko merely sitting up in bed, in a suite decorated with placards reading 'Bed Peace' and 'Hair Peace'. Few papers could understand, any more than could their progressively exasperated readership, how two people cocooned thus in the casual squalor of rock star hyper-luxury, had any relevance to burned babies in Vietnam or Biafra's living skeletons. Even calling it, with that so-fashionable suffix, a 'Bed-in' could not avert savage criticism of 'the most self-indulgent demonstration of all time'. But the press was, as always, unable to deliver the ultimate rebuff. It could not stay away. 'Day Two of the Lennon Lie-In', ran a British headline. 'John and Yoko Are Forced Out by Maria the Maid.'

They continued their journey to Vienna for the first television showing of their film *Rape* – an action they depicted being performed by reporters and TV cameras. Later, in the Sacher Hotel's sumptuous Red Salon, they staged a second 'happening'. This time, the press found them crouching on a table top inside a bag. It was, so John said, a demonstration of 'bagism' or 'total communication', in which the speaker did not prejudice the listener by his personal appearance. More 'bagism', he suggested, would generate more peace throughout the world. The British *Daily Mirror* spoke for the whole world in mourning 'a not inconsiderable talent who seems to have gone completely off his rocker'.

•

The loss of NEMS Enterprises had not discountenanced Allen Klein. The episode, indeed, had served Klein by revealing shortcomings in John Eastman which even his brother-in-law seemed to acknowledge. For it was with Paul's tacit agreement, or non-disagreement, that Klein began a counter-attack designed to extricate the Beatles from the hold of the Triumph Investment Trust.

A week after Triumph's takeover of NEMS, Klein visited the bank's Chairman, Leonard Richenberg. There followed what Richenberg subsequently described as 'various vague and threatening noises'. According to Klein, the old NEMS company owed the Beatles large sums in unpaid fees from road shows dating back as far as 1966. They would forget these arrears if Triumph agreed to give up its 25 per cent of their earnings Richenberg had bought up with NEMS. Richenberg's response showed him a worthy adversary. He requested Klein in words of one syllable to go away. No more successful was Klein's offer of a million pounds outright for Triumph's stake in the Beatles. Richenberg merely repeated his request to his visitor to depart.

Sir Joseph Lockwood, Chairman of EMI, was Klein's next point of attack. Sir Joseph, a few days later, received a note, signed by all four Beatles, requiring that henceforward their record royalties were not to go to NEMS–Triumph but were to be paid direct to Apple. The letter was timely, since EMI was on the point of paying out Beatles' record royalties in the region of £1.3m.

Leonard Richenberg had received a similar notification. He wrote back to Neil Aspinall, tersely rejecting the Beatles' claim that their contract with NEMS had expired when the *management* agreement did, in 1967. There remained the nine-year EMI contract, signed in January 1967, under which all record royalties were to be channelled via NEMS. Triumph Investments were thus entitled to collect their 25 per cent for seven more years.

At EMI, Sir Joseph Lockwood faced the uncomfortable alternatives of breaking a manifestly binding legal obligation to NEMS–Triumph or alienating the affections of the four individuals on whom his company's fortunes largely rested. Sir Joseph, with great wisdom, elected to do neither. Triumph then sought a High Court order to freeze the £1.3m pending the obviously protracted legal battle over it.

The application was heard on 2 April in the High Court before Mr Justice Buckley. Counsel for Triumph, Jeremiah Harman, QC, said that the Beatles had 'fallen under the influence of Mr Allen Klein, an American of somewhat dubious reputation'. The judge, though inclined to agree, refused to freeze the money officially since, he said, EMI themselves would obviously not release it until the dispute was settled.

It was therefore left to Klein and Richenberg – in an atmosphere now tinged by mutual respect – to slug out a deal between them. Richenberg agreed to relinquish Triumph's 25 per cent of Beatles earnings in exchange for £800,000 cash plus a quarter of the suspended £1.3m. Triumph would buy out the Beatles' 10 per cent of NEMS for just under half a million pounds-worth of the bank's own very desirable stock.

Klein could thus go back to the Beatles claiming to have turned defeat into victory. If they had not managed to acquire NEMS, at least NEMS had no further control over them. He had bought them freedom, in other words, from one cabal of 'men in suits'. The Robin Hood of Pop, in his crumpled white polo-neck sweater, was one deal up on his rivals in the Apple camp. And if Allen Klein knew anything, he would soon be two deals up.

•

Dick James was always first to admit that he was one of the luckiest men alive. Pure chance had brought Brian Epstein to his office that morning long ago in 1962. Pure chance had ordained that James be there in person, to soothe Brian's ruffled feathers and listen to the demonstration disc he carried in his briefcase. So by pure chance it came about, as the voices pealed round his dusty Denmark Street cubbyhole, that Dick James, the so-so crooner, average song plugger and now struggling music publisher, realised he was on his way to his first million.

He had seized on that luck, of course, with some prescient fair-dealing. As publisher of the early Lennon–McCartney hits, he could have been greedy, and lost them. Instead, he looked to the long term. He saw not only quality but quantity. So Heaven whispered in James's ear, prompting him to offer Brian a deal unprecedented in Tin Pan Alley. He would set up a song publishing firm, exclusively for Lennon–McCartney music. It was piquant to remember Brian's disbelieving gratitude when Northern Songs was formed. 'Why are you doing all this for us?'

When the company came into existence in 1963, Dick James and his partner Emmanuel Silver between them owned 50 per cent. John and

Paul had 20 per cent each and Brian, 10 per cent. James administered the company through his own Dick James Music Ltd. Ironically, he himself only ever published two Lennon–McCartney songs – the first one he ever heard, 'Please Please Me', and the B-side 'Ask Me Why'. It was as a middleman that he grew wealthy, husbanding a store of hit songs that piled up faster almost than an old-time Tin Pan Alley plugger could count.

The Beatles laughed at James for his tubby shape, his bald head, his constant pleas for more nice *tuneful* numbers like 'Michelle' and 'Yesterday'. His knowledge of the music business and its manifold dodges merged into the invisible shield that Brian Epstein built around them. It was James who, on the eve of a new Beatles single, would circulate every American record station with dire legal admonitions not to break the release embargo. It was James who, after the initial chaos, maximised their American impact by ensuring that other singers and groups did not cover Lennon–McCartney material to excess.

In 1965, Northern Songs had been floated as a public company. Twenty-five per cent of its 2s (10p) shares were offered on the London Stock Exchange at 7s 9d (38p) each and all instantly snapped up – in financial as well as Beatles terms an instant number one hit. Three thousand shareholders henceforward would turn to the record charts as well as the *Financial Times* to check on the health of their investment.

After the flotation, Dick James and his partner held 23 per cent of Northern Songs. John and Paul held 15 per cent each; NEMS Enterprises held 7.5 per cent, and George and Ringo between them, 1.6 per cent. By 1967 – the year when two Beatles albums, *Revolver* and *Sgt. Pepper*, between them brought profits near the million pound mark – shares in Northern had quintupled their 1965 value.

For any investor, the company's pièce de résistance were the 159 Lennon–McCartney copyrights, and John and Paul's contractual commitment to carry on composing until 1973. James, however, worked hard to create a wider catalogue. By buying up moribund firms like Lawrence Wright Ltd, Northern Songs acquired such diverse musical properties as 'Les Parapluies de Cherbourg'; 'Among My Souvenirs'; and the theme from television's *Coronation Street*. James, indeed, worked for Northern somewhat at the expense of Dick James Music Ltd. But he was happy. Everyone in Tin Pan Alley said so. He reminded himself all the time how lucky he was.

Just lately, Dick James had been a little less happy than before. It was not that Lennon–McCartney music had declined in quality. 'Hey Jude', in 1968, became a publishing success second only in worldwide sales to 'Yesterday'. The trouble was the increasingly erratic behaviour of one half of the publishing credit, and its effects on that sensitive organ the London Stock Exchange. John Lennon's espousal of the Maharishi, his involvement with Yoko, his 'bagism', his nudity – above all, his drug conviction – each produced disquiet among Northern's shareholders and fluctuations in its share price. As John's song publisher, James could be tolerant. As Managing Director of a public company with 3,000 shareholders to consider, he fretted.

Lately, too, his relationship with 'the boys' had grown somewhat strained. The deal which had seemed so miraculous in 1963 had, by 1969, become a source of vague resentment. The Beatles felt, quite simply, that James owned too large a share in their music. Nor was their resentment assuaged by James's habit of sending out inexpensive Christmas gifts such as plastic DJM monogrammed playing cards. A frosty reception had greeted him when he visited Twickenham studios during the *Let It Be* sessions.

As Northern Songs grew in prosperity, Dick James had received many offers for his 23 per cent. Of these, the most persistent came from Lew Grade, Britain's most famous showbiz mogul, whose ATV network was already a minority shareholder, and who, in the dear dead music-hall days, had been James's own theatrical agent. 'He'd been romancing me to sell out to him ever since Brian's death,' James remembered. 'It was a standing joke between us. "Oh *no*," I'd say, "not *that* again, Lew!"'

It was the addition of Allen Klein to an already unstable Beatles landscape which suddenly changed James's mind. In March 1969, without prior warning, he sold his 23 per cent of Northern Songs to ATV for something over one million pounds.

That the deal went through in secret was, as James would later admit, 'rather unfortunate'. In fairness, both John and Paul were out of the country on their respective honeymoons. John read the news in the papers on 28 March, during his Amsterdam Bed-in. Paul found out a few days later in America. The news by then was that ATV, with 35 per cent of Northern Songs under its belt, had bid £9.5m for the rest of the company.

John and Paul contacted one another, united in fury that Dick James had sold them down the river. It would have been fruitless to point out – had anyone dared try – that Northern Songs had long ago ceased to be theirs, but was the legitimate prey of whichever shareholder could gain the upper hand. All they knew was that, behind their backs, a major stake in their music had gone to a man who, with his large bulk and still larger Havana cigar, epitomised the hated breed of 'men in suits'. The conciliatory noises which Lew Grade was already making might just as well have been the snarl of an alligator on the banks of the Zambesi.

Allen Klein was recalled from holiday in Puerto Rico to formulate plans for the Beatles themselves to oppose ATV's takeover of Northern Songs. The Eastmans, though still advising Paul, figured little in the subsequent drama. Paul, once again, was willing to let Klein act for him, in the troubleshooting capacity that was still unconfirmed by any written contract.

Klein's strategy was that the Beatles, already owning 31 per cent of Northern Songs, should publicly offer £2m for the further 20 per cent which would give them a majority shareholding. The money was to come partly from the Beatles' own coffers, partly from a merchant banker, Henry Ansbacher & Co. Two Beatles companies, Subafilms and Maclen, together scraped up almost £1m. Ansbacher's would provide the remaining £1¼m, on collateral furnished by Apple shares and John Lennon's entire stock holding in Northern Songs. Paul – though he had recently increased his own Northern shareholding – refused to pledge any shares as security. Allen Klein completed the bond by guaranteeing £640,000-worth of ABKCO Industries' share in the MGM film corporation.

There now began seven weeks of business meetings, long and tortuous enough to surfeit even Allen Klein, in the winding course of which John and Yoko drifted, like rumpled white wraiths, through the grim purlieus of Threadneedle Street. John – to begin with, at least – enjoyed the negotiations. 'It's like playing Monopoly,' he said, 'but with real money.'

A third element in the ATV–Apple struggle had by now shown its hand. This was a consortium of City broker firms which, over several months, had quietly built up its own stake in Northern Songs to 14 per cent. To capture the company, ATV or the Beatles must buy out – or, at least, win over – the consortium. And from the beginning, it was clear the consortium, which included the Howard and Wyndham theatre chain, was inclined to favour the Beatles.

The main stumbling block to what might otherwise have been an instantly done deal was Allen Klein. For the Robin Hood of Pop was currently enjoying a spell of notoriety in London's financial world just as intense as his recent one in New York's. The *Sunday Times*'s Insight investigative unit had just published a lengthy piece headlined 'The Toughest Wheeler-dealer in the Pop Jungle', delving into Klein's recent exploits, from the Cameo-Parkway shares furore to his activities as the alleged saviour of the Rolling Stones. Insight also revealed how the Stones themselves had begun to turn against him, complaining that only a small portion of the $1.25 million advance he had wrung from Decca two years earlier had yet found its way into their bank accounts. There was also an impending lawsuit against Klein from the band's ex-manager Andrew Loog Oldham over Oldham's £1 million pay-off. From having pressed

Klein on the Beatles as their only possible hope, the Stones were now urging them to have nothing to do with him.

Klein did his best to reassure the nervous City consortium that if they joined up with the Beatles to purchase Northern Songs, he would personally play no part in either the negotiations or the company's administration. He gave the same assurance in typically salty terms at a press conference which, the *Financial Times* said, 'must have set some kind of a record for unprintable language'. This promise was repeated two days later in a message to Northern's shareholders from Henry Ansbacher's. If their takeover bid were accepted, neither Klein nor the bankers themselves would play any part in the company's management. The board would be strengthened by the appointment of David Platz, head of the powerful Essex Music Corporation, as Chairman. As a further inducement, John and Paul would extend their songwriting contract with Northern beyond its present 1973 expiry date.

By mid-May, Lew Grade was ready to concede defeat. The Beatles had successfully wooed the consortium, both with assurances of Klein's non-participation and also promises of directorships for the Howard and Wyndham theatre faction. Then, at the very last minute, the pact dissolved. John pulled the plug on the negotiations, announcing he was, 'sick of being fucked about by men in suits sitting on their fat arses in the City'.

The consortium melted into Lew Grade's open arms – if not as sellers yet, then as fully committed allies. On 20 May, ATV achieved effective control of Northern Songs. Grade expressed delight at having acquired a cache of songs that would 'live for ever' and hopes for an amicable future working relationship with their creators.

That same day's papers announced that Allen Klein had now officially been appointed the Beatles' business manager. Earlier reports that he would receive 20 per cent of their earnings were described as 'exaggerated'.

•

The agreement had been signed on 8 May. It bore the names of only three Beatles: John, George and Ringo. Paul still had not refused outright: he said he wanted more time – as Klein had repeatedly promised he should have – to go through the management document with John Eastman and his English lawyer. But the others, John especially, had lost patience with Paul's 'stalling'. Klein now told them he needed the signed agreement urgently to take back to New York to present to his ABKCO board. When the four Beatles met at Abbey Road on 9 May, the deed had been done. 'I see you've outvoted me,' Paul said.

So Allen Klein and ABKCO Industries Inc moved in to 3 Savile Row, W1. Shortly afterwards within the house, a soft and regular sound became audible. It was the sound of Apple executives perishing under the axe. Ron Kass, Head of Apple Records; Denis O'Dell, Head of Apple Films; Peter Asher, Head of A & R; Brian Lewis, head of the contracts department, all left the Beatles' employment with as much dispatch as if a medieval catapult had propelled them through the white front door. It was the first phase of Klein's promised economy drive to those he condemned as pampered and unproductive management figures. That Kass and Asher between them were responsible for selling some 16 million records on the Apple label did not for one instant stay the hand of their turtlenecked executioner.

After unnecessary management figures on Klein's death list came friends and dependants. The scythe swept upward through Apple's subdivisions: through Magic Alex and his electronic workshop; through Zapple, the 'spoken word' label; through Apple Retail, Apple Publishing and the Apple Foundation for the Arts. In vain did the victims appeal to their good friends John, Paul, George or Ringo. The Beatles had suddenly become as remote as Tudor monarchs after signing warrants of execution. So it was even when Klein fired Alistair Taylor, Brian Epstein's original NEMS assistant, and a long-time friend and fixer to each of the four. Taylor, when his sentence was pronounced, spent a whole day on the telephone, trying to reach John or Paul, to have his dismissal confirmed first-hand. Neither was available to discuss the matter. 'The Beatles,' John would admit, 'are the biggest bastards in the world.'

Klein's original intention was that not a single Apple executive should survive to stand between the Beatles and him. He even succeeded, for a short time, in toppling their two closest aides, Neil Aspinall and Peter Brown. Both were on the Apple board of directors, itself a gallows mark. 'I gave Klein the perfect excuse,' Peter Brown says. 'We were just coming up to the annual general meeting. I told him that all the directors had to resign as a formality and then be re-elected. Neil and I both resigned, but we weren't re-elected. We thought the Beatles wouldn't ditch us, but they did.'

Here at least Klein had gone too far. The Beatles could not function without Peter Brown, their immaculate Minister of Court. And Neil Aspinall, their oldest, truest, straightest friend, proved invulnerable to the headsman's axe. For Neil, Klein's coming was ultimately beneficial: it removed the weight of worry he had shouldered as road manager to the whole Apple fiasco. At first, when the burden went, Neil could not believe it had gone. He dreamed strange dreams, that only a road manager to the Beatles could dream: of running in fear from some unknown pursuer, with both arms full of precious silver fish. The more he ran, the more his pursuer gained on him; as tightly as he tried to hold the silver fish, they always slipped from his grasp.

Gone was the holiday atmosphere of 3 Savile Row. Rather than showing up for work and leaving whenever they pleased, staff were now expected to clock in and out just like any other wage slaves in the unenchanted world outside. The perks they had formerly enjoyed – the food, the drinks, the drugs, the free gifts, the unlimited taxi-rides – were all terminated. Nothing could be bought for the company without a purchase order signed by Klein or his lieutenant, Peter Howard. Charge accounts that had nourished hundreds dried up all over the West End.

It was no more than the way most hard-nosed American businesses were run, but Klein had a special genius for making people afraid of him. Everyone, from secretaries upwards, felt themselves under the same nervous compulsion: to prove simultaneously that they were essential to Apple and that they posed no obstacle or threat to Klein. Even those he moved upward carried a kind of stigma. Jack Oliver, Ron Kass's young deputy, found himself suddenly in Kass's job as Head of Apple Records, yet with no feeling that he had been promoted. 'I was told: "You're shit, you know that don't you, but this and this needs doing so get on with it."'

Klein had annexed Peter Asher's old office on the second floor, opposite Derek Taylor's press department. It only added to the terror felt throughout 3 Savile Row that this office remained empty for several days each week, while Klein was in New York dealing with ABKCO Industries business. Then at some unguarded moment in the late afternoon of a day when he appeared to be absent, he would return. Jimmy Clark, on the front doorstep, would hurriedly straighten a dove-grey back. The chauffeur-driven car would draw up and disgorge a squat figure that, even in its walk of a few yards to the front door, could not bear to break off its study of balance sheets or *Billboard* magazine. Margo Stevens and the other members of the doorstep brigade had already formed their own conclusions without seeing his scary sidekick, Pete Bennett. As the door closed on Klein, one of them would dart forward and shout 'Mafia!' through the letterbox.

Klein, in fact, despite the 8 May agreement, was still not absolutely sure of his position. How could he be until all four Beatles recognised him as their saviour? John Eastman remained on the scene, representing Paul and supposedly co-operating with ABKCO Industries in what had been described to the press as a 'warm, workable relationship'. Riven as he was with contempt for Eastman, Klein recognised that the relationship, if never warm, if barely workable, had to continue for the present. Sooner or later, he hoped to pull off a coup major enough to dazzle Paul out of his new fraternal obligations, and so complete the equation of Klein's heart's desire. Meanwhile, he contented himself with responding to Eastman's many challenging and provocative inter-office memos in a tone of Groucho Marxist sarcasm. 'Dear John . . . I am on a diet, so stop putting words in my mouth . . .'

A still greater incentive to Klein existed in the three-year contract which John, George and Ringo had signed with ABKCO Industries. This, indeed, gave Klein 20 per cent of their income – but only such income as was generated after his management began. Benefits gained through the NEMS and Northern Songs deal did not fall within the scope of the contract. To earn his 20 per cent, as well as prove himself to the Eastmans and Paul, he must make a major killing in the field where he had strewn so many, earlier corpses. Klein's next targets, in other words, were the Beatles' English and American record companies.

Sir Joseph Lockwood was surprised, shortly afterwards, to be visited at his EMI office by Klein and all four Beatles. They had come, Klein announced, to 're-negotiate' the nine-year contract which Brian Epstein had signed with EMI in 1967. 'I said: "All right, we can talk about it," Sir Joseph recalled. "Provided both sides get some benefit, there's no harm in re-negotiating." Klein said: "No, you don't understand. *You* don't get anything. *We* get more."

'I told them to get out. They went, looking very sheepish. Paul was pulling faces behind the others' backs, as if to say, "Sorry, it was nothing to do with me."

'My assistant was very worried. "You shouldn't have sent them off like this," he said. I said, "It's all right. I recognise the sort of man Klein is. He'll be back in half an hour." And sure enough, half an hour later he rang me to apologise.'

At 3 Savile Row, Klein and the Beatles – excepting Paul – went into conference again. Margo and the other girls were beginning to recognise those conferences by the lights burning late in the big top floor window. In the Press Office, Derek Taylor's light projector cast its wriggling coloured shapes over the wall. Journalists, still waiting for interviews, strained to catch scraps of gossip among insiders who were now all far on the outside.

'—they're just puppets now. I took something in to John and he just said: "Give it to Klein."'

'—they've calmed down a bit. They're eating scrambled eggs.'

'—you know what happened to that note you sent in? Screwed up into a ball and thrown across the room.'

•

On 26 May, in a suite at the Queen Elizabeth Hotel, Montreal, John and Yoko staged a second, even more ambitious Bed-in. They had meant to hold it in the Bahamas but they decided on Canada as being closest to the country at which their Peace Campaign was chiefly aimed (and which John, through his drug conviction, was now prohibited from entering). The Montreal Bed-in lasted seven days: it included an extended visit from Dr Timothy Leary, live broadcasts to Canadian and US radio stations, a hook-up with insurgent students at Berkeley University and an encounter with right-wing humorist Al Capp whose racist digs against Yoko almost got him thrown out on his ear. The climax was the recording at John and Yoko's bedside of the newly written campaign anthem 'Give Peace a Chance' with a chorus that included Timothy Leary, Murray the K, Tommy Smothers, a rabbi and a troupe of bald-headed, bell-ringing, chanting Radha Krishna Temple singers.

It was the prelude to two months in which John, with Yoko at his side, consciously set out to saturate the media with their demonstrations, their slogans – above all, with themselves as a living slogan: 'Mr and Mrs Peace'. For John, the campaign was tinged with aggressive satisfaction. He was turning the tables on the press, exploiting them in precisely the way he, as a Beatle, used to be exploited. He said so in a voice that still incised through the curly apostle beard, the woolly thought, the inherent heart-sinking fatuousness of representing sitting up in bed in a luxury hotel as a political, humanitarian act. 'The Blue Meanies, or whatever they are, still preach violence all the time in every newspaper, every TV show and every magazine. The least Yoko and I can do is hog the headlines and make people laugh. We're quite willing to be the world's clowns if it will do any good. For reasons known only to themselves, people print what I say. And I say "peace".'

In June, the campaign moved to 3 Savile Row. The front ground-floor office formerly occupied by Ron Kass was commandeered by John and Yoko for their own company, Bag Productions, and their continuing saturation of a still-acquiescent press. In a rooftop ceremony, before a somewhat bemused Commissioner for Oaths, John changed his name, dropping the Winston his mother gave him as a talisman against Hitler's bombs; becoming, instead, John Ono Lennon. Yoko became Yoko Ono Lennon. John was delighted to realise that their combined names contained nine letter O's, since nine had always been his lucky number.

Ron Kass's elegant salon, next to the front door, took on the appearance of an hotel bedroom during a Bed-in. Hand-lettered Peace slogans and Lennon drawings papered the panelled walls. Newspapers, dirty plates, Magic Markers and Gauloises packets submerged the chaste white telephones. In the Georgian fireplace, a plastic doll which had somehow escaped the King's Road napalm holocaust, stood on its head in a mess of cigarette ends. Yoko sat at the large executive desk with John a little to one side of her. The journalists were brought in at 15-minute intervals.

Sooner or later, in each interview, the talk would turn from Peace and bagism to a question far more deeply significant to Western civilisation. Was John truly, as he had said, reduced to his 'last £50,000'? Yes, he said. 'All that stuff about us being millionaires is only true on paper, you know. All we've really got is our houses, our cars and this place. In the old days with Northern Songs, you used to get a cheque occasionally. There's a deal now where a certain percentage of our royalties is paid into this place. So I haven't had any income for about two years. It's all been bloody *outcome.*

'Allen's putting it right for us now. We've made a lot of mistakes, but we're still here. The circus has left town, but we still own the site.'

The presence of John and Yoko downstairs gave a new complexity to the already complex 'vibes' gripping 3 Savile Row. Fear of Klein required that clerical staff should look brisk and businesslike, and sit behind their IBM typewriters like stenographic mice. Fear, no less well-founded, of the chief and ever-present Beatle demanded their help in collecting acorns to be sent by John and Yoko as a peace gesture to all world leaders from President Nixon to the King of Yemen. Since early summer is not acorn season, a country-wide appeal had to be launched. One elderly spinster sent in two dried-up specimens she had kept for 40 years in a silver box. An entrepreneur, well-versed in the principle of Beatles supply and demand, offered a supply at £1 per acorn.

His Peace Campaign, in fact, aroused John to a belligerence frequently vented on this or that awe-struck Apple employee, unable to tell him, for instance, how to fly-post the whole of London with Peace slogans. Ever since the *Two Virgins* fiasco, he had suspected the whole house of intent to sabotage his and Yoko's personal projects. He suspected it even more now that their second album, *Unfinished Music No. 2 – Life with the Lions*, had gone on release. The cover this time showed Yoko in hospital after her miscarriage, with John in his sleeping bag beside her bed. The tracks were screech and electronic scribble, and a few seconds' heartbeat from the baby that had not survived. John bitterly resented the fact that the album was not mentioned in Apple's current radio promo.

And yet none of the Beatles, however artfully approached, would let slip a word against Yoko. 'People think they're mad, both of them,' Ringo said, 'but that's not Yoko. That's just John being John.'

On 30 May, Apple released a single which at once seemed to show the Beatles reconciled to Yoko, and Yoko herself to be capable of figuring in an art form that was quite intelligible. This was 'The Ballad of John and Yoko', a diary of the pair's recent peregrinations from the Amsterdam Hilton, 'talking in our beds for a week' and 'eating chocolate cake in a bag' in Vienna, to 'honeymooning down by the Seine' when Peter Brown sent word that they could 'get married in Gibraltar, near Spain'. There were echoes of the media attacks on Yoko ('The newspapers said . . . she's gone to his head') of the '50 acorns tied in a sack' as well as of a horribly prophetic late-night conversation with 'the wife' about how 'when you're dead, you don't take nothing with you but your soul'. '*Christ*, it ain't easy!' ran the refrain, so guaranteeing worldwide bans on airplay. 'The way things are going, they're going to crucify me.' As a gesture of apparent unity, the song was credited to Lennon–McCartney and its performance to the Beatles.

In fact, 'The Ballad of John and Yoko' had been recorded by John virtually single-handed. George and Ringo were both out of the country. The drumming, overdubbed later, was Paul's.

•

It had been a typical gesture by a personality which, though outmanoeuvred, outvoted and furiously affronted by the events of the past months, still followed its old vocation of presenting the Beatles as a united and invulnerable front. It was no less symbolic of Paul's belief that the Klein era must pass and that, meantime, there was one safe refuge from him. Not even Allen Klein could harm the Beatles in any sphere where they made music together.

Early in July, Paul asked Ringo to drive up and have dinner with him and Linda at Cavendish Avenue. He had by then given up trying to dissuade John or George from appointing Klein. Ringo was, perhaps, a different story. Ringo had gone along with the others, saying that Apple needed 'a hustler'. But Paul evidently still had hopes of the solid common sense which, in so many ways, had given the Beatles their inner strength and balance.

The evening, however, did not turn Ringo against Klein so much as against Linda. 'It seemed that as soon as I started saying, well maybe Klein wasn't so bad and we should give him a chance, Linda would start crying. In a few minutes, I'd be saying the same – well, maybe he *isn't* so bad – and Linda would start crying again. "Oh, they've got you, *too*," she kept saying.'

Apple, Paul's brainchild, his living Magritte, his 'Western Communism', was now repugnant to him. London was becoming almost as bad. The girls outside his gates showed increasing hatred of Linda: they broke into the house not just to look now but to steal the new Mrs McCartney's clothes and photographic prints. When money began to vanish, even Paul's tolerance became exhausted. One day, he and Linda pretended to go out, then kept watch on the house from a garden across the street. Unfortunately, it was the moment chosen by Margo Stevens, his longest-standing admirer, to leave a bunch of flowers on the front step. 'Suddenly, Paul ran up and started shaking me. "It's *you* all the time, isn't it?" he kept shouting. I was terrified. I said, "No – I only wanted to leave some flowers." I think he could see how much he'd frightened me. He stopped shaking me and started stroking my hair.'

Late in July, Paul got in touch with George Martin. It was now five months since Martin had worked on the *Let It Be* album. According to Paul, no one had yet been able to face editing the hours of ramshackle playing. The book that was to have accompanied the disc had been written, but then heavily censored in proof by EMI. The film, originally intended for television, was now to be a full-length cinema feature, and so impossible to release before early 1970. The album, when edited, must therefore be held over to accompany the film.

Then Paul made a surprising request. The Beatles, he said, wanted Martin to produce an album for them 'the way we used to do it'. Martin, remembering his latter experience, responded cautiously. 'I said: "If the album's going to be the way it used to be, then all of you have got to be the way you used to be." Paul said: "Yeah, we will. We promise. Only please let's do the album."'

So it happened, in July and August 1969, as the decade began to wear out, that its chief creators agreed to turn back the clock a little way. John suspended his Peace Campaign. George broke off from recording the chants of the London Radha Krishna Temple. Ringo interrupted his burgeoning film career. Paul steeled himself to remain in London a little longer. The four Beatles met, for the last time, at Abbey Road.

19

'Everybody saw the sunshine'

On 22 July 1969, human beings first set foot on the moon. It was an oddly anticlimactic moment. Fictive representations of the great event for half a century past had imagined a planet inhabited by bellicose little green men, not the dead white wilderness that later close study had revealed. Story-tellers in print and film alike had failed to realise, too, that as rocket science advanced, other technologies would keep step with it. Consequently, no one expected that when a first moon-landing finally came, it could be televised to the whole world exactly as it happened; that, shown on black and white screens for hour after hour, it would gradually lose its initial stupendous fascination, becoming commonplace and ultimately even boring; so that by the time astronaut Neil Armstrong took his carefully scripted 'One small step for Man – one giant leap for Mankind', he would seem less like history's greatest explorer since Columbus than a kind of intergalactic disc jockey.

So, in their expiring months, the Sixties turned from the dusty feathers of the past and shuffled reluctantly towards a new world shaped by the myriad tools and by-products of space exploration: computers, microchips, digital clock-faces, digital typefaces, non-stick saucepans, moon boots, clingfilm, the expression 'We have lift-off'.

For millions of the young, paradoxically, that moonshot summer was devoted to getting as close as humanly possible to earth. In June came the Woodstock free festival when, on a small farm in upstate New York, a four-day pageant of top American and British rock acts was watched by a non-paying crowd of 450,000, their spirits undampened by periodic rain and the sketchiest of life-support facilities; good-humoured even in their message to a government that still wished to export their young men as cannon-fodder to Vietnam. 'There ain't no need to wonder why,' sang the giant open-air chorus led by Country Joe Fish. 'Hey, whoopee, we're gonna die!'

After Woodstock, the exotic notion of playing music for nothing spread like wildfire through the small, mutually imitative top echelon of rock bands. Doing a free concert was an easy way of becoming patron saints to the hippy subculture, who would afterwards buy their records by the million at full price; it also symbolised a widespread breakaway from the control of old-fashioned, money-motivated managers. Late that June, London saw its first free rock festival when Eric Clapton and his new 'supergroup' Blind Faith performed in Hyde Park before a crowd estimated at 150,000. That event also passed off as happily and peacefully as had Woodstock, and was followed by news of one still larger and more impressive. The Rolling Stones would give a free concert, also in Hyde Park, on 5 July.

It would have been hard to imagine a one-off live performance more unlike the one the Beatles had given for 30-odd people among the Apple chimney-pots in biting January cold. Half a million Stones fans massed around Hyde Park Corner to watch the band give the most riveting show of their career to date, fronted by Mick Jagger in what seemed to be an Edwardian little girl's white party frock. The concert was also a rite of mourning for Brian Jones, their recently dumped instrumental genius, who had been found dead in his swimming pool three days earlier. Jagger read a funerary passage from Shelley's *Adonais* – the signal for hundreds of symbolic white butterflies to be released – before settling down to simulate fellatio with a hand microphone.

In August came the most remarkable of all Britain's free rock festivals, convened on the sleepy, 1950s-ish Isle of Wight and headlined by Bob Dylan, whom the organisers had tempted out of Beatle-like seclusion by stressing the island's associations with his favourite poet, Alfred Lord Tennyson. After what proved a short, disappointing performance, Dylan was helicoptered away to what the press knew only as 'a destination near London'. It was in fact Tittenhurst Park, the rambling stately home in Sunningdale, Berkshire, now occupied by John Ono Lennon and Yoko Ono Lennon. As Dylan and John greeted each other in the gusts from the rotor-blades, it was hard to say which of them had changed more out of all recognition.

Thunderous with alfresco guitars, perfumed with joss and pot, sparkling with sunshine and acid, it was as if this last summer of the Sixties truly could, and would, go on for ever. Young people lying half-naked in the grassy heat, romping in water, foam or mud to the free sounds, for hectare after hectare, had found *Anno Domini*'s nearest equivalent to the Garden of Eden. Though their power was soon to dissipate, if it ever really existed at all, they could point to this one irrefutable achievement. Never again in their lifetime would youthful crowds of half a million and more congregate together without wanting to harm each other or smash up the environment.

But the season was already changing. And the great guiding beacon for harmless joy in the past six-year golden age was being appropriated for darker purposes. From Los Angeles came news of random multiple murder on a scale previously associated only with gangland violence. A young movie actress named Sharon Tate, pregnant wife of Polish director Roman Polanski, and six friends had been hacked to death at Tate's luxury home by a hippy named Charles Manson and his 'family' of largely female disciples. With his vaguely artistic as well as criminal tendencies, Manson was exactly the type who, a few months earlier, might have come begging at Apple's still-open door. He was also the first fan-turned-fiend; the prototype of Mark David Chapman and George Harrison's future stalker, Michael Abrams. Under questioning, Manson claimed to have received 'guidance' to commit his atrocities from two songs on the Beatles' *White Album*, 'Piggies' and 'Helter-Skelter' – the latter title having been found scrawled on walls throughout Sharon Tate's home in her and her fellow victims' blood.

•

Not all Apple creatures had perished under Allen Klein. In the Press Office there were still plastic birds, dipping and dipping their beaks around a shallow water-tray. The Press Office, likewise, continued to function, though at what inscrutable whim of Klein's Derek Taylor could not claim to understand. Sometimes in mid-afternoon, when his department became too crowded and the Scotch and Coke fumes too uproariously thick, Taylor would raise himself in his scallop-backed throne, push the hair off his eyes and shout, 'Clear the room now! I mean it!' After one such dismissal, wandering in the sudden space behind Carol Paddon's desk, he paused by the water tray and studied the nodding birds. 'Those beaks are going mouldy,' he remarked gloomily. 'No one told us they'd do that when we bought them. They cost us £1 each.'

Derek Taylor was a frustrated writer. But, unlike most frustrated writers, he had talent. Often he would have dismissed his court simply for the purpose of fighting his way back the few inches across his desk to the typewriter that stood there. He wrote a great deal during Apple's last year: essays and soliloquies and memoranda to himself, all on a theme as constant as the pressure on him from above, below and sideways. Why do I work for the Beatles? And why, of all the complex emotions produced by working for the Beatles, is the commonest one simple fear?

'Whatever the motivation,' Taylor typed, 'the effect is slavery. Whatever the Beatles ask is done. I mean, whatever the Beatles ask is tried. A poached egg on the Underground on the Bakerloo Line between Trafalgar Square and Charing Cross? Yes, Paul. A sock full of elephant shit on Otterspool Promenade? Give me 10 minutes, Ringo. Two Turkish dwarfs dancing the Charleston on a sideboard? Male or female, John? Pubic hair from Sonny Liston? It's early closing, George (gulp), but give me until noon tomorrow. The only gig I would do after this is the Queen. Their staff are terrified of them, and not without reason. They have fired more people than any comparable employer unit in the world. They make Lord Beaverbrook look like Jesus.'

Then the music would begin again, and Taylor, and Mavis Smith, and Carol Paddon – who was afraid to go on holiday lest her job should vanish – each remembered why they were sitting here. The stagnant sea of journalists and TV men remembered, or almost did. Taylor said the same thing into the telephone a dozen times each day. 'It's called *Abbey Road*. Yes – the studios are in Abbey Road. It's an album just like they used to make. They sound the way they sounded in the old days.'

Something had stopped the elements diverging, and restored them to their old unsurpassable balance. *Abbey Road* was John Lennon at his best, and Paul McCartney at his best, and George Harrison suddenly reaching a best that no one had ever imagined. It was John's anarchy, straight and honed. It was Paul's sentimentality with the brake applied. It was George's new, wholly surprising presence, drawing the best from both sources. It was a suite of glorious new songs, not warring internally as on the *White Album* but merging their irreconcilably different viewpoints into a cohesive and balanced whole, and performed with the tautness and unartificiality they had sought for so long. It was the moment, caught again and crystallised, even in the flux of an expiring decade. It was hot streets, soft porn and hippydom fading into a hard reality. It was London here and now, and Liverpool then, and the Beatles, dateless and timeless in a sudden, capricious illusion of perfect harmony.

It echoed throughout 3 Savile Row on 11 September, then a date just like any other, as the Apple house girded itself to face whatever ructions this day might bring, its green carpets vacuumed smooth, its still-empty upper suites savoury with the aroma of furniture polish. Here was the opening track, 'Come Together', with its hissing percussion and all-too-obvious echoes of the Lennons' bedroom. Here was 'Maxwell's Silver Hammer', another cutie-pie Paul song, but this time with an undertow of viciousness that made people wonder if a Japanese performance artist might have been, even unconsciously, on his mind. 'Bang-bang Maxwell's silver hammer came down on her head . . . Bang-bang Maxwell's silver hammer made sure that she was dead . . .' Here was the ritual Ringo track, a children's song called 'Octopus's Garden', as happy and optimistic as Ringo somehow remained, yet still with a wistful subtext of longing for the Beatles to be 'under the sea . . . knowing they're happy and they're safe'. Here was 'Because', featuring the sweetest and closest group harmony since 'Here, There and Everywhere', from a lyric jotted down by

John on the reverse of one of John Eastman's most reproachful inter-office memos.

In the ground-floor office of Bag Productions, the first visitors were led in to meet John and Yoko. They were not journalists; they were two blind, middle-aged Texan girls in pink and orange taffeta ball gowns. Each was led across to touch John, then Yoko led them to the group of four perspex cabinets blocking the fireplace. It was the hi-fi system which John had ironically christened The Plastic Ono Band, and even credited with the playing of 'Give Peace a Chance'. Each blind girl's hand in Yoko's touched the featureless robots hopefully, like a shrine.

Next came the day-long queue of reporters, primed with questions about Peace; about John's interest in the A6 murder case, but mainly about the two films he and Yoko had shown that week at the Institute of Contemporary Arts. The first was *Rape*; the second, entitled *Self-Portrait*, was a 42-minute study of John's penis both in partial and full erection. 'Anything that gets a reaction is good,' he told the *New Musical Express*. 'People are just frozen jellies. It just needs someone to do something to turn off the fridge.' Yoko sat beside him, eating brown rice from a bowl with a long wooden spoon. She interjected only to regret that no serious critical comment had been directed at their film of John's penis. Or, as Yoko innocently said, 'The critics wouldn't touch it.'

George and Ringo were both at Savile Row that day. For Ringo, the errand was straightforward. He had come in to give Peter Brown details of the house he wanted to sell, having bought it from Peter Sellers a few months previously. Now he was tired of its extensive parkland, its private cinema and sauna baths and wide frontage, with fishing rights, on the River Wey.

'Do you want some apple jelly?' he asked Neil Aspinall.

'Apple *jelly*?' Aspinall echoed suspiciously, as if it were code for some new narcotic.

'Yeah, we've got hundreds of apples lying round our orchard,' Ringo said. 'So Maureen's made pots and pots of apple jelly.'

George arrived, accompanied by his assistant Terry Doran to do a photographic shoot for a German magazine named *Bravo*. He was suddenly in demand, thanks largely to the song which, by common consent, was one of *Abbey Road*'s very best. George had written it months before while sitting in his friend Eric Clapton's garden. Forgetting his mantras and sitars, he had entitled it 'Here Comes the Sun', and in that simplicity at long last touched a chord of the mystical. Perhaps its ultimate accolade was that, on first hearing it, most people mistook it for a 'John' song, lead-sung by John. In the same way, years of exposure to Paul's melodic gifts had borne fruit in a ballad called 'Something', the first-ever George song chosen for a Beatles single as the A-side.

Upstairs, the *Bravo* photographer was waiting patiently beside a set banked high with flowers in Hare Krishna yellow and orange. An elderly workman staggered in, carrying a box containing the disconnected components of an eight-armed Hindu deity. Between them the photographer and he began to assemble the figure, trying to figure out which arm went into which socket. Even George seemed impressed by the thoroughness of the preparations. 'If I'd known it was going to be like this, I'd have washed me hair,' he said. As the shoot was about to start, he decided that his blue denim shirt and jeans were not a suitable outfit. A Press Office secretary was sent to the nearby Mr Fish boutique to buy half a dozen silk shirts for him to choose from. As he looked through them, he tried to answer an English journalist's question, the same old one – how had Apple managed to go so wrong? 'It was like a game of Chinese whispers, really,' George said. 'We said one thing, it was passed along among lots of other people, and what came back to us wasn't anything like we'd meant.'

The Beatles ceased to exist that afternoon, when Anthony Fawcett, John and Yoko's personal assistant, picked up a ringing telephone from the debris of papers and plates. It was a Canadian entrepreneur, asking if John and Yoko would attend a rock and roll revival concert in Toronto the following day. John took the telephone from Fawcett: he would go, he said, but only if he were allowed to perform. Within hours, the Plastic Ono Band had metamorphosed from perspex robots into an ad hoc supergroup consisting of John, Yoko, Eric Clapton, Klaus Voorman and Alan White. A charter airliner was booked to carry them, if John got up in time and did not take fright at the last minute at the thought of appearing with an unrehearsed band before an audience of thousands.

In the studio, George was still being photographed by *Bravo* magazine in his chosen Mr Fish shirt, against the Hindu idol and the banked yellow flowers. Ringo wandered in to say hello and, as a keen photographer himself, to check out the professional camera equipment being used. 'You want to use a zoom lens through that prism,' he advised the *Bravo* photographer.

'Do you fancy going to Australia to play?' George asked him in ironic reference to John's impending 24-hour Canadian visit.

'When do we get back?'

'Tomorrow.'

Two floors down, the Press Office was, as usual, plunged into darkness, speckly with psychedelic light-shapes, crowded with expectant, seated figures and reverberant with the aural sunshine of the Abbey Road album. In one corner, Mal Evans's discovery, the Iveys – now renamed Bad Finger – sat, like very young pantomime pirates, awaiting news of their first release on the Apple label. Mary Hopkin, a sweet, frail, bewildered girl, passed through with her even more bewildered Welsh parents. Neil Aspinall came in to say that the Plastic Ono Band had got away to Canada on the second charter airliner bidden to stand by after they missed the first one.

Now on *Abbey Road*, the Apple house heard the voice which had first imagined it, and argued to launch it, and which had now abandoned it, leaving only a song lyric behind as explanation. 'You never give me your money,' sang Paul to the manager he would not recognise. 'You only give me your funny paper . . .' He had contrived to make the album that was an act of reunion serve also as an outlet for his bitter frustration, even though, being Paul, he could only do so in hints, between the smiles of one who still hated to admit any unpleasantness.

By late afternoon, after its umpteenth play, it was as though *Abbey Road* told the Beatles' whole life story in miniature, from the effortless good sex of 'Come Together' to the finish of side two, where the narrative splintered into unfinished scraps and intros that led nowhere – the mystical 'Sun King', the Sergeant-Pepper-ish 'Mean Mr Mustard', the Scouse wisecracking 'Polythene Pam' ('she's the kind of a ge-erl who reads the *News of the We-erld* . . .') the memory of some relentless groupie in 'She Came in through the Bathroom Window'. Here, if not in real life, Paul had the last word, with his tender cradle-song 'Golden Slumbers'; his little wink and nod ('Her Majesty's a pretty nice girl . . .') to the monarch who would one day knight him; his coded warning to those who had beaten him that they would 'carry that weight a long time . . .' Here, prematurely, from Paul was an epitaph for the band that would never be bettered:

> And in the end, the love you take
> Is equal to the love
> You make.

That September, in the heady aftermath of festivals and free concerts, Paul made one last effort to reunite the others on stage again. His idea now was that they should play at small clubs, unannounced, perhaps even in disguise. Ringo supported the idea and George, though non-committal, did not refuse outright. But John told Paul bluntly he must be daft. 'I might as well tell you,' John continued, 'I'm leaving the group. I've had enough. I want a divorce, like my divorce from Cynthia.'

He had reached his decision while flying back with Yoko, Eric Clapton and Klaus after their tumultuous welcome at the Toronto rock 'n' roll festival. Standing up there with Yoko and the robots, singing any words that came into his head, he had realised that ceasing to be a Beatle need not strike him blind. 'Cold Turkey', his new song, named for heroin's withdrawal horrors, was written to renounce an even worse addiction. He would never again be hooked by 'Yesterday' or 'Ob-la-di, Ob-la-da'. All that remained was to do what his idol Elvis Presley had never been able to, and 'break out of the palace'.

What restrained him was an urgent plea from Allen Klein not to jeopardise the deals Klein still hoped to do on behalf of the Beatles as a unit. For Klein, at that very moment, was on the brink of an unequivocal coup in respect of their record royalties. Having failed to browbeat EMI, he had set about browbeating their American label, Capitol. Bob Gortikov, Capitol's President, under pressure from Klein, was proving less inflexible than Sir Joseph Lockwood. But clearly, for John to announce his resignation would seriously weaken Klein's bargaining position. John, therefore, agreed to keep silent – even to the other Beatles – until the Capitol deal was done.

It was a promise he found impossible to keep when Paul, in another long boardroom wrangle, brought up the subject of live performing again. A furious row developed, with John railing bitterly at Paul for his 'granny' music, especially 'Ob-la-di' and 'Maxwell's Silver Hammer', on the *Abbey Road* album, which John had particularly detested. He told Paul he was sick of 'fighting for time' on their albums, and of always taking the B-sides on singles. Then, rather tactlessly, he pointed at George as perennial victim of the Lennon–McCartney 'carve-up'. Paul replied that only this year had George's songs achieved comparable quality with theirs. George interrupted resentfully that songs he had recorded this year were often those he had written years earlier but not been allowed to release. He added that he had never really felt the Beatles were backing him. As John rounded angrily on George, Paul made a sudden, quiet plea to them to remember how they had always overcome disagreements in the past. 'When we go into a studio, even on a bad day, I'm still playing bass, Ringo's still drumming and we're still *there*, you know.'

Paul could not believe that John's resignation was anything other than a fit of temperament – like George's during the *Let It Be* sessions. When the white Rolls-Royce moved off down Savile Row that afternoon, it had been agreed not to dissolve, for the time being. Not long afterwards, a slightly stunned President of Capitol Records agreed to Allen Klein's demand for an unheard-of royalty of 69 cents on each Beatles album sold in America. Derek Taylor spoke to Bob Gortikov shortly after Gortikov ended his last session with Klein. 'We would have done the deal anyway,' Gortikov said, 'but did he have to be so *nasty* about it?'

According to Klein, the deal with Capitol swung Paul in his favour at last. 'Paul congratulated me on the agreement. He said, "Well, if you *are* screwing us, I can't see that you are."' Paul's version, sworn subsequently in a High Court affadavit, was that, on the contrary, he felt uneasy to think the Beatles had received a massive royalty increase at the very moment when their future together was so uncertain. Also, by that time, he had ceased to believe anything Klein said. The most public and PR-conscious Beatle retreated into complete seclusion, with Linda and their newborn daughter, Mary, on his farm in Argyllshire.

With the Capitol deal, Klein was assured of his 20 per cent. He could now turn his attention back to the five-months stalemate over Northern Songs and Lew Grade's ATV network. Grade, having gained effective control of Northern, now hoped to woo the Beatles into accepting him as a sort of supercharged Dick James. His plan was to buy out the Howard and Wyndham consortium's blocking 14 per cent, but to persuade John and Paul to retain their 31 per cent, and extend their songwriting contract beyond the present expiry date in 1973.

Late in October, ATV finally bought out its consortium partner, bringing Lew Grade's share of Northern to slightly more than 50 per cent. Hours afterwards, it was announced that John and Paul, and Ringo, were selling their combined 31 per cent shareholding to ATV. The news, when it reached Apple – by a tip-off from the *Financial Times* – sounded very like defeat. Allen Klein, interviewed during his customary afternoon breakfast, claimed it as a victory. A threatened lawsuit against Northern for £5m in 'unpaid' Beatle royalties helped to persuade ATV to pay cash rather than stock for the Beatles' holdings. Klein could thus congratulate himself on having enriched John and Paul by about a million and a half pounds each, and Ringo by £80,000.

The American release of *Abbey Road*, together with Paul McCartney's disappearance, now produced one of Beatlemania's strangest and sickest by-products. A Detroit disc jockey claimed to have received a mysterious telephone call telling him that Paul McCartney was, in fact, dead, and that corroboration could be found in the *Abbey Road* cover photograph. This, though it might appear a somewhat unimaginative shot of the four Beatles walking over a St John's Wood zebra crossing, actually, the mystery caller said, represented Paul's funeral procession. John, in his white suit, was the minister; Ringo, dark-suited, was the undertaker, and George, in his shabby denims, the gravedigger. Still stronger funereal symbols were divined from the fact that Paul himself walked barefoot, out of step with the other three and smoking a cigarette right-handed. The clinching clue alleged was a Volkswagen car parked in the background, plainly showing its numberplate '28 IF' – or Paul's age *if* he had lived.

Picked up by other disc jockeys, elaborated by Beatles fanatics, the rumour swept America, growing ever more earnestly complex and foolish. One faction claimed that Paul had been murdered by the CIA. Another – the most powerful – claimed he had been decapitated in a car accident and that actor William Campbell had undergone plastic surgery to become his double. Scores of further 'clues' to support this theory were discovered in earlier Beatles albums – in the scraps of gibberish and backwards tapes; the fictional 'Billy Shears' mentioned in *Sgt. Pepper*, and various macabre John Lennon lines from 'A Day in the Life' and 'I Am the Walrus'. It was said that by holding the *Magical Mystery Tour* EP cover up to a mirror, a telephone number became visible on which Paul himself could be contacted in the Hereafter. The number, in fact, belonged to a *Guardian* journalist, subsequently driven almost to dementia by hundreds of early morning transatlantic telephone calls.

In America, an industry grew up of 'Paul is Dead' magazines, TV inquests and death discs – 'Saint Paul', 'Dear Paul', 'The Ballad of Paul' and 'Paulbearer'. It was all something stranger than a hoax: it was a self-hoax. Even when Paul himself surfaced on the cover of *Life* magazine, the rumours did not abate. Consequently, Beatles record sales in America in October 1969 rose to a level unequalled since February 1964. *Abbey Road* was to sell five million copies, a million more even than *Sgt. Pepper*. The Beatles, not Paul, had died; yet how could that be when they seemed bigger and better than ever?

•

John kept his promise to say nothing of the break-up. And in a strange way, his and Yoko's continuing notoriety served as camouflage. In November, he renounced his MBE, taking it from the top of his Aunt Mimi's television set and sending it back to the Queen as a protest against Vietnam, the war in Biafra and the failure of 'Cold Turkey' to remain in the British Top Twenty. Though that final flippancy made the gesture futile, it was not without a certain coincidental irony. For the statesman who had bought his own popularity with that same small, pink-ribboned medal still reigned at 10 Downing Street. What Harold Wilson had started with the Beatles he had continued less and less discerningly, showering MBEs, CBEs, knighthoods and peerages on any cheap entertainer who might cadge him a headline or a vote.

All politicians had learned something from Harold Wilson. In Canada, Prime Minister Trudeau held talks with John and Yoko to hear their plan to turn 1970 into 'Year One for Peace', commemorated by another vast open-air concert in Toronto. *Rolling Stone* magazine named John as 'Man of the Year'. 'A five-hour talk between John Lennon and Richard Nixon,' said *Rolling Stone*, 'would be more significant than any Geneva Summit Conference between the USA and Russia.'

In Times Square, New York, and prominent places in half a dozen other American cities, vast billboards carried a cryptic seasonal message. 'War is Over if You Want it. Happy Christmas From John and Yoko.' In London, the *Beatles Monthly* ceased publication. Princess Margaret attended the premiere of a new film, *The Magic Christian*, featuring Ringo in a small cameo part. In Campbeltown, Argyllshire, Paul put the final touches to an album he had tried to make already, with *Revolver*, *Sgt. Pepper* and *Let It Be* – an album for no one but Paul.

Before 1970 had even arrived came an event foreshadowing the new face of rock music. The Rolling Stones decided to conclude their current money-soaking American tour by giving another free show, this time on a motor-racing track in Altamont, California. The event quickly turned into a nightmare, thanks to the drunken brutality of the Hell's Angels who had been hired as 'security'. Its climax was the fatal stabbing of a young black spectator while Mick Jagger vainly appealed to the crowd to 'cool out' and love one another. Goodbye Sixties; welcome to the future.

•

Three Savile Row already felt the vibes of the new decade. A house which had stood elegantly intact for two centuries before the Beatles' coming seemed to decide deep within itself that the effort was no longer worthwhile. The rear promontory began to subside, throwing an ugly crack slantwise across the cordon bleu kitchen wall. The apple-green carpets were scuffed and threadbare. The deep leather sofas were cracked and split. Most of the framed golden discs on the staircase wall had been stolen. On the front stairs, the oil painting of lion cubs was torn at one corner where someone had tried to wrench it from its frame.

Though the front door frequently stood wide open, no invaders seized the chance to stampede through it. The Apple Scruffs in their front-step purdah had risen above such immature displays. Now they wore badges, denoting seniority and precedence; they had their own magazine, even their own notepaper, headed '*Steps*', *3 Savile Row*. Margo, their leader, had crossed the ultimate threshold on their behalf: she now worked inside Apple as a teamaker. She had served George with cheese and cucumber sandwiches and Ringo with a one-egg omelette. She had seen how ordinary, how rather pale and pockmarked, were the gods whom she had worshipped for the last three years of her life, in all weathers.

The Press Office continued functioning, but in broad daylight and a quiet that grew steadily more ominous. John had unilaterally fired the whole department, transferring his publicity arrangements to the Rolling Stones' press agent, Les Perrin. Derek Taylor had left, at George's kindly insistence, to finish the book he had been trying to start since 1968. Carol Paddon was fired for telling the *Daily Sketch* the truth, that Apple was 'just an accounting office now'. Mavis Smith, the ex-Ballet Rambert dancer, and Richard DiLello, the 'House Hippy', stayed on for the present. All round the room, on the desk supporting a scarlet torso; on the desk with the light show projector; on the desk next to the nodding birds, one by one the telephones stopped ringing.

•

It was in such a dismal morning-after spirit that the Beatles' *Let It Be* project limped, at last, towards a conclusion. Klein had sold the film to United Artists, and expected it to open in London in late spring. The album tapes, recorded a year earlier, had been exhumed from Apple's now sepulchral basement studio. There remained only the job of making an LP record from those uncounted hours of rehearsing, improvising, joking, jamming and angry argument.

With the Beatles' consent, Klein had brought in the American producer Phil Spector to do that sifting and editing job which they themselves could not face. Spector's girl groups and 'wall of sound' technique had been among their earliest and strongest influences: he was, at the same time, renowned for Gothic over-elaboration and triumphant bad taste. His appointment to doctor what had begun as an 'honest, no nonsense' Beatles album only confirmed the weary indifference they now felt to their music, as well as to each other.

Spector laboured, and an album duly went to EMI for pressing. It was, inevitably, a strange, inconclusive affair. Half of it chronicled the sessions as they had happened, with tuning-up noises and parody announcements by John, amid sycophantic laughter from the film crew. The other half had been remixed and augmented by Phil Spector in his own inimitable way. An acetate went to each Beatle accompanied by a long letter from Spector, justifying what he had done but assuring them he would make whatever changes they wished.

When Paul played the acetate, he found that his ballad 'The Long and Winding Road' had been remixed, then dubbed with a violin and horn section and topped with a sickly celestial choir. Paul tried to contact Spector, but could not. He wrote to Allen Klein, demanding the restoration of his original version, but to no avail. It was the final affront of the Klein era that the most tyrannically particular and perfectionist Beatle should find he no longer controlled even the way he sang his own songs. Paul decided at last to stop fighting against fighting.

He had completed his solo album in Scotland, with no editor but Linda and no help but from Linda, that untried musician, on backing vocals. In March he returned to London and rang up John, breaking a silence of almost six months.

'I'm doing what you and Yoko are doing,' Paul said. 'I'm putting out an album and I'm leaving the group, too.'

'Good,' John replied. 'That makes two of us who have accepted it mentally.'

Paul then notified Apple, or what remained of it, that he wanted his solo album, *McCartney*, to be released on 10 April. The date was vetoed by Klein and all the three other Beatles as clashing with the release of *Let It Be*, and also Ringo's first solo album, *Sentimental Journey*. Paul, suspecting Klein of sabotage, appealed directly to Sir Joseph Lockwood at EMI. Sir Joseph said he must accept the majority decision.

Ringo well-meaningly visited Cavendish Avenue to add his personal explanation to letters he had brought from John and George, confirming that Paul's solo debut would have to be postponed. Ringo, in his own subsequent High Court affadavit, described his dismay when Paul 'went completely out of control, prodding his fingers towards my face, saying, "I'll finish you all now," and, "You'll pay!" He told me to put on my coat and get out.'

The outburst showed Ringo, at least, what a gigantic emotional significance the *McCartney* album had for Paul. It is a testament to his eternal good nature that, after Paul threw him out, Ringo went straight back to John and George and talked them into giving Paul his way. Ringo's *Sentimental Journey* LP was brought forward and *Let It Be* put back so that *McCartney* could appear, as Paul now agreed, on 17 April.

Its release gave Paul the opportunity to do what John had been dissuaded from doing the previous October. Included with the album was a smiley yet barbed 'self-interview' in which he made clear that he was leaving the Beatles – at least, as clear as Paul could make anything:

> *Q:* Are all these songs by Paul McCartney alone?
>
> *A:* Yes, sir.
>
> *Q:* Did you enjoy working as a solo?
>
> *A:* Very much. I only had to ask me for a decision and I agreed with me. Remember Linda's on it too, so it's really a double act.
>
> *Q:* The album was not known about until it was nearly completed. Was this deliberate?
>
> *A:* Yes because normally an album is old before it comes out. (Aside) Witness 'Get Back'.

Q: Are you able to describe the texture or feel of the album in a few words?

A: Home. Family. Love.

Q: Will Paul and Linda become a John and Yoko?

A: No, they will become Paul and Linda.

Q: Is it true that neither Allen Klein nor ABKCO Industries have been or will be in any way involved with the production, manufacturing, distribution or promotion of the record?

A: Not if I can help it.

Q: What is your relationship with Klein?

A: It isn't. I am not in contact with him and he does not represent me in any way.

Q: What do you feel about John's Peace effort? The Plastic Ono Band? Giving back the MBE? Yoko's influence? Yoko?

A: I love John and respect what he does – it doesn't give me any pleasure.

Q: Are you planning a new album or single with the Beatles?

A: No.

Q: Is this album a rest away from the Beatles or the start of a solo career?

A: Time will tell. Being a solo album means it's the start of a new career and not being done with the Beatles it's a rest. So it's both.

Q: Is your break with the Beatles temporary or permanent, due to personal differences or musical ones?

A: Personal differences, business differences, musical differences but most of all because I have a better time with my family. Temporary or permanent? I don't know.

Q: Do you foresee a time when Lennon–McCartney become an active songwriting partnership again?

A: No.

Q: Did you miss the Beatles and George Martin? Was there a moment, e.g., when you thought: 'Wish Ringo was here for this break'?

A: No.

The announcement enraged John, who had longed to quit years ago but had always kept on in the band for the sake of their common good. Now here was Paul, as self-centred as ever, not only walking out when he felt like it but also making out he was first to want to. Or as John put it bitterly, saying he'd had enough long after everyone else had left the stage.

•

On 20 May, *Let It Be*, the Beatles' last film and final appearance together, received its British premiere simultaneously in London and Liverpool.

A vast hoarding had been erected over the London Pavilion, on which four faces, fenced off from each other, stared out with expressions of faint nausea befitting this one more perfunctory ordeal. In Liverpool, a civic welcome waited in the cinema foyer; the Lord Mayor, aldermen, dignitaries and old friends. The train supposed to be bringing the Beatles pulled in to Lime Street, but they did not alight from it. Nor did they from the train after that. The civic welcome waited for the next train, and the next.

The Beatles were gone, but how could they be when the screen showed them as always: together, advancing? It was their last trick to make those tired, year-old scenes, at Twickenham studios and in the Apple basement, seem fresh and exciting, full of promise for the future that so obviously could not be. *Let It Be* was their sad fading; it was also the desperate sadness that they must fade. It was Paul and John singing 'Two of Us', rather pale and subdued like marriage partners after a terrible row, admitting they had been 'chasing paper, getting nowhere', but now seemingly in agreement about being 'on our way home'. It was Paul when he sang 'The Long and Winding Road' in its proper version, with only Billy Preston's keyboard and himself on piano: his make-believe beard, his make-believe hobo suit, his great, round, regretful eyes. It was Paul again, singing 'Let It Be', the mollifying phrase of a Liverpool mother to a fractious child, as if he forgave and had been forgiven and everything would get better now.

It was the scene in Savile Row when lights still filled every Apple window, and the big white cars drew up outside. It was the day when clamour split the Mayfair skies; when people came across rooftops and climbed down fire escapes to look, and people in the streets stared upward. It was the old soldier in a pork pie hat whom the film crew stopped and asked for comment. 'Yus – well, the Beatles, what I say is, you can't beat 'em. They're out on their own. They're good people. I say, good luck to 'em.'

It was the rooftop concert with their hair blowing into their eyes, with Ringo in a red plastic mac, George in green trousers, John in a ladies' short fur coat. It was four musicians playing together as no four musicians ever could or ever would again. It was voices singing 'The One After 909', the way they used to on truant afternoons at Forthlin Road. It was slow-motion guitars in the biting wind as John summed up their gift to their generation, all those Second World War babies who'd thought there was nothing ahead but greyness and rationing. 'Everybody had a good time. Everybody had a wet dream. Everybody let their hair down. Everybody saw the sun shine . . .' It was 'Get Back' dying into discord as the police finally found their way up to the roof, as the drumbeat failed, the electricity was turned off, and the derisive Lennon voice speaking as if in mock humility to Larry Parnes, all those years ago at the Jacaranda Club:

'I'd like to thank you very much from the group and ourselves and I hope we passed the audition.'

PART FIVE

LASTING

20

'I just believe in me. Yoko and me'

The break-up, in fact, was to stretch over 15 months, between September 1969, when John told the other three privately that he wanted out, and December 1970, when Paul confirmed the split unequivocally by beginning unilateral legal action against Allen Klein. It was an odd period of limbo, with all four Beatles leading determinedly separate lives and billions of fans still hoping, even praying, for their reconciliation.

John and Yoko initially went to ground at Tittenhurst Park, their Georgian mansion in Sunningdale, Berkshire. The house was equipped with its own private studio where John could set to work on a second solo album without fear of anyone objecting to his wife's presence or creative input. To work with him he summoned Phil Spector, who had put the chaotic *Let It Be* album into releaseable shape, albeit to Paul's unforgiving disgust. These Tittenhurst sessions included a simple voice-and-piano track that was to become John's post-Beatles masterpiece. 'Imagine no possessions', he sang wistfully, forgetful of his rambling stately home and 72-acre estate. It was also at Tittenhurst that the famous 'Imagine' video was shot, with John seated at a white grand piano in a long, white room, and a white-gowned Yoko drawing back curtains as if on the vista of their new life together.

In March 1971, the British High Court granted Paul's suit to remove the Beatles' partnership from Klein's control and place it in the hands of a Receiver, meaning that the break between the four was now legal and irrevocable. The following September, John and Yoko closed the white drapes at Tittenhurst Park for the last time and moved to America.

Their ostensible reason was to win custody of Yoko's seven-year-old daughter, Kyoko, from her former husband, the American film-maker Tony Cox. Though originally well-disposed towards John, the eccentric Cox had undergone the first of a series of religious transfigurations, and now furiously execrated his ex-wife and her ex-Beatle spouse as ungodly dope fiends. When ordinary diplomatic methods failed, John and Yoko resolved to snatch Kyoko from her father who, by a bizarre twist, had lately become a disciple of the Maharishi Mahesh Yogi. While Cox attended a course with the Maharishi on the island of Majorca, the

Lennons abducted Kyoko from the children's crèche, but were forced to return her after spending some hours in police custody.

Their lawyers' advice was to seek legal guardianship of Kyoko in the American Virgin Islands, where Yoko had obtained her divorce from Cox. The order was granted, but could only be put into effect within the United States, where Cox, his second wife, Melinda, and Kyoko were now thought to be living. The Lennons therefore would have to take up residence in America.

It was meant to be only a temporary, pragmatic arrangement, but John had already made up his mind not to return to Britain. He had had enough of its intrusive media, its racist attacks on Yoko and the business meetings he described as 'rooms full of old men, smoking and fighting'. America not only promised refuge and relative anonymity, but still had magic as the heartland of his musical first love, rock and roll. He never forgot how, as a no-hope teenager, he would stand on the Liverpool Pier Head and gaze out over the grey waves of the Atlantic ocean, excited to think that 'the next place was America'.

Going to the opposite extreme of Tittenhurst Park, he and Yoko moved into what was little more than a glorified bedsitting-room in New York's West Village. More than ever like twins in their matching convict crops and sunglasses, both were soon immersed in the harsh radical politics that had elbowed aside Sixties-style Love and Peace. For John, it was as if the Statue of Liberty had reached down and touched him personally with her transfiguring beacon. The image-fettered pop star who had once been scared to voice even mild criticism of the Vietnam War now publicly allied himself to Black Power revolutionaries like Malcolm X and Angela Davis, and icons of the 'yippie' movement Jerry Rubin and Abbie Hoffman. The one-time male chauvinist who'd kept his first wife in child-rearing purdah became a vociferous convert to the feminist movement, writing a song based on Yoko's axiom 'Woman is the nigger of the world' that would appear on his 1972 album, *Sometime in New York City*.

His songwriting style had changed absolutely, from the allusiveness of 'Strawberry Fields Forever' and 'A Day in the Life' to graffiti-simple political tracts like 'Give Peace a Chance', 'Power to the People' and 'Happy Xmas (War is Over)', which was to top radio Christmas play-lists for ever afterwards. He was determined to put his Beatle past, and all its monstrous highs and lows, totally behind him; to prove that, unlike Elvis Presley, he could 'break out of the palace'. The message was hammered home by his new, acrid solo voice on an album with the Plastic Ono Band: 'I don't believe in Beatles . . . I just believe in me . . . Yoko and me . . . and that's reality.'

Another kind of exorcism was giving a marathon interview to Jann Wenner, whose *Rolling Stone* magazine had set new standards in thoughtful and analytical rock journalism. John's testament ran to 30,000 words and was later published as a book, *Lennon Remembers*. In it, he declared he had outgrown George Martin ('he's more Paul's sort of music than mine') and alleged that some of the worst 'shit' thrown at Yoko had come from Apple's Managing Director, Peter Brown, and – surprisingly – from George Harrison. Indeed, he largely blamed his and Yoko's recent resort to heroin on 'what the Beatles and their pals were doing to us'.

But Wenner's tentative question, 'You were really angry with Paul?', brought a strangely muted response. 'No, I wasn't angry,' John replied. 'I was just . . . shit! He's a good PR man, Paul. I mean, he's about the best in the world, probably. He really does a job . . .'

Even so, his bitterness against Paul continued to fester, for reasons that even now are difficult to fathom. True, Paul had displaced him as head Beatle, but only at the very end, when he himself could no longer be bothered. As he half-told *Rolling Stone*, he was furious about Paul's public resignation from the band on the *McCartney* album when he himself had effectively quit six months earlier. Having suppressed his own decision for the band's collective good, he felt Paul had stolen his thunder – and that mainly for the sake of publicising a new record. Yet even this does not explain his later remark to Yoko that no one had ever hurt him the way Paul hurt him. It almost suggests that, deep beneath the schoolboy friendship and the complementary musical brilliance, lay some streak of homosexual adoration that John himself never realised. He might have longed to get away from Paul, but he could never quite get over him.

Paul, too, had been far more wounded than he ever showed, and no longer cared about preserving diplomatic niceties. On the second McCartney solo album, *Ram*, was a veiled reference to John's having thrown away his talent by going off with Yoko ('You had your lucky break and you broke it in two . . .'). John's *Imagine* album – despite the plea for universal peace and brotherhood in the title track – launched a thermo-nuclear strike back at Paul with 'How Do You Sleep?' a title suggesting crimes almost in the realm of first-degree murder. The McCartney references were unmistakable and, often, cruelly unjust: 'The freaks was right when they said you was dead . . . The only thing you done was Yesterday . . .' There was even a two-fingered gesture of contempt for Paul's new outdoor life with Linda on their Scottish farm. The *Ram* album's cover had shown him in rural outdoor mode, holding down a ram by its curly horns. Inside the *Imagine* album jacket was a postcard picture of John, playfully wrestling with a pig.

To his credit, John realised that his life in the Beatles, and before, had left him in serious need of psychiatric help. Before leaving Britain, he and Yoko had signed up for extensive sessions with the therapist Arthur Janov, whose Primal Scream technique encouraged patients to vent emotion with the same directness as babies and animals. Consultations with Janov in Los Angeles had plumbed the deepest sources of John's anger and anguish – his abandonment by his parents when he was a toddler; his rediscovery of his mother, Julia, when he was a teenager, only to lose her at the hands of a speeding motorist just a few yards from his Aunt Mimi's house.

Primal Scream Therapy also finally overcame the stage-fright that had built up in him throughout the late Sixties – and had ultimately prevented the Beatles from making peace onstage together again. In August 1972, he gave a show at Madison Square Garden, dressed in military fatigues and letting loose all the emotions released by Arthur Janov in a song about Julia very different from the earlier ballad of that name. 'Mother you had me . . . but I never had you . . .' Half a lifetime later, the filmed version is still almost too painful to watch.

America under the early-Seventies presidency of Richard Nixon was a very different country from the one which had welcomed and adored the Beatles in 1964. John's public support for the Black Panthers and the yippies soon engaged the attention of an FBI still under the control of the paranoiac J. Edgar Hoover (whose penchant for wearing women's dresses none then suspected). Following the earlier lead of Scotland Yard's Special Branch, extensive and often farcical FBI dossiers were compiled on the Lennons as potential subversives; they were covertly followed and their telephones were bugged. In March 1972, the US Immigration Service declared John an 'undesirable alien' on the grounds of his conviction for cannabis possession in 1968, and ordered him to leave the country within 60 days. His ensuing four-year battle, first against deportation, then for resident-alien 'Green Card' status, confirmed his exile from Britain. For he knew that, were he to leave the US with these matters unresolved, he would never be allowed back in again.

He also continued to devote himself to Yoko's pursuit of Kyoko, though now careful to give the Immigration Service no further ammunition against him. In 1972, Tony and Melinda Cox were found to be living in Houston, Texas, where Cox had applied for legal guardianship of eight-year-old Kyoko – now renamed Rosemary. When the Lennons flew to Houston and presented their Virgin Islands custody order, the court ruled Cox to be a more suitable guardian, though it did grant Yoko visitation rights. Cox, however, refused to give up Kyoko-Rosemary for even those prescribed 10 days, and received an overnight prison sentence for contempt of court. On his release, he, Melinda and Kyoko-Rosemary once more disappeared without trace.

John and Yoko had by now exchanged their New York bedsit for an apartment in the Dakota building – alternatively known as 'the Dakotas' – at the corner of West 72nd Street and Central Park West. With its Gothic towers and mildew-green roof, the place bore a strange resemblance to some grimly grand Victorian bank or orphanage back home in Liverpool. It was so named because at the time of its construction in the mid-19th century, this corner of Central Park seemed to Manhattanites as wild and unfrequented as faraway North and South Dakota. Latterly, with its forbidding exterior and relatively low rents, it had become an abode of Upper West Side bohemians, actors and film directors. Before the Lennons' arrival, it was best known as the location for Roman Polanski's urban horror classic *Rosemary's Baby*.

Despite their public inseparability, the Lennons' marriage was running into trouble. Though still obsessively jealous if he thought Yoko even noticed another man – John felt himself under no similar obligation to be monogamous. Women had always thrown themselves at him, and still did so now, undeterred by Yoko's constant proximity. His infidelities grew ever more blatant. One night, he and Yoko went out to a party at the home of a mutual friend. Within a few minutes of their arrival, John was having sex with another woman in an adjoining room within earshot of everyone at the party including Yoko.

At the end of 1973, she ejected him from their Dakota apartment, though in a way that only Yoko could have devised. Both of them, she suggested, needed a breathing space after having been together virtually non-stop for more than five years. It was arranged that John should go to the West Coast for an indefinite period, accompanied by a pretty young Chinese-American woman named May Pang who had recently begun working jointly for Yoko and him. Prior to the trip, Yoko spoke privately to May and made it clear her duties were to include those of a replacement bedfellow. John himself seems to have remained blissfully unaware of how Yoko might simply be reeling him out on a fishing-line. 'I'd been married since I was a kid. Now I was a single guy. All I thought was "*whoopee*!"'

He was to spend something like a year in Los Angeles on what he would later call his 'Lost Weekend' (after the 1940s film noir classic), living in Bel Air and hanging out with music cronies like Phil Spector, Harry Nilsson, Elton John and Elton's lyricist Bernie Taupin. His favourite tipple was Brandy Alexander, a mixture of cognac and milk that found its way to the real Lennon as surely, and rather more rapidly, than any Primal Scream Therapy. 'After two Brandy Alexanders, John was wonderful,' his TV reporter friend Elliot Mintz remembered. 'You got all the old stories . . . he was hilarious . . . delightful. But after his third, he was just a plain ugly drunk . . .' One night, he was thrown out of LA's famous folk club, the Troubadour, for heckling the Smothers Brothers as they performed onstage. Another evening, mildly stoned, he provoked the kind of put-down he himself might once have delivered, by emerging from the Troubadour men's room with a Kotex sanitary-towel clamped to his forehead. 'Do you know who I am?' he slurred at a passing waitress. 'Yeah,' she snapped back. 'You're an asshole with a Kotex on his head.'

Periodically he would get in touch with Yoko and plead for another chance, a campaign that intensified when he tired of LA and returned to New York bringing the Lost Weekend to almost a year and a half. But thus far, Yoko had remained impervious. 'I'd been married twice before and divorced,' she remembered later. 'For me, that was what happened to marriages. They ended.' She, too, returned to the life of a 'single', dating a man considerably younger than herself.

For Bernie Taupin, however, the stories of Lennon debauchery and desperation on the Lost Weekend have been much exaggerated. 'All I know is that, every time I went around with him, he was perfectly normal. I remember going with him to see Bob Marley at the Roxy, and we had a great night . . . John was always very sweet and encouraging about the things Elton and I did, especially "Your Song". And he was incredibly modest about the fantastic things he'd done. He'd say things like "Er, I wrote this song called 'Across the Universe'. I dunno if you know it . . ."'

Elton John had by now become as massive a world attraction as the Beatles had been 10 years earlier. But, for all his stature as a performer, he remained at heart an inveterate record fan whose greatest thrill was meeting the musicians who had coloured his lonely boyhood in Pinner, Middlesex. The Beatles, above all, had inspired his earliest songwriting efforts with Taupin, often in outright *Sgt. Pepper* knock-offs with names like 'Regimental Sergeant-Major Zippo'. And, by a weird coincidence, the duo had been discovered by the Beatles' former music publisher, Dick James, proving that once-in-a-lifetime luck can strike the same person twice.

As Elton got to know John better, he was dismayed to see how his greatest idol's solo career seemed to be slipping into the doldrums. And, with the generosity and altruism that was to be a feature of his career, he decided to do something about it. The next Elton single was both a homage to John and a ruse to drag him back into the limelight. At Caribou studios, 9,000 feet up in the Colorado mountains, the ultimate Seventies glam-rock star recorded the ultimate Sixties spine-tingler, 'Lucy in the Sky with Diamonds', set to a modish reggae beat but otherwise almost eerily reminiscent of John's 1967 version. The composer himself joined the back-up rhythm section under a complex but easily crackable code-name, 'the Reggae Guitars of Dr Winston O'Boogie'. That December, it became Elton's third US number one.

John so enjoyed working, and playing, with his superstar fan that when he returned to the studio to make the album that would become *Walls and Bridges,* he asked Elton in to sing back-up vocals. The result of their collaboration was 'Whatever Gets You Thru' the Night', a scattergun rocker equally infused with John's acidity and Elton's pub-pianist good humour. As they listened to the playback, John said jokingly that if it was a hit, he'd sing it with Elton live onstage. By November, 'Whatever Gets You Thru' the Night' was at the top of the US chart – as it would prove, John's only number one outside the Beatles in his lifetime.

Elton's current sell-out American tour was scheduled to end with a gala concert at Madison Square Garden on Thanksgiving night, 28 November. It was the perfect moment for John to honour his promise, though the very idea scared him almost witless. He had not performed in public since a charity appearance two years earlier; in the meantime his old enemy, stage-fright, had come back worse than ever. A brief rehearsal with Elton and his band in New York did not do much to help calm his fears. He showed up at the Garden wearing dark glasses and a black suit more appropriate to a funeral parlour than duetting with glam-rock's answer to Liberace. Waiting backstage, he was so nervous that he went into the men's room and vomited. He even temporarily forgot the order of strings on his guitar and had to ask Davey Johnstone, from Elton's band, to tune it for him.

Just before showtime, a messenger delivered two identical gift boxes, one for him and one for Elton. Inside each was a white gardenia and a note: 'Best of luck and all my love, Yoko.' 'Thank goodness Yoko's not here tonight,' Lennon said. 'Otherwise I know I'd never be able to go out there.' He had no idea that, playing Cupid as well as Svengali, Elton had also invited Yoko to the concert and that she was seated in the front row with her current date.

Midway through the concert, Elton paused at the piano in his top hat decorated with outsize pheasant feathers. 'Seeing as it's Thanksgiving,' he said, 'we thought we'd make tonight a little bit of a joyous occasion by inviting someone up with us onto the stage . . .' In the wings, still hesitating, John turned to Bernie Taupin. 'He said "I'm not going out there unless you go with me,"' Taupin remembers. 'So I went forward a little way with him, then he sort of hugged me and I said "You're on your own."'

Also in the audience was Margo Stevens, the former 'Apple Scruff' who had progressed from camping outside Paul McCartney's house to working as Elton's housekeeper. Margo has never forgotten the moment when John walked – or, rather, was propelled – onstage. The house lights went up and all 16,000 people present rose to their feet in a spontaneous cheer. Only Yoko felt the moment to be one of less than pure euphoria. 'When John bowed, it was too quickly, and one too many times,' she remembers now. 'And I suddenly thought, "he looks so lonely up there."'

The John–Elton set was brief and, progressively, brilliant. John sang 'Whatever Gets You Thru' the Night', as promised, with Elton's back-up vocals like a friendly instructor keeping him on track. Then Elton sang his revisited 'Lucy', backed by John. Within a few minutes, his confidence was sufficiently restored to take a sly dig at Paul McCartney: 'We thought we'd do a number of an old, estranged fiancé of mine, called Paul . . .' The number was 'I Saw Her Standing There', Paul's kick-off track on the Beatles' first-ever album, from the days when Lennon and McCartney songs were interchangeable and as perfect, in their way, as early Picassos. 'Everyone around me was crying,' Margo Stevens remembers. 'John was hugging Elton, and Elton seemed to be crying, too.'

After the show, Yoko and her companion came backstage for what was supposed only to be a friendly word with John and his own date that evening. 'John and I started talking at once, each of us totally forgetting the person we were supposed to be with,' Yoko remembers. 'After that, he invited me to an art exhibition. We started dating all over again.'

•

They settled down, as they thought, to grow old together in their rambling apartment on the Dakota's seventh floor. In October 1975, the US Court of Appeals finally overturned the deportation order against John, ruling that the British law that convicted him of drug possession in 1968 had been unfair by American standards and paving the way for the Green Card that would allow him to stay in the country without further harassment. At the age of 41, despite the traumatic memory of three miscarriages, Yoko became pregnant again. On John's 35th birthday, she gave birth to a son whom they named Sean Ono Lennon.

The year had seen John release two further albums – *Shaved Fish*, a compilation of existing tracks including 'Instant Karma', 'Cold Turkey' and 'Mind Games', and *Rock 'n' Roll*, a nostalgic collection of four-chord classics from his boyhood in the Merseyside dance halls. He had also briefly found another songwriting partner in Elton John's main glam-rock rival, David Bowie. The result was 'Fame', Bowie's first number one single in America.

After Sean's arrival, quite spontaneously, John decided to opt out of the music business altogether and devote himself to parenthood. With

Yoko's help, he said, he finally felt secure enough to function without the golden armour of fame. 'My whole security and identity [had been] wrapped up in being a pop star. But Yoko told me, the same way she told me with the Beatles. That was one liberation for me. The other was that I didn't have to go on making records.' He delighted in the symmetry of including Gene Vincent's 'Be-Bop-a-Lula' on the *Rock 'n' Roll* album. For he'd sung that same song for the first time onstage at Woolton village in 1957, the day he'd first met Paul McCartney. He was leaving the business at exactly the same place he had come in.

From here on, he organised his whole life around Sean, feeding him, putting him to bed, establishing a routine for the little boy as settled and healthy as Aunt Mimi once had for him. He learned to cook and even bake bread – his triumph in his first successful loaf mingled with slight annoyance that it did not receive the kind of accolades he was used to. ('I thought, "Well, Jesus, don't I get a gold record or knighted or nothing?"') Having given him the child he had so much wanted, Yoko was content to play a secondary role with Sean. While John took on the role of 'househusband', Yoko became their business brain, a role in which she proved highly, though perhaps not unsurprisingly, effective.

They began to buy up other apartments in the Dakota, including a ground-floor suite which they turned into their office, Studio One, and another merely to serve as storage space for their vast accumulation of files and videos. They also bought a harbour-side mansion on Long Island, a Florida mansion that once had belonged to the Vanderbilt family, and a farm with a collection of prize Holstein cattle in upstate New York. Even if they had elected to sit still and do nothing, there was no danger of John's exchequer ever being 'down to its last £50,000'. Despite the feverishly changing fashions of Seventies pop, Beatles albums and compilations still sold incessantly the world over. A vast annual royalty-income was channelled to John from London via the Apple office – now merely a nest of busy accounting machines, supervised by the ever faithful and honest Neil Aspinall.

John's involvement with Sean also awoke guilty memories of Julian, the son by his first wife, Cynthia, whose childhood he had almost missed in the whirlwind of being a Beatle. Now in his early teens, Julian lived in the Welsh hill town of Ruthin with his mother and her new husband, an electrical engineer named John Twist. He was already showing an interest in music, singing and playing guitar. But, so far as he knew, he had left no mark on his faraway father other than as the alleged inspiration for 'Lucy in the Sky with Diamonds'.

Soon after Sean's birth, John invited Julian to New York and, over the next few years, made concerted efforts to rebuild a relationship with him.

One of the many presents that Julian brought home to Ruthin was a portable typewriter, given to him by Yoko. Cynthia took a certain grim pleasure in using it to write her autobiography, *A Twist of Lennon*, published in 1978. But the book itself was characteristically free of rancour, ending with words from the *I Ching*: No blame.

John's only other regular contact in Britain was Aunt Mimi, the resoundingly normal and conventional woman whose virtues he unconsciously carried within him, and who still could read him better than anyone else.

Since the late Sixties, Mimi had lived alone in a waterside bungalow in Poole Harbour, Dorset. She had never wanted to leave Liverpool or, indeed, her old home in Menlove Avenue, but in the end the pressure of Beatles fans had made it uninhabitable. One night John arrived at 'Mendips' to find the house under siege and Mimi, uncharacteristically, crumpled up in tears on the front stairs. Next day, he told her to choose a new house anywhere else in the country that she fancied.

Mimi being Mimi, the bungalow was several sizes short of the place he would have bought her without a thought. Inside, all was as neat and spotless as ever. On the television set stood a photograph of John in his Quarry Bank High School cap, the happy, sunny little boy Mimi preferred to remember. In a bureau drawer lay bundles of his childhood drawings and poems, not yet the stuff of sky-high Sotheby auctions. Beside the patio window stood an anomalously expensive and naff object, a cocktail cabinet shaped like an antique globe from Asprey's, the Bond Street jewellers. Each Beatle rushed to possess such a globe in the first, free-spending days when, as Ringo said, Asprey's used to feel 'just like Woolworth's'. Mimi was keeping John's in case he should ever want it again.

Even this secluded reach of Poole Habour was not completely safe from lingering Beatlemania. Sometimes, to Mimi's annoyance, passing pleasure boats would announce 'There's John Lennon's aunt's house' over the tannoy to their passengers. At regular intervals, groups of pilgrims would turn up on her doorstep from as far away as Japan and Australia. Mimi would give them a scolding, then invite them in, just as she once had Paul McCartney and George Harrison. A few even got to stay the night in the little spare-room bed whose history they did not dream. 'This used to be John's bed, you know,' Mimi would say casually when she brought their morning cup of tea.

As John moved into his late 30s, his regular telephone calls to Mimi began to show increasing signs of nostalgia about his childhood – even aspects of it that he'd detested at the time. He asked her to send him various family mementoes, including the Royal Worcester dinner service that used to be displayed in the front hall at 'Mendips', and a photograph of Mimi's late husband, his much loved Uncle George. Once, to her amazement, the one-time incorrigible school truant and outlaw asked for his old Quarry Bank cap with its Latin motto *Ex Hoc Metallo Virtutem.*

Despite the 5,000 miles between them, aunt and nephew could have furious rows. One of their worst – on the subject of repainting the bungalow – ended with Mimi hooting, 'Damn you, Lennon!' and slamming the phone down. A little later, John rang back, anxious and contrite. 'You're not still cross with me, Mimi, are you?' he asked.

New York has always allowed its large celebrity population a surprising measure of privacy and anonymity. John and Yoko became just another famous Uptown couple in semi-disguise, walking through Central Park, standing in line for pizza or having birthday parties at Tavern-on-the-Green. In a city then among the world's most violent, John said he never felt a moment's insecurity – though in late 1979, with chilling prescience, he and Yoko donated $1,000 to a fund to equip the city's police with bulletproof vests.

Where he had once seemed thoroughly Ono-ised, Yoko now grew increasingly Lennon-ised. After Sean's birth, John took to calling her 'Mother' with a frisson of old-time northern comedians like Al Read. Yoko looked forward as much as he did to settling down before the television on Sunday evenings to watch Channel 13's imported English classic serials like Daphne du Maurier's *Rebecca.*

In the daytime, when Sean was asleep and the latest batch of loaves were safely in the oven, he would put on a Japanese happi coat and lie before his ever flickering giant TV screen, reading or watching the Central Park trees outside his window change from the heathery palette of spring through summer's deep green to the russet and radicchio blaze of autumn. On the wall above his bed hung a state-of-the-art electric guitar which he'd bought just after getting back with Yoko but had hardly ever played. Next to it was the number 9 and a dagger made out of a bread knife dating from the American Civil War, as he said, 'to cut away the bad vibes – to cut away the past symbolically'. From time to time, he would glance at the guitar and wonder if he'd ever hold it again.

He was certainly no recluse, as would later be claimed: each day he saw dozens of people and spoke to dozens more on the telephone. He made regular trips with Yoko to their other properties and took extended foreign holidays with her and Sean (sometimes travelling under the alias 'Fred and Ada Gherkin'). But for most of his former friends in the music business, he had disappeared off the radar. When Mick Jagger moved into a Central Park apartment within sight of the Dakota, he dropped John a note, asking him to telephone. But no reply ever came. The only exception was Elton John, who continued to bask in the Lennons' gratitude for bringing them back together and whom they asked to be Sean's godfather.

Elton returned from his first visit to the Dakota complex acknowledging that the world now held an even bigger shopaholic than himself. 'I couldn't believe it. Yoko has a refrigerated room, just for keeping her fur coats. She's got rooms full of those clothes racks like you see at Marks and Spencer. She makes me look ridiculous. I buy things in threes and fours, but she buys things in fifties. The funny thing is, you never see her wearing them. She's always got up in some tatty old blouse . . .' Yoko bore no resentment for such observations, nor did she even when Elton poked gentle fun at her in a birthday card to John:

> Imagine six apartments
> It isn't hard to do.
> One is full of fur coats
> The other's full of shoes . . .

John was equally cut off from the Beatles' old circle, though the fate of Mal Evans, their former roadie, caused him a certain macabre amusement. In 1976, Mal died a bizarre death in Los Angeles, shot through a motel-room door by police who feared he was about to harm a young girl he had with him. His wife, Lil, who still lived in England, afterwards received a bill from the motel for dry-cleaning the carpet on which he'd died. Without reference to Lil, Mal's body was cremated and the ashes were posted to her – but en route the package got lost. It was a sickly appropriate footnote, since Mal had been working for the Post Office in Liverpool when he first joined the Beatles' entourage.

The general mellowing of John's character finally encompassed even Paul McCartney. Though still nothing like a fan of Paul's solo output, he could not help but admire his 'old estranged fiancé's' steely determination in creating a new band, Wings, in controversial partnership with his wife Linda and winning it a world wide fame almost comparable with the Beatles' own in their heyday. Paul, too, had been mellowed, by matrimonial stability as much as solo success, and, around 1978, decided it was time to make up with John. The way John later told it, Paul took to showing up on his doorstep unannounced with a guitar, as if hoping to recreate their schoolboy songwriting sessions in Allerton 20 years earlier. John, however, had more pressing grown-up concerns, like putting Sean to bed at his scheduled time. 'I'd let [Paul] in, but finally I said to him, "Please call before you come over. It's not 1956, and turning up at the door isn't the same any more."'

In fact, John and Yoko and Paul and Linda spent several evenings together, in a friendliness one would never have predicted for that uneasy foursome of the late Apple era. The McCartneys happened to be visiting one evening when *Saturday Night Live*, America's seminal TV satire show, turned its mocking gaze on the continuing multimillion-dollar offers for a Beatles reunion. Producer Lorne Michaels jokingly put up a fee of $3,200 if the four would reconvene before his cameras. John and Paul happened to be watching, and for a moment considered jumping in a cab and turning up at the SNL studios; then they decided they were too tired to bother.

John's retirement ended as impulsively as it began. He had been intrigued to see how the British punk rock movement of the late Seventies had filled the charts with noises wilder than any he and Yoko ever created on their private tapes. Post-punk female vocalists like Lene Lovich, Chrissie Hynde and, especially, the keening and warbling Kate Bush, seemed to John to be 'doing Yoko's act from 10 years ago'. The clincher, he said, came one night in a Bermudan dance club when he heard the B52s' 'Rock Lobster'. 'I said to meself, "It's time to get out the old axe and wake up the wife."'

Pulling down the barely used guitar from above his bed, he began to write new songs at frenetic speed. But this was no longer the angry, insecure John of the early Seventies, obsessed with making propaganda points and settling scores. It was a man approaching 40 with most of his old demons apparently exorcised, celebrating the joys of parenthood, home and monogamy as he had once so despised Paul McCartney for doing. 'Beautiful Boy' was a song about Sean and all the bedtimes and bath-times they had shared. 'Watching the Wheels' was a view from his Dakota retreat, thankful he was 'no longer in the game'. 'Woman' was both an apology and a tribute to Yoko ('after all, I'm forever in your debt') while 'Starting Over' affirmed that for him their love was 'still special'.

They planned a double album of his-and-her songs, naming it *Double Fantasy* after the freesia John had seen in Hong Kong's botanical gardens. To symbolise the new beginning, he chose not to release it on the Apple label, as all his previous solo albums had been. Instead, he went to David Geffen, creator of the Asylum label and, later, inspirational driving force behind the hugely successful Warner-Elektra-Asylum conglomerate. Geffen won John to his new, eponymous label, not with huge cash advances but with a guarantee of personal care and sensitivity.

With *Double Fantasy* set for release, the doors of the Dakota, shut and padlocked for so long, were thrown open wide. The journalists who stampeded there from every corner of the world were equally astonished and charmed by the new John. Yoko had got his weight down and – for Sean's sake – even persuaded him to give up his incessant Gauloises cigarettes. Posing for *Rolling Stone*'s star photographer Annie Leibovitz, he looked more youthful than at any time since Brian Epstein first buttoned him into a round-collared suit. Even Yoko, not one for idle flattery, was moved to exclaim, 'Hey – you're even better looking now than when you were a Beatle.'

To every interviewer, from *Newsweek* magazine to BBC Radio One, he sounded the same top note of re-energised optimism. 'I am going to be 40 and life begins at 40, so they promise. And I believe it, too. Because I feel fine. I'm, like, excited. It's like 21 – you know, hitting 21. It's like, "Wow! What's going to happen next?"'

The only middling sales of *Double Fantasy* did not dampen John's spirits. His fortieth birthday behind him, he and Yoko started work on a follow-up album at New York's Hit Factory studios – a home-from-home for the Lennons now that Yoko had decorated one of its rooms like an Egyptian temple. The backing musicians were expected to share John's new healthy regimen, exchanging their normal drugs, cigarettes and booze for sushi, green tea and shiatsu massages.

The evening of 8 December 1980 John had set aside to work on one of Yoko's new tracks at the Hit Factory. Ordinarily, he preferred to hop in a yellow cab to the studio, but tonight Yoko had called up one of the limousines she kept on permanent 24-hour standby. Outside their building's Gothic front arch stood a little knot of the fans that John called 'Dakota Groupies'. As he walked out to the car, a pudgy young man in a Russian-style fur hat proffered a copy of *Double Fantasy* and asked him to autograph it. A bystander photographed John scribbling a signature while the pudgy young man looked on.

His name – henceforward destined always to be spoken in full like those of John Wilkes Booth and Lee Harvey Oswald – was Mark David Chapman. And his 25-year life history, when it came to be written, would show he was almost as perfect an example as Charles Manson of the way the sunny, smiling Sixties could turn bad.

Born in 1955, in Fort Worth, Texas, the son of an Air Force sergeant, he had spent a rootless childhood and adolescence living variously in Texas, Indiana and Virginia. A lonely, introverted boy, mocked and bullied by his schoolfellows, he sought refuge in his imagination, inventing a world populated by 'Little People' where he could enjoy both status and control. As a teenager, he got into drugs, experimented with LSD and became a devout Christian. But what coloured his mind above all was the music of the Beatles.

He was no graceless, hopeless nerd, as he would often later be portrayed. Despite meagre academic qualifications, he became for a period a valued worker for the YMCA organisation, helping to resettle Vietnamese refugees, or 'Boat People', and spending a hazardous time in Beirut during the first stages of its mid-Seventies civil war. He received commendations for his work and on one occasion had his hand shaken by President Gerald Ford. Settling in Honolulu, he was hospitalised for depression after a suicide attempt, but seemed to make a full recovery. In 1979 – in an eerie unconscious emulation of his still-unchosen victim – he married a Japanese-American woman several years his senior.

John Lennon's emergence from retirement turned Chapman's former near-worship of him into contempt first, then hatred. He felt personally betrayed that the man who had sung 'Imagine no possessions' now accumulated costly real estate and herds of prize cattle. His parallel obsession was with Holden Caulfield, the anarchic 16-year-old narrator-hero of J. D. Salinger's *The Catcher in the Rye.* The fantasy grew in his mind that, once he had made an end to John, he would step into the pages of Salinger's novel, transfigured into Caulfield.

So, on the first weekend of December 1980, he said goodbye to his wife, Gloria, and flew out of the Hawaiian sun, bound for New York with a .38 calibre handgun in his baggage. He would later tell his interrogators he had intended to shoot John during their first encounter early on the evening of 8 December. But John's niceness about signing his *Double Fantasy* album temporarily disarmed him.

John that night was in particularly good spirits, feeling that Yoko had at last begun to receive proper respect as a musician in her own right. When they left the Hit Factory and headed back to the Dakota, shortly before 11 p.m., he carried a tape of her new song, 'Walking on Thin Ice'. As he climbed out of the limo and walked under the Gothic arch, a voice softly called 'Mr Lennon?' Mark David Chapman stepped forward with the levelled .38 and pumped five shots into his back.

Inside the Dakota's entrance hall, the night doorman, Jay Hastings, heard the fusillade of shots. A moment later John staggered in with 'a horrible confused expression on his face', followed by Yoko, screaming, 'John's been shot! John's been shot!' Hastings thought it was some kind of macabre joke until John collapsed onto the floor, scattering cassette tapes around him. Hastings tore off his own tie to try to use it as a tourniquet to stem the bleeding, but did not know where to begin. He dialled 911, then knelt beside John to give what comfort he could. Within minutes, three police squad cars were at the scene. Chapman still stood on the sidewalk, calmly re-reading *The Catcher in the Rye* for the umpteenth time.

When no ambulance arrived, a police car was used to take John to Roosevelt Hospital at 59th Street and 9th Avenue. A few minutes after his arrival, he was pronounced dead.

Away across the time zones in Poole, Dorset, his Aunt Mimi awoke, switched on the radio and heard someone talking about him. Mimi's first thought, as so often down the decades, was, 'Oh, Lord! What's he done *now*?'

•

Five months later, I walked into the lobby of the Drake Hotel, having just been interviewed about the Beatles on ABC-TV's *Good Morning America* show. Awaiting me at the front desk was a message to call a number I did not recognise. 'Studio One,' said the voice that answered. A moment later, another, so-familiar, voice came on the line. 'Hi, this is Yoko. What you said about John was very nice. Maybe you'd like to come over and see where we were living.'

I remember how glorious was that spring afternoon of what now must be termed New York's good old days. Balmy sunshine lightened even the Dakota's drab stonework and the heavy iron vases along its Central Park facade, now cheerily planted with red geraniums. Outside the Gothic arch on West 72nd Street, tourists with cameras lingered around America's most famous assassination site after Deeley Plaza. Another Liverpool-Victorian touch is a kind of small sentry-box with a coppery metal finish, from which a security guard keeps 24-hour watch. Its occupant was bundled firmly inside it, as though too squeamish to look at the killing place, barely 10 feet away.

Everything possible had been done to mitigate the pain and shame of this seemingly ultimate Manhattan tragedy. Despite psychiatric opinion that he might be schizophrenic, Mark David Chapman – arrayed in two bulletproof vests to protect him from tit-for-tat reprisals by Lennon fans – had pleaded guilty to second-degree murder. He was now serving '20 years to life' in New York State's Attica Penitentiary where, seven years earlier, 43 inmates had died during the worst riot in US prison history. Ironically, one of John's first stage appearances after settling in America had been a charity concert for the Attica riot's bereaved wives and children.

I had not seen Yoko since the Apple era's final days – and, indeed, at first hardly recognised her. Grief had played the cruel trick it does on so many widows of making her look better than her years. The formerly unkempt frizzy hair was now tied back as neatly as any lady lawyer's or Wall Street banker's. In place of her old, trying-too-hard mini-skirts and hot-pants were sleek black trousers, high-heeled boots, a black shirt and loosened tie. The face which once seemed so implacably humourless frequently softened into smiles, even when discussing the most painful things. The once-flat little voice was full of John's sayings and phraseology, and cosy north-of-England usages like 'cuppa tea'.

She admitted feeling that with John's death, his whole character had somehow been subsumed into her. Having enjoyed 20–20 vision all her life, she suddenly found herself as myopic as he used to be. She also developed his raging sweet tooth. 'John was the one who loved chocolate; I hardly ever used to touch it. But on the day after he was killed, all I wanted to do was eat chocolate. Elton [John] was so sweet; he sent me an enormous chocolate cake. My diet went crazy for about a month – nothing but chocolate and mushrooms.'

We talked for almost two hours in Yoko's office at Studio One, a long, high-ceilinged room decorated with small trees, white sofas and pastel-shaded Art Deco lamps. She sat behind a huge inlaid desk, in a chair modelled on the throne of Pharaoh Tutankhamun. The ceiling was a trompe l'oeil panorama of lazily drifting clouds. 'Above us only sky', I couldn't help thinking.

She still had not come to terms with no longer being hated – with having changed overnight from a figure of poisonous ridicule to one of monumental tragedy. As she told me, hundreds of messages continued to pour into the Dakota each day, a goodly number from women who, as teenage Beatles fans, had once screamed 'Chink' and offered her yellow roses with the thorns uppermost, but who now wished to thank her for making John happy according to his lights, and to sympathise in her inexpressible loss.

She could even smile bleakly at the horrible irony of John's being taken just as he was feeling so fit and rejuvenated, and new doors seemed to be opening on every side. 'After all those years of not smoking and losing weight and trying to keep healthy by eating the right foods . . . Since December, I've been telling Sean, "Eat whatever you like. It doesn't matter."

'And he was so happy. Both of us were. A few days before it happened, I remember thinking, "This is all so good. I wonder how long it can go on being as good as this."'

She referred to the other former Beatles wrily as 'the in-laws', something else she must have picked up from John. There was no disguising her profound bitterness against Paul McCartney, though she said no more than repeating John's cryptic remark about how much Paul had 'hurt' him. It had also deeply offended her that, after John's death, Ringo was the only ex-Beatle to fly to New York and offer her his condolences personally.

After our talk, Yoko sent me on a tour of the seventh-floor apartment where she and Sean still lived together. My guide was Fred Seaman, the same assistant who signed the polite turn-down I had received when I first asked the Lennons for an interview. I remember thinking that he seemed the ideal factotum for someone like Yoko in her present circumstances: soft-footed, soft-mannered, infinitely attentive, caring and trustworthy.

And so, five months later than I could have wished, I finally got to see where they were living. I saw the vista of high-ceilinged white rooms with their stunning view of skyscrapers set down as though at random among the Central Park treetops. From the Strawberry Fields memorial garden directly below came a succession of small glints and flashes as visitors used pocket mirrors and other shiny objects to heliograph messages of sympathy to Yoko.

I saw the kitchen where John had learned to bake bread, a cosy domestic nucleus no different from any other wealthy New Yorker's apart from the wall painting of himself, Yoko and toddler Sean in Superman costumes, soaring upward hand-in-hand. I saw the room devoted to Egyptian relics, including a full-size gold mummy in a case, and the bentwood hatstand on which John had hung his old school cap, and the Yoko artworks and sculpture dating back to their first cautious, awkward encounters in London. A thin perspex column supporting four silver spoons bore the inscription 'Three spoons, Y.O. 1967'. I remembered how John always used to say that what attracted him first had been the humour in her work. Maybe it really was there all along.

I saw the little side room where he used to lie and 'watch the trees change colour', now empty but for some cardboard cartons and the giant-screen TV set he'd had specially shipped from Japan. Along the hall was a triangular-shaped room, full of circular clothes racks and resembling some ghostly boutique. Here with the care of a museum curator – the last quality one would have suspected in him – John had preserved everything he'd ever worn since the Sixties, from Swinging London military tunics and cloaks to agitprop fatigues, with their attendant floppy-brimmed fedoras, denim caps, boots and shoes. I even saw, or fancied I did, the knitted scarf that Stu Sutcliffe, 'the fifth Beatle', had given him *circa* 1961. The same thought kept recurring as I followed Fred Seaman around: this is the only time I'll ever see all of this.

For the most part, Yoko played her new role as rock's most tragic widow with a restraint of which few had ever suspected her capable. Her replies to the grieving millions were limited to brief, dignified communiqués, asking them to keep alive John's ideals of peace and brotherhood, and entreating some space to mourn him in private. She became a familiar, forlorn figure in Central Park, walking the paths she and John once had arm-in-arm, wrapped in a white fur coat and dark glasses to hide the tears none yet had seen, nor ever would.

Yet under the widow's weeds, the old performance artist had lost none of her compulsion to shock. Two years after John's death, she released a solo album called *Seasons of Glass* whose cover showed the bullet-shattered and bloodstained glasses he had still been wearing in his dying moments. Many were offended by what seemed tasteless and cynical exploitation, though some were willing to interpret it as an extreme form of therapy.

Yoko had made it clear she was not willing to settle for merely being the guardian of the Lennon shrine, but that she intended to continue the careers in which John had so encouraged her. She put her artworks on display at leading galleries, few of which could now refuse her, and went on releasing albums. Without John to give them melody and accessibility – much as Paul McCartney had once done for him – their sales were never spectacular. But Yoko harboured no doubts concerning her musical talent. In 1990, John's solo music was collected in a memorial four-CD set. When Yoko's collected work appeared soon afterwards, the set ran to six CDs.

She made efforts to reinforce the new, favourable view of her, taking Sean on a trip to Liverpool in 1983 to visit Beatles landmarks like Strawberry Fields, and returning in 1990 for a concert to mark the fiftieth anniversary of John's birth. More positive vibes were created that same year when, helped by Sean, she re-recorded 'Give Peace a Chance' as a protest against the Gulf War. At other times, she seemed to show her old total disregard for public and media opinion. John's public was deeply offended when she allowed his name to appear on a range of mugs, plates and jigsaw puzzles. Uncomfortable echoes of *Seasons of Glass* were stirred at a Yoko exhibition in Los Angeles when a replica of John's broken and bloody glasses went on display bearing a price tag.

But Yoko, too, was to learn something about being exploited. In the years immediately following John's death, a succession of one-time Dakota employees – aides, gofers, tarot-readers and the like – produced trashy books on their life with the Lennons, usually portraying Yoko as a scheming, manipulative virago. The worst betrayal came from Fred Seaman, the soft-footed young man who had been one of her two most trusted personal assistants. It later emerged that, just a day after John's death, Seaman had begun walking out of the Dakota with bags full of his diaries, drawings and correspondence, and feeding them to an accomplice to be processed into a book. He was charged with theft, received five years' probation and was prevented from quoting from any of the letters or diaries in the book he persuaded a New York publisher to bring out in 1991.

In 1988, Albert Goldman published *The Lives of John Lennon*, branding John as an epileptic, schizophrenic, autistic killer, thug, wife-beater and recluse whose entire musical oeuvre had been founded on the melody line from 'Pop Goes the Weasel'. A few weeks after the book appeared, despite all my expectations I found myself back in Yoko's Studio One office with the trees, the white sofas and the chair like Tutankhamun's throne. Seated beside her was a teenage boy with oriental almond eyes but an unmistakable twist of Britishness around the mouth. I realised I was to be the first writer to meet Sean Lennon, by now aged 13.

Yoko had made no attempt to sue Goldman for his many libellous references to her, nor to bring an injunction that would have removed the book from sale. Her non-reaction was seen as further evidence of her toughness and imperviousness to criticism. But to me she confessed the book had so devastated her that she'd seriously thought of committing suicide and had been held back only by the thought of Sean. Wasn't it a mistake, I asked, for her not to have uttered a single word of denial? 'I am in the position of someone who's been punched 500 times,' she answered. 'There are so many allegations against John, I could never deal with them all in one interview. If I answer just a few, people might say "What about the others? Maybe they are true."'

I reflected, but did not say, that it seemed less than wise strategy from the many high-priced advisers at her disposal. Sean corroborated that, in his very clear memory, John had not been the volcanic domestic tyrant and recluse portrayed by Goldman, but a conscientious, loving and laughing dad.

Yoko's main biographical service to John was authorising the respected film director David Wolpert to make a documentary, *Imagine: John Lennon*, which had a worldwide cinema release also in 1988. Firmly suppressing all her own ideas about avant garde film-making, she gave Wolpert a free hand to produce a clear and comprehensive portrait which unwittingly rebutted several of Albert Goldman's crazier allegations in *The Lives of John Lennon*. Goldman had asserted, for example, that John suffered from a total lack of motor co-ordination that amounted to autism. One of the film's early scenes shows him at work in the studio at Tittenhurst Park and, with lightning reflexes, catching a wad of song-sheets as it slips off his music-stand. Yoko had told me that, in fact, he was double-jointed and could fold his limbs into the most demanding yoga positions without effort.

Wolpert's film also includes the touching scene when John confronts a young American hippy who has been found living rough in the Tittenhurst grounds. For about 10 minutes, he talks to the boy, trying to persuade him that there's nothing godlike about John Lennon nor mystical truth to be disinterred from his song lyrics. The encounter has an almost New Testament quality – Jesus this time preaching unbelief. Finally, he realises that it's hopeless and asks whether the vagrant is hungry. The answer is a shamefaced nod. 'OK,' John says to the watching musicians and security people. 'Let's give him something to eat.'

Perhaps the saddest casualty was John's elder son, Julian, for whom all of this cruelly echoed what had happened to his father at the same age, 17. Having been given away by his mother as a toddler, John had just been getting to know her again when she was knocked down and killed a few yards from Aunt Mimi's front gate. In the same way, Julian had virtually lost his father in infancy and found him again as a teenager, only to be robbed of him a second time.

The Dakota apartment, when I first saw it, had photographs of Julian and Sean displayed in equal prominence. But with John no longer around, Julian could hardly expect the same treatment from his stepmother that she gave to her own son. Although Yoko made him an allowance and still invited him on visits, their relationship quickly deteriorated. Behind her back Julian took to calling her 'Old Okey-Cokey'.

A young man named Lennon who could sing and play guitar was something the recording industry could hardly pass up. Julian's debut album, released in 1984, revealed some songwriting talent and enough of the familiar Lennon vocal rasp to compel attention. His first single, poignantly entitled 'Too Late for Goodbyes', reached number six in Britain, though, surprisingly, it failed to make the American Top 40. He appeared in Chuck Berry's film autobiography, duetting with Berry on John's old favourite, 'Johnny B. Goode', and in 1991 had a second UK number six single with the pro-environment song 'Saltwater'.

After that, his career seemed to lose momentum. He knocked about the social scene with eligible young women in London, New York and Monte Carlo, where he acquired a share in a harbourside restaurant, La Rascasse. With increasing bitterness, he accused Yoko of withholding his rightful share in his father's estate and at one point even threatened legal action against her. Though their financial differences seemed to have been quietly settled, Julian remained resentful that personal keepsakes like John's guitars had not been passed on to him. His next album, *Photograph Smile*, came out in 1998 – ironically on the same day as *Into the Sun*, the debut album of his half-brother, Sean. The critics' view was that Sean's effort had the edge.

To mark the twentieth anniversary of John's death in December 2000, Julian put a message onto his website, revealing undiminished pain and anger towards the father he almost never had. John's dedication to love and peace, he said, 'never came home to me'.

When the Rock 'n' Roll Hall of Fame gave John a Lifetime Achievement award in 1994, Paul was chosen to read the citation. His speech was an open love-letter to his old partner; at its conclusion, he embraced Yoko and Sean, symbolising an end to all the old bitterness between their two houses. A significantly short time afterwards came the Beatles' 'reunion' on record, with Paul, George and Ringo playing back-up to some John solo vocal tapes provided by Yoko, and the multi-part TV documentary firmly airbrushing out all Beatle wives and girl friends but Yoko.

That year, 1995, found me back at the Dakota for a third time. Yoko by now had a permanent man friend, an amiable antiques dealer named Sam Havadtoy, and, at 62, looked better than ever, though she had taken to chain-smoking thin, dark cigarettes. My ostensible purpose was to interview her about the album she had just made in partnership with Sean, by now aged 19. But during our talk, by looks more than words, she made it clear that the reconciliation with Paul had been for the sake of business only, and that there was still a chasm of bitterness between them.

Our conversation also touched on the subject of Kyoko, the eight-year-old daughter Yoko had lost, and who had lost her as traumatically as John had lost Julia and Julian had John. After Kyoko's father, Tony Cox, absconded from Houston with her in 1972, the two had completely vanished. All John and Yoko's subsequent efforts to trace them had been in vain. Whatever her private feelings, the subject seemed to be a closed book with Yoko, although after John's death she continued to place newspaper advertisements each year on Kyoko's birthday, appealing to her to get in touch. 'Basically,' Yoko told me with a bleakly expressionless look, 'we're not in contact at all.'

Two years later, in November 1997, Kyoko finally contacted her mother by telephone from Denver, Colorado. Now 33 and married to a devout Christian, she had given birth to her first child, a daughter, only a few days before. As she was to explain later, 'I didn't think it right to become a mother without at least letting my mother know I'm alive and well.'

Kyoko's history in the intervening years had been a bizarre one. While she and her father were moving around the world as fugitives, Tony Cox had abandoned fundamentalist Christianity and joined an extreme Doomsday sect known as The Walk. Kyoko had been submerged in the cult and taught that her mother and John Lennon were 'the personification of evil'.

It was to be no dramatic, sobbing mother–daughter reunion. For a year after her initial contact, Kyoko kept her distance, speaking to Yoko only in phone calls initiated by her. By 1998, they had built up sufficient rapport for a face-to-face meeting. Not for three years more did Yoko get to meet her granddaughter, Emi – a name accidentally reminiscent of the Beatles' original record company. Photographs of the occasion showed Kyoko to be a cosy, uncomplicated-looking woman, and Emi a pretty and secure-looking child. The entranced Yoko reportedly indicated to friends that Emi would become joint heir to the £400m Lennon fortune along with Sean.

Not all visitants from the past were quite so welcome. In 2000, the world heard again from John's killer, Mark David Chapman, serving 20 years to life in Attica. Kept largely in isolation for fear of revenge attacks by fellow inmates, Chapman had received a non-stop torrent of letters which he never answered but nonetheless filed meticulously in his cell. Although most came from Beatles fans wishing him in Hell, a good proportion were from would-be celebrity stalkers saying they were 'fans' of his, or women professing romantic interest and asking if they could visit him.

Having served the minimum of his tariff, Chapman was now eligible for parole. For an unreal moment, the possibility arose of his being back on the streets again at around the twentieth anniversary of John's death. His application was denied, however, after a press furore and a 'victim-impact' statement from Yoko saying that she, Sean and Julian would all fear for their lives if he were set free.

My last meeting with Yoko, in March 2003, brought this book to a full circle more neatly than I could ever have imagined. It was by that time four years since Paul McCartney's old family home, 20 Forthlin Road, Allerton, had been acquired by the National Trust, restored to its character during Paul's boyhood and opened to the public as a site of historical interest. But for some reason, no such sanctification had been given to 'Mendips', the mock-Tudor villa in Menlove Avenue where John was brought up by his Aunt Mimi. Though a magnet for Lennon pilgrims from all over the world, it remained in private ownership until 2002, when the death of its long-time owner finally brought it onto the property market. Various plans for the house were mooted, including one to turn it into an hotel with John's old bedroom forming part of the honeymoon suite. The idea so horrified Yoko that she bought Mendips for £150,000 and presented it to the National Trust. She also paid the £75,000 cost of its restoration and made an endowment to cover its operating costs and maintain a permanent live-in custodian.

One can now therefore belatedly examine every detail of the genteel home which that professed 'working-class hero' never got completely out of his system. Here is the 'morning room' with its defunct servants' bells where Mimi first put him as a baby, tying him into an armchair with a scarf. Here is the rather chilly formal dining-room; the comfortable front lounge, the half-timbered hallway with its Spode and Coalport china plates; the glass front porch to which Mimi banished him for so many hours of solitary guitar practice. Here is the sub-baronial staircase to the seven-by-ten foot room, with its red-quilted bed and pin-ups of Elvis and Brigitte Bardot, where he read alone for hours or drafted the first eccentrically spelt versions of songs and stories that one day would captivate the world.

Virtually everything is authentic. Family members to whom Mimi left furniture or ornaments in her will have been contacted by the Trust and persuaded to lend their bequests in perpetuity. Replicas have been needed mainly for the items that, in the last months of his life, John nostalgically asked Mimi to send to him in New York – for instance, an antique wall-clock inscribed 'George Toogood, Woolton Tavern' that belonged to his beloved Uncle George. To replace it, Yoko commissioned a custom-made exact copy. When this did not quite meet her standards, another clock was made from scratch. The front door is also a replica, the original having been bought some years ago by a Lennon fanatic in Japan.

Our meeting took place when Yoko came from New York to perform the official opening of the house under its National Trust blue plaque, and show around a group of children from John's first school, Dovedale Primary. After previous conversations at the great white Dakota apartment and under Studio One's trompe l'oeil clouds, it felt ineffably strange now to be facing her in a couple of Deco armchairs in Mimi's old front lounge.

She had recently turned seventy, but looked a good twenty years younger with her cropped, lightened hair, chic black trouser suit and trendy thick-soled boots. In *Vanity Fair* magazine some weeks earlier the social commentator Dominick Dunne, covering the latest court hearing in the Fred Seaman saga, had gone so far as to call her 'a dish'. A far cry indeed from racist taunts of 'Chink!' and 'Yellow!' and yellow roses offered to her with thorns turned uppermost.

Naturally uppermost in Yoko's mind was the current war in Iraq – the long-delayed outcome of '9/11' and George W. Bush's King Lear threats – and how fiercely John would have hated and opposed it. She had responded, just as he would have done, with giant billboards in London and New York saying IMAGINE PEACE. There was also a sense of *déjà-vu*, or *déjà entendu*, in the way some radio stations were currently banning 'Imagine' from their playlists for fear of subverting the Anglo-American war effort. But nothing could stop John's voice from getting through – even at a Paul McCartney show. During his Paris concert the following night, Paul was to be temporarily nonplussed by a spontaneous audience chorus of 'Give Peace a Chance'.

Even the spartan little bedroom upstairs, Yoko felt, could be another Lennon message to posterity. 'A lot of young people might feel they can't do much on their own because they don't have a big enough room. But I'd like to say to them: "John only had that small room, but it nurtured him enough to go out and change the world. Maybe you can do the same."' A few weeks later, she was to have her first ever American hit with a dance version of 'Walking on Thin Ice' – the song on the tape that fell from John's hands as Chapman's bullets struck him. Almost his last words, indeed, had been to predict it would do well.

I once asked Yoko what most reminded her of John, apart from his picture or his voice on record. She replied that she thought of him every time she put on a loose-fitting shirt or T-shirt. This she always did as he had shown her, tucking it tight inside the belt, then raising both arms at once to make it billow out in symmetrical folds around the waist.

Love was ever made of such commonplace detail. Even for John and Yoko.

21

'The freaks was right when they said you was dead'

The blandly indifferent smile that Paul McCartney turned on the break-up was merely camouflage for someone who hated showing weakness, betraying real emotion or admitting the world was other than the happy-go-lucky, sunshiny place he portrayed in his music. Whatever he might pretend, it was a far more devastating moment for Paul than for any of the others.

He who for years had known nothing but golden success now seemed to be staring at comprehensive failure on every front. He had failed to make a success of Apple, failed to carry through his choice of a new manager for the Beatles, failed in all his efforts to steer the band past the fatal shoals of John's indifference, failed to keep control of his own music, failed above all in his lifelong vocation as Mister Nice Guy. The three individuals who were once closer than family to him had ganged up against him, outvoted, isolated and sidelined him and were now ranged against him in implacable hostility.

Typically, it would be years before Paul revealed what an effect all this had on even his seemingly boundless confidence and self-esteem. In 2001, during a television interview with his daughter, Mary, he finally admitted having felt that with the Beatles' disintegration 'I'd lost the framework for my whole working life . . . I just didn't know what to do. I started staying up all night and staying in bed all day. I stopped shaving, I started drinking Scotch and I sort of went crazy . . . Looking back, I guess I nearly had a breakdown.'

What pulled him through was the new family life he had established with Linda, their new baby daughter, Mary, and Linda's seven-year-old daughter, Heather, whom he had always treated as his own. For months the four of them remained virtually dug in at the farm near Campbeltown, Argyllshire, which Paul had bought in 1966 while he was still with Jane Asher. The unspoilt mountain country around the tract of water known as the Mull of Kintyre was the furthest possible extreme from the urban pressures and strife of the past six years. Paul had no doubt that it saved his soul and, maybe, his sanity.

The received wisdom for years afterwards was that, in the sniping between Paul and John, both on and off their respective solo albums, Linda played only a passive, involuntary role. While understandably prompting Paul to loosen all lingering matrimonial ties with the Beatles, she was thought to have stayed firmly apart from the spats between him on one side and John and Yoko on the other. However, a long handwritten letter from John, sent from Tittenhurst Park in 1970, reveals Linda to have been in the very thick of the feud. Pointedly addressed to 'Dear Paul and Linda', it is a reply to a previous missive written by the couple in tandem, and is just as vitriolic towards him as towards her. 'I was reading your letter and wondering what cranky, middle-aged Beatles fan wrote it ... I kept looking at the last page to find out ... What the hell – it's Linda!'

John berates the two of them equally for the 'shit you and the rest of my kind, unselfish friends laid on Yoko and me since we have been together – it may have sometimes been a bit more subtle or should I say middle-class – but not often. We both "rose above it" ... quite a few times and forgave you two – so it's the least you two can do for us ... Linda, if you don't care what I say – shut up!'

Yet again he reminds them bitterly that he had been the first to want to leave the Beatles, but had agreed to stay on for the common good. In passing, he also aims a swipe at Linda's father, Lee, and brother, John, for their brief participation in the band's management and Apple. 'Mrs McCartney – the c**ts asked me to keep quiet about [wanting to quit]. Of course the money angle is important – to all of us – especially after all the petty shit that came from your insane family and God help you and Paul – see you in two years – I reckon you'll be out by then ...'

The letter ends on an almost schizophrenic note, signing off 'in spite of it all, love to you both ...' then adding a furious PS and a line of dots and exclamation marks at the further slight John perceives in their letter not having been addressed jointly to him and Yoko.

To begin with, Paul's solo output showed little sign of missing John. The *McCartney* album and its 1971 successor, *Ram* (also billed as a 'partnership' with Linda), each contained work as good as any he'd ever done inside the Beatles. In March 1971, he reached number two in the UK singles chart with 'Another Day', a narrative song about a lovelorn spinster ('Every day she takes a morning bath, she wets her hair ...') evoking both 'Eleanor Rigby' and 'She's Leaving Home'. The following August, he had his first American solo number one with 'Uncle Albert/ Admiral Halsey', a novelty number with some of the same northern music-hall atmosphere as *Sgt. Pepper*.

But having solo hits in the intervals of family and agricultural life was never going to be enough for Paul McCartney. As his spirits revived, so did his burning need to re-establish contact with the live audiences whose adulation he had been denied during his last four years as a Beatle. He had worked as unselfishly as he knew how to hold the Beatles together, and it hadn't worked. Very well then, he'd show them there could be life after the Beatles onstage as well as off; that a world-beating combo could exist that did not also feature John, George and Ringo.

In 1971, he announced he had formed a new band with the Moody Blues' former guitarist Denny Laine, drummer Danny Seiwell and Linda on keyboards and vocals. Its name – consciously evoking some thankfully liberated bird or butterfly – would be Wings.

Today, such a step by a musician only a hundredth as big as Paul was in 1971 would compel instant, comprehensive media attention. But the media back then remained still overwhelmingly obsessed by the Beatles – in particular by the notion that their differences were repairable and that, sooner or later, they would get back together. The idea of Paul McCartney in any other band was one that most music journalists found impossible to take seriously. The PR man he employed to drum up stories about Wings, rather than about recent Beatles history, found few takers up and down Fleet Street. It was as though he were starting all over again from the bottom.

Paul's response was one of extraordinary courage or hubris, depending on your point of view. If they wanted him to start at the bottom again, then he'd do it. But not just at the bottom represented by third-rate TV shows and concert venues. He'd go right down to the bottom the Beatles had got to know so intimately 10 years before when they were still playing for small change, nurtured only by chips, beer and impossible dreams.

Packing Wings and their virgin equipment into a single van, he headed north up the M1, determined to break them in by playing the same kind of small halls and clubs where the Beatles had originally honed their craft. It was done somewhat in the chaotic spirit of a modern Magical Mystery Tour, with no firmly pre-planned route or set itinerary of gigs (but also, no doubt, a highly professional appreciation of its ultimate publicity value). One day, for instance, Paul saw a sign to Nottingham University and on a whim told his driver to follow it. When they reached the university campus, a roadie was dispatched to find the secretary of the students' union. 'I've got Paul McCartney and his new band outside,' the roadie said. 'Would you like them to play for you tonight?' It would have taken an iron-willed secretary to reply, 'No thanks, I think we'll stick with our scheduled lecture on the place of the potato in Irish folklore.'

Linda's inclusion in the Wings line-up had provoked universal disbelief and derison. To the residual millions of Beatle-Paul worshippers, it seemed yet further proof of her baleful influence and grim determination to advance herself by clinging tight to his coat-tails. Despite Paul's lavish tributes to her as a creative muse, she had so far been detectable only in the faint feminine coo that now shadowed his lead vocal – a 'deified Scouse with unmusical spouse', as one British magazine called them.

Yet there she was with Paul onstage, filling the place once occupied by John Lennon, her blonde hair now cut in a modish Seventies sheaf, dressed in gaudy glam-rock shirts and waistcoats but still not smiling very much, even when waving puffy sleeves above her head to encourage audiences to clap along. In some Wings songs she took the vocal, closely backed by Paul; in others she played an elementary keyboard solo he had obviously taught her that was only a step or two on from 'Chopsticks'. Halfway through the show, he would introduce her in homely Liverpool style as 'Our Lin', though to applause never more than polite. 'What do you call a dog with Wings?' ran an unkind riddle of the time.

In fact, as Linda later admitted, it was all Paul's idea that she should join Wings, mainly so that they wouldn't be separated when the band went out on tour. She said she never felt comfortable onstage and would always much rather have stayed at home with her children and animals. She did it only because it meant so much to Paul.

Despite its huge success and cosy family image, Wings was never to be a happy or stable band. As if in reaction to the old democracy of the Beatles, Paul proved an iron-fisted autocrat. A succession of talented musicians flocked to his banner, but soon left again, frustrated by his dominating ways and refusal to share the limelight with anyone but 'Our Lin' and her Chopsticks solo. Even the talented and crucial Denny Laine was given no percentage of the band's earnings, simply receiving a wage of just £70 per week (though Paul later raised this to £70,000 per year and paid off Laine's outstanding income tax). 'It was inevitable,' a former Wings associate comments. 'You had a leader who was a multi-instrumentalist, a perfectionist – and a former Beatle. Other than John, George and Ringo, he wasn't going to regard anyone else as nearly in his league.'

On record, too, Wings had a bumpy take-off. For their debut single Paul chose to air his Hibernian Catholic roots in an overt political statement whose title, 'Give Ireland back to the Irish', could hardly have been worse timed. When the record appeared in 1972, the so-called 'Provisional' IRA were escalating their campaign of sectarian murder in Northern Ireland and were soon to extend indiscriminate mass-murder to the British mainland. The simplistic sentiments of 'Give Ireland back to the Irish' seemed all too much in tune with hooded thugs now bombing and knee-capping in the name of Republicanism. Like John Lennon with 'I Am The Walrus' five years earlier, Paul found himself banned by the BBC and so deprived of any significant airplay within the UK.

His heavy-handedly ironic response was to make Wings' follow-up single a song no one on earth could accuse of being politically controversial. This was the nursery rhyme 'Mary Had a Little Lamb', in a setting which he had originally devised to sing to his daughter, Mary, while he put her to bed. 'La-*La*' ran its chorus – then, by way of a change, '*La*-la'. When Wings premiered the single on American television, there were sarcastic comments even from the talk-show hosts who introduced them. 'Once upon a time, Paul McCartney recorded songs like "Eleanor Rigby" and "Hey Jude". Now here he is with his new group and "Mary Had a Little Lamb" . . .'

Wings' continuing struggle to be taken seriously was further illustrated that same year, 1972, when Paul agreed to provide a title song for the latest James Bond film, *Live and Let Die*. Having written the song, he went into the studio off his own bat to record it with Wings, using the Beatles' old producer, George Martin, to score and produce it. A justifiably excited Martin then played the result to the Bond films' American co-producers Harry Salzman and Albert 'Cubby' Broccoli. 'Great demo,' they enthused. 'Now . . . who are we going to get to make the *record*?' It took all Martin's powers of persuasion to convince them that Paul McCartney's imprimatur could take Bond to a new, younger market and that they shouldn't call up Shirley Bassey or Lulu. 'Live and Let Die' became a top 10 single for Wings and was rated the best Bond theme since John Barry's original one for *Dr No* in 1962.

This breakthrough was consolidated by their 1973 album *Band on the Run*, whose packaging was both an oblique allusion to their spell as motorway-wandering outsiders and a throwback to *Sgt. Pepper* in-jokiness. The cover showed a melodramatically slinking posse of cloaked 'fugitives' including the Hollywood actor James Coburn, the television interviewer Michael Parkinson and the gourmet-soon-to-be-Liberal MP Clement Freud. Two tracks from the album, its title song and 'Jet' – a number likewise hinting at bonds triumphantly burst and the accelerator now pressed down flat – each became huge-selling singles.

From here on, Wings would compete with David Bowie, Elton John, T-Rex and Queen as the surest crowd-pullers of 1970s glitter rock. Their 1976 American tour sold out every venue, and found no chat-show hosts sniggering now. For Paul it was an especially sweet triumph, coming as it did exactly 10 years after the Beatles' farewell concert in San Francisco.

Although Allen Klein had retained managerial control of John, George and Ringo until 1973 (as he did of the Rolling Stones until 1975), Paul had the further satisfaction of seeing 'the Robin Hood of Pop' finally go down with an arrow in his back. In 1977, two years after Klein finally ended all connections with the Beatles, he was charged on six counts of income tax evasion by the US Internal Revenue Service. Thanks mainly to incriminating testimony from his old associate, the scary Pete Bennett, he was convicted of failing to declare income made from the illicit sale of promo Beatles albums. He was fined $5,000 and sent to prison for two months.

From here on, the new brand of McCartney songs rolled forth in the new, faintly mid-Atlantic McCartney voice that had Linda's insubstantial harmony clinging permanently to its underside like barnacles to a ship's keel. They were always catchy, always pleasant, always empty of real content and lacking that extra effort and edge that used to come from John peering over his shoulder.

The honed perfection of a lyric like 'Eleanor Rigby' or 'Yesterday' was replaced by sloppy first drafts of half-thoughts: 'Silly Love Songs', 'Listen to What the Man Said' or 'Let 'Em In', the latter merely a rambling name-check – reminiscent of John's on 'Give Peace a Chance' – from 'Martin Luther' (King) and 'Phil and Don' (Everly) to McCartney family members like 'brother Michael' and Auntie Jin. Clunky rhymes got through that John would have mocked to the skies ('The county judge/held a grudge . . .') The relentless journey to the middle of the road that had begun with 'granny tunes' like 'When I'm Sixty-Four' took another less-than-giant step when he agreed that Wings should record the theme music for television's naffest soap opera, *Crossroads*. To Beatle-Paul fans (now being fast overtaken by Wings-Paul ones) his *Crossroads* instrumental seemed the nadir – but they were soon to be proved wrong.

In 1977, inspired by the tract of water near his Argyllshire farm, and gratefully recalling its healing properties during his post-Beatles depression, he wrote a ballad entitled 'Mull of Kintyre'. Recorded at dirge-like tempo, with full bagpipe accompaniment, it seemed to have all the appeal of Fort William on a wet afternoon. Reviewers in the domestic pop press (who then still aspired to a degree of literacy) were unanimous in calling it the dreariest, blandest solo McCartney production yet. It stayed at number one in the UK for nine weeks, sold two million copies and was to remain Britain's top-selling single until Band Aid's 'Do They Know It's Christmas?' in 1984.

•

With Wings now triumphantly spread, Paul set up a publishing company, MPL (McCartney Productions Ltd). The organisation was as small and low-key as Apple had been diffuse and flamboyant, operating from one unshowy office in London's Soho Square and another in New York. The

New York end was run by Linda's brother John, with frequent recourse to the legal expertise of her father, Lee – the very management team, in fact, that Paul had once proposed should run the Beatles.

The new company was not long in pulling off a major publishing coup. In 1975, the song catalogue of Buddy Holly, the Beatles' first great idol and inspiration, was put up for sale by Holly's former manager, Norman Petty. For a knockdown price of less than $1 million, MPL snapped up the rights to Holly's music in the US and Canada. So moved was Paul to have become the custodian of 'That'll Be the Day', 'Peggy Sue' and all the rest that he decreed an annual 'Buddy Holly Week' of Holly-related concerts and events that was to be faithfully observed for some years afterwards. Norman Petty himself came over from New Mexico to inaugurate the first Buddy Holly Week; at the celebration lunch, he presented Paul with the cufflinks Holly had been wearing at his death in a plane crash in February 1959.

That was just the beginning for MPL, whose body may have been small but whose mouth quickly proved as large and ever open as that of an angler fish. Over the following years, often acting on advice from Lee Eastman, it gobbled up the publishing for a succession of hit stage shows including *A Chorus Line*, *Grease*, *Annie* and *Hello Dolly*, as well as for innumerable standards and even TV theme music, notably that for Lucille Ball's 1950s comedy show, *I Love Lucy*.

Paul had always fought shy of the rock star's lifestyle. Now, as his new band rocked the world, as he found his wealth growing far beyond any he had ever known as a Beatle, his personal life became proportionally more modest. By the mid-Seventies, he and Linda and their growing brood had left London, keeping on his old St John's Wood mansion as a pied-à-terre but settling permanently in a small house near Rye, Sussex. Given that those were far safer, less media-intrusive times, it was still an extraordinarily unpretentious and accessible roost for a multimillionaire ex-Beatle. It had neither security fences nor patrolling guard dogs; for many years, indeed, the entrance to its front drive did not even have gates. 'It wasn't much more than a hole in the hedge,' remembers one McCartney fan who trekked down for a look. 'I used to think how many cars passed that gate each day without ever knowing Paul was there.'

The interior was equally unshowy, save for Paul's growing collection of modern art. Ever the autodidact, he had developed a passion for twentieth-century American painters like Jackson Pollock and Willem de Kooning (the latter, fortuitously, a client of Lee Eastman's). The knack for cartooning that he himself had had since schooldays now developed into full-blown painting, though as yet for purely recreational purposes.

His house might look open and accessible, but Paul guarded its privacy as fiercely as if it were surrounded by razor wire and searchlights. Most people, and almost all journalists, thought he lived in the rather larger and more opulent mill house nearby that he'd turned into a recording studio. Even some of his closest professional colleagues never got to see inside his real home. A public relations man who worked closely with him during the late Seventies remembers being kept firmly at arm's length in this way. When they needed to discuss something, the PR man would drive down from London, wait in his car outside the house and Paul would emerge and talk to him there.

After Mary in 1969, Linda bore two more children: Stella (*b.* 1971) and James (Paul's baptismal name, *b.* 1977). Together with Linda's daughter Heather, they grew up in an atmosphere of absolute parental love and security, with a father who could not have been more hands-on. Unlike most rock-star kids, however, none was in the least spoiled: all four were born in National Health maternity wards, attended local state schools and were firmly inculcated with the old-fashioned Liverpudlian virtues of politeness, considerateness and respect that their grandfather, Jim McCartney, had unknowingly bequeathed them.

Linda immersed herself in family and country life, proving to be a devoted mother and an increasingly skilful cook (witness that rather patronising album track, 'Cook of the House'). Under her influence, Paul became both a vegetarian and an animal rights enthusiast, proselytising to the extent of hanging GO VEGGIE banners above the stage at Wings concerts – so fuelling the worst fears of Beatle-Paul fans who'd wondered what 'she' would do to him next.

From their Sussex neighbours, the couple won esteem for their refusal to come on like rock and roll royalty and their obvious love and respect for the surrounding countryside. The only waves they made in the community came from their fierce opposition to the local hunt – and flat refusal to allow it to cross their land. When the district's only NHS hospital was threatened with closure, Paul stepped in and donated enough money to keep it going.

Despite her crowded new domestic life, Linda persisted with her photography, snapping her husband, children, animals and surroundings at every opportunity and putting together a Christmas calendar made from the best of her year's shots. Friends may have reacted more politely, but around London's record and pop management companies the ceremonial hand-delivery of Linda's yuletide calendar would invariably be met by groans or exaggerated retching noises.

At some moment in the mid-Seventies, British pop journalists ceased referring to Wings' front man as 'Paul' and instead dubbed him 'Macca'. Though merely a contraction of 'McCartney', vaguely evoking both his

Irish and Liverpool working-class heritage, it perfectly fitted the new and very different persona that came more clearly into definition with each seven-league leap of solo success. Whereas 'Paul', in Beatles times, had suggested almost saintly softness and charm, 'Macca' suggested something altogether tougher and more synthetic; a perhaps-not-too-distant cousin to Formica. Whereas Paul had been adept at concealing his prodigious vanity from the world, Macca sometimes let it show as helplessly as a 'flasher' in a raincoat on Clapham Common. Whereas Paul had steered a largely trouble-free path through the minefields of pop stardom, Macca at times would seem almost hell-bent on blundering into the most obvious trip-wires.

His and Linda's devotion to family values did not prevent them from still indulging the emblematic habit of Sixties flower children. They used marijuana, both at home and while travelling with Wings. And, alas, there was now no magic shield to protect pot-smoking ex-Beatles from retribution.

John Lennon has gone down in history as the band's most reckless drug-user; in fact Paul in the post-Beatles years would be busted more times, and more spectacularly, than John ever was. It happened twice in 1972 for cannabis possession – first in Sweden, then on the McCartneys' Scottish farm. Another bust came in 1984 while they were holidaying in Barbados; the following day, when they and their children arrived back at Heathrow airport, further cannabis was found in Linda's luggage.

But worst by far was the Tokyo bust of January 1980, an episode almost suggesting that the new Macca-Paul was bent on a subconscious course of hara-kiri. In the whole addle-brained history of pop stars and forbidden substances, it's hard to find anyone else who has acted so stupidly or paid so scary a price.

His reputation at that moment, ironically, was at an all-time high. A month earlier, he had organised a series of London concerts, headlined by Wings, to aid refugees in Kampuchea, formerly Cambodia – a gesture of altruism still comparatively rare among pop superstars which in effect prepared the ground for Bob Geldof and Live Aid four years later. Hence that breathless moment of almost-Beatles reunion, with George and Ringo reportedly willing to appear onstage with Paul if it would send more milk and penicillin to the Kampuchean refugees, but John flatly deflating the whole idea and remaining firm even against pleas from the UN's Secretary-General.

Wings then departed on a world tour, of which the high point was to be their first ever performances in Japan. Despite Paul's huge fan base there, he had been repeatedly denied a Japanese visa as a result of his 1972 drugs-busts. Now, thanks to intense diplomatic and entrepreneurial lobbying, not to mention his current high standing with the UN, he was to be allowed in at last.

The celebratory atmosphere of the visit was to be short-lived. When Paul arrived at Tokyo airport, customs officers found 219 grammes of marijuana in a toilet-bag placed on *top* of the clothes in his suitcase. He was arrested, charged with possession – an offence carrying a maximum seven-year sentence – and then thrown into prison. Only after nine days of further intense diplomatic activity (with frantic Japanese girls wailing '*Paur! Paur!*' below his cell-window) did the authorities release and instantly deport him.

He arrived back in Britain more chastened than his public had ever seen him, pale, hollow-eyed and visibly shaken by prison conditions which he compared, with a ghost of his old flippancy, to *The Bridge on the River Kwai*. About the offence itself he said nothing, so adding further fuel to a rumour that the marijuana had actually belonged to Linda and that he'd taken the rap for her, just as Mick Jagger had for Marianne Faithfull in the famous 'Mars bar' bust of 1967.

The other members of Wings were understandably outraged at the worldwide notoriety their leader had brought down on their heads. After Paul, the band's main instrumental lynchpin had been Denny Laine, an insouciant character who always seemed able to ride the Macca bossiness and egotism. But now even Laine had had enough and quit the band without notice – so making its break-up inevitable – afterwards writing a song, 'Japanese Tears', which attacked Paul in terms almost as bitter as John's 'How Do You Sleep?' It's difficult to think of another major music star who has been so many times slagged off in songs by fellow performers.

After this traumatic and demeaning episode, there would be no more glimpses of the real McCartney for a long time to come. Even the shock of John's murder, eight months later, produced no public sign of the devastation – and, possibly, remorse – that he was suffering. 'Yeah, it's a drag, isn't it?' he said to the besieging media pack as off-handedly as if it were something no more serious than a record slipping out of the Top Ten.

Words often come out wrongly at moments of anguish. No one could possibly blame him for not producing a polished sound-bite to express what a huge part of his life Mark David Chapman's bullets had blown away. Just the same, there was something vital missing from his public response, just as there was from George Harrison's. The people whose greatest gift next to music had been the gift of the gab, who had always known just the right thing to say at any given moment, now astonished the grieving world with their gaucherie and gracelessness. More tellingly, neither appeared to think the tragedy sufficiently important to rearrange their lives for. Of the three remaining ex-Beatles, only Ringo immediately dropped everything and flew to New York as a public gesture of support for John's family and affirmation of their old brotherhood.

From here on, Paul would seem intent on proving he didn't need Wings any more than he had the Beatles. And so his public seemed to reassure him. In 1989 and again in 1993, he undertook world tours, accompanied by Linda and an unnamed backing band, and dispensing with most of Wings' flashy glam-rock effects. Both tours combined brought him an ecstatic audience numbering around 2.5 million; on a single night in Rio de Janeiro during the first, he played to a crowd of 184,000.

No one better symbolised the dawning era of brotherhood and co-operation among rock stars – or was more adept at turning it to his personal advantage. During the early Eighties, he recorded duets with two major black performers, in each of which he managed to express deference and respect to his co-vocalist while at the same time shamelessly hogging the mike. With the former Motown prodigy Stevie Wonder in 1982, he recorded 'Ebony and Ivory', a plea for racial harmony with rhymes ('piano keyboard' and 'Oh, Lord' for instance) that one would hardly have expected from the writer of 'Eleanor Rigby'. With Michael Jackson – soon to be as big to the Eighties as the Beatles had been to the Sixties – he recorded 'The Girl Is Mine' (1982) and 'Say Say Say' (1983), once more all but suffocating an inimitable stylist with McCartney syrup and over-embellishment. This new fraternal spirit also made him forget his yah-boo *McCartney* cover notes and bring Ringo to play on his 1982 *Tug of War* album.

Since the Family Way and Black Dyke Mills Band days, people had been urging him to try his hand at writing classical music. In the early Nineties, seemingly with no new pop worlds left to conquer, he decided the time had come. He may have had no formal training in classical theory or scoring – but he was Paul McCartney. The result was *The Liverpool Oratorio* drawing on recognisably the same childhood echoes as had 'Penny Lane' and 'Eleanor Rigby'. It received its world premiere at Liverpool's Anglican cathedral in 1991, performed by a full symphony orchestra conducted by Carl Davis, with the vocal part sung by Dame Kiri Te Kanawa. The occasion also included perhaps the ultimate McCartney vanity shot: the composer silhouetted against the cathedral nave, hands nonchalantly in pockets, as if the whole vast sandstone edifice had been raised to glorify him alone.

Though deserving no epithet much stronger than 'pleasant', *The Liverpool Oratorio* was received with as much critical rapture as a long-lost work by Bach or Handel: it went on to play in London at the Royal Festival Hall and in New York at Carnegie Hall, and to assume a permanent place in the classical repertory.

Not everything he touched, however, was to turn instantly to the gold of million-selling records. In 1984, MPL had moved into feature films with *Give My Regards to Broad Street*, a $9 million project inspired by the imminent closure of London's Broad Street railway station. As the lamely punning title (on *Give My Regards to Broadway*) suggested, it was Paul's pet project; like *The Magical Mystery Tour* 17 years earlier, it revealed his fatal tendency not to think things through properly but believe he could just wing it on McCartney pied-piper magic. He himself was said to have largely written the 'script', which concerned a famous pop star's picaresque quest for some lost demo tapes, but was above all a device for putting Paul McCartney, soft-focused to mid-Sixties youth and prettiness, in the dead centre of almost every frame. As in *Mystery Tour*, various accomplished actors and performers wandered in and out of shot, obviously wondering what the hell it was all about but still tickled beyond measure to be working in Beatle Heaven.

The subsequent reviews made *Magical Mystery Tour* seem like a smash hit by comparison and brought Paul his first public ridicule on British TV's *Spitting Image* puppet show. As a big-eyed Macca figure sat in a restaurant, his waiter announced 'Your turkey, Sir!' and dumped a film-can labelled *Give My Regards to Broad Street* onto his plate.

More successful MPL film projects were an animated feature about Rupert Bear and a television documentary on the Beatles' old idol Buddy Holly, released in 1985 and including the first ever intimate glimpses of Holly from his family, his fellow musicians and his widow, Maria-Elena. Yet here again, Macca could not bear to stay off-camera: as well as introducing the film, he made several incidental appearances including a lengthy – and poorly prepared – soliloquy on Holly's compositional methods. It was noticeable, too, that he chose not to be filmed in his own home but in the deliberately neutral setting of a hay barn. Even when talking of the music closest to his heart, he could not 'open the door and let 'em in'.

Supremely successful though he was on so many fronts, there remained one glaring gap among his myriad possessions, acquisitions and holdings. This ultimate creative control freak might have the satisfaction of controlling everything from Buddy Holly's songbook to *Grease* and *I Love Lucy*. Yet, ironically, he did not control his own earliest work, the songs he had written for the Beatles under the democratically unspecific 'Lennon–McCartney' byline. 'I Saw Her Standing There', 'Love of the Loved', 'I Want to Hold Your Hand', 'Do You Want to Know a Secret',

'Eight Days a Week' and all the dozens more of John and Paul's perfect primitive paintings still belonged to Northern Songs, the publishing company Dick James had sold from under their feet at the height of the Apple crisis in 1969.

Northern's original buyers, Lew Grade's ATV network, had in turn sold the company on to the Australian mogul Robert Holmes à Court. In 1985, it unexpectedly came on to the market again. Swallowing his old rancour against Yoko, Paul contacted her and persuaded her of the wisdom of their making a joint bid. But while the two and their lawyers argued over strategy, Northern was snapped up in a $47.5 million deal – by none other than the Eighties *wunderkind* Michael Jackson.

Even the canny Macca was stunned by the speed and duplicity with which his former recording partner, and supposed good friend, engineered the coup. He was later to give his own wry account of it, perfectly mimicking 'Jacko's' childlike lisp. 'Michael asked me one day how you went about buying a song catalogue, and I gave him all kinds of advice. The next time I saw him, he said "I'm gonna buy *your* songs, Paul."'

All of the former Beatles had attracted criticism for their seeming indifference to Liverpool's desperate economic plight during the recession-hit Seventies and early Eighties. With his well-founded reputation for being 'careful', to put it no stronger, Paul had always seemed the least likely benefactor of his home city or his alma mater, Liverpool Institute Grammar School. During the late Seventies, his former English teacher, 'Dusty Durband', wrote to ask his support in a school reconstruction appeal. Mr Durband was disappointed – and annoyed – to receive a cheque back for just £1,000.

A radical change of mind came in the mid-Nineties after it was reported that Liverpool Institute, already closed for some years, now faced actual demolition. Paul became the moving spirit in the old grammar school's £13 million transformation into the Liverpool Institute for the Performing Arts (LIPA for short), a project which, perhaps more than any other, was to symbolise the city's economic revival and regenerated self-belief. It was opened by the Queen in 1996, with an unfamiliarly dark-suited Macca beside her. Not since 1964 had any Beatle made so triumphant a homecoming.

By this point, it seemed that the McCartney name automatically shed magic in whatever context it occurred. In 1995, Paul's younger daughter Stella graduated from St Martin's School of Art and began an ascent in the couture world destined to be as meteoric as her father's in the musical one. Even more to Paul's satisfaction, Linda had at long last achieved recognition in her own right by skilfully blending her dietary principles with her prowess as 'Cook of the House'. The Linda McCartney range of vegetarian frozen foods with accompanying recipes, launched in 1991, now adorned major supermarkets throughout both the UK and America.

In the Queen's Birthday Honours of 1997, Paul became the third British pop singer to receive a knighthood (after the saintly Cliff Richard and Live Aid's organiser Bob Geldof). The award came in the dying days of John Major's sleaze-ridden and clapped-out Tory government, and could be seen as a desperate bid for popularity by playing the well-worn Harold Wilson card; even so, none could deny Paul had long been in line for some public recognition more substantial than his 1965 MBE. Significantly, his chequered history of drugs-busts and brief Japanese incarceration seem never to have been an issue when 10 Downing Street consulted with Buckingham Palace about the award.

Becoming 'Sir Paul' was just one of the honours now showering on him thicker than jelly beans at an old-time Beatles Christmas show. His family home, the modest council house in Forthlin Road, Allerton, was acquired by the National Trust and opened to the public, creating an historic shrine of the little front room where John and he used to huddle with their guitars and Buddy Holly records after bunking off from school. He was invited to join leading politicians and diplomats as a weekend guest at Highgrove, the Prince of Wales's country seat. He even had a variety of rose named after him.

•

The whole rose-tinted idyll came crashing around his ears when Linda was diagnosed with breast cancer.

The disease is never other than cruel and arbitrary in its toll on women often still in the prime of life. And in this case, like so many others – and so much else in the Beatles' story – history was horribly repeating itself. Breast cancer had also struck down the other essential woman in Paul's life, his mother Mary, when he was only 14. Ironically, on Linda's public appearances with Paul she looked smilier and more vibrant than her hyper-critical public had ever seen her before. Only the close cropping of the former luxuriant blonde hair gave a clue to the ordeal she was suffering.

Linda's greatest solace in those grim and increasingly less optimistic months was the explosive success of her daughter Stella in the fashion world. In 1997, just two years after graduating from St Martin's School of Art, Stella joined the Parisian couture house of Chloe as chief designer in succession to Karl Lagerfeld. She was already becoming an international celebrity in her own right, with her peaky Paul face, her plunging necklines and her penchant for walking hand in hand with female rather than male escorts. She designed clothes with a rummage-sale raggetiness no sane woman would ever wear but which flew into the glossy fashion mags as instantaneously as her father had once burnt up the Top Ten. At her first Paris show – arguably the most highly publicised since Yves St Laurent's debut in the pre-Swinging Sixties – Linda and Paul were among the host of rock and movie celebrities cheering her from the catwalk-side.

Linda died in April 1998 at the McCartneys' ranch near Tucson, Arizona, a retreat whose existence had been kept secret from all but their closest friends and associates. In a misguided attempt to preserve the ranch's incognito, Paul's spokespeople initially announced that Linda had died several hundred miles to the west, in Santa Barbara, California. The truth emerged only when Santa Barbara's municipal authority began asking why the death had not been registered with them.

It was barely seven months since Diana, Princess of Wales had been killed in a Paris car crash, unleashing a wave of hysterical mourning throughout Britain. An appetite still remained for a blonde-haired female martyr, and Linda McCartney perfectly fitted that bill. Forgetting their old hostility, the media extolled her campaigns for vegetarianism and animal rights in much the same terms as Diana's for AIDS and land-mine victims. For a brief, surreal moment, she became a kind of mini-'People's Princess', lauded with the same crazy disproportion as she had formerly been denigrated.

For Paul, paradoxically, losing Linda meant stepping back into limelight brighter than any he had known for more than a decade. Rock, as a rule, tends to create widows; here was the music's first A-list widower. For the first time ever, he showed pain and vulnerability to the world, which in turn responded with an affection greater than any he had received in all his previous decades of relentless winning. To one interviewer he recalled how he had comforted Linda's final hours by making her picture them both riding their favourite horses through their favourite countryside. To another he revealed that, in 29 years of marriage, they had never spent a single night apart.

Two memorial services for Linda were held, one in London, the other in New York. It might have been expected that the widow of Paul's oldest friend and still much-missed partner might have been asked to the New York service, especially after the reconciliation he had so publicly proclaimed at the Rock 'n' Roll Hall of Fame ceremony four years earlier. But Yoko was excluded from the list. An additional memorial was a Linda McCartney solo album, compiled by Paul in an obvious attempt to win her the musical credibility she'd been denied in her lifetime. Entitled *Wide Prairie*, it brought together various Linda vocal tracks from the Wings era, including 'Cook of the House'. Though it was widely and earnestly reviewed, not even the most ardently pro-McCartney critic could find much more to say than 'nice try'.

But the period of mourning was to end rather abruptly. Early in 1999, Paul began to be seen in public with 32-year-old Heather Mills, a prominent figure in the now interdependent worlds of show business and charity. Though initially he smiled away their meetings as pure coincidence, the subterfuge was short-lived. That summer, while Heather was being interviewed on a TV chat show, Paul made a 'surprise' appearance, took her hand and announced that they were in love.

His new love's background was, to say the least, an unusual one. Born and raised on Tyneside, she was a self-confessed juvenile delinquent who claimed to have fled from a violent, tyrannical father to work on a fairground on London's Clapham Common and live rough 'under the arches' at Waterloo station before turning her looks and spectacular figure to account as a glamour model and playmate of the Arab billionaire Adnan Khashoggi. As a teenager, she had been arrested for stealing jewellery, but had been let off with probation owing to her troubled family circumstances.

Her autobiography, *Step by Step*, recounted further traumatic youthful experiences – among them, being held prisoner as a seven-year-old by a paedophile swimming teacher and being almost murdered by a knife-wielding lesbian flatmate. She made an early first marriage, to a Middlesex businessman named Alfie Karmal who had encouraged her to progress from Soho club waitress to pin-up, a career in which she would later claim to earn as much as £200,000 per year. She became pregnant but lost the baby through an ectopic pregnancy and, not long afterwards, left Karmal for a Slovenian ski instructor. At the age of 25, she was run over by a police motorcyclist who had been hurrying to a so-called 'emergency' involving Diana, Princess of Wales. Her left foot was almost severed, and surgeons had no choice but to amputate the leg just below the knee.

Whatever might subsequently be said of Heather, no one could deny her courage or unstoppable determination. She designed her own prosthetic leg, with which she was soon able to run, dance, even ski with the same freedom she had before her accident. She would recall with hilarity how, on one early ascent in a ski lift, her prosthetic leg came loose and sailed down the slopes below with the ski still attached to it. Nor could her spirit be dampened even by the crushing advice of a female social worker immediately after she lost her leg. 'You'll have to face it, dear,' the social worker told her. 'You're never going to be attractive to men again.'

'I could lose both my arms and both my legs,' Heather replied, 'and I'd *still* be more attractive to men than you are.'

In fact, she was always to maintain that men were never turned off by her leg and that every one of her boy friends had asked her to marry him 'inside a week'. She was determinedly frank and open about the prosthesis, showing it to any interviewer who wanted to see it, once even whipping it off and waving it under the nose of American radio talk-show host Larry King.

Following her accident, she tried to make a career as a television presenter, appearing on various regional programmes but never winning any permanent spot. Her involvement in charity work began at the same time, drawing directly and indirectly on the traumas of her own past. She became a campaigner for the homeless, for amputees and – like Diana, Princess of Wales – for the victims of land-mines left behind by wars in Asia and Africa.

A television colleague of that era describes her as 'one of the shrewdest and most calculating women I've ever met. Whatever misfortune is being talked about, Heather has suffered it – from homelessness to ectopic pregnancy. But I have to admire her. Once, after she'd appeared on *The Richard and Judy Show* with a homeless girl, she had the girl to stay with her for about two weeks, even though her current boy friend was coming over to see her from New Zealand. The three of them were together in Heather's house, plus her terrier.

'When she went to Cambodia to see land-mine victims with the Duchess of Kent, she met a girl who'd lost both arms and both legs. Heather took the girl under her wing, and she's now working in the Anglia Television newsroom.

'Her attitude was that in her life she'd sunk to the very bottom, so she deserved only the very best. And Paul McCartney was the ultimate notch on the bedpost.'

The new relationship had a galvanic effect on Paul, blowing away the clouds of sadness that had engulfed him since Linda's death. To escape media harassment, he and Heather took to spending weekends at a borrowed cottage on the Cliveden estate in Berkshire – the famous scene of John Profumo's first meeting with Christine Keeler, now transformed into a luxury hotel. Heather tempted him back to parties and even discos where – as one friend reported – 'they danced together like a couple of teenagers'. As proof of her beneficial influence, he declared he had even given up using marijuana for her sake.

The announcement that they planned to marry brought a sharp change to this initially friendly perception of Heather. To be sure, the ructions surrounding Paul's wedding to Linda, 30 years earlier, would sometimes seem mild by comparison. Heather was portrayed as an opportunistic gold-digger, out to stake her claim on a McCartney fortune which – after the phenomenal success of the Beatles' *1* album – was on course to make him pop's first-ever billionaire. (To this charge, she made the somewhat surprising reply that if she'd been out for money alone, she would have gone for someone 'richer than Paul'.)

The media pack quickly tracked down her former husband, Alfie Karmal, who did not need much persuasion to describe a 'damaged' person who, he said, had left him without warning after their five-year-relationship, trashing their home by way of farewell. The childhood friend with whom she claimed to have been held prisoner by the paedophile swimming teacher dismissed her account as 'crap'. Her stepfather, John Stapley said that her memories of fairground life on Clapham Common were likewise part of the 'fantasy world' she had created from her past. It was whispered that even the best part of her career, her work for land-mine victims derived merely from an ambition to be seen as a substitute Princess Diana. Fellow campaigners questioned her claims to have been appointed a United Nations ambassador for land-mines and even to have been short-listed for a Nobel Peace Prize. One of her former TV colleagues was surprised to see her on BBC2's *Ready, Steady, Cook* programme, claiming to have been a vegetarian every bit as devout as Paul 'for the past 17 years'. 'When I worked with her a few years back, her diet used to be almost all protein,' her ex-colleague says. 'She used to tuck in to huge bits of steak.'

Most crucially, Paul's children – particularly his three grown-up daughters – were said to be horrified by his choice of a former swimwear model to replace their mother (and one sharing the name of their mother's oldest child to boot). Paul himself dropped his sunshine mask sufficiently to admit there were 'difficulties' about Heather within the family and that she could be 'bossy' at times, but at the same time made it clear that these factors had no effect on his resolve to make her the next Lady McCartney. From then on, he became as determined to win acceptance for Heather as he had once been to win it for Linda. So that nobody around him should mistake his wishes, he granted her a power and influence of which even Linda had never dreamed. At his concerts, Heather became the first person in history to give him critical notes on his performance – and have them earnestly listened to. 'Paul always has to prove his point, and he doesn't care how far he goes to do it,' says an associate. 'I've never known anyone so determined to cut off his nose to spite his face.'

She on her side showed little of the meekness and deference he had always been used to from Linda. Early in 2002, staff at a Miami hotel reported overhearing a furious row between them, in which Paul allegedly shouted, 'I don't want to marry you any more.' A hotel team equipped with metal-detectors was then mobilised to search the bushes below their room after Heather had apparently hurled her £15,000 engagement ring through its open window. Heather's explanation was that Paul and she had simply been 'having a laugh' and playing 'catch' with the ring.

The approaching nuptials brought further allegations of dissent and discontent among the McCartney children. Stella was reportedly furious at not having been asked to design Heather's wedding dress, her soon-to-be stepmother considering her clothes 'too tarty'. Instead, Heather announced, she would be 'creating' her own Chantilly lace bridal gown with the help of London couturiers Avis and Brown. Mary McCartney, a rising portrait photographer – whose subjects had already included Tony and Cherie Blair – was said to feel equally slighted because she hadn't been asked to do the wedding pictures.

The ceremony took place on 11 June, in Glaslough, County Monaghan, the part of Ireland from which Paul's maternal ancestors had originally sprung. Apart from the best man, his younger brother Michael, it was a very different occasion from the simple register office ceremony at which he'd married Linda in 1969. This time the cost was around £1 million and the setting was Castle Leslie, a medieval pile whose eccentric owner, 87-year-old Sir Jack Leslie, was famous for performing Madonna's 'Like a Virgin' in local pubs. Offers of £1.5 million from *Hello!* magazine and £1 million from *OK!* for exclusive photo access had both been refused: instead, a single colour shot of the newlyweds was issued to the media, with all reproduction fees paid to Heather's principal charity interest, Adopt a Minefield UK. The guests, including Eric Clapton, the Ringo Starrs and Sir George Martin, were asked to donate £1,000 each to the charity in lieu of wedding presents.

Paul's stepdaughter Heather and his son James were both significantly absent from the celebrations. Stella and Mary did attend, albeit with the kind of stuck-on smiles in which their father used to specialise as a Beatle. It would later be claimed that the new Lady McCartney had expressed willingness to sign a prenuptial agreement limiting her claim on Paul's assets to £20 million in the event of a divorce. But he had refused to consider it. Somewhat undermining the media-free atmosphere, the day's events were filmed for inclusion in a documentary about the bridegroom's ongoing American tour. With the slightly whingey tone that can flavour her public statements, Heather was to say that media attention – surely not unexpected either to her bridegroom or herself, and not always unwelcome – had made her wedding year 'the worst of my life'.

After their honeymoon, the couple settled in Brighton, where Heather had already lived for some years. Reports soon began to emerge of a besottedly attentive new husband, preparing hummus sandwiches for her packed lunches, being a perfect host to her friends at dinner-parties, massaging the stump of her amputated leg when it became painful or inflamed, and 'dancing around the room like Fred Astaire'. In May 2003 Heather announced that she was pregnant.

•

To have written pop music's equivalent of the works of Shakespeare, to be a billionaire, a knight of the realm, a national monument, the name of a rose and still, after all these years, among the half-dozen most famous faces on the planet might be thought more than enough to satisfy the most ravenous ambition. But it seems not to satisfy Paul.

Despite the almost incalculable pile-up of achievement behind him, he still works at being a star as though he has everything to prove, still churns out the glib, vacuous songs of his maturity, still cracks the whip as unrelentingly over musicians and technicians at his recording sessions, still pushes, promotes and hypes for all he's worth, and gets miffed when there's no phone call summoning him back on to *Top of the Pops*. The one-time master innovator scans the output of single brain-cell rappers and ninth-hand boy bands, hoping to pick up tips that will make his next product more appealing to modern teenagers. The all-time classic endlessly ponders and frets over how to be 'contemporary'.

From time to time he allows us to see how, even if you are as huge and rich and loaded with honours as Sir Paul McCartney, you can still be plagued by insecurities that no ocean of adulation can drown; old grudges and frustrations that poison the most golden triumph; little niggles that just never go away. Despite all that being a Beatle bestowed on him, he plainly continues to feel he received less than his proper share, in terms of both money and credit. In the mid-Eighties he went to the band's old record company, EMI, and demanded a larger share of their collective royalties than that paid to his two fellow survivors and John's estate. George, Ringo and Yoko joined forces to sue him and the matter was settled quietly out of court.

Someone else who had written a ballad like 'Yesterday' and lived to see it challenge Irving Berlin's 'White Christmas' as the world's most covered song might well feel only pride and satisfaction in that achievement. But not Paul. In 2000, while the hardback version of the *Beatles Anthology* was in preparation, he asked Yoko if the credits for 'Yesterday' could be changed from 'Lennon–McCartney' to 'McCartney–Lennon' since he had written it without any input from John. He even claimed John's precedence on the credit meant the Lennon estate had received a greater share of the song's royalties.

Yoko's refusal to consider the idea put the Beatles-watching community, for once, unequivocally on her side, for it was an elemental part of Beatles history, and of their ineluctable charm, that songs were historically credited to 'Lennon–McCartney', whichever of them had been the dominant or exclusive composer. The two had always been absolute creative equals no matter whose name came first; indeed, on the Beatles' first album and early hit singles like 'From Me to You', their byline had appeared as 'McCartney–Lennon'. If John received an undeserved half-credit for Paul songs like 'Yesterday' and 'Let It Be', then so did Paul for John songs like 'Norwegian Wood' and 'Strawberry Fields Forever'.

He had already received one chance to rearrange the credit to his liking when several of his Beatles songs featured on the *Wings Over America* album in 1976. Another came in 2002 with the live album of his latest American tour, which included 'Yesterday', 'Eleanor Rigby', 'Can't Buy Me Love' and 'Hey Jude'. On the Wings album, he had simply reversed the credit; this time, as if to ram the point home, it read 'composed by Paul McCartney and John Lennon'. Even long-time McCartney fans expressed themselves dumbfounded by the pettiness of it. 'He just can't bear anyone to think he didn't write "Yesterday" or "Let It Be" on his own,' observed one. 'And it was also a sign he doesn't care any more who knows his real feelings about Yoko.'

Yoko had never publicly spoken a word against him, and had gone along with many of his schemes – such as his plan to reissue the *Let It Be* album in its intended 'raw' state without the Phil Spector overdub that so offended him in 1970. But with his unilateral rewriting of the Lennon–McCartney credit, word came out of the Dakota building that Yoko had had enough and was considering legal action against him. He responded with a 700-word statement, claiming that the Lennon–McCartney formula had been agreed by John and Brian Epstein behind his back, but with the half promise it might be changed sometime in the future. He also said that Yoko had initially agreed to let him rearrange the credit, but then had changed her mind.

The statement almost descended to inarticulacy in Paul's simultaneous determination to get his way, yet still keep the boy-next-door smile on his face. '. . . This isn't anything I'm going to lose any sleep over, nor is it anything that will cause litigation, but it seems harmless to me after more than 30 years of it being the other way round for people like Yoko who have benefited and continued to benefit from my past efforts to be a little generous and to not have a problem with this suggestion of how to simply map out for those who do not know who wrote which of the songs.' The inclusion in his stage show of a tribute song to John – allegedly written just after John's death – did little to moderate the widespread negative reaction. Even his fellow survivor, the normally tractable Ringo, expressed puzzlement and faint disgust: 'I think the way he did it was underhanded. I thought he should have done it officially with Yoko . . . It was the wrong way to go about it.' The furore eventually persuaded Paul against any further interference with the credit.

The whole episode illustrated the extent to which, a generation after John's death, Paul still feels driven to compete with him, still hankers for the dividend of love and esteem that John drew from their partnership. It has never ceased to rankle that, from their earliest Beatles days John was typecast as the the 'arty', 'avant garde', 'intellectual' one while he himself was considered merely the 'nice' one. Every interview he ever gives fulminates against this gross misconception, stressing what difficult books and art he used to relish in those days, how he helped Barry Miles and John Dunbar put the trend-setting Indica Gallery together, how he was at the Sixties' cutting edge in London while John was being a Nowhere Man in the Weybridge stockbroker belt.

In recent times, the focus of his ambition, perhaps even more than music, has been showing us how wrong we were all those years ago. Together with his songwriting, John won lasting fame as a poet and an artist. Dammit then, Paul will prove himself to be an artist and a poet of a hundred times the size. And if you are Paul McCartney, with unlimited fame and funds and nothing on your horizon but yes-men, you can do it.

His collected poems, *Blackbird Singing*, appeared in 2000, heralded by mobbed book-signings and appearances at literary festivals, and greeted by plaudits from established poets such as Adrian Mitchell and Paul Muldoon. The poems dated back to 1965, with the most recent batch written during Linda's final illness. A few had the simple directness of his best song lyrics, seasoned by the wisdom of personal loss. But others demonstrated how an unfinished thought or half-coined phrase that may get by in a song lyric shrieks pure embarrassment from the printed page. 'Tears are not tears', ran the most widely quoted lines, 'They're balls of laughter dipped in salt.'

His painting – long a private hobby and beneficial therapy – has been the subject of even more determined hype. In his breezeblock-sized authorised biography, *Many Years From Now*, an entire chapter was devoted to his views on Art, his formative influences as a painter, even the kinds of paints, canvases and brushes he favours.

The 2001 Royal Academy Summer Exhibition included a blobby-blue and red Paul McCartney abstract in a kind of rock and roll corner also featuring work by David Bowie, Rolling Stone Ronnie Wood and the late Ian Dury. A year later, he had his first solo exhibition at Liverpool's Walker Art Gallery. Once again, no critic quite had nerve enough to spell out the differences between an amateur and a professional, though a glance at the Stuart Sutcliffe painting owned by the same gallery would have made the point well enough.

Echoes of John continue to turn up in McCartney music seemingly light years away from the Beatles. The title of his *Flaming Pie* album, for instance, was a quotation from John's long-ago *Mersey Beat* article, 'A Short Diversion on the Dubious History of Beatles' ('It came in a vision – a man appeared on a flaming pie and said unto them "From this day on you are Beatles."'). Paul's appropriation of the quote caused extreme dismay to even hardcore Beatles loyalists. 'He's achieved everything he possibly could as Paul McCartney,' said one. 'Why couldn't he leave that last little bit of John alone?'

For a long time he was reluctant to discuss the Beatles years, saying things like 'Yeah, they were a good little band' with the same brand of studied understatement Earl Mountbatten used when he described being Viceroy of India as 'great fun'. Now the story is a central part of every show and interview he gives, always in carefully sanitised form, with himself the focus of every scene. So familiar and formulaic have his anecdotes become that his fans refer to them by number. 'Paul did number 21 and 37 on Parkinson last week,' they will report to each other, or 'There was quite a good version of number 14 on Radio 2 on Saturday.'

As a sexagenarian he remains enviably slim and youthful, though the still-abundant hair is now dyed (as Heather has confirmed) and the pixie face has begun to wilt around the jawline, turning him more each day into a facsimile of his father, Jim. His manner remains that of an ebullient boy-next-door, gazing on the limitless excitement and promise of Beatledom for the very first time, raising both thumbs into the air and chortling '*Great!*' Indeed, he turned down a Lifetime Achievement award in the 2002 Brits because he said it would imply he was now old and past it, with all his best work behind him.

Modest and decorous throughout his 29 years with Linda, he now did not seem to mind when Heather proclaimed how many times each night they had sex.

He spent most of 2002 on an American tour, filling major arenas across the continent and featuring more than ever previously 'studio only' Beatles songs such as 'Blackbird', 'Hello, Goodbye' and 'It's Getting Better'. The tour, by then subtitled 'Back in the World', moved on to become his first journey through the UK for 10 years, then on to Europe to venues including Rome's Colosseum. It also included 'Here Today', his tribute to John (which, as the lyric rightly says, would probably have made John laugh) and a version of 'Something', played on George's beloved ukulele.

By Paul's own predictable account, he was just your ordinary musoe, one of a great band, going 'Wow' and 'Hey, cool!' when the audience roared for him. However, after each night's concert on the tour's US leg, the band were required to assemble and give him a 'spontaneous' ovation as he came out through the backstage area. Heightening the sense of Wings circa 1971, he and they all boarded a bus together, which first delivered Paul to the local airport to fly back to his Arizona ranch, then dropped the others at their hotel.

The 'ordinary musoe' had issued his American concert promoters with a 12-page list of backstage demands recalling the egomaniacal 1970s, when top groups would demand Napoleon brandy, Can-Can dancers in their dressing room or dishes of M&M chocolates consisting only of red ones. Though Paul's requirements could be classified as matters of conscience, stemming from his vegetarianism and animal rights beliefs, they still took superstar imperiousness into a new and surreal realm. The stretch limos provided for him must not have leather seats. The soft furniture in his hotel suites and dressing rooms must not have covers of real – or even artificial – animal skin. Not only must Sir Paul himself never be served with meat or meat by-products, but they also were banned from all the tour's production offices and backstage areas. The flowers in his dressing room must come only from 'reputable florists', must include at least one arrangement of pale pink and white roses and another of Casablanca lilies as well as the star's own favourite freesias, and should avoid 'weedy' things and pot plants with too-visible trunks. So lordly was the ordinary musoe's attitude, according to one tour member, that when former President Bill Clinton paid him a visit, Sir Paul didn't even trouble to rise from his seat.

In February 2002, he became potentially the world's highest-paid entertainer when he was offered $4 million to play in Las Vegas for a single night. The city was facing heavy losses after cancellation of the world heavyweight title-fight between Mike Tyson and Lennox Lewis: in the whole wide world of twenty-first-century entertainment, there seemed only one comparable heavyweight, one name guaranteed to pay out the mega-jackpot.

And did it make him happy? Who knows?

22

'It don't come easy'

In December 1969, Eric Clapton set off on a British and European tour with his American protégés, the folk-rock duo Delaney and Bonnie. Among their backing group – billed simply as their 'Friends' – was a rhythm guitarist whose bushy beard, wide-brimmed Stetson hat and buckskin jacket gave him a more than passing resemblance to Buffalo Bill Cody. He seemed anxious to avoid attention, keeping always to the back of the stage, playing only essential chords on his state-of-the-art red guitar. Among the crowds who cheered for 'the Great God Clapton' each night, few even recognised his shy, shrinking stage companion as George Harrison.

These were days long before rock superstars made elaborately modest 'surprise' guest appearances in their friends' shows. Asking George out on tour was a pure act of kindness on Clapton's part, to take his best friend's mind off the turmoil within the Beatles and encourage his first steps in the solo career that now seemed inevitable.

So George, very reluctantly and nervously at first, joined the tour, travelling with Clapton and Co. at the back of their bus, staying at drab railway hotels and each night, in Birmingham or Newcastle upon Tyne, becoming a little more used to facing a live audience once again. Most therapeutically of all, perhaps, in these far-northern climes, Clapton proved to be far more instantly recognisable than he. One lunch-time, as the two sat together in a motorway cafe near Sheffield, a passing waitress stared suspiciously at Clapton, then turned to George. 'He *is* famous, isn't he?' she queried. 'Oh, yeah,' George replied in his deadpan monotone. 'That's the world's most famous guitarist . . . Bert Weedon.'

After a few days of sharing Clapton's juvenile high spirits – food-fights with the late-night hotel buffets, races with wind-up toys on their dressing-room floor – the gaunt, bearded face was beginning to look noticeably more cheerful. The buckskinned figure at the back of the stage was almost grooving, even reaching for single-string licks during the medley of rock and roll classics that closed each show. 'I'd forgotten what a gas it is to play live,' he told Clapton gratefully. 'That Little Richard medley is in E, isn't it?'

George may have been little more than a bystander, with Ringo, in the central battle for the soul of the Beatles, but he had still been deeply affected by the months of feuding and intriguing, the wearisome board meetings and tense recording sessions, and the final, unavoidable compulsion to side with one of his two former closest friends in outvoting and marginalising the other. As he admitted in 'Here Comes the Sun', 'It's been a long, cold, lonely winter . . . it seems like years since it's been clear.'

John and Paul each had a wife to go to when the group was no more. But George had no such anchor to his existence. His six-year marriage to the bewitching former model Patti Boyd was already running into trouble, largely the result of his serial infidelities and northern male arrogance. 'He could be just horrible to Patti,' remembers one of their friends. 'George would say he was hungry, so Patti would make a wonderful meal . . . then he'd turn round and say he didn't want it.' Patti, who genuinely loved him, stayed with him in the misguided belief that he might still one day change back into the light-hearted charmer who had wooed her on the set of *A Hard Day's Night*; he stayed with her mainly from inertia, and because he had other, more pressing problems to deal with than that of changing his woman.

It was in this insecure, restless frame of mind that his eye fell on the 'Apple Scruffs', his own name for the female fans who haunted the individual Beatles' front gates, EMI's studios and the steps at 3 Savile Row. Among them was Carol Bedford, the Texan girl who had arrived from Dallas to join the sisterhood a few months earlier and now lived in a shared flat not far from Abbey Road. In their brief doorstep exchanges, Carol had impressed George with her humour, articulateness and lack of sycophancy. She sensed they were developing a rapport – though never dreaming that the ultimate fantasy of every Apple Scruff was about to come true for her.

'One day, while I was at EMI studios, the roadie Mal Evans came up and asked me where I lived. I thought he might be the one who was interested, so I refused to tell him. Then later, while I was standing at the bus stop, George came along in his Mercedes. "Fancy meeting you here," he said, and offered me a ride home.'

With all his experience as a Beatle, Carol expected him to be the smoothest and most nonchalant of seducers. Instead, she found he was almost as paralysed by nerves as she was. 'When we got to where I lived, George switched off the engine, then he pulled down his hat-brim, turned up his collar and sank down low in his seat so that no one passing would recognise him. I tried to get out of the car but couldn't get the door open, so he had to lean over to do it for me. Then the scarf I was wearing got caught somewhere. As I was trying to pull it free, I accidentally hit George in the face and knocked his hat off.'

She presumed that first uncomfortable encounter would be their last one, but a week or so later, George overcame his seigneurial inhibitions so far as to call round at her flat. He gave no advance warning, however, and Carol happened to be out at the time. 'When I came home, my flatmate told me this guy had been asking for me and that he seemed very shy and nervous. She didn't have to say any more for me to know who it had been.'

Despite his nerves he tried again, and this time did find Carol at home. 'He sat on my bed for about half an hour, and we talked. I kept thinking to myself "He must have been in so *many* girls' flats, all over the world . . ." I offered to make him a cup of tea, but was so nervous that I dropped the box of matches all over the floor. George knelt down and helped me pick them up.'

At the time he still had not fully recovered from a car accident some weeks earlier in which both he and Patti had been involved. 'Patti had been hurt worse than George and was still having to stay home,' Carol remembers. 'I asked George how she was and he said "She's got to have plenty of peace and quiet, so I'm playing the drums really loudly in the next room." That's when I realised what a rocky state their marriage was in.'

Although obviously attracted to Carol, even in these private surroundings, George still made no move on her. What chiefly seemed to inhibit him was the risk of sexually transmitted disease – mild enough in that pre-AIDS era, but still a major deterrent for someone who'd been a musician on Hamburg's Reeperbahn. 'He asked me if I'd ever had VD, or passed on NSU [non-specific urethritis]. And he also got incredibly uptight when I told him he smoked much too much. If I'd had the pressures he did, he told me, I'd be a chain-smoker, too. He was telling me about his last medical check-up after the accident and what his doctor had said. He reminded me of a little boy who'd skinned his knee and was coming to his mother for comfort and reassurance.'

His kerb-crawling for Apple Scruffs was not the only bizarre infidelity Patti Harrison would have to endure. Not long afterwards, the couple visited Tittenhurst Park, the mansion in Henley-on-Thames which Ringo and Maureen Starr had taken on after John and Yoko's departure for America. Over dinner, George suddenly blurted out that he was in love with Maureen. A few days later, Patti came home to find him and Maureen in bed together. For such a gross and meaningless betrayal of two old friends, his only explanation was a shrug and the single word 'Incest'.

•

To musician friends like Eric Clapton, George compared his release from the Beatles when it finally came to 'recovering from a six-year dose of constipation'. At long last he was free of the Lennon–McCartney stranglehold that had always kept his contribution to the band's oeuvre so pitifully small. Never again would John patronise him or Paul try to boss him or George Martin lead him to a studio piano and spell out the solo he was expected to replicate on his guitar.

Certainly, in the immediate aftermath of the break-up, he seemed like nothing so much as a brilliant genie, billowing forth from the bottle that had confined him and towering triumphantly over those who had so unfairly held him captive. His first solo project was no mere two-sided album like John's and Paul's but a grandiose three-record set whose title, *All Things Must Pass*, could be read either as a philosophical generalisation or as a heartfelt sigh of relief that the 'long, cold, lonely winter' was finally at an end. The album projected a completely new George, no longer the grimly earnest sitar-bore of 'Within You Without You' but a lighter, more open-hearted character who seemed to have found the perfect balance between his cherished Indian mysticism and high-octane commercial pop. Its perfect synthesis was 'My Sweet Lord', a global chart smash destined for eternal life as an anthem to simple faith that crossed all religious boundaries, equally valid whether chanted in a Himalayan ashram, played on the organ of an English parish church or chanted at sundown by an imam from a minaret.

In the wake of *All Things Must Pass* came a chance to prove the genuineness of his affinity with the Indian subcontinent and his exhortations to universal brotherhood. In the easterly part of Pakistan's two separate segments, a secessionist movement had declared independence from larger and richer West Pakistan, setting up a provisional government and renaming their country Bangladesh. The Pakistani Army had responded with genocidal cruelty, indiscriminately slaughtering college students, women and children as well as independence fighters. In a land already awesomely impoverished, something like two million refugees were fleeing in panic to seek refuge over the border in neighbouring India.

George conceived the idea of an all-star charity concert and live album to raise money for relief aid. As a Beatle, he doubtless would have turned the project over to his Apple minions to manage, or mismanage, as best they might. But in his new, can-do persona, he took over its organisation personally, ringing up superstar friends to enlist their support, persuading hard-nosed managers and record companies to sanction the appearance of their multimillion-dollar talents, unprecedentedly, for free.

There were, in the end, two concerts for Bangladesh at New York's Madison Square Garden in August 1971, featuring George in company with, among others, Bob Dylan, Leon Russell, Ringo Starr and Ravi Shankar. It was an historic event that gave rock the first inklings of dignity and altruism that would culminate with Live Aid 14 years later. It was no less a personal accolade for George, demonstrating in what high regard he was held by the foremost names in the business. Rock concert audiences would never again be quite so high-minded, nor so over-anxious to prove themselves just as *au courant* with Eastern mysticism as were their idols. During one show, as Ravi Shankar and his musicians finished tuning up for their sitar set, they were surprised to receive an earnest round of applause.

Ironically, the star management most difficult to square over the concerts for Bangladesh proved to be George's own. The High Court-appointed Receiver who – thanks to Paul McCartney – now administered the Beatles' partnership, was empowered to receive each ex-Beatle's solo earnings as well as their continuing income as a group (£4 million in 1970). The Receiver, James Spooner, was therefore less than thrilled to learn that George intended donating his royalties from the live album directly to the Bangladesh relief effort. Before the gift could be made, there had to be lengthy enquiries to satisfy Mr Spooner that it would not impact adversely on the other Beatles' income tax situation. The individual permissions of John, Paul and Ringo also had to be given in writing. It was to take a further High Court ruling, seven months after the event, for George's spontaneous act of generosity to be finally sanctioned.

His humanitarian instincts were not confined to people far away. In 1972 – a time when few British pop stars other than Elton John interested themselves in good works – he set up a charity called the Material World Foundation (named after his album *Living in the Material World*) which gave support to a range of causes from the arts to children with special needs. He could be generous to friends, notably the Beatles' former publicist, Derek Taylor, whom he helped to buy a mill house in Suffolk.

It was in every way a brilliant start to his new life in the new decade. But as time passed, a terrible truth slowly became apparent. 'My Sweet Lord' and the other songs bountifully packed onto the six sides of *All Things Must Pass* had almost all been written by George from inside the Beatles, when the genius of Lennon and McCartney could not help but rub off a little on him. Without John and Paul to stimulate as well as frustrate him, he would never produce work even approaching such quality again. To make matters worse, 'My Sweet Lord' was accused of plagiarising a 1964 song called 'He's So Fine' by an American female group, the Chiffons. Though George denied any conscious plagiarism, the three notes that made the central 'hook' in both songs were clearly identical. The resulting ligitation dragged on for years and took its most bizarre turn when Allen Klein, the Beatles' displaced manager, acquired the copyright of 'He's So Fine', seemingly just for the satisfaction of prolonging the lawsuit against George.

Even more bizarre was the conclusion, reached years down the line, after a British court had decided against George and he had been obliged to pay a six-figure sum in compensation. He himself acquired the copyright of 'He's So Fine', and so was free to plagiarise it or not, as he chose.

The Apple experience had not stifled his desire to have his own record label on which he could both enjoy total artistic freedom and also foster new talent. In the mid-Seventies, he finally found the right parent company in America's A & M, a label co-founded by Herb Alpert (of Tijuana Brass fame). So was launched Dark Horse Records, its name consciously congratulating a long-time outsider who was now the music industry's odds-on favourite.

Ironically, however, the establishment of Dark Horse saw his solo career begin a gradual and seemingly irreversible decline. His albums were critically panned, and sold in decreasing quantity. He began to alienate concert audiences by his self-importance and his heavy-handed attempts at lecturing and preaching. His 1974 American tour was a failure so resounding that he never again went on the road in America, nor any other Western country. He had the satisfaction, at least, of seeing 'Something', his Abbey Road song, mature into a classic whose originality no one questioned and which over time would be covered by vocalists of every stamp from Frank Sinatra to Shirley Bassey.

His continuing unhappy marriage to Patti, meanwhile, had produced one of rock's strangest ever love-triangles. Eric Clapton had become infatuated with Patti years earlier but, as George's best friend, felt honour-bound not to pursue her. His classic song 'Layla', on the pseudonymous *Derek and the Dominoes* album, was both a love letter to Patti and a lament for his own tied hands: 'I tried to give you consolation . . . when your old man let you down . . .' In 1974, Patti finally left George, subsequently divorcing him and marrying Clapton. Despite all this, the two guitar soulmates managed to stay friends; George even attended Patti and Eric's wedding. 'If my wife's going to run off with someone,' he said, 'I'd rather it was with a guy that I love.'

Thereafter, he seemed to content himself with the life of a landed gentleman-hippy, retreating into Friar Park, the 120-room Gothic mansion near Henley he had bought for £200,000 in 1970. The house, built by an eccentric named Sir Frankie Crisp, would have made a perfect alternative school for Harry Potter with its myriad sooty turrets, grotesque gargoyles and light switches fashioned like monks' skulls. Although George went on releasing albums at regular intervals, he devoted himself mainly to restoring Friar Park's vast grounds, which encompassed a lake with stepping stones set near the surface so that he could enjoy the feeling of walking on water. He also began a relationship with Olivia Arias, a secretary in the American office of his Dark Horse label. They married in 1978, a month after the birth of their only child, Dhani.

In 1980, he published *I, Me, Mine*, a limited edition pictorial autobiography retailing at £175 per copy and including colour facsimiles of his song lyrics as he had first handwritten them on sheets of hotel or office stationery; one even reproduced a burn he had made on it with his cigarette. Also reproduced was the cheque for £1 million he'd had to write in August 1973 in 'part payment' to the hated taxman.

John Lennon's murder in 1980 had a profound effect on George, although – like Paul – he was unable to react with more than inappropriate Merseybeat flipness. He said that a late-night phone call had woken him with the news, he'd gone back to sleep, 'and when I woke up next morning, it was still true'. With reflection he could only add the mock-tabloid cliché that he was 'shocked and stunned'. In fact, he was probably the worst affected of the three survivors, having never rebuilt bridges with John the way Paul and Ringo had. He knew, too, that John had been furious with him over the scant references to their early friendship he had made in *I, Me, Mine.*

He tried to make amends with a 'tribute' song, 'All Those Years Ago', which recalled his teenage hero-worship of John ('I always looked up to you') and hit out, rather too late, at those who had treated him 'like a dog'. It was, however, little more than a hasty doodle, sung at the anomalously cheerful tempo of a Boy Scout camp-fire song and not a patch on the Elton John–Bernie Taupin Lennon tribute single, 'Empty Garden', released soon afterwards.

The main effect of the tragedy on George was hugely to increase the secretiveness and suspicion that had always been so deeply embedded in his nature. From now on, he would be haunted by the fear that some Chapman figure – characterised as 'the devil's best friend' in 'All Those Years Ago' – might ultimately come gunning for him, too. He installed elaborate security systems at Friar Park and brought in his older brothers, Harry and Peter, as security chief and head gardener respectively. 'Before John's death, the front gates had always stood wide open,' a former associate recalls. 'But afterwards, they were always shut and locked.'

In the early Eighties, a wholly unexpected new career beckoned thanks to his friendship with Michael Palin and other members of the Monty Python comedy team. He was especially close to Eric Idle, whose post-Python fantasies included a 1977 documentary send-up of the Beatles called *The Rutles*. One scene parodied the plundering of the Apple house, with a TV interviewer speaking to Palin outside the front door while figures in the background gambolled off with TV sets and furniture. Demonstrating a little-suspected ability to laugh at himself, George took the role of the interviewer.

Idle, Palin, John Cleese and company had since moved from television into cinema films with Monty Python's *Life of Brian*, a project originally financed by the Beatles' old parent company, EMI. Not until filming had begun in Tunisia did EMI's chief executive, Lord Delfont, realise he was funding a breathtakingly sacrilegious skit on the story of Christ. Delfont immediately pulled the plug, leaving the cast and unit marooned on location. Hearing of their plight, George weighed in to help them, mortgaging Friar Park to raise the £4 million necessary for the film's completion. 'Python helped keep me sane while the Beatles were breaking up,' he told Idle and the others, 'so I owed you this one.'

The *Life of Brian* went on to make a fortune at the box-office and bring George properly into the film business as part-owner of a new company called HandMade. His partner was a former merchant banker named Denis O'Brien, to whom he had originally been introduced by the comedian Peter Sellers. Tall, dapper and persuasive, O'Brien subsequently took over the financial management of both George and the Python team.

On the surface, HandMade appeared a spectacular success, releasing 23 films in 10 years and taking most of the kudos for the British cinema's strong revival during the early and middle Eighties. Their slate included lasting classics like *Mona Lisa*, *The Long Good Friday*, *Withnail and I*, Terry Gilliam's *Time Bandits* and Alan Bennett's *A Private Function*, though there were also such notable turkeys as *Shanghai Surprise* starring Madonna. One of the more surreal moments in that era was seeing Madonna appear at a press conference with George – once a king of press conferences the world over – as her silent, scowling minder.

In 1987, his long-dormant recording career suddenly revived by a collaboration with Jeff Lynne, formerly of the Electric Light Orchestra, a Birmingham band sometimes called 'the Beatles of the Seventies'. From the *Cloud Nine* album, produced by Lynne, came a single, 'Got My Mind Set on You', which took George to number one in America and number two in Britain. The following year, he and Lynne teamed with Bob Dylan, Tom Petty and Roy Orbison as 'the Traveling Wilburys', a kind of corn pone Sergeant Pepper band playing laid-back acoustic country-rock which they self-deprecatingly termed 'skiffle for the Eighties'. The Wilburys released a hit album and brought Orbison back to prominence as a seminal rock artist in the last months before his death.

Meanwhile, HandMade Films was proving an even more painful financial experience for George than Apple Corps had been a decade and a half earlier. The company's projects were financed chiefly by bank loans supposedly guaranteed by him and his partner, Denis O'Brien. In fact, as he belatedly discovered, he was usually the sole guarantor. Most banks were happy to trust in the solvency of a former Beatle but then one – Barclays – demanded an audit of George's affairs and brought to light a deficit of something like £20 million. In yet another eerie echo of Beatles history, George received the same warning John Lennon once had: that if he carried on like this, he'd soon be bankrupt. The possibility even loomed of having to sell his beloved Friar Park. He launched a $25 million lawsuit against Denis O'Brien, also adopting the now familiar Beatles tactic of pillorying him in a song ('Lying O'Brien'). But by the time the American courts had decided in George's favour and awarded him $11 million, O'Brien had filed for bankruptcy. 'George was traumatised by the HandMade experience,' one former associate remembers. 'It wasn't so much the money he lost as the feeling of personal betrayal. In fact, I'd go so far as to say that all the health troubles he suffered later really started here.'

It was mainly George's urgent need of cash that helped bring about the Beatles' reunion on their 1995 *Anthology* project – although of the three survivors he proved conspicuously the least charming. Most bitterly did he seem to resent the fact that they had received no collective national honour beyond their MBE each in 1965. 'After all we did for Great Britain, selling all that corduroy and making it swing,' he sneered, 'they gave us that bloody old leather medal with wooden string [sic] through it.'

Charm was, indeed, the most notable deficiency in these later years. Despite his own late burst of chart success, he began to come across like some old curmudgeon in a chimney-corner, voicing detestation of new musical styles like rap and Britpop and affecting not to listen to anything recorded later than about 1976. He even spat some venom at Oasis, a band who made their adoration of the Beatles clear in almost every note they played. True, they released a track whose title unwittingly copied his *Wonderwall* album – but he, of all people, might have understood about that. Liam Gallagher, their volatile front man, became incensed enough by George's negative comments to vow to thump him one if ever they should meet.

Though private and publicity-shy he never became a recluse in the

Howard Hughes mould, as would later be alleged. He followed Formula 1 racing and also became an obsessive fan of the 1940s musical entertainer George Formby, who used to sing in a squeaky northern accent, playing a ukulele. George took his own Formby-style ukulele with him wherever he went and frequently attended conventions of Formby soundalikes, though he always shunned equivalent gatherings of Beatles fans. 'He was rubbish on the ukulele,' remembers Mal Jefferson, an old school friend and fellow Merseybeat musician who occasionally met him at George Formby conventions. 'I saw him play once, and then get slaughtered by a nine-year-old lad.

'Afterwards, I offered to buy his uke' off him and, to my amazement, he agreed. "But I paid two grand for it," he said. "I've got to get back what I paid. I need every penny at the moment. I've just lost forty million with HandMade Films." As a joke, I wrote him out a cheque for £2001 – but George said, "Thanks very much" and stuffed it into his pocket.'

At the time of the *Anthology* came a brief period of rejuvenation, when he took to combing his hair back in the same Teddy-boy style that used to get him into such trouble at Liverpool Institute. But as time passed, he looked less like a one-time world idol than some modern Worzel Gummidge, in his old parkas and shapeless gardening hats. Despite his public reconciliation with his former Beatles colleagues, his bitterness towards Paul continued to fester. In a Radio 2 interview during the late Nineties, he was heard griping about how 'Paul McCartney ruined me as a guitarist', still apparently unable to recognise the inestimable luck of having lived and worked alongside such provocative talent.

He remained a devotee of Transcendental Meditation and, despite all John's mockeries and fulminations, had never turned against Maharishi Mahesh Yogi. Despite losing the Beatles as figureheads, 'TM' and the Maharishi had prospered in Britain; they now owned Mentmore House, former country seat of the Rosebery family, where they were rumoured to teach their followers to fly in rooms with shock-absorbing mattresses nailed around the walls. They had also produced a political wing, the Natural Law Party, which fielded a huge array of parliamentary candidates in the 1992 General Election. They hoped that George himself might stand, thereby guaranteeing at least one NLP MP in Parliament. He declined, but showed his support by giving his first ever solo concert in the UK and donating its proceeds to their election campaign.

His greatest asset proved to be his marriage to Olivia, not a rock star's cipher wife but a woman of character and compassion, who became deeply involved in charity work to help orphans in Romania. Though George no longer engaged in casual affairs, as he had when he was with Patti, Olivia still found life with him anything but a bed of roses. The rockiest moment occurred when a Los Angeles prostitute known only as Tiffany identified him as one of her clients, alleging that while a sexual service was performed for him, he was playing his ukulele and singing a George Formby song. But Olivia stood by him, becoming – in one insider's words – 'the bedrock of his existence'. Together they proved model parents, raising their son Dhani in comparative normality – and totally out of the media spotlight. Despite his ambivalence towards 'the material world', George acquired several properties overseas, including estates in Maui and the West Indies, and travelled by private Gulfstream jet.

In 1997, while gardening at Friar Park, he noticed a lump had appeared in his neck. Its cause was found to be a cancerous tumour in his throat, the result – as he himself acknowledged – of a lifetime's heavy smoking. After an operation at the Margaret Hospital in Windsor followed by a course of radiation therapy at Royal Marsden in London, he was pronounced to have made a complete recovery. He himself told the media he was completely fit again and had taken to heart this warning never to smoke again.

On 30 December 1999, the 'devil's best friend' he had feared for so long finally called on him. It was, indeed, an eerily exact replay of the December night 17 years before when Mark David Chapman had murdered John Lennon. A similarly deranged Beatles fan, 34-year-old Michael Abrams, broke into Friar Park, believing himself to be on 'a mission from God' to murder George. His intended victim later recounted how his first instinct on coming unexpectedly face to face with Abrams was to shout his old Sixties peace mantra, 'Hare Krishna!' As the two grappled at the foot of the main staircase, Abrams stabbed George four times in the body with a knife. 'I felt my chest deflate and the flow of blood to my mouth,' George said later. 'I truly thought I was dying.'

So he certainly would have done but for his wife Olivia who, like an avenging angel, laid into Abrams with a poker and the base of a lamp while her husband lay, bleeding and helpless, on the ground. Her later testimony would uncannily recall Yoko's description of the 'horrible confused' look in John's eyes after Chapman had pumped five shots into him. Olivia was likewise to remember how, as George lay bleeding among his meditation cushions, 'he was very pale and . . . staring at me in a really bizarre manner'. The struggle continued until police arrived and overpowered Abrams. 'I should have got the bastard better,' muttered the intruder as he was led away.

The Apple office, through Neil Aspinall, initially played down the seriousness of the incident. Not until Abrams' trial at Oxford Crown Court 11 months later was its full horror revealed. Olivia appeared as a witness though George, still seemingly traumatised by his ordeal, was allowed to give evidence by written statement. After Abrams had been sentenced to be detained indefinitely in a secure psychiatric unit, a statement was read on George's behalf by his son, Dhani, by now 22 and an almost exact replica of his father at the same age.

The attack inevitably deepened George's paranoia over personal privacy, to the point where he seriously considered leaving Britain altogether and settling in either America or the West Indies. Security at Friar Park was immediately strengthened, with guard dogs and, it was rumoured, ex-para bodyguards added to the existing razor-wire fence, electronic front gates and video surveillance system that had failed to stop Abrams entering the house. His stable-door security mania even extended to the police officers who had rescued him from Abrams. PC Matt Morgans, who had cradled him in his arms until medical help arrived, later gave an interview to the local newspaper, the *Henley Standard*. George was so incensed by the interview that he threatened an official complaint against his rescuer.

According to George's Henley neighbour, Sir John Mortimer, there was a sick aftermath to the episode – one which revealed how far Britain had travelled as a society from the loving, sunny Sixties. A car full of people drove past Friar Park's gates, loudly cheering because George had been attacked. Other anonymous sickos sent flowers to his would-be killer in hospital.

In March 2001, a routine check-up at the Mayo Clinic in Rochester, Minnesota, revealed cancerous cells in one of his lungs. He underwent surgery and was said by his doctors to have made 'an excellent recovery'. He himself assured the media, in his familiar mordant way, that he had 'no plans to die'. But he seems to have realised already that the writing was on the wall. Most of that following summer was spent in Switzerland, at a villa near Lugano's San Giovanni clinic, where he was receiving treatment from the world-famous oncologist Professor Franco Cavalli. Partnered by his son Dhani, he wrote and recorded a new song, 'Horse to the Water', for inclusion on an r & b album also featuring Jools Holland, Van Morrison and Sting. With typical graveyard humour, he copyrighted the song to 'Rip 2001 Ltd'. 'He never felt sorry for himself,' Dhani was to recall. 'We took the view "be here now" and made the most of our time. He used to say "Oh, you're going to have to finish all these songs." I'd say, "Well, not if you do it first. Get off your arse and finish them."'

Aware that the end could now not be far away, he set about making arrangements for his departure and healing the two major emotional breaches in his life. There was a reconciliation with his older sister, Louise, now in her seventies, to whom he'd barely spoken since she lent her name to an Illinois bed-and-breakfast called the Hard Day's Night. He also got together with Paul McCartney, ending the chill that had never really abated since Paul had tried to boss him around on the *Let It Be* sessions. Hugging one another as they never had even as boyhood cronies, they agreed how little all such things matter in the end.

Nor did the eerie repetitiveness of Beatles history cease with his death on the last day of November. As with Linda McCartney three years earlier, the quest for privacy created some initial confusion about where the event had happened. Initially, it was reported to have been at the Laurel Canyon mansion of Gavin de Becker, a security consultant who specialises in providing safe houses for celebrities. On the death certificate, however, it appeared as '1971 Coldwater Canyon', an address which proved fictitious. The discovery brought faint echoes of a time when all Beatles output was thought to carry hidden subtexts and messages. For 1971 was the year of George's greatest triumph, the concerts for Bangladesh. As in Linda's case, too, the ruse brought a threat of official prosecution which hung over Olivia Harrison until she filed an affidavit stating the true address six months later.

In fact, the place where George died had symbolised a Beatles reunion perhaps more significant than any in the previous 20 years. He had been staying at 9536 Heather Road, Beverly Hills, a property owned by Paul McCartney and loaned to George as a last sanctuary which the media would never find. With him at the last, as well as Olivia and Dhani, were his two favourite Indian gurus, Mukunda and Shayamsundra, chanting the same 'Hare Krishna' mantra that used to echo through the lush-carpeted corridors of the Apple house and up and down Oxford Street. Olivia requested a worldwide minute's silence as a mark of respect. (One could imagine George somewhere, fuming over the fact that John got a full five minutes' silence in 1980.) At Varanasi, India, hundreds gathered beside the River Ganges, expecting his body to be brought there and cremated according to Hindu custom. But, like so many watchers outside Apple in days of yore, they were doomed to disappointment. Cremation had been quietly carried out in LA, immediately after his death.

His obituaries touched levels of hysteria and hyperbole remarkable even for the early twenty-first century. He was lauded, not only as a towering figure in popular music but also as a philanthropist, a visionary, a mystic, even a messiah. On BBC radio, the former Traffic drummer Jim Capaldi said that if Christ had been reborn into the world, He could just have easily written the opening line of 'While My Guitar Gently Weeps'.

His estate was valued at £99 million, a figure said not to include his properties in Hawaii, Switzerland and Italy. Everything was left to Olivia, in trust for Dhani. Neither his sister Louise nor his surviving brother Peter received a penny.

On the first anniversary of his death, his closest musical blood brother headlined a memorial concert at London's Royal Albert Hall which eerily recreated that 1969 concert billing of 'Eric Clapton and Friends'. It also brought a further reunion of the Beatles' surviving, uncontentious half, with Paul McCartney and Ringo Starr instantly agreeing to join Clapton's ensemble. Before the show, tickets with a face value of £150 were changing hands for up to £1,000.

George was not great; just an average guitarist who got incredibly lucky. But he was also an indispensable part of the greatest engine for human happiness the modern world has known. The pity was that it never seemed quite enough for him.

•

Of the four Beatles, Ringo Starr may have had the least natural talent with which to sustain a solo career. But what he did have was an enormous fund of goodwill, both inside the music business and outside. Whereas John, Paul and George, in their different ways, all had to battle to prove themselves as individual performers, there was general, unspoken agreement that Ringo *had* to make it.

The conflict and bitterness of the break-up seemed not to have affected his essentially happy, optimistic nature nor in any way compromised the affection which all the other three still felt for him. Apart from that one atypical loss of self-control at Cavendish Avenue, even Paul had never shown him hostility nor said a bad word about him. Rather as divorcing parents worry about the children, so all three felt concern about how Ringo would fare without them around to look after him. To be sure, it was probably the one point on which they all agreed. The little unselfishness and team-spirit they had left they focused on him.

Thanks to these helping hands from all directions, Ringo's post-Beatle career looked potentially bigger than either John's or Paul's. In 1970, following Beatles practice for some years past, he put out two albums: the country-flavoured *Beaucoup of Blues*, recorded in Nashville, and *Sentimental Journey*, a collection of standards aimed mainly at pleasing his mum. The more than a little help from his superstar friends spawned two massively successful singles, 'It Don't Come Easy' in 1971 and 'Back Off Boogaloo' in 1972, both his own compositions, produced by George Harrison and warbled in the same chewy lead vocal style, as though he were simultaneously masticating egg and chips.

In 1973 came the *Ringo* album, which, amazingly, brought him two

American number one singles: 'Photograph' and a cover version of Johnny Burnette's 'You're Sixteen'. The album's numerous celebrity sidemen included not only George but both other concerned 'parents', John and Paul, playing on separate tracks. A year afterwards came a third successful album, *Goodnight Vienna*, including a hit cover version of the Platters' 'Only You'. With George simultaneously triumphing in the American singles charts and John and Paul's relatively small impact there, the Beatles' long-eclipsed 'second division' seemed to have turned the tables with a vengeance.

Following his droll cameo appearances in the Beatles' own films and Terry Southern's *Candy*, a screen acting career seemed to beckon even more alluringly than Ringo's musical one. Those early comparisons with Keaton and Chaplin seemed justified when, also in 1973, he co-starred with David Essex and Adam Faith in *That'll Be the Day*, a nostalgic evocation of the seaside holiday camps he used to play with Rory Storm's Hurricanes, before John rang him at Skegness and offered him Pete Best's old chair in the Beatles. The previous year had seen his debut as a documentary director with *Born to Boogie*, a film about his close friend the glam-rocker Marc Bolan. Then suddenly in the mid-Seventies, it was as if a turbo-jet had been removed from Ringo's back. His albums were recorded with ever decreasing energy and conviction – like the spiritless *Rotogravure* of 1976 – and sold in ever decreasing quantities. He refused to appear in the sequel to *That'll Be the Day*, turning instead to Hollywood, which cast him in a series of increasingly dire pot-boilers. He became best known as a guest on TV talk shows, always jokily sidestepping the only question that interested his audience: what had it been like to be a Beatle?

His marriage to Maureen in the end lasted for 10 years – though it probably never recovered from Maureen's fling with George – and by the early Seventies, the two of them were living separate lives on separate continents. In 1970, Ringo began a relationship with American model Barbara Bach, his co-star in a risible movie called *Caveman*. Their marriage in 1981 was attended by Paul and Linda McCartney and George and Olivia Harrison, proof of Paul's and George's undimmed fondness for him and a symbolic act of togetherness in the aftershock of John's murder.

In the early Eighties, Ringo's artistic fortunes sank to their nadir. Signed to the RCA label in 1981, he made an album called *Stop and Smell the Roses* which failed to register despite further fraternal contributions from Paul and George. Its follow-up, *Old Wave*, was considered too feeble for release either in America or Britain. Over the next decade, his main public exposure would be on children's television and video as narrator of the Reverend W. Awdry's Thomas the Tank Engine stories.

As with so many of his contemporaries, decades of heedless rock-star life finally began taking their toll when he entered his forties. Even his buoyant spirits could not completely protect him against the slump in his prestige other than with juvenile steam-railway enthusiasts. Despite his delicate stomach, he had always been a heavy drinker; now his consumption of champagne and table wines increased to several bottles per day, with Barbara usually matching him glass for glass. In 1988, they entered a drying-out clinic together, which not only saved their health but also seemed to consolidate a marriage which few had expected to last.

Following this internal spring-clean, Ringo's enthusiasm for drumming returned, with a consequent small revival in his career. In 1989 he went back on the road, leading (shades of Rory Storm!) an 'All-Starr Band' including distinguished sidemen like Billy Preston, Dave Edmunds and Nils Lofgren and featuring his own elder son, Zak, as back-up drummer. A successful US and Japanese tour that year was followed by a less successful European one in 1992. The once modest and self-knowing character who, as George Martin noted, 'couldn't do a roll to save his life', now billed himself unblushingly as 'the World's Greatest Rock 'n' Roll Drummer'.

His 25 per cent share of Apple meant he never had to work again unless he wanted to. By the Nineties, he had moved to the tax haven of Monaco, acquiring a top-floor apartment in a luxury sea-front block overlooking the famous Sporting Club. Barbara and he took a full part in the principality's jet-set social life, were received by its ruler, Prince Rainier, and, especially after their internal laundering, could often be seen strolling along Avenue Princess Grace hand in hand, in matching black outfits, as if making their virtuous way to some Quaker meeting house.

Both Ringo's sons, Zak and Jason, went on to become rock drummers, both creditably refusing to exploit his celebrity to advance their careers and always working under their real family name of Starkey. Zak in particular turned out to be a brilliant performer although, ironically, his role model was not his father but the manic Keith Moon of The Who. Far from resenting this, Ringo even arranged for Moon to give Zak lessons. And no one could have been prouder when, long years after Moon's death from suicidal alcohol and drug abuse in 1978, The Who recruited Jason to be drummer on some of their various comeback tours.

Perhaps the greatest surprise of all was Ringo's former wife, Maureen, the former mousy little Liverpool hairdresser who, after the divorce, might have been expected to sink into comfortably maintained obscurity.

Instead, Maureen went on to marry Isaac Tigrett, the founder of the Hard Rock Café chain, and then to present Tigrett with a baby daughter, Olivia. Ringo remained on good terms with her and close to all three of their children. The original family not only survived but provided each other with crucial love and support in the double ordeal that was soon to come.

In 1995, Ringo and Maureen's fashion designer daughter, Lee, by then 25, was rushed to a London clinic to have fluid removed from her brain. Diagnosed with a brain tumour, she underwent radiation treatment at the Brigham and Women's Hospital in Boston, Massachusetts and, after several agonising weeks for her parents and brothers, was pronounced to be in the clear. Late that same year, Maureen herself was found to be suffering from leukaemia. Again, the prognosis seemed favourable, especially after an apparently successful bone-marrow transplant from her son Zak. But by Christmas, the illness had shown itself to be incurable. Maureen died in January 1996 with Ringo as well as her children at her bedside.

In 2000, Ringo bought a property in Cranleigh, Surrey, mainly to be near Jason and his girl friend Flora who had by now presented him with two grandsons, Louis and Sonny. Coincidentally, their near neighbour in north London happened to be Paul McCartney's daughter Mary, herself the mother of a son, Arthur, by her TV producer partner Alistair Donald. The Beatles grandchildren were often to be found playing together, establishing who knows what early links for bands far into the future.

That 5 November, the villagers of Cranleigh asked the newly arrived celebrity in their midst to be guest of honour at their Guy Fawkes night firework display. It must have seemed small stuff to Ringo, after all the red carpets that had been unrolled for him all around the world, but he turned out good-naturedly enough on the village green to give the signal for the display to start, then stood and watched the Catherine wheels, the Roman candles, the little rockets whooshing only halfway to Heaven. As he advances into his sixties, the only cloud on his horizon seems the health of his daughter Lee who, in late 2001, was reported to be having further hospital treatment in Boston for a second brain tumour called an ependymoma.

He may have been no more than history's most famous bit-part player, but still, his must be the last word about it all. Look at the *Beatles Anthology* television documentary, that laughably incomplete and doctored account. Fast-forward through bland, self-deluding Paul and crabby George until you find Ringo, playing his usual cameo role on some sun-soaked LA balcony, his close-cropped hair and grey-grizzled beard giving him an almost uncanny resemblance to the Palestinian leader Yasser Arafat.

Not only is he the funniest, most honest and self-knowing of the survivors; he is also the only one willing to show real emotion. Tears glisten in the big mournful eyes as he says that for him, above all, the Beatles will always be 'just four guys who loved each other'.

Which perhaps best sums up the whole story.

Index